CRIME RECONSTRUCTION

CRIME RECONSTRUCTION

W. Jerry Chisum, BS
Brent E. Turvey, MS

AMSTERDAM • BOSTON • HEIDELBERG • LONDON
NEW YORK • OXFORD • PARIS • SAN DIEGO
SAN FRANCISCO • SINGAPORE • SYDNEY • TOKYO
Academic Press is an imprint of Elsevier

Acquisitions Editor: Jennifer Soucy
Acquisitions Editor: Mark Listewnik
Editorial Assistant: Kelly Weaver
Project Manager: Sarah M. Hajduk
Cover Designer: Eric DeCicco
Cover Printer: Phoenix Color
Interior Printer: The Maple-Vail Book Manufacturing Group

Elsevier Academic Press
30 Corporate Drive, Suite 400, Burlington, MA 01803, USA
525 B Street, Suite 1900, San Diego, California 92101-4495, USA
84 Theobald's Road, London WC1X 8RR, UK

This book is printed on acid-free paper.

Library of Congress Cataloging-in-Publication Data
Chisum, W. Jerry (William Jerry)
    Crime reconstruction / W. Jerry Chisum, Brent E. Turvey.
        p. cm.
    Includes bibliographical references and index.
    ISBN 0-12-369375-6 (hardback : alk. paper)   1. Criminal investigation.   2. Forensic
sciences.   I. Turvey, Brent E.   II. Title.
    HV8073.C515 2006
    363.25—dc22

                                                                    2006010167

British Library Cataloguing in Publication Data
A catalogue record for this book is available from the British Library

ISBN 13: 978-0-12-369375-4
ISBN 10: 0-12-369375-6

For all information on all Elsevier Academic Press publications
visit our Web site at www.books.elsevier.com

Printed in the United States of America
07 08 09 10   9 8 7 6 5 4 3 2 1

TABLE OF CONTENTS

COVER ART DETAILS

1. Victim's glasses found in his back yard at an arson-homicide crime scene. These glasses were dropped by the victim, who had been shot in both the face and the leg. The glasses established a portion of the victim's route as he exsanguinated, and that they were dropped subsequent to his injuries, as indicated by the presence of blood. They also established that for the final moments of his life, while he was moving around, he could not see. These issues were significant to the overall reconstruction of the crime.

2. An x-ray of a golf ball in the mouth of a domestic homicide victim. Cause of death was asphyxiation. The x-ray shows the depth of the placement of the golf-ball, as well as the absence of other injury to the victim's skull and jaw. The victim also suffered insertions of other foreign objects into her skin and bodily orifices, such as other golf balls, golf tees, and a steak knife. Taken together, these elements created a compelling picture of a unique expression of anger in a domestic homicide.

3. Shoes found outside a residence covered in soot from an arson-homicide. The absence of soot beneath the shoes evidences that they were in place before the fire burned the residence. The nature and condition of the shoe evidence demonstrates that the victim, found in the home, was not wearing them at the time of their death.

4. A fire burning with the timer in the foreground. This was set up as part of an experiment conducted to test theories developed in a fire investigation.

5. Photo of a purple fiber. This fiber was collected from the nude body of a victim in a sexual homicide. In conjunction with other physical evidence, the presence of this purple fiber told investigators that the victim was transported or stored after death while in contact with something woven with purple wool fibers. This could be compared to suspect clothing, blankets, or transfer in suspect residences and vehicles.

PREFACE

A HOLISTIC APPROACH TO CRIME RECONSTRUCTION

W. Jerry Chisum and Brent E. Turvey

> Relating to or concerned with wholes or with complete systems rather than with the analysis of, treatment of, or dissection into parts. Emphasizing the organic or functional relation between parts and the whole.
> —*Holistic*, Dictionary Definition

> What is the nature of the whole, and what is my nature, and how this is related to that, and what kind of a part it is of what kind of a whole.
> —Marcus Aurelius Antoninus, 167 CE, *Meditations, Book II*

Holistic crime reconstruction is the development of actions and circumstances based on the system of evidence discovered and examined in relation to a particular crime. In this philosophy, all elements of evidence that come to light in a given case are treated as interdependent; the significance of each piece, each action, and each event falls and rises on the backs of the others. More evidence gives rise to more meaning, and less evidence necessarily allows for the resolution of less meaning. The final reconstruction is a function of this system, of how much evidence there is, and whether and how it interrelates and maintains its consistency.

A system of related evidence and any conclusions based thereon are like a mechanical engine or a biological organ, with few if any extraneous parts working judiciously, and in harmony, toward a desired end. If one of the parts fails, then the whole system suffers and may fail. With evidence and its interpretation it is precisely so. Interpretations must be compatible, working in concordance to support each other. Or at the very least not working against each other. Bloodstain pattern interpretations must not contradict the ballistic analysis, trace evidence must not contradict the conclusions of the arson investigator, DNA evidence must not contradict the conclusions of the fingerprint examiner, and so forth. A concordance of the evidence must be apparent. The reason for this is straightforward. Although it can be forgotten in a climate that seeks and rewards certain conclusions (namely the climate of the courts), all science, and even forensic science—

especially forensic science—is grounded in skepticism. It necessarily follows that a finding out of harmony with any of the others in its system should call one or all into question.

ORIGINS: THE FORENSIC GENERALIST

The foundation for holistic crime reconstruction doctrine was introduced more than a century ago, with the 1894 publication of *Handbuch fur Unter-suchungsrichter als System der Kriminalistik (Criminal Investigation: A Practical Textbook for Magistrates, Police Officers and Lawyers)* by the legendary Austrian jurist Dr. Johann (Hans) Baptist Gustav Gross. The goals of this manual were formative and ambitious: to establish principles of scientific investigation and to provide for the birth of the scientific investigator. The manual was a broad success with international appeal, achieving no less than five English editions (1906, 1924, 1934, 1949, and 1962). It also provided the basis for the practical work later undertaken by French scientist Dr. Edmund Locard when he established what is considered to be the world's first police crime laboratory in Lyon, France, in 1910. Despite the passage of time and advances in technology, the philosophies of *System der Kriminalistik* remain a touchstone of forensic knowledge and wisdom to the present day.

The approach to crime reconstruction advocated by Dr. Gross, and subsequent students of his work, was to assign such duties to a scientific investigator—what would be referred to in more modern language as a forensic generalist. The scientific investigator was to be a professional schooled broadly in the subjects of crime, criminals, and the scientific methods of their identification, apprehension, and prosecution. Their role was to understand how the system of evidence and details of a case could be established, how they could be related, and how they could be inter-preted. This holistic method, branded by dispassion and an adherence to science, would ideally free the scientific investigator from the constraints of politics, cronyism, and emotional bias.

The philosophy of Hans Gross was mirrored in many subsequent pub-lished works and aspired to in numerous crime labs throughout the United States.

THE FORENSIC GENERALIST FADES

At present, the forensic generalist is all but a memory and until recently (Turvey, 1999; Inman & Rudin, 2000; Savino & Turvey, 2004) had not made an honest appearance in forensic science textbooks since DeForest,

Gaensslen, and Lee (1983). More curiously, some forensic professionals become angered when generalists are described, let alone remembered. There is more than one reason for the disappearance of the generalist and related professional sensitivity. We focus on the three most apparent: over-specialization, diminished crime lab budgets, and the false paradigm of sides.

THE GROSS FACTS

Forensic generalists and forensic specialists alike are a requirement for informed forensic case examination, laboratory testing, and crime recon-struction to occur. A forensic generalist is a particular kind of forensic sci-entist who is broadly educated and trained in a variety of forensic specialties. They are "big picture" people who can help reconstruct a crime from work performed with the assistance of other forensic scientists and then direct investigators to forensic specialists as needed. They are experts not in all areas, but in the specific area of evidence interpretation. According to DeForest et al. (1983, p. 17),

> Because of the depth and complexity of criminalistics, the need for specialists is inescapable. There can be serious problems, however, with overspecialization. Persons who have a working knowledge of a broad range of criminalistics prob-lems and techniques are also necessary. These people are called generalists. The value of generalists lies in their ability to look at all of the aspects of a complex case and decide what needs to be done, which specialists should be involved, and in which order to carry out the required examinations.

Specialization occurs when a forensic scientist has been trained in a spe-cific forensic subspecialty, such as an area of criminalistics, forensic toxi-cology, forensic pathology, or forensic anthropology. Specialists are an important part of forensic science casework, with an important role to fill. Traditionally, forensic specialists provide the bricks, and forensic generalists have traditionally provided the blueprints.

In the modern forensic system, the majority of forensic scientists have become so specialized in their analytical functions that they are no longer in possession of the gross facts in the cases they work. This is a source of both angst and embarrassment to some crime lab personnel, because they would prefer that their analyses be better informed. Still others would prefer to retain the appearance of overall forensic authority that knowing the full case facts allows. Nowadays, a piece of evidence is brought to a crime lab or examiner, it is examined using a specific method, test, or procedure as the requesting agency dictates, a report of findings is written, and the overall context may or may not be known or even sought. Without the gross facts of a case, and at least some knowledge of assembling them, crime reconstruction cannot occur. Not participating in this process, for lack of skill, time, or invitation, has become a sore point for some in the community of forensic science specialists.

UNDERFUNDED AND UNDERSTAFFED

In terms of money, government crime laboratory budgets nationwide rarely allow for the full suite of forensic specialties, with, for example, trace evidence units vanishing in the shadow of the forensic titan that DNA has become because of its acceptance by the courts. Money, after all, is allocated for those areas of forensic science that the court has embraced. Money is not allocated for areas of forensic science that the court shows disinterest. Also, money for research is often a luxury that cannot be afforded at all.

Furthermore, government labs have faced severe budget and personnel shortages in recent years. There are several interwoven reasons for this. First, the demand for lab services has increased with the growing national profile of forensic science thanks to the popular media. More law enforcement officers are coming to understand that forensic evidence can help their cases, more juries are expecting it at trial, and as a result government crime labs are being asked to do more examinations on more evidence. Second, practice standards in many regions have evolved to meet the needs of crime lab certification. Nationwide, many of the larger government crime labs and lab systems are suffering excruciating independent reviews and scrambling to meet the criteria set by the American Society of Crime Lab Directors Laboratory Accreditation Board (ASCLD/LAB) in order to claim this coveted credential in court. To meet ASCLD/LAB criteria, more of the diminishing lab budget must be spent on quality control, adequate workspace, and adequate evidence tracking and storage. Additionally, each person must complete a proficiency test on each type of evidence he analyzes each year. This slows the amount of time forensic scientists have to work on case material and can, in extreme cases in which there are staff shortages, put the examination of evidence on hold for periods of time. The accreditation process is not easy, and it even requires some labs to simply start over and build entirely new multimillion-dollar facilities. This to say nothing of the requirement to hire more adequately qualified personnel, bringing front and center the problem of too few qualified candidates available with less money to pay them. Additionally, new forensic analytical techniques are not encouraged because they must be "proven methods"—

refinements of methods are not allowed. This works against the intention of the scientific method and stamps out the spark of creativity because many of the past advances in crime lab analysis were the result of "experimentation" with actual case materials and trying something new. Third, the public funding of state crime labs constantly suffers at the hands of wary voters who tend to lack enthusiasm for raising taxes to help fund education, let alone forensic science.

With all of these factors at work, many government crime labs do not have the time, the resources, or the personnel to perform their regular analytical casework. As a consequence, backlogs have mounted in almost all areas of forensic analysis. In this environment, the extra time and commitment required for crime reconstruction is an added expense that becomes difficult for administrators to justify.

THE PARADIGM OF SIDES

The paradigm of sides challenges forensic scientists on two fronts, presenting a false choice in which they are invited to abandon their chosen profession for advocacy. First, there is the obvious division between the prosecution and the defense. More than a few forensic scientists work in an environment that rewards them for thinking and behaving as though there is a morally right side of the courtroom and a morally wrong side of the courtroom. By choosing fidelity to one side of the courtroom over another, the forensic scientist not only loses that which defines science, namely objectivity, but the forensic scientist also presumes a role in court not meant for any expert or witness—that of the trier of fact. It is not the place of the forensic scientist to decide who is worthy of a defense, who is legally or actually guilty, or how they should be punished. These are moral and legal conclusions, which brings us to the second part of the paradigm of sides: the division between scientific fact and legal truth. The forensic scientist is an educator to the court. It is the role of the forensic scientist to establish scientific fact and explain what it means to an investigator, attorney, judge, or jury in the context of a given case. Moreover, the scientific facts should be the same no matter which side the forensic scientist is working for. It is the role of the judge and jury, not the forensic scientist, to form legal conclusions about who is guilty of what, and what the penalty should be based on the totality of evidence.

Although often confused, scientific fact and legal truth are not the same thing. Scientific fact is established through careful examination using the scientific method. Legal truth is determined by the trier of fact, based on available and admissible evidence, as well as their understanding of the law. This is made abundantly clear in cases of wrongful conviction, in which a person may be found legally guilty of a crime without having actually committed it. Juries do not, consequently, determine the ultimate facts of a case, only the legal facts. This distinction becomes important when one considers the roles played in our justice system by directed verdicts, appellate courts, supreme courts, gubernatorial pardons, and DNA exonerations, all of which have the power to influence or overturn a juries estimation of the facts and its final verdict. Subsequently, the abilities of a forensic scientist are not measured in arrests, convictions, or even acquittals, as will be made evident throughout this work. Forensic science, although a servant to court, must serve itself first in order to have any intrinsic value. When science chooses a side other than itself in any conflict or dispute, it is no longer science but advocacy.

The majority of forensic scientists have no trouble understanding the gravity involved in navigating the paradigm of sides on this level and would rather resign from a case or an agency than sacrifice their objectivity and integrity. The true forensic scientist knows that his first onus is to his profession, and that if there is no science, there can be no forensic science.

This community understanding is all well and good until it is remembered that a fair number of forensic scientists work in government crime labs that are housed within, or directly supervised by, police agencies or district attorney's offices. In terms of the actual reconstruction of crime, police and prosecutors are faced with the reality that the scientists they employ may not always agree with their theories regarding a case. In fact, in some instances, the evidentiary findings of the crime lab may hamper or even disprove an important point upon which a police or prosecution theory is built. For some government agencies, this internal evidence-based self-correction is a welcome adjustment to the course of a criminal investigation and any future prosecution. However, history has shown that this is not always so. Not all government crime labs enjoy an open or healthy relationship with their law enforcement and prosecutorial supervisors. Also, a significant number of government agencies remain hesitant to put their scientists in a position in which they can reconstruct the crime in its entirety and then be called by the defense as witnesses against them.

The paradigm of sides presents the forensic scientist with a false choice between prosecution or defense; between scientific fact or legal truth. Pressure to choose can be brought to bear in many ways—personal, professional, and financial. Furthermore, the pressure on a forensic scientist in such environments, to be part of the "team" and help "get the bad guys," can be seductive and overwhelming to the point of assimilation. As discussed later in this book, the rewards for assimilation are great, and the consequences for failing to assimilate can be equally great.

Overspecialization, diminishing budgets, and the paradigm of sides—in such ways the practice and implementation of crime reconstruction has, with some exceptions, faded from many crime labs and been moved into the hands of others.

The authors view this with neither frown nor favor, but rather agree to recognize that it is so; all manner of reconstruction opinions find their way into court from a variety of sources. However, in many instances, it has become clear that scientific reconstructions are being subverted and even intentionally excluded. Consequently, with its departure from the crime lab, the practice of crime reconstruction is in no small danger of losing its footing on the ascending ladder that is the employment of scientific principles to evidence interpretation. Under no circumstance should this situation be acceptable. As such, the need for the development of this textbook becomes apparent.

MODERN CRIME RECONSTRUCTION

Modern forensic science and crime reconstruction is slowly becoming the work of police technicians trained inexpensively through short courses and lectures, as opposed to formally educated forensic scientists shepherded by mentors of quality experience. The difference between the two is significant. Forensic scientists do not just test or examine evidence and then record the results; they are meant to explore, understand, and explain its significance. Thornton (1997, p. 3) provides a succinct and accurate description:

> The single feature that distinguishes forensic scientists from any other scientist is the certain expectation that they will appear in court and testify to their findings and offer an opinion as to the significance of those findings. The forensic scientist will testify not only to what things are, but to what things mean.

This is the very heart of crime reconstruction—not just what, where, and when, but also how and why.

The reconstruction of a crime from physical evidence is the culmination of a long and methodical process. It is the last step in the analytical journey each piece of physical evidence takes from the moment it is recognized at a crime scene. Those steps occur in roughly the same order for each item of evidence:

1. Recognition
2. Preservation

3. Documentation
4. Collection
5. Transportation
6. Identification/classification
7. Comparison
8. Individuation
9. Interpretation/reconstruction

Traditionally, the specific duties are broken down as follows:

Detective/investigator/forensic technician
1. Recognition
2. Preservation

Forensic technician (aka crime scene technician)
3. Documentation
4. Collection
5. Transportation

Forensic scientist/criminalist
6. Identification/classification
7. Comparison
8. Individuation
9. Interpretation/reconstruction

The problem is that these forensic titles and roles are often mixed, misunderstood, or outright confused, sometimes over many generations of professionals in a given system. As a result, forensic job titles abound, with more than one to describe the same set of duties—crime scene investigator, crime scene technician, forensic investigator, evidence technician, forensic technician, laboratory technician, laboratory specialist, forensic specialist, forensic analyst, forensic scientist, criminalist, etc. What is important to remember about titles is that they are administrative and not necessarily suggestive of a particular background, education, training, or expertise. It is the work that defines the professional. It is education, training, experience, and the quality of work products that define expertise.

For the purposes of this text, it is important to become disentangled from this avalanche of jumbled titles and return to classic definitions for the purpose of clarity.

A *technician* is one who is trained in specific procedures, learned by routine or repetition. A forensic technician is trained in the specific procedures related to collecting and even testing evidence found at crime scenes. This is without any need for employing or even understanding the scientific method and the principles of forensic science. This describes the police technicians documenting crime scenes and collecting evidence, and more than a few of the forensic personnel working in government crime labs.

A *scientist* is someone who possesses an academic and clinical understanding of the scientific method and the analytical dexterity to construct experiments that will generate the empirical reality that science mandates. A *forensic scientist* is one who is educated and trained to examine and determine the meaning of physical evidence in accordance with the established principles of forensic science, with the expectation of presenting her findings in court. This describes fewer and fewer of those practicing forensic science in government crime labs.

As the authors have experienced on countless cases, it is technicians, investigators, and ultimately attorneys who are actually providing a majority of crime reconstructions in court, often with little understanding of forensic science or the scientific method, to say nothing of the natural limits of physical evidence. Crime lab personnel are performing any necessary laboratory analysis, but police and prosecutors are taking the final step to explain events and their relationships in court. This has the net effect of elevating the lay testimony of investigators and forensic technicians to that of the forensic scientist and of reducing the expert findings of the forensic scientist to the level of the technician.

Without the proper scientific foundation, technicians and detectives performing crime reconstructions may do so without a sense of what good science is and what constitutes the difference between assumptions, opinions, theories, and facts. To say nothing of failing to understand the actual science beneath the methods or instruments they employ in the search for evidence, a reality that often causes their explanations of false positions and false negatives to be works of useful fiction. In a related fashion, they also tend to fail with regard to grasping the necessity for testing their theories, and for continually attempting to falsify them against the revelations of experimentation and newly developed information. A scientist knows that confirmation of one's theories is easy to find, especially if that is all one seeks. Good science is not about trying to prove one's theories but, rather, working tirelessly to disprove them through falsification (Popper, 1963).

HOLISTIC CRIME RECONSTRUCTION

This textbook is aptly titled *Crime Reconstruction*. It is not a manual intended to explain the technical mechanics of searching or processing crime scenes or to delineate the rote procedures related to instrumental laboratory analysis. There are plenty of texts available that adequately cover these very important considerations, without which reconstruction would be impossible. As already discussed, holistic crime reconstruction is the development of actions and circumstances based on the system of evidence discovered and examined in relation to a particular crime. It is best conceived as the function of a forensic generalist. Our purpose is to educate students and prepare generalist practitioners of the forensic sciences as to the manner in which interpretations regarding evidence may be legitimately achieved and expressed.

As we have suggested, not everyone agrees with the forensic generalist model. One of the philosophical arguments against the generalist is that "one cannot be an expert in everything." As already stated, we do not propose that to perform crime reconstruction one needs to be an expert in all forensic disciplines. We propose that forensic reconstructionists must become an expert in only one: *the interpretation of the evidence in context.* If students wish to pursue further knowledge about examination and analysis in a particular discipline, then there are several excellent publications that are available for that purpose. However, there has never been a textbook devoted only to the interpretation of evidence in context—the proofs, the perils, and the prevarications. Consequently, those studying and performing crime reconstruction have perhaps lacked some advanced measure of informed guidance on the subject. It is our collective goal to assist with filling that void.

Crime reconstruction, to be accurate, must be based on a close scientific examination of the physical evidence and the surrounding environment. These examinations must be the result of applying the scientific method. Interpretations of the meaning of subsequent results must be clearly derived by logic and critical thinking. We will try to explain these concepts so that students can understand that crime reconstruction is not just mere observation and speculation. We will also give students several ways to approach the problem of how reconstruction may be competently performed. Throughout this work we have included reconstruction techniques, interpretation guidelines, and even practice standards.

Also, students will come to appreciate that the crime scene is a dynamic location; it does not remain virginal or static, as a "frozen moment of time," but rather it is constantly subject to change. The greater the time interval between the crime, the documentation, and examination of the scene, the greater the changes may be. These changes we have referred to as *evidence dynamics.* To be ignorant of the problems inherent in the interpretation of the evidence due to evidence dynamics can result in serious misinterpretation errors.

Different areas of physical evidence offer opportunities for reconstruction. Bloodstains, firearms, arson, and trace evidence all contribute to the whole. We have included chapters on each of these types of evidence by some of the leading experts in these fields.

Finally, there are chapters on ethics and expert testimony so that students may understand how to comport themselves professionally and what truly waits for them in the courtroom. The perspectives of the forensic scientist and the attorney are provided. As readers will come to appreciate, these considerations are far from trivial.

It is important for students of forensic science to learn that no one discipline can truly stand alone in a reconstruction. Each form of evidence must be in agreement with the other forms that are present. Each part must be meticulously established and then considered not just on its own but also in its place as part of the greater whole. What is it, how does it fit, and what does it mean in context—these are the questions asked by a reconstructionist.

Given this holistic approach, the authors have come to view reconstruction as the work of one who is sufficiently educated, trained, and experienced to understand the total body of forensic evidence and analysis in a case. That is, again, the forensic generalist. The generalist–reconstructionist, it must be understood, need not know how to perform all of the forensic examinations that were conducted. They need not have the ability to operate a camera to view a photograph; they need not have the ability to extract DNA and amplify it to comprehend a DNA analyst's report; they need not have the ability to perform an autopsy to understand the cause and manner of death, and appreciate the trajectory of the projectiles that passed through the body. Rather, they must be able to understand what the results of forensic examinations are, how they were reached, what they mean, and how they may be integrated to create of picture of events. Integration of findings is key because crime is best reconstructed when forged by a collaboration of the forensic evidence, and not a reliance on one single examination or discipline. To rely on one piece of evidence, or one theory, without placing it in context is not only potentially misleading but also a disservice to the justice system that the forensic scientist ultimately serves. It is our collective hope that this text will be worthy of that service and will assist the next generation of forensic generalists with the difficult tasks that are before them.

REFERENCES

DeForest, P., Gaennslen, R., and Lee, H. (1983). *Forensic science: An introduction to criminalistics.* New York: McGraw-Hill.

Gross, H. (1906). *Criminal investigation*. Madras, India: Ramasawmy Chetty.

Gross, H. (1924). *Criminal investigation*. London: Sweet & Maxwell.

Inman, K., and Rudin, N. (2000). *Principles and practice of criminalistics: The profession of forensic science*. Boca Raton, FL: CRC Press.

Popper, K. (1963). *Conjectures and refutations*. London: Routledge & Keagan Paul.

Thornton, J. (1997). The general assumptions and rationale of forensic identification. In D. L. Faigman, D. H. Kaye, M. J. Saks, and J. Sanders (Eds.), *Modern scientific evidence: The law and science of expert testimony* (Vol. 2). St. Paul, MN: West.

Savino, J., and Turvey, B. (2004). *Rape investigation handbook*. Boston: Elsevier.

Turvey, B. (1999) *Criminal Profiling: An Introduction to Behavioral Evidence Analysis*, London: Elsevier Science.

ACKNOWLEDGMENTS

W. Jerry Chisum

I had great intentions to write a book about crime reconstruction when I retired; I knew I would have lots of time. That is always the thought that nonretirees have; after retirement you wonder how you ever had time to work. I stopped writing on the original project with Academic Press and gave up. Then Brent got me going again and was constantly cajoling and encouraging me to do my parts. He was the driving force behind this book.

The thoughts that I express are not always original. We are all a product of our education and experiences, and every writing reflects contact with many persons. However, there is one person who contributed greatly to my development. Joe Rynearson and I taught law enforcement about evidence and crime reconstruction for 25 years. Joe and I used to have discussions into the wee hours about cases, crime reconstruction, and interpretations. We discovered many myths were existent in the field; however, we never took the time to publish except in the book *Physical Evidence and Crime Scene Reconstruction*, which Joe has rewritten several times. For those discussions and making me think, I thank Joe.

Finally, I must recognize the efforts of my wife, Bona. She would ask me every time I took a break if I had done enough for the day. She pushed me to complete the book this time. She has put up with my behavior for almost 50 years, but this book did take a lot of time and attention away from her.

Thank you Bona, Joe, and Brent.

Brent E. Turvey

In graduate school, we were taught what kinds of evidence to expect, how to find it, how to collect it, and what it meant under the best circumstances. It is an important lesson that in actual casework, seldom are we dealing with evidence under the best circumstances. Working cases, one finds this out rather quickly, and with the same speed reaches out to one's betters for advice.

I was both personally and professionally fortunate that the betters within my reach included Jerry Chisum and John Thornton. It was a privilege to work with John on a number of cases early in my career—watching how far was far enough when working with incomplete and inadequate evidence, as was often the case. It is one thing to read his work, unravel his philosophy, but to participate with him in the reconstructive process, at a scene or around a meeting table, had value that cannot be measured.

It was Jerry, however, who first told me to go back and study the original publications of Hans Gross, cited often in this text as a touchstone of forensic scientific thought. After he retired from the California Department of Justice, it was Jerry who continued to counsel me through difficult evidence and issues in my casework.

At one point in 1998, John asked that Jerry and I meet with him at a restaurant in Monterey to discuss a particular problem in the forensic community—examiners who take the evidence too far, by leaps and bounds. Causes and motives were discussed, from apathy to ignorance to bias. Solutions were discussed as well. For me, this textbook represents our first joint effort to approach any of these issues in a meaningful fashion.

This textbook was rendered for those students and practitioners of forensic science who do not have what I had—who are perhaps newly minted and do not have trusted mentors to call in the late evening hours when entangled by difficult evidence under difficult circumstances. By my count, they are many in number, and they are in need of both information and the permission to use it. These are the professionals whom I wish to acknowledge. If they did not exist, there would be no reason to write this book.

To the contributors of this work, I say that this was a job well done and an important service to the forensic science community. We can all be proud of the final result. We can all share the credit for this tremendous accomplishment. What we have done will serve our students for years to come.

Most important, I express the feelings that I have for my friends and colleagues, who shepherded me through the governance of this project: Jerry Chisum, John Thornton, Eoghan Casey, Michael McGrath, Wayne Petherick, and Craig Cooley. Without these individuals of tremendous heart, intellect, and ability in my work and in my life, this textbook could not have happened. It is the most important thing I have done in my entire professional career, and I am grateful that we came together to make it happen.

ABOUT THE AUTHORS

EOGHAN CASEY, MA

Eoghan Casey investigates network intrusions, intellectual property theft, and other computer-related crimes and has extensive experience analyzing and interpreting digital evidence. He has assisted law enforcement in a wide range of criminal investigations, including homicide, child exploitation, cyberstalking, and larceny. He also has extensive information security experience. As an information security officer at Yale University from 1999 to 2002, and in subsequent consulting work, he performed vulnerability assessments; deployed and maintained intrusion detection systems, firewalls, and public key infrastructures; and developed policies, procedures, and educational programs. He has written numerous articles and is the author of *Digital Evidence and Computer Crime: Forensic Science, Computers, and the Internet* (2nd ed.); editor of *Handbook of Computer Crime Investigation: Forensic Tools and Technology*; and coauthor of *Investigating Child Exploitation and Pornography: The Internet, Law and Forensic Science* (all published by Elsevier). He is currently Senior Consultant and Computer Forensic Examiner with Stroz-Freidberg.

W. JERRY CHISUM, BS

William Jerry Chisum has been a criminalist since 1960. He studied under Dr. Paul L. Kirk at U.C. Berkeley, worked in San Bernardino, and set up the Kern County Laboratory in Bakersfield. After joining the California Dept. of Justice, he took a leave of absence (1971–73) to work at Stanford Research Institute. He has been President of the California Association of Criminalists three times, and has also served as President of the American Society of Crime Lab Directors. In October of 1998, he retired from 37 years of public service but continues working as a private consultant.

In addition to practicing as a criminalist, he spent 25 years teaching law enforcement with National Crime Investigation and Training in several states. He also taught forensic scientists at California State University,

Sacramento and the California Criminalistics Institute. He has lectured/taught in England, Taiwan, Australia, and Tanzania. He has several publications in journals and books on Forensic Science.

CRAIG M. COOLEY, MS, JD

In 2000, Craig Cooley received his MS in forensic science from the University of New Haven–Sacramento. He was subsequently accepted to DePaul University College of Law in Chicago. He worked his way through law school as an investigator with the Office of the State Appellate Defenders Death Penalty Trial Assistance Division from 2001 to 2004. After receiving much acclaim for his published research on forensic science, miscarriages of justice, and forensic reform, he went on to receive his JD from the Northwestern University School of Law in 2004. He then passed the bar exam and went to work for the Capital Habeas Unit of the Law Offices of the Federal Public Defender in Harrisburg, Pennsylvania. He is currently Assistant Federal Defender with the Federal Public Defenders' Capital Habeas Unit for the District of Nevada (Las Vegas-CHU).

RAYMOND J. DAVIS, BS

Raymond J. Davis is a forensic scientist with 33 years of experience in general criminalistics, and he holds a degree in chemistry from California State University, Sacramento. He has testified in more than 1600 criminal and civil cases throughout the states of California, Washington, Alaska, and Oregon. He has worked in both private and public sector laboratories. He is the author and presenter of the "Courtroom Presentation of Evidence" training classes offered throughout the United States since 1988. He retired from the Department of Justice Jan Bashinski DNA Laboratory in Richmond, California, and currently lives in Eagle, Idaho.

JOHN D. DeHAAN, PhD

Dr. John D. DeHaan has been a criminalist for more than 32 years. He has worked at county, state, and federal forensic labs. He is a native of Chicago and has a bachelor of science degree in physics from the University of Illinois at Chicago. He has been involved with fire and explosion investigations for more than 30 years and has authored dozens of papers on fires, explosions, and their investigation and analysis. He is best known as the author of the textbook *Kirk's Fire Investigation* (now in its sixth edition). He has a doctorate from the University of Strathclyde in Glasgow, Scotland, with a dissertation on the reconstruction of fires involving flammable liquids. He is a member of the National Fire Protection Association (NFPA), and served on its 921 Technical Committee from 1991 to 1999. He is also a member of the International Association of Arson Investigators (IAAI) and serves on its Forensic Science Committee. He holds a diploma in fire investigation from the Forensic Science Society (United Kingdom) and one from the Institution of Fire Engineers (United Kingdom). He is a fellow of the American Board of Criminalistics in Fire Debris Analysis and a member of the Institution of Fire Engineers. He retired from the California Department of Justice in December 1998 and is now the president of Fire-Ex Forensics, Incorporated, based in Vallejo, California. He continues to consult on fire and explosion cases throughout the United States, Canada, and overseas.

DONNA KIMMEL-LAKE

Donna Kimmel-Lake is an evidence specialist and crime scene investigator with the Napa, California, Sheriff's Department, having previously served in that capacity with the Contra Costa County, California, Sheriff's Department. She has 17 years of experience in crime scene processing, from the most trivial crimes to the most complex homicides. She is active in teaching and in International Association for Identification matters. She is the founder of the Crime Scene Investigators of California study group. She directs the Napa County Evidence Laboratory.

BRUCE R. MORAN, BS

Bruce R. Moran is a criminalist/firearms examiner in the Criminalistics Unit of the Sacramento County District Attorney's Laboratory of Forensic Services in Sacramento, California. He is a recognized expert in firearm and toolmark examination and crime scene investigation/reconstruction, and he currently serves as a team leader on the Crime Scene Response Unit. He has practiced in the forensic science field in California for more than 29 years. He holds a bachelor of science degree in forensic science and a minor in chemistry from California State University, Sacramento. He earned ABC Diplomate status in 1990. He has a broad background in the forensic sciences but has special interest in firearms examination and crime scene investigation and reconstruction. He is a Distinguished Member of the Association of Firearm and Toolmark Examiners and is an active member of the International Association for Crime Scene Reconstruction. He is also a member of the California Association of Criminalists, the International

Association of Blood Pattern Analysts, and a Life Member of the International Association for Identification. He has provided training for forensic scientists, law enforcement professionals, and prosecuting and defense attorneys in the field of general criminalistics, crime scene investigation/reconstruction, and firearm and toolmark identification and served as an adjunct professor at California State University, Sacramento, in 1997 and the University of New Haven forensic science masters program in 2000. He has also presented papers and workshops on these topics at professional meetings in the United States, Europe, and Asia. He has served since 1993 as an instructor for the Department of Justice–California Criminalistics Institute in Sacramento on the topics of firearm and toolmark examination and identification, and he has been a forensic subject matter expert/consultant for the Cold Case Homicide Investigation course offered by the California Department of Justice–Advanced Training Center since 2000.

JOHN I. THORNTON, PhD

Dr. John I. Thornton is Emeritus Professor of Forensic Science at the University of California at Berkeley. He is board certified in criminalistics. He has 20 years of experience in operational crime laboratories. He has participated in crime scene processing and crime reconstruction in cases from Hawaii to Massachusetts and Alaska to Florida. He has taught physical evidence methods in Colombia, India, Mexico, Israel, and China. He has served as president of the California Association of Criminalists, chairman of the Criminalistics Section of the American Academy of Forensic Sciences, and chairman of the Ethics Committee of the California Association of Criminalists.

BRENT E. TURVEY, MS

Brent E. Turvey spent his first years in college on a pre-med track only to change his course of study once his true interest took hold. He received a Bachelor of Science degree from Portland State University in Psychology, with an emphasis on Forensic Psychology, and an additional Bachelor of Science degree in History. He went on to receive his Masters of Science in Forensic Science after studying at the University of New Haven, in West Haven, Connecticut.

Since graduating in 1996, Brent has consulted with many agencies, attorneys, and police departments in the United States, Australia, China, Canada,

Barbados and Korea on a range of rapes, homicides, and serial/multiple rape/death cases, as a forensic scientist and criminal profiler. He has also been court qualified as an expert in the areas of criminal profiling, forensic science, victimology, and crime reconstruction.

In August of 2002, he was invited by the Chinese People's Police Security University (CPPSU) in Beijing to lecture before groups of detectives at the Beijing, Wuhan, Hanzou, and Shanghai police bureaus. In 2005, he was invited back to China again, to lecture at the CPPSU, and to the police in Beijing and X'ian.

He is the author of *Criminal Profiling: An Introduction to Behavioral Evidence Analysis, 2nd Edition*, which has been translated into Chinese and adopted by their police services for training at the CPPSU. He is also co-author of the *Rape Investigation Handbook* (2004) with Det. John O. Savino of the New York Police Department's Manhattan Special Victim Squad. He continues in private practice as a Forensic Scientist, Criminal Profiler, and Instructor with Forensic Solutions, LLC.

CHAPTER 1

A HISTORY OF CRIME
RECONSTRUCTION

W. Jerry Chisum, BS and Brent E. Turvey, MS

The palest ink is better than the best memory.
—Chinese Proverb

The present reaps what the past has sown, and the future is
the product of the present.
—Buddha

There are few disciplines whose labors are as culturally resonant as those of
the historian. Without the historian, we would lose track of everything we
have been, errors and achievements alike, and become entrenched hope-
lessly in an immediate, immature culture that lacks sufficient foundation to
learn or grow. That is to say, without the historian we risk losing our history
and we compromise the value of our future. We are forever condemned to
making the same errors we have made in the past. The historian allows us
to learn from our experience and build upon it.

History, the chronicling and study of past events, is a quiet but feared
discipline. History reminds us where our knowledge and wisdom came from
when we lose sight of those who cut the path. History teaches us what has
been lost to fire and fancy, despite conquering or dominant ideologies that
would leave us ignorant of all that came before. History collects, history
records, and history remembers. And it patiently waits for unsatisfied minds
to discover it.

From this it may be rightly inferred that the purpose of studying history
is not to learn dry facts for later academic recitation in order to appear intellectual. The study of history is about going back to see what has come before
in order to honestly gauge where we are right now and, it is hoped, why.
The study of history is about digging beneath and beyond cultural and institutional indoctrination because what you know, and what you've been told,
are not always so.

The study of history is for critical thinkers—those who will not
blindly and politely accept what they have been handed by someone claiming to be an authority. It is for those who would rather come to understand
things and their relationships for themselves. It is for those who understand

the value of hunting down information and sourcing it out, and who would prefer not to be led by the hand into intellectual servitude. It is a bold and dangerous journey that can educate, inspire, and inflame a lifetime of study.

Crime reconstruction is the determination of the actions and events surrounding the commission of a crime. A reconstruction may be accomplished by using the statements of witnesses, the confession of a suspect, the statement of a living victim, or by the examination and interpretation of physical evidence. Some refer to this process as crime scene reconstruction; however, the scene is not actually being put back together as it was; only some of the actions and sequences of events are being established. When working at the evidentiary level, this is in no small part because of the natural limits to what forensic science is capable of. Consequently, the term crime scene reconstruction is at best an inaccurate description of what forensic science is actually able to contribute to the cause of justice.

Some go further and confuse crime reconstruction with the specific task of *crime scene processing* and the overall field of *crime scene investigation*. As we have discussed, and will explain further in other chapters, these are not the same thing. Suffice it to say that reconstruction is performed by forensic scientists and is based on the evidence processing that is done at the scene, the results of the scene investigation, and the subsequent analysis of physical evidence.

Ardent scholars will attest that there can be no one definitive history of any subject, and crime reconstruction is not an exception. Crime reconstruction has many components, many practitioners, and many students. Every reconstruction specialty has a history of practitioners; every practitioner has a history of students; every student has a history to discover and study.

The purpose of this chapter is to examine a history of crime reconstruction from the view of the forensic generalist, as described in the Preface. The generalist understands that crime reconstruction is the result of objectively examining a whole related system of evidence rather than a narrow, specialized portion. Not just the evidence as it was found in the scene but also the results of all subsequent forensic examinations. Not just the technical process of collecting of bits and pieces with tape and spray but also the methodical, scientific examination of evidentiary relationships, their origins, and their ultimate meaning within the case. The generalist considers the totality of the known evidence and only then frames theories regarding the actions and circumstances of a crime, steered by good science and the scientific method and with no investment in the outcome. The generalist then tests those theories and the theories of others against the evidence, using a framework of analytical logic and critical thinking in order to determine the facts.

From this perspective, there are certain individuals whose work, theories, and publications are of considerable and particular value to understanding the history of crime reconstruction, not to mention their enormous contribution to the other professions inhabiting the various forensic disciplines. Deliberate students are strongly encouraged to make use of the references at the end of this chapter and explore more of the details of this limited history for themselves.

DR. JOSEPH E. BELL (1837–1911)

> From close observation and deduction, gentlemen, you can make a correct diagnosis of any and every case. However, never neglect to ratify your deductions, to substantiate your diagnosis with the stethoscope, and by other recognized and every-day methods of diagnosis.
>
> —Dr. Joseph Bell (as quoted in Freeman, 2004)

Dr. Joseph Emory Bell (Fig. 1.1) was a surgeon at the Royal Infirmary and a professor at the University of Edinburgh Medical School during the 19th century. He reportedly had a great facility for both observation and inference with regard to assessing patients in his keep. As the previous quote

Figure 1.1
Dr. Joseph E. Bell.

indicates, he also believed in testing theories and what can only be described as the scientific method where final conclusions were concerned. The discipline of careful observation and inference is one that he religiously impressed upon his students.

The following account of Dr. Bell is set forth in an essay by Dr. Harold Emery Jones (1904):

> All Edinburgh medical students remember Joseph Bell—Joe Bell—as they called him. Always alert, always up and doing, nothing ever escaped that keen eye of his. He read both patients and students like so many open books. His diagnosis was almost never at fault.
>
> "This, gentlemen" announced [Professor Bell], "contains a very potent drug. To the taste it is intensely bitter. It is most offensive to the sense of smell. But I want you to test it by smell and taste; and, as I don't ask anything of my students which I wouldn't be willing to do myself, I will taste it before passing it round."
>
> Here he dipped his finger in the liquid, and placed it in his mouth. The tumbler was passed round. With wry and sour faces the students followed the Professor's lead. One after another tasted the liquid; varied and amusing were the grimaces made. The tumbler, having gone the round, was returned to the Professor.
>
> "Gentlemen," said he, with a laugh, "I am deeply grieved to find that not one of you has developed this power of perception, which I so often speak about; for if you watched me closely, you would have found that, while I placed my forefinger in the medicine, it was the middle finger which found its way into my mouth."

Dr. Bell was an accomplished lecturer, served as the personal surgeon to the Queen when she visited Scotland, and published several medical textbooks in his lifetime. However, he is perhaps best remembered for the association he enjoyed with one of his students, Sir Arthur Conan Doyle, author and creator of the fictional character Sherlock Holmes. Dr. Bell, who wrote the foreword for at least one of the Sherlock Holmes adventures, is widely regarded as the primary inspiration for that fictional character and his uncanny deductive abilities.

Arthur Conan Doyle first met then 39-year-old Dr. Joseph Bell in his capacity as a lecturer in 1877. It was Doyle's first year of medical school. By the end of Doyle's second year, Dr. Bell selected him to serve as a clerk on his ward at the Royal Infirmary in Edinburgh. Reflecting later on the inspiration for Holmes, his scientifically inclined protagonist, Doyle (1989) wrote:

> I thought of my teacher Joe Bell, of his eagle face, of his curious ways, of his eerie trick of spotting details. If he were a detective he would surely reduce the fascinating unorganized business [of detective work] to something nearer an exact

science. I would try [to see] if I could get this effect. It was surely possible in real life, so why should I not make it plausible in fiction? It is all very well to say that a man is clever, but the reader wants to see examples of this—such examples as Bell gave us every day in the wards. The idea amused me.

Of the Sherlock Holmes stories, and of Arthur Conan Doyle in specific, Dr. Bell wrote with some pride:

Dr. Conan Doyle has made a well-deserved success for his detective stories, and made the name of his hero beloved by the boys of this country by the marvelous cleverness of his method. He shows how easy it is, if only you can observe, to find out a great deal as to the works and ways of your innocent and unconscious friends, and, by an extension of the same method, to baffle the criminal and lay bare the manner of his crime. There is nothing new under the sun.

Dr. Bell's method of medical diagnosis was in essence a reconstruction of ailment by careful observation of behavior and symptoms, an encyclopedic knowledge of disease, and a tireless study of the habits of men. The chief lesson to his students was attention to all details at all times, and scrupulous ratification of theories through a firsthand investigation of fact. This, among other things, inspired Conan Doyle to develop what may be referred to as the Holmesian method of crime reconstruction.

At this point it is perhaps necessary to concede that some may regard the inclusion of a fiction writer and his mentor in any history of crime reconstruction as an error in judgment, but this is not the case. The situation is not comparable to modern-day authors, where pulp novels and nonfiction true crime are spun out to horrify readers and glorify crimes and criminality. These were professionals, educated in all that medicine and science had to offer in their day. Each Sherlock Holmes story was a carefully crafted lesson in the application of science and deductive reasoning, with cases solved by investigative ability and attention to detail. The error would be failing to admit their direct and inspirational roles in forensic history, as we will explore further.

SIR ARTHUR CONAN DOYLE (1859–1930)

Crime is common. Logic is rare.
—Sherlock Holmes in *The Adventure of the Copper Beeches*

Arthur Conan Doyle (Fig. 1.2) was born in Edinburgh on May 22, 1859. He received a Jesuit education and then went on to study medicine at the

Figure 1.2

Dr. Arthur Conan Doyle as a young man.

University of Edinburgh Medical School under Dr. Joseph Bell in 1877. Throughout his education, he enjoyed good stories and reading, and he was inspired by authors such as Edgar Alan Poe and Bret Harte. During his second year at medical school, while working as an assistant for Dr. Bell, he was able to pen no fewer than two short stories of his own for publication— *The Mystery of Sasassa Valley* and *The American Tale*.

While in his third year at medical school, Doyle was offered the post of ship's surgeon on the Hope, a whaling boat on its way to the Arctic Circle. He took the position and followed the crew to Greenland, where they hunted for seals. A young man in his early twenties, he was disgusted by the brutality of it. However, he was fascinated and thrilled by the whale hunt that followed, to the point of later writing a story integrating his experiences called the *Captain of the Pole-Star.*

In 1880, he returned to medical school and completed his studies a year later, receiving a bachelor of medicine and master of surgery degree. After a difficult beginning marked by near bankruptcy, Dr. Arthur Conan Doyle's hard work eventually paid off and his private practice began to earn him a comfortable living.

In 1886, Conan Doyle split his time between his medical practice and his writing of the first story that was to launch the fictional career of Sherlock

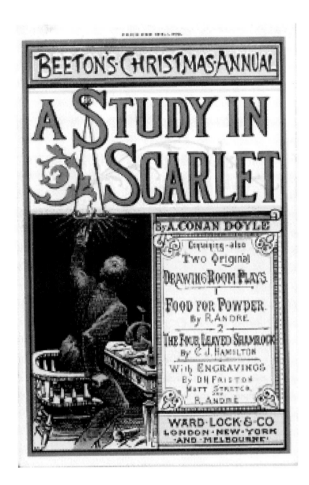

Figure 1.3

A Study in Scarlet, published in November 1887 as the main part of Beeton's Christmas Annual.

Holmes, *A Study in Scarlet*, published in 1887 (Fig. 1.3). It has been widely theorized that the name "Sherlock Holmes" was chosen based on the American jurist and fellow doctor of medicine, Oliver Wendell Holmes, and Alfred Sherlock, a prominent violinist.

In *A Study in Scarlet*, through the character of Dr. John Watson, Conan Doyle outlined the evidence-based method of inference and deduction that would become the defining element of Sherlock Holmes' fictional reconstruction casework (Doyle, 1887):

> Like all other arts, the Science of Deduction and Analysis is one which can only be acquired by long and patient study, nor is life long enough to allow any mortal to attain the highest possible perfection in it. Before turning to those moral and mental aspects of the matter which present the greatest difficulties, let the inquirer begin by mastering more elementary problems. Let him, on meeting a fellow-mortal, learn at a glance to distinguish the history of the man, and the trade or

profession to which he belongs. Puerile as such an exercise may seem, it sharpens the faculties of observation, and teaches one where to look and what to look for. By a man's finger-nails, by his coat-sleeve, by his boots, by his trouser-knees, by the callosities of his forefinger and thumb, by his expression, by his shirt-cuffs—by each of these things a man's calling is plainly revealed. That all united should fail to enlighten the competent inquirer in any case is almost inconceivable.

Of this first effort by Conan Doyle, the British author David Stuart Davies (2004) wrote regarding the nature of the evidence-based inferences within:

Doyle establishes Holmes' mystifying detective brilliance in the early pages... Sherlock Holmes is more than just an armchair observer. He actively pursues clues in a dynamic manner which characterizes all his subsequent investigations. In addition to engaging in analytical reasoning, he studies the wheel marks of a hansom cab, examines elaborate patterns of footprints, identifies cigar ash, flings himself to the ground in search of clues, and in the end engages in a step by step summary of his methods—a staged finale that became an indispensable element of the mystery story format. In this novel, amongst his other habits and traits, we learn of Holmes' violin playing—"Low melancholy wailings"—his chemical experiments and his love of strong tobacco.

Conan Doyle's protagonist also held fast to the principle of eliminating unnecessary bias and reducing preconceived theories in reconstructions. Through Holmes, he chastised those impatient for results in the absence of evidence (Doyle, 1887):

My companion was in the best of spirits, and prattled away about Cremona fiddles and the difference between a Stradivarius and an Amati. As for myself, I was silent, for the dull weather and the melancholy business upon which we were engaged depressed my spirits.

"You don't seem to give much thought to the matter in hand," I said at last, interrupting Holmes's musical disquisition.

"No data yet," he answered. "It is a capital mistake to theorize before you have all the evidence. It biases the judgment."

The second Sherlock Holmes story, *The Sign of the Four*, was written for *Lippincott's Magazine*, and other subsequent stories were written for *The Strand Magazine*. In carefully woven plots, Conan Doyle continually referenced observation, logic, and dispassion as invaluable to the detection of scientific facts, the reconstruction of crime, and the establishment of legal truth. In *The Sign of the Four*, Sherlock Holmes gave further voice to Conan

Doyle's understanding and appreciation of scientific objectivity (Doyle, 1890):

> Detection is, or ought to be, an exact science and should be treated in the same cold and unemotional manner. You have attempted to tinge it with romanticism, which produces much the same effect as if you worked a love-story or an elopement into the fifth proposition of Euclid.

Conan Doyle specifically referred to the concept of "reconstructing the events," or the crime, in more than a few of his stories. In these stories, there was a heavy emphasis on establishing or refuting suspect statements with physical evidence. For example, in "The Crooked Man," a conversation takes place between Holmes and Watson that describes a Socratic style of theory elimination through observation, scientific examination, and discussion (Doyle, 1893):

> Holmes pulled a large sheet of tissue-paper out of his pocket and carefully unfolded it upon his knee.
>
> "What do you make of that?" he asked.
>
> The paper was covered with the tracings of the footmarks of some small animal. It had five well-marked footpads, an indication of long nails, and the whole print might be nearly as large as a dessert-spoon.
>
> "It's a dog," said I.
>
> "Did you ever hear of a dog running up a curtain? I found distinct traces that this creature had done so."
>
> "A monkey, then?"
>
> "But it is not the print of a monkey."
>
> "What can it be, then?"
>
> "Neither dog nor cat nor monkey nor any creature that we are familiar with. I have tried to reconstruct it from the measurements. Here are four prints where the beast has been standing motionless. You see that it is no less than fifteen inches from fore-foot to hind. Add to that the length of neck and head, and you get a creature not much less than two feet long—probably more if there is any tail. But now observe this other measurement. The animal has been moving, and we have the length of its stride. In each case it is only about three inches. You have an indication, you see, of a long body with very short legs attached to it. It has not been considerate enough to leave any of its hair behind it. But its general shape must be what I have indicated, and it can run up a curtain, and it is carnivorous."

Later, in "The Abbey Grange," Holmes reconstructs a crime for Watson based on the careful observation of tool marks and bloodstain patterns (Doyle, 1904):

"Man, Watson, man. Only one, but a very formidable person. Strong as a lion—witness the blow that bent that poker! Six foot three in height, active as a squirrel, dexterous with his fingers, finally, remarkably quick-witted, for this whole ingenious story is of his concoction. Yes, Watson, we have come upon the handiwork of a very remarkable individual. And yet, in that bell-rope, he has given us a clue which should not have left us a doubt."

"Where was the clue?"

"Well, if you were to pull down a bell-rope, Watson, where would you expect it to break? Surely at the spot where it is attached to the wire. Why should it break three inches from the top, as this one has done?"

"Because it is frayed there?"

"Exactly. This end, which we can examine, is frayed. He was cunning enough to do that with his knife. But the other end is not frayed. You could not observe that from here, but if you were on the mantelpiece you would see that it is cut clean off without any mark of fraying whatever. You can reconstruct what occurred. The man needed the rope. He would not tear it down for fear of giving the alarm by ringing the bell. What did he do? He sprang up on the mantelpiece, could not quite reach it, put his knee on the bracket—you will see the impression in the dust—and so got his knife to bear upon the cord. I could not reach the place by at least three inches—from which I infer that he is at least three inches a bigger man than I. Look at that mark upon the seat of the oaken chair! What is it?"

"Blood."

"Undoubtedly it is blood. This alone puts the lady's story out of court. If she were seated on the chair when the crime was done, how comes that mark? No, no, she was placed in the chair after the death of her husband. I'll wager that the black dress shows a corresponding mark to this. We have not yet met our Waterloo, Watson, but this is our Marengo, for it begins in defeat and ends in victory. I should like now to have a few words with the nurse, Theresa. We must be wary for a while, if we are to get the information which we want."

Dr. Joseph Bell would go on to write of the Sherlock Holmes character, and of the importance of acumen facilitated by science:

Mere acuteness of the senses is not enough. Your Indian tracker will tell you that the footprint on the leaves was not a redskin's, but a paleface's, because it marked a shoe-print, but it needs an expert in shoe-leather to tell where that shoe was made. A sharp-eyed detective may notice the thumb-mark of a grimy or bloody hand on the velvet or the mirror, but it needs all the scientific knowledge of a Galton to tender the ridges and furrows of the stain visible and permanent, and then to identify by their sign-manual the suspected thief or murderer. Sherlock Holmes has acute senses, and the special education and information that make these valuable; and he can afford to let us into the secrets of his method.

Seventy years after the creation of the Holmes character, Jurgen Thorwald would reflect on Conan Doyle's hero as the prototypical generalist (Thorwald, 1966, p. 234):

> Sherlock Holmes was the harbinger of a kind of criminological investigation which did not fit into any of these special [forensic] disciplines, and which ultimately far surpassed them in range. What Holmes did was to avail himself of all the chemical, biological, physical, and technological methods which were springing up at the turn of the century.

Not unlike like the intense proliferation of popular forensic science oriented television programs today, the public became enamored with the stories and the character and could not get enough of either. The intense international success of the Sherlock Holmes series eventually became a great burden for Conan Doyle. Ironically, he felt the stories were too commercial, and he wished to be remembered for more serious works. With great hope for closing this chapter of his life and moving on to other challenges, Conan Doyle killed off the Sherlock Holmes character in *The Final Problem*, which was published in late 1893. As a consequence, it has been reported that approximately 20,000 readers cancelled their subscriptions to *The Strand.*

Several years later, during the Boer War, Conan Doyle volunteered and served as a doctor at a field hospital in Bloemfontein, South Africa. There he learned of death from war and disease firsthand. Subsequently, he wrote *The Great Boer War*, a 500-page chronicle published in October 1900. It was a report of the state of the war and also a commentary on the organizational shortcomings of the British forces.

After the war, Conan Doyle took stock and wrote a new Sherlock Holmes story, a prequel called *The Hound of the Baskervilles*. It was published in August 1901 and was an instant international success. In 1902, King Edward VII knighted Conan Doyle ostensibly for services rendered to the Crown during the Boer War. However, it has long been rumored that the king, an avid fan of Sherlock Holmes, bestowed the honor on Conan Doyle as a reward for stories told and with the hope of more stories to come.

Sir Arthur Conan Doyle (Fig. 1.4) did not disappoint his fans. In 1903, he brought Sherlock Holmes back to life in a new series of stories beginning with *The Return of Sherlock Holmes.*

Sir Arthur Conan Doyle's work with fictional crime fighting did not just entertain and inspire others, although that would have been enough to heavily influence the forensic sciences, specifically crime reconstruction, forever; it also had practical applications in his own work outside of writing

Figure 1.4

Sir Arthur Conan Doyle.

and medicine. Conan Doyle, it is often forgotten, was a chief architect of the concept of post-conviction case review in the early 20th century and a firm believer in overturning miscarriages of justice.

This included the case of George Edalji, an Indian who had been wrongly convicted of mutilating and killing sheep, cows, and horses. In 1903, someone was inflicting long, shallow cuts to these animals in the Great Wyrley area of the United Kingdom, under cover of night, causing them to bleed to death. Anonymous letters were written to the police, taunting them and identifying the offender as George Edalji, a local Indian solicitor. Edalji was arrested and a trial was held. He was found guilty and he was sentenced to seven years in prison. However, there was a public outcry that an injustice had been done and that Edalji had been framed for reasons of race. Ten thousand people signed a petition protesting the conviction, demanding his release from prison. As a result, he served only three years, but the conviction stood.

In 1906, Sir Arthur Conan Doyle learned of the Edalji case, became deeply concerned about the circumstances of the conviction, and set about to examine the facts for himself. The forensic evidence and the context of the crimes all pointed away from Edalji's involvement, and Sir Arthur Conan Doyle became determined to educate the public. The British government took notice in more ways than one ("The George Edalji Case," 2005):

As he reviewed the facts it seemed to Conan Doyle that the evidence was overwhelming. Edalji was innocent. The bloody razors found in the Edalji home were later discovered to be merely rusty razors. The handwriting expert who testified that Edalji's handwriting matched the writing on the taunting letters was discovered to have made a serious mistake on another case causing an innocent man to be convicted. The mud on George's boots was of a different soil type than that of the field where the last mutilation took place. The killings and letters continued after Edalji was prosecuted.

And then there was the final piece of evidence that Conan Doyle gathered. The evidence that he saw in an instant the first time he set eyes on George Edalji. Conan Doyle stated, "He had come to my hotel by appointment, but I had been delayed, and he was passing the time by reading the paper. I recognized my man by his dark face, so I stood and observed him. He held the paper close to his eyes and rather sideways, proving not only a high degree of myopia, but marked astigmatism. The idea of such a man scouring fields at night and assaulting cattle while avoiding the watching police was ludicrous. . . . There, in a single physical defect, lay the moral certainty of his innocence."

Conan Doyle wrote a series of articles for the *Daily Telegraph* about the Edalji case. He outlined everything in great detail. These articles caught the public's attention and that caught the attention of the British government. At that time there was no procedure for a retrial so a there was a private committee meeting to consider the matter. In the spring of 1907 the committee decided that Edalji was innocent of the mutilations, but still found him guilty of writing the anonymous letters.

Conan Doyle found anything less than a finding of innocent on all charges a miscarriage of justice, however the decision made a huge difference for Edalji. The Law Society readmitted him. Edalji was once again able to practice as a solicitor.

It is important to note that partially as a result of this case the Court of Criminal Appeal was established in 1907. So not only did Conan Doyle help George Edalji, his work helped to establish a way to correct other miscarriages of justice.

It should be remembered that when he discovered the likely culprit in the crimes (a school student and butcher's apprentice) and made it known, Conan Doyle began to receive anonymous threatening letters.

Also, the panel that was eventually appointed to investigate Conan Doyle's new evidence in the Edalji case was made up of three commissioners, one of whom was a cousin to the original lead investigator. Conan Doyle was disgusted by their slander of Edalji and their collusion to protect each other's reputations even while being forced to pardon him for crimes he clearly had not committed. Conan Doyle's involvement with the Edalji case left him more than a little jaded, to say the least.

In 1909, a German named Oscar Slater was tried and convicted in Edinburgh for murdering an elderly woman named Marion Gilchrist with a hammer the year before. Miss Gilchrist had been bludgeoned to death, her personal papers had been rifled through, and a diamond brooch had been stolen. That case came to Conan Doyle's attention as well, and once again he was compelled to investigate. What he learned did not require much deduction, only observation and the force of indefatigable publicity ("The Oscar Slater Case," 2005):

> While it was true that Slater did possess a small hammer it wasn't large enough to inflict the type of wounds that Miss Gilchrist had sustained. Conan Doyle stated that a medical examiner at the crime scene declared that a large chair, dripping with blood, seemed to be the murder weapon.
>
> Conan Doyle also concluded that Miss Gilchrist had opened the door to her murderer herself. He surmised that she knew the murderer. Despite the fact that Miss Gilchrist and Oscar Slater lived near one another, they had never met.
>
> *The Case of Oscar Slater* caused some demand for a new trial. However the authorities said the evidence didn't justify that the case be reopened. In 1914 there were more calls for a retrial. New evidence had come to light. Another witness was found that could verify Slater's whereabouts during the time of the crime. Also, it was learned that before Helen Lambie [Gilchist's only servant] named Slater as the man she'd seen in the hallway the day of the murder she had given the police another name. Unbelievably, the officials decided to let the matter rest.
>
> Conan Doyle was outraged. "How the verdict could be that there was no fresh cause for reversing the conviction is incomprehensible. The whole case will, in my opinion, remain immortal in the classics of crime as the supreme example of official incompetence and obstinacy."

The matter probably would have ended there in 1914, but in 1925 a message from Oscar Slater was smuggled out of Peterhead Prison, addressed directly to Conan Doyle. In it, he begged Conan Doyle not to forget his case and also to make one last effort to free him. Reinvigorated, Conan Doyle began lobbying once more, writing everyone he knew in the media and government.

As a result of the renewed interest, an investigative journalist in Glasgow named William Park published a book about the case that brought public interest in the Slater case to a fever pitch. The story was in every news-paper. Helen Lambie was subsequently sought out and found living in the United States; she then confessed during an interview that she had actually known the real murderer, just as Conan Doyle had suggested years before. She further confessed that the police had talked her out of this initial iden-tification and persuaded her she was mistaken. In short, she confessed to falsely accusing Oscar Slater of a crime she knew he did not commit to protect someone of her acquaintance who she refused to name.

Mary Barrowman, a 14-year-old girl at the time of the murder who claimed she bumped into a man under a lamppost running from Gilchrist's apartment on the day of the murder, also came forward. She confessed that she had, under some pressure by police, tailored her eyewitness identifica-tion to match the accused.

In 1927, having been contacted by Conan Doyle, the secretary of state for Scotland ordered the release of Oscar Slater. Eventually, an appeal was granted. However, officials still refused to admit to any wrongdoing and would not suggest corruption or blame other officials for any breakdowns or wrongdoing. Slater's conviction was ultimately overturned on a techni-cality, allowing the authorities to save face. According to Gildart and Howell (2004, p. 3),

Arthur Conan Doyle had always been convinced of Slater's innocence. An inquiry into the verdict in 1914 had upheld the original decision, but in 1927 Conan Doyle sent to [Prime Minister J. Ramsay] MacDonald a copy of a newly published book by William Park, *The Truth about Oscar Slater*. This suggested both the weakness of the prosecution's case and that the police had suppressed inconvenient evidence. Discussions between MacDonald and the secretary of state for Scotland, Sir John Gilmour, preceded Slater's release on 15 November 1927. The Court of Criminal Appeal for Scotland had only been inaugurated the preceding year and had no power to deal with cases that predated its foundation. However a single-clause bill was passed that permitted Slater to appeal [championed by Arthur Conan Doyle]. [Lord Craig Mason] Aitchison appeared for Slater before the High Court of Jus-ticiary in July 1928. He spoke for 13 hours, claiming that "the Crown's conduct of the case was calculated to prevent and did prevent a fair trial" [*The Times*, 10 July 1928]. The verdict was given on 20 July. The court ruled against the defense claim that on the basis of the evidence offered at the original trial the jury had acted unreasonably. Similarly new evidence did not justify the overturning of the origi-nal verdict. However the appeal was allowed on the ground that the judge in 1909, Lord Guthrie, had misdirected the jury; he had underlined the prosecution's emphasis on Slater's unattractive character. The defendant had allegedly lived off prostitution. This was held to have weakened the presumption of innocence [*The*

Times, pp. 10–13, 21 July 1928; Marquand (1977) 412–13; for a location of the trial in the context of anti-Jewish prejudice see Barber (2003)].

Though it was not the absolute exoneration Conan Doyle's efforts sought, an innocent man was set free, the level of public debate on the justice system was raised, and the creation of the Court of Criminal Appeal was successfully leveraged.

Sir Arthur Conan Doyle was far more than the creator of a popular fictional character. He was a medical doctor and a scientist. He was a forensic practitioner and a forensic reformer. He believed in logic, he believed in the scientific examination of evidence, and he taught these philosophies through his stories, which remain inspirational to forensic scientists of modern day. When he died in 1930 of heart disease, it was not without having helped to create much of the philosophical forensic landscape that we currently find ourselves navigating.

The late Stuart Kind, former director of The Metropolitan Police Lab (Scotland Yard Laboratory), wrote the following (Kind, 1977, p. 12): "Even the forensic scientist himself owes his existence and attitudes a good deal more to Conan Doyle, and a good deal less to Newton and Darwin, than he is usually prepared to admit."

DR. JOHANN (HANS) BAPTIST GUSTAV GROSS (1847–1925)

A thousand mistakes of every description would be avoided if people did not base their conclusions upon premises furnished by others, take as established fact what is only possibility, or as a constantly recurring incident what has only been observed once.

—Dr. Hans Gross (1906)

Johann (Hans) Gross (Fig. 1.5) was born on December 26, 1847, in Graz, Austria. He studied criminology and the law, and he eventually came to serve as an Examining Magistrate of the Criminal Court at Czernovitz. It was during this time that Gross observed firsthand the failings of apathetic and incompetent criminal investigators, as well as criminal identifications made by flawed and biased eyewitness accounts. He also became painfully familiar with the continuous stream of false suspect, eyewitness, and alleged victim accounts that poured into his office as a regular matter of course. These experiences led him to the conclusion that because people were essentially unreliable, and investigators were often their own worst enemy, a methodical, systematic way of determining the facts of a case was needed.

Figure 1.5
Dr. Hans Gross.

It is not known whether the works of Conan Doyle directly inspired Gross, but both men were moving in precisely the same direction at precisely the same time. In 1893, the same year that Conan Doyle killed off the Sherlock Holmes character, Gross finished his seminal work, *Handbuch fur Untersuchunsrichter, als System der Kriminalistik* [*Criminal Investigation, A Practical Textbook for Magistrates, Police Officers, and Lawyers* (Gross, 1906)]. It was a watershed event in which Gross proclaimed the virtues of science against intuition, and a systematic approach to holistic crime reconstruction against uninformed experience and overspecialization. Specifically, Gross wrote on the importance of objectivity and theory falsification when seeking to reconstruct events. A good example includes the following passage (Gross, 1924, p. 21):

> Carried away by zeal and the desire to bring the case to some conclusion, the Investigating Officer has proceeded too fast and without the calm and prudence requisite to such inquiries, and so all his work has been in vain. There is but one way to avoid this, to proceed "steadily," be it at a walk, at a trot, or at the charge; but in

such inquiries a halt must from time to time be made and instead of going forward he must look back. He will then examine one by one the different points of the inquiry, taking them up in order from the beginning. He will analyze each acquired result even to the smallest factor of those apparently of the least importance, and when this analysis is carried to its furthest limits, he will carefully verify each of these factors, from the point of view of its source, genuiness, and corroboration. If the accuracy of these elements be established, they may then be carefully placed one with another and the result obtained examined as if viewed for the first time. The case will then generally assume quite another complexion, for at the outset the sequence was not so well known; and if it has a different aspect from at the first each time the matter is so revised, the question must be asked whether it is in proper adjustment with the whole argument which has been formulated and whether there is any mistake to rectify. If the whole result is defective, the Investigating Officer must confess, "My calculation is false, I must begin all over again."

The success of this groundbreaking textbook was, without exaggeration, unparalleled in the history of forensic science and crime reconstruction. The forensic community as it existed, perhaps made fertile and hungry by the works of Conan Doyle, enthusiastically devoured *System der Kriminalistik*. It achieved a fifth edition and was translated into eight languages by 1907. This included versions in French, Spanish, Danish, Russian, Hungarian, Servian, English, and Japanese, each with an overwhelmingly supportive foreword written by a forensic contemporary impatient to see it printed and adopted in his respective country.

To illustrate the appeal and impact of this text, the words of M. Gardeil, professor of criminal law at Nancy, describing Gross in the introduction to the French translation, may be of some use:

An indefatigable observer; a far-seeing psychologist; a magistrate full of ardour to unearth the truth, whether in favor of the accused or against him; a clever crafts-man; in turn, draughtsman, photographer, modeler, armourer; having acquired by long experience a profound knowledge of the practices of criminals . . . he opens us the researches and experiences of many years. His work was no dry or purely technical treatise; *it is a living book, because it has been lived.*

Although Conan Doyle's vision had been ultimately idealistic and fictional, *System der Kriminalistik* was quite practical and quite real. The blueprint for scientific investigation, and the generalist, was cast by Gross and then embraced by those working cases. As written by Thorwald (1966, pp. 234–235):

You had only to open Gross's book to see the dawning of a new age. . . . Each of his chapters was an appeal to examining magistrates (his word for criminologists) to avail themselves of the potentialities of science and technology far more than they had done so far.

Gross became a professor of criminal law at the University of Czernovitz, a professor of criminology at the University of Prague, and later a professor of criminal law at the University of Graz. With the success of *System der Kriminalistik* as a platform, he launched other professional ventures that continue to contribute significantly to the development of forensic science. In 1898, Gross began serving as the editor for the *Archiv fur Kriminalanthropologie und Kriminalistik*, a journal to which he was a frequent contributor. He also introduced the forensic journal *Kriminologie*, which still serves as a respected medium for reporting improved methods of scientific crime detection. In 1912, he established the Museum of Criminology, the *Kriminalmuseum*, at the University of Graz. According to the Graz Tourism Bureau (2005),

In 1912 a dream came true for Hans Gross: The "Imperial Criminological Institute" was opened at the University of Graz. It was the first of its kind in the world. For Gross, it was the culmination of an 18-year struggle to have criminology recognized as a serious academic discipline. But it was worth it. He earned a place in history for himself as the "founder of scientific criminology" and one for his "Graz school of criminology" as a model for similar institutes around the world. Hans Gross said the real center of the Institute was the museum.

Some authors have credited the formulation of modern criminalistics as a discipline to Hans Gross, in no small part because he coined the term *Kriminalistik* and placed a heavy emphasis on the examination of the various forms of physical evidence by respectively qualified expert scientists as an indispensable part of the forensic process (DeForest, Gaennslen, & Lee, 1983, p. 12). However, a criminalist (actually a criminologist by international definition), by his usage, would have been one who studies crime, criminals, and the scientific methods of their identification, apprehension, and prosecution. The modern term *criminalist* is used in the United States to describe a particular type of analytical forensic scientist and is therefore far narrower in scope.

Regardless, there is a curious legacy to Dr. Hans Gross and his collective publications. In the first half of the 20th century, he was highly regarded by U.S. authors and widely cited in works of criminal investigation, forensic science, and crime reconstruction. In the last quarter of the 20th century, actual references in such texts waned, and his work was barely mentioned at all. However, this did not stop many authors from republishing his ideas relating to reconstruction as though they were novel. As a consequence, many of the forensic students and reconstruction professionals minted within the past 20 years have no idea who Hans Gross is, let alone that he helped to forge and professionalize the field they have chosen.

The significance of *System der Kriminalistik* cannot be understated. It was the first comprehensive textbook to systematically cover the integrated philosophy and practice of scientific criminal investigation, forensic analysis, and crime reconstruction. Its philosophies have not been diminished by the passage of time and should be required study for any student of these subjects.

DR. ALEXANDRE LACASSAGNE (1843–1924)

Dr. Alexandre Lacassagne was a professor of forensic medicine with the faculty of medicine at the University of Lyon, France. In 1880, he became the director of the Lyons Institute of Forensic Medicine. He was a medical doctor, an anthropologist, and a fervent advocate of combining science with criminology. According to Thorwald (1966, p. 281), Lacassagne also planted very specific ideas in the minds of his students about the potential importance of what we now refer to as trace and transfer evidence in the investigation and reconstruction of crime:

> He had encouraged some of his students to make studies on clues that few or no criminologists had hitherto considered. Thus, he proposed the idea that the dust on clothing, or on people's ears, noses, and fingernails, could provide information on the occupations and whereabouts of suspects.

DR. EDMOND LOCARD (1872–1966)

> I must confess that if, in the Police Laboratory in Lyon, we are interested in any unusual way with this problem of dust, it is because of having absorbed the ideas found in Gross and Conan Doyle, and also because certain investigations in which we have been involved have happened, so to speak, to force the issue.
>
> —Dr. Edmond Locard (1929)

Edmond Locard was born in 1872 in Saint-Chamond, France (Fig. 1.6). He was a student of Dr. Lacassagne. In time, he became a doctor of medicine and a master of law, and he would eventually replace Lacassagne as the director of the Lyons Institute of Forensic Medicine.

In 1908, having been educated by Lacassagne and inspired by the works of Gross and Conan Doyle, Locard traveled the world to better study how

Figure 1.6
Dr. Edmond Locard.

police agencies in major cities were incorporating the scientific method and trace evidence analysis into their investigation and reconstruction of crime. During the next two years, he would visit agencies and colleagues in Paris, Lausanne, Rome, Berlin, Brussels, New York, and Chicago. To his dismay, he found no true police crime labs or even scientific detectives, and the majority of police agencies remained steeped in *Bertillonage* (a form of personal identification based on a system of body measurements and photography of features). The only real question that existed, Locard found, was whether fingerprinting should become the new standard for personal identification, over Bertillonage, as had been declared necessary in 1893 by Gross in *System der Kriminalistik* (1906).

In 1909, the Institut de Police Scientifique et de Criminologie was formally created at the University of Lausanne, Switzerland, under the direction of Professor Rudolph A. Reiss (1875–1929). It was the first university to deliver a degree in forensic science (criminalistics) covering all major subjects. Professor Reiss had originally offered courses in forensic photography, scene of crime investigation, and identification, and he had been involved in forensic casework since at least 1903. The institute developed from the success of those courses and his tireless efforts.

In the summer of 1910, after having visited with Professor Reiss, Locard returned to Lyon and persuaded the prefects of the Rhone Department to provide him with two rooms in an attic of the Law Courts and two Surete officials as assistants. (The French Surete Nationale was a plainclothes undercover unit developed to keep strict surveillance over all ex-convicts and known criminals living in and migrating into the city; to pursue all law-breakers and make arrests; and to prevent criminal activity before it occurred. In Locard's day, the Surete Nationale, which was separate from the local police, was assuming a lot of police functions, and this alliance protected his lab politically.) The arrangement was what Locard wanted, but the actual accommodations were not the best, as described in Thorwald (1966, p. 283):

> The laboratory was reached through a gloomy entrance hall from which one corridor led to the prison and a dirt-stained door into the dusty caves and archives. Every day Locard climbed the steep winding staircase leading to his laboratory four floors up.

This marked the creation of what has become regarded as the world's first police crime laboratory, as it was housed under the auspices of law enforcement and staffed by law enforcement agents. However, contrary to some publications, this was not the world's first forensic science laboratory. The first forensic science labs were private, often specialized, and tended to be housed in universities, as Locard had experienced in Switzerland with Reiss. For example, one of the earlier forensic science labs of record was established in 1868; the French Institut de médecine légale de Paris (Paris Institute for Forensic Science).

In any event, once in place at his lab in Lyon, Locard took to the task of implementing everything he had learned from the publications of Hans Gross, from the stories of Conan Doyle, from his study and travels, and from his devotion to forensic science and crime reconstruction. These efforts included foundational research, publications, and the development of practice standards in dust analysis, detailed in Locard (1929), and fingerprint examination, as described by Clark (2005):

> Dr. Edmond Locard ... established the first rules of the minimum number of minutiae necessary for identification.
>
> He is also known as the father of Poreoscopy, which is the study of pores that appear in the fingerprint ridge, and their use in the individualization process. Dr. Locard also realized the value of the shape of the ridge as being permanent, and he should also be known as the father of Edgeoscopy.
>
> Locard went beyond the variations of the individual friction ridge path which Sir Francis Galton noted as he defined those friction ridge events. The variations

of the individual friction ridge features which he noted, has evolved into "Ridge-ology," which is a coined phrase describing the use of those features in the fingerprint identification process. Dr. Locard should also then be known as the father of "Ridgeology."

Locard also helped establish one of the first forensic science professional organizations. In 1929, after the death of Prof. Reiss, Locard returned to Lausanne and gathered with his European forensic scientist colleagues to form The International Academy of Criminalistics.

His contributions to the forensic sciences were nothing short of massive, as summarized in Söderman (1957, p. 25):

> He put the analysis of handwriting on a firmer footing, systematized the analysis of the dust in the clothes of suspects, invented a modified method of analyzing blood stains, and invented poroscopy, whereby the pores in the papillary ridges of fingerprints are used as a means of identification.

However, Locard is most famous for the forensic axiom that bears his name: Locard's Exchange Principle. It has been misstated, misrepresented, and misattributed over the years by those lecturing and writing authoritatively on the subject. Confusion in the forensic science community and among students has resulted.

A reference from Locard found in *La Police et Les Méthodes Scientifiques*, in the original French, may be of use to understand what he actually meant (Locard, 1934, pp. 7–8):

> A recherche des traces n'est pas, autant qu'on pourrait le croire, une innovation des criminalistes modernes. C'est une occupation probablement aussi vieille que l'humanité.
>
> Le principe est celui-ci. Toute action de l'homme, et *a fortiori*, l'action violente qu'est un crime, ne peut pas se dérouler sans laisser quelque marque. L'admirable est la variété de ces marques. Tantôt ce seront des empreintes, tantôt de simples traces, tantôt des taches.

Translation:

> Searching for traces is not, as much as one could believe it, an innovation of modern criminal jurists. It is an occupation probably as old as humanity.
>
> The principle is this one. Any action of an individual, and obviously, the violent action constituting a crime, cannot occur without leaving a mark. What is

admirable is the variety of these marks. Sometimes they will be prints, sometimes simple traces, and sometimes stains.

In 1935, a Spanish translation of this same general principle was provided in Locard (1935, p. 107):

> Al malhechor le es imposible actuar, y sobre todo actuar con la intensidad que supone la acción criminal, sin dejar indicios de su paso.

Translation:

> To the criminal, it is impossible for him to act, and mainly to act with the intensity that supposes criminal action, without leaving indications of his step.

The principle has been adapted and adopted in its English translation by the forensic science community in the United States. As stated by Dr. John Thornton, a practicing criminalist and a former professor of forensic science at the University of California (UC) at Berkeley (Thornton, 1997, p. 29),

> Forensic scientists have almost universally accepted the Locard Exchange Principle. This doctrine was enunciated early in the 20th century by Edmund Locard, the director of the first crime laboratory, in Lyon, France. Locard's Exchange Principle states that with contact between two items, there will be an exchange of microscopic material. This certainly includes fibers, but extends to other microscopic materials such as hair, pollen, paint, and soil.

By recognizing, documenting, and examining the nature and extent of evidentiary traces and exchanges in a crime scene, Locard postulated that criminals could be tracked down and then later associated with particular locations, items of evidence, and persons (i.e., victims). He regarded this postulation as both obvious and ancient, and he likened the recognition and examination of trace evidence to hunting behavior as old as mankind (Locard, 1934, p. 7). The prey, for example, in the normal course of drinking at a watering hole, leaves tracks and spoor and other signs that betray their presence and direction; the hunter deliberately seeks out this evidence, picks up the trail, and follows. Every contact leaves a trace that may be discovered and understood. The detection and identification of exchanged materials is interpreted to mean that two objects have been in contact. This is the cause-and-effect principle reversed; the effect is observed and the cause is concluded. Understanding and accepting this principle of evidentiary exchange makes possible the reconstruction of contacts between objects and persons. Consequently, the incorporation of this principle into evidentiary interpretations is perhaps one of the most important considerations in the reconstruction of crime.

It is true that Locard concerned himself chiefly with organizing and systematizing methods of analyzing prints, traces, and stains. He wrote extensively on how to identify and individuate dust, how to identify and individuate fingerprints, how to analyze and interpret handwriting, how to analyze and interpret blood stains, etc. However, a careful read of his publications reveals that his goals were ultimately those of reconstructing crime through the skills brought to bear by a forensic generalist. As Locard (1934, p. 6) explained, "Criminalistics [forensic science] seeks tools everywhere, in biology, physics, and more particularly chemistry, and proposes solutions to every problem brought up by the criminal investigation." Consequently, he organized and systematized methods of physical evidence analysis in order that reasonable and well-founded reconstruction interpretations might be possible. After all, what is the point of seeking out dust or prints or other traces if one does not wish to examine them, or interpret the meaning of their presence?

EDWARD OSCAR HEINRICH (1881–1953)

> The camera never lies, but a camera in the hands of a liar is a dangerous instrument.
>
> —Edward O. Heinrich (as quoted in Block, 1958, p. 37)

Edward Oscar Heinrich (Fig. 1.7) was born in 1881 in Clintonville, Wisconsin. At age 18, he became a licensed pharmacist in Tacoma, Washington; he worked hard and saved his money, aspiring to a college education and becoming a chemist. In 1908, he realized that goal and graduated from the UC Berkeley with a bachelor's degree in chemistry. Soon thereafter, he moved back to Tacoma, where he worked for the city as a chemist and sanitary engineer for the next nine years. This position gave Heinrich his first exposure to forensic casework—it involved frequent requests for investigative assistance from both the police and the coroner's office.

Applying chemistry to casework taught Heinrich the limits of specializing. He learned that to be of use—to fully reconstruct events—a forensic scientist must have at least a general working knowledge of as many forensic specialties as possible. As a result, he continually made a study of ballistics, geology, physics, photography, hairs, handwriting, paper, and inks; he read every reference text and article he could get his hands on. In essence,

he made a forensic generalist of himself, and his reputation grew with the successful employment of his methods to both criminal and civil cases.

In 1916, Heinrich became the chief of police in Alameda, California, and reorganized the department from top to bottom in terms of criminal files, fingerprints, and the employment of more modern investigative techniques. During that time, after the onset of World War I, he also lent his services to U.S. Army intelligence, providing training and performing forensic analysis.

Only a few years later, Heinrich would open his own private lab in Berkeley. To augment his practice, he became a member of the UC Berkeley faculty where he lectured on the subject of criminal investigation and served as a research associate in police science. When Heinrich began his private forensic casework, his methods were the exception and not the rule (Block, 1958, pp. 41–42):

> Scientific work was little known and often ridiculed. Plodding, without definite direction, took its place—chasing here and there for information, trying to find someone who might know something about the crime.
>
> In every way Heinrich's approach was quite opposite.
>
> That approach—his methodology—was one of the unique features of his whole career.

"Understand this first," he usually said. "Crime analysis is an orderly procedure. It's precise and it follows always the same questions . . .

"Precisely *what* happened? Precisely *when* did it happen? Precisely *where* did it happen? *Why* did it happen? *Who* did it?"

. . .

"It's all like a mosaic, and every fact must be evaluated before it can be fitted into the pattern. In that way, every fact as it is developed and equated becomes a clue."

Heinrich would dedicate his life to advancing the cause of scientific investigation and reconstruction through the employment of his methods, despite any opposition. As recalled in Walton (2004, p. 5):

In Berkeley, the work of Edward Oscar Heinrich laid the foundation for the future of professional forensic sciences. From his laboratory, Heinrich repeatedly demonstrated the value of scientific examination of trace evidence as his meticulous inspections provided the necessary links between the crime and suspects. As a result, his work was in demand by prosecutors and defense attorneys alike throughout the West.

According to Heinrich, the crime scene always contained a variety of clues, and it was up to a scientific investigator to find and accurately interpret them (Walton, 2004). Those interpretations could be combined to form a reconstruction of events that established both contacts and actions. Evidence, to Heinrich, was the only reliable witness to a crime (Block, 1958, pp. 43–44):

In the test tube and crucible or through the lens of the microscope and camera I have found in my own practice the evidence of poison, the traces of the deadly bullet, the identity of a clot, the source of a fiber, the telltale fingerprint, the differing ink, the flaw in the typewriter, the slip of the pen upon which I have turned in dramatic scenes of our courts the rightful title to an estate, of the liberty, even the life, of an individual.

Clues thus found and verified as physical facts definitely related to an action become of enormous importance to clarifying erroneous observations of eyewitnesses.

Heinrich did not regard the interpretation of evidence and its reconstruction as something within the ken of the average person or investigator. He regarded reconstruction as an ordered, disciplined, and scientific practice borne out of tireless dedication to one's personal education, experience, and research (Block, 1958, p. 44):

> It is a matter of understanding the scientific aspects of ordinary phenomena. Rarely are other than ordinary phenomena involved in the commission of a crime. One is confronted with scrambled effects, all parts of which separately are attributed to causes. The tracing of the relationship between isolated points of fact, the completion of the chain of circumstances between cause and effect, are the highest functions of reason—to which must be added the creative imagination of the scientist.

Heinrich died in 1953 at the age of 72, with many of the techniques and philosophies that he had practiced adopted in police crime labs throughout the United States. His sheer force of dedication to the forensic sciences inspired many and accomplished much by way of instruction and example.

DR. PAUL L. KIRK (1902–1970)

> This is evidence that does not forget. It is not confused by the excitement of the moment. It is not absent because human witnesses are. It is factual evidence. Physical evidence cannot be wrong; it cannot perjure itself; it cannot be wholly absent. Only its interpretation can err.
>
> —Dr. Paul Kirk (1953, p. 4)

Paul Leland Kirk (Fig. 1.8) was born in Colorado Springs, Colorado, in 1902. He was first and foremost a scientist, but he was also a man of practical application as opposed to pure theory. He was educated at Ohio State University, where he received an A.B. in chemistry; the University of Pittsburgh, where he received an M.S. in chemistry; and the University of California, where he received a Ph.D. in biochemistry.

From 1929 to 1945, Kirk served as a professor of biochemistry at UC Berkeley. Later in his career, he would tell students that he was initially drawn to forensic science in his early teaching days when a biochemistry student approached him with a question about a deceased dog and whether or not it could be determined if the dog had been poisoned. Investigating this issue peaked Kirk's forensic curiosities. Soon after, he was contacted by authorities to examine the clothing of a victim of rape—they wanted to know whether or not anything on the clothing could be found, at the microscopic level, to associate the victim with her attacker. Kirk's discovery of fibers from the attacker's shirt, and the subsequent conviction of the rapist,

Figure 1.8

Dr. Paul Kirk. Source: John E. Murdock, ATF Forensic Lab, Walnut Creek, CA.

sealed his interest and secured his reputation for solid results based on careful examinations. Subsequently, in 1937, Kirk assumed leadership of the criminology program at UC Berkeley. The program gained momentum and grew in its reputation under his charge.

In 1939, during World War II, it was believed that Nazi scientists were developing an atomic bomb. In response, the United States initiated its own top-secret atomic weapon program overseen by the Army Corps of Engineers in June 1942 (a year and a half before formally entering the war). This was done in order to develop the atomic bomb first and gain the upper hand in a war that had already consumed Europe and Asia and would most certainly involve the United States directly at some point. This covert effort would become known as the Manhattan Project.

Theoretical physicist Robert J. Oppenheimer was asked to direct research on the Manhattan Project at a remote site in Los Alamos, New Mexico, which would later become the Los Alamos National Laboratory. He set to the task of identifying top scientists and engineers from universities nationwide—to fill a room with the smartest people available and get them working. Because of his extensive knowledge and ability with work done at the microscopic level, Dr. Paul Kirk was among them. From 1942 to 1945, Kirk was on leave from his university teaching duties to the Manhattan Project, where he helped to develop the process for isolating fissionable plutonium.

In 1945, Kirk returned to UC Berkeley and reconnected to his interest in forensic science. He formalized a major in technical criminology that year. In 1950, Chief Vollmer established the school of criminology, and Kirk was appointed to chair the criminalistics department. According to DeForest *et al.* (1983, p. 15), "The program grew to be well-known, and Kirk developed a substantial reputation in forensic science, devoting his time to instruction, research, and casework." In 1953, Kirk published the first edition of *Crime Investigation*, a treatise on criminal investigation, crime reconstruction, and forensic examination that endures to this day as a foundational industry standard with few equals (Kirk, 1953). In the preface, he describes arriving at the same precipice as all who studied forensic science before him, and he calls once again for the education of forensic generalists (p. v):

> LeMoyne Snyder, in his excellent book, *Homicide Investigation* [Snyder, 1944, pp. 269–271], includes a short chapter, "Why I Wrote This Book," which should be required reading for all law enforcement agents. The situation described there, involving a lack of coordination, communication, and understanding, was one in which conscientious but untrained and incompetent officials did everything possible to make the crime impossible of solution, and little if anything to aid in its solution. The possible implication that this situation is characteristic only of homicides is, unfortunately, not true. Far too many crimes of all types are "investigated" as he describes. His reasons for writing the book apply equally to the writing of this one, which aims only to attack the same fundamental problem but on a broader basis.
>
> This volume is not intended as a guide for specialists. Rather, it is written with the needs of police investigators, general criminalists in smaller police laboratories, and students of criminalistics and police science in mind.

Kirk also supported the validity of Locard's Exchange Principle for use in reconstruction work, and he refined it to a point so keen that his words are frequently confused for those of Locard (Kirk, 1953, p. 4):

> Wherever he steps, whatever he touches, whatever he leaves, even unconsciously, will serve as silent witness against him. Not only his fingerprints or his footprints, but his hair, the fibers from his clothing, the glass he breaks, the tool mark he leaves, the paint he scratches, the blood or semen he deposits or collects. All of

these and more bear mute witness against him. This is evidence that does not forget.

However, Kirk also argued for caution in the interpretation of evidentiary exchanges. Unlike Gross or Locard before him, Kirk was not so enamored with forensic science that he misunderstood its limitations and potential abuses. On establishing the identification of an object's source, he makes it clear that it is an endeavor with inherent hazards, to include the examiner, under even the best conditions (Kirk, 1953, p. 16; revised in Kirk & Thornton, 1970, p. 10).

> In the examination and interpretation of physical evidence, the distinction between identification and individuation must always be clearly made, to facilitate the real purpose of the criminalist: to determine the identity of source. That is, two items of evidence, one known and the other unknown, must be identified as having a common origin. On the witness stand, the criminalist must be willing to admit that absolute identity is impossible to establish. Identity of source, on the other hand, often may be established unequivocally, and no witness who has established it need ever back down in the face of cross-examination.
>
> It is precisely here that the greatest caution must be exercised. The inept or biased witness may readily testify to an identity, or to a type of identity, that does not actually exist. This can come about because of his confusion as to the nature of identity, his inability to evaluate the results of his observations, or because his general technical deficiencies preclude meaningful results.

Kirk also shared the views of Gross and Locard regarding issues of witness reliability, physical evidence, and crime reconstruction, explaining (Kirk & Thornton, 1970, p. 33),

> The utilization of physical evidence is critical to the solution of most crime. No longer may the police depend upon the confession, as they have done to a large extent in the past. The eyewitness has never been dependable, as any experienced investigator or attorney knows quite well. Only physical evidence is infallible, and then only when it is properly recognized, studied, and interpreted.

Paul Kirk is perhaps best remembered for his involvement in the infamous Sam Sheppard case. On July 4, 1954, 31-year-old Marilyn Reese Sheppard, approximately 4 months pregnant, was found murdered on a twin bed in the bedroom of her home in Bay Village, a suburb of Cleveland, Ohio. After a hasty and flawed investigation, fraught with preconceived theories, her husband, Sam Sheppard, was arrested for the crime. On December 21, 1954, a jury convicted him of second-degree murder (intentional but without premeditation).

On January 22, 1955, Kirk visited the Sheppard home to examine the scene and collect evidence in preparation for an appeal on behalf of the Sheppard defense. Subsequently, he wrote a reconstruction report detailing his findings related to bloodstain pattern analysis and the presence of a third person at the scene. Although Sheppard's motion for a new trial and appeal were denied in 1955, a U.S. District Judge overturned his conviction in 1964, agreeing that intense media coverage had led to an unfair conviction. In 1966, the U.S. Supreme Court eventually reviewed the case and upheld that decision.

Later that same year, Sam Sheppard was put on trial again, and this time Paul Kirk was allowed to testify. According to Chisum (2000):

> The first person to really study the bloodstain patterns in the Sam Sheppard case was Professor Paul L. Kirk from UC Berkeley.
>
> . . .
>
> The identification of a person through their blood was of primary interest to Paul and was the focus of much of his research after the Sheppard case. However, he died prior to the discoveries that led to his dream of individualization of blood.
>
> He rediscovered blood spatter interpretation. He conducted many experiments in a closed room with a bucket of blood and various tools. He tried to establish the cause of different patterns. He was not the first person to experiment with blood in this manner, however, there was about a 30-year gap in the field. Kirk's affidavit in this case is still looked upon as one of the milestones of blood spatter interpretation.
>
> Paul Kirk did testify in the second trial, which resulted in an acquittal for Dr. Sheppard.

Kirk's involvement in the Sheppard case as an expert for the defense publicly and professionally embarrassed Dr. Samuel Gerber, a senior member of the American Academy of Forensic Sciences (AAFS) who worked the Sheppard case for law enforcement and believed Sam Sheppard to be guilty. As explained in Chisum (2000):

> Dr. Sam Gerber, M.D., was the coroner in Cuyahoga County at the time of the [Marilyn Sheppard] murder and for several more years. He was a very powerful person in the county and in the forensic field. He knew how to work the system to his advantage. He was also vindictive as shown by his personal attacks on Prof. Paul Kirk. Many believe he was behind the movement that kept Dr. Kirk out of the American Academy of Forensic Sciences.

Subsequently, Kirk was not allowed to join the AAFS because of his findings in the Sheppard defense, their impact on Sheppard's acquittal, and Gerber's influence.

In 1969, Kirk broke more forensic ground with the publication of *Fire Investigation*. This work was intended to bring the basic principles and methods of fire scene investigation and reconstruction down from the language of highly technical journal publications to ordinary criminal investigators and forensic generalists. Today, in the able hands of Dr. John DeHaan, it survives as a worthy industry standard (DeHaan, 2002).

After his death in 1970, Kirk's student and colleague Dr. John I. Thornton finished the manuscript for the second edition of *Crime Investigation* (Kirk & Thornton, 1970) and gave sole credit for the ideas expressed within as those of Kirk, stating (p. v), "Those of us involved in editing and rewriting served only to tidy up the work a bit, performing a type of literary janitorial service; the essential character of the text is decidedly that of Dr. Kirk."

Paul Kirk left behind a valuable body of work and a legacy of skilled students from all over the world. Since his passing, a fair number of those students have helped to shape the forensic science universe in the best possible sense, each in their own right, with several contributing to the development of this text. Also, ironically, the highest honor that one can now earn in the criminalistics section of the AAFS is the Paul L. Kirk Award.

THE BROADER THEME

It is evident that the history of crime reconstruction is built on a succession of inspiration, expectation, and disappointment. Each of the fathers of forensic science entered the profession, in one fashion or another, both inspired by something and to repair something. They came in search of science and, finding it lacking, set about to make things right. The broader theme of their collective work is that physical evidence is of the greatest value when establishing the facts of a case, but it must be cautiously and dispassionately interpreted. In that endeavor, education in the sciences and the scientific method are not to be discarded as impractical but, rather, embraced as essential to defining the quality of subsequent examinations and interpretations.

Moreover, and not less important, is the lesson that the forensic sciences will advance only in the hands of able students and practitioners. Crime reconstruction is a complex process; the less someone knows about it, the simpler it seems. Consequently, the fathers of forensic science made it clear that crime reconstruction should not be the responsibility of anyone unable to reach with the full extension of all that science, analytical logic, and critical thinking has to offer.

These are lessons that current and future reconstructionists would do well to remember and keep close in their casework, testimony, and teaching.

REFERENCES

Block, E. (1958). *The Wizard of Berkeley.* New York: Coward-McCann.

Chisum, J. (2000, December). A Commentary on Bloodstain Analyses in the Sam Sheppard Case. *Journal of Behavioral Profiling,* 1(3).

Clark, D. (2005). Dr. Edmond Locard, the Father of Ridgeology. *Latent Fingerprints.* Retrieved June 21, 2005, from http://www.latent-prints.com/Locard.htm

Davies, D. (2004). *A Study in Scarlet—An Introduction.* London: The Sherlock Holmes Society of London. Retrieved from http://www.sherlock-holmes.org.uk/News/Articles/David_Stuart_Davies/A_Study_in_Scarlet_An_Introduction.htm

DeForest, P., Gaennslen, R., & Lee, H. (1983). *Forensic Science: An Introduction to Criminalistics.* New York: McGraw-Hill.

DeHaan, J. (2002). *Kirk's Fire Investigation* (5th ed.). Englewood Cliffs, NJ: Prentice Hall.

Doyle, A. C. (1887, November). A study in Scarlet. *Beeton's Christmas Annual.*

Doyle, A. C. (1890, February). The Sign of Four. *Lippincott's Magazine.*

Doyle, A. C. (1893, November). The Memoirs of Sherlock Holmes: The Crooked Man. *The Strand Magazine.*

Doyle, A. C. (1989). *Memories & Adventures.* Oxford: Oxford University Press.

Doyle, A. C. (1904, September). The Return of Sherlock Holmes: XII. The Abbey Grange. *The Strand Magazine.*

Freeman, T. (2004). *Dr. Joseph Bell.* London: The Sherlock Holmes Society of London. Retrieved from http://www.sherlock-holmes.org.uk/The_Society/Arthur_Conan_Doyle/Joseph_Bell.htm

The George Edalji case. (2005). *The Chronicles of Sir Arthur Conan Doyle.* Retrieved June 21, 2005, from http://www.siracd.com/life_case1.shtml

Gildart, K., & Howell, D. (2004). *Dictionary of Labour Biography* (Vol. 7). Hampshire, UK: Palgrave Macmillan.

Graz Tourism Bureau (2005). *Hans Gross Criminological Museum.* Retrieved April 14, 2005, from http://cms.graztourismus.at/cms/beitrag/10005851/47303/

Gross, H. (1906). *Criminal Investigation.* Madras: G. Ramasawmy Chetty.

Gross, H. (1924). *Criminal Investigation.* London: Sweet & Maxwell.

Jones, H. (1904). The original of Sherlock Holmes. In A. C. Doyle (Ed.), *Conan Doyle's Best Books in Three Volumes: The Sign of the Four and Other Stories.* New York: Collier.

Kind, S. (1977). *The Scientific Investigation of Crime.* Harrogate, England: Forensic Science Services.

Kirk, P. (1953). *Crime Investigation.* New York: Interscience.

Kirk, P. (1969). *Fire Investigation: Including Fire-Related Phenomena: Arson, Explosion, Asphyxiation.* New York: Wiley.

Kirk, P., & Thornton, J. (Eds.). (1970). *Crime Investigation* (2nd ed.). New York: Wiley.

Locard, E. (1929). The Analysis of Dust Traces, Part 1. *Revue Internationale de Criminalistique,* I(4–5), 176–249.

Locard, E. (1934). *La Police et Les Methodes Scientifiques.* Paris: Les Editions Rieder.

Locard, E. (1935). *Manuel de Tecnica Policiaca.* Barcelona: Imprenta Claraso.

The Oscar Slater case. (2005). *The Chronicles of Sir Arthur Conan Doyle.* Retrieved June 21, 2005, from http://www.siracd.com/life/life_case2.shtml

Snyder, L. (1944). *Homicide Investigation.* Springfield, IL: Charles C Thomas.

Söderman, H. (1957). *Policeman's Lot.* London: Longmans, Green and Company.

Thornton, J. I. (1997). The general assumptions and rationale of forensic identification. In D. L. Faigman, D. H. Kaye, M. J. Saks, & J. Sanders (Eds.), *Modern Scientific Evidence: The Law and Science of Expert Testimony* (Vol. 2). St. Paul, MN: West.

Thorwald, J. (1966). *Crime and Science.* New York: Harcourt, Brace, & World.

Walton, R. (2004, Spring). The Legacy of Edward Oscar Heinrich. *Bancroftiana: The Newsletter of the Friends of the Bancroft Library,* No. 124, p. 5.

CHAPTER 2

CRIME RECONSTRUCTION— ETHOS AND ETHICS

John I. Thornton, PhD

We are interested in physical evidence because it may tell a story. Physical evidence—properly documented, properly collected, properly analyzed, and properly interpreted—may establish the factual circumstances at the time a crime occurred. In short, the crime may be reconstructed. Our principal interest is ultimately in the reconstruction, not the evidence per se. We are interested in DNA, in gunshot residues, in blood spatter, in firearms evidence, in friction ridge evidence, only insofar as these materials enable us to reconstruct the crime incident.[1] It is the story, rather than the evidence, that will be applied to the ultimate determination of justice. The crime scene has a certain character, a certain essence. It has been given form and has been shaped by the laws of nature and by the vagaries of human conduct. The crime scene is an entity of sorts. It has its own ethos, as do the processes by means of which the scene is reconstructed.

Ethos pertains to the valid essence of something, with equal emphasis on the "valid." The Greek word ethos (ηΘΟς, *character*) means character, and it is not just coincidence that it is the root of the word "ethics" as well. The dictionary definition of ethos is the moral, ideal, or universal element in something, as opposed to that which is subjective or emotional in its appeal. A premise here is that there is a "thing" called a crime scene, but there is also a "thing" termed crime reconstruction. As with the crime scene, the crime reconstruction has a character, an ethos. Also, along with the ethos is an ethic—a moral obligation to maintain the integrity of the processes by means of which the reconstruction is accomplished. In short, the ethics of crime reconstruction represent an imperative to "get it right."

"Getting it right" involves more than guessing correctly. It necessitates a systematic process. It involves the proper recognition of the evidence, the winnowing of the relevant wheat from the irrelevant chaff, and the precise application of logic, both inductive and deductive. The process is not trivial.

[1] Some clarification of terminology may be appropriate. In this discussion, an *event* is a single occurrence, action, or happening. An *incident* is a series of related events, contemporaneous in time and for which responsibility may generally be assigned.

Unless the reconstruction honors the truth, it will be a perversion of reason and unsuited for any use we may have of it. And here we must speak of fundamental truth, not just the perception of it by the observer. Recklessness or malfeasance in the process of crime reconstruction will fall in the domain of ethics, but simple misfeasance may be at play as well. Sincere but misguided beliefs do violence to the ethos of crime reconstruction. We must pursue the ethos of the reconstruction, and the ethics.

Is it unethical to be mistaken in a crime reconstruction? It is if the mistake was avoidable. It is if the mistake has arisen from haste, bias, recklessness, succumbing to outside pressure, or an ignorance of logical pitfalls.

A goodly bit of what passes for crime reconstruction falls within the domain of commonsense deductions. For example, blood in one part of a room but in no other would indicate that a victim had not visited other areas after being stabbed. A bloody shoeprint with a sole design different from that of the victim might be that of the assailant. (However, it may have arisen after the incident when medical intervention was attempted.) Commonsense deductions of this sort—derived from everyday experience—do not require formal training in logic, but it is nevertheless logic that is the engine for conclusions such as these.

We use commonsense logic so often and so casually that we generally gloss over many complexities. As a consequence, commonsense logic can be treacherous. Premises may be misapplied, incomplete, or uncertain, and fallacies of logic may be compounded.

But logic has its underpinnings, which are, well, logical. Formal logic, as opposed to casual logic masquerading as common sense, is an exceedingly powerful tool, and one not to be ignored or given short shrift. The crime reconstructionist would be well advised to gain some conversancy with the subject, both to solve problems correctly and to avoid a misapplication of logic—that is, to avoid engaging in fallacies of reason.[2] The point here is that the employment of weak or fallacious logic will almost invariably result in a weak or fallacious reconstruction of the crime.

Apart from popular fiction—the Sherlock Holmes stories leading the list—logic has not been stressed in written accounts of crime reconstruction. For reasons that are not altogether recoverable, the professional literature on crime scene processing and criminal investigation has not devoted much attention to the subject. But it is not too late to raise the topic.

Logic is the science that evaluates arguments. (Note that it is considered a "science" in that it makes use of the scientific method. The scientific method, in its simplest form, involves the formation of hypotheses and the testing of those hypotheses through attempts at falsification.) An argument

[2] A good place to start would be Hurley (2002).

as used here does not mean a verbal fight but, rather, a group of premises that claims to support a conclusion. Premises are statements that set forth the reasons or evidence for an idea. Conclusions are the statements that the evidence is claimed to support or imply. For logic to work properly, the parent premises must be valid and the conclusion must follow from valid premises. This places a great premium on the ability of the crime reconstructionist to develop true, rational premises; if this is not accomplished, the arguments will be invalid. Certainly arguments exist in which the premises do in fact support the conclusion, but there are arguments that do not support the conclusion, even though they are believed, and therefore claimed, to do so. It is the process of distinguishing between true arguments and false arguments that we call logic.

Frequently, it is supposed that crime reconstruction involves only deductive reasoning. In practice, however, both deductive and inductive arguments are employed. A deductive argument is one in which it is impossible for the premises to be true and the conclusion false. A deductive argument is therefore something to be striven for. An inductive argument is one in which it is merely unlikely that the premises are true and the conclusion false. Inductive arguments are those that necessitate some measure of probabilistic reasoning. Often, crime reconstruction is framed in terms of deductive reasoning, but in fact most reconstructions involve a mix of both deductive and inductive arguments. Many conclusions must certainly be couched in probabilistic (i.e., "likelihood") terms, and inductive reasoning is much more common than many crime reconstructionists would care to admit. Simply put, we are forced into it.

Valid logic is generally synonymous with the casual and sometimes elusive commodity that we call common sense. In its application, it cannot be haphazard. The scene reconstructionist has the professional and ethical obligation to interpret the scene correctly. The imperative to read the scene correctly burdens the reconstructionist to avoid engaging in lapses of proper logic. Valid conclusions based on valid logic are essential. The avoidance of fallacy is also essential. Avoidance of fallacy has historically been given short shrift in discussions of crime reconstruction.

Fallacies of logic are a conspicuous peril to the crime reconstructionist. Many fallacies are subtle and reach out to ensnare the reconstructionist who is oblivious to them, operating under a bias that obscures them, or so hurried as to cut corners. Fallacies of logic are typically not considered in any discussion of the crime reconstruction; they should be, since they must be avoided at all costs. Failure to avoid them will inevitably result in a corrupt reconstruction.[3] Failure to avoid them may lead to a lapse in professionalism—a lapse in ethics.

[3] In some instances, we are actually encouraged to accept fallacies. Advertisers, in their marketing strategy, willingly advance fallacies of logic in order to promote their product. In our everyday lives, we can scarcely avoid exposure to instances of corrupt logic.

Fallacies of logic are generally categorized as fallacies of relevance; fallacies of weak induction; and fallacies of presumption, ambiguity, and grammatical analogy. Some examples are useful.

FALLACIES OF LOGIC

I. Fallacies of relevance: Fallacies of relevance are those where the arguments are based on premises that are *logically* irrelevant, although they may have considerable *psychological* relevance. Conclusions may *appear* to follow from the premises but do not follow logically.

A. Appeal to force (*argumentum ad baculum*): An argument is supplied to one person by another, along with a statement—implicit or explicit—that something adverse will happen to the second person if the offered conclusion is not accepted. In the most raw form, this may be a clear threat: "Clearly the suspect displayed premeditation. If you don't agree, forget about my support for a raise." Here, it is abundantly clear that the person making the threat is engaging in unethical behavior, and the person receiving the threat would incur unethical behavior if he or she succumbed to it. But this fallacy could be much more subtle, along the lines of, "Bill, forget about documenting all of those bloodstains. If we don't finish up in the next ten minutes all of the restaurants will be closed."

B. Appeal to pity (*argumentum ad misericordum*): The appeal to pity may be directed by the person making the argument, but the appeal may be directed toward some third party as well. "Bill, if you conclude that the scene was processed improperly, you will jeopardize Jim's reputation and possibly his job. You know that he only has six months before retiring."

C. Appeal to the people (*argumentum ad populum*): This appeal commonly takes some form of the "Don't you want to get on the bandwagon?" "What do you mean, you aren't convinced that the fingerprint in evidence isn't that of the suspect? Several other examiners have already verified the identification." This becomes a fallacy when the appeal is to the emotions and enthusiasm of the reconstructionist rather than a legitimate appeal to more carefully scrutinize the basis of the claimed identification. A converse fallacy—an argument *against* the people—exists when the emotions of the reconstructionist are fanned to stigmatize a particular group of people. "What can you expect from that group of gang-bangers?"

D. Argument against the person (*argumentum ad hominem*): This may occur when a conclusion is advanced, with another person responding by directing attention not to the first person's argument but to the *character* of the first person. This may be abusive: "The defense consultant has a detailed crime reconstruction, but consider how much he is being paid to say what he is saying!" It may be more subtle: "Bill is entitled to his opinion, but in the past 20 years he has made no attempt to keep up with recent developments!"

E. Accident: The fallacy of accident applies to situations in which a principle is applied to a particular instance but in which the principle cannot be reasonably expected to apply. This fallacy is termed an "accident" because some "accident" prevents the otherwise valid rule from applying. "It is well established in law that a person is innocent until proven guilty. The suspect hasn't been found guilty yet, so let's ignore the fact that he has blood on his clothing."

F. Straw man: The straw man fallacy is a type of misrepresentation where one person distorts another argument for the purpose of more easily attacking it, then attacks the reformulated argument, and then asserts that the original argument has been effectively discredited.

G. Missing the point (*ignoratio elenchi*): Missing the point occurs when the premises support one conclusion, but another conclusion is drawn. "No expended cartridge cases were found at the scene. The shooter must have picked them up" (dismissing the possibility that a revolver was used).

II. Fallacies of weak induction

A. Appeal to unqualified authority (*argumentum ad verecundiam*)
"The witness, who has never touched a gun and is terrified of them, states that she thinks the firearm used in the crime was a revolver. I guess we have to go with that."

B. Appeal to ignorance (*argumentum ad ignorantiam*)
"No one has ever come forward to say that the subject ever lost his temper, or even raised his voice in anger. Therefore he just isn't capable of killing his children."

C. Hasty generalization (*converse accident*)
"Half the scumbags living within a six-block radius have a drug habit. The other half must be dealing drugs."

D. False cause
"The crime rate is steadily rising. Clearly the police are falling down on the job."

E. Weak analogy
"A landlord can enter an apartment to check on its condition. So the police don't need a search warrant to enter if they are only interested in the condition of the premises and aren't really searching for anything."

III. Fallacies of presumption, ambiguity, and grammatical analogy
  A. Begging the question (*petitio principii*)
     "This crime obviously took a good deal of planning. Of all our suspects, only Suspect A is a meticulous nerd, so he must be the perpetrator."
  B. False dichotomy
     The fallacy of false dichotomy occurs when a statement offers two alternatives, but two alternatives only. The classical fallacy is the question: "Have you stopped beating your wife?" The fallacy results from the alternatives not being exhaustive. A similar fallacy occurs with complex questions: "Where did you stash the murder weapon?"
  C. Suppressed evidence
     The fallacy of suppressed evidence occurs when a premise ignores a vital piece of evidence that outweighs the evidence actually presented and results in an entirely different conclusion. For example, "The scene shows no sign of forcible entry. Therefore the crime must have been committed by a member of the family." (This ignores the fact that entry may have been accomplished without force.)
  D. Equivocation
     The fallacy of equivocation occurs when a conclusion hinges on a concept that is used in two different senses in the same argument. For example, depending on how it is used, the word "bad" may have two connotations. "The victim had a bad experience. Therefore she must have been a bad person."
  E. Amphiboly
     The fallacy of amphiboly occurs when an ambiguous statement is misinterpreted, and the conclusion is then based on the faulty interpretation. For example, "Witness A told Informant B that he had made a very bad mistake. If he was able to admit that, then he is probably being truthful in his account of other details."
  F. Composition
     The fallacy of composition occurs when a narrow attribute, truthful in isolation, is applied to a broader proposition. For example, "The witness was known to have liked ice cream cones, and liked liver and onions as well. Therefore he would have liked a liver and onion flavored ice cream cone."
  G. Division
     The fallacy of division is the opposite of the fallacy of composition. It occurs when a conclusion involves an application of an attribute, truthful in its own right, from a broad proposition to a specific instance. For example, "Members of the gang wear red to show their affiliation. The victim was wearing red. Therefore he must have been a gang member."

Note, however, that although the progression of logic is defective in this instance, there are other instances in which this application of an attribute is legitimate. There is no lapse in logic to the reformulation of the previous statement as "The victim was a gang member. That explains why he was wearing red."

Apart from lapses in logic, where else does the process of crime reconstruction go awry? Several possibilities present themselves: (1) deliberate but legally ordained deception on the part of police investigators, (2) the outright fraud, (3) the hurried, (4) the inexperienced, and (5) the honest reconstructionist subjected to pressure.

DELIBERATE DECEPTION

Something must be said about the police practice of misrepresenting evidence in order to induce a confession from a suspect. In the interrogation of a suspect, police investigators may claim to have reconstructed a crime in such a fashion as to implicate a suspect, when in fact they are bluffing. This is duplicitous but has been consistently condoned by our courts and tolerated by our society.

It should be understood, however, that crime reconstruction rendered for this purpose is fiction. Some elements may be reported truthfully, but the component linking the suspect to the crime is not credible, and the police investigator knows well that it is not. This is not actually crime reconstruction, any more than the mystery writer conjuring up a story engages in crime reconstruction. There is no ethical obligation on the part of the investigator to correctly and truthfully represent the reconstruction since deception has set the tone in the first place. But this practice is outside the penumbra of crime reconstruction as understood by ethical crime reconstructionists. This traditional police procedure, although not considered unethical in terms of our developed culture, stands off to the side of ethical crime reconstruction.

THE FRAUD

In every profession and in every aspect of human endeavor there are a few individuals who misplace their ethical compass. Often, this is the reason that a crime has occurred in the first place. It would compound the tragedy if this occurred in crime reconstruction as well. Within the ranks of those responsible for crime reconstruction, there have been a very small number of outright dishonest people, but alas the number has not been zero.

Occasionally, someone is caught falsifying evidence, testifying untruthfully, or engaging in some activity that is not only unethical but also downright illegal. These people do not belong in the cadre of crime reconstructionists; they belong in jail. The community of crime reconstructionists should be perpetually alert to the possibility of malfeasance and should be merciless in the condemnation of corrupt professional practices. But certainly there is nothing that could be said here that would totally prevent these occasional lapses, any more than the Ten Commandments has vanquished all crime and social evils.

HASTE

In crime reconstruction, an "honest mistake" may have terribly severe consequences. Innocent people may be implicated, and guilty ones exonerated. As developed elsewhere in this discussion, a mistake resulting from carelessness may be elevated to an ethical concern. In discussing ethics in connection with document examination, Hilton (1976, p. 780) states that most ethical dilemmas arise from carelessness or lack of thoroughness resulting from haste.

THE INEXPERIENCED

More deserving of our tolerance, but a threat nevertheless, is the tyro—the inexperienced or the beginner who is unfamiliar with the unique role that the crime reconstructionist plays in the legal system. Many of these will be honest, capable people who are suddenly called upon, with little experience and perhaps less training, to make judgment calls that may affect the conduct of an investigation. Some of these people may have an inescapable responsibility to conduct crime reconstruction (e.g., police investigators) but simply are inexperienced. Others may be brought to the table because of their particular expertise (e.g., engineers, physicians, dentists, chemists, physicists, and geologists) who are coincidentally called upon to perform some activity that is necessary for a particular investigation.

These people may have an incomplete grasp of the proper ethical stance to assume. From where would they learn of it? Whatever ethics they bring to the reconstruction will consist of their preconceived notions of how the world is put together, how it operates, and how it ought to act. This places a great premium on the ability of the crime reconstructionist to "get it right."

To these concerns may be added a sincere but misplaced desire to please the agent or agency that has requested an examination—that is, to fulfill the confirmatory function that is expected of the examiner, even in the absence of external pressure.

THE HONEST CRIME RECONSTRUCTIONIST SUBJECTED TO PRESSURE

It is essential that the crime reconstructionist deliver an opinion that will not plant a false impression in the mind of, well, anyone. Not in the mind of the recipient of an oral report or the reader of a written one. Not in the minds of the jury, the trial judge, or a journalist. The implication of this is that on some occasions the reconstructionist must be prepared to thwart the will of the entity on whose behalf the reconstructionist has been called and to resist any pressure exerted by that agency.

The crime reconstructionist employs the scientific method. But practicing the scientific method within the confines of the legal system instantly precipitates certain potential problems. Certain of these problems arise from the crime reconstructionist operating within a police agency. Some investigators view an undifferentiated community of convicted criminals, suspects, defendants, and potential suspects as the enemy, to be vanquished as quickly as possible and with the use of whatever tool is at hand. If they can use proper science to apprehend and convict a miscreant, fine. If they cannot do it with proper science and must resort to improper or indifferent science, that is OK too. If the crime reconstructionist must work within this milieu, it is likely that sooner or later there will be an attempt on the part of even an erstwhile investigator to pressure the reconstructionist into an opinion that favors the investigator's perception of the case.

Pressure from attorneys, on both the prosecution and defense side, may be even more relentless, as their canon of ethics allows them, within bounds, to be insincere. Attorneys are legitimately propagandists of a particular point of view. They are advocates, and they want their views to prevail. Until they are told differently, they may wish to enlist the reconstructionist in their efforts. Apparently no one ever bothers to tell them in law school that the crime reconstructionist is not their trained seal.

This is an aspect of a basic dilemma between law and science. Crime reconstruction is, or certainly it should be, an application of the scientific method. Science takes as its fundamental goal the establishment of truth. Crime reconstruction, as the handmaiden of the legal process, takes as its goal the pursuit of justice. Truth and justice are not enemies, but they are not the same thing, and this has caused and will continue to cause a certain tension between the two disciplines.

Perhaps the best way to avoid having anyone apply pressure for a particular finding is not to give that anyone any reason to believe that they would be successful in doing so. If a police investigator believes that he and the reconstructionist are kindred spirits in helping to stamp out the dark forces of evil, this notion will be acted upon and even exploited. If, on the other hand, the investigator has reason to believe that the reconstructionist will refuse to succumb to suggestion, fewer attempts will be made and those that are made are likely to be feeble and perhaps even jocular. Police investigators should be made to understand that crime reconstruction is more than a casually offered surmise, and that the crime reconstructionist must honor a high standard of objectivity.

The way to avoid being pressured by attorneys to put the best face on the evidence—that is, the best face as they perceive that face to be—is not to yield the first time. If the crime reconstructionist demonstrates a manner of professional chastity and does not yield the first time, it will establish the tenor of the relationship between the attorney and the reconstructionist on terms that the attorney will have to accept. Attorneys do not invite others to shape and form their canon of ethics. It is only fair that they should not dictate how crime reconstructionists should approach their own ethical stance.

RECONSTRUCTION BASED ON UNEVALUATED SURMISE

A crime reconstruction is an opinion. It must be based on the evidence, but there is a component of the reconstructionist's experience as well—experience born of common sense and experience born of training. However, the issuance of an opinion where experience is substituted for defensible fact is treacherous. An opinion that is not subjected to testing is nothing but a surmise. There is an obligation to test an opinion. This may be as abbreviated a process as projecting the evidence against a gestalt of past experience and against a standard of plausibility, or it may require something considerably more. Reasonable tests may simply not be available in the armory of techniques available to the reconstructionist. However, if tests are available, the most rigorous among them should be selected and applied. The evidence should be evaluated in light of that testing before an opinion is advanced to whatever agent or agency has requested the reconstruction.

How may one guard against this potential pitfall? Three measures present themselves:

1. By setting appropriate thresholds by means of which a rational mind may be convinced of a fact. These thresholds must be set fairly high and approached

with healthy skepticism. This skepticism must be applied to experience as well.

2. If a theory or hypothesis of how the crime occurred cannot be tested or evaluated fully, then that theory or hypothesis should be clearly labeled as tentative; any opinions delivered should be accompanied by appropriate qualifications.

3. Recognizing that the physical evidence may not tell the whole story of what happened, but only isolated bits of the entire drama.

A CANON OF ETHICAL CONDUCT FOR THE CRIME RECONSTRUCTIONIST

The establishment of a canon of ethics, and the enforcement of that canon, is more or less universally construed as contributing to the maturity of a profession.

Canons of ethics tend to be one or the other of two kinds—a very abbreviated code, which in essence says, "Thou shalt do no wrong," and detailed codes, which set forth the specific types of activities that a profession would wish to encourage and those it would wish to proscribe. Ethical codes have been developed for police professionals, such as the *Law Enforcement Code of Ethics* (International Association of Chiefs of Police, n.d.), and for forensic scientists (American Academy of Forensic Sciences, n.d.; California Association of Criminalists, n.d.). The *Journal of Forensic Sciences* has published a symposium on ethical conflicts in the forensic sciences. Portions of those codes are applicable to crime reconstruction, but an ethical code that focuses particularly on crime reconstruction has not been put forward. The following discussion is an attempt to do so.

In practice, those involved in crime reconstruction soon develop a local reputation among investigators, prosecutors, defense attorneys, and judges. Some are seen as honest and unbiased; others are seen as tilting toward one or the other of the contestants. It is far easier to maintain the former reputation, once achieved, than it is to rebut the latter.

As discussed previously, the very nature of the legal system invites a certain amount of pressure being placed on the crime reconstructionist. It is exceedingly rare for this pressure to be applied crassly, as in "If you don't write a report stating that the suspect was deliberately lying in wait for the victim and then shot him in cold blood, we will take it as a sign that you are unhappy with your job here." More often, it is much more insidious, as in "What do you mean that you can't say that the suspect was lying in wait? He almost said as much in his statement." The way to deal with this sort of pressure, from whomever, is to communicate fully—to talk about what you will be able to prove, to talk about what you would be able to justify in your reconstruction and what you would not. It is generally helpful to deflect the conversation away from you, the reconstructionist, and back to the specifics of the evidence present at the scene. It is not about you, it is about the evidence—what it is capable of showing.

One simple device that may assist the crime reconstructionist in the maintenance of a proper professional stance against external pressure is a printed statement of ethical behavior posted conspicuously in his or her office. A consulting reconstructionist could have it posted on his or her Web site. This may read something along the lines of

1. As a practicing crime reconstructionist, I pledge to apply the principles of science and logic and to follow the truth courageously wherever it may lead.
2. As a practicing crime reconstructionist, I acknowledge that the scientific spirit must be inquiring, progressive, logical, and unbiased.
3. I will never knowingly allow a false impression to be planted in the mind of anyone availing themselves of my services.
4. As a practicing crime reconstructionist, it is not my purpose to present only that evidence which supports the view of one side. I have a moral and professional responsibility to ensure that everyone concerned understands the evidence as it exists and to present it in an impartial manner.
5. The practice of crime reconstruction has a single professional demand— correctness. It has a single ethical demand—truthfulness. To these I commit myself, totally and irrevocably.
6. The exigencies of a particular case will not cause me to depart from the professionalism that I am required to exercise.

It is hoped that the crime reconstructionist would have embraced these covenants in any event and that they are not just for show. Nevertheless, a published display will serve notice to everyone that the reconstructionist is unlikely to be receptive toward efforts to encroach upon these principles. In short, this posted statement may prevent someone from attempting to manipulate the reconstructionist. Additionally, when faced with any ethical dilemma, the crime reconstructionist should seek the counsel of other professional colleagues or should seek the aid of a professional organization that has established ethical guidelines.

REFERENCES

American Academy Code of Forensic Sciences (n.d.). *Bylaws and Code of Ethics*. Available at www.aafs.org

California Association of Criminalists (n.d.). *Code of Ethics.* Available at www. cac.news.org

Curran, W. (1980). Ethical standards. In W. Curran, A. McGarry, and C. Petty (Eds.), *Modern Legal Medicine, Psychiatry, and Forensic Science.* Philadelphia: Davis.

Hilton, O. (1976). Ethics and the Document Examiner Under the Adversary System. *Journal Forensic Science,* 21(4):779–783.

Hurley, P. (2002). *A Concise Introduction to Logic.* Belmont, CA: Wadsworth.

Peterson, J. (1989). Symposium: Ethical Conflicts in the Forensic Sciences. *Journal Forensic Science,* 34(3):717–793.

International Association of Chiefs of Police (n.d.). *Law Enforcement Code of Ethics.* Available at www.iacp.org

Interpol (n.d.). *Code of ethics.* Available at www.interpol.int

OBSERVER EFFECTS AND EXAMINER BIAS: PSYCHOLOGICAL INFLUENCES ON THE FORENSIC EXAMINER

Craig M. Cooley, MS, JD and Brent E. Turvey, MS

> Men generally believe quite freely that which they want to be true.
> —Julius Caesar, from "(H)omines fere credunt libentur id quod volunt."
> G. J. Caesar, Caesar's commentaries on the Gallic War 155 (51 BCE)

> Our assumptions define and limit what we see, i.e., we tend to see things in such a way that they will fit in with our assumptions even if this involves distortion or omission. We therefore may invert our title and say "Believing Is Seeing."
> —Johnson (1953, p. 79)

> [T]he history of science generally, and the history of psychology more specifically, suggests that more of us are wrong longer than we need to be because we hold our theories not quite lightly enough.
> —Robert Rosenthal as quoted in Zuckerman (1992)

Paul L. Kirk (1974, p. 4), pioneering criminalist, wrote, "Physical evidence cannot be wrong; it cannot be perjured; it cannot be wholly absent. *Only in its interpretation can there be error*" (italics added). This passage is of particular interest to forensic scientists because they are defined by their interpretive role with regard to physical evidence. The challenge is that much of what forensic examiners (i.e., forensic scientists and reconstructionists) are confronted with represents ambiguous stimuli—evidence that might be interpreted in more than one way depending on a variety of subjective influences.

When asked about bias, the majority of forensic examiners claim that they are entirely objective when performing their analyses, or that they try very hard to be. They also hold firm that their employer, their emotions, and their personal beliefs gain no influence on their final conclusions.[1] To admit otherwise would be professional suicide, as objectivity and emotional detachment are prized above all other traits in the course of a forensic examination. One could even argue that these are the defining traits.

Given the professed objectivity of forensic examiners, and their scientific training, it could be asked how bias may yet persist in their results. This is a perfectly reasonable question. Some forensic examiners claim that it does not, and that an objective aspect combined with scientific training is

[1] For instance, according to the renowned Dr. Henry Lee (1993), "The adversarial relationship between the state and a defendant tends to place the forensic experts engaged by one side or the other into an adversarial relationship. . . . Nevertheless, most forensic scientists, regardless of who employs them or engages their services, think of their results as entirely objective and try not to allow themselves to be forced into adversarial roles. . . . In most areas of forensic scientific inquiry, this task yields an objective set of results which is in no way altered by the fact that one side or the other has engaged a scientist's services."

sufficient to cure most, if not all, ills that may infect their examinations and subsequent results. However, this is untrue because it ignores a fundamental principle of cognitive psychology—the pervasive existence of observer effects.

As cognitive psychologists have repeatedly documented, tested, and proven, "[T]he scientific observer [is] an imperfectly calibrated instrument" (Rosenthal, 1966, p. 3). Their imperfections stem from the fact that subtle forms of bias, whether conscious or unconscious, can easily contaminate their seemingly objective undertakings. *Observer effects* are present when the results of a forensic examination are distorted by the context and mental state of the forensic examiner, to include the examiner's subconscious expectations and desires.

Identifying and curtailing this kind of bias is a considerable task when one takes into account the forensic community's affiliation with both law enforcement and the prosecution. Specifically, this association has fashioned an atmosphere in which an unsettling number of forensic professionals have all but abandoned objectivity and have become completely partial to the prosecution's objectives, goals, and philosophies (Giannelli (1997) discusses how the forensic community's structural configuration has created many pro-prosecution forensic scientists). They may even go so far as to regard this association as virtuous and heroic, and believe any alternative philosophy to be a manifestation of something that is morally bankrupt. So strong is the influence of this association between forensic science and law enforcement that some forensic examiners have even deliberately fabricated evidence, or testified falsely, so that the prosecution might prove its case; however, this is the extreme end of the spectrum (Bales (2000) discusses many instances concerning FBI examiners).

It is fair to say that the majority of practitioners in the forensic science community routinely acknowledge the existence of overt forms of conscious bias. That is, they generally recognize and condemn forensic ignorance, forensic fraud, and evidence fabricators when they are dragged into the light and exposed for all to see. Moreover, the forensic community seems to realize that in order to effectively serve the criminal justice system, they must immediately eliminate individuals, procedures, or circumstances that call into question examiner objectivity and neutrality (although this may be called into question in some specific cases, when forensic science organizations essentially fail in their duty to regulate membership and essentially protect inept and unethical examiners).

Although the forensic community is attenuated to the potential for extreme forms of outright fraud and overt bias, it tends to be wholly unaware when it comes to understanding and accepting that well-documented forms of covert bias can taint even the most impartial scientific examinations. This is disheartening for the simple reason that covert and subconscious biases represent a far greater threat to the forensic community than do the small percentage of overtly biased, dishonest, or fraudulent forensic examiners.

To grasp the elusive yet powerful nature of subconscious bias requires a brief lesson in cognitive psychology. *Cognitive psychology* is the psychological science that studies cognition, the mental processes that are believed to underlie behavior. This includes examining questions about the workings of memory, attention, perception, knowledge representation, reasoning, creativity, and problem solving.

The following is a well-established principle of cognitive psychology: An individual's desires and expectations can influence their perceptions, observations, and interpretations of events. In other words, the results of one's observations are dependent on at least two things: (1) the object or circumstance being observed and (2) the person's state of mind. Cognitive psychologists have coined several terms to describe this phenomenon, including *observer effects*, *context effects*, and *expectancy effects* (Neisser, 1976; Risinger et al., 2002; Rosenthal, 1966; Saks et al., 2003). This chapter uses all three to describe different manifestations of subconscious examiner bias, but readers may consider them essentially interchangeable.

PURPOSE

The purpose of this chapter is to remedy the omission of observer effects as a subject of study in the practitioner-oriented forensic science literature for the benefit of all forensic examiners. Furthermore, it is hoped that this will foster discussion of the subject by those practicing now and in the years to come. We begin by covering the predominant observer effects that may influence forensic examiners: prescreened evidence, single sample testing, attorney–investigator communication, contradictory findings, and selective reexamination. Mechanisms for dealing with observer effects are then outlined, including awareness, evidence lineups, blind testing, and filtering domain-irrelevant information. The ultimate goal of this chapter is not to convince forensic examiners that they are inherently biased and should therefore change careers. Rather, it is to help them realistically identify the potential influences of observer effects in their own work and ultimately blunt them to the extent that this is possible.

OBSERVER EFFECTS

As Professor D. Michael Risinger and colleagues (2002, p. 9) explained in their groundbreaking law review article on observer effects in forensic science, many different forms of observer effects exist: "At the most general level, observer effects are errors of apprehension, recording, recall, computation, or interpretation that result from some trait or state of the observer." As mentioned previously, these covert biases are more concerning than deliberate fraud and misconduct because they are often misperceived, or even thought of as beneficial, and therefore tend to go undetected. Consequently, in order to blunt their impact, scientists or researchers must be aware that these influences exist and can indeed significantly influence their analyses. Once conceded, they can be studied and understood; once understood, they can be addressed and even mitigated. The vast majority of scientific disciplines accept the need to blunt examiner bias and observer effects as a given and it is reflected in their published research. Put simply, "[s]ensitivity to the problems of observer effects has become integral to the modern scientific method" (Risinger et al., 2002, p. 6).

The observer effect phenomenon should be of particular concern to forensic scientists, especially reconstructionists, because so much of their role involves the selective recognition, documentation, and interpretation of physical evidence, the meaning of which hinges on objectivity in their observations. In this regard, forensic examiners have tremendous authority and an immense responsibility. If their examinations are distorted in any fashion, the results can be catastrophic for everyone concerned. It naturally follows that developing and imparting an understanding of observer effects would rate high in the consideration of forensic scientists when interpreting evidence and teaching their students. Sadly, as already mentioned, this is not the case.

Subconscious observer effects are not discussed in any of the major forensic science texts (Ashbaugh, 1999; De Forest et al., 1983; Fisher, 1999; Heard, 1997; James and Nordby, 2003; Lee et al., 2001; Saferstein, 2001) or treatises (Saferstein, 2002, 2004; Seigel et al., 2000), although Inman and Rudin (2000) provide perhaps the closest to a serious discussion in several sections of their exploratory treatise, *Principles and Practice of Criminalistics*. Likewise, no forensic science programs, undergraduate or graduate, regularly teach students about (1) observer effects in general and (2) how these effects may thrive in a government crime lab that is annexed with a law enforcement or prosecutorial agency.

Despite the lack of specific mention in major forensic texts and forensic science curricula, one could perhaps argue that forensic scientists have conducted comprehensive experiments designed to better learn the circumstances under which observer effects arise in their work and how examiners may take pains to tame them. In other words, one could argue that just because observer effects are not mentioned in books and classrooms does not mean that forensic scientists are necessarily ignorant of the subject. Regrettably, this argument cannot be made because no such experimentation has taken place. The forensic sciences are among the very few "scientific" disciplines that have failed to concede the existence and impact of observer effects, let alone study them. This is no small omission, as will be discussed later.

Because the forensic community has generally ignored this basic principle of cognitive psychology and good research methodology, by failing to account for subconscious examiner influences on research and casework, the following tends to be true:

- Forensic examiners are unaware that observer effects do exist and can impact their examinations, or
- Forensic examiners naively profess to be aware of subconscious observer effects yet, at the same time, refuse to admit that anything could possibly impact their conclusions; they claim that they have been trained to be objective and can, by exercising a unique will power, purge their minds of any impurities (conscious and subconscious alike) that may taint their analyses.

With respect to the latter situation (i.e., "these effects cannot distort my analysis"), what forensic examiners are in fact claiming is that their training montage consists of learning a special ability that is denied all other scientific disciplines, which makes them invulnerable to subconscious influences. This position is not defensible, although many upper tier forensic scientists continue to profess otherwise.

For instance, it appears that some forensic pathologists may adhere to the latter position (i.e., "I can disregard any biasing evidence so my conclusions will not be distorted"). Consider the following passage from a commonly referenced forensic pathology textbook (Di Maio and Di Maio, 1993, p. 14):

[The police] prefer the charlatan who tells them what they want to hear to the expert who tells them unpalatable truths or that conclusions cannot be made. One of the characteristics of the unqualified expert in forensic pathology is an ability to interpret a case in exquisite detail. This "expert" sets the time of death, plus or minus a few minutes, accurately positions the deceased, and gives detailed analysis of the events surrounding the death and precise deductions about the

[2] Similarities can be seen in the following statements: "Although the laboratories are intended primarily to assist the police, the work is carried out under the sole control of the director who makes his reports as an entirely independent investigator, that is to say irrespective of whether they favor the prosecution or the defense; they may therefore, be used subsequently in Court by either side" (Grant, 1941, p. 16); "For forensic science practitioners to perform their function properly within the legal system, they must exercise independence and integrity. Stated simply, forensic scientists cannot be biased for or against an investigation in which they are involved. The job of each practitioner is to champion his or her expert opinion based on accepted, properly performed scientific inquiry. Forensic scientists who understand their roles in a democratic criminal justice arena help to protect individual rights and freedoms while ensuring that justice is delivered" (Fisher, 1993, p. xxiv). Although Grant and Fisher both state the obvious—forensic scientists must be neutral and objective—they seem to suggest, particularly Fisher, that only overt biases, such as purposeful fraud or misconduct, can destroy an examiner's neutrality and objectivity. As this chapter highlights, such a suggestion is sorely misinformed. An examiner's objectivity and neutrality can be unknowingly and easily compromised in a variety of ways in today's publicly funded crime labs. Consequently, forensic scientists will "help protect individual rights and freedoms" once they acknowledge that they, like their scientific counterparts in every other scientific discipline, can fall prey to context effects.

[3] Dr. Selavaka made these comments to Cooley immediately after their panel discussion for the "Toward a Model Death Penalty Code: The Massachusetts Governor's Council Report" symposium at Indiana University School of Law. See "Symposium: Toward a Model Death Penalty Code" (2005).

assault. If the police have expressed prior opinions, it is not uncommon for the opinions of the "expert" to agree almost in complete detail with the police hypotheses. The experienced forensic pathologist tends to hedge, knows there may be more than one interpretation of a set of facts, and is more "wishy-washy" than the charlatan.[2]

While conceding that law enforcement suggestion and pressure represent major conscious obstacles for the "unqualified" forensic pathologist, Di Maio and Di Maio claim that the "qualified" forensic pathologist will have the necessary skill and resilience to remove any bias from the information he or she received prior to rendering a final autopsy report. The authors do not explain how this is actually accomplished, only that it is.

Similarly, one of the authors of this chapter (Cooley) served as a scientific evidence panel member at a death penalty symposium at the Indiana University School of Law. The author's presentation registered concern with the panel regarding the forensic community's misunderstanding of, and even indifference toward, the need to acknowledge and deal with subconscious influences on evidence interpretation (a.k.a. observer effects). Immediately following the panel discussion, a copanelist approached the author and said, "I have never heard of observer effects or examiners' biases. However, even if these effects do exist they cannot and do not affect my interpretations because I am an objectively trained scientist" (C. M. Selavaka, personal communication, September 10, 2004).[3] The panel member was and remains a PhD educated chemist who serves as director for a large state police laboratory system. The copanelist's second claim (i.e., "observer effects cannot taint my analysis"), like the "qualified" forensic pathology argument, demonstrates a general ignorance pertaining to the subconscious nature and potential influence of observer effects.

As Risinger et al. (2002, p. 51) explain, the notion that observer effects can be willed away is unfounded:

Every field that has considered the problem has concluded that it cannot be solved merely by trying to will it away. When everyone from Nobel prize winners to average citizens, who informally subject themselves to homemade "blind taste tests," take steps to make sure their judgments are not distorted by extraneous context information, then it is hard to conceive of what it is that makes forensic scientists think they are immune from the same effects.

Neglect and misunderstanding toward observer effects have prevented and continue to prevent the forensic community from developing procedures that could minimize their impact. With no preventative measures in operation, these imperceptible effects thrive in an environment that provides two powerful ingredients for the distillation of subconscious examiner influence—ambiguity and expectation. As a result of this collective ignorance and inaction, even the most neutral forensic examiners may offer conclusions that are imprecise, erroneous, or misleading, even when achieved through validated forensic techniques.[4]

"HUSHED" CONVERSATIONS AND THE THIRD RAIL

At this point, it is natural for students of forensic science to ask why the forensic community has neglected to openly discuss or study observer effects and their impact. Especially since every other legitimate science has done so. Many "hushed" conversations with colleagues across the legal and scientific spectrum throughout years of forensic practice lead the authors to an inescapable conclusion. Mention of the existence of overt bias is enough of a sore point among some law enforcement and prosecution-employed laboratory personnel, without having to concede the existence of subconscious and ultimately unknown observer effects. Furthermore, many forensic scientists and reconstructionists are employed directly by police agencies or by crime labs affiliated with, or under the direction of, law enforcement (to include the prosecution). Consequently, open discussion and study of examiner bias has long been considered a "third rail" in the forensic community. A brief explanation is warranted: The third rail is the method of providing electrical power to a railroad, such as a mass transit system, by means of an exposed conductor. Anyone who makes the mistake of touching the third rail is instantly killed by a surge of electricity. So it is with the issue of observer effects and their influence on subconscious examiner bias because such a discussion necessarily involves critical review of the actions and motives of both law enforcement and prosecutorial agencies. These are not professional communities that are generally perceived as receptive of criticism or review, and they are frequently hostile to external or independent efforts involving either.

The hostility of law enforcement toward open discussions of bias would not ordinarily be a problem for a scientific community, except, again, law enforcement actually employs a majority of the forensic scientists and reconstructionists whose subconsciously influenced results are at issue. Therefore, this is not an ordinary scientific community—the community that employs the forensic examiner is also the community that puts him at risk for observer effects. Any forensic examiner who raises this issue fears touching

[4] As Professor Michael J. Saks (2003) explains, "Indeed, such distortions will be more ubiquitous and more insidious precisely because they are not intended and their presence goes unnoticed."

the third rail—being the object of hostility and derision within the law enforcement and government lab community and losing not only his job but also his friends and, in some cases, his professional identity.

To be perfectly blunt, this situation cannot be allowed to continue. The inability to have an open discussion about the the impact of observer effects among forensic examiners, independent of agency or employer, severely hampers the professional growth of all forensic sciences. Good science works to account for bias—it does not ignore it or profess that it does not exist.

SUBJECTIVITY AND EXPECTATION IN FORENSIC SCIENCE

As mentioned previously, observer effects are governed by the fundamental principle of cognitive psychology that asserts that the subconscious needs and expectations shape both perception and interpretation. In a forensic science context, this includes what is recognized as evidence, what is collected, what is examined, and how it is interpreted. The ingredients necessary for the examiner to fall prey to this kind of bias are as follows:

1. The forensic examiner must be confronted by an ambiguous stimulus (a crime scene or an item of evidence) that is open to varying interpretations.
2. The forensic examiner must be made aware of an expected or desired outcome (Neisser, 1976).

To be clearer, this form of bias is characterized by the "tendency to resolve ambiguous stimuli in a manner consistent with expectations" (Thompson, 1996).

CONFRONTING AMBIGUITY AND SUBJECTIVITY

In a forensic science context, *ambiguity* becomes a factor when evidence or circumstances are incomplete, murky, and equivocal (Phillips et al., 2001). *Subjectivity* becomes a factor when identifications and interpretations rest on the examiner's experiences or beliefs (Thornton and Peterson, 2002). These factors are problematic when a forensic interpretation is premised on an examiner's belief that his or her experience is all that is required to render an identification.

Consider also that the majority of forensic examinations involve at least three layers of subjectivity: evidence collection, evidence quantity and quality, and a lack of articulated standards for qualifying the results of comparative analysis and identifications.[5]

The first subjective layer is the collection of evidence. What is collected and provided to the forensic examiner for analysis is perhaps one of the most subjective processes that inhabit the realm of forensic science. Presented with a crime scene, police investigators and technicians collect and submit evidence to the forensic scientist for examination and interpretation. At best, it represents an incomplete picture of the evidence that was left behind in the wake of a crime: Investigators cannot recognize everything and they cannot collect everything. At worst, it represents evidence collected in accordance with a specific preconceived theory that police investigators are seeking to bolster. Often, this is done in concert with ignoring or simply omitting facts and evidence that might point the forensic examiner away from the desired conclusion. The forensic examiner is given what attorneys and investigators deem of importance to their case and often nothing further. Quantity and quality of the evidence aside, what is collected and subsequently considered evidence can and does have an impact on the subsequent examination.

The second layer of subjectivity involves the quantity and quality of the evidence provided. As already explained, unlike the vast majority of practicing scientists, many forensic examiners have no control over the quality or quantity of their evidence. Depending on the abilities of local crime scene personnel, the quantity of evidence collected will vary dramatically. In some instances, the examiner will have an abundance of evidence to examine; in others, the examiner may find the sample sizes less than desirable—sometimes to the point where no significant examination or testing can be performed. With respect to the quality of evidence, forensic examiners must frequently perform forensic assessments on physical evidence that is of substandard quality. The quality of evidence can be compromised by a variety of agents and/or circumstances, which have been described as *evidence dynamics* (see Chapter 6). The very nature of the evidence may prohibit meaningful interpretation. Determining whether and when the physical evidence is of sufficient quantity and quality to allow for meaningful examination and interpretation can add further subjectivity to the process when minimum thresholds are not established.

A third layer of subjectivity occurs when forensic examiners are determining whether two pieces of physical evidence are "consistent with" or "match" each other. This is often accomplished by identifying an unspecified number of corresponding points of similarity during a comparative analysis. The majority of forensic disciplines do not require their examiners to isolate a specific number of matching points before they claim an

[5] *Identification sciences* are those that answer the question "What is it?" *Comparative analyses* are those that answer the question "Who or what does this belong to?" For example, the first identifies a visible pattern on a surface as a fingerprint with particular individuating characteristics; the second involves its comparison to potential sources.

[6] Consider the wide-ranging point "system" in fingerprinting, see *Commonwealth v. Hunter*, 338 A.2d 623, 624 (Pa. Super. Ct. 1975) (14 points); *United States v. Durant*, 545 F.2d 823, 825 (2d Cir. 1976) (14 points); *Alexander*, 571 N.E.2d 1075, 1078 (Ill. App. Ct. 1991) (11 and 14 points); *State v. Starks*, 471 So.2d 1029, 1032 (La. Ct. App. 1985) (12 points); *People v. Garlin*, 428 N.E.2d 697, 700 (Ill. App. Ct. 1981) (12 points); *Garrison v. Smith*, 413 F. Supp. 747, 761 (N.D. Miss. 1976) (12 points); *State v. Murdock*, 689 P.2d 814, 819 (Kan. 1984) (12 points); *Magwood v. State*, 494 So.2d 124, 145 (Ala. Crim. App. 1985) (11 points); *State v. Cepec*, 1991 WL 57237, at *1 (Ohio Ct. App. 1991) (11 points); *Ramirez v. State*, 542 So.2d 352, 353 (Fla. 1989) (ten points); *People v. Jones*, 344 N.W.2d 46, 46 (Mich. Ct. App. 1983) (ten points); *State v. Jones*, 368 S.E.2d 844, 846 (N.C. 1988) (ten points); *Commonwealth v. Ware*, 329 A.2d 258, 276 (Pa. 1974) (nine points); *State v. Awiis*, 1999 WL 391372, at *7 (Wash. Ct. App. 1999) (eight points); and *Commonwealth v. Walker*, 116 A.2d 230, 234 (Pa. Super. Ct. 1955) (four points). See also Epstein (2002).

[7] Determining whether the match is a coincidental match—examiners are essentially asking how probable is it to find a match by pure chance.

[8] Phillips et al. (2001) state, "[W]ith the exception of such areas as biological fluids . . . the forensic sciences possess little empirical data to assist examiners in interpreting the meaning of their test results and affixing a probability or confidence to their findings"; and "Ordinarily, the examiner does not have access to a database that assists in quantifying the rarity of the marks, or which even records them, but must rely on memory of other samples viewed in the past" (p. 299).

[9] Thornton and Peterson (2002, p. 2) state, "Most forensic examinations are conducted in government-funded laboratories,

absolute identification between two items.[6] Likewise, forensic examiners regularly utilize varied criteria that are typically not published or even articulated (Phillips et al., 2001). Interwoven with this process is the probabilistic determination that a match or event is not coincidental.[7] DNA aside, the results of comparative analysis and identifications are too often manifestations of an examiner's experience rather than logical inference, empirical study, and published research.[8] Without established evidentiary thresholds and practice standards for evidentiary interpretation, forensic examiners are able to make apparent scientific interpretations of evidence that are actually based on what they feel and believe, rather than on what has been proven or disproved by their methods.

The occurrence of ambiguous physical evidence, as well as evidence that is susceptible to subjective interpretation, opens the door for subconscious observer effects to influence examiner results. However, it is the lack of examiner confidence coupled with expectation that invites them inside.

THE LURE OF EXPECTATION

Forensic examiners are regularly put into situations in which they are privy to information that can easily cultivate conscious or unconscious expectations. The most common expectation developed is that a suspect or defendant must be guilty of something, if not the crime they are accused of. The occurrence of this expectation is not surprising when one considers, again, the structural alignment of publicly funded crime labs. The overwhelming majority of, if not all, public crime labs are annexed with the very police and prosecutorial agencies to which they provide assistance.[9] The primary objectives of these parent agencies are to identify, prosecute, and convict the guilty. Working in a pro-prosecution environment, where a suspect's guilt is both suspected and even anticipated, it is easy to see how and why some forensic examiners can subconsciously develop certain preexamination expectations that may influence their results.[10] This section discusses specific forensic science and law enforcement practices that are capable of inducing these potentially biasing expectations.

Single Sample Testing

For the most part, when investigators turn over evidence to forensic examiners, it typically falls into three groups:

1. Samples taken from the crime scene
2. Samples taken from the victim
3. Samples provided by the suspect

Single sample testing in the forensic sciences has been shown to directly affect whether an examiner's report will associate the suspect with the crime scene or the victim. For instance, in one published study, researchers found that fewer than 10% of forensic reports failed to associate a suspect to the crime scene or the victim (Peterson et al., 1984). Stated conversely, 90% of forensic reports inculpated the suspect in some fashion. As Professor D. Michael Risinger of Seton Hall Law School and his colleagues (2002, p. 47) explain:

> This high rate of inculpation comes from the fact that each piece of evidence connected with any suspect has a heightened likelihood of being inculpatory, since investigators do not select suspects or evidence at random, but only those they have some reason to think were connected to the crime. Thus, forensic scientists have a continuing expectation that the evidence before them is inculpatory.

The emphasis here is on the existence of a continuing expectation of inculpation because of past results and an examiner's propensity for generalizing: Nine times out of ten the hairs match, the fingerprints match, or the DNA matches—so odds are it's probably going to match this time.

Single sample testing is eerily similar to an eyewitness "show-up," which is an identification procedure in which an eyewitness is presented with a single suspect for comparison and identification (Technical Working Group for Eyewitness Evidence, 1999). Eyewitness research has continually recognized an assortment of shortcomings associated with this form of identification (Wells et al., 1998). Considering forensic examiners and eyewitnesses perform comparable identification and comparison tasks, the same weaknesses that surface during eyewitness show-ups can undoubtedly emerge during single sample forensic evaluations (Risinger et al., 2002). The most obvious is the expectation that the samples submitted to the forensic examiner will, in some way, inculpate the defendant because this is usually the case.

Note that the possibility of examiner error is diminished in such circumstances by the use of analytical logic, the scientific method, and empirical research. However, single sample testing becomes problematic in the context of ambiguous and subjectively interpreted evidence. This is necessarily exacerbated when results are predicated entirely on examiner experience, as is the case with some reconstruction interpretations.

Prescreened Evidence

Even the most scrupulous reconstructionist can be undone by resting solid conclusions on incomplete information. As already discussed, forensic

usually located within law enforcement agencies, and typically for the purpose of building a case for the prosecution."

[10] Miller (1987, pp. 157–158) states, "In criminal investigations, the police generally have little or no doubt regarding the suspect's guilt. Their preoccupation lies with obtaining sufficient proof for a conviction. That attitude may be communicated to the forensic examiner through personal interaction or through the written synopsis accompanying the evidence to be examined. It is conceivable that the forensic examiner may unconsciously believe that the suspect must be guilty or the police would not have made the arrest. Such unconscious beliefs may potentially create prejudice, bias, and stereotypes on the examiner's part regarding conclusions about the evidence. The occurrence of belief transferals from one to another person has been well documented in the social-psychological literature."

examiners, especially those working for state agencies, are often fed a narrow amount of physical evidence from attorneys and investigators that may or may not be sufficient to render fully informed reconstruction interpretations. Commonly, they will not have visited the crime scene and viewed its context and will not have collected the evidence themselves. In such instances, they are forced to rely on the efforts of law enforcement-employed crime scene technicians who, working directly under the influence of detectives, have decided what is important and what is not based on an initial and perhaps incorrect theory of the crime.

One retired crime scene investigator wrote the following to express concerns regarding this practice in a discussion on the need for increased forensic science education on the part of crime scene personnel (Wally Lind, retired crime scene analyst, public e-mail communication with Turvey):

> Detectives have theories, and detectives usually decide what gets lab tested. Detective theories can be wrong and unfair to the victim and defendant. Detective[s] don't send in evidence to learn what happened, they send it in to support their theories. And, unfortunately, the defense has no say in what gets lab tested by the state.

This circumstance creates a situation in which, from the start, the forensic scientist or reconstructionist is disadvantaged. Unless they are given unfettered access to the crime scene when possible, and full crime scene documentation, they cannot be certain that enough forensic data have been collected to answer the questions presented by the available evidence in a meaningful or faithful manner. What they are generally provided is a narrow picture of evidence that has been preselected by investigators because of its value to furthering the cause of a particular theory. Subsequently, any expectation on the part of forensic examiners that they are getting everything relevant to their analysis is more than likely unwarranted.

Far from being an argument that forensic scientists are too disadvantaged to perform reconstructions because they lack first hand knowledge of the scene as it was found, quite the opposite is true. Forensic scientists evaluate not just the scene but the nature and quality of the evidence processing and documentation efforts. The jury, it must be remembered, will also be asked to make determinations about events using the same evidence, without having gone to the scene. If the nature and quality of the scene processing and documentation efforts are insufficient for the forensic scientist to reconstruct certain events, the same must be true for the lay juror. When crime scene technicians and investigators have not sufficiently processed or documented the scene to enable a reconstruction, for whatever reason, the jury needs to have this brought to their attention.

Prescreening of evidence may also occur in an environment in which there exists an expectation on the part of investigators that forensic scientists and reconstructionists have a strong desire to help their cause. That is, they may expect that forensic examiners will do whatever they can with whatever they are given to make a connection between the victim, the suspect, or the crime and prove their theory. Unless forensic examiners establish unequivocal and unwavering evidentiary thresholds for their examinations, they may find themselves unable to resist the temptation to perform analyses and render conclusions under these circumstances, even when the evidence is insufficient.

Irrelevant Data: Communication between Investigators and Examiners

When forensic examiners are presented with a new case, they typically receive evidence and contextual information in one of two ways. Either they meet directly with the lead investigator and have a conversation, or the pertinent case information is forwarded to them via mail, e-mail, courier, or facsimile. Both circumstances are equally capable of inducing examiner expectation.

Unlike investigators, forensic examiners have a duty to act with restraint in regard to the information they consider when performing analyses and forming conclusions. As Risinger et al. (2002, p. 28) explain:

> When the forensic scientist is exposed to, relies on, or is influenced by any information outside of her own domain, she is abusing her warrant, even though she may honestly believe that such information makes her conclusion more reliable, and even, or especially, if she is right about this.

This brings us to the question of how forensic examiners come into contact with domain-irrelevant information. For the most part, they do not receive only the physical evidence when assigned a new case. Rather, the lead investigators frequently supplement their forensic examination requests with detailed crime scene and investigative reports. For instance, Miller (1987, pp. 157–158) wrote:

> In the examination and identification of human hair . . . investigators usually submit the questioned and known suspect hair samples along *with a synopsis of facts surrounding the investigation* [italics added]. The main purpose of the synopsis is to provide information to the examiner that may assist in the analysis. The synopsis

usually contains the facts and circumstances leading to the arrest of a suspect. In some cases, the synopsis may even include eyewitness accounts, other forms of physical evidence collected in the case, and admissions or confessions made by the suspect.[11]

As the scenario suggests, investigative reports and correspondences regularly convey superfluous information about the crime, the victim, and the defendant. For instance, examiners may be told that other physical evidence inculpates the defendant, or they may be told what investigators anticipate based on case theories and witness statements. In short, forensic scientists are frequently made privy to "potentially or irrefutably inculpatory evidence in a case" (Saks, 2000). Although investigatively relevant, much of this information is unnecessary when performing many forensic examinations, particularly comparative analysis and identifications. More significantly, these superfluous facts make murky forensic evaluations even murkier because they convey and implant the hopes, beliefs, and expectations of the investigator.

Case Example: Boots and Proctor

Consider the case of Christopher Boots and Eric Proctor. Boots and Proctor were charged in 1986 and convicted in 1987 for the 1983 execution-style slaying of a convenience store clerk in Springfield, Oregon [see *State v. Boots*, 767 P. 2d 450 (Or. App. 1989), *rev'd*, 780 P. 2d 725 (Or. 1989); *State v. Proctor*, 767 P. 2d 453 (Or. App. 1989)]. Aside from some dubious and ultimately discredited bloodstain pattern analysis results that failed to convince a grand jury in 1984 (the criminalist admitted during a deposition that he had used the same ruler to scrape blood from the victim's and then the suspect's clothing for blood on the same day), the only physical evidence linking Boots and Proctor to the crime was described by forensic scientists as two flakes of double-base smokeless gunpowder located on Proctor's pants. A criminalist with the Springfield crime lab analyzed the first flake of possible gunpowder in 1983. The test, which consumed the particle, was positive for oxidizers. Oxidizers are certainly found in gunpowder, but they are also in fireworks, matches, fertilizer, car paint, and many other substances. A photo of the flake could not be located. The criminalist discovered a second alleged gunpowder flake in 1986, this time sending half of it to the FBI crime lab in Washington, DC, to verify his conclusion that it matched particles found on the victim (Teichroeb, 2004). In addition to forwarding the evidence, he enclosed the following letter to the FBI laboratory (Risinger et al., 2002, pp. 35–36):

[11] In his book, *Bones: A Forensic Detective's Casebook* (Ubelaker and Scammell, 1992), Douglas Ubelaker, a forensic anthropologist for the Smithsonian Institute, details how, on numerous occasions, he received extensive case information from the FBI when the FBI requested his services. Realizing that "being influenced by someone's expectations" is a major threat to forensic examiners, Ubelaker developed a system in which he would only read the information necessary to log in the evidence sent to him.

As per our phone conversation of March 6, 1986, I am submitting the partially burned flakes of double base powder out of our Oliver homicide.

This is a murder case that took place in June 1983. The killer or killers entered a local 7–11 store in the late evening hours and forced the young male clerk into the back room (cooler) and broke a full 10 ounce bottle of Orange Crush over his head and then shot him in the head three times with a .22 caliber weapon (probably a Hi-Standard revolver). Due to some interagency problems the case to date has not been prosecuted, but will be soon.

Going through the trace evidence, some of which had been analyzed by SEM-EDAX, I found a partially burned double base powder flake on one of the planchets. The flake was originally found on the trousers of one of our suspects. We want, if possible, for you or Ed to compare this flake (B) to some partially burned flakes (A) found on the body of our victim. The only difference between the treatment of the flakes is that flake B has been carbon coated to prepare it for SEM work.

Exhibits:

Both A and B are sandwiched between the glass slides and clearly circled and labeled. (I have tried to get them to move by tapping the slide but they appear to be stationary.)

(Sample A) Several partially burned flakes of double base powder from the victim.

(Sample B) One piece of partially burned flake of double base powder from the trousers of a suspect.

Request:

If possible, please compare A to B.

Time is of the essence now because of a lawsuit one of the suspects is bringing against the police department for false arrest.

I would appreciate any help you can give. Thank you very much.

/S/

The FBI lab produced a confirmatory result. An FBI supervisor testified at both criminal trials that the particle was double-base gunpowder (Teichroeb, 2004).

Also linking Boots and Proctor to the crime was the bloodstain pattern analysis performed by the Oregon criminalist. According to the record [*State of Oregon v. Eric A. Proctor*, 94 Or. App. 720, 767 P. 2d 453, Or. App., Jan 11, 1989],

[The criminalist] collect[ed] and identify[ied] . . . high velocity blood spatter from defendant's [Proctor's] shirt. Not expecting to find blood spatter in his forensic examination, [the criminalist] scraped and vacuumed the surface of the shirt and examined the resulting debris microscopically, looking for hairs and fibers that might serve as evidence linking defendant to the crime. He discovered that the debris contained blood particles of a size and shape consistent with high velocity blood spatter caused by the impact of a bullet into a nearby bloody target. The technique [the criminalist] employed to collect the sample was not one that would ordinarily be used to determine the presence of blood spatter.

According to further reports (Teichroeb, 2004, p. A1),

> At the criminal trials, [the criminalist] testified that he'd found "high-velocity blood spatter" on both men's clothes—the type of spatter that could only have come from being in close proximity during the shooting of victim Raymond Oliver. He said [at trial] a renowned blood-spatter expert had agreed with his conclusion, something the expert later denied in an affidavit.
>
> [The criminalist] also told the jury he'd found two flakes of double-base smokeless gunpowder on Proctor's pants.
>
> That was the only physical evidence tying the men to the crime. The rest of the prosecution's case relied on testimony from police informants, including two who later recanted their statements.
>
> . . .
>
> DNA testing in 1994 on the 10–12 remaining blood particles determined that all but one particle did not match the victim, according to court documents.
>
> The plaintiffs' experts attributed the one matching particle to contamination after [the criminalist] admitted during a deposition that he'd used the same ruler to scrape both the victim and suspects' clothing on the same day—and had failed to wear gloves.[12]
>
> The state argued that the single matching particle was proof that Proctor was linked to the crime.

The case against Boots and Proctor totally collapsed after an anonymous tip led investigators to the real perpetrator. Richard Kuppens, whose fingerprint was later discovered on duct tape from the victim's body at the crime scene,[13] confessed before killing himself in October 1994. His coconspirators told investigators they had never met Boots and Proctor. In November 1993, after spending eight years in prison, Boots and Proctor were set free and eventually sued the state of Oregon, settling for $2 million in 1998 (Teichroeb, 2004).

Case Example: Stephen Casey

George Castelle (1999), a public defender from West Virginia, provides another excellent example. This is a case from the files of the infamous

[12] This procedure is wrong when looking for trace evidence, including hairs and particularly for fibers because microscopic fibers could adhere to the ruler at any time. The ruler must be cleaned or preferably a different one utilized. Also, wearing gloves is a safety issue, and they should always be worn when handling evidence. The gloves must be changed when going from one garment to another even from the same person.

[13] Remarkably, during closing arguments, Proctor's defense attorney argued that this unidentified fingerprint belonged to the real killers (see *State v. Proctor*, 767 P.2d 453, 455 (Or. App. 1989): "An unidentified fingerprint was recovered from the masking tape used to bind the victim. Defense counsel contended in closing argument that the fingerprint on the masking tape, which belonged to neither defendant nor to the victim, was most probably the fingerprint of the actual killer."

criminalist Fred Zain.[14] Stephen Casey was arrested and charged with sexually abusing a five-year-old child. Prior to the West Virginia crime lab obtaining the physical evidence, Zain resigned from the lab and accepted a position with the Bexar County Medical Examiners Office in San Antonio, Texas. Once the West Virginia crime lab received the physical evidence, technicians who examined a carpet sample could not identify any semen stains on the carpet. Investigators had hoped that the carpet sample would contain the offender's semen (a.k.a Mr. Casey's semen). Undeterred by the crime lab's failure to discover inculpatory evidence, investigators sent the carpet sample off to Zain in San Antonio. The carpet sample was accompanied by the following letter (Castelle, 1999, p. 12):

> Mr. Zain:
> This is the carpet that we discussed via Public Service. The W. Va. State Police Lab was unable to show any evidence of sperm or blood being present on it.
>   The suspect was arrested for 1st Degree Sexual Abuse on a five-year-old female. Any evidence you can find pertaining to this crime will greatly increase our chances of conviction.
>   Thank you,
>   Det. R. R. Byard
>   Huntington Police Department

Like the letter sent by the criminalist in the Boots and Proctor case, the letter to Zain contains both domain-irrelevant information and expectation cues, the irrelevant data being that the West Virginia lab failed to identify any semen and that the defendant was being charged with sexually abusing a five-year-old. Both pieces of information are completely irrelevant to whether Zain can identify a semen stain and whether that semen stain is consistent with the defendant's semen. The expectation cue is fairly obvious: "Any evidence you can find pertaining to this crime will greatly increase our chances of conviction." As might be expected, Zain succeeded where his West Virginia counterparts had failed; he found semen.

    The Fred Zain affair was perhaps the worst scandal in the history of the West Virginia State Police Crime Lab. A West Virginia State Police investigation identified as many as 182 cases that were affected by his work. Beyond the expense of investigating and prosecuting Zain, and retrying cases related to him, West Virginia has paid at least $6.5 million to settle lawsuits by wrongfully convicted defendants. Zain was ultimately put on trial for perjury in numerous serology cases, for tests not performed ("dry-labbing"), and for fraud regarding the misrepresentation of his credentials. He died in December 2002 of colon cancer before convictions could be secured.

[14] See Matter of Investigation of West Virginia State Police Crime Laboratory, Serology Div., 438 S.E.2d 501 (W.Va.1993), which discusses at length Zain's fraudulent conduct and incompetence.

Case Example: The FBI Crime Lab and the 1997 Office of the Inspector General's Report

The Office of the Inspector General's (OIG, 1997) investigation of the FBI laboratory identified various incidents in which examiners relied on domain-irrelevant information when forming their conclusions. Among the most brazen incidents detailed by the OIG's report was the testimony in the 1996 World Trade Center bombing case. An explosives expert in the FBI crime lab's explosives unit claimed to have identified the main charge as a urea nitrate bomb. His conclusion, however, was not premised on any physical evidence from the bombing scene but on "speculation based on evidence linking the defendants to that explosive" (p. 11). The OIG report (pp. 128–129) condemned the practice of relying on scientifically irrelevant data:

> [The expert] portrayed himself as a scientist and rendered opinions as an explosives expert. As such, he should have limited himself to conclusions that logically followed from the underlying data and the scientific analyses performed.... He should not have based his opinions, in whole or in part, on evidence that was collateral to his scientific examinations, even if that evidence was somehow connected to the defendants.... By basing his urea nitrate opinion on the collateral evidence, [he] implicitly accepted as a premise the prosecution's theory of guilt. This was improper.[15]

[15] The "report concluded that an examiner from the lab's explosives unit had erred by purporting to identify the particular explosives used in the World Trade Center and Oklahoma City bombings. The error stemmed from the examiner's reliance on information that was tied to suspects but not relevant to his scientific analysis" (Bales, 2000, p. 51).

In a strikingly similar case in which a defendant was charged with creating a large quantity of explosive material by stripping it out of detonating cord, the FBI examiner (OIG, 1997, p. 30):

> acknowledged that his identification of PETN on the tools was based in part on the fact that stripped detonating cord was found in the defendant's garbage. In his interview with the OIG, [the expert] observed that given this information, he presumed the material on the knife was PETN.... Rudolph failed to distinguish between the separate and distinct roles of an investigator and a forensic scientist.

With the OIG report condemning the practice of basing a scientific opinion on improper information, one would assume that the forensic community might respond by encouraging the practice of limiting the types of information conveyed to forensic examiners. Unfortunately, for the most part, the forensic community has yet to embrace such a view. For instance, consider the following passage from a forensic science textbook (Netzel, 2003, pp. 165–166):

Association with a law enforcement agency is critical to most government laboratories, but should never influence the outcome of a scientific investigation. Vital to a laboratory's role in an investigation is access to information and physical evidence at the crime scene. Without legal access to a crime scene, a laboratory will be severely hindered in performing its function during an investigation. *Also, a free exchange of information between law enforcement agencies and the laboratory is necessary* [italics added]. Without an official association, this exchange of information could be difficult. Individuals who believe that a forensic scientist should work independently of investigative information are misled. *No scientist in any discipline should choose to work without having as much information as possible about his assignment* [italics added]. Knowledge of certain facts will assist the criminalist in determining what questions should be addressed by his examination.

. . .

As a part of the criminalist's role in an investigation, he must utilize his own ability to ask questions and investigate the information already available. A solid approach to being a case examination, particularly a major case, would include review of crime scene reports, diagrams and photographs, evidence collected, statements of suspects and/or witnesses, and, of course, information in police reports. . . . Most of the information that aids the criminalist comes from asking questions of the law enforcement investigator. *Gaining as much information as possible about a situation will not alter scientific results* [italics added].

Specific to comparative analysis and identification procedures, it is true that more information regarding the evidence and how it was found is of vital importance. However, general contextual information regarding the results of other forensic examinations, the statements of suspects, and the expectations of investigators is not. Without clear delineation between the type of information that is necessary to an identification scientist and the type that is not, the suggestion that any and all available information be sent their way is troubling (of course, the problems for the reconstructionist are far greater precisely because they require all of the available contextual information and analytical results; this is discussed later).

A document examination textbook stated the following about what information should be considered before rendering an opinion (Dines, 1998, pp. 4–5): "Before an attempt by the examiner to identify handwriting, the investigator should consult and [obtain] as much circumstantial evidence as possible about the case." Again, no delineation as to what should be screened and why—just send everything.

Inman and Rudin's text (2000, pp. 248–249) advocates a somewhat similar position, although it is more upfront about the dangers this may pose:

Typically the analyst knows something about the history of the evidence up until the time it enters the laboratory, and will interpret the results based on that history. Forensic scientists are generally familiar with the need to interpret evidence in the context of the history of the sample prior to its collection and preservation. But before the results are interpreted, and even before any analysis occurs, the criminalist must define the relevant questions. *The more the analyst knows about the case, the better she can direct and refine the questions so that the answers are both useful and relevant* [italics added].

The argument, made mostly by attorneys, against the analyst knowing the circumstances of a case, is that such knowledge may introduce subconscious, or worse yet malicious bias, leading to prejudiced interpretation of the results. Superficially, this would seem to be a credible thesis. However, we believe that the advantages gained as a result of an informed analysis substantially outweigh the concerns. Furthermore, a series of checks and balances can and should be employed to *ensure that alternate explanations for the data are duly considered* [italics added]. Moreover, we submit that bias is most likely to enter a case and do the most damage at the level of the question being asked, rather than in the interpretation of results.

Although we applaud Inman and Rudin for discussing the "how much should a forensic examiner know" issue, their analysis and explanation is somewhat limited. First, it is not simply defense attorneys who make the claim that scientific observers should screen the information they consider before rendering a conclusion. Rather, cognitive psychologists have studied this phenomenon for years and have documented, time and again, that having too much biasing information can create a conscious or subconscious expectation regarding the results. These can create expectations that can easily contaminate an examiner's objectivity. Instead of impartially interpreting evidence and accepting the good with the bad in terms of their stated hypothesis, the expectation, in effect, creates an internal set of blinders.

Second, unlike reconstructionists who require access to other experts' reports and crime scene findings in order to integrate and corroborate final results, there is no reason why forensic identification examiners (e.g., DNA analysts, fingerprint examiners, toolmark examiners, or handwriting examiners) need to know as much about the case as possible. Their primary objectives are not to establish events, sequence actions, or determine the nature of broad associations like their reconstructive colleagues. Rather, they are called on to answer a basic question: Does the print, pattern, toolmark, or handwriting related to the crime associate the print, patterns, tools, or penmanship associated with the suspect, and to what degree? This question can be answered without having to refer to the results of other forensic experts working on the case and without consideration of extraneous case theories. Relying on such information can only increase the likelihood that the identification examiner's results will be tainted.

Luke May, a forensic science pioneer, warned of this in his book, *Crimes Nemesis*, written in 1936. According to May:

> In the classroom of the School of Scientific Police at the Palais de Justice in Paris is a truism: "The eyes see in things only what they look for, and they look only for what is already in the mind."
>
> This might well be a universal warning in crime detection, for often the most significant bit of evidence is overlooked or misinterpreted because someone has jumped to a premature conclusion. The detective who quickly reconstructs a crime without sufficient supporting evidence is very liable to spend days, weeks, and perhaps months on a wrong scent in a vain effort to make evidence fit his personal version of what happened at the scene of the crime. Unconsciously, perhaps, he may try to convict an innocent victim who he believes committed a crime while the real perpetrator takes advantage of the wild-goose chase to make a clean get-away.
>
> To face a crime with an open mind—a mind willing to believe and disbelieve even its own senses, sometimes willing to admit and desert one line of investigation for another, is one of the most difficult tasks of the detective. He is human, and like all other humans he is subject to personal prejudice.

Although Inman and Rudin's (2000) minimization of the context effect issue is problematic, they do provide an excellent illustration of how certain types of evidence or information can affect an individual's interpretation of ambiguous stimuli (e.g., bloodstain patterns) (p. 183):

> One example of such an overinterpretation occurred in a case involving two suspects accused of torturing and shooting the clerk at a Stop 'N Rob convenience store. A detective from another jurisdiction, who had attended several bloodstain pattern interpretation workshops, was retained to prepare a reconstruction based on the blood patterns at the scene. He wrote an 11-page report, including every movement of the victim and suspects over a 30- to 45-minute time period. He included in his reconstruction a 5-minute time period where all activity ceased for the three individuals, basing this on a photograph of what he interpreted as a blood clot. He concluded that the victim was shot, bled for a period of 5 minutes on the floor, and then was beaten by the assailants. How did he arrive at this detailed reconstruction? He was given one suspect's confession, who indicated that they had shot the victim, sat around eating sandwiches and mocking him for 5 minutes, and then beat him for good measure. The detective used this as a starting point for his reconstruction, and picked out stains from the crime scene photographs that

appeared to him to be clotted blood. As a nonscientist, he couldn't quite comprehend the criticism that it was not possible to distinguish between a blood clot and a bloodstain based on a photograph. Happily, he did not include a reconstruction of the suspect's meal, although perhaps only because no blood was involved in it.

Although they coin this phenomenon "overinterpretation," what they are actually describing in this scenario is the "expectancy effect." This example is excellent because it illustrates what can happen when the forensic examiner is given what is probably the most prejudicial information in a case, the defendant's statement, before rendering her opinion. After reading the defendant's statement, the bloodstain expert became fixated on one explanation for events. In effect, what the bloodstain expert did was the antithesis of science, as he started with an explanation (i.e., the defendant said the crime occurred in this manner) and then dredged through the evidence to find any bloodstains or evidence that would tend to support his explanation. What he found was something that he could use to justify the conclusion, even though it was impossible to see. He saw it because he needed it to support the foredrawn conclusion.

Again, as Luke May (1936) warned, "The eyes see in things only what they look for, and they look only for what is already in the mind."

Contradictory Findings

When more than one forensic expert is involved with the examination of physical evidence in a given case, there is the possibility that they will reach different or conflicting results. When two or more forensic examiners achieve contradictory findings, reevaluations of the evidence will typically ensue. Occasionally, after reevaluating the physical evidence and considering the contradictory findings, some forensic examiners will alter and even tailor their original conclusions so that all inferences drawn from each member of the forensic team are in accord.[16] This form of opinion "editing" is easily influenced by expectation bias. Both factors that cultivate expectation bias are present—an ambiguous stimuli that is capable of multiple interpretations and the awareness of a desired or expected outcome.

Selective Reexamination of Evidence

The occurrence of contradictory forensic interpretations is not unheard of among government-employed laboratory analysts working separately but on the same case, as already suggested in the previous section. When this happens, prosecutors and investigators will occasionally seek out the forensic examiner whose interpretation is inconsistent with their preferred theory

[16] What they should do is look for an explanation that removes the conflict between the findings. That is, both findings are consistent with an alternative hypothesis that may be tested.

of the case. Once in direct contact, they will confront the contrary examiner, stating that the examiner's results are at odds with another examiner's conclusions and the theory of the case. They may further emphasize that this contradiction, if not corrected, will appreciably weaken the state's case against the defendant.

Having laid this foundation, the prosecutor or investigator will then ask the examiner to reevaluate the evidence; reinforcing the fact that if conclusion "X" is reached, the case against the defendant will be substantially stronger. The contamination present within this scenario is easily identified; by explaining to the examiner that a certain conclusion is favored (e.g., a more inculpatory finding), prosecutors and investigators are attempting to lure the examiner to tamper with their initial conclusions. Once again, both factors that can nurture observer effects are present—an ambiguous stimuli that is capable of multiple interpretations and the awareness of a desired or expected outcome.

Although this kind of bias-inducing interaction may be fairly easy to recognize, the impartiality that it fosters is potent. The mere act of soliciting a particular examiner to reassess his conclusions will automatically distort any new conclusions. *Cherrypicking*, as it is commonly referred to, invites reconsiderations of only those conclusions that are not preferred by the police and prosecutor [see Peterson and Conley (2001), who discuss cherrypicking in the legal and scientific context]. Conclusions that they favor, that help the prosecution of the accused, are not sent back for reconsideration.[17]

Consequently, if the preferred conclusion is incorrect and the nonpreferred conclusion is correct, selective reexaminations where the examiner succumbs to observer effects essentially add forensic strength to a potential wrongful conviction. Because the incorrect conclusion is not reevaluated, it cannot be identified and corrected.

Also, the examiner in such cases is made aware that other, more desired, conclusions were reached. It is the examiner's awareness of a more desired outcome that makes this type of interaction and request susceptible to observer effects. The reexamination request along with the irrelevant information may compel an examiner to doubt and weaken her conviction concerning initial (correct) conclusions. Worse, it may lead the examiner to abandon her original (correct) conclusion entirely and move to agree with the examiner who proffered the incorrect, yet preferred, conclusion.

[17] On a related issue, state and federal labs must always be on guard when contacted by an agency that has access to a local laboratory. Are they "lab shopping," hoping to find the results they want because the local lab did not agree with their theory? In such instances, if a case is submitted from a jurisdiction or agency that has its own lab (and the evidence is not part of an investigation into that lab), then it is advisable to require that the local lab submit the evidence along with a letter from the director explaining why the state or federal lab should perform any necessary examinations. This policy creates a record that only those shopping for results would prefer to avoid.

RECOMMENDATIONS TO BLUNT OBSERVER EFFECTS

To decrease bias, conscious and unconscious alike, the forensic science community must utilize the same checks and balances already adopted by other scientific communities. The ensuing discussion focuses on three of the more important procedural reforms that would curtail observer effects in forensic science and crime reconstruction: awareness, filtering domain-irrelevant information (blind testing), and evidence lineups.

AWARENESS

Awareness of observer effects, their subconscious nature and undeniable influence on perception, is a first and necessary step. Forensic examiners have a duty to understand which of these influences may persist in their environment and to adjust their professional manner and practices to guard against them when possible. This begins with admitting their potential existence and becoming more than just literate on the subject. However, awareness is only the beginning.

FILTERING THE IRRELEVANT

As already shown, too much of the wrong kind of information can bias the way that a forensic examiner perceives and interprets the evidence he is provided. Once the problem of observer effects is admitted and understood, forensic examiners in each forensic discipline must come to an agreement regarding which kinds of information are actually required in order to competently perform their analysis. Furthermore, they should also be able to create a list of the kinds of information that might bias or influence their analysis and whether it may be filtered or not. The inability of any forensic examiner to perform this basic task suggests that they have become lost in the geography of observer effects and are unable to distinguish what they do as an objective form of forensic analysis with an articulable methodology.

The authors propose the following: *Identification scientists* (those forensic scientists concerned with making identifications through evidence examination and comparison) should have as little information about the extraneous circumstances surrounding any item of evidence they are given as possible. They are concerned with *what* and *who*, not *how*. To perform competent and informed comparisons, they require the questioned evidence they are examining, its known history, the circumstances of the collection, and the known evidence to which they are comparing it. They should otherwise be as blind as possible and further barred from having or even perusing any information related to:

- Victim statements and background
- Witness statements

- Suspect statements
- Investigative theories
- Attorney theories
- The results of other forensic examinations
- The nature of the offense

The DNA analyst does not actually need to know whether the suspect has confessed in order to compare short tandem repeat (STR) profiles; the hair examiner does not need to know that the victim was a five-year-old girl who was sodomized; and the fingerprint and firearms examiners do not need to know that others have already confirmed a match between two prints or projectiles.

Arguments that support the need for gathering and considering extraneous case information related to the identification scientist's examinations seek to facilitate the following: (1) locating or developing evidence that may have been missed, (2) formulating hypotheses regarding potential transfers, and (3) helping triage evidence through the lab. These are all perfectly legitimate goals that should be the function of either a forensic generalist or a forensic specialist who will not be involved in making any related identifications. That is, only disinterested forensic examiners, whose minds are necessarily blind to biasing influences, should be responsible for making forensic identifications.

With respect to proficiency testing (a.k.a. performance testing), some contend "the logistics of full-blind proficiency tests are formidable" (National Research Council, 1996, p. 79). While true in many situations, its practical implementation is by no means impossible.[18] Likewise, developing a system that filters out all unnecessary domain-irrelevant data before identification scientists perform their evaluations is also possible [Cook et al. (1998) discuss the "filtering" process system that has been developed in the United Kingdom's Forensic Science Service]. As with all things, if we want to get it done, we will find a way to get it done. That a solution to a big problem might be difficult is not a legitimate reason for setting it aside.[19]

Generalist–reconstructionists, on the other hand, must indeed have "everything they can get their hands on" with respect to the crime scene and the physical evidence. They are concerned not with *who* but with *how* and *why*. Their task is to gather the evidence, and the results of any subsequent examinations, and establish what may be known to separate opinion and speculation from defensible scientific fact. They may even benefit greatly from hard information about both the victim and the suspect because the issue of *what* or *who* may already be firmly established in the case at hand.

[18] Considering that the forensic community "deals mostly with inanimate objects, the blinding procedure will be simpler than in fields that work with humans and animals, such as biomedical research and psychology. Those fields must construct double-blind studies, while forensic science needs only single-blind procedures" (Risinger et al., 2002, p. 1).

[19] Blind and nonblind tests are conducted if the lab is accredited through the American Society of Crime Lab Directors (ASCLD). This proposal would make blind tests far easier to administer.

They should be blind, however, to information that might create an expectation regarding their findings, and they should actively work to screen any theories about the case that come from human sources, such as investigators, attorneys, witnesses, and suspects. These theories regarding events will be compared against the results of the reconstruction and should not be used to build it. It must be admitted, however, that this level of screening may not always be possible. The very context of the reconstructionist's involvement in a case often precludes the ability to screen case theories as they come flowing in. This reality makes the necessity of developing and firmly adhering to scientific practice standards all the more vital to maintaining what Thornton referred to in the previous chapter as the reconstructionist's "professional chastity." It also increases the importance of being able to rely on sufficiently thorough and objective crime scene processing efforts and, as well as sufficiently blind results from forensic identification scientists, when forming reconstruction conclusions.

EVIDENCE LINEUPS

A procedural reform for crime lab employees that can further minimize subconscious biasing influences among the identification sciences involves the employment of "evidence lineups" (Miller, 1987; Risinger et al., 2002). In an evidence lineup, multiple samplings are presented to the forensic examiner. However, some samples are "foils."[20] Forensic examiners would be blind to which samples constitute the foils and which samples constitute the true questioned evidence. For instance (Risinger et al., 2002, p. 48):

[20] Professor Saks and colleagues employ this word; see Risinger et al. (2002).

> [A] firearms examiner might be presented with a crime scene bullet and five questioned bullets labeled merely "A" through "E." Four of those bullets will have been prepared for examination by having been fired through the same make and model of firearm as the crime scene bullet and the suspect's bullet had been. The task for the examiner would then be to choose which, if any, of the questioned bullets was fired through the same weapon as the crime scene bullet had been.

As already discussed, many forensic examinations are currently the equivalent of eyewitness identification show-ups. In both situations, only one suspect or sample is presented to the examiner; because of the selective nature of this process and the often high rate of past identifications that have been positive, the environment works to reinforce the expectation of a match. Evidence lineups would serve to help resolve this particular influence and may even identify biased examiners who are unaware that they are being unduly influenced.

RESTRUCTURING THE PUBLIC CRIME LAB

In order to curb the conscious and subconscious influences that expectation can set against the forensic examiner's purpose, public crime labs are well advised to return to the practice of employing forensic generalists (actual forensic scientists, not lab technicians) to perform the following duties:[21]

1. Responding to crime scenes
2. Assisting forensic specialist with processing evidence at the crime lab
3. Forensic evidence triage
4. Crime reconstruction

The crime lab should therefore be given statutory authority to respond to specific kinds of crime scenes and take sole charge of evidence processing duties. This is not some new idea or radical concept. For example, the medical examiner or coroner is statutorily responsible for the body of the victim at the scene and for determining the cause and manner of death (arguably, to reconstruct the death). Likewise, a forensic generalist could be responsible for the body of physical evidence that establishes any element of the crime, with the lab given statutory obligation and authority to reconstruct events. This would allow police to focus on their investigative function, and it would clearly delineate the scientific investigation of the evidence from law enforcement efforts to identify and apprehend suspects.

At the crime lab, a generalist unit should take custody of the evidence. A supervising generalist, who knows the true capabilities and consequences of their lab and its analytical efforts, should be assigned to each case. Their primary function and philosophy should be to aggressively disprove every theory that is presented to them (a disconfirmatory, Popperian mind-set). They would seek to resolve the following questions and to perform a forensic triage of the evidence collected:

- Which questions are pertinent to the case and whether the evidence can answer them
- Whether the evidence is of sufficient quality and quantity for meaningful testing
- Whether an item of evidence can be examined at the lab or must be sent to another facility
- Which laboratory sections an item of evidence needs to be sent to
- Which specific forensic examinations should be performed
- Which ordering of forensic examinations will be the least destructive

[21] It should be noted that, currently, nonscientific police personnel, with little or no training and education in science, forensic science, or proper evidence collection procedures, most commonly performs these duties.

In the performance of these duties, the supervisory generalist would listen to many case theories, have contact with police investigators and attorneys, and act as a barrier between these influences and the examining criminalists in the rest of the lab. That is, the forensic specialists working in the other sections of the crime lab would be blind to the information and theories provided to the generalist from outside agencies. They would perform the analyses requested by the supervisory generalist and then render their objective results in a written fashion.

With respect to instrumentation, a technician may certainly be trained to run an instrument and test samples under the direction of forensic scientists. This is sometimes both necessary and useful. However, a qualified forensic scientist must perform the interpretation of any results. A distinction must be made between the function of the technician and the function of the scientist. It is a distinction that is currently so blurred that many can no longer see it or even understand it.

Subsequent to specialist tests and analysis, the senior generalist would aggregate these and assign a generalist–reconstructionist from the generalist unit to perform crime reconstruction duties. This reconstruction would be based on the results of the crime scene investigation, instrumental analysis, and other objective forensic examinations. As with the forensic specialists, the generalist–reconstructionists would be blind to the various case theories until the results of their reconstruction were complete. If their results failed to address specific questions of value to the case, as determined by the supervising generalist (who knows all the proposed theories), they could revisit these through directed experimentation.

It is important to bear in mind that there is room for judgment with respect to the examination of evidence submitted to the crime lab. That is, not all samples would require this level of triage and treatment. Drug analysis, blood alcohols, and serial number restorations are among the many simple tests done in the lab that do not require this level of sophistication to adequately blind the forensic specialists.

With respect to findings, both generalists and specialists must believe that they have sufficient support from their supervisors to form conclusions that do not go beyond their understanding of good science. They must know that their jobs are not at risk when they offer findings that may conflict with the expectations of others in positions of authority.[22] Consequently, their job, pay, workload, and hours must not be a reflection of how helpful their findings have been to police or prosecutors. This means no bonuses for assisting with an arrest and no citations of merit or promotions for assisting with a successful prosecution or a reliable track record of the same. Moreover, their performance reports should never reflect or be based on whether

[22] In some jurisdictions, police and prosecutors bypass the scientists who are employed in the public laboratory. The prosecution does not want to hear that its theory is not supported by science, so they hire "outside experts" who have no scientific background, do not understand the scientific method, and can be counted on for confirmatory results. These "witnesses having other rationalized explanations" can seem very impressive until one closely examines their work product. Unfortunately, the lab scientists are not generally able to openly criticize such individuals because that would jeopardize the prosecution, the scientist's job, or the relationship with the prosecutor. Not to mention the potential for being sanctioned if they step out of line and act in a manner not serving the best interests of their agency. This is a circumstance that must be remedied.

their findings assist or fail to assist a successful prosecution. Their performance reports should instead be based on how well they follow the scientific method, how well they present their logic, their writing skills, their verbal skills (i.e., court testimony), and how well they meet their individual goals.

CONCLUSION

There can be no doubt that observer effects exist and subconsciously influence an untold number of forensic examiners. The pervasive failure of the forensic science community to confront this and design safeguards speaks volumes with regard to what James Starrs (1991), professor of forensic science, refers to as "institutional bias":[23]

> Institutional bias in the forensic sciences is manifested by the policies, programs, or practices of an agency, an organization or a group, whether public or private, or any of its personnel which benefit or promote the interests of one side in a courtroom dispute, while either denying or minimizing the interests of the other side.

To correct institutional bias, which accounts for many of the unwanted observer effects discussed in this chapter, it may be time to consider separating the forensic scientist once and for all from police culture. In other words, it may be time to consider separating all state crime lab systems physically, philosophically, and fiscally from law enforcement and to advocate for the creation of wholly independent state divisions of forensic science that are publicly funded but available to all.

The idea is not new. Kirk and Bradford (1965, pp. 22–23) advocated for independent crime labs four decades ago:[24]

> An independent operation, not directly a part of any other law enforcement agency, but available to all, would certainly find it easier to maintain the high degree of scientific objectivity that is so essential to good operation. It is very probable that the quality of service furnished would be higher than is now possible, because there would be no dependence on budgets of the other organization with their inevitable competition for available funds, and there would be no question of comparable rank of personnel, which is a problem in some organizations under the common American system.

Although the United Kingdom and some government labs in Australia have embraced what may be described as an independent configuration [see

[23] See also Lee (1993), who states, "Many laboratories are housed within police or federal law enforcement agencies. Laboratories that operate under the supervision of police departments or prosecutors' office are *generally not available to the defense*"; Thornton and Peterson (2002, p. 2), note, "Most forensic examinations are conducted in government-funded laboratories, usually located within law enforcement agencies, and *typically for the purpose of building a case for the prosecution*".

[24] Similarly, Professor Starrs (1993) urged that the "inbred bias of crime laboratories affiliated with law enforcement agencies must be breached." Professor Gianelli (1997) also advocated for independent crime labs, stating, "These laboratories should be transferred from police control to the control of medical examiner offices, agencies that are already independent of the police."

Wilson (1994) for the various independent agencies in Australia and National Public Radio (2003) for the United Kingdom's system], the U.S. forensic science community has perpetually rebuffed such an arrangement.

However, change may be forthcoming because of the increasing number of crime lab problems that continue to surface throughout the United States. For instance, Governor Ryan's Commission on Capital Punishment endorsed establishing an independent crime lab in Illinois ("Report of the Governor's Commission on Capital Punishment," 2002). Likewise, (former) Houston Police Chief C. O. Bradford and Harris County District Attorney Chuck Rosenthal have both acknowledged that the problems with the Houston Police Department crime lab may merit creating an independent statewide agency (Khanna, 2003). Not only is this idea feasible but also, in some states such as Virginia, it has already been done. In the end, "forensic science service must be independent, perceived to be independent, and confidently taken to be independent" (Samuel, 1994). Specifically (Peter Neufeld, Innocence Project codirector, as quoted in National Public Radio, 2003):

> What [we] really want to do is not simply create an artificial independence, but [we] want to change the entire *mind-set* of the people who work in these laboratories so they can be proud that they are independent scientists and not simply cops in lab coats.

The desire for scientific independence is a universal in that it is shared by all of those who want the most reliable and objective examinations from the forensic scientists they employ. Only the mechanisms for achieving scientific independence seem to vary. It is hoped that this discussion of observer effects, and their remedies, has contributed to this much-needed airing of issues that continue to divide forensic scientists from themselves.

ACKNOWLEDGMENT

We recognize the contribution of coeditor W. Jerry Chisum to this chapter. Without his advice and edits, its completion would have been lacking, if not impossible.

REFERENCES

Ashbaugh, D. R. (1999). *Quantitative–Qualitative Friction Ridge Analysis: An Introduction to Basic and Advanced Ridgeology*, Boca Raton: CRC Press.

Bales, S. (2000). Turning the Microscope Back on Forensic Scientists, *Litigation* 26:51.

Castelle, G. (1999, May). Lab Fraud: Lessons Learned from The "Fred Zain Affair." *Champion,*: 12.

Cook, R., Evett, I. W., Jackson, G., Jones, P. J., and Lambert, J. A. (1998). A Model for Case Assessment and Interpretation. *Science & Justice*, 38:151.

De Forest, P., Gaensslen, R. H., and Lee, H. (1983). *Forensic Science: An Introduction to Criminalistics*, New York: McGraw Hill Co.

Dillon, D. J. (1998). Book Review. *Scientific Sleuthing Review*, 22:4–5.

Di Maio, D. J., and Di Maio, V. J. M. (1993). *Forensic Pathology*, Boca Raton: CRC Press.

Epstein, R. (2002). Fingerprints Meet Daubert: The Myth of Fingerprint "Science" Is Revealed. *Southern California Law Review*, 75:605.

Fisher, B. A. J. (1993). *Techniques of Crime Scene Investigation, (5th ed.)*, Boca Raton: CRC Press.

Fisher, B. A. J. (1999). *Techniques of Crime Scene Investigation, (6th ed.)*, Boca Raton: CRC Press.

Giannelli, P. C. (Spring, 1997). The Abuse of Scientific Evidence in Criminal Cases: The Need for Independent Crime Laboratories. *Virginia Journal of Social Policy & Law*, 4:439–470.

Grant, J. (1941). *Science for the Prosecution*, London: Chapman & Hall.

Heard, B. J. (1997). *Handbook of Firearms and Ballistics: Examining and Interpreting Forensic Evidence*, New York: John Wiley & Sons.

Inman, K., and Rudin, N. (2000). *Principles and Practice of Criminalistics: The Profession of Forensic Science*, Boca Raton: CRC Press.

James, S. H., and Nordby, J. J. (2003). *Forensic science: An Introduction to Scientific and Investigative Techniques*, Boca Raton: CRC Press.

Johnson, M. L. (1953). Seeing's Believing. *New Biology*, 15:60–79.

Khanna, R. (2003, April 3). HPD Chief Proposes Independently Run Crime Lab. *Houston Chronicle*, p. 1.

Kirk, P. L. (1974). *Crime Investigation, (2nd ed.)*, New York: John Wiley & Sons.

Kirk, P. L., and Bradford, L. W. (1965). *The Crime Laboratory: Organization and Operation*, New York: Charles C Thomas Pub. Ltd.

Lee, H. C. (1993). Forensic Science and the Law. *Connecticut Law Review*, 25:1117–1124.

Lee, H. C., Palmbach, T., and Miller, M. (2001). *Henry Lee's Crime Scene Handbook*, London: Academic Press.

May, L. S. (1936). *Crime's Nemesis*, New York: The Macmillan Company.

Miller, L. S. (June, 1987). Procedural Bias in Forensic Science Examinations of Human Hair, *Law and Human Behavior*, 11(2):157–163.

National Public Radio (2003, May 15). *Crime Labs*, Reported by Larry Abramson, Morning Edition.

National Research Council (1996). *The Evaluation of Forensic DNA Evidence*, Washington, D.C., National Academy Press.

Neisser, U. (1976). *Cognition and Reality: Principles and Implications of Cognitive Psychology*, New York: W. H. Freeman & Co.

Netzel, L. (2003). The forensic laboratory. In S. H. James and J. J. Nordby (Eds.), *Forensic Science: An Introduction to Scientific and Investigative Techniques*, Boca Raton: CRC Press, pp. 163, 165–166.

Office of the Inspector General (1997, April). *The FBI Laboratory: Investigation into Laboratory Practices and Alleged Misconduct in Explosive-Related and Other Cases.* Washington, DC: U.S. Department of Justice.

Peterson, D. W., and Conley, J. M. (2001). Of Cherries, Fudge and Onions: Science and its Courtroom Perversion, *Law and Contemporary Problems*, 64(4):213–240.

Peterson, J. L., Mihajlovic, S., and Gilliland, M. (1984). *Forensic Evidence and the Police, 1976–1980,* Washington DC: United States Department of Justice, National Institute of Justice, Grant Number 82-IJ-CX-0064.

Phillips, V. L., et al. (2001). The Application of Signal Detection Theory to Decision-Making in Forensic Science. *Journal of Forensic Science*, 46:294–298.

Risinger, D. M., Saks, M. J., Thompson, W. C., and Rosenthal, R. (January, 2002). The Daubert/Kumho Implications of Observer Effects in Forensic Science: Hidden Problems of Expectation and Suggestion, *California Law Review*, 90(1): 1–56.

Rosenthal, R. (1966). *Experimenter Effects in Behavioral Research,* New York: Appleton-Century-Crofts.

Saferstein, R. (2001). *Criminalistics: An Introduction to Forensic Science, (7th ed.),* Upper Saddle River, NJ: Prentice Hall.

Saferstein, R. (Ed.) (2002). *Forensic Science Handbook:* Vol. 1 *(2nd ed.),* Upper Saddle River, NJ: Prentice Hall.

Saferstein, R. (Ed.) (2004). *Forensic Science Handbook:* Vol. 2 *(2nd ed.),* Upper Saddle River, NJ: Prentice Hall

Saks, M. J. (Summer, 2000). Banishing Ipse Dixit: The Impact of Kumho Tire on Forensic Identification Science, *Washington and Lee Law Review*, 57:879–886.

Saks, M. J. (2003). Ethics in Forensic Science: Professional Standards for the Practice of Criminalistics. *Jurimetrics: Journal of Law, Science and Technology*, 43: 359–363.

Saks, M. J., Risinger, D. M., Rosenthal, R., Thompson, W. C. (2003). Context Effects In Forensic Science: A Review and Application of The Science of Science To Crime Laboratory Practice in the United States. *Science and Justice*, 43:119.

Samuel, A. (April, 1994). Forensic Science and Miscarriages of Justice, *Medicine, Science, and the Law*, 34:148–150.

Siegel, J. A., Knupfer, G. C., and Saukko, P. J. (Eds.) (2000). *Encyclopedia of Forensic Science* (Vols. 1–3), London: Academic Press.

Starrs, J. E. (1991). The Forensic Scientist and the Open Mind. *Science and Justice*, 31:111–134.

Starrs, J. E. (1993, Winter). The Seamy Side of Forensic Science: The Mephitic Stain of Fred Salem Zain, *Scientific Sleuthing Review*, 17:1–8.

Symposium: Toward a Model Death Penalty Code: The Massachusetts Governor's Council Report (2005), Panel Discussion, *Indiana Law Journal*, 80:1.

Technical Working Group for Eyewitness Evidence, U.S. Department of Justice (1999). *Eyewitness Evidence: A Guide For Law Enforcement.* Washington, DC: U.S. Department of Justice.

Teichrobe, R. (2004, December 27). Forensic Scientist in Crime Lab Tied to Wrongful Convictions in Oregon. *Seattle Post-Intelligencer*, p. A1.

Thompson, W. C. (1996). DNA Evidence in the O. J. Simpson Trial. *University of Colorado Law Review*, 67:827–845.

Thornton, J. I., and Peterson, J. L. (2002). The General Assumptions and Rationale of Forensic Identification. In D. L. Faigman et al. (Eds.), *Science in the Law: Forensic Science Issues*, St. Paul, MN: West Publishing, pp. 26–27.

Ubelaker, D., and Scammell, H. (1992). *Bones: A Forensic Detective's Casebook*, New York: Harper-Collins.

Wells, G. L., et al. (1998). Eyewitness Identification Procedures: Recommendations for Lineups and Photospreads, *Law and Human Behavior*, 22:603.

Wilson, P. (1994). Lessons from the Antipodes: Successes and Failures of Forensic Science. *Forensic Science International*, 67:79–83.

Zuckerman, A. A. S. (May, 1992). Miscarriage of Justice—A Root Treatment, *Criminal Law Review*, 323–332.

CHAPTER 4

PRACTICE STANDARDS FOR THE RECONSTRUCTION OF CRIME

W. Jerry Chisum, BS and Brent E. Turvey, MS

When the liberty of an individual may depend in part on physical evidence, it is not unreasonable to ask that the expert witnesses who are called upon to testify, either against the defendant or in his behalf, know what they are doing.
—John I. Thornton, in Kirk and Thornton (1970, pp. v–vi)

Many that live deserve death. And some die that deserve life. Can you give it to them? Then be not too eager to deal out death in the name of justice, fearing for your own safety. Even the wise cannot see all ends.
—J. R. R. Tolkien (1954)

Practice standards for crime reconstruction are those basic foundations and precepts that set the limits of evidentiary interpretation. As provided by Thornton (1997, p. 18), for all forensic scientists, they include working toward a reduction of bias, the employment of analytical logic and the scientific method, and forming definite hypotheses and conclusions in accordance with the known evidence. The danger is that these ideas appear so basic and seem so uncomplicated, with familiar terms and assumed definitions, that many fail to actually comprehend them. Most of us have heard of the scientific method and understand that it is something good; most us have heard of bias and understand that it is something bad; and most of us believe that our approach is logical—whether it is or not. However, the extent to which these ideas are truly studied, appreciated, and incorporated within the forensic community leaves much to be desired.

The purpose of this chapter is to provide forensic examiners with a baseline of subjects they need to study; of mental skills they should develop; and of steps they should take to better ensure accuracy, reliability, and proficiency in their findings. It builds upon concepts found in the existing literature. It is also written from the perspective that most practicing reconstructionists would probably have a great deal of enthusiasm for strict adherence to standards that embrace diminished bias, analytical logic, and the scientific method, if only they understood what these things are.

IS CRIME RECONSTRUCTION A SCIENCE?

Crime reconstruction is a forensic discipline based on the forensic sciences, the scientific method, analytical logic, and critical thinking. But is the discipline of reconstruction a science in its own right? This requires some discussion. The first problem is consistency with terms and usage between forensic professionals, as described in Moenssens (1997):

> One of the recurring problems we must face in the law of opinion evidence is that the words "scientific evidence," as they have come to be used by courts, lawyers, and legal commentators, do not necessarily connote that the evidence is arrived at purely by mathematically verifiable scientific principles. Indeed, courts are not always in agreement on whether a particular forensic practice is to be called "scientific" or not. Much opinion testimony that has been by common usage labeled as "scientific evidence," involves aspects wherein standard and measurable rules govern certain determinations. It also involves evaluations that are much more a matter of art and interpretation, yielding an opinion that is rarely quantifiable, despite the fact that defined methodologies for conducting examinations exist. Forensic disciplines may prescribe the use of certain protocols and measurements for some phases of the analytical process, but when it comes to interpreting the meaning of the evidence in court it often becomes a matter of judgment based on the expert's considerable experience.

Education in the sciences and specialized training help define a *scientist*, not just experience, and even this is not enough. Though it often escapes notice, a scientist is actually defined by their adherence to the scientific method when solving problems such as how something works, why something does not work, or how something happened. Anyone who fully comprehends and diligently employs the scientific method is a scientist, lab coat or not. Though these seemingly limited criteria may appear to the uninitiated as a lowering of the bar, they actually raise it. A degree requirement, for example, even in the hard sciences, in no way ensures student exposure to, or comprehension of, the scientific method. The emphasis, again, is on full comprehension and diligent employment of the scientific method; all the college degrees in the world combined with a lifetime of experience do matter unless it shows in one's work. This will be discussed later in this chapter and will be a theme that runs through every page of this text.

A *forensic scientist*, as discussed in the preface of this work, is one that examines and determines the meaning of physical evidence in accordance with the established theories and principles of forensic science, with the expectation of presenting his findings in court. This presumes the use of the scientific method, analytical logic, and critical thinking.

The *scientific method* is a way to investigate how or why something works, or how something happened, through the development of hypotheses and subsequent attempts at falsification through testing and other accepted means. It is a structured process designed to build scientific knowledge by way of answering specific questions about observed events through analysis and critical thinking. Observations are used to form testable hypotheses, and with sufficient testing hypotheses can become scientific theories. Eventually, over much time, with precise testing marked by a failure to falsify, scientific theories can become scientific principles. The scientific method is the particular approach to knowledge building and problem solving employed by scientists.

Scientific knowledge is any knowledge, enlightenment, or awareness that comes from examining events or problems through the lens of the scientific method. The accumulation of scientific knowledge in a particular subject or discipline leads to its development as a *science*. The classic definition of a *science*, as provided by Thornton (1997, p. 12), is "an orderly body of knowledge with principles that are clearly enunciated," as well as being reality oriented and having conclusions susceptible to testing.

A strong cautionary is needed here. The use of statistics does not make something scientific. The use of a computer does not make something scientific. The use of chemicals does not make something scientific. The use of technology does not make something scientific. Science is found in the interpretations. Was the scientific method used to synthesize the knowledge at hand, and has that knowledge been applied correctly to render interpretations, with the necessary humility. The relationship of scientists, the scientific method, and science is thus: Scientists employing the scientific method can work within a particular discipline to help create and build a body of scientific knowledge to the point where its theories become principles, and the discipline as a whole eventually becomes a science. And the discipline remains a science through the continued building of scientific knowledge.

Crime reconstruction as a discipline is ripe for development as a science; however, its scientific theories have, arguably, yet to achieve the necessary level of empirical maturity. As we will discuss in this chapter, crime reconstruction is reality based, there is an orderly body of knowledge that exists in the literature, there are generally accepted theories and practice standards, and reconstruction conclusions reached through the scientific method are susceptible to verification through independent peer review and testing. Where the discipline falls short is in the realm of empirically established scientific principles that are clearly enunciated, but this hardly distinguishes it from the majority of the forensic sciences (for discussions, see Inman and Rudin, 2000; Jonakait, 1991, 1994; Thornton, 1994). In other words, the vast majority of forensic sciences do not have principles or even practice standards for interpretation that are clearly enunciated, and those claiming otherwise should be asked precisely what these are while under oath.

In any event, there is much good forensic science theory in crime reconstruction, and as described in this text it is often based on sound scientific methodology. There is simply not enough published research to establish a clear body of scientific principles. This will take more time, more data, and more research. Consequently, courts rightly perceive the discipline of crime reconstruction as an area of specialized knowledge.

OVERSIMPLIFICATION AND OCCAM'S RAZOR

Before we can discuss crime reconstruction practice standards, we must deconstruct the popular yet mistaken assumption that it is a simple and certain enterprise based solely on careful observation and experience.

Oversimplification occurs when a complex situation is described in simplistic terms that neglect its complexity in order to achieve a greater measure of certainty. These days oversimplification has become commonplace in entertainment, political rhetoric, and even journalism. But it has no place in the justice system.

Oversimplification is too common a vice in the forensic disciplines, from scene processing to laboratory analysis to crime reconstruction. It manifests itself in the supplanting of a formal scientific education with short courses, rote technical training, and learning on the job. It manifests itself with appeals to experience instead of scientific fact. It manifests itself in the form of appeals to common sense for the sake of intellectual ease. It manifests itself when reconstructionists admonish others not to get "bogged down by all the facts," when the facts actually provide the context needed for an informed and accurate interpretation. It manifests itself in these forms and others, wherever there is a desired conclusion and the full weight of the scientific method is perceived to be the long way or the wrong way.

Those with a basic grasp of logic and reasoning might stop us right here and invoke *Occam's razor*. They might suggest that the scientific method reveals simplicity, and that complexity relates directly to improbability—the more complex a theory, the less probable—given Occam's razor.

Occam's razor is an often misstated principle that, ironically, has been reduced for mass consumption to the point of misapplication. Not uncommonly, it is stated as something along the lines of "all things being equal, the simplest explanation is most often the correct one." Although this interpretation of Occam's razor sounds good and has the virtue of popping up in a television show or movie every now and again, it is inaccurate.

Pluralitas non est ponenda sine neccesitate. Translation: *Entities should not be multiplied unnecessarily;* or *plurality should not be posited without necessity.* In the 14th century, a Franciscan friar named William of Occam used this principle so frequently in his writings on religious philosophy that modern scientists and logicians have come to call it "Occam's razor." It is a fine concept and has been used to provide a basis for scientific modeling and theory building. Generally, it may be summoned as a reminder to choose the least blended hypotheses from any of otherwise equivalent test models or reasoning—to remove the extraneous and the nonessential from interpretations. The secret to unlocking Occam's razor is determining what of one's hypothesis is necessary to an interpretation and what is not. Occam, for example, assumed the existence of God in all modeling and theory building. Not all modern scientists would be willing to make this assumption, nor would most be eager to factor it into their reconstructions of crime.

Sir Isaac Newton (1642–1727) wrote, "We are to admit no more causes of natural things than such as are both true and sufficient to explain their appearances." Ernst Mach, an Austrian physicist and philosopher in the early 1800s, advocated this version of Occam's razor in what he called the principle of economy, stating, "Scientists must use the simplest means of arriving at their results and exclude everything not perceived by the senses." Here, Mach and Newton have given us permission to ignore the possibility of extraterrestrials, bigfoot, and other phenomenological explanations not yet proven by science when formulating an interpretation of evidence or events. In the principle of economy, the senses provide the basis for what is acceptable and necessary. Therefore, interpretations for events should first be attempted in terms of what is already known, which we call the accepted facts.

Today, some philosophers and scientists suggest as an axiom that "the explanation requiring the fewest assumptions is most likely to be correct." This is not precisely Occam's razor but rather a shade of the law of parsimony, developed by Sir William Hamilton (1788–1856), who wrote (Hamilton, 1853, p. 580):

> Without descending to details . . . there exists a primary presumption of philosophy. This is the law of parsimony; which prohibits, without a proven necessity, the multiplication of entities, powers, principles, or causes; above all, the postulation of an unknown force where a known impotence can account for the phenomenon.

This is a more rational evolution of both the principle of economy and Occam's razor, and it recognizes that not all conclusions are created equal. Some involve more unnecessary details and make more unfounded assumptions than others. The key to unlocking an interpretation with the law of parsimony is deliberately cleaving established facts from irrelevant information and unfounded assumptions.

Fewer blended theories, less phenomenology, and fewer assumptions. This is all a far cry from the fatuousness of "don't get bogged down by the facts" and "the simplest explanation is most likely correct." Occam's razor and its progeny are important tools but not to be used as a substitute for reason, or specifically as an excuse to ignore relevant information because it makes a preferred conclusion easier to prove.

We would do better to recall Albert Einstein's cautionary, which provides, "everything should be made as simple as possible, but not one bit simpler." In other words, we are encouraged to embrace both the complexity of reality and the simplicity of direct logical reasoning without irrelevent encumberances.

Reconstruction is particularly susceptible to oversimplification because many of those currently involved, as discussed in the Preface, do not come from a scientific background of any kind. Consider this explanation of crime reconstruction from an instructional piece written by an authority on crime scene processing and investigation (Baldwin, 2005a):

> The reconstruction of crime scenes is a misnomenclature. You are in reality interpreting the information that you find by examining and processing the scene for evidence. This evidence will then permit you to make factual statements in regards to your findings.
>
> . . .
>
> You will be able to reconstruct the crime scene in court if you remember that the "reconstruction" is your interpretation of the factual evidence in the case.

On the surface, this may not seem like a bad way to proceed. Go to the crime scene, look at the evidence, make observations, call them facts, and that is a reconstruction. Simple.

But simplicity is actually the problem here, as several crucial steps are absent from this method. The bare observations of a crime scene technician are painted as a factual interpretation of events, and it is further suggested that this be offered as "factual evidence" of a reconstruction in court. The first problem is that it advocates a confirmatory mind-set, intentionally or otherwise. There is no accounting for how facts are to be separated from assumptions. There is no discussion of what is to be made of the evidence after it has been collected and sent off for examination or how the results of that examination must be factored into the reconstruction. There is no stated concern for evidence dynamics. There is no consideration for rigorously seeking to disprove one's interpretations. In other words, the scientific method is absent. There is only blind faith in the experience and judgment of the scene technician.

This approach is explained in greater detail as Baldwin goes on to further confuse reconstruction and scene processing, and offer that it is a simple, intuitive process made easy by experience, conducted solely in a place where scientists are unwelcome (2005b):

> There is nothing difficult about processing crime scenes. They are actually very simple. . . . Yes we [CSIs] can "read" the scene and our experience tells us what needs to be done, no forensic scientist that sits in a lab all day can do any of this.
>
> . . .
>
> Just because someone thinks crime scenes should be processed by only those with a scientific background doesn't necessarily mean it should be done that way. CSI's are trained to process crime scenes in there [sic] entirety while forensic scientists are trained to process and analyze evidence. Two different worlds. I don't want a FS [forensic scientist] at my crime scene, they get in the way.

Scene interpretation and crime reconstruction, in this mode of thinking, are simplistically reduced to experience-driven observation, intuition, and surmise. There is, moreover, a clear and utter disdain for science at the crime scene. Subsequently, there is no consideration for eliminating bias, theory falsification, or theory revision. Experience is heralded as the final word on interpretation, and the contributions of forensic science are scorned outright as impractical.

The process that Baldwin (2005a) describes is referred to as an "informal reconstruction" by author and reconstructionist Ross M. Gardner, a retired investigator for the U.S. Army Criminal Investigation Command. As explained in Gardner (2005):

> The primary responsibility of the crime scene technician is to collect pertinent evidence and document the scene, thus they report these observations and actions as lay witnesses. But crime scene analysis/reconstruction is conducted in two distinct venues . . . on scene as the scene is processed (an informal reconstruction) and then after the fact (the formal reconstruction), when all of the forensic data is available. The second a technician arrives on scene, they begin that informal reconstruction. . . . The technician walks into a scene, typically with incorrect information (e.g., told it's a stabbing when in fact it's a shooting); they don't

know the extent of the scene, they don't know squat other than something happened.

It is that informal reconstruction that most often gets police organizations in trouble. This happens when they form a consolidated theory early on and are unable or unwilling to alter it as they encounter new evidence refuting their original position.

The reason that the so-called "informal reconstruction" actually "gets police organizations in trouble" is because it is not a reconstruction at all. As conceded by Gardner, it is at best a hypothesis about some of the events that may have occurred, based on untested assumptions, awaiting verification through careful forensic examination, laboratory analyses, and the delicate swing of analytical logic. Failing to appreciate this, those without a scientific background are prone to treat their initial intuitions as conclusions and then selectively process the scene or look for other evidence in a way that tends to confirm what they believe. This in turn affects the total picture of evidence that is sent up the line to criminalists at the crime lab.

A reconstruction of events is not as simple as observation and conclusion based on experience. There are steps in between that must be followed to ensure a measure of reliability and accuracy. A reconstruction must be a conclusion regarding what has occurred or not based on a consideration of the forensic sciences, the scientific method, and analytical logic. Anything offered without this foundation is a guess, no matter how many years of experience one stacks beneath it for support. The confusion of guesswork and intuition for forensic fact is something that the reconstructionist must remedy in her work. The notion of "formal" and "informal" reconstruction based on experience and intuition very much misses this point, and it contributes to the problem of oversimplification by lowering the bar well beneath the watermark of sound scientific methodology.

Evidence interpretation is a complex process, and the less one understands about the nature of physical evidence, the principles of forensic science, analytical logic, and the scientific method, the simpler crime reconstruction may seem. In that spirit, we explain these and related issues further so that reconstructionists may have them available in their intellectual tool kit.

THE POLITICS OF BIAS

Bias, as we are using the term, refers to a preference or an inclination that inhibits judgment to the point of impartiality. In the forensic disciplines, bias manifests itself in the form of preferences for or against particular theories, methods, suspects, agencies, or sides of the courtroom. Whether we care to admit it or not, bias exists and can find its way into the results of our examinations. The only way to mitigate bias is to first recognize its parentage and then work toward methods that minimize common points of impact, which is no small part of what this work seeks to accomplish.

A good barometer for the presence of bias, and even inability, is anger. Wherever there is bias or ignorance, there is also fear of its discovery. As a consequence, anger is a nearly universal Pavlovian response to any unwanted inspection or review. The only purpose that anger serves, aside from telegraphing fear, is to intimidate others by making them uncomfortable. This is a particularly sinister problem in the realm of forensic science, in which dispassion and objectivity are prized above all else. Bias, both seen and unseen, can have horrendous consequences for justice, as explained in James and Nordby (2003, p. 4):

> When emotions overcome reason, a zealous forensic scientist may intentionally or inadvertently deny real justice. Results are misinterpreted, or worse, falsified. Such flawed science may not be easy to spot, since it can only appear through the results of the scientific investigation.

A true forensic scientist does not get angry at the prospect of admitting potential bias and working diligently to smother its sources. They understand that bias can creep in, and they want to see it eradicated where possible. They are not out to help authorities catch bad guys, protect an agency, protect a reputation, or protect a client. Their first onus is to dispassionately establish the objective facts of a case as may be determined by a careful and thorough examination of the evidence, and not to a particular institution, employer, or side. They work to establish the scientific facts and their contextual meaning with no investment in the outcome of their analysis. The completion of their job is to educate courts and juries with these findings, not to advocate for or against the guilt of an accused. Though some may expect otherwise, forensic scientists, including reconstructionists, are well equipped to assist in educating those who make legal determinations. However, they do not make legal determinations themselves.

None of this is to say that the findings and interpretations of forensic scientists, reconstructionists in particular, are unimportant. In many cases, quite the opposite can be true. As explained by the court in *People of the Philippines v. Aguinaldo* (1999):

> When physical evidence runs counter to testimonial evidence, conclusions as to physical evidence must prevail. Physical evidence is that mute but eloquent manifestation of truth which rate high in our hierarchy of trustworthy evidence.

In other words, the physical evidence of what happened is often afforded more weight than any witness, victim, or suspect account because sometimes people are mistaken, and sometimes people lie. Physical evidence, as Dr. Paul Kirk explained, cannot lie; physical evidence can only be misinterpreted and misrepresented by the less knowledgeable, the less competent, and the morally destitute (Kirk, 1953, p. 4). The subsequent responsibility of the reconstructionist to diminishing bias and enhancing objectivity is considerable.

ZEALOUS ADVOCATES

In mystery novels, the homicide detective reconstructs the crime and deduces the identity of the guilty person. However, in actuality, the homicide detective seldom has the scientific background necessary to build a reconstruction on his or her own. For the majority of detectives, the use of physical evidence is secondary to the interview and interrogation of the witnesses and suspects. Theirs is commonly a mind-set of chasing suspects as a fox goes after a rabbit, and once focused they are regularly undeterred until a capture has been made. Concern for this form of bias is echoed by Gardner (2005), who admits that impartiality within this community remains a problem:

> We (police supervisors of which I used to count myself as) have done a poor job of teaching impartiality across the board. There are still many police officers and criminal investigators who think they work for the DA or who think their job is to put people in jail. Our job has and always will be investigating and reporting crime and then bringing the people we think are involved to justice. Juries and judges (our communities) decide if they really are "bad guys" and what to do with them, a.k.a. justice.

District attorneys (DAs), Gardner reminds us, have their own agenda. They want to convince the jury of the guilt of the defendant, a belief that may be based on evidence, emotion, politics, or any combination thereof. However, the interpretation of the evidence does not always favor the prosecution. District attorneys, in preparation for prosecuting a case, put together a theory of the crime. The less reconstruction done by forensic scientists, the more this role falls to the DA. Without the proper tools, this can have disastrous results, especially when the defense lacks the good sense or resources to independently investigate and understand the evidence.

Attorneys are zealous advocates—that is their nature and function. The prosecutor zealously seeks to convict the defendant by making the crime more heinous in nature. The defense zealously seeks to exonerate the defendant by minimizing the prosecution's arguments and evidence. Both will theorize about how the crime occurred with different objectives. Both cannot be correct and, lacking a scientific reconstruction, both will probably be wrong. The case theories of attorneys are alternatives and should be examined against the evidence (Chisum 2002, p. 93).

At this point, it bears mentioning that attorneys should not direct the forensic scientists' work. They may have particular questions or particular issues, but scientific methodology and conclusions remain the strict domain of the forensic scientist. Misunderstandings and miscommunications often occur when attorneys seek the services of forensic scientists because attorneys work in a professional domain that is essentially binary in nature. Evidence either supports or fails to support a legal finding of guilt or innocence, and through their efforts attorneys either win or lose the case. The findings of the forensic scientist are not binary—they are multivalued and independent of legal determinations. Very seldom is anything in science black or white. Rather, it is often some shade of gray along an almost infinite continuum. Those practicing in the legal professions need to recognize that forensic scientists are professionals in their own fields, as attorneys are in theirs. Respect must be had for the differences in their desired ends.

There is another component adding tension to the strained relationship between forensic science and the law. In any criminal legal proceeding, the prosecution often has its own stable of police officers and police scientists working directly or indirectly under its administration. This circumstance can create the false impression that only forensic scientists working for the prosecution are on the right or just side of the conflict, protecting society and speaking for the victim. This is an impression that many prosecutors are happy to encourage and that many police scientists are infrequently quick to correct. The defense expert is often regarded as the one "wearing the black hat" or on "the Dark Side" in the words of prosecutors, police officers, and public-employed forensic scientists. This can help create the false impression that the forensic scientists working for the defense are on the wrong or unjust side of a conflict, out to protect the defendant. This is also a false impression that many prosecutors are pleased to encourage.

As already explained, for the true forensic scientist there are no sides to a case. There is only what the evidence supports or fails to support. The problem is that the nature of the adversarial process can pressure even well-intentioned forensic scientists to forget this, enabling them to become advocates bent on getting the bad guy. The phrase that has been used to describe this occurrence is "cops in lab coats"—those in police laboratories who try to make their results match their agency's case against the accused. According to Dr. Elizabeth Johnson, a private forensic DNA analyst, formerly DNA section chief for the Harris County, Texas, medical examiner's office ("DNA Testing", 2003):

> [It is] a problem that's found in many cities when crime labs are located in police departments and analysts can feel pressured to be "cops in lab coats"—trying to make the science match the police department's case.
>
> "Too much of the time the police or the detectives come in and they submit evidence and they stand around and visit for a while and start telling chemists their version of what happened in the crime," says Johnson. "That's a dangerous situation."

David McBride, the former chief of police in Oklahoma City, Oklahoma, who oversaw the recently embattled police crime lab there before scandal broke out, has publicly admitted that this kind of bias is far too common, and ("Under the Microscope", 2002)

> could happen anywhere that a forensics lab is attached to a police agency, and that is the case in most large American cities. He says it creates scientists who consider themselves cops in lab coats.
>
> "I think there's an inherent potential conflict there," he says. "And I don't know that that's always healthy for the criminal justice system."

This problem is also described in James and Nordby (2003, p. 4):

> While crime laboratory scientists may pride themselves as being "independent finders of fact," most operate under police jurisdiction or administration, and many scientists, perhaps unconsciously, develop the attitude that they work exclusively for the police or prosecutor.

This particular form of bias creates a confirmational environment, in which forensic scientists are rewarded, often directly, through promotions, bonuses, or letters of appreciation, for their certainty and for their assistance with successful prosecutions (Saks, 1998):

> No other fields are as closely affiliated with a single side of litigation as forensic science is to criminal prosecution. . . . The institutional setting of forensic science promotes habits of thought that more closely resemble the thinking of litigators than of scientists. While science pursues knowledge through disconfirmation, prosecutions are won by confirmatory proofs. This confirmatory bias dominates the

thinking of most forensic scientists. Where science advances by open discussion and debate, forensic science has been infected by the litigator's preference for secrecy. Tests of the proficiency of crime laboratories are conducted anonymously, kept secret, and are not routinely published. It is ironic that while studies of the effectiveness and accuracy of so many professional enterprises are available in published literature, the same is not true of a field whose sole purpose is to do some of the public's most public business.

Some regard confirmatory, pro-prosecution bias a problem that begins with inexperience and continues for lack of exposure to actual science, as in Moenssens (1993):

> This special issue [pro-prosecution bias] demonstrates that even where crime laboratories do employ qualified scientists, these individuals may be so imbued with a pro-police bias that they are willing to circumvent true scientific investigation methods for the sake of "making their point."
>
> . . .
>
> Unfortunately, this attitude is even more prevalent among some "technicians" (nonscientists) in the crime laboratories, for whom the presumption of innocence disappears as soon as police investigative methods focus on a likely suspect. These individuals, who are frequently trained to do forensic work on the job after obtaining an undergraduate degree in chemistry or biology, are bestowed with the job title of "forensic scientist" after only a short time in their crime laboratory function. Their pro-police bias is inconsistent with being a scientist. In fact, the less of a scientific background a lab person has, the less critical that person is likely to be in terms of investigating the validity of claims made by other laboratory personnel. These are the "experts" who typically jump on the bandwagon of anything new that comes down the pike, and will staunchly advocate its reliability, even in the absence of any objective investigation and validated experimentation.
>
> Again, many of these individuals do good work in the field in which they have been trained, but their bias is often so strongly pro-prosecution that they may lack the kind of objectivity and dispassionate judgment that one expects of a true scientist, be it forensic or otherwise.

Such attitudes, and a bias, are perpetuated by a slough of popular television shows and docudramas, in which forensic scientists are portrayed as a part of the law enforcement team, and sometimes the whole affair, wielding science like a badge to push suspects into confessions and even make arrests. This powerful imagery, given an air of authenticity by consulting law enforcement officers and police scientists whose names roll in the credits, contradicts everything that good forensic science is about.

Even when the forensic scientist does maintain an aura of impartiality, the system may cause him to contribute a biased result. In many circumstances, unless the forensic scientist has gone to the crime scene and knows what evidence has been collected, or may have been present but uncollected, she will be limited to receive and analyze only that which is given to her. The evidence they are provided is selected by the investigator in support of a particular theory or by the prosecutor in support of a conviction. The forensic scientist is given the evidence with a specific request for analysis. They should ask, "What is the purpose of this analysis?" or "What is the question you are trying to answer with this test?" Only then can they, and not the nonscientist, ascribe meaning to the evidence. As long as the forensic scientist receives only selected evidence and selected information about a case, the analyses and conclusions of that scientist may be biased at least to that extent.

On the other side of the spectrum, there are private forensic experts who will testify to any position for the right amount of money or prestige, rightly labeled by some as "hired guns" or "whores of the court." Such individuals will offer whatever conclusion or interpretation helps their employer, regardless of whether it contradicts something they have testified to before. This practice also contradicts good science because a true forensic scientist will prefer to give his client "bad" news before anyone else does—to realistically educate the client regarding the nature and the strengths of the opposition's evidence.

The paradigm of sides within the forensic science community has and continues to rend its members because of their need to secure or maintain employment, relationships, friendships, and fidelities with those outside, but in control of, the forensic realm. In other words, bias toward one side of the courtroom or the other is often about politics—the politics of a too often subordinated group, forensic scientists, in relation to their vested interest colleagues and employers to whom they are commonly beholding. Science exercised on behalf of the law is forensic science; science exercised on behalf of politics, personal or professional, is not science at all—it is a form of propaganda. Rising above this through soundness of reason and methodology is a tremendous challenge and an awesome responsibility.

TAKING STEPS

A first step to hefting the weight of bias is accepting that forensic science as a pursuit or profession does not belong to just one side of the courtroom. It does not belong to the state, it does not belong to the court, it does not belong to the police, and it does not belong to attorneys. Forensic science as a course of study may be pursued by anyone, and it belongs to objective professionals who should be working together to better their disciplines rather than allowing politics to divide them. Consequently, there is no "dark side" of the courtroom to serve, only dark forensic scientists—forensic scientists who conceal, obfuscate, and otherwise distort forensic results behind a cloak of false prowess and false certainty. Such individuals are recognizable from their use of the argument that "education, training, and experience" is the sole basis for their reasoning and conclusions without the willingness or ability to explain precisely how and why.

Another step is accepting that forensic scientists serving clients on both sides of the courtroom provide a necessary balance to the process of evidentiary examination and interpretation, in terms of independent evaluation, replication and overall peer review. A forensic expert testifying for one side, with none on the other, as often occurs, can leave the courtroom in a state of imbalance. It can telegraph a message to the jury that the side with the lab coats has the best grasp of the facts and the most viable case theory. Without an independent review of findings, the reliability and validity of any theory cannot be reasonably assured.

True forensic science, true evidence interpretation, is not emotional. It does not become enraged or annoyed by doubt or disbelief—it questions itself and invites skepticism through reexamination. More to its purpose, forensic science in the absence of independent review exists in an unrefined form that is arguably not fit for court. It is this step, after all, that has historically been proven to identify errors, ignorance, misapplications of method, and outright fraud.

The next steps involve learning how to observe, how to reflect, and how to make valid inferences. To accomplish this we must marry the complexity of evidence discovered in the wake of criminal behavior to the simplicity of logic and reason.

THINKING ABOUT THINKING

Forensic science is about the search for scientific fact and, subsequently, scientific knowledge—that is, facts and knowledge developed through the scientific method. The French philosopher Denis Diderot (1713–1784) wrote of knowledge, and of reflection, in what may be described as his take on the scientific method (Diderot, 1753):

> There are three principal means of acquiring knowledge available to us: observation of nature, reflection, and experimentation. Observation collects facts; reflection combines them; experimentation verifies the result of that combination. Our

observation of nature must be diligent, our reflection profound, and our experiments exact. We rarely see these three means combined.

In the writings of Diderot, as for us all, reflection is a vital ingredient for tempering thought and reason. Thoughts and reason that surface without reflection are often the result of mental habit, personal belief, or prejudice masquerading as insight (otherwise known as intuition).

Much of government funded forensic science occurs in circumstances that do not allow for reflection, contemplation, or experimentation, for lack of funding, time, or intellectual dexterity. Consequently, a careful student of forensic casework and testimony will find no small amount of the conclusions that modern forensic scientists profess in their reports and testimony to be based on raw experience, incomplete evidence, unchecked assumptions, untested theories, poor on the job training, and oversimplified arguments. This occurs, and is allowed to occur, because those with vested interests and authority encourage forensic findings that serve their purposes. To paraphrase Diderot, they drink deeply from the sweet wines that flatter them, and sip carefully at the bitter taste of scientific fact. As long as forensic science is "overseen" by vested individuals and organizations, there will remain little incentive for competence, rigor, or reflection apart from the individual professional compass (James and Nordby, 2003, p. 4).

All this to say there is a responsibility to reflect on theories and findings before ascribing meaning to them, and certainly before throwing them into a report of our conclusions. Reconstruction is, again, complex. We are meant to brood and deliberate over the quality of our inferences and invite others to do the same.

THE SOCRATIC METHOD AND THE SCIENTIFIC METHOD

We invent our myths and our theories and we try them out: we try to see how far they take us. And we improve our theories if we can. The better theory is the one that has the greater explanatory power: that explains more; that explains with greater precision; and that allows us to make better predictions.

—Karl Popper (1965, p. 192)

The *Socratic method* is an approach to knowledge building and problem solving based on discussion and debate. Practitioners seek explanations by identifying assumptions in their arguments and eliminating that which is not true or cannot be proven. Hypotheses are generated and conceptually tested or challenged based on what is known. It commonly involves two or more people engaged in the debate of a specific issue. In this fashion, the strongest explanations of circumstances or events survive, whereas the weakest are killed off by a succession of contradictory facts or counter-examples (Windelband, 1958, p. 96).

The *scientific method* is another particular approach to knowledge building and problem solving based on the development of empirically testable hypotheses that are assaulted by experiments intended to falsify them. Each of the contributors to this text will cover their incorporation of the scientific method in the following chapters, however, it is useful to discuss the general steps involved.

The first step in the scientific method is *observation*. An observation is made regarding some event or object. This observation then leads to a specific question regarding the event or object, such as where it originated from or how it came to possess certain traits.

The second step in the scientific method is attempting to answer the question that has been asked by forming a *hypothesis*, or a guess, regarding the possible answer. Often, there is more than one possible answer.

The third step in the scientific method is *experimentation*. Of all the steps in the scientific method, this is the one that separates scientific inquiry from others. Forensic scientists design experiments intended to disprove their hypotheses. Once again, forensic scientists design experiments intended to disprove their hypotheses, not to prove them.

At least one major forensic science text that provides readers with discussions of crime reconstruction as a process has failed to emphasize this crucial aspect of the experimentation or "testing" phase in theory development. Rather, crime reconstruction is presented in an overly simplified fashion for use by investigators looking to prove their theories (Baker and Napier, 2003, p. 538; Miller, 2003, pp. 128–129). These joined works collectively leave the door open for a confirmatory bias. Reconstruction conclusions regarding crime-related actions or events are not intended to absolutely "verify," "confirm," or "prove" investigative theories. Rather, they are meant to support or refute investigative theories. The words "support" and "confirm" are worlds apart. One suggests assistance, and one suggests finality. This difference may sound semantic to some, but it is not.

The purpose of forensic science and crime reconstruction is to test investigative theories and subsequently provide independent support or opposition. The key word is *independent*. If the job of the forensic scientist is merely to work toward confirming law enforcement theories, then there is no point in performing an analysis. Confirmation is always easy to find if that is what one looks for—all one needs to do is ignore everything that works against the prevailing theory and embrace everything that even remotely supports it. But that is not what the scientific method is about. The absolute corner-stone of the scientific method is *falsification*:

SCIENCE AS FALSIFICATION

—Sir Karl R. Popper (1963, pp. 33–39)

These considerations led me in the winter of 1919–20 to conclusions which I may now reformulate as follows.

1. It is easy to obtain confirmations, or verifications, for nearly every theory—if we look for confirmations.
2. Confirmations should count only if they are the result of risky predictions; that is to say, if, unenlightened by the theory in question, we should have expected an event which was incompatible with the theory—an event which would have refuted the theory.
3. Every "good" scientific theory is a prohibition: It forbids certain things to happen. The more a theory forbids, the better it is.
4. A theory which is not refutable by any conceivable event is nonscientific. Irrefutability is not a virtue of a theory (as people often think) but a vice.
5. Every genuine test of a theory is an attempt to falsify it, or to refute it. Testability is falsifiability; but there are degrees of testability: Some theories are more testable, more exposed to refutation, than others; they take, as it were, greater risks.
6. Confirming evidence should not count except when it is the result of a genuine test of the theory; and this means that it can be presented as a serious but unsuccessful attempt to falsify the theory. (I now speak in such cases of "corroborating evidence.")
7. Some genuinely testable theories, when found to be false, are still upheld by their admirers—for example by introducing ad hoc some auxiliary assumption, or by reinterpreting the theory ad hoc in such a way that it escapes refutation. Such a procedure is always possible, but it rescues the theory from refutation only at the price of destroying, or at least lowering, its scientific status. (I later described such a rescuing operation as a "conventionalist twist" or a "conventionalist stratagem.")

One can sum up all this by saying that the criterion of the scientific status of a theory is its falsifiability, or refutability, or testability.

If a hypothesis remains standing after a succession of tests or experiments fail to disprove it, then it may become a *scientific theory*.

Scientific theories that withstand the test of time and empirical study eventually become *scientific principles*. Although there is no universal agreement as to whether and when a scientific theory crosses this line to become a scientific principle, there is universal agreement that no such principles exist in forensic science or crime reconstruction. This does not, however, completely diminish their value or contribution to the cause of justice.

A scientific theory, developed with the assistance of the scientific method, has a greater degree of reliability and acceptance than mere observation, intuition or speculation. With regard to crime reconstruction, this may be explained in terms of establishing what has not occurred, and what may or may not be supported by the evidence, as opposed to absolutely confirming a specific event or sequence of events.

To use a simple example, imagine a ball of clay. It is perfectly spherical except for a flattened area on one side. We theorize that the ball was dropped onto a flat surface causing it to become flattened. To test this theory we take several clay balls of the same diameter and weight and drop them from various heights. We then examine the flattened area on each. When we find one with a flattened area equal to that on the original, we postulate they were both dropped from approximately the same height.

Are there alternative solutions? Of course, the ball may have been molded that way in the first place. Could it have been pressed with a flat object? No, it would cause two flat sides—we can try this experiment to show this result. Could the area have been cut off? We can examine the surface of the clay to determine whether or not there has been a surface change. We can imagine several different ways of cutting—knife, razor blade, laser, etc. Each would change the surface characteristics in a distinctive fashion, leaving behind a particular pattern or tool mark.

To eliminate alternatives, we need to do experiments. If experiments about one part of the evidence cannot determine which alternative is correct, then we must expand our experiments to other parts of the evidence or we need to research the background of the subject. In the previous simplified example, we have two alternative solutions: The ball was made the way we found it, or it fell from a determined distance. To eliminate one of the alternatives we could examine the flat surface where the ball was found. We could place preflattened balls on the surface and we could drop spherical balls from the predetermined height to the surface. We then determine if we can see a difference in the amount or type of residue remaining when the balls are removed. We may even leave the balls on the surface to determine if the time in contact makes a difference. We then look back at the original surface to see which of our experiments reproduces the characteristics we find.

When we are left with only one alternative, then we conclude our hypothesis must be true. Or, as stated by the fictional Sherlock Holmes, "Eliminate all other factors, and the one which remains must be the truth" (*The Sign of Four* by A. Conan Doyle, 1888).

This is the scientific method. We make an observation; we theorize or state a hypothesis; and we conduct experiments, which support or negate our hypothesis. The problem is designing the correct experiments; we must be able to identify alternative solutions and design the experiments to distinguish between the various hypotheses without letting our personal biases and prejudices favor one or the other. Although we try to be objective, we must recognize that there are factors that we do not realize are present that influence our decisions. As stated by Kuhn (1977), "Subjective criteria, such as 'individual biography and personality,' play an overwhelming role in scientific decision making." We are not able to completely eliminate these "subjective criteria" from our thought processes, but we must be aware that they are present. This will be discussed further in other chapters.

INDUCTIVE AND DEDUCTIVE REASONING

There is much confusion on the subject of inductive and deductive reasoning. This is perhaps a product of using dictionaries to define terms rather than more learned references. It is also perhaps a product of the desire to present inductive/statistical inferences as more certain than they actually are. The concepts, however, are fairly straightforward and simple, and not open to a lot of debate with respect to certainty.

Deductive reasoning, strictly speaking, involves arguments made where if the premises are true, then the conclusions must also be true. In a deductive argument the conclusions flow directly from the premises given (Walton, 1989, p. 110). Or, as DeForest et al. (1983, p. 2) describe it, "In deductive logic, a conclusion follows inescapably from one or more of the premises. If the premises are true, then the conclusion drawn is valid." This formulation, from a forensic science perspective, is shared and expounded upon by Thornton (1997, p. 13), who considers induction and deduction subjects that too many forensic scientists are only vaguely familiar with:

> Induction is a type of inference that proceeds from a set of specific observations to a generalization, called a premise. This premise is a working assumption, but it may not always be valid. A deduction, on the other hand, proceeds from a generalization to a specific case, and that is generally what happens in forensic practice.

Providing that the premise is valid, the deduction will be valid. But knowing whether the premise is valid is the name of the game here; it is not difficult to be fooled into thinking that one's premises are valid when they are not.

Forensic scientists have, for the most part, treated induction and deduction rather casually. They have failed to recognize that induction, not deduction, is the counterpart of hypothesis testing and theory revision. They have tended to equate a hypothesis with a deduction, which it is not. As a consequence, too often a hypothesis is declared as a deductive conclusion, when in fact it is a statement awaiting verification through testing.

Understanding the presumptive nature of inductive hypotheses is where many reconstructionists fall down in their analysis. Rather than take the time to test or falsify their hypotheses, it is not uncommon to see such unfinished thinking in reports and testimony masquerading as conclusive findings. As will be discussed further in the practice standards section of this chapter, reconstructionists have an obligation to carefully delineate between inductive hypotheses and deductive conclusions.

CRITICAL THINKING

There are many definitions for the term *critical thinking*. Their unifying concept is that critical thinking tends to involve indiscriminately questioning assumptions in arguments that we encounter in any context. This means rigorously questioning the assumptions beneath the reasoning and opinions of others as well as our own.

Paul and Scriven (2004) note:

Critical thinking is the intellectually disciplined process of actively and skillfully conceptualizing, applying, analyzing, synthesizing, and/or evaluating information gathered from, or generated by, observation, experience, reflection, reasoning, or communication, as a guide to belief and action.

Sadly, most of the students encountered by the authors have no idea what critical thinking is, what it involves, or how it can be useful in problem solving. In fact, it is extremely likely that most students reading this text will have never formally encountered the concept of critical thinking.

For the purposes of forensic science and crime reconstruction, the application of critical thinking to casework means a staunch refusal to accept any evidence or conclusions without sufficient proof. It involves the careful and deliberate determination of whether to accept, reject, or suspend judgment about any information or related findings. It means skeptical gathering of evidence, skeptical examinations, and the skeptical interpretation of results. This includes the following:

1. Evaluating the nature and quality of any information and its source
2. Recognizing bias
3. Separating facts from opinions
4. Distinguishing between primary sources of information (unaltered—direct from the source) and secondary sources of information (altered—interpreted or summarized through someone else)
5. Synthesizing information

The problem with critical thinking is that in some circumstances it is easier, and perhaps more realistic, to accept what others have told us or shown us rather than to investigate matters for ourselves. There may also be harsh consequences for questioning information or findings when they come from those who perceive themselves as our betters (or our supervisors). Although this can be true as a practical matter, it does not make arguments based on uncritically accepted information or conclusions more reliable. Reconstructionists are warned to embrace the limitations, and accept the consequences, of that which is accepted uncritically when conducting their analysis.

NO GOOD REASON: LOGICAL FALLACIES IN CRIME RECONSTRUCTION

If it was so, it might be; and if it were so, it would be; but as it isn't, it ain't. That's logic.

Tweedledee, in Lewis Carroll's *Through the Looking Glass, and What Alice Found There*, London: MacMillan (1872)

Perhaps the most revealing indicators of the absence of analytical logic and the scientific method in a crime reconstruction are the presence of logical fallacies in forensic conclusions. Logical fallacies are errors in reasoning that essentially deceive those whom they are intended to convince. This does not mean that the fallacious reconstructionist is being intentionally deceptive. What it does mean is that some reconstructionists lack the intellectual dexterity to know whether and when their reasoning is flawed.

Forensic practitioners of all disciplines would do well to learn more about fallacies in logic and reasoning in order to avoid them in their own work as well as identify them in the work of others. Common logical fallacies in crime reconstruction, and the forensic sciences in general, include, but are certainly not limited to, the following:

Suppressed evidence or card stacking: This is a one-sided argument that presents only evidence favoring a particular conclusion and ignores or downplays the evidence against it. It may involve distortions, exaggerations, misstatements of facts, or outright lies. This is not an acceptable practice for any forensic practitioner.

EXAMPLE

In 2002, Special Agent Kathleen Lundy of the FBI crime lab, an expert in comparative bullet-lead analysis, testified in a criminal case against Shane Ragland, who was ultimately convicted in the 1994 shooting death of Kentucky football player Trent DiGiuro. Under oath in court, she knowingly gave false testimony that the Winchester company had melted its own bullet lead until 1996, when in reality Winchester had stopped the practice in 1986. She did so to bolster her conclusion that two bullets had come from the same batch of manufacturing lead and could therefore be linked to the same person. She knowingly and purposefully gave the false information to help buttress the confidence of her otherwise weak conclusions. Lundy claimed that she gave the false testimony under pressure coming from the many recent challenges to her area of expertise—she feared that her testimony might be disallowed and that her field might lose credibility with the courts (Taylor, 2002, p. A1):

"I cannot explain why I made the original error . . . nor why, knowing that the testimony was false, I failed to correct it at the time," Lundy wrote in a May 28 internal FBI memo. "I was stressed out by this case and work in general. I had been under a great deal of professional pressure for over a year and had considered resigning. This pressure was increased by new and repeated challenges to the validity of the science associated with bullet-lead comparison analysis. These challenges affected me a great deal, perhaps more than they should have. I also felt that there was ineffective support from the FBI to meet the challenges."

Racked with guilt, Lundy informed her superiors of what she had done. According to Post (2005):

Lundy was subsequently terminated by the Bureau, but not before her superiors tried to convince her that she hadn't really lied, according to interviews conducted by the U.S. Department of Justice's Office of the Inspector General, Case No. O & R 20022003.

The federal authorities declined to prosecute her for any wrongdoing; however, the State of Kentucky took a slightly different view. She was charged and pleaded guilty to false swearing in Fayette County District Court. She received a 90-day suspended sentence and a $250 fine.

On November 18, 2004, the Kentucky Supreme Court overturned the conviction of Shane Raglund.

Figure 4.1

Sandra M. Anderson and her dog, Eagle.

Appeal to authority: This kind of argument occurs when someone offers a conclusion based on the stated authority or expertise of themselves or others. This kind of reasoning can be fallacious when the authority lacks the expertise suggested; when the authority is an expert in one subject but not the subject at hand; when the subject is contentious and involves multiple interpretations with good arguments on both sides; when the authority is biased; when the area of expertise is fabricated; when the authority is unidentified; and when the authority is offered as evidence in place of defensible scientific fact.

EXAMPLE

In *Wisconsin v. Kupaza* (2000), Sandra M. Anderson (Fig. 4.1), an internationally famous dog handler, testified that her dog, Eagle, made a positive hit on the defendant's vehicle for decaying biological material. The significance of this finding was to support the theory that the defendant had used his vehicle to transport the victim's dismembered, decaying body.

However, a Luminol test failed to react positively to anything in the vehicle. To explain this discrepancy, Ms. Anderson testified that her dog's nose was more sensitive than any form of scientific testing, and that it was still reasonable to assume that the body had been transported in the defendant's vehicle. She testified to this without any actual knowledge of the sensitivity or nature of Luminol testing or of the anatomy, physiology, and sensitivity of her dog Eagle's nose. The court allowed this testimony.

However, Anderson is not a forensic scientist and holds no forensic credentials of any kind. She is, as stated, a dog handler. For her to offer testimony on issues of forensic science, forensic testing, and evidentiary interpretation was out of place, to say the very least.

It is of interest that in March 2004, Anderson pleaded guilty to five felony charges, including obstruction of justice and making false statements to federal authorities for planting biological evidence in numerous criminal cases throughout Michigan and Ohio. Her dog would find the planted evidence and this would be used to bolster law enforcement theories of foul play. She was sentenced to 21 months and order to pay $14,500 in restitution to various law enforcement agencies that she defrauded.

It is common for forensic experts of all kinds to offer their years of experience as evidence of accuracy. However, experience and accuracy are not necessarily related. Though skill and ability are potential benefits of age and experience, it does not follow that those with experience will necessarily gain skill or ability, let alone be ever accurate in their examinations. As explained by Thornton (1997, p. 17), summoning experience instead of logic and reasoning to support a conclusion is an admission to lacking both:

> Experience is neither a liability nor an enemy of the truth; it is a valuable commodity, but it should not be used as a mask to deflect legitimate scientific scrutiny, the sort of scrutiny that customarily is leveled at scientific evidence of all sorts. To do so is professionally bankrupt and devoid of scientific legitimacy, and courts would do well to disallow testimony of this sort. Experience ought to be used to enable the expert to remember the when and the how, why, who, and what. Experience should not make the expert less responsible, but rather more responsible for justifying an opinion with defensible scientific facts.

In other words, the more experience of quality and substance one has, the less one will need to tell people about it in order to gain their trust and confidence—the quality of one's experience is demonstrated through the inherent quality of one's methods and results.

Furthermore, experience in finding, collecting, and/or packaging evidence (a.k.a. crime scene processing) is not related to experience interpreting the meaning of evidence in its context (a.k.a. crime reconstruction). This would be an appeal to false authority. As explained in O'Hara (1970, p. 667), the role of crime scene investigator and the role of evidence interpretation should not intersect:

> It is not to be expected that the investigator also play the role of the laboratory expert in relation to the physical evidence found at the scene of the crime. . . . It suffices that the investigator investigate; it is supererogatory that he should perform refined scientific examinations. Any serious effort to accomplish such a conversion would mutilate against the investigator's efficiency.
>
> . . .
>
> In general the investigator should know the methods of discovering, "field-testing," preserving, collecting, and transporting evidence. Questions of analysis and comparison should be referred to the laboratory expert.

In addition, although he emphasizes cooperation between crime scene investigators and forensic scientists, Lee (1994) is in agreement with this separation of collection and interpretation duties. He details crime reconstruction as a process of systematic evidence examination based on adherence to the principles of forensic science and the scientific method, something necessarily beyond the training of the average crime scene technician (pp. 191–201).

Appeal to tradition: This kind of argument reasons that a conclusion is correct simply because it is older, traditional, or "has always been so." It supports a conclusion by appealing to long-standing, institutional, or cultural opinions, as if the past itself is a form of authority.

EXAMPLE

The basic assumption of fingerprint examination is that each human fingerprint is unique and identifiable because of the way they are formed and because nature never repeats itself.

In *Utah v. Quintana* (2004), Raymond Michael Quintana appealed his conviction for burglary on the basis that fingerprint examination methods lack empirical research and study, and necessarily fails the state's threshold reliability test for scientific evidence. The court held that the threshold reliability test for scientific evidence only applies to new and novel forms of evidence. The court of appeals explained to Mr. Quintana that fingerprint evidence, because of its history of acceptance by the courts,

need not meet the same rigorous standards of reliability. In other words, the reliability of fingerprint
examination methods may be assumed because that
is the way it has always been.

Notably, one of the concurring judges suggested
that trial courts should be directed to instruct juries
about the existing weaknesses of fingerprint examiner training and identification protocol.

Fingerprint experts have claimed for years that fingerprints are individual
because "no one has ever seen two alike in all the prints collected." The
absurdity of that statement is lost on the nonscientist. It is not conceivable
that each fingerprint collected had been compared to "all other prints." Not
until the computer and automated latent print searches were available was
there any way to compare more than a few individual prints. The computer
systems pick out the most likely matches, those having the most geometri-
cally spaced matching points. The means is at hand for verification of the
individuality of fingerprint or the ability to put fingerprints in the same
realm as DNA by offering statistical statements, but this has not been undertaken to the best of the authors' knowledge.

Argumentum ad hominem, a.k.a. "argument to the man": The argument attacks an
opponent's character rather than an opponent's argument. Because of its
effectiveness, it is perhaps the most common logical fallacy. Even if true, it is
important to note that arguments against character are not always relevant to the
presentation of scientific conclusions, logic, and reasoning.

EXAMPLE

Arguing that a conclusion based on science and reasoning is invalid because the forensic examiner lacks
experience or is an alcoholic.

Although a forensic examiner may or may not be
experienced, and may or may not be an alcoholic, it
is the examiner's methods and findings that should
be scrutinized. The scientific method, though often
enhanced by the skill that can come with experience, does not falter simply because of youth or inexperience. Moreover, for alcoholism or any other
form of addiction to be relevant in an argument, a
causal connection must be shown. This connection
would exist if perhaps owing to the addiction the

forensic examiner were shown to have been negli-
gent or to have committed fraud in order to per-
petuate or conceal his addiction.

It would be intellectually dishonest to suggest
that any forensic conclusions must be wrong solely
because the examiner is an alcoholic and a drug
addict. However, it is fair to observe that these circumstances can lead to fraudulent behavior that
should cast doubt on his casework and initiate an
independent review of his related findings. The distinction here is the call for a review to determine if
there are errors, rather than an immediate and
untested conclusion that there must be errors.

Emotional appeal: An attempt to gain favor based on arousing emotions and/or sympathy to subvert rational thought.

EXAMPLE

In April 1998, during a pretrial interview, a supervisory criminalist told defense attorney Stephanie Adraktas that no report had ever existed that failed to match the DNA profile of her client, on trial for rape, to the DNA on a victim's vaginal swabs. This was because of the discrepancies in his lab notes. The criminalist had in fact authored such a report, which failed to match the defendant because of a simple error he had made in the testing process. Instead of admitting to the error, he destroyed the report and lied about its existence to the defense attorney under questioning. When he finally admitted to the error and to his attempts at concealing it, he argued, among other things, that the pressure of expert testimony had simply gotten to him, and that relentless defense attorneys were in part responsible for his actions: "We were facing on a monthly basis people who were trying to destroy our reputations."

In September 2000, the criminalist resigned from the crime lab in lieu of being fired.

Obviously, feeling stressed and pressured are not legitimate mitigating circumstances for the commission of fraud by a forensic expert to help bolster the case against any defendant.

Circulus in probando, a.k.a. circular reasoning: An argument that assumes as part of its premises the very conclusion that is supposed to be proven.

EXAMPLE

An armed suspect is shot to death by police snipers after a prolonged standoff involving hostages. The negotiators on the scene declare that the suspect was not rational and acted bizarre, mentally scattered, and paranoid during attempts at communication. Alcohol and cocaine are found near his body. Police theorize that he was abusing alcohol and cocaine, and they release this information to the media as a factor in the suspect's mental state and subsequent irrationality and death. Several weeks later, a forensic toxicology report is released that provides that the suspect's body tested negative for alcohol and cocaine metabolites. However, instead of indicating that alcohol and cocaine were not found, the absence chemical indicators are listed on the report as a "false negative." The report is supplemented with the written explanation that the negative laboratory findings are in error because of the investigative discovery of alcohol and cocaine at the scene, in concert with the suspect's reported behavior.

In this example, forensic science (in this case toxicology) is asked to assist with reconstructing the *why* part of the deceased suspect's aberrant scene behavior. The investigative assumption is that the suspect's behavior must have been drug related. The scientific tests that are performed fail to support this assumption and are subsequently written up in the lab report as false negatives based purely on investigative findings. The problem is that the investigative findings represent theories that lab tests are meant to verify through science. Investigative theories that are disproved by scientific testing must be abandoned, and not the other way around.

Cum hoc, ergo propter hoc, or "with this, therefore because of this": When one jumps to a conclusion about causation based on a correlation between two events, or types of event, that occur simultaneously.

EXAMPLE

A crime scene technician arrives at an outdoor location where a body has been found. The victim is a prostitute, and the location is a secluded wooded area, accessible by vehicle, frequented by prostitutes and their customers for the purposes of engaging in clandestine sexual activity. Within 20 feet of the body, the technician locates 15 condoms, one of which is found underneath the victim. All are collected and submitted for analysis. A DNA database finds a matching profile for the sperm fragment of the condom discovered under the victim's body; it belongs to a registered sex offender. The sex offender is arrested and put on trial.

In this example, the suspect is arrested because he has been identified as associated with the scene and because he is a known sex offender, but not because he has been directly associated with the victim or the murder. To associate the victim with the suspect, her DNA profile would need to match the DNA profile of the epithelial cells found on the outside of the condom with his DNA found on the inside. That is the first test. This same test would need to be run on all of the condoms collected. To associate the offender with the homicide would require other circumstantial evidence because the victim could easily have visited the location more than once with multiple customers who also immediately discarded their condoms.

Just because a condom is found at the scene of a homicide where a prostitute has been killed does not by itself prove that the person who wore it is the killer. How it got there is just as important as finding it because it may or may not be related to the crime. This connection may not be assumed.

Post hoc, ergo propter hoc, or "after this, therefore because of this": When one reasons to a causal conclusion based solely on the alleged cause preceding its alleged effect.

EXAMPLE

A crime scene technician finds a stain on a bed sheet where a rape is known to have occurred. It is tested and determined to be semen. The conclusion is drawn that this stain must be related to the rape because it was found subsequent to the rape. In reality, there are other explanations for the semen stain in the example provided, including recent consensual or autoerotic sexual activity.

Hasty generalizations: When one forms a conclusion based on woefully incomplete information or by examining only a few specific cases that are not representative of all possible cases.

EXAMPLE

A woman is murdered in her home, and her body is found face down in the bedroom in a pool of blood. The cause of death is multiple stab wounds to the chest and exsanguination. Blood is found in the bedroom, in the bathroom, and in the hallway. DNA testing is performed on the blood in the bathroom, and it matches the DNA profile of the victim. A reconstruction of events is offered in which it is assumed that the blood in the bedroom and in the kitchen also belongs to the victim.

Although it may be a safe bet that the blood in the bedroom belongs to the victim because of the nature of her death, it is not safe to assume anything. All discrete areas of blood must be tested and their origin confirmed before inclusion in a reconstruction of events.

Sweeping generalization: When one forms a conclusion by examining what occurs in many cases and assuming that it must or will be so in a particular case. This is the opposite of a hasty generalization.

EXAMPLE

A criminal profiler testifies in court regarding a staged crime scene. A man has been found shot to death in his home, and the profiler believes that the crime scene was staged to appear like a burglary gone wrong. The profiler provides in her report that, according to FBI statistics, in the majority of residential burglary cases the burglar will not enter a residence if a car is parked in the front driveway. Since the victim's car was in the front driveway, and clearly visible to all, this leads to the conclusion that it is unlikely that the killer was a burglar, and that the crime scene was staged.

This conclusion not only assumes that statistical probability translates into a fact that may be assumed for every case but also inappropriately assumes that all burglars think and act alike.

False precision: When an argument treats information as more precise than it really is. This happens when conclusions are based on imprecise information that must be taken as precise in order to adequately support the conclusion.

It bears mentioning that presenting precise statistics or numbers in support of an argument gives the appearance of scientific accuracy when this may not actually be the case. Many people find math and statistics overly impressive and become easily intimidated by those who wield numbers with ease. This is especially true with DNA evidence, whose astronomic statistical probabilities are often presented by those without any background in statistics and without full consideration of the databases that such probabilities are being derived from.

EXAMPLE

A criminalist testifies that a hair found on a victim's body and a hair sample taken from a known suspect "match" with respect to physical characteristics. The criminalist further testifies that the probability of a match is 1 in 10,000.

The word "match" when used in this fashion does not prove that the hairs must have come from the same person, and the use of statistics to support this is evidence of outright fraud. The use of any probabilities is contrary to the fact that there is not and never has been a well-established probability theory for hair comparison.

In the advent of varying DNA databases and subsequent statistics of impressive weight being read in court to bedazzled jurors, and the outright fabrication of statistics related to hair comparisons, the cautionary offered in Kirk and Kingston (1964) is more appropriate now than ever: "Without a firm grasp of the principles involved, the unwary witness can be lead into making statements that he cannot properly uphold, especially in the matter of claiming inordinately high probability figures." A more specific criticism of forensic practices was provided in Moennsens (1993):

Experts use statistics compiled by other experts without any appreciation of whether the database upon which the statistics were formulated fits their own local experience, or how the statistics were compiled. Sometimes these experts, trained in one forensic discipline, have little or no knowledge of the study of probabilities, and never even had a college-level course in statistics.

Those using statistics to support their findings have a responsibility to know where they come from, how they were derived, and what they mean to the case at hand, before they form conclusions and certainly before they testify in court.

PRACTICE STANDARDS

It should not need to be mentioned that all forensic practitioners have a duty to strive for objectivity, competence, and professionalism in their work. Forensic examiners should want their findings to be accurate and their methods to be reliable. There are few forensic practitioners who would disagree with Lee (1993), who provides, "Perhaps the most important issue in forensic science is the establishment of professional standards. An assessment is needed of standards of practice in the collection, examination, and analysis of physical evidence." Practice standards define a minimum threshold of competency. They also help define a practitioner's role and outline a mechanism for demonstrating their facility. They are a compass for diligent practitioners to follow and a screen against which those who have lost their way can be delayed and educated.

As this suggests, the purpose of defining practice standards is not only to help professionals achieve a level of competency but also to provide independent reviewers with a basis for checking work that purports to be competent. Practice standards set the bar and are a safeguard against ignorance, incapacity, and incomprehension masquerading as science and reason. In a field in which the most common argument tends to be that conclusions are accurate simply because of how many years a practitioner has been on the job, the need for providing practice standards should be self-evident.

The major published works that cover both forensic science and crime reconstruction may be aggregated to assist in defining basic yet essential practice standards that apply to forensic practitioners of almost every kind (Bevel and Gardner, 1997, 2001; Chisum and Rynearson, 1997; DeForest et al., 1983; DeHaan, 2002; Gross, 1906; Inman and Rudin, 2000; Kirk, 1953; Kirk and Thornton, 1970; Lee, 1994; Locard, 1934; O'Connell and Soderman, 1936; O'Hara, 1956, 1970; Saferstein, 2001; Thornton, 1997; Turvey, 2002). In these collected texts authored by practitioner–educators, the scientific method, analytical reasoning, and objectivity are prized above all else, whereas emotion, intuition, and other forms of bias masquerading as knowledge are shunned. With the assistance of these works, the following generally accepted practice standards may be offered:

1. **Reconstructionists must strive diligently to avoid bias.**

Dr. Paul Kirk wrote of crime reconstruction, "Physical evidence cannot be wrong; it cannot be perjured; it cannot be wholly absent. *Only in its interpretation can there be error*" (Kirk and Thornton, 1970, p. 4). With this simple observation, Kirk was referring to the influences of examiner ignorance, imprecision, and bias on the reconstruction of physical evidence and its meaning. The evidence is always there, waiting to be understood. The forensic examiner is the imprecise lens through which a form of understanding comes.

Specifically, there are at least two kinds of bias that objective forensic examiners need to be aware of and mitigate in their casework in order to maintain their professional lens—observer bias and confirmation bias. These were discussed in previous chapters but bear repeating here for our purposes.

Observer bias may be described as the conscious or unconscious tendency to see or find what one expects to see or find. In a practical sense, this means that the forensic examiner can develop an expectation of findings based on information and opinions learned from the popular media, witnesses, and the opinions and findings of others. These influences are particularly insidious because, unlike overt fraud, they can be subconscious. Unless intentionally screened or recognized by the examiner in some fashion, influences can nudge, push, or drag examiner findings in a particular direction.

Confirmation bias may be described as the conscious or unconscious tendency to affirm previous theories, opinions, or findings. It is a specific kind of observer bias in which information and evidence are screened to include those things that confirm a position and to actively ignore, not look for, or undervalue the relevance of anything that contradicts that position.

It commonly manifests itself in the form of looking only for particular kinds of evidence that support a given case theory (i.e., suspect guilt or innocence) and actively explaining away evidence or findings that are undesirable. As stated previously, this can be the selection of the evidence to examine by persons advocating a particular theory or by persons interested in "watching the budget" so that potentially exculpatory evidence is not selected for analysis because that would cost more money or require too much time.

Wrestling with confirmation bias is extremely difficult, often because it is institutional. Many forensic examiners work in systems in which they are rewarded with praise and promotion for successfully advocating their side when true science is about anything other than successfully advocating any one side. Consequently, the majority of forensic examiners suffering from confirmation bias have no idea what it is or that it is even a problem. Many even come to believe that they are a valuable member of a prosecutor's team and that winning a case is the measure of a job well done.

What must be understood by all forensic examiners is that the primary value of forensic science to the legal system (the forensic part) is their adherence to the scientific method (the science part), and that this demands as much objectivity and soundness of method as can be brought to bear. Success in the forensic science community must be measured by the diligent elimination of possibilities through the scientific method and peer review, not through securing convictions. As Professor Brian Parker (Personal Communication, 1972) states, "The job of the crime lab is to prove the investigator wrong."

2. Reconstructionists are responsible for requesting all relevant evidence and information in order to perform an adequate reconstruction.

Reconstructionists must define the scope of evidence and information they need to perform an adequate reconstruction, partial or otherwise, and make a formal request from their client, employer, or the requesting agency. Upon receiving that evidence, they must determine what has been made available and what is missing. This basic task is incumbent upon every forensic examiner.

When a reconstructionist is not able to base his findings on complete information as he defines or understands it, this must be made clear as part of his conclusions.

Basic requests for information must include

- A list of all agencies that responded to the crime scene and/or have assisted in the investigation to date
- All available crime scene documentation, including collection and security logs, notes, sketches, and photos
- All available investigative reports and notes from all responding/assisting agencies
- All available forensic reports, notes, and laboratory findings from all responding/assisting agencies
- All available medical reports and notes, including trauma-grams and injury photos
- All available medical examiner reports and notes, including trauma-grams and autopsy photos
- All relevant investigative and forensic testimony from any court proceedings to date
- A list of all witnesses to the crime or crime scene
- Any documentation of witness and suspect statements, including recordings, transcripts, and investigative summaries

3. Reconstructionists are responsible for determining whether the evidence they are examining is of sufficient quality to provide the basis for a reconstruction.

The harsh reality is that crime scene processing and documentation efforts are often abysmal if not completely absent. Crime scenes throughout the United States are commonly processed by police-employed technicians or sworn personnel with little or no formal education, to say nothing of training in the forensic sciences and crime scene processing techniques. The inservice forensic training available to law enforcement typically exists in the form of half-day seminars or short courses taught by nonscientists who, on their own, in no way impart the discipline and expertise necessary to process crime scenes adequately for the purposes of reconstruction.

In order to determine whether evidence is of sufficient quality to provide the basis for a reconstruction, the most important considerations are the following:

- The ability to identify the item of evidence.
- The ability to conceptually if not literally place the item back in the crime scene where it was found in relation to the other items of evidence. This is done through competent sketches and related written and photographic documentation. Memory is not a reliable substitute for hard documentation.
- The ability to identify every person who handled the item subsequent to its collection. Is the chain of evidence secure and complete?
- The ability to identify every test that was performed on the item, who performed them, and the results.

If crime scene documentation and processing efforts are not sufficient to the task of allowing for the reconstructionist to establish the previously mentioned considerations, then those efforts were at best inadequate. Reconstructionists must make note of such deficiencies in their analysis and factor them into their conclusions, and may even need to explain that they cannot derive certain conclusions because of them.

It is important to note that the reconstructionist cannot know absolutely everything about any item of evidence. Nobody can. The challenge is to consider all that is known when performing a reconstruction and be prepared to incorporate new information as it may come to light. This means appreciating that new information about any item of evidence, or its history, may affect any conclusions about what it means.

4. Reconstructionists must, whenever possible, visit the crime scene.

It is highly preferable that the reconstructionist visit the crime scene. The following are examples of the kind of information that may be learned:

- The sights, smells, and sounds of the crime scene, as the victim and the offender may have perceived them.
- The spatial relationships within the scene.
- Observe and experience potential transfer evidence first-hand. Vegetation, soil, glass, fibers, and any other material that may have transferred onto the victim or suspects may become evident or may transfer onto the reconstructionist, providing examples of what to look for on suspect clothing or in suspect vehicles.
- The attentive reconstructionist may discover items of evidence at the scene previously missed and subsequently uncollected by crime scene technician efforts. This is far more common than many care to admit, and it is one of the most important reasons for visiting the crime scene.

In many cases, it will not be possible for the reconstructionist to visit the crime scene. This occurs for a variety of practical reasons, including time limitations, budgetary limitations, legal restrictions, the alteration of the scene by forces of nature, or the obliteration of the scene by land or property development. If the reconstructionist is unable to visit the crime scene for whatever reason, this must be clearly reflected in the findings.

It is not disputed that the primary reason for documenting a crime scene is to provide for later reconstruction efforts. Therefore, the inability of the reconstructionist to visit the scene does not preclude reconstruction efforts across the board. Competent scene documentation by forensic technicians may be sufficient to address the issues in question, or it may not. Each case is different and must be considered separately and carefully with regard to this issue.

5. Reconstruction conclusions, and their basis, must be provided in a written format.

Hans Gross referred to the critical role that exact, deliberate, and patient efforts at crime reconstruction can play in the investigation and resolution of crime. Specifically, he stated that just looking at a crime scene is not enough. He argued that there is utility in reducing one's opinions regarding the reconstruction to the form of a report in order to identify problems in the logic of one's theories (Gross, 1924, p. 439):

> So long as one only looks on the scene, it is impossible, whatever the care, time, and attention bestowed, to detect all the details, and especially note the incongruities: but these strike us at once when we set ourselves to describe the picture on paper as exactly and clearly as possible.
>
> . . .
>
> The "defects of the situation" are just those contradictions, those improbabilities, which occur when one desires to represent the situation as something quite different from what it really is, and this with the very best intentions and the purest belief that one has worked with all of the forethought, craft, and consideration imaginable.

Moreover, the reconstructionist, not the recipient of the reconstructionist's opinions (i.e., investigators, attorneys, and the court), bears the burden of ensuring that her conclusions are effectively communicated. This means writing them down. This means that the reconstructionist must be competent at intelligible writing, and reports must be comprehensive with regard to examinations performed, findings, and conclusions.

Verbal conclusions should be viewed as a form of substandard work product. They are susceptible to conversions, alterations, and misrepresentations. They may also become lost to time. Written conclusions are fixed in time, easy to reproduce, and are less susceptible to accidental or intentional conversion, alteration, and misrepresentation. An analyst who prefers verbal conclusions as opposed to written conclusions reveals preference for conclusive mobility.

Apart from their relative permanence, written conclusions also provide the reconstructionist with the best chance to memorialize methods, conclusions, arguments, and the underlying facts of the case. This includes a list of the evidence examined, when it was examined, and under what circumstances. Generally, a written report should include, but need not be limited to, the following information:

- A preliminary background section, describing the reconstructionist's involvement in the case.
- A chain of custody section, describing and detailing the evidence that was examined or included in the reconstruction.
- A descriptive section, in which the reconstructionist thoroughly describes examination and consideration of the facts and evidence.
- A results section, in which the examiner lists any results and conclusions, including their significance and limitations.
- The intended user of the end result is the jury: The report should be worded so that there is no question in the mind of the reader as to what is being said. This means writing in lay language and keeping it simple. Although occasionally there are professors on juries, there are more homemakers who married young and raised families. Do not make your report confusing by using long words or complicated sentences.

If a reconstruction cannot be written down in a logical form, easily understood by its intended user, then apart from having no value it is also probably wrong.

6. Reconstructionists must demonstrate an understanding of science, forensic science, and the scientific method.

The current national educational requirements for forensic scientists, which are agency specific and therefore nonexistent, fall short of ensuring that practitioners understand not only science and the scientific method but also basic research and statistical methods. All forensic scientists, including reconstructionists, must have a working knowledge of these subjects. It has been said, and it is true, that "if there is no science, there can be no forensic science" (Thornton, 1997, p. 17).

At a minimum, this means the reconstructionist must be educated in the fundamentals of science and the scientific method by an actual scientist. According to Thornton (1997, pp. 15–16), "A measure of scientific education and a university degree in a scientific discipline will ordinarily meet that test."

It further means that the reconstructionist must be educated in the forensic sciences by practicing forensic scientists. If their work involves the interpretation and presentation of statistical data, it means at least basic university-level coursework in that subject as well. Too many are learning these subjects informally, on the job, or from nonscientists and are consequently bringing their ignorance to case examination and then into court.

7. Reconstruction conclusions must be based on established facts. Facts may not be assumed for the purpose of analysis.

Many examiners are willing to provide a certain reconstruction of events based on experiential comparisons to unnamed cases, factual guesses and assumptions, or nonexistent physical evidence. If the underlying facts have not been established through investigative documentation, crime scene documentation, the examination of physical evidence, or corroborating eyewitness testimony, then any reconstruction of those facts is not a reliable or valid inference of events. This includes hypothetical scenarios.

8. Reconstruction conclusions must be valid inferences based on logical arguments and analytical reasoning.

In the process of establishing the facts that are fit for analysis, facts must be sifted and distinguished from opinions, conjectures, and theories. Inductive hypotheses must further be delineated from deductive conclusions, and conclusions must flow naturally from the facts provided. Furthermore, the reconstruction must be reasonably free from logical fallacies and incorrect statements of fact.

9. Reconstruction conclusions must be reached with the assistance of the scientific method.

The scientific method demands that careful observations of the evidence be made and then hypotheses generated and ultimately tested against all of the known evidence and accepted facts. Subsequently, the reconstructionist must provide not just conclusions but all other postulated theories that have been falsified through examinations, tests, and experiments. Falsification, not validation, is the cornerstone of the scientific method. Theories that have not been put to any test, or that appear in a report or in courtroom testimony based on rumination and imagination alone (i.e., experience and intuition), should not be considered inherently valid or reliable.

10. Reconstruction conclusions must demonstrate an understanding of, and clearly distinguish between, individuating findings and all others.

The concept of identification and individuation is often misunderstood. *Identification* or *classification* is the placement of any item into a specific category of items with similar characteristics. Identification does not require or imply uniqueness. *Individuation* is the assignment of uniqueness to an item. To individuate an item, it must be described in such a manner as to separate it from all other items in the universe (Thornton, 1997, p. 7).

In the presentation of findings, reconstructionists will find themselves using statements that suggest varying degrees of confidence. Vague terms or terms of art, such as "probably," "likely," "identify," "match," "consistent with," and "reasonable degree of scientific certainty," are among those used to qualify the certainty of findings. Unchecked, this language can be misleading to those it is intended to assist. Confidence statements must be qualified and discussed to the point of absolute clarity. Without clarification, findings may be misunderstood, misrepresented, and misapplied.

If the reconstructionist provides individuating findings of any sort, the nature of the uniqueness and how it was established must be clearly presented. When the reconstructionist has given his findings, there must remain no question as to whether the findings are individuating and no question as to how this was determined. The purpose of presenting findings is to clarify the evidence, not muddle it.

11. Reconstructionists must demonstrate an understanding of establishing the conditions of transfer (Locard's Exchange Principle and evidence dynamics).

Identifying and individuating physical evidence is only one part of crime reconstruction. Equally important is the need to establish the source of evidence and the conditions under which it was transferred to where it was ultimately found. Reconstructionists must not be quick to oversimplify complex issues, such as the examination and interpretation of physical evidence, or to disregard those circumstances that can move, alter, or obliterate that evidence.

12. Any evidence, data, or findings on which reconstruction conclusions are based must be made available through presentation or citation.

It is not acceptable for the reconstructionist to provide conclusions based on phantom databases, phantom data, phantom research, phantom evidence, or unseen comparisons. Data, research, and evidence must be detailed to the point where others reviewing their work may easily locate or identify it. Data, research, and evidence that cannot be duplicated or identified by the court in some fashion should not find its way into forensic conclusions.

These minimum practice standards should be applied to the evaluation of any method of crime reconstruction, both the general and the specialized, in order to show due diligence. If a reconstructionist is able to meet these standards, then a minimum threshold level of professional competency has indeed been achieved. Subsequently, the recipients of their conclusions may be assured that whatever the findings, they may be independently investigated and reviewed for reliability, accuracy, and validity. It bears pointing out that a reconstructionist who fails to climb even one of the rungs prescribed will not have reached this threshold. In failing they should have their findings questioned, as well as subsequent reports and testimony viewed with disfavor by the court. This will be echoed in the chapters that follow.

It is important to clarify that these practice standards do not leave anyone behind, but they do require everyone to show their work. Reconstructing crime is not easy or rote, and it is not supposed to be. Conclusions must be earned and that means competency must be demonstrated and peer review embraced. A reconstructionist has a duty to formulate her conclusions with the full reach of everything that forensic science, the scientific method, and analytical logic have to offer. Without these tools, reconstructionists are at risk of not being able to recognize forensic and scientific illiteracy in themselves or others.

To the uninitiated, these practice standards may seem too many or even too harsh. It may also seem as though the authors and contributors of this text are interpreting the forensic science and crime reconstruction literature in favor of objective forensic science and in opposition of everything else. To these and similar criticisms we offer this: First, crime reconstruction is a subdiscipline of the forensic sciences because it is forensic in nature and purports to be scientific in its practice. Second, those who wish to practice any form of crime reconstruction under that umbrella are obligated to know something of both the scientific method and forensic science. Third, if it seems that the authors and contributors of this text lean quite far in favor of practicing the scientific method and impartial evidence-based analysis above all else, it is because we mean to.

These practice standards may also raise the ire of some forensic examiners who have been reconstructing crime based on intuition and experience, perhaps for years, and who are unaccustomed to explaining themselves or their methods apart from stating their vast experience. If peer review and criticism are not welcome at a conclusion's doorstep, if instead such visitors are met with hostility and derision, then something other than science dwells within. To be clearer, the absence of the scientific method and logical inference in any reconstruction should not be a point of pride because it is ultimately evidence of ignorance. A reconstruction in the absence of the scientific method, analytical logic, and critical thinking is called a guess. A courtroom is no place for ignorance or guessing. Consequently, it is not unreasonable to expect that anyone reconstructing crime in such a manner be prepared to explain why.

REFERENCES

Baker, K., and Napier, M. "Criminal personality profiling." In S. James and J. Nordby (Eds.), *Forensic Science: An Introduction to Scientific and Investigative Techniques*, Boca Raton, FL: CRC Press, 2003.

Baldwin, H. (2005a) "Crime Scene Processing Protocol," *Forensic Enterprises*, Accessed June 4, 2005; URL: http://www.feinc.net/cs-proc.htm

Baldwin, H. (2005b) E-mail Communication to Public Discussion Forum, ICSIA-PublicForum@yahoogroups.com, Accessed June 7, 2005; URL: http://groups.yahoo.com/group/ICSIA-PublicForum

Bevel, T. and Gardner, R.M. *Bloodstain Pattern Analysis: With an Introduction to Crime Scene Reconstruction*, Boca Raton: CRC Press, 1997.

Bevel, T. and Gardner, R.M. *Bloodstain Pattern Analysis: With an Introduction to Crime Scene Reconstruction, 2nd Edition*, Boca Raton: CRC Press, 2001.

Chisum, W. J. "An introduction to crime reconstruction." In B. Turvey (Ed.), *Criminal Profiling: An Introduction to Behavioral Evidence Analysis*, (2nd ed.). London: Elsevier, 2002.

Chisum, W. J., and Rynearson, J. M. *Evidence and Crime Scene Reconstruction* (5th ed.). Shingletown, CA: Shingletown Press, 1997.

DeForest, P., Gaensslen, R., and Lee, H. *Forensic Science: An Introduction to Criminalistics.* New York: McGraw-Hill, 1983.

DeHaan, J. *Kirk's Fire Investigation* (5th ed.). New York: Prentice Hall, 2002.

Diderot, D. (1753) "On the interpretation of nature, no. 15." In L. Crocker (Ed.) *Diderot's Selected Writings*, New York: Macmillan, 1966.

"DNA Testing: Foolproof?" *CBS News*, May 29, 2003; "DNA Testing: Foolproof?" CBS News, 60 Minutes II, May 28, 2003; URL: http://www.cbsnews.com/stories/2003/05/27/60II/main555723.shtml

Gardner, R. (2005) "One Man's Opinion." E-mail Communication to Public Discussion Forum, ICSIA-PublicForum@yahoogroups.com, Accessed June 15, 2005; URL: http://groups.yahoo.com/group/ICSIA-PublicForum

Gross, H. *Criminal Investigation.* Madras: Ramasawmy, 1906.

Gross, H., *Criminal Investigation*, London: Sweet & Maxwell, Ltd, 1924.

Hamilton, W. *Discussions on Philosophy and Literature, Education and University Reform.* Edinburgh, UK: MacLachlan & Stewart, 1853.

Inman, K., and Rudin, N. *Principles and Practice of Criminalistics: The Profession of Forensic Science.* Boca Raton, FL: CRC Press, 2000.

James, S., and Nordby, J. *Forensic Science: An Introduction to Scientific and Investigative Techniques.* Boca Raton, FL: CRC Press, 2003.

Johnson, Elizabeth "DNA Testing" 2003.

Jonakait, R. "Forensic Science: The Need for Regulation," *Harvard Journal of Law & Technology*, 109:1991.

Jonakait, R. "Real Science and Forensic Science," *Shepard's Expert & Scientific Evidence Quarterly*, Winter 1994.

Kirk, P. *Crime Investigation.* New York: Interscience, 1953.

Kirk, P., and Kingston, C. "Evidence Evaluation and Problems in General Criminalistics," *Journal of Forensic Sciences*, 9:434–437, 1964.

Kirk, P., and Thornton, J. (Eds.) *Crime Investigation* (2nd ed.). New York: Wiley, 1970.

Kuhn, T. S. "Objectivity, value judgment and theory choice." In *The Essential Tension.* Chicago: University of Chicago Press, 1977.

Lee, H. Forensic Science and the Law, Law Review, 25:1117, 1124, 1993.

Lee, H. *Crime Scene Investigation.* Taoyuan, Taiwan: Central Police University, 1994.

Locard, E., *Manuel De Technique Policière: Les Constats, Les Empreintes Digitales. 2nd Ed.* Paris: Payot, 1934.

McBride, David. "Under the Microscope," 2002.

Miller, M. "Crime scene investigation." In S. James and J. Nordby (Eds.). *Forensic Science: An Introduction to Scientific and Investigative Techniques*, Boca Raton, FL: CRC Press, 2003.

Moenssens, A. "Novel Scientific Evidence in Criminal Cases: Some Words of Caution," *Journal of Criminal Law and Criminology*, Spring 1993.

Moenssens, A. "Handwriting Identification Evidence in the Post-Daubert World," *UMKC Law Review*, Winter 1997.

O'Connell, J. and Soderman, H., *Modern Criminal Investigation*, New York: Funk & Wagnalls Co., 1936.

O'Hara, C., *Fundamentals of Criminal Investigation*, Springfield, IL: Charles C Thomas, 1956.

O'Hara, C. *Fundamentals of Criminal Investigation*, (2nd ed.). Springfield, IL: Charles C Thomas, 1970.

Parker, Brian, D. Crim., JD, Professor of Forensic Science, UC Berkeley, 1968–1970; California State University, Sacramento, 1973–1985. Statement made to one of the authors (Chisum), July 21, 2005.

Paul, R., and Scriven, M. (2004) "Defining critical thinking," *Foundation for Critical Thinking*; Accessed URL: http://www.criticalthinking.org/aboutCT/definingCT.shtml

People of the Philippines v. Rodrigo Loteyro Aguinaldo, GR No. 130784, Oct. 13, 1999.

Popper, K. *Conjectures and Refutations*. London: Routledge & Keagan Paul, 1963.

Popper, K., *Conjectures and Refutations: The Growth of Scientific Knowledge*. (2nd ed.). New York: Basic Books, 1965.

Post, L. "FBI Bullet Test Misses Target: Court Rejects Test; FBI Has Suspended Use," *National Law Journal*, April 4, 2005.

Saferstein, R. *Criminalistics: An Introduction to Forensic Science*. (7th ed.). Upper Saddle River, NJ: Prentice Hall, 2001.

Saks, M. "Merlin and Solomon: Lessons from the Law's Formative Encounters with Forensic Identification Science," *Hastings Law Journal*, April 1998.

Taylor, L. "Ragland Case Lie Sparks Call for FBI Review; Expert Admitted to Perjury about Bullet-Lead Tests," *Lexington Herald Leader*, July 20, 2002, p. A1.

Teichrobe, R. "Oversight of Crime-Lab Staff Has Often Been Lax," *Seattle Post-Intelligencer*, July 23, 2004.

Thornton, J. "Courts of Law v. Courts of Science: A Forensic Scientist's Reaction to Daubert," *Shepard's Expert & Scientific Evidence Quarterly*, Winter 1994.

Thornton, J. "The General Assumptions and Rationale of Forensic Identification." In D. L. Faigman, D. H. Kaye, M. J. Saks, and J. Sanders (Eds.). *Modern Scientific Evidence: The Law and Science of Expert Testimony*, Vol. 2. St. Paul, MN: West, 1997.

Tolkien, J. R. R. *The Lord of the Rings: The Fellowship of the Ring*. Boston: Houghton Mifflin, 1954.

Turvey, B. *Criminal Profiling: An Introduction to Behavioral Evidence Analysis*. (2nd ed.). London: Elsevier, 2002.

"Under the Microscope," 60 Minutes II, July 24, 2002; URL: http://www.cbsnews.com/stories/2001/05/08/60II/main290046.shtml

Utah v. Raymond Michael Quintana, Utah Court of Appeals, Case No. 20030471-CA, 2004 UT App. 418, 2004.

Walton, D. *Informal Logic: A Handbook for Critical Argumentation*. New York: Cambridge University Press, 1989.

Windelband, W. *A History of Philosophy*. New York: HarperCollins, 1958.

Wisconsin v. Peter Kupaza, Sauk County, Case No. 00-CF-26, 2000.

CHAPTER 5

METHODS OF CRIME RECONSTRUCTION

W. Jerry Chisum, BS and Brent E. Turvey, MS

To know that you do not know is the best.
To pretend to know when you do not know is a disease.
—Lao-Tszu, Chinese philosopher (604–531 BC)

Here is my lens. You know my methods. What can you gather yourself . . . ?
—Sir Arthur Conan Doyle (1892)

Crime reconstruction requires the ability to put together a puzzle using pieces of unknown dimensions without a guiding picture. The next logical question is only this: How? It is a question that should occur to everyone and should be asked frequently of any reconstructionist. The answer is not always apparent from the results. More accurately, the answer is not always forthcoming when asked. This is in no small part because competent and proficient reconstruction comes to some forensic scientists with ease, to some with difficulty, and to others not at all.

There are several different approaches to the problem of reconstruction. However, the specific approach used by the reconstructionist is not the entire answer to the question. There is consideration of ethics, bias, practice standards, the crime scene investigation, evidence dynamics, and other issues that inhabit the pages of this text. Each shapes and influences the methods used and the inferences made. The purpose of this chapter is to describe some of the more successful conceptual approaches to crime reconstruction and, ultimately, provide more organization to the reconstructionist's toolbox.

Stuart Kind (1986) suggests that there are two kinds of reconstructionists—the *scientist* and the *historian*. He defines the historian as the intuitive reconstructionist who, based on his experience, will see the overall picture and form a theory of what happened. On the other side of the reconstruction coin is the *scientist*, who will see the pieces and traces of events and arrange them carefully into a whole. The historian will look at a crime scene and describe what happened, and then he will search for the details that prove that "theory." The scientist will look at the details and piece them together until he has the overall scene reconstruction. Either way, the methodology used must be fully understood by the reconstructionist and be easily explained to a jury. Therefore, it must be premised on clear logic and relate to what is known by people who do not understand investigative processes or science.[1]

More important is that all of the evidence encountered must either support or fail to nullfiy the reconstructionists final conclusions. This cannot be emphasized enough. The interpretation of an individual item of evidence must be consistent with the other known items. If it is inconsistent, then that interpretation must be eliminated as a possible explanation for the events. Simple theories are useless when they are not supported or outright contradicted by the facts.

CRIME RECONSTRUCTION AND EXPERIENCE

The most common method of crime reconstruction is to base interpretations on experience. Dr. Hans Gross (1924) emphasized the importance of learning from experience in the late 19th century. He wrote that the scientific investigator must take pains to learn from everything he observes, not only in his work but also in his daily life. And question everything; question why something has happened, or what has caused it to happen—then investigate.

The reconstructionist, Gross posited, must learn to see effects from causes and then reverse the process and establish causes from the effects. When similar events occur at a later time, the reconstructionist should then be able to extrapolate what she has learned about effects and infer the potential causes responsible. The learning and the discipline urged by Gross should make it clear that he was not advocating the value of raw and uneducated experience but, rather, experience tempered with extensive learning and what he referred to as an "encyclopaedic knowledge."

As this suggests, experience is not unimportant, but it can lead the naïve, ignorant, or inept reconstructionist astray when taken in isolation as gospel. Regardless of the quality of our experiences, and our capacity to learn from them, the experiences we have in everyday life prepare us to make inferences about the possible causes of the effects we see only when we seek to learn from them. Consequently, the use of one's experience as a knowledge base for developing reconstruction hypotheses and theories, or for inferring the cause from an examination of the effects, is commonplace. It is consequently important to bear in mind that not all experience is equal, not all experience is sufficiently instructive, and not everyone learns from his or her experiences.

For these same reasons, it also unacceptable to argue "in my experience" as a sole premise to explain how and why an event must have occurred. Any

[1] One of the authors (Chisum) was asked on the witness stand about the clotted blood on the suspect's clothing. Could it have been from rinsing the knife used by the other defendant? He replied, "no, as any parent knows who has rinsed a child's cut under the faucet. The bloodstains that might splash back on the clothing are very different in nature from these stains." The jurors nodded their heads; they could relate to a cut being rinsed.

inference regarding an event must be supported by factual details submitted to thoughtful analysis and rigorous logic. The thoughtful reconstructionist will also prepare citations from the published literature in support of their interpretations when necessary, as they may be asked to support the basis of their knowledge in court. The purely "experience-based reconstructionist" may give examples of his conclusions to demonstrate how he reconstructs but often will not be able to show the logic and science behind his methods. They will also be unable to cite the literature in support of their findings. The absence of such "long division" in his work is in effect an absence of science.

Perhaps one of the more valuable discussions of this issue can be found in the writings of Dr. John Thornton (1997, p. 17), a contributor to this text as well as a learned colleague:

> Virtually everyone agrees that an expert's bare opinion, unsupported by factual evidence, should be inadmissible in a court of law. And yet, precisely that sort of testimony is allowed every day in courts throughout the country by judges who believe that every statement uttered by a person with a scientific degree or employed by an agent, called "scientific" is therefore a scientific opinion. Courts permit expert testimony from those with specialized knowledge. But how is a court to gauge such knowledge? The answer generally lies in the education and experience of the prospective witness. A convenient means is to look for a measure of scientific education, and a university degree in a scientific discipline will ordinarily meet that test.
>
> With an educational requirement satisfied, a court will then look at experience. But experience is very difficult to evaluate. The more experience the better, but rarely is there any effort exerted to distinguish between 10 years of experience and 1 month of experience repeated 120 times, or 1 month of experience spread out over 10 years. Furthermore, some experts exploit situations where intuition or mere suspicions can be voiced under the guise of experience. When an expert testifies to an opinion, and bases that opinion on "years of experience," the practical result is that the witness is immunized against effective cross-examination. When the witness testifies that "I have never seen another similar instance in my 26 years of experience . . . ," no real scrutiny of the opinion is possible. No practical means exists for the questioner to delve into the extent and quality of that experience. Many witnesses have learned to invoke experience as a means of circumventing the responsibility of supporting an opinion with hard facts. For the witness, it eases cross-examination. But it also removes the scientific basis for the opinion.
>
> . . .
>
> Testimony of this sort distances the witness from science and the scientific method. And if the science is removed from the witness, then that witness has no

legitimate role to play in the courtroom, and no business being there. *If there is no science, there can be no forensic science.*

Experience is neither a liability nor an enemy of the truth; it is a valuable commodity, but it should not be used as a mask to deflect legitimate scientific scrutiny, the sort of scrutiny that customarily is leveled at scientific evidence of all sorts. To do so is professionally bankrupt and devoid of scientific legitimacy, and courts would do well to disallow testimony of this sort. Experience ought to be used to enable the expert to remember the when and the how, why, who, and what. Experience should not make the expert less responsible, but rather more responsible for justifying an opinion with defensible scientific facts.

Failure to appreciate the limitations of bare experience untempered by analytical logic, critical thinking, and the scientific method can lead some analysts to wrongly believe that they should learn and be able to conclusively "read" the events that have transpired in a crime scene simply by standing in it and looking around. It may further confuse some analysts into believing that scientific examinations and scientific inquiry are an impractical investigative burden, as opposed to a necessary form of theory validation or exclusion. This kind of vanity reconstruction, based on presumed expertise from years of experience performing various tasks, is simply that—vanity substituting for scientific inquiry. Courts that allow any form of reconstruction testimony to proceed along these lines contribute mightily to stalling the development of crime reconstruction as a scientific discipline, by failing to demand more of witnesses.

REASON, METHODS, AND CONFIDENCE

As detailed in Chapter 4, the reconstructionist must be capable of critical thinking.[2] That is, the reconstructionist must have the ability to discern fact from speculation, must be able to postulate or theorize alternative solutions for events, must be able to connect facts together, and must further make informed judgments about what questions are important to ask of the evidence in the case at hand.

The process may be regarded as something like this:

- Observe the evidence of events and related clues
- Determine what might be learned of events from each observation
- Postulate what the clue or observation means in light of the crime
- Propose alternative explanations for events
- Eliminate alternatives with analytical logic, critical thinking, and experimentation
- Sequence events until the picture is completed

[2] Critical thinking is a purposeful, reflective, and goal-directed activity that aims to make judgments based on evidence rather than conjecture. It is based on the principles of science and the scientific method. Critical thinking is a reasoned, interactive process that requires the development of strategies that maximize human potential (Old Dominion University, School of Nursing faculty minutes, 1997).

Put this way, it seems deceptively simple.

Sir Arthur Conan Doyle, through his fictional characters Sherlock Holmes and Dr. John Watson, showed how one could derive information regarding events from close observation and attention to detail. He claimed it was a form of deductive logic. Though no offense is meant to Doyle, it is relatively easy to use deductive logic when you can contrive the facts to fit a single theory of "whodunit" in a fictional story. The use of deduction in actual casework, in which multiple theories may explain known events, is much more difficult.

In 1933, Henry T. F. Rhodes described a case from 1817 England and proposed how "modern criminal investigation" could have solved the crime (p. 54):

> Nothing more is really claimed for the reconstruction quoted here than that it illustrates how scientific methods can be linked to the reconstruction of a crime real or supposed. It illustrates too the elementary process indicated by Sherlock Holmes—when you have eliminated all the impossible solutions then the solution or one of the solutions remaining, however apparently improbable, must be the right one.

He wrote of his approach (p. 58):

> It is merely a question of fitting the known parts together and endeavoring to fill in the missing parts as far as possible and is so far as those unknowns are directly and inevitably deducible from the known. This is a scientific conception. Neither in mathematics nor chemistry, nor criminal investigation is it always necessary to establish all the facts independently. If it is given that $x + y = 2$ it cannot be said that we know everything about x and y, but we can demonstrate as a matter of certain fact that $x + y - 2 = 0$.
>
> That is the object of this kind of reconstruction. If certain facts are definitely established it may well, and generally be true that certain conclusions are inevitably deducible from them. There are even circumstances in which a picture of the affair, accurate in all essentials, can be reconstructed from comparatively few facts.

Rhodes claimed that the reconstruction of events should become obvious using his method. His explanations for events, however, are really more of a reductive justification of his theories. This is because life and events are not always susceptible to explanation through an equally balanced equation. One event can have multiple causes, and even with the best evidence it is not always possible to distinguish which of those actually happened.

Perhaps Edward Oscar Heinrich, the famous "Wizard of Berkeley" described in Chapter 1, was familiar with the work of Rhodes. He practiced crime reconstruction in the 1930s and 1940s. He consulted on cases throughout the world and was sought after for his ability to identify clues, put them together, and explain events through discrete forensic evidence with great clarity. He described his methods to the press after working a missing person case in San Francisco (as quoted in Block, 1958; pp. 42–44):

> Crime analysis is an orderly procedure, it's precise and it follows always the same questions that I ask myself. Let's consider what they are:
>
> Precisely *what* happened? Precisely *when* did it happen? Precisely *where* did it happen? *Why* did it happen? *Who* did it?
>
> The average investigator seems to give immediate attention to the *why* and *who* but he takes what happened for granted . . . . We simply must analyze the method of the crime before we can analyze its purpose and look for the criminal . . .
>
> It's like a mosaic, and every fact must be evaluated before it can be fitted into the pattern. In that way, every fact as it is developed and equated becomes a clue.
>
> . . .
>
> One clue always is present after the commission of a crime. That one is the criminal's method. Every person in his every act in daily life leaves some impress of his method of procedure. So the criminal. Although he aims to keep his character and his identity a secret, yet the mechanism of the crime, that is, precisely how it was committed, exposes his knowledge, his skill, and his habit. Among these, typical, symptomatic actions appear that limit an investigation to a particular individual or to a small group.
>
> . . .
>
> In the test tube and crucible or through the lens of the microscope and camera I have found in my own practice the evidence of poison, the traces of the deadly bullet, the identity of a clot, the source of a fiber, the telltale fingerprint, the differing ink, the flaw in the typewriter, the slip of the pen upon which have turned in dramatic scenes of our courts the rightful title to an estate, of the liberty, even the life, of an individual.
>
> . . .
>
> This work of mine—it is not mysterious. It is a matter of understanding the scientific aspects of ordinary phenomena. Rarely are other than ordinary phenomena involved in the commission of a crime. One is confronted with scrambled effects, all parts of which separately are attributable to causes. The tracing of the relationship between isolated points of fact, the completion of the chain of circumstances between cause and effect, are the highest functions of reason—to which must be added the creative imagination of the scientist.

As this passage demonstrates, Heinrich used more than just scientific laboratory analysis in his investigations. He employed the natural sciences to establish facts, develop reconstruction theories and solve cases. But he also combined this with an early form of criminal profiling as well. He understood, like Gross before him, that the more one understood of the criminal's actions, the more one understood of the crime. Both Heinrich and Gross argued that the physical evidence could tell a great deal about possible suspect characteristics, and narrow the investigative field of suspects to a more manageable level.

Charles O'Hara was a New York City police detective who turned to writing textbooks out of sincere frustration regarding both the lack of objectivity and the lack of basic investigative knowledge among his contemporaries. In 1956, he wrote *Fundamentals of Criminal Investigation*, which was adopted for use in both police academies and colleges throughout the United States. In that text, he states (p. 55):

> Subsequent to the search of the scene of the crime an effort should be made to determine from the appearance of the place and its objects what occurred and, particularly, what were the movements and methods of the criminal, since this latter constitutes part of the modus operandi. The process of ascertaining the circumstances of a crime is known as reconstructing the crime. . . . From a study of the evidence in this manner it is often possible to make useful inferences which may be synthesized into a reasonable theory.

O'Hara goes on to describe what he calls *physical reconstruction* as the reconstruction of the physical appearance of the scene, involving both evidence and any available witnesses as participants. This is separate from *mental reconstruction*, in which the investigator tests his theory for logic and consistency. He cautions (p. 56):

> No assumptions should be made concerning actions which are not supported by evidence. The theory finally developed by the investigator should provide a line of investigative action but should not be stubbornly pursued in the face of newly discovered facts which are not consistent with it.

O'Hara has given his method as observation, hypothesis, and testing against the evidence—this is a crude form of the Scientific Method. This is also the same basic process suggested by Conan Doyle. O'Hara does not, however, try to explain how reconstructionists should develop, formulate, or falsify hypotheses.

In 1983, Joe Rynearson and W. Jerry Chisum published the first edition of their text, *Evidence and Crime Scene Reconstruction*, for the course they had been teaching on the subject since 1976. Rynearson has continued to update the text periodically. One of the primary changes in each edition has been the treatment of how reconstruction is actually performed. Early efforts were primarily case oriented, showing examples and hoping the students could understand the process. The text discussed the "Sherlockian" philosophy of finding and eliminating alternatives. Then it explained the logic used by putting it into flowcharts. It further discussed the roles that evidence plays in reconstruction as a classification scheme. This scheme is discussed later because it is the basis for understanding reconstruction. It was introduced at several forensic science professional meetings and conferences throughout the late 1970s and early 1980s.

Subsequent to the Chisum and Rynearson text, other reconstructionist practitioners began to write about what they thought the process of crime reconstruction should involve. For example, Jerry Findley and Craig Hopkins wrote an overview of reconstruction in 1984. They describe it as (pp. 3–4):

> the process of applying logic, training, experience, and scientific principles to:
>
> (1) The crime scene itself (i.e., location, environment, condition, etc.)
> (2) Physical evidence found at a crime scene.
> (3) The results of examinations of physical evidence by qualified experts.
> (4) Information obtained from all other sources in order to form opinions relative to the sequence of events occurring before, during, and after the criminal act.
>
> In essence, reconstruction is the sum total of the investigation demonstrated in its tangible form.

These authors discuss the degrees of certainty on a scale of 1 to 10, with 1 being mere speculation and 10 an absolute certainty. They suggest that the larger the information base, and the better the information, the closer the reconstructionist can be to a 10; however, reconstructions will usually fall short of this ideal goal.

They also enumerate the concepts that they explain (Findley and Hopkins, 1984, p. 12): "There are 5 sources of information, 5 tests of a witness' story, 2 types of reconstruction, 7 requirements and 3 goals of a reconstruction." They further stress caution in reconstructions, stating, "The investigator must not try to reconstruct with insufficient or unreliable information or jump to a conclusion before all the data is available" (p. 15). We have a great deal of enthusiasm for this specific sentiment, which is in accordance with our previously rendered practice standards.

However, we reserve a measure of respect for the practice of assigning a specific numeric value to the confidence of what is ultimately an opinion.

Numeric values look a lot like math, and many consider math among the hardest of the hard sciences. This and similar practices may have the unintended (or perhaps intended) consequence of making opinions look more certain or reliable than they actually are without the burden of showing any underlying work. This is due to the fact that there is no established means of consistently assigning numeric value to reconstruction certainty—such an assignment is a function of the reconstructionist's subjective judgment and experience, not a function of any particular mathematics. Assigning a numeric value, or even a statistical probability, to reconstruction certainty is ultimately misleading.

In reality, the known evidence in a case

- supports a reconstruction theory;
- does not support a reconstruction theory;
- refutes a reconstruction theory; or
- is inconclusive.

Consequently, of any theory a reconstructionist may say only that it is

- Supported by/consistent with the physical evidence and known circumstances. This is used for describing results that favor a particular theory or explanation of events.
- Inconsistent with/eliminated/disproved by the physical evidence and known circumstances. This is used for describing results that show the facts are out of alignment with a particular theory or explanation of events.
- Inconclusive or not disproved/not eliminated by the physical evidence and known circumstances. This is used for addressing alternatives that remain untested or examinations that result in inconclusive results.

EVENT ANALYSIS

Tom Bevel and Ross M. Gardner initially wrote separate articles regarding the technique they use to perform crime reconstruction. They advocate the methods espoused by the military, based on naval research. They have since published these in *Bloodstain Pattern Analysis, With an Introduction to Crime Scene Reconstruction* (1997). In this text, they describe what is referred to as *event analysis.* They state (p. 20), "Reconstruction is the end purpose of analysis; it requires not only the consideration of the events identified, but whenever possible the sequence of those events." Bevel and Gardner delineate event analysis as follows:

- Collect data and using all evidence establish likely events.
- Establish from the data specific snapshots or event segments of the crime.
- Consider these event segments in relationship to one another in order to establish related event segments.
- Order or sequence the event segments for each identified event.
- Consider all possible sequences and, where contradictory sequences exist, audit the evidence to determine which is the more probable.
- Final order or sequence of the events themselves.
- Flowchart the overall incident based on the event and event segment sequencing.

One caution that is made by Bevel and Gardner is that there is no way to be certain of one's conclusions regarding a reconstruction. The analysis may be logical and based on scientific facts, but, like the conclusions of an archeologist, there is no true standard to which we can compare our results (pp. 20–21).

This is certainly true, and it is perhaps one of the greatest limits of crime reconstruction. There are always unknowns with regard to the evidence—holes in the sequence or gaps in timing that cannot be filled. The physical evidence provides a record, but it is ultimately limited to itself. For instance, we may be able to say a person is in a certain location at one time, then in a different location at another time. However, it may be impossible to determine the precise route taken from one place to another, the time elapsed, or the manner of travel.[3] Also, there is often no true record of the total event that we can consult to ascertain whether our conclusions are valid. We have only our science, or logic, and our reasoning to guide us through the evidence so that we may explain its strengths and limits to others. And ultimately what cannot be shown with the evidence is as important as what can.

Apart from an incomplete record in the evidence, another barrier to full reconstruction is complexity combined with enormity: The amount of evidence and the sequence of events may simply be too overwhelming.

We take a somewhat different approach. We look to the physical evidence based on its role in the crime. This approach allows each item to be evaluated for what it can contribute to the reconstruction of the overall incident or crime. We further break down the crime into segments, as will be explained later.

THE ROLE OF EVIDENCE: RECONSTRUCTION CLASSIFICATIONS

The essence of analysis is the breaking down of complex problems and information into its component parts. In crime reconstruction, the information

---

[3] This is why animation of a crime is prejudicial. One cannot know these details. The animator and reconstructionist seldom have the information that would enable them to provide the details necessary to make one event connect to another.

is in the form of physical evidence, and the complex problem to resolve is what happened during the commission of the crime.

Crime reconstruction requires that evidence be broken down and examined in a different mode, and with a different goal, than may be familiar to many forensic specialists. Most classification schemes that describe forensic evidence are based on the type of analysis being performed, the section of the laboratory involved (trace evidence, biological evidence, serological evidence, drugs, firearms, toxicology, etc.), or even the type of crime that produced it. These classifications may assist with the process of triaging evidence as it comes into the crime lab, and perhaps even shed some small amount of light on its context. In crime reconstruction, however, these classifications are not very informative. The reconstructionist needs to consider evidence with regard to the role it plays in the crime and what it can establish regarding the events that have taken place.

The following evidence classification provides basic types of evidence in terms of the fundamental "who," "what," "when," "where," "how," and sometimes "why" questions that are the focus of crime reconstruction:

- Sequential
- Directional
- Locational
- Action
- Contact
- Ownership
- Associative
- Limiting
- Inferential
- Temporal
- Psychological

It should be noted that one piece of evidence may and likely will fit into more than one of these categories in any given case.

Sequential evidence is anything that establishes or helps to establish when an event occurred or the order in which two or more events occurred. Examples:

- A footprint over a tire track shows that an individual person was present subsequent to the vehicle passing.
- Blood found under the glass from a broken window at a burglary/murder establishes that the window was broken after the blood was deposited. This may

call witness statements into question and begin to suggest the possibility of staging (this phenomenon is discussed in Chapter 12).

- Radial fracture patterns in plate glass from multiple gunshots, used to establish the firing sequence.

Directional evidence is anything that shows where something is going or where it came from. Examples:

- Footprints may be used to help indicate potential direction of travel.
- Projectile trajectory analysis can help establish the origin and direction of bullets, spears, arrows, and other missile weapons.
- Bloodstain pattern analysis can be used to determine the direction of blood that is dripped, cast, smeared, spattered, wiped, or swiped.
- Wound pattern analysis can be used to determine the direction of abrasions and other injuries to the skin via an examination of piled epithelium; the epithelium piles in the direction of the object traveling across the skin which creates the abrasion.

Locational/positional evidence is that which shows where something happened, or where something was, and its orientation with respect to other objects at the location. Examples:

- A single fingerprint inside the passenger window could indicate that a particular person was inside a vehicle at some point. However, if the fingerprint is pointed down and at the top of a window that rolls down, it may only mean that the person reached inside the glass to speak to the driver.
- The orientation of a tool mark on a door or window may indicate a potential point of offender entry into a scene, and subsequently suggest the need to look for other transfer evidence from the offender at that location.
- Bloodstains or spatters can indicate where a victim was injured or where the victim, offender, or even bystanders may have been standing, sitting, or lying. They can also be used to help determine where intermediate objects may have been located, by virtue of void patterns.
- Livor mortis is the settling of the blood in the lower (dependent) portion of the body, causing a purplish-red discoloration of the skin. When the heart is no longer beating, red blood cells sink in accordance with gravity into the tissue. This discoloration does not occur in the areas of the body that are in contact with the ground or another object because the capillaries are compressed. Livor mortis becomes fixed after roughly 10 hours and may be used to determine whether or not a body has been moved subsequent to this if inconsistent with the victim's final resting position.

- Indentations in a carpet show where a chair was normally sitting and can indicate that it was moved.
- A pile of cigarette butts in one location can show the location of someone laying in wait.

Action evidence is anything that defines anything that happened during the commission of the crime. This may seem a basic issue, but it is crucial when establishing the elements of a crime as required by law. Misinterpretation of action evidence at any point during the reconstruction can provide for criminal charges brought against an innocent defendant and failure to charge a guilty party with the totality of the crimes that have been committed. Examples:

- Bloodstains and patterns indicate an injury to the offender or a victim or that a blood source was moved rapidly resulting in cast-off patterns.
- Gunshot wounds, bullet holes, and cartridge casings indicate that a firearm was discharged.
- Sharp force injury indicates that a sharp force weapon was used (knife, sword, razor, box-cutter, etc.).
- A broken window with glass on the floor next to the door lock indicates that the window was broken to gain entry (of course, this can be staged as well).

Contact evidence is something that demonstrates whether and how two persons, objects, or locations were at one point associated with each other (the importance of contact and association is discussed more thoroughly in Chapter 7). Examples:

- Trace evidence such as hairs, fibers, soil, and glass may be used to suggest an association between persons, objects, and locations.
- A fingerprint on a glass can be used to indicate that a particular person was holding it at one point.
- The victim's blood on the soles of the suspect's shoes indicates contact with a location where the victim was bleeding.
- Two toothbrushes and two wet towels would indicate that two persons were residents (conversely, only one indicates a single occupant).

Ownership evidence is something that helps answer the "who" question with a high degree of certainty. It includes any evidence that may be connected to, or associated with, a particular person or source. It also includes individuating forms of physical evidence. Examples:

- Written signatures
- Driver's licenses
- Credit cards
- Computer IP addresses
- PIN numbers
- Mail
- E-mail
- Serial numbers
- Vehicle identification numbers
- DNA
- Fingerprints

Associative evidence is usually a form of trace evidence that can be identification or ownership evidence. The finding of common materials on the suspect and victim, the suspect and the scene, or the scene and the victim is used to suggest contact, in accordance with Locard's Exchange Principle. Although associative evidence indicates certain or potential contact between persons or environments, it cannot by itself indicate when that contact occurred. This requires the presence of other circumstantial evidence. Examples:

- A bloody footprint on linoleum places a person at the scene.
- Fibers found on a body that match the fibers in the trunk of a vehicle.
- Double-base gunpowder found on both the suspect and the victim.
- Vegetation found in the trunk of a vehicle suspected of hauling a body that is consistent with the vegetation found at the crime scene and on the body.

Associative evidence takes on a higher degree of importance when there is more than one type involved. For example, if all the previous examples were discovered in one case, the reconstructionist would first be inclined to postulate that the vehicle (associated with the crime via fibers and vegetation) was used to transport the body. If the owner of the vehicle were also the person whose bloody footprint was discovered on the floor, and the blood belonged to the victim, the tightening circle of associations would increase the importance of this evidence.

Limiting evidence is that which defines the nature and boundaries of the crime scene. Determining the nature and limits of the crime scene is perhaps one of the most difficult tasks in crime reconstruction. It is made difficult by the fact that reconstruction is most often performed after the scene is released, and that first responders, without any forensic training, often determine scene limits by arbitrarily throwing up barrier tape wherever it seems appropriate. This may or may not reflect the actual limits of the scene and the evidence. By the time crime scene investigators (CSIs) realize that there is evidence outside of the tape, it is often already trampled upon by a variety of well-meaning crime scene personnel. Examples:

- Points of entry and exit to and from a scene.
- Walls inside a building.
- Doors inside a building.
- Geography and landscape of an outdoor scene.
- Fences on a piece of property.
- Location of the known scene (indoor, outdoor, vehicle, etc.).
- The confines of a vehicle (car, truck, boat, cruise ship, etc.).
- The beginning and end of blood trails.
- The beginning and end of drag marks.
- The location of items dropped by the offender when fleeing the scene.
- The absence of any evidence that should be there given the known action evidence that specifically suggests a secondary scene. This includes the absence of blood at a scene where the victim has exsanguinated, the absence of teeth on the ground from a victim whose teeth were knocked out during a fight, and so forth.

Limiting evidence is important because it helps establish whether there are secondary crime scenes and whether the evidence search area must be expanded to include other nearby locations.

Inferred evidence is anything that the reconstructionist thinks may have been at the scene when the crime occurred but was not actually found. Examples:

- A contact gunshot to the face of a victim produces a quantity of blood on the table where she was sitting. A void pattern is formed on the table with a specific outline. It is inferred that the package of cocaine described by a witness was consistent with this outline and may have been removed after the victim was shot.
- A deceased victim is found without his wallet.
- A deceased married victim is found without his wedding ring.
- A deceased female is found outdoors without her underwear.
- A victim is found stabbed to death in her residence, but the knife is not found.
- A victim is found shot to death in his residence, but the gun is not found.

It is important when dealing with inferred evidence to refrain from assuming that the offender must have removed it from the scene, even when the reconstructionist knows precisely what it is. For example, a witness or even crime scene responders may have stolen a victim's cash or wallet from the victim's body, and a female victim found without underwear may simply not be in the habit of wearing underwear. These questions must be asked, and their answers known, before informed inferences regarding what the offender may or may not have removed from the scene can be made.

Temporal evidence is anything that specifically denotes or expresses the passage of time at the crime scene relative to the commission of the crime. Examples:

- It is known that the electricity was turned off at a main switch to a home. The victim was shot during this time. The electricity was turned back on. The clock in the bedroom was one that reset itself to midnight. Therefore, to establish the time of death, the time that the crime lab looked at the clock was subtracted from the present time to give the time when the clock was turned back on.
- A clock is knocked off a nightstand during a struggle, affixing the time.
- A new stick candle is lit during the commission of a crime. It is discovered still burning with only half of the wax remaining. The length of time it takes to burn this candle half way may be established via experimentation with a candle of precisely the same type.
- A bowl of ice cream is placed on a kitchen counter just prior to the commission of a murder. It is barely melted when police arrive. The more expensive the ice cream, the less air is injected into it during its manufacture and the longer it takes to melt. The length of time it takes to melt may be established via experimentation with ice cream of precisely the same brand and flavor.
- A forensic pathologist uses the decrease in body temperature, rigor and livor mortis, analysis of the vitreous humor, and examination of the gastric contents to determine a victim's approximate time of death.
- A forensic entomologist uses the life cycle of insects found on a deceased body to approximate how many days the victim's body has been susceptible to those insects.

Psychological evidence (i.e., motivational evidence) is any act committed by the perpetrator to satisfy a personal need or motivation. This type of evidence is more commonly the province of the criminal profiler and the behavioral scientist. Examples:

- An offender murders his wife in their bedroom and stages the scene to appear as though it were a burglary gone wrong (issues related to staging are examined thoroughly in Chapter 12). This is done to conceal his otherwise obvious connection to the crime and the crime scene.

- An offender tortures his victim, sexually, to satisfy a sadistic motivation.
- An offender records his attack of a victim to both humiliate the victim and relive the event later for fantasy purposes.
- An offender beats his victim repeatedly with the butt of a pistol out of rage.
- An offender binds and gags a victim during an attack at a private location where no one would hear the screams to prevent the victim from disrupting the offender's fantasy of victim compliance.

Ultimately, there are no bright yellow lines between these evidence classifications. In fact, it may be more useful for reconstructionists to consider these more like questions to ask of each item of evidence. What can this tell us about sequence? What can this tell us about contact? What does this tell us about action? What does this tell us about ownership? In this way, evidence relationships are less likely to be lost, and the fullest picture of events may be allowed to emerge.

CREATING TIME LINES

There are several ways to create and use a time line when reconstructing crime. Bevel and Gardner, for example, use a relative time line to set specific events in order. However, the reconstructionist can also use the time line without specifying particular events. We have found that it is often of great value to begin a reconstruction by placing the general elements of the crime in order.

By breaking the crime down into small events, or isolating specific segments, the reconstruction may become less daunting, and events may become more apparent. Rynearson (1997, pp. 102–104), for example, takes the approach of breaking the total sequence of the crime into "elements" that are present in a variety of crimes. This scheme is similar to that proposed by Hans Gross in the 1890s, but it has been added to and modified by Rynearson and Chisum. In their work, they propose that evidence is anything that assists in proving or disproving any theory about any element of the crime. All these elements are not necessarily present in all crimes. However, serial crimes with a sexual component tend to include all of them:

- Fantasy—The person thinks about the offense.
- Planning—The person plans what he is going to do.
- Contact—The person chooses a way to approach a victim.
- Control—The person takes control of the victim.

- Offense—The act against the victim.
- Defense—The resistance of the victim.
- After—What to do with the evidence of the crime.
- Flight—Leaving the scene.
- Alibi—Making an excuse for the time.
- Fantasy—Remembering; then it starts over.

Investigators at the scene tend to concentrate on the evidence of the offense and the flight. Once conceptualized, it is not typically difficult to establish the evidence of each. This is the starting point of a reconstruction (Ryenarson, 2002, pp. 171–176).

Subsequently, a time line allows the reconstructionist to conceive and maintain focus on the overall picture of the crime, without forgetting that there are details requiring attendance. When the reconstructionist identifies a discrete event, it is placed where it fits within the elements of the crime. This provides the foundation for the sequence of events and keeps them in order. In this fashion, the time line expands from a sequence of general elements to a sequence of discrete events.

With this basic concept of elements forming a skeletal time line, the next steps of the reconstruction require synthesizing knowledge from the evidence and keeping it organized in a meaningful fashion. The reconstructionist must exercise personal choice here and utilize those methods that are most useful and appropriate to his or her own intellectual dexterity. Consider the following.

MIND MAPPING

Mind mapping is a method of linking seemingly random and unconnected thoughts to create a diagram of what one knows about a subject. This approach is useful for getting one's ideas together when the evidence is unclear and the picture of the crime is essentially fuzzy. Most commonly, a single piece of paper is used on which the reconstructionist writes down the primary problem (a blank whiteboard will also do), for example, a decedent's name. Next, one writes down clothing, weapon, injuries, activities, and times as starter categories for information around the name. Then the reconstructionist can add one-word descriptors of what is known in those categories. Other categories may surface. It is important to let one's mind wander during this process, to reflect and ruminate about the known evidence and the scene. To that purpose, the scene photos and diagrams should be handy. Finally, the reconstructionist can connect these thoughts and impressions with lines to show relationships or time sequences. The result is a collection of ideas regarding what one knows or needs to know about the evidence in one's case. These may be used to direct further investigation, create hypotheses, and construct experiments.

Mind mapping is a visual technique that is used to gather ideas for the solution of a problem or to establish relationships. It uses one word to stimulate thoughts and ideas, and it goes in any direction necessary. It is recommended that the reconstructionist utilize color markers, diagrams, charts, and other necessary visual aides to stimulate ideas. This same basic practice can also be accomplished with 3×5 cards or with photos. A line of one color shows relationships, such as "this blood is from the victim (red), this blood is from the suspect (blue)." Or it can be a combination of various photos, report quotes, and relationships. This same approach can be used in a group setting by "brainstorming" over the evidence (see Chapter 4).

Faye Springer, a criminalist with the Sacramento District Attorney's Forensic Laboratory, uses 3×5 cards in her alternative method of mind mapping. She writes a description of an item of evidence on a card. Then she writes down what can be determined regarding that item. When all the evidence is listed, she determines if there are relationships between items; included in the relationships are exclusions as well as positive relationships. She then proceeds with the scientific method by eliminating the impossible through logic and reasoning.[4] The methodology is simple, requiring nothing more than a package of 3×5 cards, a pen, and plenty of room to spread the cards out.

Additionally, The Brain (available at www.thebrain.com) is a software package that allows the reconstructionist to mind map a case on the computer. This software has been used extensively by one of the authors (Chisum). Facts are put into "thoughts," and relationships become easier to see as these thoughts are connected to each other. Text, photos, and references can be added either as notes or as files. It is a very useful way of organizing, preserving, and perpetuating the mind mapping process throughout a case.

[4] Faye explained this methodology to Jerry Chisum at the California Department of Justice Laboratory when he was her supervisor in 1993.

PERT CHARTING OR FLOW DIAGRAM

The program evaluation and review technique (PERT) is a project management tool first developed by the U.S. Department of Defense's U.S. Navy Special Projects Office in 1958 as part of the Polaris submarine-based ballistic missile project. It is essentially a method for analyzing the tasks involved in completing a given project, specifically the time needed to complete each task, in order to identify the minimum time needed to complete the total project.

Figure 5.1

A PERT chart.

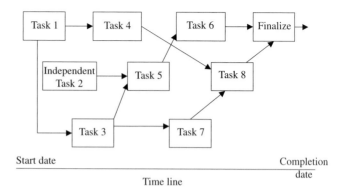

Figure 5.1 is an example of a PERT chart with two (2) different beginning tasks and a total of nine (9) tasks to be completed in the order indicated by the arrows. The dates for each task would be indicated on the time line.

The PERT chart technique can be adopted for crime reconstruction. This technique is a method of putting the "events" in order. The chart would be simpler than that shown in Figure 5.1 but it would also reflect decisions or alternatives to each box.

[5] A bullet will be wiped by the first layer of cloth (or other material) it enters. This leaves a black ring of lead, grease, and powder residues. Subsequent layers will not have this ring.

CASE EXAMPLE

By W. Jerry Chisum

Several years ago, I had a case involving whether a man was shot with a high-power rifle in the front of the jaw or the back of the head exiting the other side. I used a flowchart to help me reach a conclusion. The witness changed her mind from one day to the next so that the case went from voluntary manslaughter (front) to first-degree murder (back).

I was able to view the body prior to the autopsy, which I could not attend. However, I was able to get the body X-rayed in the time between the funeral and the interment. I had the victim's clothing and had a conversation with the detectives. One of them informed me that the sheriff/coroner had put his finger into the back of the neck to feel the size of the hole. They also showed me a photograph of a probe through the head prior to the pathologist arriving.

When I first looked at the shirt, I noted there was a hair that was protruding root first from the hole in the neck. I also noted that there was no black ring surrounding the hole in the outer layer of the shirt collar.[5] For this reason, I became "stubborn" and wanted to conduct tests to determine for certain the true direction of the shot. The sheriff was adamant that it was to the back.

There was a small hole in the back of the neck and a large stellate hole at the point of the chin. The doctor performing the autopsy (not a forensic pathologist) concluded that the victim had been shot in the back because the tissue at the edges of the hole was tucked in, and because he found dark particles in the section of tissue from the neck. He stated the particles were gunpowder. He withdrew his opinion upon learning that the wound had been probed and that the "gunpowder particles" were actually bits of lead.

The first approach was to try to reenact the crime. The path of the bullet, from where the shooter was sitting along through the victim's head, was established. A man of the same height was used as a model; however, the path through the head was the same if he was standing with his back to the shooter or bent over toward the muzzle. This simple experiment did not aid in the determination.

The sheriff/coroner offered that he hunted a great deal, had much experience killing animals, and it is always little hole in and big hole out. I explained to him this generalization was not true in close shots due to cavitation, and because the shot was to the mouth there were other dynamics that could also affect the size of the hole. This is ultimately an example of "experience" giving the wrong answer because it is the wrong experience; the effects of distance shots are different than those in close shots.

The X-ray showed lead in a teardrop pattern with the V shape pointing toward the chin. The teeth were pushed back at an angle with the crowns pointing to the back and the roots forward. All these facts demonstrated a force starting at the apex of the V, at the chin. Therefore, I was able to conclude that the victim had been shot in the front and the defendant's story was actually supported by the evidence.

ROLE PLAYING

Role playing is a process in which participants engage in animated, free-form hypothesis development, and theory revision regarding the potential actions of individuals involved in an event or a series of events. They may use props; they may revisit the scene; they may approximate victim or offender choices and responses. It is an exploratory and dynamic effort intended to gauge action and event feasibility. Its greatest value is that it can assist with answering the question of whether or not something could have happened in a particular way given the known evidence and physical limitations.

As the reconstructionist examines the evidence in a case there will be questions raised about many issues. For example, can an alleged victim shoot himself in a specified location with a particular gun; can he tie himself up in the manner in which he was found at the scene; what position was the victim in when he received a particular injury or created a particular transfer pattern? These possibilities can be tested in role-play exercises.

However, the reconstructionist must remember the formation of alternative solutions. Just because the victim could not have pulled the trigger if the gun was held in the conventional manner does not eliminate the possibility of self-infliction. It may have been held or positioned in an unconventional fashion. To explore and eliminate alternatives, the reconstructionist may need to position herself as the victim was, in a similar environment, with the same type of weapon used. And if the reconstructionist wishes to eliminate the possibility that a victim tied himself up, she can get similar material, re-create similar circumstances, and attempt to tie herself up in the presence of a witness. This is basic role playing.

Here again, victimology becomes important. It would be extremely embarrassing to argue something on the stand regarding a victim's carriage or deportment and then find out that the victim's body mechanics would not allow such a position to be attained. The victim may be too large or too small, too tall or too short. If the victim has a physical handicap (nonfunctioning or missing limbs, inability to walk, inability to hear; etc.), the reconstructionist may be putting the victim in an impossible position. On the other hand, if the victim is an athlete (e.g., gymnast, body builder, or marathon runner), the victim may be able to achieve positions that others cannot.

Attaining a plausible reenactment, or the refutation of a particular theory, is the ultimate goal of role playing.

REENACTMENTS

Occasionally, a physical demonstration of some kind is needed to fully and accurately relay a reconstruction theory.

A reenactment is a process in which the participants mimic the actions involved in a specific event or series of events. Rather than being a free-form and exploratory form of hypothesis development and theory revision, a reenactment is fixed and is intended to educate or convince others.[6]

The danger of some reenactments, especially those involving computer animation, is that they may present a theory of the crime as though it is the one and only way that events could have happened.[7] For this reason, the full crime must not be reenacted because this level of certainty is rarely possible. A full reenactment, it must be remembered, necessarily involves a great deal of unguarded conjecture and speculation. It is therefore more useful and objective to present the short segments of events that are firmly grounded in the evidence and not attempt to fill the evidence voids with experience-oriented guesswork.

THE CRIME SCENE

As previously explained, the reconstructionist should attend the crime scene if possible. However, this effort should be forensic science-oriented and be

[6] The author (Chisum) had a defense attorney and his investigator climb on a table in court to demonstrate the way blood was deposited on a defendant's shirt. This was offered to disprove the theory of the prosecution regarding the manner of blood staining. When they were in the position described by the prosecution witnesses, it was impossible to deposit the blood patterns. The jury was effectively convinced by this simple reenactment.

[7] Computer-generated reenactments, often inappropriately referred to as computer reconstruction or even as a form of crime reconstruction, are commonly produced by putting a case theory into animated form on a computer using compelling graphics and animations. The problem with this is that many who interpret the evidence for such animations are not actually trained in forensic science and present nonscientific theories in a format that appears scientific by virtue of its association with computer technology.

entirely detached from the police investigation with respect to role and responsibility, as explained in Chapters 2–4. The first question that will be asked by police technicians who consider the crime scene their territory may be "why?"

Ironically, the crime scene is attended by a multitude of responders from various agencies, only a few of which have even minimal training and education in scientific methodology or forensic science. These include the vast majority of police technicians (a.k.a. CSIs) and medicolegal death investigators in cases of homicide. These also include police investigators, who are in charge of the scene from the law enforcement perspective and who have often advanced because of political considerations as opposed to a demonstration of investigative skill (many detective units with low solve rates are in fact carried by one or two tireless investigators of tremendous skill, without which the majority of the unsolved crimes in their jurisdiction would remain so).

Additionally, the medical examiner or coroner may or may not attend the crime scene personally, depending on schedules and backlogs.[8] Also, police technicians may not respond to nonhomicide scenes unless requested specifically by a detective or police officer. Moreover, detectives and investigators may not actually respond to a nonhomicide crime scene unless it is considered a major case; in many cases, an investigator will not be assigned to a case at all—rather, its resolution will be left to patrol.

All this to say that unless a forensic scientist with a generalist background attends a crime scene, and assists in determining which evidence needs collecting and which tests should be run, the results of crime scene processing can and do vary widely with respect to quality. In the absence of informed judgments made by forensic scientists at the scene, processing efforts are left in the hands of police officers, police investigators, and police technicians who are largely without scientific or forensic expertise and who tend to approach evidence at the scene from a confirmatory mind-set (discussed in Chapters 3 & 4). Although this practice is administratively useful because it is less expensive than having qualified personnel work the evidence, it ultimately results in no science or, worse, bad science.

We have each worked many cases and have assisted with processing many crime scenes in conjunction with law enforcement agencies. We have also performed similar work for the defense, after law enforcement has released the scene. Our conclusions are the same: To be blunt, modern-day crime scene processing efforts are in need of major reform. There are some notable and even heroic exceptions, but few if any agencies seem to regularly employ and subsequently require qualified personnel

[8] Medical examiners must be board-certified forensic pathologists with a medical degree. Depending on the jurisdiction, the coroner may or may not be a doctor and may or may not have any forensic training. In some jurisdictions, the coroner may be a sheriff, mortician, or justice of the peace with no formal education and no forensic science background. The more rural the jurisdiction, the more likely this scenario.

at the crime scene. Rather, it is commonly believed, and regularly practiced, that new personnel can and should learn scene-processing duties on the job from other police officers, all with little or no scientific background.

In other words, crime scene processing is so low in priority to many law enforcement agencies that prospective scene personnel need only have a high school diploma or GED, a valid driver's license, and no criminal record. Once hired, crime scene technicians commonly look forward to low pay, long hours, and less than rewarding working conditions in terms of both agency politics and limited funding for equipment and training. Because many in law enforcement perceive that crime scene processing is a simple task that anyone can perform, literally anyone is doing so.

Given this state of affairs, the need for an objective forensic scientist at the crime scene should be apparent. This is, admittedly, an ideal that exists only in some jurisdictions to limited extent, and in others perhaps never. For those who would at this point still ask "why," it is probable that no explanation would suffice. But we offer the following reasons, based on years of seeing crime scene processing done poorly or not at all in jurisdictions throughout the United States:

- The forensic generalist has the education and training to understand the science behind the chemical tests and instrumental analysis that will be performed on the evidence, and knows not just what needs to be collected but also how and why.
- The forensic generalist is better qualified to interpret the meaning of evidence and subsequently recognize which evidence will be of greatest importance to both support and refute any investigative theories.
- The forensic generalist will not chase a particular theory and will engage in the thorough documentation of what is at the scene, as well as what is not. The whole concept of negative documentation is something that routinely escapes police technicians for lack of understanding why they are doing what they are doing.
- The forensic generalist is free to collect evidence and speculate about the case external from the direction of a lead police investigator, who may have a strong propensity to direct collections that seek to confirm particular theories of the case without consideration of others.
- The forensic generalist has a better appreciation of the capabilities and limitations of the public lab, as well as those of any commonly utilized private labs.
- The forensic generalist will have a better understanding of the impact of collection and storage methods on particular kinds of evidence.

One could go on and on, but the message is essentially the same. Technicians are commonly poorly trained and poorly educated personnel whose understanding of the science beneath their tasks is necessarily limited by law enforcement employment practices. Also, their understanding of how to collect evidence is commonly derived from, and limited to, written procedures prepared by lab scientists or other police personnel. And that's when they've read them which is rare. Their lot is not to ask why but to follow orders in the chain of command from police supervisors. Again, there is much room for reform in the realm of crime scene processing.

If unable to respond to the scene, as is the case for most forensic scientists, the reconstructionist may still be able to visit it at a later time. It is best to do this after a thorough examination of the scene documentation as well as the results of forensic analysis. Visiting the scene prior to this will waste valuable time. The more the reconstructionist knows about the crime and the evidence during such a visit, the more specific and informed questions will be asked of it. Even so, the totality of the available evidence and information may or may not be sufficient to answer the questions that must be answered to adequately reconstruct one or more elements of the crime.

Also, it is important for the reconstructionist to have evidence in context with regard to other evidence, related circumstances, and even victim history. In other words (Erzinçlioglu, 2000):

> Evidence presented in isolation may lead us to very different conclusions from those we would have reached had we been given some other evidence at the same time. . . . Evidence suggests there are valid questions that need to be addressed. . . . Let us not complicate matters unnecessarily. . . . The mind has the tendency to select evidence most in keeping with its expectations and to ignore the evidence that is not.

Regarding crime reconstruction, unlike the identification sciences, less information is not better—as long as it is the right kind of information. The nature of the information sought to educate the reconstruction must also embrace the issue of examiner bias and context effects as discussed in Chapters 3 and 4. The reconstructionist must therefore take care to screen and separate out law enforcement theories regarding suspects. Furthermore, the reconstructionist must accept that witness and suspect statements are theories to test with the evidence, not inputs for the reconstruction. Corroboration is good, but scientific evidence must stand on its own in that process. Science must be used to test investigative theories and witness veracity, not the other way around.

One way to consciously separate out theories is by writing them down. Write a paragraph or two that summarizes the existing theories of what happened and where they came from (detectives, witnesses, suspects, supervisors, colleagues, students, patrolmen, lawyers—anyone with a theory). Now examine the videos, photos, and reports with the thought of disproving each of those theories. Ask the following: Is there any evidence that shows that any part of the theory could not have happened in the manner that the theory requires? This approach may sound a bit backward to the uninitiated, but it is actually the scientific method being applied to a hypothesis in a logical manner. The reconstructionist who is unfamiliar with this practice will find it not only enjoyable but also revealing and even educational.

A *truth table*, or veracity table, is a good method for testing the veracity of the multiple theories inhabiting a case. It is based on the previous suggestion that alternative theories for events be written down. This is accomplished by creating a table with the theories across the top and then the observations, clues, and physical evidence along the side. Using the case from Chapter 9, these are the following case theories (Table 5.1):

1. The "victim's" story: She was walking along the sidewalk when a car pulled up and four other women got out and threw her to the sidewalk. She was held face down and her shirt cut, then her back cut. She states she felt the blood running down her back. She struggled against them and broke free and ran home. She called the police.
2. Staged the crime, cut her shirt. Realized she needed to be bleeding when police arrived so cut herself.

The list could go on to cover all the observations made. When an "F" for "false" is present, that hypothesis is false and can be eliminated or modified. This is a simple example. A major case could have several columns of theories.

Table 5.1

Truth Table

Evidence	Victim's story	Staged crime
Back is cut	T	T
Shirt is cut	T	T
Still bleeding 1.5 hours later	F	T
Clothes not scuffed or soiled	F	T
Cuts not serious	?	T
No blood on shirt	F	T

The truth table is a simple way to test hypotheses and present the results of your analysis to others. Alternative theories to an event can be tested against other events, or the whole may be tested at once. This is a useful tool for an investigation; however, caution must be exercised if it is used in court presentations. There is a fine line between determining the alternative that is best supported by the facts and using the results in an attempt to address the ultimate issue. The reconstructionist may use a truth table for testing hypotheses and developing viable theories but not for trying to show guilt or innocence. That is a legal determination and not a scientific one.

The use of a truth table is an effective tool for showing the inconsistencies of the evidence with the prosecution's case, regardless of the side employing the reconstructionist. If this occurs, then the charges against the defendant may be modified or dropped, as was done in the previous example.

This does not always occur, however, and in such cases the reconstructionist is urged not to surrender her professional chastity, as mentioned by Thornton in Chapter 2. In the past, and even in some public lab systems today, when a forensic examiner had a case in which the prosecutor ignored his findings and proceeded to prosecute, his professional ethics were tested. The dilemma that forensic scientists faced as public employees was that the prosecutor had tremendous influence over their jobs. If one's superiors are prosecution oriented, one might have lost her job if she complained or leaked any information to the defense.

Discovery laws (the compulsory disclosure of pertinent facts or documents to the opposing party in a court action, usually before a trial begins) are intended to relieve today's publicly employed forensic scientists of that problem. The defense should receive a copy of their report. If the prosecutor ignores their input, the defense can choose to call them or not depending on the strategy it has chosen. If, however, they do not complete their findings and write a report subsequent to the discovery motion, the prosecutor may not reveal it unless called on to do so by the court. Therefore, it is important that all publicly employed forensic examiners write their reports in a timely manner to help ensure that both sides are equally informed of the findings.

However, there is still the matter of pressure to change the language in one's reports or leave things out of one's reports. In such ways, the professional chastity of the publicly employed forensic scientist remains at risk. For those still concerned with navigating this issue, a reread of Chapters 2 & 3 is perhaps in order.

CASE EXAMPLE

By W. Jerry Chisum

This case shows how the reconstructionist approaches a problem—how bloodstains can reveal many things about positions; how one must be careful to know just how the blood sheds from the body; and that one must weigh all stories against the physical evidence. It also demonstrates how the reconstructionist must change the answer to fit the facts and not change (or ignore) the facts to fit a particular answer. This is a civil case involving a wrongful death suit.

A young man is going home one night; it is raining and he sees a woman run across the street in front of him at a stop sign. He stops and asks her if she needs a ride. She points to his other side. He turns and sees an angry looking man approaching. Another car pulls up behind and a witness gets out.

There are two versions of the story at this point.

The defendant says the angry man jerked his car door open. The defendant jumped out and tried to intimidate the smaller man, as he was 6′ 2″ and the angry man was approximately 5′ 8″. They grappled; the next thing he knew, he was on the ground face down. The angry man was on his back holding him down.

The defendant claims he was grabbed by the eye and his head was pulled back. There was someone kicking him; he was afraid they would kill him if they connected with his throat or under his nose. He had a knife in his pocket. He pulled it out and opened it one handed, reached over his shoulder and stabbed at the person on top. There was an immediate release of the pressure. He rolled over and the angry man walked away.

There was a witness there who had pulled up. The defendant thought the witness was the one kicking him, so he threatened the witness with the knife by waving it back and forth. The witness drove off, so he got in his vehicle and left.

Later that night, the defendant heard that the man he stabbed had died. He turned himself and his clothing into the police. The woman, who was the girlfriend of the decedent, supported this story in her initial interview.

The witness claimed he came on the scene just after the driver had jumped out of his car. He said the driver ran over to the decedent and knocked him down, drew his knife, and plunged it into the chest of the decedent. The witness was a bouncer and had been a martial arts student for years, so he ran over and, using a martial arts throw, reached across the chest of the assailant and threw him to the side. The witness claims he helped the decedent up but did not realize the extent of the injury. He said the crazy guy (the driver) started at him with his knife, waving it back and forth and threatening him. The witness subsequently got into his car and left the scene. He claims he drove around the next block and called 911 from a convenience store. The witness claims he then returned to the scene and rendered first aid until the paramedics arrived.

The girlfriend was told by her mother's attorney that the story she told to the police would not help her or her boyfriend. From that point on, she adhered to the story told by the witness.

The decedent was a state champion wrestler in high school. He was a very jealous person and had instigated numerous fights in response to someone looking at or flirting with his girlfriend. Additionally, the decedent and his girlfriend had been fighting that evening, and he had been drinking. She was walking away from him at the time the incident started.

The decedent was stabbed in the first intercostals space on the right, nicking the side of the aorta. He walked 85 feet before he collapsed. There was a lot of blood on the shirt of the defendant, but only three drops (it had stopped raining) between the scene and the body.

There were three phone calls to the 911 dispatcher prior to the witness's call. One of those calls was from a friend of the decedent (at who's residence the decedent had been drinking) who ran a block to the body and then ran back to call.

The witness did not drive to the convenience store; he walked. He lived just a half a block from where the incident occurred. The first officer at the crime scene knew the witness. The officer said he did not see him there, and that no one gave first aid because the paramedics arrived soon after. The witness was actually a friend of the decedent and his girlfriend. They had been to the bar where he worked that evening.

The clothing was submitted to the laboratory for examination. DNA was relatively new at the time, but it was used to determine that it was the decedent's blood on the defendant, as well as on the shirt from the witness.

The plaintiff's expert witness opined that blood spurted out of the decedent's chest due to arterial pressure as the decedent lay on his back at the scene. The aorta was nicked or cut on the side. The aforementioned expert further opined that the blood would spurt as though from a garden hose as a result of that nick. There were a few small droplets on the left sleeve/chest area of the defendant. This, the expert claimed, was the spurt that follows the knife out of the injury. They had marked three of the drops as to directionality. They also claimed that the blood on the witness's shirt came from arterial spurting as well.

Figures 5.2 and 5.3 show how the droplets on the shirt were marked by the prosecution and then by the author. These drops do not go in one direction. Blood does not spurt out in a tiny stream from a chest wound as the knife is withdrawn; in fact, knives used to stab people in the chest seldom have enough blood on them to see without a microscope or with chemicals. This pattern is explained by the

Continues on next page

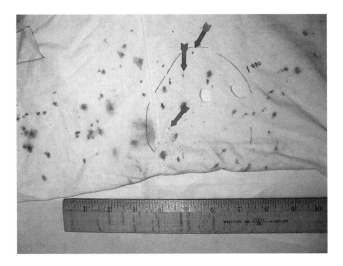

Figure 5.2

This is the sleeve of the defendant's shirt. The directionality of some of the blood drops on the sleeve has been marked by the plaintiff's expert.

Figure 5.3

The directionality of additional blood drops by the author shows the different directions the blood was traveling. These different directions do not support the theory of the plaintiff's expert.

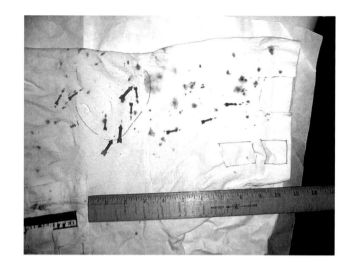

Continued

defendant waving his bloody hand and knife while threatening the witness. By marking only a few, the plaintiff's witness was ignoring the facts that did not fit his theory.

The witness submitted this shirt (Figure 5.4). He claimed to have reached across the chest of the defendant to throw him off. Yet there are no large transfers of blood on this shirt. There are several drops on the chest area. These are consistent with the blood cast off the knife blade when the defendant was threatening him.

Blood does spurt out a cut artery with each heartbeat, like water out of a pulsating sprinkler. However, when the artery is cut on the side, the spurting is into the chest, not out a narrow channel that is 3 inches through muscle tissue.

The clothing of the decedent was not cut by the stab wound. His shirt and T-shirt were over the wound; therefore, they were pulled up at the time he was stabbed. The wound will drain when it is down, but when the person is standing, sitting vertically, or lying on his back, the blood will stay in the chest. This collapses the lungs and puts pressure on the heart.

The right side of the defendant's shirt (Figure 5.5) is heavily bloodstained. It is on the right sleeve and down the front of the shirt. This shows that the decedent was above the defendant at the time he was bleeding and the defendant had turned toward him. There are small drops on the back of the outside collar. These were the first drops shed after the stabbing. The decedent stood up at this point and the blood gushed out in a couple of heartbeats. When he stood completely, he did not spurt any more blood.

The jury stated that the witness, the bouncer, was clearly a pathological liar. They also believed that he was making things up as he went along. They further suggested that they might leave the courtroom if he took the stand again. They did find for the plaintiff, however, and awarded $1 in punitive damages.

Why was the witness lying? He had taken martial arts since he was 10 years old. He wanted to be a hero. We believe he could not face the fact that when he had a chance to become one, he fled and left a young woman with a "crazed killer," as he described the defendant. He believed his story after he told it enough times.

Figure 5.4

This is the shirt worn by the witness. There is a lack of bloodstains that should be present if he did as he said. The small spots on the front of the shirt are "cast off" from the knife being waved in front of him.

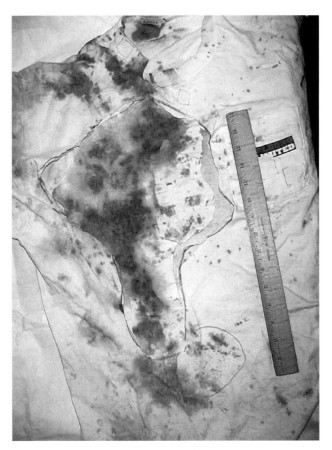

Figure 5.5

This is the shirt worn by the defendant. The large blood pattern on the right side shows how the blood poured from the injury down onto the defendant as the decedent stood. Sent under separate email.

This case illustrates why it is important that the reconstructionist establish the facts using the evidence and then test the stories of all the actors in whatever role they purport to take in the incident.[9]

THE NATURE OF RECONSTRUCTION

No matter how complex, problem solving is a function of thinking and reasoning; it involves the recognition that one does not immediately know how to move from a given state (ignorance) to a desired state (enlightenment). Crime reconstruction is a form of evidence interpretation based on the application of advanced problem recognition and solving skills; however, there are limits to our understanding of how the mind works. Far more research is necessary before we can speak with absolute certainty regarding how it is that the human mind recognizes and sorts the patterns in the evidence that help us compose our theories. Creativity and imagination, for example, are components that elude quantification. In other words, how we form and inform our hypotheses is not always understood, but how we test, support, or disprove them must be.

The tools described in this chapter are essentially methods for organizing one's thoughts and reducing complex problems to manageable ones. They will help the reconstructionist identify and answer questions about the evidence and allow her to explain the results of her examinations to others. As presented, these tools presume an adherence to critical thinking, analytical logic, the scientific method, and the practice standards discussed in Chapter 4.

There is no one true method for reconstructing crime; however, there are many valid and invalid techniques. Only a small number of them have been mentioned in this chapter. The viability of any technique is measured by the extent to which the reconstructionist adheres to the scientific method, analytical logic, ethics, and a willingness to show his work and support his conclusions in a way that can be understood and replicated by others. The reconstructionist has a duty to explain not only her results but also how they were derived and how everything else in consideration was eliminated.

CRITICAL/CREATIVE THINKING EXERCISES

Answering the questions that present themselves in reconstruction casework requires thinking beyond the rules that we too often assume must be present. In other words, reconstructionists need to see causes and effects, actions and consequences, from multiple perspectives and learn to think

0	0	0
0	0	0
0	0	0

Figure 5.6
Exercise 1.

outside of the box. The following is a series of exercises designed to help the reconstructionist learn precisely that.

EXERCISE 1

Connect the nine dots in Figure 5.6 using only four straight lines. The lines must be a pathway; that is, you cannot lift your pencil from the paper.

EXERCISE 2: DIRT

Calculate the amount of dirt in a hole in the ground that is 2 feet deep and 8 inches in diameter.

EXERCISE 3: MOUNT EVEREST

Before the discovery of Mount Everest, what was the tallest mountain in the world?

EXERCISE 4: CUT THE PIE

Cut a pie into eight pieces using only three cuts.

ANSWERS—SORT OF

1. Do not read into the rules what is not there. To solve this problem, you must literally think outside the box.

2. Zero cubic inches. Reread the problem. What is the definition of a hole? The dirt has been removed; if not it is not a hole.

3. Just because something is not found does not mean it is not there. Mount Everest has always been the peak with the highest elevation above sea level.

4. Reread the rule. You assume too much. The lines do not have to be straight. Bonus: cut the pie into eight equal pieces using three straight cuts.

REFERENCES

Bevel, T., and Gardner, R. M. *Bloodstain Pattern Analysis, With an Introduction to Crime Scene Reconstruction.* New York: CRC Press, 1997.

Block, E. B. *The Wizard of Berkeley.* New York: Coward-McCann, 1958.

Chisum, W. J., and Rynearson, J. M. *Evidence and Crime Scene Reconstruction.* Redding, CA: Shingletown Press, 1983.

Doyle, A. C. The Adventure of the Blue Carbuncle, *Strand Magazine,* January 1892.

Erzinçlioglu, Z. *Every Contact Leaves a Trace: Scientific Detection in the Twentieth Century.* London: Carlton Books, 2000.

Findley, J. F., and Hopkins, C. S. Reconstruction: An Overview, *Identification News,* October 1984.

Gross, H. *Criminal Investigation.* London: Sweet & Maxwell, 1924. (English translation of earlier work).

Kind, S. *Scientific Investigation of Crime.* self-published, 1986.

O'Hara, C. *Fundamentals of Criminal Investigation.* Springfield, IL: Charles C Thomas, 1956.

Rhodes, H. T. F. *Clues and Crime.* London: Murray, 1933.

Rynearson, J. M. *Evidence and Crime Scene Reconstruction* (5th ed.). Redding, CA: Shingletown Press, 1997.

Ryenarson, J. M. *Evidence and Crime Scene Reconstruction* (6th ed.). Redding, CA: Shingletown Press, 2002.

Thornton, J. I. The general assumptions and rationale of forensic identification. In D. Faigman et al. (Eds.). *Modern Scientific Evidence: The Law and Science of Expert Testimony,* Vol. 2. St. Paul, MN: West, 1997.

CHAPTER 6

EVIDENCE DYNAMICS

W. Jerry Chisum, BS and Brent E. Turvey, MS

If we don't collect evidence and we don't store it properly, then the science is useless.
—Richard Rosen, Professor of Law, University of North Carolina–Chapel Hill (as quoted in Zerwick, 2005)

Crime reconstruction is an exacting process that often yields imprecise results containing evidentiary holes, sequential gaps, and alternate possibilities. This is not necessarily evidence of poor science and examiner inability. Establishing and revealing evidentiary frailty, however, can be an indication of scientific honesty. Forensic scientists are responsible for remembering, and reminding others, that what the evidence supports is often just as important as what it does not.

The more we learn about physical evidence—how it can be affected by external forces and distortions—the more we come to appreciate that it is not necessarily an abiding and precise record of actions and events. Even under the best circumstances, physical evidence must be interpreted through successive layers of necessary and uncontrollable influences. As a consequence, though it is often the most objective record of events, physical evidence and reconstructive interpretations can infrequently be expressed in terms of absolute certainty.

The purpose of this chapter is to discuss those necessary and uncontrollable influences, which we refer to as evidence dynamics,[1] and how reconstructionists must make efforts to account for them in their interpretations.

[1] Evidence dynamics as a formal concept was first described by the authors in Chisum and Turvey (2000). Portions of that article have been used to develop the current chapter.

EVIDENCE DYNAMICS

Crime reconstruction efforts are concerned with interpreting the physical evidence of the effects of actions and events related to the commission of a crime. However, frequently missing from this analysis is the recognition and consideration of those influences that can change physical evidence prior to, or as a result of, its collection and examination. The general term *evidence dynamics* has been developed by the authors to refer to any influence that adds, changes, relocates, obscures, contaminates, or obliterates physical evidence, regardless of intent. This term was deemed appropriate because all forms of physical evidence are at the mercy of environmental change, activity, and time.

Evidence dynamics are at work even before the crime happens and also during the interval that begins as physical evidence is being transferred or created. They continue on and do not stop affecting the evidence throughout its life, until it has been completely destroyed. For those who are familiar with such influences, and account for them in their analyses, this terminology is intended to provide a necessary and useful descriptor. As we will discuss, an appreciation of evidence dynamics is requisite, and often pivotal, to any examinations done by the laboratory and to the subsequent reconstruction of the events of the crime.

DYNAMIC INFLUENCES: PREDISCOVERY

Crime reconstructions are too often built on an *assumption of integrity*—that evidence left behind at a scene is guarded and vestal prior to the arrival of police investigators and other responders. This assumption involves the mistaken belief that taping off an area, limiting access, and setting about the task of taking pictures and making measurements somehow ensures the integrity of the evidence found within. Subsequently, any conclusions reached through forensic examinations of that evidence are wrongly assumed to be a wholly reliable lens through which to view the crime. Though reconstruction is made easier with this assumption, it is not made more accurate.

Reconstructionists must accept that each item of evidence at a crime scene will go through some or all of the following before it is actually recognized:

1. Transference or creation at the scene
2. Changes due to time (blood and semen dry; dead bodies decompose, stiffen, and equalize with room temperature)
3. Changes due to the environment (rain, heat, cold, and wind)
4. Alteration/destruction/creation by individuals involved in their duties
   First officer(s) at the scene
   Paramedics
   Other law enforcement or related personnel
5. Recognition or discovery that it is evidence (sometimes only after stepping on it or in it)

Each of these processes, legitimate and uncontrollable alike, has the potential to leave its mark on the evidence—to alter it in some irretrievable way.

Consider the following forms of evidence dynamics:

THE OTHER SIDE OF THE TAPE

The placement of crime scene security tape by first responders sets into motion a series of expectations and events that defines the scope of all evidence processing efforts. Under the best circumstances, first responders may fully grasp the complexity of the crime scene and the involvement of surrounding areas; they may be limited by natural barriers in the environment such as active freeways, cliffs, or bodies of water; they may have inaccurate preconceived ideas about where the crime occurred; or they may simply be misinformed about the nature of events. Under the worst circumstances, they may simply lack proper training or concern with regard to the importance of the physical evidence.

This concern is explained in plain but effective language by Eddie-Joe Delery a forensic examiner for the New Orleans Police Department's crime lab (personal communication with Turvey, July 23, 2005):

> Every time I roll up on a scene and see the tape coming off the back of a patrol car, tied to a telephone pole or something like that, I just shake my head. Everybody's so worried about searching inside that tape, by the time they realize the crime took place on the other side of it they've walked all over the evidence. And that's if they didn't park their vehicle on it.

The limiting effect of crime scene tape is tremendous. First responders have a duty to understand and implement competent barrier efforts; scene technicians have a responsibility to understand and implement competent search and collection efforts. Each must grasp the dangers of setting up the tape and working only on one side of it.

When relevant, the reconstructionist is advised to consider whether the tape accurately defined the scene and whether subsequent evidence search and collection efforts reflect the most informed picture of the evidence given the nature of the crime. If, for example, evidence was found outside the tape and search efforts were not expanded accordingly, this might suggest an incomplete investigative and processing effort.

THE CRIME SCENE

Before the crime occurs, the area where it eventually takes place may already contain items that are "evidence" of everyday activities, such as cigarette butts, beer or soft drink cans, fibers, evidence of recent sexual activity, old bloodstains—the potential list is endless. The reconstructionist has a responsibility to differentiate between these preexistent items and actual evidence of the crime. That is, each item of evidence must somehow be associated with the crime; its association may not be assumed merely by establishing its presence in the scene.

The person who "recognizes" the evidence at a crime scene must also have the ability to make this distinction or there will be useless items collected as though they are relevant and relevant items ignored as though they are useless. Mistakes in this effort can result in a reconstruction that is not only erroneous but also may point to the wrong actions and even the wrong suspect.

EXAMPLE

One of the authors (Turvey) recently worked a post-conviction case out of Oklahoma where a very highly regarded bloodstain analyst examined what he thought was high velocity blood spatter on a car believed to be associated with a shooting death. The bloodstain analyst testified at trial, in the pre DNA era, that the bloodstains on the car door almost certainly came from a shooting incident, and assumed that they were associated with the homicide. The defendant, Richard Tandy Smith, was convicted. Eighteen years later, DNA proved that the substance was indeed blood, but that it did not match the homicide victim in the case. The bloodstain was unrelated to the homicide, and its origins have been lost to time.

OFFENDER ACTIONS

The actions of an offender during the commission of the crime, and in the postoffense interval, directly influence the nature and quality of evidence that is left behind. These can include precautionary acts, ritual or fantasy, and staging (Turvey, 2002).

- *Precautionary acts* involving physical evidence are behaviors committed by an offender before, during, or after an offense that are consciously intended to confuse, hamper, or defeat investigative or forensic efforts for the purposes of concealing the identity of the perpetrator and/or his connection to the crime, or even the crime itself. This includes disposal of the body, clipping victim's fingers or removing their teeth or fingers to prevent identification, cleaning up the blood at the scene, picking up shell casings—essentially anything that changes the visibility, location, or nature of the evidence.
- *Staging* of the crime scene is a specific type of precautionary act that is intended to deflect suspicion away from the offender. Staging often involves the addition, removal, and manipulation of items in the crime scene to change the apparent "motive" (see Chapter 12).
- *Ritual* or *fantasy* may also influence the offender's actions during a crime and can include postmortem mutilation, necrophilia, and purposeful arrangement

of a body or items in a scene. Fantasy may also be involved with items found in the suspect's home environment that show planning or pre-/postincident fantasies.

VICTIM ACTIONS

The victim's activities prior to a crime may result in artifacts that are mistaken for evidence that is related to the crime. The actions of a victim during an attack and in the postoffense interval can also influence the nature and quality of evidence that is left behind. This includes defensive actions, such as struggling, fighting, and running, which can relocate transfer evidence, causing secondary transfer. The victim's actions may also include cleaning up a location or their person after an attack.

EXAMPLE

A woman reversed the murder scene in the film *Psycho* and stabbed a man in the shower. She was going through his pants in the next room when he came out of the bathroom and attacked her. Blood from his injuries cast off all over the walls. The bloodstain evidence was very confusing due to the actions of the victim.

EXAMPLE

A woman had sex with her boyfriend in his vehicle. He dropped her off at her apartment. As she entered her bedroom, she surprised a burglar. A struggle ensued causing tears in her clothing before the burglar strangled her and fled. The boyfriend was suspected of the "rape/homicide." His DNA was found in her vagina. This would be considered absolute proof of his guilt in many courts.

Fortunately, the boyfriend had an alibi; he was stopped for DUI a couple of blocks from the house. He was in police custody during the time the screams were heard by the neighbors. In this case, the victim's actions prior to a crime caused "false evidence" to be present that could have resulted in an "ironclad case" against the innocent boyfriend had he not had a strong alibi.

SECONDARY TRANSFER

Transfer evidence, as discussed in Chapter 7, is produced by contact between persons and objects (Cwiklik, 1999; Lee, 1995). Secondary transfer refers to an exchange of evidence between objects or persons that occurs subsequent to an original exchange, unassociated with the circumstances that produced the original exchange.

EXAMPLE

The body of an adolescent female was found on a couch in her home where she lived with her mother and younger brother. She was wearing only a shirt and bra at the time of discovery. She was determined to have died of "asphyxia secondary to manual strangulation." She had a history of sexual abuse, suggested by the absence of her hymen and numerous anal scars, as well as a history of promiscuity. The DNA of one of her mother's lovers was found on her perineum, in the form of sperm.

Given the location and circumstances of the crime, the precise conditions of this exchange could not be reliably established. One possibility is that the suspect was engaged in some form of sexual activity with the victim, and that sperm transferred to her perineum as a result. However, the suspect and the victim's mother had sexual relations in the mother's bed, where the victim had been playing previously with her brother. There were also reports that the suspect and the victim's mother may have had sexual relations on the couch, where the victim would have been sitting. Additionally, a review of the crime scene video shows several evidence technicians moving evidence around on the couch and other locations and then touching the victim's body in multiple locations, examining her body as it is being photographed, with and without gloves.

Given these circumstances, and the victim's history, the following are potential evidence transfer relationships in this case:

- From the suspect to the victim during a forced sexual assault
- From the suspect to the victim during a consensual (but unlawful) sexual encounter
- From the couch to the victim's perineum
- From the mother's bed to the victim's perineum
- From the scene technician's fingers to the victim's perineum

WITNESSES

The actions of witnesses in the postoffense/prediscovery interval can influence the nature and quality of evidence that is left behind. This includes actions taken to preserve victim dignity, as well as the deliberate theft of items from the scene upon discovery of an incapacitated or deceased victim. It also includes any other well-intentioned yet destructive efforts. Consider the following example from a burglary in Palm Beach, Florida ("Police Blotter: Burglary," 2004):

> A man dressed in black, with a burgundy scarf covering his face, robbed a store at gunpoint in the 300 block of North Main Street, taking about $57. Police could not process the crime scene because an employee had contaminated it by putting everything back in its place before they arrived.

WEATHER/CLIMATE

The meteorological conditions (e.g., temperature, precipitation, and wind) at a crime scene can influence the nature and quality of all manner of evidence that is left behind. This includes the destruction or obliteration of evidence, as well as the effects of climate on body temperature and decomposition. Inclement or extreme weather in particular can destroy evidence, destroy crime scenes, and in some cases prevent responders from getting to the scene altogether. If too much time elapses under such conditions, the chance to locate, secure, and retrieve evidence may be lost. A corpse in the water may bloat and eventually disintegrate. A hard rain may wash away footprints in the soil.

There are rare exceptions to the destructive properties of weather, however. For example, extreme cold may inadvertently preserve the body of a murder victim that becomes frozen in an outdoor disposal scene. This may keep areas of injury from decomposing and preserve DNA evidence for testing. Extreme heat and dryness, on the other hand, may mummify a corpse and cause it to shrivel.

DECOMPOSITION

Naturally occurring rates of decomposition can obscure, obliterate, or mimic evidence of injury to a body. Because of this, in combination with the smell and revulsion experienced by examiners, there is a perception that everything else has decomposed as well. Consequently, the clothing from a decomposed body will normally receive less attention for trace or transfer evidence. This is a mistake because hair, fiber, and other synthetic transfer evidence can endure well beyond biological material.

As previously mentioned, the rate of decomposition is affected by climate. With respect to body temperature, it changes to meet room or environmental temperature after death. In a freezer, this means a decrease; in a heated indoor or outdoor environment, this means an increase. This change affects the rate of decomposition as well as the onset and duration of both rigor mortis and livor mortis (Knight, 1996).

EXAMPLE

A woman's near decapitated body was found in her bed. Her body temperature taken at the morgue indicated she had died approximately four hours after the detectives arrived at the scene. This determination was made by calculating expected heat loss. Confronted with this glaring contradiction, further investigation was initiated. It was eventually learned that the body had been lying on a heated waterbed; it had not cooled.

INSECT ACTIVITY

The actions of flies, ants, beetles, and other insects can obliterate or mimic the wounds on a body. They may also move, remove, or destroy the transfer evidence. The evidence of their activities may also appear to the inexperienced to be evidence of torture.

EXAMPLE

An adolescent female was missing for approximately two weeks before investigators found her body. It was located in a slightly concealed area of foliage behind an unoccupied residence. Her deceased body had been placed inside of a piece of recently discarded carpeting, beneath a heavy metal water tank, and then covered by several more layers of older discarded carpeting.

According to the autopsy report, and visible in the autopsy photos, the victim's underwear was found in her mouth. The cause of death was determined to be "asphyxia by gagging" possibly in combination with a violent blow to the victim's jaw as evidenced by a fracture to the mandible.

The question arose as to whether there was evidence of manual or ligature strangulation. Due to the overall advanced state of decomposition, and the fact that maggots had consumed the soft tissue associated with the neck, a determination on this issue was not possible. In the absence of evidence to examine, one cannot make a legitimate determination as to whether or not manual or ligature strangulation occurred. This did not exclude the possibility that it may have occurred; merely that it could not be established and therefore should not be assumed for the purposes of analysis.

ANIMAL PREDATION

The feeding activities of all manner of indigenous wildlife, from ants to mice, coyotes, and bears, can relocate body parts, obliterate patterns, and further obscure, obliterate, or mimic injury to a body.

EXAMPLE

A man was found in an alley with his throat opened and his eyes gouged out. When he was undressed it was found that he had injuries to his exposed ankles and wrists as well. He also had electrocardiograph (ECG) patches on his chest.

Investigation revealed that he had experienced chest pains earlier in the day and went to the hospital. They had him "under observation" after running an ECG. He walked out on his own, up the block into the alley. He subsequently died from a heart attack. The injuries were from rats gnawing on the dead body.

FIRE

In cases in which fire is involved, intentional or otherwise, the result can be the burning and obscuring of all manner of physical evidence related to criminal activities, as well as its potential destruction.

In cases involving arson, evidence of the actions of the offender may be obscured if not eliminated (concealing homicide, concealing theft), but evidence of the arson may remain (see Chapter 10).

EXAMPLE

A young female arrived at her older boyfriend's home, where he lived with his elderly mother and two teenage children. A confrontation ensued. The boyfriend and his mother, who were the only ones home at the time, were both killed, dying of exsanguination from multiple gunshot wounds.

The boyfriend's body was found outside of the residence with an associated blood trail. After the girlfriend removed some items of value, she set both the house and the body of the boyfriend on fire, separately.

Some of the actions and circumstances involved in the crime were evident, given the body outside of the home, associated transfer evidence, and blood patterns. However, a sequential reconstruction of the shots fired within the house, as well as the relative positions of the shooter and the victims, was significantly impaired. This was due to the movement and destruction of walls, furniture, flooring, household items, the body of the mother, and blood evidence in the scene. A crime analysis of the case by one of the authors (Turvey) reads in part,

> Precise reconstruction efforts are hampered in this case due to the numerous destructive and evidence-altering variables that were imposed upon the scene in the interval after the deaths occurred and before it was safe for forensic efforts to take priority. These destructive and evidence-altering variables and elements,

documented in part by a video made of this scene during and after suppression efforts were engaged, include, but are not limited to:

- the destructive nature of the fire itself, which involved both stories and many rooms in the house;
- the destructive nature of the suppression efforts, which involved water being pumped into the home at approximately 1000 gallons per minute, the destruction and movement of items in the home for both suppression and salvage purposes, as well as unintentional damage that may have been caused by heavy fire hoses in various locations within the home;
- the number of personnel venturing in and out of the home during and after suppression efforts, which some estimate may have been more that 50 individuals.

THE FIRST RESPONDER/POLICE PERSONNEL

The duty of the first responder on the scene is to protect life, not to preserve evidence. They must first protect their own life and then the lives of others by giving first aid and determining that potential suspects are no longer a threat to personal or public safety. That is, the officer cannot protect public safety if incapacitated; therefore, the officer must first ensure his own safety by searching the premises for suspects, bombs, or other hazards. The officer cannot worry about footprints or fingerprints during this search. After that, the officer must render aid to victims and establish that the scene is secure from further danger. The first officer should be interviewed, if not at the scene then before the reconstruction is finalized.

Additionally, detectives and other law enforcement personnel should know to refrain from touching evidence at the scene before it is properly documented. When possible, a strict "hands in the pockets" policy must be enforced among those not saving lives, documenting, or collecting evidence. Their actions may relocate evidence, obliterate patterns, cause transfers, and add artifacts to the scene.

When relevant, the reconstructionist must avail herself of all reports and notes detailing such activities to prevent misinterpretation. If no such documentation exists, the reconstructionist should realize that there is a serious gap in the reliability of the evidence and must so qualify her report. Moreover, it is arguably the duty of the reconstructionist to document and report the absence of such vital scene documentation, as well as any other failings or shortcomings in scene processing efforts. In this way, misrepresentations of the evidence by overly certain examiners or legal professionals may be prevented.

FIRE SUPPRESSION EFFORTS

In cases in which fire is involved, there may be suppression efforts made. These efforts typically involve the use of high-pressure water, heavy hoses, and perhaps chemicals. The job of the fire suppression personnel is to put out the fire; evidence is secondary to this concern. Any of these activities, alone or in concert, can relocate or destroy the evidence, obliterate patterns, cause potentially misleading transfers, and/or add artifact evidence to the scene (see Chapter 10).

THE EMERGENCY MEDICAL TEAM

The actions of emergency medical personnel engaged in life-saving activities at the crime scene may relocate and destroy evidence, obliterate patterns, cause transfers, tear clothing, and add artifacts. Additionally, they may intentionally inflict therapeutic injuries to the victim, such as cuts or punctures. This is expected and necessary.

Should a victim be transported to a medical facility, treatment rendered there can also change the nature of injuries. This will cause problems for subsequent examination and interpretation of the injuries at autopsy. Again, this is expected and should not be misinterpreted.

When relevant, as with first responders and law enforcement personnel discussed previously, the reconstructionist must avail himself of all reports and notes detailing these activities to prevent misinterpretation. If no such documentation exists, the reconstructionist should request that it be sought and created.

EXAMPLE

A youth was stabbed several times by rival gang members. He ran to a home but collapsed in its walkway. A photo of the scene taken prior to the arrival of the EMT team shows a distinct blood trail, and that the victim was lying face down. Subsequent photos show the five EMTs working on the body on his back. He had been rolled over onto the blood pool. It subsequently became impossible for bloodstain pattern interpretation to be used to reconstruct the events leading to the death of the youth.

SECURITY

Proper scene security must be maintained at all times. This means limiting access to only necessary personnel and controlling it by means of a security officer who logs the entry times, exit times, reason for entry, and duties performed of each person who passes through the tape. This is a basic concern that is part of every scene processing training course and program that the authors have encountered. However, it is still regularly ignored. Sometimes, a reminder is needed.

EXAMPLE

The author (Chisum) was called out of a forensic science seminar and sent to a crime scene in the Oak Park area of Sacramento by the bureau chief. There were two bodies buried in the back yard of a local residence. The suspect, Morris Solomon, was killing local prostitutes. One was found in the closet of the house; then later these two were found in the back yard.

Upon arrival, it was noted that there was a tape across the sidewalk keeping the public out and the officer was taking names of people entering the crime scene. However, the scene had several detectives walking around the property and interfering with the criminalists and ID personnel. The officer in charge was located and asked if he would like some crime scene management suggestions. He replied that he would.

An additional tape was placed across the entry to the back yard. No one was allowed beyond that tape unless they were actively engaged in documenting the scene, assisting with the cleaning out of the gravesites, or recovering the bodies. All persons entering this part of the scene were required to put on protective gear (i.e., gloves and face masks). A trash bag was placed at the barrier for these items when the scene was left. The porch overlooked the scene, so it was still visible for those who needed to see the operation.

Morris Solomon was convicted of six murders, including these two. He probably committed others.

However, gentle reminders may not be enough. In one case, a Minneapolis police sergeant became so disturbed by the lack of security at a double homicide scene that he wrote an e-mail to his supervisors to make an official record (Chanen and Collins, 2005, p. 1B):

A Minneapolis police sergeant sent an e-mail to his supervisors questioning why nonpolice personnel were walking around a taped-off crime scene where two men were shot to death in a north Minneapolis restaurant nearly two weeks ago.

Members of the Police Community Relations Council (PCRC) were given copies of the e-mail that Sgt. Robert Berry sent to police administration and Fourth Precinct supervisors relating his concerns about the crime scene following the March 4 fatal shootings of Frank Haynes, 21, and Raliegh Robinson, 68, both of Minneapolis.

PCRC member Ron Edwards said the e-mail suggested that the crime scene may have been contaminated by unauthorized people.

In his e-mail, Berry said "people moved freely" and could have destroyed evidence. He said one woman was "confidently walking beyond the crime scene tape, as a number of others had, then passed by an officer and into a door leading into the restaurant from the south side."

Berry said officers were hesitant to question those entering the site because they were concerned about creating controversy.

"The officers do not know who should or should not be allowed inside these scenes. Some of them were flat out ignored when they inquired about a person's presence inside the perimeter," Berry said in the e-mail. "This should never be the case."

Several community leaders were seen walking around the crime scene that stretched for blocks more than an hour after the shooting occurred at 3010 Penn Av. N. Some of them stood beside Police Chief Bill McManus behind the crime scene tape as he answered questions from reporters.

Lt. Lee Edwards, head of the homicide unit, said at Wednesday's meeting that the scene was not contaminated, but he did cite other sites that hadn't been properly secured. He told attendees that police officials have already addressed internally the issues Berry raised. Capt. Rich Stanek said there still may be times when people will be allowed behind crime tape.

Although administrators may think that there are legitimate reasons for passing unchecked into or through the tape when one is not directly involved in the processing effort, this is entirely mistaken and can add to the evidence or even obliterate it.

EXAMPLE

In the *Onion Field* (see the book by Joseph Wambaugh), the chief of the criminal division of the Kern County Sheriff's Office, Loren Fote, was prevented from entering the crime scene by a deputy sheriff who had never met him. Instead of entering the scene, complaining, or retaliating against the deputy, the chief gave him a commendation.

Once aid has been rendered and danger has been eliminated, the scene may be secured. Subsequently, the search for evidence may begin. The dynamic influences on physical evidence do not end with its recognition, however.

DYNAMIC INFLUENCES: POSTDISCOVERY

Crime reconstruction is at the end of, and dependent on, a long line of necessary investigative and forensic processes. Each item of evidence collected from a crime scene will go through some or all of the following steps after it has been recognized:

1. Protection (from the environment and those in it)
2. Documentation (notes, sketches, photos, video, etc.)
3. Collection/packaging/marking
4. Preservation before delivery to lab and in lab
5. Transportation (to the forensic lab)
6. Identification (as a general kind of evidence based on its properties)
7. Comparison (to knowns, unknowns, and controls)
8. Individualization (as a unique piece of evidence)
9. Interpretation (consideration with other evidence from the case)
10. Disposition (storage/destruction/loss/deterioration)

As with prediscovery influences, each of these processes has the potential to leave its mark on the evidence. A crime scene in high-traffic public areas such as sidewalks and subways can wreak havoc on evidence collection efforts, even to the extent that law enforcement may refuse to process it if too much time has passed. Packaging items of clothing in plastic may result in static electricity pulling away valuable fiber evidence or bacterial growth causing degradation of biological or botanical evidence. Transportation may shake and jar a dead body, causing fluids to purge from the injuries or the mouth and nose. Examination may result in the intentional sectioning and destruction of evidence portions. Reconstructionists must consider these and related influences and attempt to account for them in their interpretations.

Consider the following incarnations of evidence dynamics:

FAILURE TO SEARCH OR RECOVER

Even when the prediscovery evidentiary influences have been accounted for or even avoided, it is still possible that crime scene personnel may fail to adequately recognize the true scope of the scene and perform an adequate search for evidence. This can result in areas at or related to the scene that are insufficiently searched and documented to support reconstruction interpretations. It can also result in evidence that is missed entirely. Consider the following comments made by a chief of police to his evidence technicians with respect to this issue, from a major headline-grabbing case. It involves evidence missed, potential animal predation, and failure to conduct a thorough search (Cella, 2002, p. 1):

> D.C. Police Chief Charles H. Ramsey yesterday said his investigators "blew it" in searching the site where Chandra Levy's remains were found, after private detectives this week discovered another bone just yards away in Rock Creek Park.
>
> The chief met with members of his forensics team to determine why the 12-inch shin bone wasn't discovered by any of the police teams combing the area during a weeklong search. Private investigators working for the Levy family said they found the bone within 25 yards of where Miss Levy's skull was recovered by police May 22, nearly 13 months after the former federal intern disappeared.
>
> Police spokesman Sgt. Joe Gentile said that during a preliminary review of investigative procedures the team shared with Chief Ramsey photographs, maps, and charts created at the scene.
>
> "It appears that department technicians did not pass over the bone during the original search," Chief Ramsey said in a statement issued last night. "There appears to be a greater likelihood that the bone was reintroduced to the area by wildlife."
>
> That theory corresponds with a description of the bone by Cmdr. Christopher LoJacono of the D.C. Police Forensic Science Division, who said Thursday that the bone showed "substantial animal activity." Police also said the bone was found within three feet of what appeared to be an animal's den.
>
> Sgt. Gentile said after the preliminary review that no one stands to be disciplined, though an assessment of how police missed the bone during the original search continues.
>
> Chief Ramsey said discovery of the leg bone was no reason to reopen the medical examiner's investigation of the death of Miss Levy, 24. D.C. Chief Medical Examiner Jonathan L. Arden declared her death a homicide based on circumstances surrounding the discovery of her remains, but could not determine a cause.
>
> Chief Ramsey said investigators would return to the spot where Miss Levy's remains were discovered in an attempt to locate any more evidence that might have been overlooked.
>
> He said 85 percent of Miss Levy's remains have been recovered, but that parts of her pelvis, left leg, and foot were still missing when police ended their search.
>
> "There's no guarantee that another bone might not surface," Chief Ramsey said.
>
> Sgt. Gentile said investigators would search with cadaver dogs tomorrow and perform a grid search with a platoon of cadets Monday.

The nature of this kind of influence is to deprive the police investigation and the forensic investigation of the most complete picture possible. The failure to recognize evidence, the failure to conduct a complete and thorough search the first time through, and the failure to document the entirety of the scene each represent a missed opportunity to learn more about the crime. Recovering from these can be time-consuming, expensive, and, to some extent, impossible.

EVIDENCE TECHNICIANS

Evidence technicians [a.k.a. crime scene investigators (CSIs)] are charged with evidence recognition, preservation, documentation, collection, and transportation. They are expected to locate and protect physical evidence without damaging it, without causing potentially misleading transfers, and without adding artifact evidence to the scene. They are expected to document and preserve, as much as possible, any pattern evidence. They are also expected to collect and package the evidence in a manner that preserves it for subsequent analysis and interpretation.

An important step in this process is documenting the scene prior to entering so that any changes that do occur as a result of their efforts are evident to those interpreting the documentation at a later time.

EXAMPLE

The clothing of a homicide victim was torn, and there were obvious foreign fibers present on the sheets of the bed where she was raped and strangled. The sheets were wadded together and placed into a large polyethylene bag. The static generated in placing the blanket in the same bag first caused the foreign fibers to jump off the sheets. Many of them were lost. Plastic bags must never be used for biological evidence or for items that may have microscopic (trace) evidence.

As an extreme example, consider the case of an Essex County crime scene investigator who was indicted for stealing cash from a homicide victim's body and then trying to cover it up (Hepp, 2005):

An Essex County crime scene investigator stole $8,380 from the pockets of a murder victim in 2002, then tried to replace the cash with newer bills when state investigators asked him to turn over the evidence, authorities charged yesterday.

John J. Cosgrove, an investigator with the Essex County Prosecutor's Office crime scene unit since 1995, was indicted by a state grand jury yesterday on charges of official misconduct, theft, tampering with evidence, and tampering with public records.

Cosgrove, 33, of Edison, faces up to 20 years in state prison and $100,000 in fines if convicted, authorities said. The Essex County Prosecutor's Office suspended him without pay last May.

According to the indictment, Cosgrove was investigating the slaying of Dennis Fiore outside a Bloomfield Avenue cafe in Newark on the night of July 11, 2002, when he and the medical examiner found $8,380 stuffed in the pockets of the victim's shorts.

Cosgrove took the cash and made a note of it in his preliminary report, Division of Criminal Justice spokesman John Hagerty said. But it disappeared somewhere between the crime scene and the state's Regional Medical Examiner's Office in Newark where the autopsy was performed.

"All the evidence is packaged by CSI at the scene and taken to the autopsy," Hagerty said. "Once the autopsy is completed, the victim's clothes and personal effects are entered into inventory as evidence and forwarded along with an evidence list to police. When Newark Police Department got the evidence and the inventory list, there was no evidence of cash."

The missing cash went unnoticed until 2003, when the State Police and Division of Criminal Justice's organized crime and racketeering bureau got involved in the murder investigation because Fiore may have had ties to organized crime, Hagerty said.

As part of that investigation, state detectives asked to review all evidence, photos, and records collected during the homicide investigation, authorities said. After reading Cosgrove's preliminary crime scene report they asked to look at the cash, but it wasn't in Newark's evidence locker when they checked in May 2004.

The detectives called Cosgrove at the county's crime scene unit office, located about ten minutes away, and he told them the money was locked in a safe there, authorities said.

When the detectives arrived they noticed Cosgrove had an envelope thick with cash that he carried with him as he went to the safe, a state law enforcement source said. Cosgrove returned from the safe minutes later and handed over what he said was the evidence, according to the source.

"The problem was in the money that he turned over—It had dates that did not agree with the year in which Fiore was killed," the source said. "They were too new."

Harvey said Cosgrove's action was especially egregious because it could affect the prosecution of Fiore's murderer.

"The court and the jury is entitled to evaluate the case based upon the evidence collected at the crime scene and elsewhere," Harvey said. "That evidence should not be impaired or destroyed."

CORONER/MEDICAL EXAMINER

The actions of the coroner or medical examiner while removing the body from the scene can alter evidence, obliterate patterns, cause potentially misleading transfer, and add artifact evidence to the scene. Influential events include the physical removal of the body from the location where it was discovered, the placement of the body into a "body bag," transporting the body from the scene, storing it, and reopening it for examination at a later time. These actions may change pattern evidence on the body and clothing of the victim, and they may relocate or destroy potentially valuable transfer evidence.

EXAMPLE

Photos taken of the deceased show isolated blood-stain patterns on the clothing of the victim of a rape homicide. She had been sexually assaulted and her throat was cut. The patterns on her underwear appeared to be bloody transfers from a hand. The coroner refused to remove the clothing at the scene.

When the panties were submitted to the laboratory they were soaked in the victim's blood from transporting her in the body bag. The patterns were destroyed as well as making it impossible to isolate the stains for identification purposes.

PREMATURE SCENE CLEANUP

When a crime occurs in a public place, especially one that is highly visible or well traveled, there is sometimes an irresistible urge to clean up any signs of extreme violence left in the wake, including bloodshed, body parts, and brain matter. If done prematurely, this will hamper crime scene investigation efforts.

Consider the following example of a coroner openly criticizing police and EMS personnel for precisely such premature cleaning and potential evidence loss (Silver, 2003):

> Allegheny County Coroner Dr. Cyril H. Wecht yesterday suggested that the crime scene where a high school student was found shot to death last week was inadvertently tainted, possibly complicating efforts to determine whether Dion Hall committed suicide or was killed by police.
>
> During a news conference, Wecht said firefighters who hosed down blood from Chartiers Avenue in Sheraden Thursday night should not have done so before a criminalist from the coroner's office had a chance to examine the evidence.

"It's entirely possible that the slug from the boy's head was lying there in the blood," Wecht said. "The slug may have been washed down a sewer or somewhere."

Police have not recovered the bullet that killed the 17-year-old Langley High School junior.

Also, Wecht said the .357-caliber revolver in Hall's hand should not have been removed. And a blanket that police saw covering Hall as he allegedly hid in a van was not over the body when the coroner's staff arrived. Wecht said that blanket is now in police custody.

"I would have preferred that something like that blanket which was on that boy should not have been removed," Wecht said. "That is something that we want to see."

Investigators recovered five fragments from Hall's brain—four from the bullet jacket and one from the bullet itself. Wecht said it was likely that an analysis could determine whether those fragments came from the specific gun found in Hall's hand.

Though it is important for scene personnel to be courteous and professional toward bystanders and the public, it is equally important for the scene to be documented properly. This means being firm in the resolve to remove nonessential personnel and civilians from the scene so that they are not able to influence processing efforts. This also means being patient—Do not be in a hurry to process the scene, remove the body and other evidence, or to get rid of anything.

PACKAGING/TRANSPORTATION

As already suggested throughout this chapter, the manner in which evidence is packaged and transported will have an effect. Clothing evidence with wet stains, for example, should not be folded in such a manner as to transfer the stains to other parts of the garment. They must be removed and dried or preferably wrapped in butcher paper so the stains cannot transfer. Also, whenever possible, avoid placing multiple items of evidence in a single package, under a single number. This provides for potential cross-contamination and confusion with evidence tracking.

Svensson and Wendel (1974, p. 35) offer further suggestions:

Evidence which is to be sent to a laboratory for further examination should be packaged in such a way that it does not run the risk of breaking, spoiling, or contamination which might destroy its value as evidence.

Containers should be tight and, depending on the nature of the material, strong enough that they will not break in transit.

If the evidence consists of several objects they should be packaged in separate containers or wrapped individually in paper. Each item should be clearly marked as to contents and then packaged in a shipping container. Loose evidence is thereby kept from contaminating other evidence. In some cases, it may be necessary to fix articles to the container separately so as not to come in contact with each other. Bottles and other glass vessels which contain liquids should not be packaged with other evidence, since they may break and contaminate other material.

Whatever specific evidence collection guidelines are adopted, they must preserve the evidence in transport, prevent cross-contamination, prevent spoilage, and provide for later identification. If evidence collection guidelines fail in any of these respects, then they are insufficient to the purposes of forensic science in general and crime reconstruction in specific.

STORAGE

Evidence storage is a subject that is infrequently discussed because it is often the source of extreme angst for police departments and their respective crime labs. Commonly, they do not have enough space to store the evidence they collect or sufficient and qualified personnel available to keep it properly inventoried. Deficiencies in this area can be disastrous, resulting in evidence lost or destroyed, and cases dismissed.

The following examples are taken from the public record. Although they may be embarrassing to some, the authors believe that we must read them and be aware that the public is reading them as well. They portray an image of forensic science that the community is uninformed and inattentive—an image that is spreading and creating a credibility gap. It is our job to learn from these examples and take steps to prevent further occurrences.

In Revere, Massachusetts, inclement weather and flooding during 2004 unexpectedly disrupted evidence storage at one particular police storage facility. This was an unforeseeable event that nevertheless left a mark on the evidence while in storage (Rosinski, 2004):

> Torrential downpours that flooded roads and rivers also poured into the Revere police station yesterday, soaking boxes of evidence from unsolved homicides and rapes, authorities said.
>
> "Shelves of evidence of major felony cases—homicides and sexual assaults—were damaged and destroyed. The water is dripping on them like a shower," Revere police Capt. Dennis Collyer said. "Frankly, it's a disgrace."

Water was dripping from the ceiling onto boxes of evidence stored in a second-floor room, including one sealed box of physical evidence from a 1979 double-fatal shooting and multiple rape kits.

The situation in Massachusetts, as described, is quite different from the circumstances uncovered at the Houston Police Department (HPD) crime lab. The problems in the HPD system are representative of chronic, system-wide laboratory failure. Apart from their many other problems, the HPD crime lab has suffered from evidence storage nightmares that range from evidence overcrowding to incompetent storage practices and even to rats. According to the independent investigator's report (the following are selected outtakes; Bromwich, 2005),[2]

[2] The independent investigator's reports are posted on the investigation's Web site at www.hpdlabinvestigation.org.

In March 2002, Mr. Bolding estimated that there were 19,500 sexual assault kits received by HPD that had never been processed, some dating as far back as 1980.[53] During our tours of the Property Room, we were struck by the number of unprocessed rape kits currently being stored in the Property Room's freezers.[54]

The Property Room is located at 1103 Goliad Street and is comprised of two main areas. One area houses central receiving; the evidence tracking system; the administrative area; file storage; a vault for high value evidence; and property storage areas for firearms, knives, digital equipment, and small item evidence. Although this area is air-conditioned, it remains susceptible to high heat and humidity.

The second, and much larger, component of the Property Room consists of a large, single-floor warehouse and an annexed three-story warehouse, known as the Volker Building. Most of this area has shelving containing evidence and property stored in bins and boxes, as well as tools, bicycles, and other large items of evidence. We observed that some of the boxes stored in this area are marked with biohazard labels. This area is not air-conditioned and is subject to extreme heat and humidity. The floors are dirty and dusty. Currently, the area lacks space for the storage of additional property.[60] This area also houses two walk-in freezers containing sexual assault kits and other biological evidence.[61]

The Property Room facility has two major deficiencies as a property storage facility—(1) inadequate storage space and (2) lack of humidity and temperature control. In addition, the facility has had major ongoing maintenance problems over the last 15 years, which have included roof leaks, faulty electrical wiring and lighting, inoperable elevators, asbestos concerns, and the need for new windows and doors. Managers of the Property Room have documented these major facility issues.

The roof at 1103 Goliad Street was repaired in 2004, but many of the other problems with the facility still exist. Even if repairs are made to the present facility, it may not be adequate for the proper storage and handling of evidence due to the lack of temperature and humidity control and inadequate storage space.

. . .

Beginning in the early 1980s, the Property Room allowed various divisions of HPD to store items on the third floor of the Volker Building. The items stored on the third floor were considered to be under the control of the divisions that deposited the items and were not logged or inventoried by the Property Room. The Crime Lab was one of the divisions that stored items on the third floor of the Volker Building. The items stored by the Crime Lab included evidence as well as nonevidentiary items, such as excess office furniture. The evidence was stored in envelopes and boxes placed inside larger white boxes, which were stacked against a wall and under several windows.

In the 1980s and 1990s, the Volker Building's roof was in poor condition and experienced leaks. Rainwater leaked through the windows and roof, damaging some of the evidence stored by the Crime Lab. In addition, rats were present on the third floor, and they ate through a number of envelopes and boxes containing evidence.

In early 2000, the Property Room began to run out of space to store the evidence in its custody. Divisions storing property on the third floor of the Volker Building were asked to remove their property to free up space. When Crime Lab personnel came to the Property Room to remove the Lab's property, they took the contents of the damaged white boxes of evidence and placed the items in 283 new, large cardboard boxes. Each of the 283 boxes contained multiple pieces of evidence from multiple cases. Some boxes contained evidence from as many as 100 cases. The evidence dated from the 1960s to the early 1990s.

Once the evidence had been placed into the 283 boxes, Crime Lab personnel tagged the boxes to transfer custody to the Property Room so that the boxes could remain there. In doing so, the Crime Lab personnel identified each box by the incident number related to only one of the many items of evidence contained in each box, which misleadingly suggested that each box contained evidence related to only a single case. In fact, each box contained evidence relating to many cases. At some point, two of the 283 boxes were checked out of the Property Room by Crime Lab personnel. The pieces of evidence contained in these two boxes were individually tagged as individual pieces of evidence, and checked back into the Property Room. Thus, these two boxes ceased being part of the original 283-box collection.

On September 21, 2000, the Property Room received a routine destruction order to dispose of certain evidence. The evidence subject to the order was contained in one of the 281 remaining boxes. Coincidentally, the incident number related to the evidence subject to the destruction order was the incident number that happened to be listed on the outside of the box. Because the Property Room personnel believed, based on the box's label, that the box contained evidence related only to the one incident identified in the destruction order, Property Room personnel destroyed all of the box's contents. Subsequently, it was determined that this box contained evidence from 33 cases in addition to the one case identified on the box label.

In November 2003, the remaining 280 boxes were moved from the Property Room to a section of the 24th floor of the HPD headquarters, located at 1200 Travis Street, to protect the evidence from further degradation. On August 1, 2004, the Inspections Division began cataloguing and tagging the evidence contained in the original 283 boxes of evidence. Approximately 8000 individual evidentiary items have been identified in the boxes. We will continue reviewing this area, and we will provide additional information regarding Project 280 in future reports.

. . .

The storage of biological evidence has been an ongoing problem for the Property Room. The primary issue is the lack of sufficient temperature-controlled space for the storage of such materials. Prior to 1998, the Property Room stored sexual assault kits and other bodily fluid evidence in a freezer for a period of 18 months. After 18 months, the evidence was moved to air-conditioned areas within the Property Room for long-term storage. By 1998, the Property Room was running out of space in the freezers as well as the air-conditioned storage area. In March 1998, the head of the Property Room, Ron Cobb, asked Mr. Bolding if it was necessary to provide air-conditioned storage for this evidence after the initial 18-month period of storage in the freezer. In a March 18, 1998, memorandum to the captain of HPD's Homicide Division, Mr. Cobb relayed the response he had received from Mr. Bolding:

> "[T]here is **NO** need to provide air-conditioned storage for any type of body fluid evidence after the original freezer period of 18 months. [Mr. Bolding] related that he has taken evidence that was stored on the third floor of this building (which reaches extremely high temperatures in the summer), and has achieved successful DNA testing."

On April 1, 1998, in reliance on the information received from Mr. Bolding, Property Room personnel began relocating sexual assault kits and other biological evidence to general property storage areas. The general property storage areas are not air-conditioned and, therefore, are subject to high humidity and temperatures.

Both of the Property Room's freezers are overloaded and additional storage space is needed. Some biological evidence is commingled with other general evidence and stored in the general property room storage areas. This practice raises serious concerns about proper storage of biological evidence.[62] HPD has advised us that it expects delivery very soon of an additional freezer, which has been on order for several months, to the Property Room.

53. In a letter to Council Member Shelley Sekula-Gibbs, M.D., dated May 22, 2002, Chief Bradford stated that "current estimates indicate that there are 7200 sexual assault cases dating back to 1992 with usable DNA evidence at HPD which have not been processed."

54. The Property Room freezer currently contains 2233 rape kits, most of which (2116) date from the period 2000 to present. Of the kits in the Property Room freezer, 112 are from the 1990s and 5 predate 1990. Approximately 7886 sexual assault kits are being stored at HPD headquarters at 1200 Travis Street. In sum, HPD is currently storing over 10,000 sexual assault kits.

60. HPD is attempting to address overcrowding in the Property Room by storing evidence at the 1200 Travis Street building and exploring the alternative of auctioning items through the Web site www.propertyroom.com.

61. During a tour of the Property Room, one freezer appeared not to be maintaining the proper temperature, and we observed a considerable amount of water on the floor around the freezer. HPD advised us that the freezer was subsequently inspected and that it did not malfunction. HPD has suggested that the water we observed may have been attributable to condensation.

62. For example, in May 2004, water caused damage to 10 to 12 boxes of evidence due to a roof leak. Nine of these boxes contained clothing with possible biological evidence. The wet clothing was removed and hung to dry before being checked back into the Property Room.

Forensic scientists from all disciplines should study the reports written by the independent investigator of the HPD crime lab. They are a model of both forensic negligence and forensic incompetence with respect to these and other more staggering revelations.

Those with questions about evidence packaging and storage are encouraged to contact the American Society of Crime Lab Directors (www.ascld.org) because it has developed related standards and protocols for labs seeking accreditation.

EXAMINATION BY FORENSIC EXAMINERS

The purposeful actions of forensic scientists will remove evidence, obliterate patterns, may cause potentially misleading transfers, and can add artifact evidence. Forensic examination involves opening the packaged evidence, exposing it to the "lab" environment,[3] exposing it to the forensic examiner, and submitting it to procedures that may require its physical separation or even destruction. Although the last is often unavoidable and even expected, the first two can introduce unknown, unexpected, and questionable results when proper procedures are absent or ignored.

Consider the following examples:

[3] The "lab" environment is really any place that the evidence is opened and examined. This may be a secure forensic lab with forensic examiners in protective clothing, or it may be a back office in a police department shared by a CSI unit with a folding table in the middle on which they examine evidence as well as eat their lunch. The reconstructionist is better off knowing which is the case.

The Washington State Patrol Crime Lab
("WSP Crime Lab Slip Up," 2004)

The Washington State Patrol's crime labs have recurring problems with DNA contamination and errors, an investigation by the *Seattle Post-Intelligencer* has found.

Through public records requests and interviews with defense attorneys and experts, the paper found that forensic scientists made mistakes while handling DNA evidence in at least 23 cases during the past three years. Human error is apparently the main problem.

In eight of the 23 faulty cases, forensic scientists tainted tests with their own DNA. They made mistakes in six others, ranging from throwing out evidence swabs to misreading results. Tests were contaminated by DNA from unrelated cases in three instances, and between evidence in the same case in another. The source of contamination in five other tests is unknown.

The WSP contends strict protocols make sure the incidents only represent a fraction of the 1400 DNA cases handled each year.

"We're as good as any lab and probably better than many," said Barry Logan, director of the crime labs.

Although the labs only recently set up a mandatory reporting system for mistakes, officials are "100 percent certain that with all the precautions we catch everything," said Gary Shutler, who supervises the lab system's DNA work.

Cells in the human body contain a copy of a person's unique DNA, or deoxyribonucleic acid, which determines a person's eye color, height, and other inherited characteristics. A DNA match is considered infallible proof of guilt or innocence in many crimes.

Illinois State Police Crime Lab (Armstrong and Mills, 1999, p. 1)

After 15 years in prison for a rape and murder he insists he didn't commit, Anselm Holman thought DNA testing would finally set him free.

Instead, a blunder by the Illinois State Police crime laboratory not only threatens to cost Holman a chance to prove his innocence, but almost certainly will bring additional scrutiny by defense attorneys who say the lab has made repeated mistakes in recent years.

In the Holman case, a forensic scientist at the crime lab committed what forensic scientists call an extraordinary error: contaminating a semen smear on a microscope slide by somehow transferring his own DNA into the evidence. The situation has confounded experts, who note that one of the nation's premier crime labs, based in Connecticut, even tried and failed in an experiment to deliberately contaminate DNA evidence by sneezing into a sample and by putting hair, blood, and skin cells into it.

It's unclear how the contamination in this case occurred, but Holman's lawyers say the scientist who performed the test told them he was not wearing gloves. That, according to experts, violates fundamental laboratory procedures for such testing.

. . .

Prosecutors acknowledge the mistake occurred but say they will continue to assume Holman is guilty in the absence of evidence that exonerates him.

. . .

Moses Schanfield, chief of a forensic genetics lab in Denver, said he had never heard of a case in which a DNA sample had been contaminated by the analyst's own DNA.

"This shouldn't happen," Schanfield said. "It should cast a good deal of questions about the people doing the profile as well as the laboratory."

Added John Gerdes, a Denver scientist who testified for the defense in the O. J. Simpson criminal trial: "I can't believe that he didn't wear gloves. And it's not only to protect yourself, but also to prevent contamination. That's absolutely standard. It's unbelievable."

Crime lab officials and Cook County prosecutors disclosed the contamination error to Holman's attorneys at a meeting two weeks ago.

"They were very embarrassed; they were ashen," Betten said. "It was a dark day."

Crime lab officials couldn't say how it happened, but the forensic scientist who performed the tests, Aaron Small, offered a possible explanation during that meeting, the lawyers said.

"I said to him, 'How did your DNA get into this evidence?'" Ruebner said. "And he said, 'I handled the slide without gloves. I may have touched my nose and then the slide.' He did not believe he was bleeding at any time when he handled the slide, but he thought perhaps he may have had a small cut that could not be seen or wasn't bleeding due to the roughness of the slide."

Small, 29, has worked for the state since 1992, according to state records. He declined comment Monday, referring questions to a supervisor.

"We've worked dozens of cases, into the hundreds of cases, and not seen contamination," [James Kearney, laboratory director for the Illinois State Police Forensic Science Center in Chicago] said. "Does that mean there might be a case out there where contamination might occur? Yes, I think that's possible."

Kearney said he doesn't know of any other case where contamination like this has occurred in the Illinois lab.

PREMATURE DISPOSAL/DESTRUCTION

At some point, an item of evidence may be slated for lawful disposal or destruction. Cases may be adjudicated, statutes of limitation may run out, and biological or chemical hazards may exist that make such measures necessary. However, physical evidence must not be destroyed before proper documentation and forensic examination have taken place. Unfortunately, those charged with the custody of evidence are commonly prone to neglect, mistakes, and ignorance with respect to the performance of these duties.

Consider the following examples, and the consequences:

New Orleans Police Department Crime Lab (Perlstein, 2004)

Alcee Brown faced the possibility of life in prison when he arrived in court last week on an aggravated rape charge. When he got there, though, he learned that the New Orleans Police Department had inadvertently helped his case by destroying critical pieces of evidence.

As a result, prosecutors Tuesday offered Brown the opportunity to plead guilty to a lesser charge of forcible rape and to serve 30 years in jail. Brown, 36, promptly accepted.

There is no way to determine how many future cases may be compromised by the Police Department's improper destruction of evidence, but an NOPD internal report this week suggests that problems are likely to crop up for years. And, the report says, missing evidence, like that in the Brown case, probably will go unnoticed until prosecutors try to retrieve the items for trial.

The voluminous report, as thick as several telephone books, lists 55 open murder cases that have been rendered virtually unsolvable because all evidence was mistakenly destroyed.

In the past year, cold-case detectives had zeroed in on suspects in two of those killings, but the disposal of key evidence left the detectives empty-handed and their cases all but scrapped, the report says.

In addition, some or all evidence was improperly destroyed in 2500 rape cases, but poor record-keeping has made it impossible to determine how many were still prosecutable.

The scope of the problem was acknowledged earlier this month by Police Superintendent Eddie Compass in a Dec. 3 disciplinary letter to Capt. Michael Sauter, former commander of the Central Evidence & Property Division.

An evidence room purge, which took place from 1999 until 2002, led to the "unauthorized and illegal destruction of an unknown amount of items including but not limited to narcotics, rape kits, DNA evidence, and weapons submitted by investigating officers as evidence in criminal cases," Compass wrote.

"The exact amount and type of evidence cannot be determined because you failed to enter all evidence into a computer database," Compass continued.

Glendale Police Department, Arizona (Alonzo-Dunsmoor, 2005)

An *Arizona Republic* review of police records has found that two Glendale police officers destroyed evidence in sexual-assault cases and failed to investigate hundreds of domestic-violence cases.

As a result, the acting police chief said, prosecutions never took place in 191 cases, some involving reported sexual assaults against children and disabled people.

. . .

The cases date as far back as 1998, but police officials never disclosed the actions of then-Detectives Jeff Horsley and Kristian Grube to the victims or outside law enforcement agencies. Investigations of the officers' misconduct were handled internally.

. . .

Both police officers were reassigned and suspended, but they are still working for the Glendale Police Department. Both declined requests for interviews.

. . .

Horsley, an 11-year police veteran, worked in the sex-crimes division from December 1999 to July 2002 but did not properly investigate at least 59 sexual-assault cases, destroyed at least 30 videotapes that were evidence in those cases, and closed out incomplete cases without explanations, according to an internal investigation.

. . .

The audit found that 38 of the 59 cases assigned to Horsley didn't go anywhere. Horsley destroyed evidence in some of those cases or waited as much as a year before following up on a reported crime, records say.

. . .

In one case, the audit found, Horsley logged clothes and a sexual-assault kit as evidence. Just six days after the complaint, he authorized the release of the clothes to the victim and the destruction of the rape kit. The case remained open, but Horsley didn't pick up on it for another two years. He eventually submitted the case for prosecution without any evidence or documented interviews. Prosecutors turned down the case.

. . .

It's unclear whether the outcome would have been different in those 38 cases had Horsley not dumped evidence in the trash at his home or if he had worked and properly documented the cases. Other detectives picked up the remaining 21 cases.

Los Angeles Police & Sheriff's Department ("Police Accidentally Destroy DNA Samples," 2002)

Police Department and sheriff's employees unaware of changes in state law destroyed DNA samples from thousands of open sexual assault cases, law enforcement officials have admitted.

A statute passed last year permits prosecution of certain sex offense cases within ten years of the crime, as opposed to the previous six.

But police and sheriff's officials said officers apparently unaware of the change had destroyed biological evidence in cases filed earlier than 1996.

The lost evidence could affect as many as 4000 cases in city and county jurisdictions, said the district attorney's forensic science director.

The "cleaning" that took place at the New Orleans Police Department crime lab has been attributed largely to miscommunication and ignorance. However, the practice of specifically targeting untested rape kits for destruction has been criticized, by some, as an intentional effort to prevent private post-conviction testing that could result in an overturned conviction or even an exoneration.

To account for these postdiscovery influences, a record must be kept of the people, places, and processes that the evidence has endured since the time of recognition at the scene. This record is usually referred to as the *chain of custody*. Even though a reliable chain may be established, physical evidence may have been altered prior to or during its collection and examination. Unless the integrity of the evidence can be reliably established, and legitimate evidentiary influences accounted for, the creation of a chain of evidence does not by itself provide acceptable ground on which to build reliable forensic conclusions. It is, however, a good start, and without it evidence should not be considered sufficiently reliable for courtroom opinions.

CHAIN OF CUSTODY/CHAIN OF EVIDENCE

The chain of custody is the record of everyone who has controlled, taken custody of, or had contact with a particular item of evidence from its discovery to the present day. It has tremendous importance with respect to providing context for, and a record of, any scientific examinations. It also has considerable value with respect to establishing the origins of, and influences on, evidence presented in court.

For some items of evidence, a chain of custody may not be known or established prior to its recognition. Investigators may have to work hard in order to establish how it got where it was found. For other items, the chain of custody prior to recognition may be readily evident and undisputed. Accepting these limitations of the evidence, and working within them when interpreting the elements of the crime, is part of the normal investigative and forensic process.

The official chain of custody typically begins with the person who first found the item of evidence. In this way, potential evidence transfer, evidence contamination, and evidence loss are tracked. Because of the increase in potential influences on the evidence, the fewer people handling the evidence, the better. As described in O'Hara (1970, p. 69):

> The number of persons who handle evidence between the time of commission of the alleged offense and the ultimate disposition of the case should be kept at a minimum. Each transfer of the evidence should be receipted. It is the responsibility of each transferee to insure that the evidence is accounted for during the time that it is in his possession, that it is properly protected, and that there is a record of the names of the persons from whom he received it and to whom he delivered it, together with the time and date of such receipt and delivery.

O'Hara gives more specific instructions regarding the creation of the chain (p. 78):

> Evidence should be properly marked or labeled for identification as it is collected or as soon as practicable thereafter. The importance of this procedure becomes apparent when consideration is given to the fact that the investigator may be called to the witness stand many months after the commission of the offense to identify an object in evidence which he collected at the time of offense. Indeed, defense counsel may require that the complete chain of custody be established, in which case each person who handled the evidence may be called to identify the object.

Photographs and measurements of the evidence that document its condition and location in the crime scene are also an important and commonly overlooked part of the chain of custody. Those looking for doubt can, in some cases, legitimately suggest weakness in a chain of custody that does not have this level of documentation.

As already shown, not everyone enthusiastically participates in the process of rendering a solid chain of evidence. Moreover, even when it is considered to be of importance, there is no guarantee that those responsible will know what they are doing. It is therefore not uncommon for the various chains of custody in a given case to be inconsistent, weak, and, for some items, nonexistent.

Consider the following case example of a chain of custody in utter confusion, from evidence to interviews, and the consequences:

THE CASE OF JAMIE PENICH

In 2001, Jamie Penich, a 21-year-old junior majoring in anthropology at the University of Pittsburgh, was in Korea studying at Kiem Yung University for a semester. Penich and seven other students had traveled to Seoul for a weekend of sightseeing. Some of them, including Penich, went dancing and drinking at Nickleby's, an expatriate bar frequented by U.S. military in Seoul's party district, to celebrate St. Patrick's Day.

Penich was found dead in her hotel room at approximately 8 A.M. on March 18, 2001. Though initial police reports indicated she was strangled, her autopsy report determined that she had been stomped to death. There were imprints of jogging shoes on her chest, and she had sustained extensive head, neck, and facial injuries. U.S. Army CID became involved because they suspected a U.S. soldier had committed the crime. They investigated the scene, the suspects, and the evidence.

As reported in *Stars & Stripes* (Kirk, 2001),

[Forensic scientist Brent] Turvey criticized the evidence collection and investigation methods in the Penich case, citing gathering up garments from the crime scene and placing them all in the same container as irregular.

Korean police brought two pieces of evidence collected at the crime scene—a black jacket and a brown pullover—to a lab in the same bag, Korean forensic officials said. Turvey said that evidence should not have been clumped together.

"Every item of clothing—every shoe, every sock—should have its own bag," Turvey said. "You should never ever put two items in the same bag."

Penich's roommate in the hotel said the jacket completely covered Penich's face when she found the body. Two other witnesses said they remember Penich's face was covered with what they believed to be her black jacket.

The jacket is not seen over Penich's head in numerous crime scene photos shared with *Stars and Stripes*, or in the autopsy report. In some photos, the jacket is seen near Penich's body.

. . .

Another area of contention is whether Penich was sexually assaulted or had intimate relations with her attacker.

Lee Won-tae, chief medical examiner and director of the Department of Forensic Medicine in Seoul, said he's worked more than 800 murder cases. He said that evidence collection hinges on the quality of the detective.

"Sometimes, they [investigators] are very highly qualified," Lee said. He said he considers the Yongsan Police Department officials good at collecting evidence.

Lee said his lab was unable to get a DNA fingerprint from semen samples on two pairs of underwear belonging to The Netherlands woman and Penich, respectively. During the autopsy, investigators also took a sample from Penich's body that tested positive for semen.

Lee said it was not unusual to not recover DNA. Turvey agreed, but said it could be a case of inexperience.

"I would say that's very possible [to not get DNA results] if the lab doesn't have experience doing that kind of test," Turvey said. "Another lab with more experience may be able to find something."

Turvey also questioned the role of U.S. investigators.

One soldier originally suspected in the murder told *Stars and Stripes* that U.S. Army Criminal Investigation Command, known as CID, agents came to his barracks room to check his clothing. They donned goggles, turned off the room lights, and scanned the clothes with a special light, he said.

"They told me it was to see if [my clothes] had any body fluids, traces of blood," he said.

The agents found nothing, the soldier said, and allowed him to keep his clothes.

"This is ridiculous and speaks to the horrible level of training in forensic science on the part of CID investigators," Turvey said. "The clothes should simply have been taken and submitted to a lab for analysis. Investigators should not be doing that kind of thing themselves."

Marc A. Raimondi, chief of public affairs for CID in Virginia, said CID agents are well trained.

"We are better trained than any federal law enforcement agency in the country," he said.

According to Raimondi, agents routinely use a Polilight[4] to find biological fluids and stains. The light uses selected wavelengths across the visible spectrum to fluoresce or identify stains or latent fingerprints for analysis.

Turvey said that method might not show all traces of fluids that could be present. Investigators can use other methods to detect blood, and clothes can be analyzed for fibers, he said. "There are so many things they can do with evidence," Turvey said. The soldier said CID agents returned a few weeks later to confiscate his clothing.

It is flawed when evidence is not collected immediately and retained, Turvey said. Delaying evidence collection makes analysis more problematic, he said.

[4] A Polilight is a full-spectrum light source that has narrow band filters and it can be dialed to very small wavelengths. This is a good tool for finding the presence of semen, saliva, vaginal secretions, and other bodily fluid stains. It also shows fibers very well. Most CSIs will not have access to this piece of equipment.

Eventually, the FBI reinterviewed 20-year-old Kenzi Snider, a fellow student and traveling companion who had befriended Jamie Penich during their time together at Kiem Yung University. She was back in the United States at the time. FBI agents claim that Snider ultimately confessed to the crime during their interview; however, that interview was not recorded (Arnold, 2002).

[FBI Special Agent Mark] Divittis and [U.S. Army Criminal Investigations Division Agent Mark] Mansfield conducted the two-day interview [of Snider] along with another federal investigator.

The inability to answer even one of these questions represents a broken link in the chain of evidence and may call into question subsequent interpretations. The answers to these begin to address the issue of evidence dynamics, and subsequently a clearer picture of influences is established. As a result, the reconstructionist may learn whether and when uncertainty, equivocation, or reexamination are warranted.

CONCLUSION

The failure to consider *evidence dynamics* as a part of any crime reconstruction process has the potential to provide for misinterpretations of physical evidence and inaccurate or incomplete interpretations. Any subsequent use of the reconstruction would have a diminished foundation and relevance, compounding the harm in legal, investigative, and research venues. It is the responsibility of forensic scientists to perform reconstructions of the circumstances and behaviors involved in a crime with diligence, and to be aware of the possibility of *evidence dynamics*, in order that their interpretations reflect the most informed and accurate rendering of the evidence. Evidence dynamics do not always preclude a meaningful reconstruction, but reconstruction interpretations are questionable when evidence dynamics have been ignored.

REFERENCES

Alonzo-Dunsmoor, M. "2 Officers Botched Hundreds of Cases," *The Arizona Republic,* July 25, 2005.

Armstrong, K., and Mills, S. "DNA Sample Error Puts Case on Line, Lab on Spot," *Chicago Tribune,* July 27, 1999.

Arnold, L. "Snider Discusses Confession to Killing: Hearing to Decide if Former MU Student Will Be Tried for Murder," *The Herald-Dispatch,* October 3, 2002.

Bromwich, M. R. *Third Report of the Independent Investigator for the Houston Police Department Crime Laboratory and Property Room,* June 30, 2005.

Cella, M. "Police 'Blew It' in Missing Levy Bone; Ramsey Begins Review of Search," *The Washington Times,* June 8, 2002.

Chanen, D., and Collins, T. "Sergeant Raises Questions about Site of Slayings," *Minneapolis Star Tribune,* March 17, 2005.

Chisum, W. J., and Turvey, B. "Evidence Dynamics: Locard's Exchange Principle & Crime Reconstruction," *Journal of Behavioral Profiling,* 1(1), January 2000.

Cwiklik, C. "An Evaluation of the Significance of Transfers of Debris: Criteria for Association and Exclusion," *Journal of Forensic Sciences,* 44(6):1136–1150, 1999.

Hepp, R. "Investigator Faces 20 Years in Tampering," *Newark Star Ledger,* March 19, 2005.

Jae-Suk, Y. "Kenzi Snider Acquitted in Murder of Jamie Lynn Penich," *Associated Press,* June 19, 2003.

Kirk, J. "U.S. Forensic Scientist Says Investigation of Student's Murder Was Flawed," *Stars & Stripes*, May 24, 2001.

Knight, B. *Forensic Pathology.* (2nd ed.). Oxford: Oxford University Press, 1996.

Lee, H. (Ed.) *Physical Evidence.* Enfield, CT: Magnani & McCormick, 1995.

O'Hara, C. *Fundamentals of Criminal Investigation.* (2nd ed.). Springfield, IL: Charles C Thomas, 1970.

Perlstein, M. "Evidence Purge Likely to Haunt NOPD: Report Suggests Fallout Will Last for Years," *New Orleans Times-Picayune*, January 11, 2004.

"Police Accidentally Destroy DNA Samples," *San Diego Union Tribune*, July 31, 2002.

"Police Blotter: Burglary," *The Palm Beach Post*, November 24, 2004.

Rosinski, J. "Heavy Rains Wash Away Roads, Police Evidence," *Boston Herald*, April 2, 2004.

Silver, J. D. "Sloppy Police Work Charged Evidence Moved, Missing in Teen Death, Wecht Says," *Pittsburgh Post-Gazette*, May 14, 2003.

Svensson, A., and Wendel, O. *Techniques of Crime Scene Investigation.* (2nd ed.). London: Elsevier, 1974.

Turvey, B. *Criminal Profiling: An Introduction to Behavioral Evidence Analysis.* (2nd ed.). London: Elsevier, 2002.

"WSP Crime Labs Slip Up," *Spokesman-Review*, July 23, 2004.

Zerwick, P. "Tainted Evidence? Appeal in 1993 Capital Case Questions Blood Tests on a Mixed Bag of Clothing," *Winston-Salem Journal*, August 29, 2005.

CHAPTER 7

TRACE EVIDENCE IN CRIME RECONSTRUCTION

John I. Thornton, PhD and Donna Kimmel-Lake

Etiam capillus unus habet umbram. ~ Even a single hair has a shadow.
—Publilius Syrus (~100 BC)

The reconstruction of a crime may proceed along several lines. Living witnesses may provide an account of what took place at the time the crime occurred. Surveillance cameras may have captured the action on tape or digital media. But witnesses need not be verbal, human, or even living. Witnesses may be dead and therefore uncommunicative, and witnesses may take on countless inanimate forms. The fundamental premise is that a criminal act generates a record of itself, and it is the responsibility of the reconstructionist to interpret it.

Truly there is no limitation as to what might constitute the physical evidence that helps us to tell the story of what happened at the time of the crime. Anything, tangible or intangible, can be physical evidence. In one case the physical evidence may be as large as a truck, or it may be so small that a microscope is needed to see it. In another case it may be as offensive as the odor of a decaying body, or it may be as subtle as a faint whiff of gasoline lingering after a fire.

For two reasons, the small bits of evidence may have significance beyond that which is commensurate with their size. First, their occurrence may arise from processes that describe the activities that generated them. Fracture, broadcasting of fine particles, and adhesion of foreign particles come to mind. Second, their size makes them inconspicuous. Any actor in the drama that we will call a crime is likely to be oblivious to the existence of this minute evidence, and even if he or she were aware, would be more or less powerless to do anything about it. These traces may provide information by means of which the factual circumstances at the time the crime occurred may be established. We call these materials *trace evidence*. It is an extremely broad category of physical evidence.

No one has stated the situation better than Dr. Paul Kirk, one of the principal forensic scientists of the 20th century. Turvey, in his introductory chapter to this work, commented on Kirk's development of the significance of physical evidence, but some amplification of Kirk's statements is appropriate here. Kirk (1953, p. 4) wrote:

> However careful a criminal may be to avoid being seen or heard, he will inevitably defeat his purpose unless he can also control his every act and movement so as to prevent mutual contamination with his environment, which may serve to identify him. The criminal's every act must be thoroughly reasoned in advance and every contact guarded. Such restraint demands complete mental control. The very fear of detection, which must almost always be present, will make such control next to impossible. Wherever he steps, whatever he touches, whatever he leaves—even unconsciously—will serve as silent evidence against him. Not only his fingerprints and his shoeprints, but also his hair, the fibers from his clothes, the glass he breaks, the tool mark he leaves, the paint he scratches, the blood or semen that he deposits or collects—all these and more bear mute witness against him. This is evidence that does not forget. It is not confused by the excitement of the moment. It is not absent because human witnesses are. Physical evidence cannot be wrong; it cannot perjure itself; it cannot be wholly absent. Only in its interpretation can there be error. Only human failure to find, study, and understand it can diminish its value.

Kirk's words hold as true today as they did when they were first written, more than a half-century ago. We might add, though, that it is not just the criminal that leaves traces; the evidence may tell us how victims, witnesses, medical personnel, and police officers have influenced the scene (see Chapter 6).

Trace evidence has the potential of great utility in establishing associations that lead to a reconstruction, but only if the evidence is recognized and properly interpreted. If it is not acknowledged and not recognized, it is lost just as surely as if it had never existed. Furthermore, if it is not interpreted correctly, it will do violence to any effort to reconstruct the crime. One may easily argue that evidence that is misinterpreted is worse than no evidence at all.

Another caveat is appropriate here as well. Although trace evidence may assist enormously in the reconstruction of crime, it may not provide answers that will result in a complete reconstruction. Any reconstruction, whether based on trace evidence or any other type of evidence, is much like looking at a tapestry from the back side. The essence of the scene may indeed be understood in general terms. In some instances, it may be understood in definitive terms. In other instances, the evidence may simply not provide the clarity that we would need for a full reconstruction. We may not be able to reconstruct every nuance and movement from an event. In these instances, the reconstructionist must take pains to explain why isolated elements of the reconstruction cannot legitimately be bridged. If a reconstruction is overextended and cannot be supported when subjected to severe scrutiny, a miscarriage of justice may occur. At the very least, the trust and confidence placed in the reconstructionist will be diminished.

It is possible to develop an array of common types of trace evidence, and we will do so eventually. But it cannot be stressed enough that any such list is necessarily open-ended. Exigencies of a given case may vault an exceedingly obscure type of evidence into a position of prominence. Indeed, the more obscure the evidence, the greater may be its probative value. The other side of this coin, however, is that a rarely encountered form of evidence may not be recognized for what it is and what it may signify, or the crime reconstructionist may not know how to deal with it or, worse, may misinterpret it. Ignorance, or the type of bias resulting from parochial beliefs, may be at play.

It is not practical to discuss here the unique, once-in-a-lifetime presentations of rare forms of trace evidence, other than to say that they do exist. Subsequently, the reconstructionist must exercise constant vigilance and then be willing to adapt. Examples? Certainly. Two will suffice, both from actual cases. In the first case, the crime scene was a "dump site." A body was found in a remote location. There was no indication that the victim was killed there. Rather, it seemed much more likely that the victim was killed elsewhere and transported to the scene. A few dry pine needles on the body were noted, but pine trees and pine needles were not otherwise present at the scene. A suspect was developed, and in the trunk of his car a number of dry pine needles were found. Under a stereoscopic microscope, an actual physical match was established between the fracture edges of portions of needles from the body and from the vehicle trunk. The significance of this to the case is patent. The effort that this must have required on the part of the analyst was necessarily staggering, but it paid off.

In another case, a roof-top burglary of a supermarket occurred. To avoid breaking a window or door and thereby tripping an alarm, the burglars chopped a hole in the roof and lowered themselves down on a rope. In the process, a jar of peanut butter was broken, and one of the burglars stepped in the peanut butter. The crime scene investigator knew this because of a poorly defined shoe impression in the remaining peanut butter. Later the same night, several suspects were stopped. One of them had some brown material smeared on the bottom of his shoe. Peanut butter? Well, maybe. If it were peanut butter, this would be an excellent form of associative evidence. The investigator could probably taste it, but it probably is not a very good idea to taste every brown material on the bottom of every shoe. At this point, the case became a research project. What, besides peanuts, makes something peanut butter? What are the appropriate protocols for the analysis of peanut butter? The analyst must now go to the library and learn about peanut butter—its composition and profitable avenues of analysis.

The point here is that many trace evidence cases may devolve into a full-blown research project. Neither the investigator in the field nor the analyst in the laboratory can be expected to know much about peanut butter, and looking under "p" for peanut butter in the index of a textbook on physical evidence is not going to help, either. In instances such as this, the reconstructionist must be prepared to embark on a campaign to understand the evidence. The effort may appear daunting, and it may well be formidable, but that is in fact what the evidence cries out for, and that is in fact what the evidence deserves. Other examples of how trace evidence may provide essential information in crime reconstruction may be found in Petraco (1986), and trace evidence in general has been reviewed by DeForest (2001). In many instances, it is the trace evidence, rather than the dramatic DNA analysis or the noble firearms evidence, that brings coherency to the reconstruction and allows the case to be fully understood. In the broad landscape of physical evidence, it is the trace evidence that provides the poetry.

But what of the more prosaic forms of trace evidence? Although some overlap may occur, trace evidence tends either to associate a person with a crime scene or to tell us what happened. Examples of the former are a fingerprint or the DNA extracted from a spatter of the victim's blood on the clothing of a suspect. An example of the latter is a trail of blood from one location to the place where the victim collapsed. The evidence may occasionally serve both functions, and it is prudent not to make too much of a distinction between the two. Some cases are of the "whodunit" variety, whereas others are more properly the "howdunit" type. Both are the subject of the crime reconstruction.

A number of physical evidence types represent the bulk of trace evidence and consequently will be discussed here. As Turvey and Chisum emphasized in the Preface, this is not a textbook on the technical mechanics of processing crime scenes or of procedures carried out in the forensic laboratory. But it is essential, however, that any person engaged in any aspect of crime reconstruction appreciate what trace evidence can contribute to the reconstruction process and what associations can be made. Commonly encountered forms of trace evidence include

- Fingerprints
- Blood and semen

- Hair
- Fibers
- Paint
- Glass
- Soil
- Dust
- Footwear and tire tracks
- Gunshot residue
- Tool marks
- Projectile wipes
- Explosive residue
- Automobile light "on-or-off"

For anyone attempting crime reconstruction, this array of trace evidence categories should represent a portion of the furniture of their consciousness. It should be understood that although any enumeration of trace evidence categories is bound to be arbitrary, a convention of sorts does exist. Tire tracks are often excluded from such a list and are viewed as something other than trace evidence, despite the undeniable fact that they are indeed evidence, and they may exist as only a trace. Many would exclude fingerprints, preferring that they be placed in a separate category. But then if we were to live in a Spanish-speaking country, we would speak of *huellas dactilar*, finger "traces."

FINGERPRINTS

Although now challenged by DNA typing, fingerprints—friction ridge identification, actually, to include palm prints and foot sole prints—have historically been considered as the ultimate in personal identification. We refer to the "fingerprint region" of an infrared spectrum—that is, the portion of the spectrum that possesses the greatest amount of individuality and character. Until recently, the results of DNA typing were referred to as a "DNA fingerprint."

Fingerprints can establish with virtual certainty that (1) a person was present at the crime scene, (2) had previously touched something that was left at the crime scene, or (3) touched something that was originally at the crime scene as established by other means but was removed and found elsewhere. Any or all of these possibilities may have such impact on a crime reconstruction as to eclipse other considerations.

A fingerprint identification may not put all issues to rest, however. Legitimate prior access to the scene or to an object may be relevant. If the fingerprint is visible, and in blood, it may establish that the deposition of the fingerprint was contemporaneous with the crime. If the fingerprint is a latent print, however, the question of persistence and durability may enter into the discussion. Moreover, a latent fingerprint on a porous surface, such as paper, will persist indefinitely—for years. Assuming that a sufficient amount of material to constitute a fingerprint was deposited to begin with, a latent fingerprint on a nonporous surface, such as glass or metal, will last more than a year if protected from light and air exchange. On the other hand, one night's dew on a nonporous surface may effectively destroy a latent print.

Although fingerprints are an excellent means of personal identification, they may be the subject of unrealistic expectations on the part of the lay public and even on the part of some police investigators. It is very difficult to develop good fingerprints on latex rubber gloves, a firearm whose surface is already oily, or a cement brick. Furthermore, the presence of a fingerprint is conclusive evidence of contact, but the absence of a fingerprint is not conclusive evidence that contact has not taken place. While on this subject, we may engage in a short discursion that is relevant not only to fingerprints but also to many other evidence categories. A cliché that is developing some currency in our language and culture, and thereby finding its way into some courtrooms, is that "absence of evidence is not evidence of absence." As a sound bite, this has a nice ring to it. It is often uttered in a tone of authority, as if the validity is beyond cavil. In truth, it depends mightily on the circumstances. If one were to wake up in a mountain cabin and see that there were no tracks in the snow outside, one would reasonably conclude that a bear had not paid a visit during the night. In this instance, an absence of evidence would clearly be evidence of absence.

In the future, DNA typing may play a role in fingerprint evidence. In the United States, there has been little attempt to subject fingerprints to DNA extraction techniques for the purposes of typing. In the United Kingdom, however, this approach has been used for several years with considerable success. If epithelial cells from the finger are deposited on a surface along with the oils and perspiration that have historically been sought, DNA may be potentially recovered and typed. The work in the United Kingdom has shown that five to 20 cells are sufficient for a "low copy number" DNA typing. (By way of comparison, nuclear DNA typing of the sort employed for blood and semen analysis requires on the order of 150 to 160 cells.) The appeal of DNA typing in fingerprint work is that it may be applicable to the numerous instances in which a latent fingerprint has insufficient clarity to enable an identification to be made by conventional means.

BLOOD AND SEMEN

Blood and semen have special significance because they occur in crimes of particular gravity. DNA typing of blood and semen has developed, with respect to both sensitivity and specificity, to the point that a few microliters is capable of establishing the identity of the donor to a practical certainty that often satisfies the "who" aspect of a crime reconstruction (Rudin and Inman, 2002).

In addition, the interpretation of the nature, pattern, and distribution of bloodstains often satisfies the "how" aspect. Bloodstain pattern interpretation has practically evolved into a science of its own. Blood in flight obeys very definite laws of physics, and a bloodstain pattern may indicate the circumstances in which the blood was shed. Drops of blood accelerated by gravity alone (i.e., a "trail" of bloodstains) can be distinguished from the spatter caused by blunt force impact or the fine mist caused by a gunshot discharge. Considerations of distance and directionality may establish the relative positions of victim and assailant. Smears may indicate contact of a bloodstained object with other parts of the scene.

Techniques also exist for the detection of exceedingly small amounts of blood, such as might be expected if an effort has been made to clean up a crime scene. Chemical tests can show blood that has been diluted to the extent, roughly, of a shot glass of blood in a railroad tank car of water, and blood can be demonstrated on cotton clothing that has gone through a normal machine washing with detergent (although the DNA typing may not be possible under such extreme circumstances, nor may one be able to determine whether or not it is human blood as opposed to animal blood). Also, it is not uncommon to find bloody mop swipes or bloody shoeprints at scenes where "cleanup" has taken place.

HAIR

Hair is commonly encountered in crimes of violence because it is rather easily lost by forceful contact. It will persist at the scene indefinitely, and it may provide information as to the following:

1. Animal or human hair? If animal, the species may be determined. Closely related species, such as dog and wolf, may not be distinguished, however.
2. Forcefully pulled out or otherwise? The "otherwise" may be the loss of the hair with little forceful removal or the natural loss of the hair with essentially no force (i.e., the hair has just "fallen out" on its own accord). If the hair has been forcefully removed and has a tag of tissue remaining on the root sheath, it may

be successfully characterized by means of nuclear DNA, with the splendid discrimination provided by that type of analysis.

3. Similarity with respect to color, length, and microscopic features? This rests partly on commonsense considerations. A thick, black, curly hair an inch long will not have originated from a person with 18-inch long blond hair. From the microscopic appearance of a hair, it may be possible to eliminate a particular person as having given up the hair, but it is never possible from a microscopic examination to unequivocally identify a person. The most that can be said is that the evidence hair is "consistent with" having originated from a particular person. This statement would need to be followed by a qualifier in which it was stressed that the hair would be consistent with having originated from many other people as well. It may be possible in some instances to determine the race of the donor of the hair and whether the hair is from the scalp or pubic area. This, however, is somewhat treacherous, and most analysts approach this with considerable diffidence.

4. Did the hair originate from a particular person? Hair may be subjected to the type of analysis referred to as mitochondrial DNA analysis. This is a different type of analysis than the DNA analysis of blood and semen (nuclear DNA). The mitochondrial genome is much smaller than that displayed by nuclear DNA, and consequently the number of polymorphisms available for discrimination between individuals is much smaller. Mitochondrial DNA is conveyed by the maternal parent and, although delivering useful information, does not provide the awesome statistics given by DNA analysis of blood and semen. Additionally, it cannot distinguish between persons in the same maternal lineage. Despite certain shortcomings, however, mitochondrial DNA is now considered to be the best method for addressing the issue of whether an evidence hair came from a particular person.

FIBERS

Fiber transfer is often a good indicator of contact. They are easily lost from a parent garment (or cordage), because of static electric charge they tend to remain in place wherever they come to rest, and they will persist in a given location for a long period of time. Associations of garments, typically framed as victim's clothing and suspect's clothing, may be established by appropriate laboratory testing. Information may be provided as to the following:

1. Type of fiber? Microscopic examination of a fiber will establish whether the fiber is natural (e.g., cotton), animal (e.g., wool), or synthetic (e.g., nylon, polyester, or acrylic). Instrumental techniques exist for the analysis of a single

fiber to assist in the identification of synthetic fibers. Principal among these is Fourier transform infrared microspectrophotometry (FTIR). (This is an expressive word; "metry" pertains to measurement, "photo" to light, "spectro" to appearance, and "micro" in this context means small. So microspectrophotometry is a means of measuring the appearance of light on small specimens. Infrared microspectrophotometry is applicable to the analysis of a wide range of organic trace evidence categories.)

2. Did the fiber originate from a particular source? This question can never be answered unequivocally, excepting in the obvious case in which a physical match can be established between the torn edges of shards of cloth. But the color of the fiber may be compared, as can the type and diameter of the fiber, the presence or absence of any delusterants applied to the fiber, and the chemical nature of any dyes used to color the fiber.

PAINT

Traces of paint may assist in establishing that contact has taken place between a painted source and some other. If the other object is painted as well, the possibility exists of a cross-transfer of paint in both directions. The presiding question, generally, is whether a given sample of paint originated from a given object. Some instances may arise in which a physical match can be established between a paint chip and the location on the object from which the fragment was lost. This would constitute unequivocal proof of the origin of the paint fragment.

Paint may also be assessed on the basis of color, number of layers, sequence of layers, relative thickness of layers, and chemical type. Instrumental techniques exist for dealing with microscopic fragments. The principal instrumental approach is FTIR, which is suited for the characterization of paint regarding chemical type (e.g., acrylic or alkyd) and to resolve certain specifics of polymer composition. Additionally, databases exist for automotive paint composition.

GLASS

Glass occurs at crime scenes with moderate frequency because it is so well represented in architectural situations (e.g., windows) and in beverage bottles, and because it is so easily broken. Minute particles of glass may be embedded in a suspect's shoes or may be found in his or her clothing. It is generally possible, even with trace particles, to determine whether the glass originated from ordinary soda-lime-silica window glass, tempered glass from commercial business establishments, tempered glass from automobile side or rear windows, beverage bottles, or automobile headlights.

Physical matches may be established with larger fragments, and microscopic fragments may be characterized on the basis of density, refractive index, dispersion, fluorescence, and elemental composition. A good match in physical and optical properties between evidence and exemplar will not conclusively prove that a fragment originated from a particular source, but it will permit the opinion that it is very likely.

SOIL

Soil from a crime scene may be compared with soil from a suspect's shoes or clothing, soil from the tires or undercarriage of a vehicle, or soil on a tool. Only a few milligrams of soil is needed to conduct a comparison of color, texture, mineral composition, and behavior in a density gradient. Microscopic examination may reveal distinctive pollen grains or highly characteristic diatoms. In these ways, various soils may be compared and even identified for the purpose of establishing possible origins.

DUST

Dust is composed principally of very finely divided mineral particles and vegetable material, although it may involve literally anything. Locard, in an early discussion of dust as trace evidence, stated broadly "All chemical substances may be met with" (1930, p. 280). In other words, one may expect to encounter anything when examining the minute particles that comprise dust. The uniqueness of dust, and hence its probative value as evidence, is determined by the uniqueness of parent materials from which the dust is derived, but it tends to be quite variable. Apart from minerals and vegetable and fabric fibers, frequently encountered materials include micrometer-sized particles of epithelial cell fragments, fragments of insect exoskeletons, fly ash from industrial applications, scales of butterflies, eggs of lower animals and insects, rubber, polymers, cosmetics, feathers, asphalt, tobacco, pollens, diatoms, and various food and spice products. A useful reference on the subject is that of Hess (1996).

Not everything that constitutes dust has significance. Cotton fibers, for example, are so ubiquitous that they are typically intentionally ignored. White and blue fibers, for example, tend to be found everywhere, but less common colors, such as purple and red, more readily generate interest. In many instances, dust may be only partly characterized as to be fundamental composition, but even a partial characterization of the dust under the microscope may establish a valuable association.

FOOTWEAR AND TIRE TRACKS

Shoeprints and tire tracks in deformable materials (e.g., mud, soft soil, clay, or snow) are typically considered as something other than trace evidence and are commonly dealt with by photography followed by casting techniques. Shoeprints and tire tracks in dust are not uncommon, however, and these are properly considered as a type of trace evidence. A comparison of the two-dimensional evidence print with test prints of footwear or tire tracks may establish an association, which in turn may facilitate a reconstruction of events. Databases exist for footwear and tire tread design.

GUNSHOT RESIDUE

Gunshot residues are of two types; both will qualify as trace evidence. We may speak of *uprange* and *downrange* residues.

Downrange residues consist of soot (at very close range) and fragments of unburned gunpowder (at close range). At a greater range, but still limited to just a few feet from the muzzle of the firearm, traces of lead, copper, and barium may be demonstrated by chemical tests performed on target materials. The size of the patterns made by soot, unburned gunpowder, and by lead and barium distributions may establish the distance separating the firearm from the target at the instant of discharge. Chemical and instrumental tests exist for confirmation of fragments of unburned gunpowder, and chemical tests exist for the demonstration of very fine particles of lead and barium.

Another type of gunshot residue consists of very small particles (<1 μm) of lead, barium, and antimony derived from the primer mixture of the ammunition. At the instant of discharge, these particles are dispersed around the firearm in a sphere roughly the diameter of a beach ball. Anything within that domain will likely be contaminated by these particles. The particles are so small that a scanning electron microscope is needed to visualize them. The scanning electron microscope used for this purpose is equipped with an energy-dispersive X-ray spectrometer to analyze candidate particles for the elements lead, barium, and antimony. If the hands of a subject are tested and show these particles, it is consistent with the following: (1) The person has recently discharged a firearm, (2) has been in close proximity (i.e., within the "beach ball" domain, although this is a conservative estimate) to a firearm when it was discharged, (3) has handled a

firearm or other object that was contaminated with gunshot residue particles from a previous or subsequent gunshot discharge, or (4) was in a room
for a long period of time in which a firearm had recently been discharged.

Uprange gunshot residue particles may be easily washed off skin surfaces
and do not persist on the skin of a living subject for more than a few hours.
On the hands of a dead subject, typically a suspected suicide, they will persist
for an extended period. On other surfaces, such as clothing, and in the
absence of strong movement that would dislodge them, they may persist
indefinitely.

TOOL MARKS

Striated tool marks (viz., scratches made by tools on a softer surface) may
be identified with certitude as having been made by a particular tool. As
described in Schell (2000):

> Pliers and screwdrivers, for instance, can be eliminated as having produced certain
> tool marks if those impressions are significantly larger or smaller than the width
> of the tools' grasping jaws or blades. Like the size and shape of a tool's working
> surface, the distance between a toothed instrument's teeth is considered a class
> characteristic. Individual characteristics, produced during manufacture and use,
> are unique to a particular tool or tool mark but can include noticeable defects such
> as missing or partial teeth, raised metal nodes or ridges, distinctive signs of wear
> or damage, or a broken tip or blade.

An area of only a few millimeters is typically sufficient to effect an identification when an evidence mark is compared microscopically with test marks
made with the suspected tool.

PROJECTILE WIPES

The penetration by bullets of walls, doors, and other more or less fixed
objects at a crime scene may be confirmed by metal wipe tests. Sensitive
chemical tests may be applied, even in the field, to confirm the presence of
lead from lead bullets or copper from jacketed bullets.

EXPLOSIVES RESIDUE

When explosive materials are detonated, much of the explosive chemical is
sundered. But small amounts of the parent material will survive. These
residues are broadcast widely and may be recovered from objects at the

scene. Although the amounts of material are small, typically they are sufficiently great to permit their identification by chemical and instrumental means.

In the past, the bulk of explosive cases have involved a very small number of explosive materials, typically smokeless gunpowder (nitrocellulose and nitroglycerine) or "black powder" mixtures of carbon, sulfur, and a strong oxidizer such as chlorate or nitrate, perhaps with aluminum "flash powder" incorporated into the mixture. With the increased incidence of state-supported terrorism, other more powerful explosives, such as dynamite, TNT, RDX, or Semtex, may be encountered with greater frequency. Analytical techniques are available for the detection of commercial and military explosives down to the microgram level.

AUTOMOBILE LIGHT "ON-OR-OFF" DETERMINATION

It has been stressed previously that depending on the circumstances, nearly anything can be physical evidence. Some types of trace evidence occupy a very narrow niche; they may be encountered rarely, but when they exist they may have a profound influence on the crime reconstruction. An example of a narrow niche type of trace evidence is vehicular light "on-or-off" determination. The reconstruction of a vehicular collision may incorporate a consideration of whether a vehicle's headlights (or taillights or turn signals) were operative at the time of the incident. A microscopic examination of the tungsten filaments, whether fractured or intact, may resolve this issue. A filament showing minute particles of glass, fused onto the filament by virtue of the heat of the energized filament, together with a glob of molten tungsten at the terminus of a fractured filament, would indicate that the light was on at the instant the glass envelope was shattered. An abrupt terminus would indicate that the filament was cold and that the light was not on. However, if the glass is not broken, the reconstructionist must make any determination of distortion or lack thereof with extreme caution. Noncollision events can cause distortion of the filament, whereas a collision may not.

TRACE EVIDENCE TRANSFER

When crime reconstruction was in its infancy, the French forensic scientist Edmond Locard introduced a concept that has had a profound influence on trace evidence interpretation. Much of the history of the Locard's Exchange Principle has been presented by Turvey in the introductory chapter to this text and will not be repeated here. But casual translation of

Locard's words has led to the generalization that every contact leaves a trace. That is not exactly what Locard said, but that is more or less how the doctrine has been passed down.

Consider the following: "The basis of this reconstruction and of contact traces was laid down by Locard (1928) (sic) who stated that when two objects come into contact *there is always a transference of material from each object on to the other* [italics added]" (Nicholls, 1956, p. 39), or "The one statement that perhaps most clearly epitomizes the pursuits of the [crime reconstructionist] is that made by Edmond Locard who said 'every contact leaves a trace.'... Certainly every contact leaves a trace; *it is up to us to detect it* [italics added]" (James et al., 1980, p. xv).

It should be recognized that Locard's doctrine is, and always has been, an assumption—not an immutable law drawn after a systematic study or experimentation. Current thought has crystallized to the point where the doctrine is viewed as a useful premise, but that any incorporation of the words "every" or "always" is inappropriate. Whereas an angora sweater can be expected to be a rich and productive source of fibers, a nylon monofilament windbreaker will not. The Locard Exchange Principle does not take into consideration issues of persistence; it does not incorporate any clear understanding of the time frame over which it may operate. In short, the doctrine may be operative in some situations, but as a practical, realistic matter it may not be applicable to others. Exchange may or may not take place, it may take place in only one direction, or it may have taken place but the exchange was not capable of being adequately followed. The phrase "every contact leaves a trace; it is up to us to detect it" may be modified to state "if a contact leaves a trace, it is up to us to detect it." That places the responsibility where it belongs and underscores the presiding issue in trace evidence: The recognition of the trace evidence is often more of a challenge than its subsequent processing. There can be no carping, however, that exchange often occurs across the contact boundary.

Consider the following: A person is struck on the head with a metal bat. Hair and blood are found on the bat. This is a one-directional transfer from the donor to the recipient, commensurate with a certain level of association. Consider then another person struck on the head with a wooden stick. Hair and blood are found on the stick, but the stick is fractured and a fragment of the stick is found embedded in the victim's scalp. This is a bidirectional transfer from two donors to two recipients, with a significantly augmented level of association.

Consider now the following: In a hit-and-run case, red paint is found on the victim's green car, and green paint is found on the suspect's car. In both instances, good accord is seen in the number of layers, the color of the layers, the sequence of the layers, the relative thickness of the layers, and the chemical type of paint. This is a bidirectional transfer with a great deal of developed information, resulting in a very strong level of association, and it should be reported that there is evidence of contact between the vehicles.

These examples illustrate that when there is a contact, and an exchange of evidence, the nature of that exchange is dependent on the materials and circumstances involved. It is the responsibility of the reconstructionist to account for this in his or her interpretations.

TRACE EVIDENCE INTERPRETATION IN CRIME RECONSTRUCTION

It is important to understand that a reconstruction does not proceed immediately from trace evidence. There is an intermediate step involved—that of association. The evidence proceeds to an association, and the association proceeds to a reconstruction. Interpretation is involved at each step, however. This process may take only an instant, as might occur in the recognition and interpretation of a blood trail from one location to the place where the victim was found, or it may take many days, as in the complex analysis of overlapping blood spatters. If the evidence is not interpreted properly, then any perceived associations will be faulty. If the associations are faulty, then the resultant reconstruction will be fallacious. As developed elsewhere in this text, there is a moral and professional responsibility on the part of the reconstructionist to interpret the evidence correctly. Subsequently, the consideration of evidence association must be tended with the utmost concern.

Crime reconstruction, it must be remembered, is not a simple or trivial endeavor. For any person wishing to pursue crime reconstruction, a useful (and humbling) exercise is to go into one's own kitchen and attempt to dispassionately reconstruct recent activities that have taken place there. This is not even a realistic reconstruction because the expected activities are familiar and to some extent known. A more challenging exercise would be to go into a neighbor's house and attempt the same thing. If these attempts at reconstruction are murky or incomplete, then how much reliance can be placed on a reconstruction in a totally unfamiliar milieu? It is a question that needs to be asked often.

In assessing the associations that may present themselves in the examination of trace evidence, whether it be in a kitchen or a crime scene or both, the work of Cwiklik (1999) stands out conspicuously with regard to placing trace transfers in clear perspective. Those involved in crime reconstruction would be well advised to become familiar with her work. Cwiklik does ratify, in a fundamental form, the Locard Exchange Principle. Using set theory as a guide, Cwiklik has proposed rational criteria for making decisions concerning the significance of trace evidence. The criteria proposed, which have been accepted by most people working in the area of trace evidence, assist in establishing contact based on corresponding sets of trace particles, for excluding contact in the absence of corresponding sets of particles, and for the recognition of instances in which prudence argues for refraining from making either an association or an exclusion. Unique in discussions in the forensic science literature of trace evidence transfer is Cwiklik's treatment of the extended array of conditional possibilities that may apply to a given situation. These include situations in which trace evidence may have been lost since the initial contact, or the possibility of secondary transfer of evidence to an object which then transfers a portion of that evidence to yet another object. Cwiklik is also the first to suggest that multiple criteria be applied simultaneously to the assessment of association, as opposed to one or two criteria applied separately or sequentially.

Cwiklik's work is particularly relevant to considerations of association and their liaison with reconstruction conclusions. She points out the nuances that are at play. With respect to validity, isolated associations may themselves be of various strengths. When compounded, or when combined with investigative and other facts of a case, a rational mind may find them relevant and convincing. Reconstruction, as the next step, involves a manipulation of those associations, with each association accompanied by its own level of certainty or uncertainty. Often, the emphasis in reconstruction is not on the strength of the conclusion as expressed by the reconstructionist but, rather, its validity.

Suffice it to say that reconstructionists would do well to study Cwiklik's formative work.

TRACE EVIDENCE AND THE FUTURE

For all elegance and utility, trace evidence is experiencing a period of decline. Many of the techniques that were originally developed to deal with trace evidence analysis came into being in connection with burglary and other crimes against property—offenses that are not currently investigated as aggressively as in the past. Many investigative agencies have channeled nearly all of their investigative efforts into crimes against the person, with homicide and sexual assault cases dominating their investigative tapestry. When blood and semen evidence exists, trace evidence is often given a subordinate role in the investigation. Although this is understandable, given the capability of DNA to discriminate among individuals, the skill inventories required for trace evidence analysis are forced into senescence. Some trace evidence categories will be encountered only rarely, whereas at the same time full competency in the identification of, for example, woods or pollen or soil minerals, requires years of study. Increasingly, training in trace evidence analysis has lost momentum. In short, trace evidence, for all its value and effectiveness, is not in vogue. This is unfortunate, given the fact that frequently it is the trace evidence that brings coherency to the physical evidence in a particular case.

It is hoped that the eclipsing of trace evidence by DNA typing is a short-term adjustment. Trace evidence will continue to have a future, but only if it is given the respect, and support, that it legitimately deserves. This is a challenge to both up-and-coming reconstructionists and those who would seek to educate them.

REFERENCES

Cwiklik, C. An Evaluation of the Significance of Transfers of Debris: Criteria for Association and Exclusion. *Journal of Forensic Sciences*, 44(6):1136–1150, 1999.

DeForest, P. What is trace evidence. In B. Caddy (Ed.), *Forensic Examination of Glass and Paint*, New York: Taylor & Francis, 2001.

Hess, K. Forensics of environmental dust. In *Environmental Sampling for Unknowns*. Boca Raton, FL: CRC Press, 1996.

James, R., Meloan, C., and Saferstein, R. *Laboratory Manual for Criminalistics*. Englewood Cliffs, NJ: Prentice Hall, 1980.

Kirk, P. *Crime Investigation*. New York: Interscience, 1953.

Locard, E. The Analysis of Dust Traces, *American Journal of Police Science*, 1. 276–298, 1930.

Nicholls, L. *The Scientific Investigation of Crime*. London: Butterworth, 1956.

Petraco, N. Trace Evidence—The Invisible Witness, *Journal of Forensic Sciences*, 31(1): 321–328, 1986.

Rudin, N., and Inman, K. *An Introduction to Forensic DNA Analysis*. (2nd ed.). Boca Raton, FL: CRC Press, 2002.

Schell, S. Firearms and Toolmarks in the FBI Laboratory, Pt. 2, *Forensic Science Communications*, 2(2), Retrieved April 2, 2000, url: http://www.fbi.gov/hq/lab/fsc/backissu/april2000/schehl2.htm

CHAPTER 8

SHOOTING INCIDENT RECONSTRUCTION

Bruce R. Moran, BS

It's not what you look at that matters, it's what you see.
—Henry David Thoreau

This chapter discusses general concepts in the investigation of shooting incidents with an emphasis on the reconstruction of events that occur at such scenes using a comprehensive approach that includes pre- and post-shooting incident considerations. Considerations for the forensic scientist are numerous in shooting incident reconstruction but are not widely discussed in the literature. I know of no published attempts to gather these shooting incident reconstruction considerations within a single writing. To this end, I have attempted to organize the discussion into a chronological progression of considerations that include (1) a philosophy of critical thinking, (2) an introduction to various specific shooting incident/firearms-related phenomenon that offer reconstructive information integrated with other forms of physical evidence, (3) practical approaches to reconstructive techniques that can be applied during the direct investigation of shooting scenes and/or resolving reconstructive issues that inevitably arise after the fact, and (4) practical considerations gleaned from a review of sources from investigative and/or physical evidence prepared by various professionals in law enforcement and forensic science.

However, within the confines of a single chapter, detailed descriptions of specific methods and procedures associated with shooting incident reconstruction are not practical. Such a comprehensive treatment would easily fill the pages of a lengthy textbook. Therefore, emphasis is placed on introducing the reader to an overall approach to shooting incident investigation and reconstruction. This will facilitate expanded vision through critical thinking and questioning that will contribute to improved recognition of potential information garnered from shooting incidents. The ideas set forth in this chapter will better equip the reader to approach these investigations and thereby recognize pieces of the puzzle that might otherwise remain mute. They will also provide the best representation of such observations with regard to the application of the scientific method. This in turn will contribute to a more successful resolution to any shooting incident reconstruction.

SHOOTING INCIDENT RECONSTRUCTION—A PROCESS

Shooting incident reconstruction is the process of identifying specific events that have occurred during a shooting. It provides explanations of how those events happened through careful consideration of investigative information and its correlation with the physical evidence. The entire process is dependent on gathering information from a variety of investigative and physical evidence sources. Additionally, the process is cyclical in that as information becomes available, questions emerge, and these questions prompt investigation, research and/or analysis, and testing of possible solutions to resolve the problems that arise. The additional information obtained by this process will in turn prompt even more questions. The information is continually evaluated and the reconstruction of the incident evolves through a process of elimination as answers to these questions are provided. The end product of this process is (1) the elimination of events that are impossible, (2) consideration of events that are improbable but possible, and (3) an offering of events that are most probable and best supported by the evaluation of the evidence available. Ideally, all possible theories, or scenarios, will be eliminated except one. In the case of shooting incidents, the process can assist in identifying key elements such as the following:

- Number of participants involved
- Number and type of firearms involved
- The manner in which a firearm was fired
- The distance from which a firearm was fired
- The location, position, and orientation of a firearm at the moment of discharge
- Direction of projectile paths within a shooting scene
- The presence and type of any intervening objects struck during the flight of bullets fired
- Location(s), position(s), and orientation(s) of participants at the moment of any discharge(s)
- Sequence of shooting events that occurred

In reality, it is the exception rather than the rule that all elements of a shooting incident are completely reconstructed. For example, the flight of fired bullets within the confines of a building, their impact with intervening objects, and terminal penetration into a wall occur within a fraction of a second and are impossible to be seen visually. However, evidence of flights is in the form of bullet impact sites, ricochets, and bullet holes, and each bullet bears witness to this instant in time and can be readily observed, documented, and studied. These observations, correlated with known principles of physics and knowledge of bullet behavior, either previously established or determined through empirical experimentation under similar conditions, can be used to reconstruct the bullet path. Repeating this process in shooting scenes where multiple shots are fired allows the reconstructionist to indirectly record these moments in time. Although these brief moments by themselves are insufficient to resolve reconstructive questions, they can provide very useful clues when correlated with other sources of investigative information and/or physical evidence present at the scene.

In other cases, there may simply be a paucity of information available to confidently reconstruct certain segments within a shooting incident. These situations often result from a lack of meaningful physical evidence (i.e., either because it was not produced or because it was not recognized, documented, and collected), unreliable witnesses or participant information that cannot be resolved through the examination of physical evidence, and/or insufficient or poorly developed investigative information. Most commonly, it is possible to exclude some but not all accounts or theories, although at worst it may not be possible to corroborate or refute any witness or participant accounts or eliminate any theories offered. Sometimes the differences between these scenarios may be insignificant; sometimes they may be considerable. What is important is that the reconstructionist can only work within the limitations of the information at hand and the limitations of the reconstruction process. Within these limitations, the reconstruction process is an evolving event in that the opinion of the reconstructionist may be modified with the addition of new information; this is discussed in more detail in the following section. Ideally, it may be possible to reasonably eliminate all but one theory or account when sufficient information is gathered and properly interpreted. There are indeed rewarding times when all the physical evidence supports one particular account or explanation of a shooting incident and refutes all other theories.

The reconstructionist may depend on the following sources of information to assist him or her in forming conclusions:

- Direct examination of the shooting scene
- Crime scene reports, photos, and diagrams
- Investigative reports, including witness and suspect statements

- Physical evidence reports, including the examination of firearm-related evidence, blood pattern interpretation, footwear and tire track evidence, trace evidence, and toxicological findings
- Autopsy reports and diagrams of deceased participants
- Medical reports of injured participants
- The results of experiments specifically conducted to test possible solutions to questions and issues identified during the course of the shooting scene evaluation

An attempt to address these sources of information is included in this chapter.

Shooting incident reconstruction is most effective when a comprehensive approach is taken. This includes considerations of events before, during, and after the shooting incident. By following a comprehensive and thorough approach to assessing a shooting incident, examining physical evidence, and correlating it with other investigative information, it may even be possible to successfully resolve unanticipated questions or hypotheses that may develop.

The reader may be wondering at this point how to best educate oneself, and what experience or background might best serve as a backdrop for becoming an effective practitioner of crime scene reconstruction. It is the author's opinion that the most successful crime scene reconstructionist will require at minimum a general understanding of all forensic science disciplines and will have the ability to integrate a variety of information sources to accomplish reconstruction goals. As a result, reconstruction is typically left to the most experienced forensic scientists graced with a generalist background or the most experienced criminal investigators having a practical understanding and appreciation of the scientific method in resolving reconstruction issues.

The late Parker Bell, a criminalist and criminal defense attorney, stated in an article written on the topic of crime scene reconstruction (Bell, 1991, p. 740):

> It is the role of the criminalist to aid the trier of fact by giving it information about the physical evidence. Because the trier of fact is concerned with the ultimate issue of what happened, the information given by the criminalist which most closely answers this question is of most value.

Bell also expressed concern in that "one criticism that may be made of criminalists today—particularly in laboratories where criminalists specialize—is that they forget the goal of the system they serve" (p. 740). I share

Bell's concerns that in light of technical advancements in the field of forensic science and in our zeal to pursue a greater degree of professionalism, the profession has moved toward increased specialization that distances the reconstructionist from the opportunity to acquire the generalist background and the way of thinking that is vital to the success of any reconstructionist. As a result, there is an increased risk of reducing independent and innovative thinking in regard to conducting shooting incident reconstruction.

The generalist seems to be a vanishing breed, and if allowed to vanish, the "big picture thinking" and holistic approaches necessary to provide a comprehensive approach to reconstruction will fade. However, there is a small but persistent voice among the ranks of present-day practitioners who understand the need to swing back toward the generalist approach to some degree, before it is too late, and strike a more appropriate balance with the benefits of specialization. The balance is not to have generalists capable of doing everything in every forensic specialty but, rather, to have every specialist maintain an understanding of everything relevant to the problem that is being considered. We owe it to ourselves and to our profession to keep this risk of narrowly focused specialization in mind so that we can maintain the forensic sciences as applied sciences within a holistic context rather than do ourselves the disservice of allowing our profession to become lost in the minutia of specialization. This concern is magnified when considering the requirements to conduct the comprehensive tasks required by the reconstructionist.

APPLICATION OF THE SCIENTIFIC METHOD (A KEY ELEMENT IN THE RECONSTRUCTIVE PROCESS)

Before continuing, it is important to establish an all-important link between the process of shooting incident reconstruction and the practice of sound science using the scientific method. The degree of success of the former is ultimately dependent on the practice of the latter. The process of shooting reconstruction is ultimately concerned with the best determination of events that have taken place and the most reliable explanation of how they have occurred in a shooting incident. To arrive at this end, however, involves systematic thinking about a problem or problems associated with the incident being investigated and, if possible, solving them. This is addressed by answering questions developed to address the problem. The answer to these questions leads the reconstructionist to a solution or, in some cases, more than one solution to the problem. Frequently, the solution may be so basic that the reconstructionist who solves the problem may not have consciously followed a predetermined process for approaching it. However, in situations that are more complex, the requirement for a formal means of problem solving becomes an essential element in reaching solutions in an efficient and reliable manner. This is when the reconstructionist gets out the heavy lifting equipment of the scientific method necessary to address such problems.

If one is to become familiar with the scientific method, then a working understanding of the definition of science is in order. Lastrucci (1967, p. 6) defines science as "an objective, logical, and systematic method of analysis of phenomena, devised to permit the accumulation of reliable knowledge." So too is the goal of the reconstructionist by which the accumulation of reliable knowledge will be employed to answer questions in a shooting incident. Lastrucci also advises that "science is an intersubjective method; it is available to any interested and competent person; it is not the special province of a favored few" (p. 6). In other words, there is no requirement to be a "scientist" to employ a scientific approach to shooting reconstruction. Rather, the scope of the scientific method can be viewed as the entire range of human interest because "it is not the field of study but the type of problem posed that determines whether or not a scientific approach can be profitably employed" (p. 17).

The scientific method is nothing more than a formal process of problem solving. What distinguishes between the scientific method and science is that the former usually leads to the latter. The scientific method consists of (1) stating the problem, or what will be investigated; (2) gathering information about the problem; (3) forming a hypothesis that attempts to provide an explanation for the problem; (4) developing controlled experiments to test the hypothesis; (5) recording and analyzing data; (6) forming a conclusion about the validity of the hypothesis; and (7) if the hypothesis is proven false, forming a new hypothesis and repeating steps 4–6 (Grzybowski et al., 2003). I submit that the reader has likely informally employed the scientific method as a routine matter when solving everyday problems.

Traditionally, the evaluation process involved in general crime scene investigation and reconstruction is based on individual expertise built on training and experience. It is founded on formally developed scientific principles developed from basic research conducted in all the physical science disciplines. The crime scene investigator and reconstructionist are generally not concerned with the formal basis for how the scientific method is used to develop scientific theory employed within the multitude of these science disciplines. Rather, reconstructionists, while performing routine casework, are engaged in applied science. For example, reconstructionists concerned with shooting incident investigation routinely make use of such fields as physics, chemistry, microscopy, trigonometry, geometry, ballistics, and pathology during the course of their work. Tests and methods employed by the reconstructionist can be linked to these recognized scientific disciplines that have been well established using the scientific method. Borrowing from these disciplines, the practitioner addresses such questions (problems) as:

1. Was this cartridge case ejected from that gun?
2. Was the bullet that struck the decedent a result of a direct impact or from a ricochet off some intermediary target?
3. How far away was the shooter when the shot was fired?
4. Was the decedent in a defensive or offensive posture when the shot was received?

Finding solutions to these types of routine problems does not require classical "basic research" using the scientific method. This might lead one to think that we are not applying the scientific method when conducting this type of investigation. However, we are indeed applying the scientific method but, in the main, not in a formally structured way. On the other hand, physical evidence encountered in crime scenes readily lends itself to formal scientific investigation when it becomes necessary to employ it to resolve reconstructive problems (Moran and Murdock, 2003). Since this chapter is concerned with the investigation of shooting incidents, events that occur from the use and/or misuse of firearms offer some special and unique opportunities to formally apply the scientific method. In this regard, Haag and Haag (2004, p. 1) rather succinctly note that:

> because of the wide variety of firearms and ammunition types, the relatively predictable behavior of projectiles and firearms discharge products, the chemistry of many of these ammunition-related products and certain laws of physics may be utilized to evaluate the various accounts and theories of how an event took place. These phenomena are used to reconstruct such things as the sequence of events, the location of one or more impacts, etc.

Using an all-inclusive approach, the reconstructionist must first focus on the issues in the case and then consider any physical evidence within the context of those issues. This is simply accomplished by asking many questions before proceeding headlong into the investigation. Whether using the scientific method formally or informally, reconstructionists must first be practical in ascertaining the specific circumstances of the case. Second, they make systematic evaluations based on those circumstances by defining the important issues and questions. Third, they must determine what is known and what is in dispute, and they must ultimately design and test possible solutions to these questions based on the information obtained from these considerations. Indeed, physical evidence in shooting scene investigations is conducive to examination and the designing of tests to address solutions to such issues using the scientific method. It should be regarded as a cross-check with which to assess various solutions, theories, accounts, or scenarios that might be offered during the reconstructive process.

Perhaps the most important consideration in the reconstructive process is that the practitioner within this discipline should not set out to "prove" anything. Rather, he or she should provide a voice that best represents the significance of information gathered, observations made, and conclusions rendered within the tenets of sound science through the application of the scientific method. Within this framework, the reconstructionist must also be prepared to consider alternatives to the most probable solution or solutions and be willing to devise examinations and/or experiments to test these lesser possibilities. If one does not follow this principle, then one is not practicing the reconstruction process for the purpose in which it is intended.

CONSIDERATIONS DURING DIRECT INVESTIGATION OF THE SHOOTING INCIDENT

Getting first-hand knowledge of the shooting is most desirable. The reconstructionist should become involved in the investigation of a shooting incident scene at the earliest opportunity so that relevant issues or questions can be identified as early as possible to maximize the potential to recognize the reconstructive value of the physical evidence. This has great advantages to both the reconstructionist providing the service and the user agency in that observations will be made within the context of the entire scene and the significance of observations will be most fully realized by direct participation in the scene investigation.

The reconstructionist should approach the shooting scene investigation with "big picture" thinking that is not limited to the task directly in front of him or her. Information regarding the conduct of participants and incidents occurring prior to, during, and after the incident being investigated can add significant insight into the significance of potential evidence to be gathered at the scene and what experiments or testing will be conducted to resolve issues. This approach reduces "tunnel vision" when considering potential evidence encountered at the shooting incident scene. Additionally, any observations made, evidence recovered, and/or examinations conducted during this process should be sufficiently documented and supported. The work should be conducted and documented in such a manner that any interested party reviewing the work product of the reconstructionist will understand what was done and why the conclusions were reached. If they wish to repeat the work, they should reach the same conclusions.

PREINVESTIGATIVE CONSULTATION

Keeping in mind the categories of questions to be answered, a preinvestigative consultation should be conducted with investigators or officers who have the greatest knowledge of the entire incident to gather as much information as possible prior to processing the scene. Gathering as much information concerning the circumstances of the incident is highly desirable because it can help focus the investigation and/or alert the reconstructionist to key considerations and/or observations that may be overlooked if such inquiries are not made early on. It is important to keep in mind at this stage that personal bias, an inescapable trait that is inherent in all human endeavors, must be set aside. Accounts provided by participants in the shooting incident, witnesses, and even explanations or hypothesis offered by investigative personnel should not be assumed as accurate or erroneous. These accounts should simply be treated as information on which some crime scene investigation steps will be made. This practice should be equally applied throughout any information gathering conducted in later stages of the reconstructive process through the review of investigative reports, interviews, or statements offered by police officers, investigators, prosecutors, plaintiffs, defense attorneys, or the defendant(s).

Such inquiry should include any information that can be obtained about the conduct of participants and any known events that occurred prior to the incident. Has any explanation(s) of discharge(s) by shooting participants and/or witnesss been offered? This might include the location and/or positions of participants during the incident. Were the shooters and/or other participants stationary or moving during the incident? What was the manner in which the participant(s) held the firearm(s)? Was the firearm held in a normal shooting position or in an awkward orientation typical of "gangland"-style shooting postures? Was the shooter standing, kneeling, or lying down when operating the firearm? What was the approximate height of the firearm during its use? Was the shooter using a barricade to support the firearm during its operation? In what way was the firearm discharged? Did the shooter arm the firearm prior to discharging it? Were any safety mechanisms manipulated prior to or during operation of the firearm? Was the firearm fired in double action or single action? Were there any observed malfunctions or problems during use of the firearm? Was the firearm discharged by being dropped or during an observed struggle with another participant? What events occurred after the shooting incident, and what was the conduct of the participants involved during this time? Answers to these types of questions serve to provide a starting point from which the reconstructionist may begin an assessment of potential physical evidence that may either support or refute this source of information in the evolving process of reconstructing events at a shooting scene.

THE WALK-THROUGH

After as much information as possible is gathered concerning the circumstances of the incident, a careful walk-through of the shooting scene should be conducted with a minimal number of personnel to assess the scene, identify items of evidence, prioritize the processing of the scene, and establish an overall plan. Suggested personnel should be the investigating officer in charge of the scene (or person most familiar with the scene), the consulting forensic investigator/reconstructionist, and a photographer (to photographically record any areas that might potentially be disturbed by the walk-through process). At the conclusion of the walk-through, the investigating officer in charge and the forensic investigator/reconstructionist should establish a plan of priorities for processing the scene to address such issues as impending weather that might destroy or hamper documentation and collection of evidence, security issues with regard to high-traffic areas, the availability of daylight, and the establishment of a team or teams of investigative personnel to most effectively process the scene. If applicable, arrangements should be made for an aerial ladder truck to conduct overhead photography and/or aerial photographs to be taken at this time.

RECONSTRUCTION WITHOUT THE BENEFIT OF PERSONAL INVOLVEMENT IN THE ORIGINAL CRIME SCENE INVESTIGATION

Direct involvement in the investigation of an original shooting incident scene as outlined previously is the ideal situation for reconstructive purposes. Unfortunately, this opportunity is by far the exception rather than the rule. Often, reconstruction issues are an afterthought of the primary investigation. It is more than likely that the reconstructionist will be approached long after the fact to address such reconstructive issues. In this situation, the reconstructionist must initially rely on the information provided by others, including police officers, investigators, forensic scientists, prosecuting attorneys, and defense counsels. This information will likely be obtained through the review of crime scene reports, diagrams, photographs, investigative reports, documented interviews, and medical/pathological reports.

Information may be offered verbally in the form of theories by police officers, investigators, prosecutors, and defense attorneys. Although these offerings are made in good faith, as previously cautioned, they should be assumed as neither accurate nor erroneous. This approach should be conducted in the spirit of remaining as objective as possible and thereby minimizing the chance of any preconceived influence that could restrict the vision necessary to consider all possibilities no matter how seemingly absurd they might be. At some point during later stages of the reconstructive process when the reconstructionist has had an opportunity to evaluate these sources of information (and possibly conduct independent examinations or tests), there will be an opportunity to form one's own conclusions.

As with the initial walk-through and preinvestigative consultation conducted at a crime scene, information gathering should be obtained through verbal inquiry as well as review of written reports and other sources of documentation. Working blindly from written reports alone, in my experience, will often limit the effectiveness of the reconstructionist. I therefore spend much time on the phone consulting with key investigators and/or the assigned prosecuting attorney and/or defense attorney to supplement information gathered from these written records in an effort to obtain a clearer overall picture of the case. To this end, some excellent questions, as suggested by Haag and Haag (2004, p. 2), should be asked in the early stages of the reconstructive process:

Tell me about this case. What are the issues?

What do you believe happened?

What do any witnesses to the incident say happened?

Did the shooter provide an explanation?

What is and what is not in dispute in this case?

What are the competing hypotheses (theories)?

What does the autopsy report reveal? (medical records if a gunshot wound without a fatality)

What other evidence has been collected beyond that which has been submitted to the laboratory?

These types of questions serve to identify key issues in the case and thereby increase the potential for recognizing the significance of any physical evidence that might be available for evaluation and can be used to cross-check other sources of investigative information.

The following sections outline in more detail physical evidence considerations to introduce various specific shooting incident or firearms-related phenomenon that offer reconstructive information integrated with other forms of physical evidence, and other sources of investigative information that are encompassed within the reconstructive process.

THE FIREARM

Proper documentation of the condition of firearms recovered at the scene is critical to the shooting incident investigator. Subtle but important observations concerning the condition of the firearm and its use during the incident are easily lost forever if a thoughtless approach to the examination is conducted at the scene. Failure to make such observations may make the difference in being able to distinguish a homicide from a suicide, offensive versus defensive postures of shooting participants, potential mechanical problems or malfunctions of the firearm, evidence that might support an intentional versus unintentional discharge of the firearm, or whether the scene was staged. Firearms should be submitted to careful visual examination followed by close-up photography to document significant observations prior to handling them. Some suggested considerations regarding the firearm at the scene (within practical limits) and during laboratory examination are provided here.

PRELIMINARY CONSIDERATIONS

Any knowledge concerning the history of the firearm prior to and after the incident may provide relevant context during direct examination of the firearm at the scene and/or examination at the forensic laboratory. Such considerations should include how the firearm was normally stored and in what condition it was prior to the incident. For example, was the firearm previously cleaned and oiled, or was it in a dirty or rusty condition? Was a loaded magazine kept in the gun or stored separately? How was the gun loaded or typically prepared for use? What was the specific manufacturer(s) of ammunition used in the firearm (i.e., bullet type and weight)? What was the source of this ammunition and is it available for examination?

LOCATION AND POSITION OF THE FIREARM

The location and position of the firearm in the scene and its relationship to other items of evidence should be carefully considered and documented during the first stages of the investigation. Observations relative to the location and position of decedents in suicides, accidental deaths, and suspicious deaths may be especially critical to the successful resolution of investigations. Subtle but important observations that can mean the difference between a genuine suicide and the detection of a staged homicide, for example, can be irretrievably missed if proper attention is not paid to these considerations. Preparation of shooting scene diagrams that are supplemented with appropriate orientation photographs is paramount to recording observations. Furthermore, these are of great value in resolving questions or issues that may develop well after the immediate crime scene investigation is completed.

TRACE EVIDENCE CONSIDERATIONS

Trace evidence, because it is typically fragile and susceptible to change or loss during handling of the firearm, should be considered and documented prior to or as soon as it is practical during the examination of the firearm at the scene. If not practical, it should be documented and preserved on the firearm in such a manner that these materials may be collected during laboratory examination at a later time. Hair, blood, and tissue may be encountered on both the exterior and the interior surfaces of the firearm. The presence of this material not only provides potential associative evidence with the source of such material but also may provide valuable information concerning the distance from the victim that the firearm was fired. This is most notable in contact, near-contact, and other close-range shooting circumstances or in situations in which there is a struggle over control of a firearm. Interpretations of the patterns of these materials are often of greater importance than their mere presence alone. For example, high-velocity impact blood spatter patterns commonly associated with gunshots on the exterior of a firearm suggest a close-range shot (Fig. 8.1). Additionally, microdroplets of blood observed inside the muzzle of the barrel are indicative of contact or near-contact range shots. Transfer stains such as swiped, wiped, or specific patterns resembling the surface from which blood has originated can be indicative of how a firearm may have been handled during or after bloodshed has occurred.

The presence of finger and palm prints may also be encountered on external and internal surfaces of the firearm. This form of trace evidence also plays a dual role in the reconstructive process from both an associative standpoint to the source of such evidence and the orientation of such prints on the firearm (Fig. 8.2) in regard to how it may have been handled by the shooter and/or other participants of a shooting incident. For example, the presence of a palm print around the grip of a handgun may suggest the

Figure 8.1

High-velocity blood spatter documented on the face of the muzzle and along the sides of the barrel of this firearm provided significant support that the gun was in close vicinity to the decedent at the time the fatal shot was fired.

Figure 8.2

The location of this thumbprint on the back of the slide of this pistol is significant in that it is in the vicinity of the expected position for pulling back the slide to arm the weapon or possibly to operate the safety lever just below it.

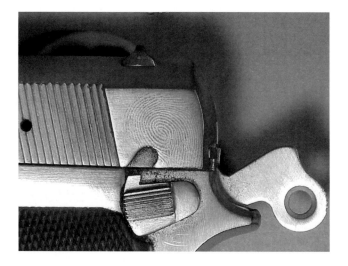

identity of the operator of the firearm, whereas the presence of fingerprints of the decedent oriented backwards on the barrel of the firearm may support statements by the shooter of the firearm that the decedent grabbed the gun during a struggle.

Gunpowder particles and residues encountered on the interior surfaces of the barrel, the chamber, and the breech suggest that the firearm has been fired since last cleaned and may provide information concerning the manufacture of the ammunition used during the incident. The presence of smoke halos around the forward surfaces of the chambers of a revolver cylinder may provide valuable information about the number and sequence of shots fired from such weapons.

Figures 8.3 and 8.4

The presence of lint inside the barrel bore as well as inside all the chambers of the cylinder of this revolver recovered at a shooting scene provides strong evidence that it was not discharged during the incident.

The existence of fibers on a firearm can provide evidence of the location where it was stored prior to the incident, such as the pocket of a particular garment worn only by one of several individuals suspected of involvement in a shooting incident. Bits of fabric caught on the tang of a hammer may support statements that the firearm became caught on such material during a struggle, causing the hammer to be inadvertently cocked without the operator's knowledge. The presence of lint in the bore or chamber(s) of the firearm may support statements that it was not fired (Figs. 8.3 and 8.4). Metal deposits in the bore may provide valuable clues about the composition of the bullet or bullets. The presence and nature of primer lacquer debris adhering to the internal surfaces of the breech may provide helpful information concerning the design of the cartridge case or cases.

The presence of materials such as paint, sheetrock, concrete, asphalt, grass debris, or soil and their location on the firearm may shed light on the type of surface or surfaces that a firearm may have come into contact with as a result of situations in which the firearm has been dropped or subjected to a hard impact of some kind. Any significant observations made should be recorded with close-up and orientation photographs prior to collection of samples.

CONDITION AND CONFIGURATION OF THE FIREARM

Careful observation concerning the condition and configuration of the firearm also plays an important role in the potential discovery of significant clues that could shed light on the circumstances of a shooting incident. These observations should be noted and documented with photographs during the course of the examination of the firearm both at the scene, within the limits of a field examination, and during more detailed examinations that can be conducted in the laboratory.

The examination should include an overall assessment of the exterior condition of the firearm. This should include an inspection of the firearm for signs of damage; broken, bent, or missing parts; or evidence of mistreatment that could affect the function of the firearm. An appraisal of any modifications to the firearm, such as obliterated serial numbers or a sawn-off barrel or stock, should be made. Signs of rust or corrosion of the finish and, most significantly, on any parts that could affect the function of the firearm should be noted. For example, corrosion between the frame of the firearm with the hammer and/or trigger can potentially influence the force necessary to pull the trigger. Modifications to internal parts of the firearm (typically observed during laboratory examination) may also play a significant role in resolving questions that arise in shooting incidents.

The configuration of the firearm should be carefully assessed, photographed, and documented prior to manipulating the action or moving any of its parts (Fig. 8.5). For example, the position of any externally set safety mechanisms or decocking levers should be noted. Additionally, the position of the hammer (cocked, half-cock, or uncocked), when present, should be documented. Load indicators present on some firearms that alert the operator of a cartridge in the chamber should be noted. The position of the slide or bolt on repeating arms should be checked. The orientation of the cylinder should be indexed with respect to the frame of revolvers prior to disengaging or removing it from the firearm. Failure to do so will result in loss of the position and sequence of any cartridges fired and/or unfired in the chambers of the cylinder or the position and sequence of tell-

Figure 8.5

Close-up photography displaying the condition of this pistol adequately documents its condition prior to handling it. The hammer is cocked, the safety is off, and the magazine is still in the pistol.

Figure 8.6

This photo, taken by investigating patrolmen, depicts a semiautomatic pistol recovered from under a bed mattress that was later identified as having fired bullets recovered during the attempted homicide of a police officer. Note that the slide "appears" to be in a rear locked position.

tale smoke halos around chambers from which fired cartridge cases have been removed.

The manner in which the firearm is loaded should also be documented. An inventory of any unfired cartridges in the magazine, their manufacturer, description, and order of loading in firearms so equipped should be conducted. It should also be noted whether the magazine is properly inserted into the firearm or separate from it. The presence/absence of an unfired cartridge or fired cartridge case in the chamber should be noted as well. Additionally, signs of malfunction of the firearm, such as a fired cartridge case caught in the breech of repeating arms, may also provide significant evidence relative to the circumstances of the case (Figs. 8.6 and 8.7). The position and sequence of any fired cartridges, unfired cartridges, or empty

Figure 8.7

This close-up photo, taken by an astute police officer, documents a jammed cartridge in the chamber of the pistol. This key form of documentation corroborated statements made by witnesses that the suspect pointed the gun at police officers but failed to fire the gun.

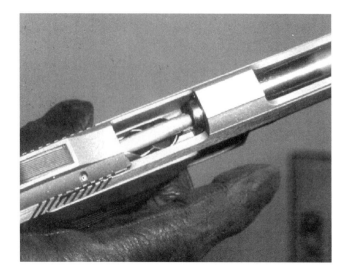

Figure 8.8

Documenting the contents as well as the position of each chamber in a revolver cylinder can make the difference between determining a homicide versus a suicide. Note the firing pin impression clearly depicted in the primer of the cartridge case at the 11 o'clock position. The remaining chambers contain unfired cartridges with no firing pin impressions.

chambers in the cylinders of revolvers should then be described as well as the direction of the cylinder rotation (Figs. 8.8 and 8.9). These observations can provide subtle but significant clues, for example, in the investigation of suspicious deaths and suicides as to whether a revolver cylinder has been manipulated after last having been fired or support evidence of post-shooting activity by participants of a shooting incident.

Figure 8.9

The presence of a powder halo or flare around the forward surface of the chamber containing an expended cartridge case provides further evidence that only one shot was fired from this revolver.

FIELD AND LABORATORY EXAMINATION OF FIRED AND UNFIRED AMMUNITION COMPONENTS

Much can be said concerning the general forensic examination of ammunition components fired from rifled firearms in terms of (1) determining the specific caliber and manufacturer of fired bullets and cartridge cases through study of their many manufacturing features; (2) generating lists of manufacturers and models of candidate firearms that could be responsible for firing bullets and cartridge cases by classifying rifling impressions appearing on the sides of fired bullets and/or cycle-of-fire markings imparted on various locations of the cartridge case resulting from their interaction with various internal parts of firearm mechanisms; and (3) comparing individualistic tool marks imparted on fired bullets and cartridge cases for the purpose of identifying a specific firearm that fired them when such guns are available for examination. This type of information is by far the most commonly requested form of investigative lead provided by the forensic science laboratory and addresses the most obvious of reconstructive questions. Unfortunately, it is my experience that the majority of requests for information stop at this level and few questions are asked concerning the interaction of the fired projectile or the ejected cartridge case with the scene or the firearm. This lack of awareness and/or interest inadvertently denies the requesting party the potential for attaching additional significance to this category of physical evidence in resolving questions about specific events that have occurred within a shooting scene.

If the reconstructionist is involved in the initial investigation of a shooting scene, a conscious effort to visually note and document the appearance of projectiles recovered should be made prior to collection and packaging. Such observations as the presence of trace evidence on the projectile, damage to the projectile surface, and overall deformation of the projectile can offer valuable information about the surfaces the projectile may have come into contact with and the manner in which the projectile interacted with those surfaces. These observations may provide immediate clues to assist the investigator in reconstructing the paths. If these observations are possible during the initial investigation of the scene, they can provide significant insight into the manner in which projectiles traveled and can lead to more thorough and complete documentation. However, such observations may not be practical at the scene and should be left to the examiner in the laboratory, who is better equipped to conduct more sophisticated examinations with the assistance of microscopes and who can rely on appropriate instrumentation and analysis to assist in characterizing trace materials. The reconstructionist can integrate this information with other information initially gathered at the scene when it becomes available.

TRACE EVIDENCE CONSIDERATIONS

When two objects come into contact with one another, there is a propensity for an exchange of materials from the surfaces of those items. This mutual exchange, known as Locard's Exchange Principle, has great potential to provide witness to the identity of surfaces that an object has come into contact with and is often applied to the examination of fired components recovered from shooting incidents with great effect. For example, the presence of red paint on the edge of a fired cartridge case mouth might suggest that it has come into contact with the only red painted surface located in a shooting scene. This information, in combination with knowledge of the firearm from which it was fired and the firearm's ejection pattern characteristics, could assist in approximating the location of the operator of the firearm at the moment the questioned cartridge case was ejected. Another example is the presence of powdered glass embedded in a fired bullet that might be confidently associated with the only bullet hole in a plate glass window among numerous bullet holes present in other items at the scene. This information could potentially shed light on the direction from which the fatal bullet was fired. Some common trace evidence materials often encountered with fired bullets are sheetrock/wallboard, glass,

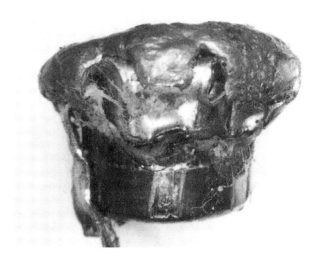

Figure 8.10

The bullet depicted in this photograph was recovered from the ground in the vicinity of a decedent who had been shot to death. One of the wound tracks was through a wound to the head. The results of DNA analysis of the tissue and comparison of hair on this bullet involved in this multiple victim/participant shooting incident revealed that it had not struck the decedent but, rather, had passed through a surviving shooting victim.

soil, asphalt, wood and plant material, bone fragments, tissue, blood, hair fragments (Fig. 8.10), paint, plastic, rubber, and natural and man-made fibers.

The order of the layers of trace materials adhering to a fired bullet, as well as their location, is indicative of the sequence of intermediary objects or surfaces it struck, passed through, or penetrated during its flight (Fig. 8.11). For example, a bullet exhibiting fabric material preceding a layer of wood fibers over a layer of wallboard material above a layer of blue paint might suggest that the projectile passed through a blue painted wall and then through a fabric surface of some kind, such as a furniture item or possibly a clothing item worn by a wounded participant involved in the incident being investigated. Given a closed set of items struck in a shooting scene, such a projectile may be conclusively associated with a particular bullet path to the exclusion of all other bullet trajectories at the scene through a process of elimination.

Even in the absence of materials that are readily observed with the unaided eye, laboratory examination of fired bullets, cartridge cases, and other ammunition components can reveal the presence of materials that can provide important clues about the nature of material(s) that these items have come into contact with at a crime scene. Laboratory analyses such

Figure 8.11

The fabric impression in the wood fibers adhering to this bullet could provide conclusive evidence that it passed through a hollow-core door before impacting the Kevlar fibers of a bullet-proof vest worn by a police officer involved in a shooting incident.

Figure 8.12

The surface appearance of this lead bullet suggests that it struck a rough textured surface (concrete) at a shallow angle (20 degrees). Analysis of microscopic particles embedded in the inclusions among the scoring marks may reveal the identity of the surface struck.

as stereomicroscopy, infrared photography, polarized light microscopy, scanning electron microscopy with energy dispersive X-ray (SEM-EDX) analysis, infrared spectroscopy, chemical tests, and serology are commonly employed to characterize such materials. This information can provide investigative clues contributing to a more thorough reconstruction of events (Rathman and Ryland, 1987). For example, the detection of microscopic pieces of material such as minerals common in soil embedded in the surface of a fired bullet might suggest contact with such a surface, and the manner in which it is embedded in the surface of the bullet may indicate the direction of impact with that surface relative to the flight path of the bullet (Fig. 8.12).

In cases in which projectiles have passed through or deflected off intermediary targets, the acquisition of reference samples from those surfaces is desirable to confirm the identity of materials that have transferred onto the projectile(s). Having a general sampling of common surfaces in a shooting scene to establish a baseline of the shooting scene environment should be considered regardless of whether it is known at the time if intermediary targets are involved. These would include samples of such common materials as carpet, wallboard, upholstery, curtains, paint, metals, asphalt, concrete, tile, and cinder block. Any observations made by examiners at the laboratory at some later time in regard to trace evidence from intermediary targets may raise the question of the source of the intermediary target that produced the trace material. Typically, by the time these laboratory observations are made it is too late to return to the scene to recover reference samples.

BULLET SURFACE DAMAGE CONSIDERATIONS

Locard's Exchange Principle can be extended beyond the transfer of trace evidence such that when two objects come into contact with one another, they may also damage or deform one another. Haag and Haag (2004, p. 50) suggested four basic substrate categories that are useful in considering potential for reconstructive information from impact surfaces: (1) unyielding surfaces, such as concrete, stone tile, or steel plate; (2) yielding/malleable surfaces (that can be further subdivided into homogeneous and nonhomogeneous in their composition), such as sand, sod, asphalt, wood, sheet metal, and sheet rock; (3) frangible, yielding surfaces (that can be further subdivided into homogeneous and nonhomogeneous in their composition) such as cinder block, bricks, and concrete; and (4) liquid surfaces (a special case of a homogeneous, yielding surface).

The appearance of surface damage to fired projectiles can add valuable indicators of the type of surface(s) struck during the bullet's flight and often supports any trace evidence that is embedded in or adhering to the bullet's surface (Rathman, 1987). It is recommended that the examiner be familiar with the morphology of surface damage to various types of bullets that have struck common materials. Conducting empirical studies in controlled conditions with such materials and/or studying the empirical work reported in the literature will go a long way toward accomplishing this.

In general, hard materials such as rough concrete, asphalt, steel plate, and linoleum will impart their texture to the bullet surface. For example, a bullet deflecting off rough concrete will likely exhibit a rough striated textured surface where it has contacted this material, whereas a bullet

Figure 8.13

The surface appearance of this lead bullet suggests that it struck a smooth surface (linoleum floor) at a shallow angle (10 degrees).

Figure 8.14

The bow wave-like pattern of scoring marks exhibited on this lead bullet is indicative of deflection off of soft yielding material, such as sand or soil. This bullet deflected off of dry loose sand at an incident angle of 10 degrees. Note the granules of sand embedded in the bullet, which could potentially be further characterized using SEM-EDX analysis.

deflecting off smooth steel plate will likely exhibit a relatively smooth textured surface within the area of contact (Fig. 8.13). A bullet deflecting off a soft forgiving material, such as soil, sand, or sod, can exhibit scoring marks in a configuration resembling bow wave-like patterns similar in appearance to the waves passing around the bow of a boat, termed the "bow effect" by Haag and Haag (2004, p. 48) (Fig. 8.14).

A bullet striking a tempered glass window at an angle will exhibit a smooth flat impact damage area oriented at an angle roughly the same as the impact angle of the bullet. When the first bullet passing through it fractures the tempered glass, the internal stresses built into the glass will frac-

Figure 8.15

The radial fractures surrounding the bullet hole in the center of this tempered glass automobile window indicate damage from the first bullet that passed through it. The two remaining bullet holes exhibiting an absence of radial fractures and surrounded by classic cube/rectangular-shaped fractures were subsequently produced. However, it is not possible to further sequence them due to the dynamics of tempered glass fracture behavior.

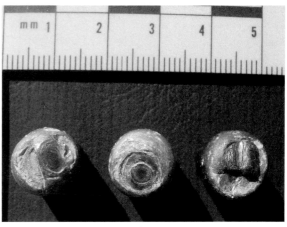

Figure 8.16

The three bullets producing the holes in the tempered glass window in Figure 8.15 exhibit damage revealing the identity of the first bullet to strike the window. The bullet in the center exhibits powdered glass embedded in the jacket surface and deformation indicating that it has struck a smooth, hard surface of the unbroken window. The bullets to each side struck the window subsequent to the first bullet because they exhibit powdered glass embedded in very irregular faceted contours resulting from impact with the prefractured cubicle-shaped glass surface.

ture into numerous small irregularly shaped cubical sections, sometimes leaving the glass in the frame. All subsequent bullets fired into the fractured tempered glass window typically exhibit an irregular-shaped impact damaged area containing a faceted appearance. This knowledge can indicate to the reconstructionist which bullet struck first (Figs. 8.15 and 8.16) and which went through the broken glass. Tempered glass as a potential impact surface is discussed further in a later section of this chapter.

Bullets passing through or impacting in a direction orthogonal (perpendicular) to certain materials with little or no lateral movement may sometimes have the texture of the impacting surface imparted on them in the form of an impression (see Fig. 8.11). For example, a bullet passing through a metal screen door may exhibit an impression of the metal screen pattern. The weave pattern of fabric on clothing items, fabric awnings, and bullet-proof vests can be imparted as an impression on the bullet. I have also observed the impressed patterns of textured plastics in automobiles imprinted on the surface.

BULLET DEFORMATION CONSIDERATIONS

The type and extent of bullet deformation is the third major consideration when gathering information about the manner in which a projectile has interacted with materials it has struck. Bullet deformation can provide an indication of impact angle, most notably with hard unyielding surfaces such as steel, concrete, and glass. Generally, when a stable bullet strikes a hard unyielding surface at an angle, it will deform in a manner such that the displacement of the bullet material will roughly mimic the angle separating the axis of the bullet and the plane of the impacting surface. This angle of deformation can be measured with simple angle measuring tools to estimate the impact angle (Fig. 8.17). The amount of deformation, given the same material and impact angle, is dependent on the impact velocity. Impact velocity is related to the distance the bullet has traveled. This relationship is useful for estimating distances of bullet travel in long-range shooting incidents.

Armed with the knowledge acquired from the previous three considerations, the reconstructionist may be in a position to identify the types of materials and the manner in which a bullet has come into contact with them during its travel. In a closed set of possibilities (which is often the case in a shooting incident), it is possible, using a process of elimination, to identify specific objects that a bullet has struck. This is useful for estimating the direction from which a bullet has traveled in cases in which information about the position of the shooter is not known. It may lead to the successful detection of bullet holes or bullet impact points not previously discov-

Figure 8.17

The deformation of this full metal jacketed bullet is an indicator that it struck a solid surface at an angle (30 degrees). An estimate of the impact angle can be made by measuring the angle of deformation relative to the long axis of the bullet.

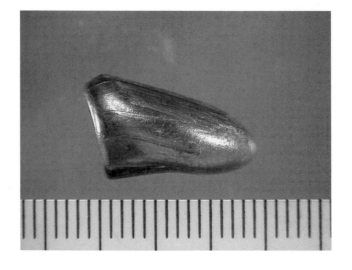

ered. Also, it could ultimately lead to an estimate of shooter position, especially when correlated with other converging clues, such as the location of fired cartridge cases, gun shot residue patterns, and footwear impressions.

DETECTION AND IDENTIFICATION OF PROJECTILE HOLES, IMPACT SITES, AND RICOCHETS

VISUAL EXAMINATIONS WITH THE UNAIDED EYE

As previously discussed, the appearance of surface damage to fired projectiles can add valuable indicators of the type of surface(s) struck during the flight of a bullet. Conversely, the appearance of the impact site by a bullet can provide clues about the composition of the projectile that struck a particular surface, the angle of impact, and the direction from which it was traveling. Methodical examination of the shooting scene should be conducted to detect the presence of projectile holes, impact sites, and ricochets. Detection of defects is typically accomplished through recognition of their characteristic appearance supplemented with chemical tests (discussed later).

Distinguishing projectile holes and defects from non-firearms-related anomalies can be difficult. It is recommended that the examiner be familiar with the morphology of projectile entry and exit holes, impact sites, and ricochet sites in a variety of common materials, such as sheetrock, wood, rubber, plastic, sheet metal, plate glass, tempered glass, laminated windshield glass, sand, soil, sod, concrete, and asphalt. Study of common defects produced by nails, screws, bolts, screwdrivers, drills, and other common household items is recommended to develop the expertise of the examiner. Study of dents and grazing damage from common household items such as hammers should also be conducted to build confidence in distinguishing these types of defects from projectile ricochets and impact sites.

The examiner should also be familiar with the following terms in regard to bullet impact behavior:

- *Perforate*: when a bullet passes all the way through an object
- *Penetrate*: when a bullet enters and remains in an object it strikes
- *Deflect*: a change in the direction of the bullet path by means of penetration or perforation of an object
- *Ricochet*: a change in the direction of the bullet path by means of impact with an object
- *Fragment*: when a bullet breaks up into smaller portions (typically resulting from impact with an object)

- *Primary impact*: the location where a bullet first comes into contact with an object during its flight path
- *Secondary/tertiary/etc. impact*: second, third, etc. location(s) where a bullet comes into contact with objects during its flight
- *Terminal point*: location where the bullet comes to final rest

CHEMICAL TESTS TO ASSIST IN VISUALIZATION AND CHARACTERIZATION OF BULLET IMPACT DEFECTS

Some of the most common materials used to manufacture bullets are lead, copper, aluminum, and copper–zinc alloys. Additionally, when a bullet is fired, it is covered with a thin layer of gunshot residue materials composed of dark organic carbonaceous by-products of burned gunpowder (nitrocellulose in modern-day gunpowder) and consumed primer constituents (e.g., barium, antimony, or lead). When determining if damaged areas are caused by bullet impact, Locard's Exchange Principle once again plays a significant role. When the bullet strikes an object, traces of the residues adhering to it, as well as the relatively soft metals that make up the bullet, are typically transferred to the margins of the hole created when such an object is perforated or penetrated. The material deposited around the margins of the hole appears as a dark-colored ring referred to as a *bullet wipe* (Fig. 8.18), indicating the first object struck. These same materials can be transferred (deposited) within the boundaries of defects on impacted surfaces caused by bullet impact or deflection (ricochet).

A number of field tests to detect metals commonly associated with projectiles (e.g., lead and copper) can be applied to suspected projectile defects to corroborate the visual identification of a suspected projectile hole, impact site, or ricochet. The most common of these tests are sodium rhodizonate reagent for the presence of lead and dithiooximide (DTO) reagent for the presence of copper. Lead in the presence of sodium rhodizonate forms a brilliant reddish-purple color (Dillon, 1990a). A color change from reddish-purple to blue with the addition of dilute hydrochloric acid increases the specificity of this test for the presence of lead (Fig. 8.19). Copper in the presence of DTO forms a mossy green color (Haag, 1989). These tests serve a dual purpose in that a positive color reaction indicates the presence of lead and/or copper as well as the distribution of these materials within or around the suspected defect. The reagents can be directly applied with sprayers in cases in which the surface in question is a light color and absorbent, such as an unpainted wood surface containing a questionable bullet hole or graze mark.[1] An alternative lifting method can be employed for dark-colored surfaces and items that are not transportable, nonporous,

[1] These tests should only be performed by laboratory personnel because there are hazards associated with the chemicals.

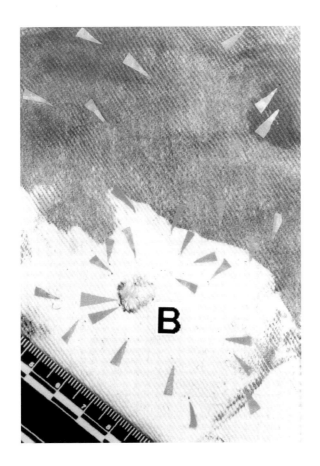

Figure 8.18

The bullet entry hole displaying classic "bullet wipe" favoring the left edge of the defect is depicted in the material of a pair of light-colored pants. Green arrows indicate the locations of gunpowder particles. The orange arrow indicates the location of a microscopic fragment of copper. These observations suggest that a copper jacketed bullet struck the garment at an angle from left to right fired from a gun at a distance of approximately 1 or 2 feet. See color plate.

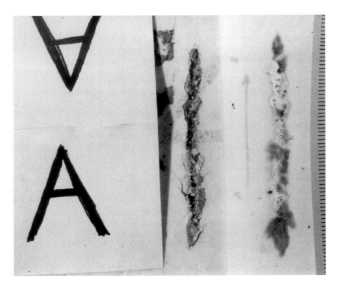

Figure 8.19

This gouge in a linoleum floor is actually a bullet ricochet site. Note the strong rosy-red color reaction associated with the presence of lead (a common constituent of bullets) along the margins of the defect as represented by the filter paper transfer treated with sodium rhodizonate reagent. This reagent can be useful in the field for detecting obscure defects that might not be recognized as damage caused by bullet impact. See color plate.

and/or remotely located or difficult to reach. The lifts can also be retained for instrumental analysis (Haag and Haag, 2004, p. 26).

These tests are fairly simple to perform, sensitive, and useful for determining whether an otherwise obscure defect may be associated with the impact of a projectile. Moreover, the presence of lead and/or copper in the immediate vicinity of a defect that resembles a classic bullet hole or impact site adds significant weight to the examiner's confidence that he or she is indeed dealing with a bullet hole or impact site. Additionally, the presence of lead only versus the presence of lead and copper or copper only in the margins of a bullet hole can also be useful in distinguishing between non-jacketed lead bullets and copper jacketed or coated bullets that have struck a questioned surface. Such knowledge is useful to the reconstructionist, for example, for including or excluding participants in a shooting incident if the type of ammunition each shooter was using can be established.

There may be occasions when the muzzle of a suspected firearm is close to a projectile defect on a questioned surface. The deposit of gunshot residues expelled from the muzzle of the responsible firearm becomes a possibility. Although it is most desirable to collect the item that is suspected of containing gunshot residue for transport to a laboratory facility where tests for such materials can be performed in more desirable conditions (clothing items in particular), there may be occasions when this is not possible. Prior to any chemical testing, complete documentation of the defect or pattern using measurements, drawings, and photographs with scales should be performed. The Griess reagent in the presence of nitrites (commonly associated with consumed modern-day gunpowder) forms a bright orange color reaction (Dillon, 1990b). The Griess reagent is facilitated by using a lifting technique on questioned areas in the field and brought to the laboratory. The resultant pattern developed using this reagent should be carefully documented and photographed with scales for potential comparison to test patterns produced by candidate firearms that may be recovered to estimate muzzle distance as well as orientation to a questioned target surface. Muzzle-to-target considerations are discussed more in-depth later.

TAPE LIFTING BULLET HOLES AND OTHER DEFECTS

Tape lifts and pre-prepared adhesive disks applied to bullet holes and impact sites prior to performing the previously described field chemical tests is a simple and effective way to collect such materials for follow-up instrumental analysis, such as SEM-EDX. Such instrumental analysis is more sensitive than the chemical tests for the detection of common bullet constituents, such as lead and copper; in addition, it is able to detect other metals that can be indicative of bullet construction, such as nickel, aluminum, steel, and molybdenum, as well as constituents of the primer material in cartridges associated with the fired bullet. Micro-infrared analysis can also be employed on such samples for characterizing organic materials associated with bullet strikes such as lubricants and burned/unburned gunpowder residues/particles transferred from the surface of the projectile to the object.

Tape lifts can also serve to supplement photographic documentation of bullet holes and defects. They are often effective in recording surface disturbance characteristics exhibited by such defects that can be used to determine bullet direction of travel, angle of impact and/or deflection, and angle of penetration or perforation. After all the appropriate photographs, measurements, drawings, and samples have been collected for the chemical tests, this method can be used to record additional surface disturbance characteristics that might not be sufficiently recorded by photographs. For example, tell-tale "boat-wave" fracture patterns in painted metal surfaces such as automobiles associated with bullet ricochets are indicative of bullet path direction (Mitosinka, 1971). These patterns can be very effectively visualized by applying fingerprint powder to the defect area. The developed pattern is then transferred using a tape lift to a latent print card as a permanent record (Figs. 8.20–8.22). Similarly, applying fingerprint powder to bullet holes and defects in general can be done using the same technique to generally supplement photographic documentation.

CASTING BULLET HOLES AND OTHER DEFECTS

Photographs are limited to two dimensions. Casting bullet defects have the added advantage of registering their three-dimensional contour. The displacement of the impacted surface (most notably in malleable materials such as sheet metal) can be permanently recorded and subsequently measured. This data is useful in estimating such parameters as bullet velocity and impact angle by comparing measurable displacement with defects in similar materials produced under controlled test conditions. Mikrosil casting material is a reliable product for recording the three-dimensional detail of such defects for further examination on most surfaces. It is also an excellent product for recording the finest details on the surface of such impacted surfaces. Casts can then be examined in the laboratory to more critically determine bullet incident and deflective angles with appropriate experimentation if the need arises. Additionally, in situations in which an identified bullet hole, impact site, or ricochet is located on an item that is

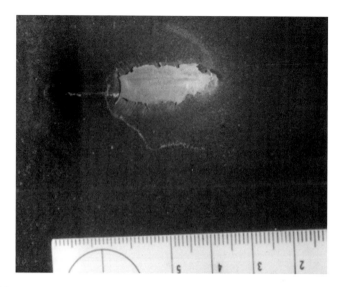

Figure 8.20

I was requested to examine a possible bullet ricochet site on the roof of a passenger car reportedly involved in a gang-related shooting incident. The two occupants of the vehicle stated that they had been fired upon from occupants of another vehicle as the vehicles were passing each other in opposite directions. The occupants further stated that the shooting was unprovoked. Officers were suspicious of the truthfulness of the statement and were interested in what could be determined about the direction of bullet travel that caused the damage to the roof of the car. The defect indeed resembled a classic ricochet site and furthermore gave positive sodium rhodizonate and DTO tests for the presence of lead and copper (respectively), suggesting that the damage had been caused by a grazing strike from a copper jacketed bullet.

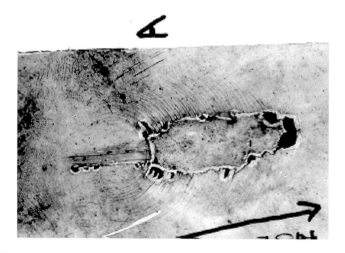

Figure 8.21

The defect area was treated with fingerprint powder and tape lifted to record the overall morphology that included characteristic boat-wave fractures in the surrounding paint. The characteristics of the defect indicated that the bullet struck the roof of the car at a very low incident angle while traveling from passenger side to driver side.

Figure 8.22

These observations did not support the statements offered by the occupants of the vehicle. Furthermore, it was demonstrated, as recorded in this photo, that the evidence supported a more likely scenario that the passenger in the front seat had fired a shot directed toward the driver side of the vehicle with his arm extending from the passenger side window. While doing this, he inadvertently struck his own vehicle during the incident.

not practical to collect, these recording techniques, in conjunction with photography and the previously discussed chemical tests, are the next best alternative for follow-up examinations at the laboratory. It may be possible to associate recovered projectiles with ricochet sites by comparing impressed and striated tool marks produced on either item resulting from one surface marking the other. There are documented accounts in which this has been accomplished by comparing the markings appearing on casts of bullet impact ricochet sites to the surfaces of recovered bullets (Patty et al., 1975).

DETERMINING THE DIRECTION OF PROJECTILE TRAVEL AND ANGLE OF IMPACT BY EXAMINATION OF BULLET HOLES, IMPACT SITES, AND RICOCHETS

Once a defect is identified as a projectile hole, impact site, or ricochet, information about the manner in which the projectile interacted with the impacted item may be obtained. Considerations about the projectile hole or impact site, such as entrance versus exit, entrance angle versus exit angle, and direction of travel, will provide useful information about reconstruction issues during the course of a shooting investigation while at the scene and for resolving issues that may develop as the investigation continues long after the scene has been processed. For example, determining the approximate direction and angle of impact in which a bullet struck an object while at the scene may provide immediate clues to assist the investigator in reconstructing the paths of projectiles. This information may serve to identify the presence of other bullet impact sites associated with the bullet's travel and greatly assist in determining from which direction a bullet was fired. This information, given a closed set of participants involved in a shooting

Figure 8.23

The oblong shape of this bullet entry hole indicates that the bullet passed through this painted sheet metal in a nonorthogonal direction. Measurement of the width and length of an oval that approximates the contours of this hole and use of trigonometry can be used to estimate impact angle. This bullet impacted the surface at 30 degrees, traveling from right to left.

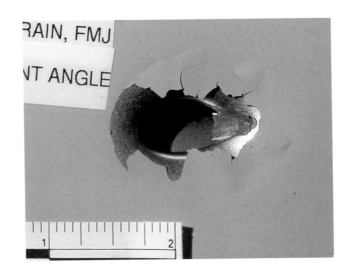

incident, may serve to include or exclude certain shooters involved when corroborated with other sources of investigative information. This information may also serve to eliminate or include certain areas or locations from which a shooter could have discharged a firearm.

The dynamics of bullet interaction with various materials and the morphology of holes, impact sites, and ricochet sites exhibited by the material surfaces struck are predictable. For example, it is a general rule that the deflecting angle of a projectile striking a hard unyielding surface such as concrete or plate steel will be significantly lower than its incident angle (Rathman, 1987). Additionally, the deflecting angle of a projectile striking a yielding surface such as sand (Haag, 1996) or water (Haag, 1979) is higher than the incident angle. Another phenomenon that is observed in low-angle impacts with sand is that departing bullets demonstrate consistent left or right deflection in accordance with twist direction of the responsible firearm (Haag, 1979). Similarly, the morphology of defects created by bullets is characteristic for various materials and can be useful for providing reconstructive information. For example, bullets striking a surface such as a painted car door (or other painted sheet metal surfaces) at a nonorthogonal angle will characteristically create an oval-shaped hole. Bullets (and spheres in the case of shotgun pellets and buckshot) have a circular component in their shape. The profile of this shape when projected over a flat surface at a given angle has a trigonometric relationship such that an estimation of impact angle can be approximated by dividing the width by the length of the oval and calculating the arcsine of this value (Barr, 2001a) (Fig. 8.23). This phenomenon can be used to make approximate estimates of impact angle in

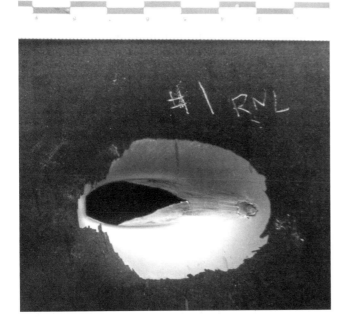

Figure 8.24

This bullet hole exhibits classic indicators of its right-to-left direction as it passed through a car door: (1) a pinch point or small area of crushed paint at the apex of the parabolic-shaped "lead-in mark" on the right side of the defect, (2) the metal at the left edge of the hole is pushed inward and in the direction of bullet travel, and (3) the remnants of boat wave fractures along the margins of the chipped paint.

other materials as well, including wood, wallboard, and other common materials encountered in shooting incidents (Barr, 2001b). Additionally, in the case of painted sheet metals, the direction of impact can be determined by examining the direction of travel of the metal. In many cases, when the bullet first engages a painted sheet metal surface, a small area of paint will be crushed into the metal surface. This *pinch point*, as termed by Haag and Haag (2004, p. 48), occurs at the entry side of the oval-shaped hole and is useful in determining bullet direction of travel (Fig. 8.24). There is also a critical angle at which a projectile of particular design striking the surface of a specific material will no longer perforate/penetrate it and begin to deflect from the surface. These thresholds, which are typically at low incident angles depending on the material and bullet design, can be quite helpful in estimating angle of impact.

In the case of ricochet sites, a number of predictably observed indicators of bullet direction can be observed given the type of surface and/or the construction of the bullet. The presence of an elliptical/parabolic-shaped transfer lead-in mark (Haag and Haag, 2004, p. 49) produced by the bullet as it first contacts a surface at low incident angle can also establish the entry side of a ricochet mark (Fig. 8.25). In some cases, impressions of the rifling characteristics on the bullet are transferred to this area of the ricochet (Hueske, 2003) that provide potential clues about the rifling characteristics of the firearm. As the bullet grazes across painted sheet metal surfaces prior

Figure 8.25

This ricochet damage on a car door was caused by a shallow angle of incidence from an impacting caliber 38 Special lead round-nose bullet moving from left to right. Note that the classic parabolic-shaped lead-in mark at the left edge of the defect and the feathered edges of the boat wave fractures also indicate direction of bullet travel.

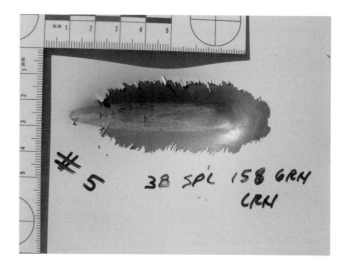

Figure 8.26

A lead bullet deflecting off of a linoleum floor surface traveling from right to left at 20 degrees produced this ricochet mark. Note that the asymmetrical extension of the graze mark favoring the lower edge, termed the Chisum trail, is caused by the left edge of the impacting bullet remaining in contact with the surface after the main body of the bullet has lifted off the surface while rotating in a counterclockwise direction from the left twist rifling of the firearm that fired it. If the asymmetry were extended to the upper side, it would indicate a right twist rifled barrel. This indicator of rifling twist direction could potentially be used to include or exclude the involvement of candidate firearms in a shooting incident.

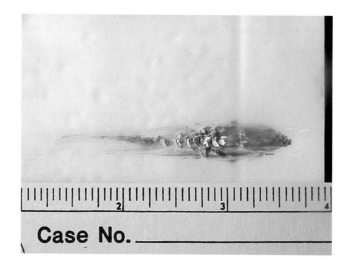

to deflection, the relatively brittle paint layer on top forms a series of fractures in a characteristic boat wave-like appearance (Hueske, 2003), giving an excellent indicator of direction. A unique ricochet mark, termed the *Chisum trail* by Haag and Haag (2004, p. 49) (named after criminalist Jerry Chisum, who first characterized it in the United States; Fig. 8.26),

occurs on flat unyielding surfaces as the bullet departs the surface. It is caused by the right or left edge of a flattened bullet remaining in contact with the surface after the main body of the bullet has lifted off the surface. This asymmetrical extension of the ricochet mark will be on the left side if the bullet was fired from a firearm having left twist rifling and on the right side in the case of a right twist firearm."

Another feature, termed *lead splash* (Haag and Haag, 2004, p. 19), is caused by the impactive spatter and vaporization of lead that deposits on the down-range side of nonperpendicular impact angles typically associated with lead bullets and jacketed bullets with exposed lead noses. It is a morphological feature that can be used for interpretation of lead projectile impact direction (see Fig. 8.31).

Glass is a very common material in both structures and vehicles, so a brief discussion of projectile deflection/perforation characteristics as well as potential for sequencing order of bullet impact is warranted. Glass is generally classified as plate glass (common in standard household windows), tempered glass (common in many household and industrial applications, such as shower doors and side windows of vehicles), and laminated "safety" glass (common in windshields of vehicles). The morphology of impact sites and holes through these classes of glass are significantly different.

PLATE GLASS

When projectiles perforate plate glass, a cone-shaped fracture (Fig. 8.27) occurs around the periphery of the hole on the downrange side of the glass. The shape of the hole will generally be round with orthogonal impact and progress to increasingly exaggerated elliptical shape as the angle of impact

Figure 8.27

The presence of cone fractures on the downrange side of bullet holes in plate glass as depicted in this photo provides a clear indicator of bullet direction.

Figure 8.28

*The radial fracture
extending from the lower
left bullet hole blocks
radial fractures extending
from the upper right bullet
hole, indicating that the
lower left hole was created
first in this plate glass
window.*

decreases (Murdock et al., 1987). Radial and concentric fractures radiate out from this cone-shaped hole and resemble a spider web (Fig. 8.28). The radial fractures are of use in sequencing the order of bullets that pass through the same sheet of plate glass. The radial fractures created by a previous bullet hole will block the progression of the radial fractures in a subsequently produced bullet hole (Murdock et al., 1987). Thus, by observing the blockage of these fractures, bullet holes can be sequenced relative to each other.

The symmetry of radial fractures that surround the bullet hole in plate glass is dependent on the angle of impact. Generally, the elongated fracture lines point away from the direction of impact. It is also possible to determine the direction of bullet travel by microscopic examination of the direction of conchoidal-shaped "rib marks" on the edges of radial and concentric fractures (Kirk, 1974). Therefore, pieces of glass should be collected for examination by the laboratory when the conical hole is missing.

TEMPERED GLASS

Tempered glass, because of internal stress, is much stronger than plate glass of the same thickness. However, when it is broken by impact, it will fracture into many small cubical- or rectangular-shaped fragments within a fraction of a second. This feature of this glass design reduces the potential for serious injury. Once broken, the window is extremely fragile, and often large portions of the window will fall out of the frame. Consequently, partial or complete loss of the fractured areas around the bullet hole(s) needed for interpretation is a common occurrence (Figs. 8.29–8.31). Even when the glass pane remains intact sufficiently to preserve projectile holes, cone fractures are extremely shallow and difficult to interpret.

The ability to sequence the order of bullets striking tempered glass is limited to only the first shot. The first bullet striking the glass will create radial fractures that propagate for a short distance around the hole and then quickly degrade into the classic cubical fracture pattern. Any subsequent bullets striking the glass will merely push sections of the prefractured glass from the pane. These subsequent holes are therefore identical in appearance (see Fig. 8.15).

The morphology of damage exhibited on the first striking bullet is significantly different from that of those which strike subsequently. Tempered glass offers a smooth, hard, impact-resistant surface; therefore, the first bullet striking it typically exhibits a smooth, flat area of deformation that is an approximate indicator of the angle of bullet impact (Rathman, 1993). In contrast, damage to the subsequent bullets that push through the prefractured glass segments exhibits significantly less overall deformation. The impacted surface is also not smooth but multifaceted in contour and typically has substantial fragments of glass embedded in it (see Fig. 8.16).

Even when substantial portions of glass are missing from a panel of tempered glass, any radial fractures that are still intact can be extrapolated back to a convergence point to accurately locate the position of the first bullet to strike the glass (Prendergast, 1994).

LAMINATED GLASS

Laminated glass is composed of two preformed sections of plate glass with a thin polyvinyl plastic layer in between. It is used primarily for windshields of vehicles. Laminated glass also poses its own unique challenges to bullet impact interpretation. Cone fractures can be used to interpret direction of bullet impact; however, it has been my experience that cone fractures can

Figure 8.29

A tempered glass passenger window was completely shot out by a load of buckshot in an officer-involved shooting. Although it was not possible to determine the locations of the projectile holes in the tempered glass, the window tinting covering the glass provided this information.

Figure 8.30

Lead splash marks surrounding the holes produced by impacting buckshot were observed in this close-up photo of the window tinting collected from the shooting scene. In this example, the splash pattern is circular in shape and suggests a fairly orthogonal direction of impact.

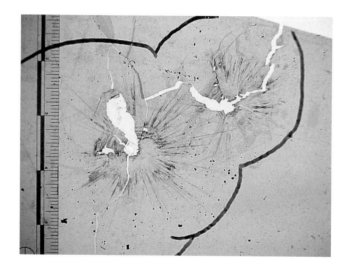

Figure 8.31

The window tinting with the registered buckshot holes was used as a template to trace the passenger window in a section of clear Plexiglas. The Plexiglas was then inserted into the window frame of the vehicle to reconstruct the location of the buckshot holes to facilitate the estimation of the projectile paths that passed into the vehicle.

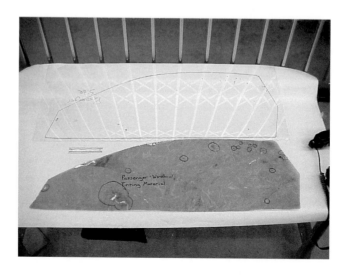

occur on both sides of the glass but are typically much more prominent on the downrange side. Because of the slope of windshield glass (typically approximately 30 degrees in most passenger vehicles), most bullets fired through them at eye level will produce oval-shaped holes. The orientation of the long axis of the oval is an indicator of bullet direction.

Laminated glass offers a hard and impact-resistant surface. Consequently, it is not uncommon for bullets to strike the glass sufficiently to fracture the glass layers on both sides of the laminate but deflect off the windshield without perforating. In the case of extremely low angles of incidence (approximately 5 degrees or less), the bullet deflects off the surface of the glass, creating a transfer mark and possibly a small area of radial cracks at the impact point and/or a series of crescent-shaped fractures resembling boat-shaped waves that provide a reliable indication of bullet direction (Van Arsdale, 1998).

Sequencing of bullet holes in windshield glass by examination of the radial fractures emanating from them is unreliable due to continued propagation of the fractures. Vibrations from later shots extend the cracks of earlier shots, giving false impressions of shot sequence (Roberts, 1998).

DETERMINATION OF PROJECTILE PATHS

Determining or reconstructing the actual path(s) that a projectile(s) has taken in a shooting incident scene will provide useful information regarding the location(s) and position(s) of participants and the location of any intermediary targets struck. For the purpose of determining projectile paths within a distance of 100 feet (absent striking an intermediary target), the investigator can assume a projectile(s) is traveling in a straight path given the accuracy and precision of the methods with which these determinations can be made. Indoor scenes are typically sufficiently restrictive in their dimensions to qualify under this condition. In these situations, the probe and string method for bullet path determination is typically used. For outdoor scenes that involve longer distances but are less than 100 feet, the laser method may be a more practical technique. For distances greater than 100–200 feet, gravity and atmospheric conditions will begin to have an effect exceeding the accuracy/precision of the previously mentioned techniques. In this case, long-range ballistic programs will be useful for estimating bullet paths.

PROBE AND STRING METHOD

This method of projectile path determination employs the use of a probe (rods of various diameters) to represent the impacting and/or exiting bullet

Figure 8.32

Probing bullet holes to represent bullet paths is most accurate when the probe connects two points. Single surfaces with projectile holes can provide useful bullet path information depending on the material and the thickness. Probes of various thicknesses and colors are being used by the author to represent numerous bullet paths through the door of this pickup truck.

path from a perforation and/or deflection from a given surface. The path represented by the probe is extrapolated with string.

TWO POINTS OF REFERENCE

Projectile paths are most accurately determined when the projectile has passed through two or more surfaces (Fig. 8.32). For example, a 6-inch residential wall of sheetrock construction that has been perforated by a projectile offers a much more dependable means of projectile path determination than a single layer of sheet metal. The probe is used to connect these two points to represent or visually illustrate the projectile path by passing the rod through the projectile hole(s). Different sized probes can be employed to accommodate variations in projectile hole diameters.

SINGLE POINT OF REFERENCE

The ability to accurately estimate projectile paths through a single surface is greatly diminished and will be dependent on the nature of the material struck and the thickness of that material. Generally, the greater the thickness of the material that a projectile has penetrated or perforated, the more confidently the bullet path estimation can be determined. A foam headrest in a vehicle provides a more dependable means of projectile path determination than a single pane of window glass.

Brightly colored string can be used to extrapolate the projectile path represented by the probe in both incoming and outgoing directions as desired.

Colored Post-it notes can be folded over the string at intervals to better visualize the paths (Figs. 8.33 and 8.34). The use of string is most applicable in indoor situations. It can also be used outdoors where distances involved are reasonably short.

Figure 8.33

Brightly colored red string was used to extrapolate the paths of buckshot that passed through a wooden sign and continued into the vehicle while the door was in the open position. This reconstruction was conducted while the vehicle was in its original position at the scene. See color plate.

Figure 8.34

This photograph illustrates the bullet path from the perspective of the shooter. Colored string with colored Post-it notes attached at 2-feet intervals for increased visibility in the photograph represent these two bullet paths. See color plate.

LASER METHOD

In situations in which projectile path distances are more lengthy, as in outdoor shooting incidents, the use of a laser device can be employed to extrapolate the estimated projectile path illustrated by either the previously described probe and string method or by direct application of the laser to represent the projectile path without the use of probes. A laser pen can be used for preliminary projectile path estimation and for guiding other examiners to likely locations to which projectiles may have traveled after passing through or deflecting from intermediary targets. For more accurate projectile path documentation, commercial laser devices on a tripod should be used (Fig. 8.35).

MEASURING IMPACT, DEFLECTIVE, AND EXIT ANGLES

Once a projectile path has been illustrated using either the probe and string or the laser method, the location as well as the path of the projectile must be documented and described. These representative paths should be photographed and the representative directions described in terms of azimuth (compass) directions and inclination angles (vertical angle). This is most conveniently accomplished using angle measurements in reference to the vertical and horizontal planes. These angles can be either directly measured using a variety of angle measuring tools (i.e., protractors for azimuth angles and inclinometers or electronic levels for inclination angles) or calculated using measurements and trigonometric functions (Fig. 8.36). Additionally, these representative bullet paths, when properly photographed in the correct planes of view, may be reliably approximated using the photographs.

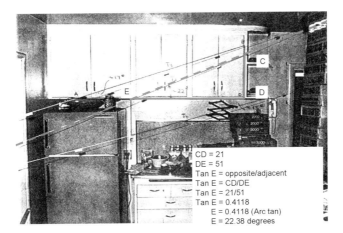

```
CD = 21
DE = 51
Tan E = opposite/adjacent
Tan E = CD/DE
Tan E = 21/51
Tan E = 0.4118
     E = 0.4118 (Arc tan)
     E = 22.38 degrees
```

Figure 8.36

When photographs are taken in proper perspective, it is possible to estimate bullet path angles. In this example, I was able to calculate inclination angles of three bullet paths progressing from right to left and downward in this photograph by using the cabinet in the background as a reference for establishing right triangles relative to the bottom edge and sides of the cabinet. In this case, the right edge (CD) and bottom edge (DE) of the cabinet formed the legs of a right triangle for the middle bullet path (dotted line). Dividing the length of CD (21 scale units) by DE (51 scale units) and multiplying this ratio against the arc tan value equals approximately 22 degrees. Careful examination of the photo reveals two other triangles drawn in by hand relative to the remaining two bullet paths.

These angle measurements and descriptions are useful for such tasks as empirically or mathematically extrapolating bullet paths and for calculating shooter positions along an established bullet path given known heights of shooting participants. I have found it difficult to decipher some verbal descriptions of bullet paths in written crime scene reports. This is because angle measurements are relative to the particular plane of reference being used. For example, the azimuth component could be described from the point of view of the shooter facing the west wall (NATO method of description) instead of using the plane of the west wall as the reference. Both of these descriptions are correct, but they are relative to these two different planes of reference. Correlation of any crime scene diagrams that illustrate the described bullet paths is very helpful in supplementing such descriptions to minimize confusion.

It should be noted that such bullet path determinations are an approximation and are subject to a number of variables that will affect the accuracy and precision of these estimates, including (1) the effect of the medium a bullet passes through or deflects from on incident versus reflective angles and (2) the variance of probe placement through projectile holes (Garrison, 1996). Studies conducted by me and experience by other examiners[2] suggest that repetitive measurements of predetermined bullet paths are usually within 2 or 3 degrees of the target value. Subsequently, it is generally acceptable to conservatively report a ±5 degree variation from the measured result as a range of possibility for estimating bullet path directions.

The investigator's ability to predict the positions of shooters in an incident is restricted to his or her ability to reproduce an accurate bullet path, as discussed previously. The string and probe method as well as the laser

[2] The following experiment directed by criminalists Chris Colemen (Contra Costa County Sheriff Department) and Bruce Moran (Sacramento County District Attorney's Office) was conducted at a California Association of Criminalists Northern California Firearms Study Group bullet path reconstruction workshop held at the Alameda County Sheriff's

training facility in Pleasanton on March 3, 2005:

A series of mock walls simulating standard sheetrock construction separated by 2 × 4 stud sections were prepared by Colemen. A total of 12 bullets were fired through the prepared wall sections at known angles. The participants were asked to measure the bullet path azimuth and vertical angle components using the probe and/or laser method. Each participant measured the azimuth and vertical components of these bullet paths using protractors and inclinometers. Twenty-eight participants working in two-person teams took a total of 312 measurements. The data was collected from each participant and summarized on an Excel spreadsheet by Colemen. It was noted that the participants' measured results were within 1–3 degrees of the target value. Maximum variation between measurements of the participants was within 5 degrees.

Note: Very similar results were obtained by approximately 25 participants in an exercise using the same experimental design conducted by Luke and Mike Haag at the Forensic Shooting Scene Reconstruction Course, Prescott, Arizona, attended by me in November 2004. It is my understanding that Mike Haag has been accumulating data from previous exercises conducted in earlier classes and intends to publish the data in the *AFTE Journal* in 2006.

method of bullet path reconstruction are essentially an extrapolation of a line between two points (e.g., entrance and exit hole in a standard residential wall). This is straightforward but does not take into account the effect of deflection angles as a function of the medium through which the bullet passed. Deflection as a result of perforating/striking an object rather than rebounding off of surfaces (ricochet) is used to describe deviations in any direction from the projectile's normal flight path (Haag and Haad, 2004, p. 48). There can be significant changes in bullet direction depending on the medium through which the bullet passes and the design of the bullet. For example, tempered glass (Thornton and Cashman, 1986) and laminated windshield glass (MacPherson and Fincel, 1996) can effect bullet deflection by as much as 10–20 degrees. Bullet path determination and resulting shooter position reconstruction are approximations, and conclusions made should be reported conservatively. It may be necessary to perform empirical tests to study the effect of a specific target material(s) on bullet deflection resulting from perforation when this consideration is significant to the resolution of reconstructive issues.

PHOTOGRAPHIC DOCUMENTATION OF ILLUSTRATED PROJECTILE PATHS

Photographic documentation of illustrated projectile paths is an essential step in the shooting reconstruction process. Proper photographic documentation of illustrated projectile paths will be important in supporting the examiner's reconstructive conclusions, providing graphic illustrations to investigators and police personnel, attorneys, the court and jury, and/or any party interested in reviewing the reconstructionist's work.

Photographs of bullet paths illustrated by either the probe and string method or the laser method should be taken to represent the azimuth and inclination components of the projectile path and parallel to the axis of the bullet path in both directions (Figs. 8.37 and 8.38). Photos should be taken at the same height as the location of the impact or exiting projectile defect to minimize photographic distortion of the projectile path. If a photograph is to be used later for measurement of inclination angles, it is essential that the film plane in the camera be in alignment with the azimuth direction of the bullet path to achieve the proper perspective for accurate measurement. Use of ladders and/or elevating equipment is essential in obtaining azimuth (overhead) views of projectile paths. At outdoor shooting scenes, it is sometimes desirable to perform overhead photography from a fire truck aerial ladder (Fig. 8.39). Overall aerial views of the shooting scene from airplanes or helicopters are also highly desirable (Fig. 8.40).

Figure 8.37

This photograph of bullet paths is taken in reference to the horizontal plane. Note that the photograph is taken at the level of the bullet entrance holes to minimize distortion.

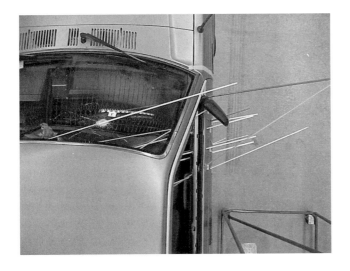

Figure 8.38

This photograph depicts bullet paths in reference to vertical plane. Note the use of a stepladder to obtain the correct perspective directly over probes.

Figure 8.39

*Overhead photographs of
shooting scenes using an
aerial ladder truck are
extremely useful in
illustrating shooter
position(s) in relationship
to other objects and/or
participants in a shooting
scene.*

Figure 8.40

*Aerial photographs of the
entire shooting scene are
recommended in outdoor
shooting scene
investigations.*

Photography of bullet paths using the probe and string method during daylight hours can be most effective when bright fluorescent-colored string for maximum visibility is used. Hanging colored Post-it notes folded over on themselves at 2- or 3-foot intervals along the string can add increased visibility.

A method to photo document projectile paths using the laser technique involves spraying the entire laser beam along the bullet path with commercial photographic fog in darkened conditions during an open shutter camera exposure, which will create a continuous beam representing the illustrated bullet path. However, the fog technique is cumbersome and susceptible to weather conditions. An alternative is to move a piece of white paper attached to a clipboard along the laser beam. When done correctly, the person spraying the fog or moving the clipboard is not seen in the photograph.

LONG-RANGE TRAJECTORY DETERMINATION

The majority of shooting incidents involve relatively short distances, the flight time of the bullet is measured in fractions of a second, and for all practical purposes the bullet is traveling in a straight line. Participants and objects in the scene that are in motion at the time shots are fired can be considered stationary during the bullet's flight (Haag and Haag, 2004, p. 83). Each shot fired registers a very brief moment in time and, in essence, amounts to a snapshot of the shooting incident.

In situations in which distances are greater than 100–200 feet, gravity and drag will begin to have an effect on the path of the bullet, causing it to curve. Additionally, as the distance traveled increases, the bullet's flight time can be lengthened to several seconds or longer and may become a significant reconstruction issue. Efforts to estimate a shooter's position therefore become significantly more difficult. This is most typically encountered in cases that involve victims struck down by wayward bullets fired by people celebrating a holiday or by hunters or target shooters who have missed their intended target. Often, the shooter has no idea that he or she has wounded or killed the victim (Figs. 8.41–8.44).

The study of bullets in motion is called *ballistics*. The term ballistics is often erroneously associated with the discipline of firearms identification (involving the determination of whether a certain firearm has or has not fired a particular bullet or cartridge case). An in-depth discussion of ballistics is beyond the scope of this chapter. In general, however, to derive meaningful information for reconstructive purposes, it is necessary to employ long-range ballistic programs to estimate these curved projectile paths.

Figure 8.41

This bullet was recovered from the floor of a child's bedroom in a residential neighborhood. Investigation revealed that it had entered through the roof of the residence.

Figure 8.42

Approximately one-half mile from this location, this 45 Auto handgun was recovered from a citizen who was reportedly firing it "straight up into the air" to scare car thieves away. I concluded that the bullet had been fired from the pistol after comparing rifling impressions on test-fired bullets to the rifling impressions exhibited on the questioned bullet.

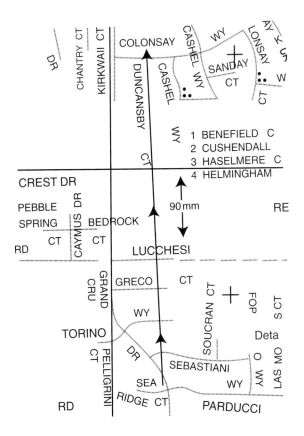

Figure 8.43

The distance the bullet traveled was estimated to be approximately 2650 feet based on calculations made from a street map between the position of the shooter and the child's bedroom.

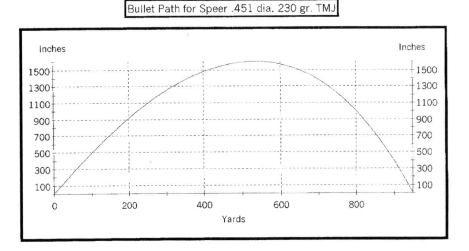

Bullet Path for Speer .451 dia. 230 gr. TMJ

Figure 8.44

Information concerning the aerodynamic flight characteristics of a caliber 45 Auto full metal jacketed bullet fired from a 4-inch barreled caliber 45 Auto pistol was used to calculate the terminal velocity of the bullet as it struck the child's residence and the angle of departure of the bullet in order to reach the child's residence from a half mile away. The calculated angle of departure was determined to be between 8 and 12 degrees. This relatively horizontal departure angle did not support statements by the shooter that he fired shots "straight up in the air."

SHOOTER LOCATION, POSITION, AND ORENTATION ALONG ESTABLISHED BULLET PATHS

THE THREE ZONES OF SHOOTER POSITION

In cases in which a bullet path can be confidently established using either the probe and string method or the laser method from bullet hole, rico-chet, and impact site evidence at the scene, it is possible to begin a process of considering various shooter locations along the bullet path and possible shooter positions/orientations at those locations. When the bullet path is on an incline either up or down, a suggested approach is to consider what I have coined as the three zones of shooter position: most probable, improb-able but possible, and impossible.

This is conducted through a process of elimination where the investiga-tor has knowledge of the shoulder height of the shooter and the maximum height that the shooter can reach. A person of the same height and build as the suspected shooter is selected to model various shooting positions along the extrapolated bullet path represented by string or a laser beam using the same type of firearm used. The model or shooter is directed to move along the extrapolated bullet path while maintaining the barrel of the firearm in exact alignment with the represented bullet path. The shoulder height and height of maximum reach are key measurements because they will be used to establish the thresholds between these three zones of possi-bility. For example, working backwards along a downward-directed bullet path to the item struck, the zones are described and associated threshold distances between these zones would be established as follows:

Zone 3: Impossible

The model or shooter is directed to move backward along the bullet path (i.e., the height of the bullet path increases as distance to the item struck increases). When the shooter reaches a point where he is unable to physi-cally align the barrel of the firearm in the bullet path as a result of (1) being unable to reach high enough to place the firearm in a position of alignment or (2) reaching some physical barrier that terminates the extrapolated bullet path such as a wall or large intervening object to the bullet path, a distance from this point to the target is measured and reported as the begin-ning of zone 3 (Fig. 8.45). Any distance greater than this threshold mea-surement would be in the impossible zone.

Zone 2: Awkward (Improbable) But Possible

This zone includes a range of distances at which the shooter is able to phys-ically align the barrel of his or her firearm with the bullet path but in a manner that is awkward and/or difficult to achieve. This typically occurs (in

These photographs depict the reconstruction of one of numerous shots fired into a vehicle involved in a homicide. The vehicle was towed back to the scene and placed in its original position using crime scene diagrams and crime scene photographs after various bullet paths were estimated using the probe and string method. The bullet recovered at the terminus of the bullet path represented by the yellow probe was identified as having been fired by a caliber 38 Special revolver. The model/shooter in these photographs was selected because he was the same height and similar in build as the suspected shooter, and the gun being used is of the same manufacturer and model as the gun identified in the case. Note the resulting three zones of shooter possibility are very short due to the extremely steep inclination angle of the reconstructed bullet path. Shallower inclination angles will result in larger ranges of distance within these zones.

Figure 8.45

Impossible: Any distance equal to or greater than the distance represented by the arrow is reported as the zone of impossibility since the shooter is no longer able to place the firearm in alignment with the reconstructed bullet path.

the case of a downward-directed shot) when the height of the bullet path exceeds the top of the shooter's shoulders. For the purpose of this example, the shoulder point shooting position is the highest elevation of natural shooting stances before the shooter is required to raise the height of the firearm above the level of the shoulders. Any level above this height precludes the ability of the shooter to obtain a normal "sight picture."

Additionally, as the height above shoulder level increases, the shooter is placed in an increasing position of awkwardness until such point as the shooter is no longer able to align the firearm with the bullet path (threshold between zone 2 and beginning of zone 3). Once the outer limit of possibility is established, the model or shooter is directed to move forward along the bullet path until the string or laser beam touches the top of the shoulder. The distance of the shooter from this location along the bullet path to the item struck is measured and the range between this distance and the threshold distance marking the beginning of zone 3 is reported as the improbable zone (Fig. 8.46).

Zone 1: Most Probable

In this downward-directed shooting example, any height lower than the height of the shoulders allows the shooter to easily achieve a number of standard shooting positions where normal sight picture can be achieved (i.e., shoulder point, kneeling shoulder point, and prone position) as the height of the bullet path decreases. The distance between the beginning of zone 2 and the item struck is reported as the probable zone (Fig. 8.47).

Figure 8.46

Improbable but Possible: The shooter is able to physically align the barrel of his or her firearm with the bullet path but in a manner that is awkward and/or difficult to achieve.

Figure 8.47

Most Probable: The bullet path is at a height equal to or lower than the top of the shooter's shoulders and can be easily achieved by the shooter in a number of standard shooting positions. The distance between the beginning of zone 2 and the target is reported.

Figures 8.45–8.47 depict an example of these zones within a relatively short distance due to the steep incline of the bullet path into the vehicle. However, as the incline of the bullet path decreases, the shooter zones of possibility will increase. In cases in which the bullet path is level or near level, this process will not be applicable and the reconstruction will be

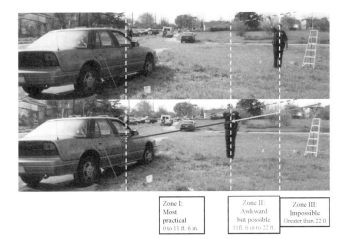

Zone I:	Zone II:	Zone III:
Most	Awkward	Impossible
practical	but possible	Greater than 22 ft
0 to 11 ft. 6 in.	11 ft. 6 in to 22 ft.	

Figure 8.48

This composite of two photos (used as a court exhibit by the author) graphically demonstrates the threshold positions between zones 1–3 of shooter location possibility with associated distances along a reconstructed bullet path using a model of similar height and build as the suspected shooter. Note that the model is standing at shoulder point in one photo and in the second photo is demonstrating the farthest point where the gun can just barely be aligned with the projected bullet path that has been extrapolated with string. The model is using the same make and model of firearm used in the incident. The ladder in the background is being used to support the end of the string representing the bullet path. The vehicle was towed back to the shooting scene and placed in its original position using photographs and crime scene measurements to conduct this reconstruction.

required to rely on other sources of investigative and/or physical evidence to estimate shooting positions along such bullet paths. I have found this method to be an effective tool for either supporting or refuting suspect or witness statements.

This process is most effective when conducted at the original shooting scene while it is still in control of investigative personnel. Unfortunately, such knowledge of the shooter in many cases is unavailable during the crime scene examination stages of such investigations. However, if appropriate measurements and crime scene photographs have been obtained during the crime scene documentation process, it is possible to return to the original scene after the fact to reconstruct the bullet path and demonstrate these zones of possibility (Fig. 8.48) and make such estimates through the use of trigonometric calculations in conjunction with scale diagrams of the scene.

FURTHER NARROWING SHOOTER POSITION POSSIBILITIES

GUNSHOT RESIDUE PATTERNS AND MUZZLE-TO-TARGET DISTANCE DETERMINATION

The investigator may be able to further limit the shooter's position within the previously described zones of shooter possibility by considering the presence of any gunshot residue patterns that have been detected on an object(s) along the bullet path. The presence of any discernable gunshot residue patterns (Figs. 8.49 and 8.50) typically restricts the muzzle of the firearm to within a distance of 4 feet from the item.

A comprehensive discussion on muzzle distance determinations is not the focus here because there are numerous treatments of this topic in the

Figure 8.49

The presence of discernable gunshot residue and/or particle patterns associated with a reconstructed bullet path can be used to further restrict shooter location within the zones of shooter possibility. As demonstrated in this reconstruction, very fine sooting is present around the periphery of the bullet entrance hole in this vehicle.

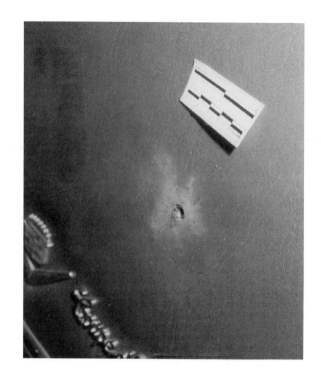

Figure 8.50

The converging information provided by the bullet path as demonstrated by the probe with the presence of the fine sooting around the bullet entrance hole suggests a muzzle-to-target distance of no more than 1 foot.

literature. However, for the purposes of general reconstructive considerations, a brief description of gunshot residue and the patterns it produces when expelled from the muzzle of a firearm and its usefulness is warranted.

When a firearm is discharged, a variety of materials are expelled from the barrel in addition to the bullet. Such firearm discharge products include fine carbonaceous particles or soot from incomplete combustion of the propellant; unburned and partially burned powder particles; metal particles stripped from the bullet; bullet lubricant; and inorganic elements from the cartridge primer, such as lead, barium, and antimony in traditional U.S. center-fire ammunition and possibly other elements in some of the recently developed lead-free ammunition formulations. The heavier materials are propelled from the muzzle as a very fine spray within the gas cloud of lighter materials emerging from the firearm. The aerodynamic qualities of this aerosol/gaseous cloud are very poor and consequently are propelled forward for a very short distance relative to the travel of the bullet. However, their distribution and general appearance on items they are deposited on will change with distance. This correlation can be used to estimate the muzzle-to-target distance. I use the following five zones of distance associated with the general appearance of gunshot residue deposits as described by Haag (2004) as a general guideline in estimating muzzle-to-target distance without the benefit of producing test patterns with the suspected firearm and ammunition:

Zone I: Contact: Contact causes blast destruction, tearing of the skin or cloth; soot and powder particles mostly on the inside of the garment and/or driven into the wound. The outline of certain parts of the firearm (e.g., barrel bushing and front sight) may be printed in the skin adjacent to the entry hole.

Zone II: Near contact (1–4 inches): Intense, dark sooting with dense deposits of unburned and partially burned powder particles located around the bullet hole; blast destruction still possible in clothing and even in skin in some cases; powder tattooing on the skin.

Zone III (3–8 inches): Some medium to light gray sooting with a roughly circular "shotgun" pattern of powder particles around the bullet hole. Powder tattooing is still possible particularly with dense and/or poorly burning powders.

Zone IV (6–36 inches): No visible sooting. Widely dispersed powder particles often loosely adhere to the receiving surface. The distribution pattern is usually circular at closer distances but may become poorly defined to nonexistent at greater distances. Chemical tests can be employed to raise latent powder or gunshot residue patterns on garments.

Zone V (3–4 feet or greater): No discernable firearms discharge products present. Bullet wiping present around the margin of the entry side of the bullet hole regardless of range.

The previous descriptions assume that the firearm was pointed perpendicular to the receiving surface. Actual distances associated with zones II–IV will vary to some extent depending on the type of firearm, the length of the barrel, and ammunition used, as well as the shape and the composition of the receiving surface. In cases in which gunshot residue deposits are produced on surfaces where the firearm is oriented in an increasingly non-perpendicular angle to the receiving surface, the overall shape of the pattern will change to an increasingly exaggerated oval shape. The distribution of the gunshot residue material will also become increasingly unevenly distributed across this overall oval pattern, with a greater density of soot or gunpowder particles being deposited on the side of the oval closest to the muzzle.

In reality, the most reliable method of estimating muzzle-to-target distance is by comparing the size, shape, and distribution of the previously described gunshot residue/particulate materials of the questioned pattern to test patterns produced at known distances using the suspected firearm and the same ammunition under the same conditions (i.e., angle and orientation).

An additional consideration involving the deposit of gunshot residue that can be helpful in narrowing the shooter location and position/orientation is the detection of aerosol or gaseous gunshot residues that escape from either the ejection port of autoloading firearms or the cylinder gap (space between the forward end of the revolver cylinder and the forcing cone of the barrel). These will deposit on items that are in contact with or within a few inches of the gun. For example, the backwards extrapolated bullet path of a bullet hole 2 feet above the floor in a hallway that passes through a doorway of another room and terminates in the opposite wall behind the door at a height of 6 feet might suggest a number of shooter possibilities in zones I and II. However, the detection of a cylinder gap pattern at the edge of the doorway leading into the hallway in close alignment with the extended bullet path would strongly suggest that the shooter fired the shot from the doorway using the edge of the door opening as a barricade as opposed to being in the hallway or farther back in the adjoining room. When the side of the revolver is in contact and/or very close to the surface of an item such as a wall or clothing, the distance between the gunshot residue pattern created by the muzzle end of the revolver and the cylinder gap pattern can give an estimate of the barrel length as well as its location and position/orientation (Figs. 8.51 and 8.52).

FIREARM EJECTION PATTERN CONSIDERATIONS

The firearm ejection pattern may also assist in further limiting the shooter's position along an extrapolated bullet path (Figs. 8.53 and 8.54). Ejection patterns are subject to numerous variables, such as the design of the firearm, the ammunition used, the height and orientation of the firearm, the nature of the receiving surface or surfaces, and the position and location of intervening

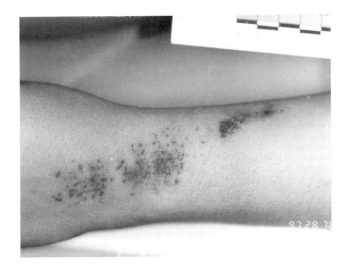

Figure 8.51

A woman was fatally shot through the head by her boyfriend at point-blank range using a 41 Magnum revolver. The bullet passed laterally through the base of the skull from left to right, exiting the decedent and deflecting off a wall switch plate. The bullet path through the head, the bullet impact site on the switch plate, and bloodstain patterns in the vicinity provided strong evidence that the decedent was in a semistanding/crouched position with her head pinned against the wall when the fatal shot was fired. The defendant claimed that the decedent "grabbed the revolver and the gun went off." This autopsy photograph depicts a linear cylinder gap gunpowder stippling/tattoo pattern on the back of the decedent's left wrist, indicating that this area of the left arm was in close vicinity to the side of the revolver frame at the moment the fatal shot was fired.

Figure 8.52

A properly scaled computer model depicting the female decedent (using Poser) was constructed and imported into one of the crime scene photographs in which the decedent received the fatal shot. The anatomical model depicts a likely position of the decedent including the orientation of the left arm in relationship to the likely location of the revolver and shooter (not shown) at the instant the shot was fired. The deposition of the cylinder gap pattern on the back of the decedent's left wrist suggested that she was attempting to parry the gun away rather than grabbing for it.

Figure 8.53

The probes illustrating the bullet paths in the side of this vehicle support statements by police officers that the suspect, while driving the vehicle, was firing his handgun in the direction of pursuing police vehicles.

Figure 8.54

The bullet paths that struck the side of this vehicle can be most reasonably achieved in the manner being demonstrated by a model of similar height and build as the suspect in this officer-involved shooting incident. Note that the pistol in question is oriented horizontally with the ejection port side up. This orientation was significant in that an ejected cartridge case was recovered inside the vehicle directly behind the driver's seat. The ejection port is on the right side of this firearm. The sideways orientation of the pistol accounts for the ejection of a cartridge case over the left shoulder of the shooter and into the restricted space behind the seat and the cab wall. Additionally, the model demonstrating this orientation noted that it was much easier to achieve this sideways orientation than a vertical orientation while seated in the driver's seat.

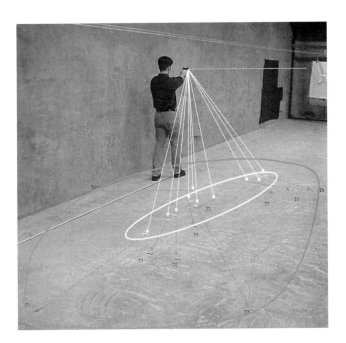

Figure 8.55

Consideration of firearm ejection patterns associated with certain firearm designs can contribute to limiting the shooter positions along an established bullet path. The small oval represents the location where ejected cartridge cases first struck the smooth concrete surface of the testing area. The larger oval represents the final resting positions of the ejected cartridge cases after bouncing on the hard concrete surface. The smaller oval represents the distribution of cartridge cases that would likely land in soft, giving surfaces, such as sand, soft dirt, or grass, where little bounce is expected. The larger oval represents the distribution of cartridge cases on hard, unforgiving surfaces, such as concrete or asphalt, where significant bounce is expected.

objects that ejected cartridge cases may strike. Generalizations made without the benefit of conducting ejection pattern tests should be done so with extreme caution. If the firearm and ammunition used are available for testing, the more variables that can be controlled, the more confidence the reconstructionist will have in reproducing an accurate representation of ejection patterns. Given adequate testing, it may also be possible to make some conclusions in regard to whether a shooter is stationary or moving when cartridge cases are ejected from a firearm (Haag, 2003).

Consideration of the receiving surface for ejected cartridge cases is also a very important factor in estimating shooter position. Generally, when conducting ejection pattern tests, I document the location where the ejected cartridge case first comes into contact with the receiving surface as well as the location of the cartridge case after it has bounced to its terminal resting place. Two resulting ejection patterns are therefore established that can be useful when correlated to a scene that has both hard surfaces, such as concrete or asphalt, and soft, yielding surfaces, such as sand, loose dirt, or grass (Figs. 8.55 and 8.56).

There is the potential for further movement of ejected cartridge cases at the scene due to rolling of cartridge cases on inclines, wind, postshooting activity of participants involved in the shooting incident, postincident activity by citizens and/or moving traffic, postincident activity of emergency personnel responding to the scene, and postincident activity by police and investigative personnel.

Figure 8.56

The presence of ejected cartridge cases associated with known ejection characteristics of the rifle used in this shooting reconstruction restricted the shooter to the area of the doorway as the most likely shooting position even though there were many shooting positions possible, both forward and rearward, along these bullet paths. This scene was reconstructed by (1) placing several boxes with bullet holes back in their original positions (in the foreground just outside of this photograph), (2) extrapolating the bullet paths using the probe and string method, and (3) illustrating the location of ejected cartridge cases documented during the initial investigation. Good measurements and photographs were the key to making it possible to accurately place the boxes and ejected cartridge cases back in their original locations.

THE PRESENCE OF INTERVENING OBJECTS ALONG BULLET PATH

The presence of a wall or other large intervening object, such as a tree or large vehicle, along the bullet path may further limit the possibilities even though the height of the bullet path is still within zones 1 or 2. The hood of an automobile may restrict a shooter's ability to fire shorter range shots into the windshield within zone 1, depending on his or her ability to reach over the hood.

GUNFIRE INVOLVING VEHICLES

Vehicles offer additional considerations for the reconstructionist. They can be involved as a platform from which gunfire can be directed as well as a receptacle for receiving fired bullets and related ammunition components. Because of their mobility, I consider vehicles a crime scene within a crime scene and treat them as a subset of an overall shooting incident.

DOCUMENTATION CHALLENGES AND RECONSTRUCTION CONSIDERATIONS INVOLVING VEHICLES—"A MOVING CRIME SCENE"

The modern-day vehicle offers a multitude of materials, including sheet metal, steel and/or aluminum support members, tempered safety glass windows, laminated glass windshields, a variety of plastics, insulation materials, foam padding, upholstery, rubber moldings, weather strips, and card stock (Garrison, 2003). These materials introduce numerous frangible, malleable, hard and soft impact surfaces that result in significant variance in both penetration and deflection characteristics (Haag and Haag, 2004, p. 65). Bullets often strike complex arrangements of internal parts concealed from view. To the unwary examiner, this may result in erroneously estimated bullet paths through the auto body components in which they are contained, if such hidden intermediary targets go undetected.

The design and styling features of vehicles offer an additional unique problem in the determination of projectile paths. Unlike the walls, floor, and ceiling in a structure or the edge of a sidewalk and a telephone pole in a street shooting, there are no true coordinate reference points available for measurement of projectile defect locations and for projectile path determination in a vehicle. Fixed reference points are required to accurately describe the location of bullet holes and impact sites.

Therefore, the examiner must create a set of artificial vertical and horizontal coordinate reference points. To accomplish this, the vehicle can be referenced to three principal axes: its longitudinal axis from front to back, its vertical axis, and a width axis. Establishing a common reference point along these three axes allows the location of bullet defects and bullet paths to be described accurately in three-dimensional space. This approach is referred to as *squaring the vehicle* (Haag and Haag, 2004, p. 66) or placing the vehicle in a box.

A technique to square the vehicle is to establish the extreme limits of the vehicle's length and width by surrounding it with lengths of string stretched tautly between four tripods acting as the corners of the box. The tripods are placed at such a position so that the string is just touching the front bumper, rear bumper, and both sides of the vehicle, with the strings parallel to the longitudinal axis of the vehicle and a plane perpendicular to the longitudinal axis (Garrison, 2003, p. 73). All measurements are then referenced to these lines. Vertical or height measurements are referenced to ground level.

An alternate method used by the author to square the vehicle is to select a location on the vehicle (such as the edge of a door) to establish a vertical reference line using a 4-foot level marked with colored masking tape (Fig. 8.57). A second reference line parallel to the long axis of the vehicle (measured from the wheel hubs of the vehicle) is also established (Fig. 8.58). A third technique to establish a midline down the length of the vehicle is to measure midway between two symmetrical points on the vehicle such as the halfway point between the outer corners of a trunk lid.

These artificial coordinate reference lines are then located in the vehicle diagram and used to locate subsequent projectile holes and defects throughout the vehicle. Defect locations can then be measured using tape measures from these references with the employment of levels and plumb bobs (Fig. 8.59). Angle measurements in both the azimuth and the vertical planes can be made using a variety of protractors, levels, and plumb bobs (Fig. 8.60). This technique lends itself well to the accurate location of bullet holes, defects, and ricochets and measurement of bullet paths at or through these

Figure 8.57

Note the vertical and axial reference lines for plotting the location of bullet defects and measuring azimuth and inclination angles of bullet paths.

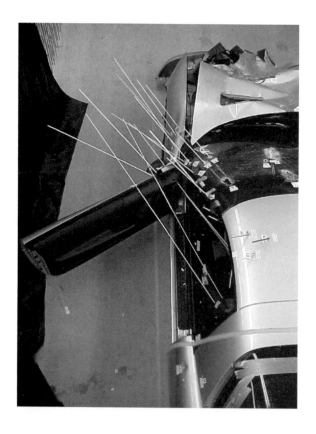

Figure 8.58

An artificial reference line is established by snapping a chalk line at known distances from the axles of the vehicle. Colored masking tape is applied to the line for better visualization, as seen in this photograph.

Figure 8.59

A 4-foot level, measuring tape, and plumb bob are used to accurately plot the location of bullet holes using the reference line. Measurements taken using this method can be used to generate accurate scaled computer-aided design (CAD) diagrams of the bullet paths through the vehicle that can be imported into other scaled CADs of the shooting scene.

Figure 8.60

A protractor is employed to measure azimuth angles of various bullet paths represented by probes in this vehicle. Note the longitudinal reference line on the ground and a parallel reference line using string between two tripods that can be slid up and down to the various heights of the probes for convenient/accurate measurement with the protractor.

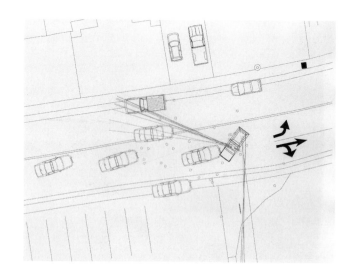

locations. It is also sufficient to plot bullet paths in computer-aided diagrams (Fig. 8.61).

Vehicles are often moving when struck by bullets or when receiving incoming bullets directed at them. Consequently, the suspension system of a vehicle, centrifugal and acceleration and deceleration forces acting on the vehicle, causes it to sway and tilt in a variety of orientations during a given period of time while the vehicle is in motion. This is complicated by the fact that the vehicle may be traveling over changing terrain while receiving striking bullets. Stationary vehicles are often not on level surfaces because they encounter crowning on roads or may be oriented in nonlevel positions when straddled over curbs or parked on uneven terrain. Tires struck by bullets may deflate and alter the level of the vehicle as well. In some cases, depending on the design of the bullet, holes created will cause total deflation of a tire within a second or two, whereas other bullet holes will cause very slow deflation lasting 15–20 minutes. All of these variables must be considered when evaluating vehicles that have been struck by fired bullets/projectiles.

It is therefore prudent for the reconstructionist to make a concerted effort to inquire about the circumstances of the shooting incident. Any knowledge about the orientation of the vehicle at the time it was struck by bullets as well as a review of any photographs or video taken of the vehicle at the scene are very useful to identify as many variables as possible prior to estimating the most probable bullet path angles (Figs. 8.62 and 8.63). Additionally, vehicles are often transported from a shooting scene prior to examination for the purpose of reconstructing bullet paths, making the previously mentioned inquiries even more important (Haag and Haag, 2004, p. 65).

Figure 8.62

Vehicles present additional challenges to the reconstruction of bullet paths due to their mobility, flexible suspension, and travel over varying terrain when receiving fired bullets. Bullet paths registered in vehicles are relative only to the vehicle at the moment it is struck in whatever orientation it may be in, given the previously mentioned conditions. Therefore, it is important to document the orientation of the vehicle while still at the shooting scene to account for as many variables as possible. In this case, I used a laser level device on a short tripod as a reference beam relative to the height of the edge of a roadway to document the longitudinal inclination of the vehicle body using the axles as reference points.

Figure 8.63

The lateral tilt of the vehicle is measured using an inclinometer at the scene to document its orientation relative to the terrain, and this can later be used to correct estimated bullet paths determined after the vehicle is towed.

In drive-by shootings, expended cartridge cases are often dispersed from the moving vehicle while at the same time the vehicle is potentially receiving bullet strikes from shooters outside the vehicle. Although challenging, the distribution of fired cartridge cases recovered at the scene can be used to reconstruct, indirectly, the approximate speeds of a vehicle (Haag, 1988) and its position in the roadway. Generally, these reconstructive estimates are made by conducting controlled experiments to create ejection patterns on the same or similar surfaces as the shooting scene with a known firearm in a known orientation and height, using the same ammunition. The resulting distribution of cartridge cases on the test surface is then compared to the distribution of cartridge cases recovered from the scene to estimate the speed of the vehicle. From reported studies (Garrison, 1993; Haag, 1988), it is generally known that increasing the speed of the vehicle increases the scatter of the cartridge cases as they continue to move to their final resting places from the launch or ejection point. Ideally, these patterns represent longer and wider ovals as vehicle speed increases (Garrison, 1993, p. 19).

Garrison (1993) suggests as a general rule for rough estimates for estimating vehicle speed while at the scene that "10 miles-per-hour means that a car or cartridge case is moving at roughly 15 feet per second, or about an average car-length per second. Twenty mph translates to two car-lengths per second, 30 mph to three, 40 to four, and so on" when cartridge cases are dropped from a moving vehicle (p. 20). Although this data does not simulate cartridge cases actually ejected from a vehicle that has the added effect of the speed and direction of the ejection forces from the firearm, such data can be helpful for conservative estimations of vehicle speed based on the distribution of cartridge cases at a shooting scene.

If the direction and approximate speed of the vehicle can be determined with some degree of confidence through investigative information, the measured bullet path azimuth angles in the vehicle and the use of trigonometry to estimate the change in azimuth angle to the speed of the vehicle can assist in estimating the approximate direction from which shots were directed. Conversely, if the shooter position outside the vehicle can be established at a fixed location through investigative and/or physical evidence such as the location of fired cartridge cases with an estimated rate of fire, the measured azimuth angles in the vehicle and the use of trigonometry can be used to calculate the change in azimuth angle to the speed of the vehicle. The reader is cautioned that these are estimates solely dependent on the reliability of the data being used to make such calculations. Such parameters in making these estimates should be well qualified and included in any conclusions made from these estimates.

RECONSTRUCTION CONSIDERATIONS INVOLVING SHOTGUN EVIDENCE

SHOTGUNS

An extensive descriptive treatment of shotgun design and shotshell construction is well beyond the scope of this chapter. However, the reconstructive information from this design of firearm and the components of ammunition utilized in them are well deserving of consideration. Shotguns differ from rifled long arms and handguns in that they are most commonly equipped with a smooth bore rather than a rifled bore.

Shotguns were originally developed for hunting of small game animals and birds by discharging numerous spherical balls or shot. The diameter of the bore of shotguns is expressed in terms of *gauge*. The most common gauges in modern-day shotgun design are 12 gauge [0.730 in. (18.5 mm)], 20 gauge [0.615 in. (15.6 mm)], and 410 gauge [0.410 in. (10.4 mm)]. Less common gauges include 10 gauge [0.775 in. (19.6 mm)], 16 gauge [0.670 in. (17.0 mm)], and 28 gauge [0.550 in. (14.0 mm)]. Additionally, the bore may contain a constriction at the muzzle end called *choke*, designed purposely to control the spread of the shot when it leaves the barrel. This is of particular significance in that it has a direct bearing on patterns of shot. The amount of restriction in increasing order is described as cylinder, improved cylinder, modified choke, and full choke, and such restrictions are typically designated on the shotgun thus equipped. Some shotguns are equipped with a polychoke mechanism that allows for adjustment of the choke restriction. The position of this mechanism should be documented by photography and notes at the scene before the weapon is touched. Shotgun bores that are rifled will have a dramatically different effect on the spread of shot as well as wads.

SHOTGUN AMMUNITION

Unlike standard cartridges that are composed of a cartridge case, primer, gunpowder charge, and, in most cases, a single projectile, shotshells present a much more complex arrangement of components, including numerous sizes and compositions of shot, shot wads, shot cups, shot collars, and buffering materials. Additionally, these components are produced in an extensive variety of configurations and various materials. However, because of the endless variety of shotshell designs and the physical dynamics of how these materials interact with the shooting scene environment, much can be gleaned from this type of evidence in shooting incidents that is helpful for reconstructing events.

DYNAMICS OF SHOTGUN EVIDENCE AT SHOOTING SCENES

Unlike single projectiles fired from a rifled firearm, a load of shot fired from a shotgun, due to its aerodynamic qualities, rapidly loses velocity and spreads outward over the distance traveled. Relatively speaking, the maximum range of shot is measured in yards and is conservatively less than 1 mile even when the largest of buckshot loads is fired, whereas single bullets from a rifled firearm can travel several miles. The rate of shot spread and resulting size of the pattern are predominantly controlled by the distance and the choke. Gauge is generally not a factor in determining the spread size. In addition to the expulsion of shot, numerous wads and buffer material are also propelled from the muzzle as well as the burned and partially burned propellant powder products. These materials travel considerably shorter distances than shot or slugs and are typically measured within inches to a few feet in the case of propellant powder and buffer material and as far as 75–100 feet in the case of some wad/shot cup designs. It is these relatively shorter range "exterior ballistics" exhibited by shotshell components that are of greatest value in shooting incident reconstruction. Furthermore, if the gun and ammunition are available, these components can be studied, measured, and used to answer specific questions developed in the reconstructive process.

A progression of very general observations concerning the ballistic characteristics of these various components with approximate distance traveled (when the surface struck is perpendicular to the direction of component travel) is described in the following sections.

Contact

Contact with a head will result in significant blast damage, causing extensive tearing of the skin and fracture of bone. Contact wounds to the trunk, however, are relatively nontraumatic in appearance (Di Maio, 1999). The entire contents of the shotshell enter the wound tract in skin and tissue or objects struck, causing a single hole. The majority of any soot and powder particles are deposited on the interior surface of the object and/or driven into the wound along with the wads and shot. Some heat searing and blackening from the hot gasses may be present around the edges of the entrance hole. An imprint of the muzzle may also be registered on the surface of the skin around the periphery of the hole.

Close Range (>0–12 Inches)

At near contact to distances of a few inches, the contents of the shotshell enter the wound tract or object struck. Dark, dense to light gray sooting with deposits of unburned and partially burned powder particles (along with buffer material, if present) are present around the single entrance hole. Blast destruction (still prominent in the skull area) (Di Maio, 1999) on skin in some cases as well as powder tattooing and/or heat damage on clothing (including melting of synthetic fabrics) occurs around the immediate region of the entrance hole.

Intermediate Range Zone I (1–2 Feet)

At intermediate range distances of 1–2 feet, the contents of the shotshell are still very likely to enter the wound tract or object struck. Sooting is likely to be greatly diminished or undetectable at this distance; however, the heavier unburned powder particles and buffer material (if present) will be deposited in a roughly circular pattern around the periphery of a single entrance hole. These particles may be embedded in the weave or loosely adhering to the fabric surface.

Intermediate Range Zone II (2–3 Feet)

At intermediate range distances of 2–3 feet, the contents of the shotshell are still very likely to enter the wound tract or object struck. The single entrance hole may begin to exhibit scalloping around the edges as the pellets begin to spread outward, but this is insufficient to create individual pellet holes (Di Maio, 1999) (Fig. 8.64). Sooting is no longer present, and heavier, more aerodynamic unburned gunpowder particles as well as buffer material (if present) are likely to be deposited in an increasingly less detectable. roughly circular pattern around the periphery of the entrance hole. These heavier particles, if present, are likely to be loosely adhering to fabric.

At this distance, it is significant to note the following observations reported by Haag and Haag (2004, p. 100) and observed by the author.

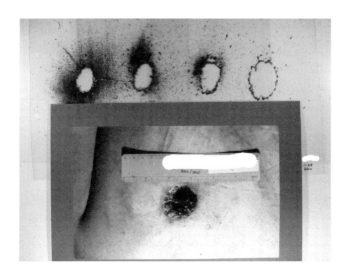

Figure 8.64

The single entrance hole created by this shotgun wound exhibits indications of the beginning of individual pellet holes at the margins. This is generally typical at distances of approximately 2–3 feet. In this case, I concluded that the muzzle-to-wound distance was approximately 2 feet after comparing the morphology of the wound pattern to test patterns produced at known distances and angle using the responsible shotgun and ammunition.

Combination wads equipped with petaled shot cups (commonly manufactured in the United States) will open as they are subjected to wind resistance and then, due to their very light weight and rear-end center of gravity, travel rear-end forward. Combination wads of this design will consistently cycle in this manner within the first 3–4 feet of travel after leaving the shotgun muzzle and therefore have significant reconstructive value. For example, the configuration of the impact marks on these one-piece wads is quite characteristic and can resolve muzzle-to-target distance questions of 1 foot versus 2 or 3 feet. These telltale rectangular "slap" marks, when they appear on skin or clothing items, strongly suggest this restricted 2- or 3-foot range of distance. At less than 1 foot, the petals have not opened, and at 3–4 feet there will be an absence of a slap mark because the wad is now fully rotated to its side and then turned on end (Figs. 8.65–8.67).

Intermediate Range Zone III (3–6 Feet)

At this distance, the shot pellets are still traveling in a tight group; however, a few pellets begin to separate to form individual pellet holes. Additionally, wads or shot cups with the least aerodynamic qualities begin to veer off from the shot column and strike the target surface, creating a variety of patterns depending on the design of the wad or shot cup and the angle at which they impact. These strike marks can often be readily observed with the unaided eye or, if associated with lead shot, can be visualized using sodium rhodizinate reagent (Fig. 8.68).

Distant Range Zone I (6–100 Feet)

At more distant ranges, the column of shot pellets will elongate as well as spread in a predictable manner with increased distance traveled. The rate of spread will be affected by the choke restriction of the shotgun bore. A general guide to these rates of spread is summarized in Table 8.1. Depending on their aerodynamic qualities, shot wads or shot cups are capable of traveling approximately 100 feet. At these distances, however, the chances of detectable strike marks are increasingly diminished. Additionally, they will often significantly veer from the path of the shot pellets and fall with little consequence to the ground.

Distant Range Zone II (>100 Feet)

Pellets will continue to spread at rates generally indicated in Table 8.1. At distances greater than 120 feet, however, the patterns become increasingly diffuse and undecipherable, and they do not provide reliable reconstructive information. Eventually, depending on the size and composition of the shot pellets, gravity and wind resistance overcome their forward movement

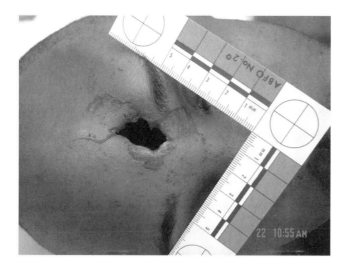

Figure 8.65

Telltale slap marks were observed around the periphery of an entrance wound to the decedent's forehead involving a .410 GA shotgun loaded with a shotshell containing #4 shot and a plastic tripetal combination wad. Powder stippling/powder tattooing can also be observed around the entrance wound. Photo printed with permission of Faye Springer.

Figure 8.66

A plastic tripetal combination wad used in shotshells fired in suspect shotgun. Photo printed with permission of Faye Springer.

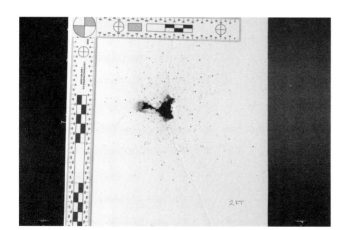

Figure 8.67

Using the suspect shotgun and the same ammunition, test patterns were produced with very similar slaps marks and gunpowder patterns at distances between 18 and 32 inches and were used as a basis to estimate the muzzle distance of the shotgun from the decedent's head at the instant the fatal shot was fired. This pattern was produced at a 24-inch distance. Photo printed with permission of Faye Springer.

Figure 8.68

Note the impression of a plastic wad in this wooden sign among several buckshot holes. Such impressions can be an indicator of distance traveled in addition to the pattern of the shot pellets.

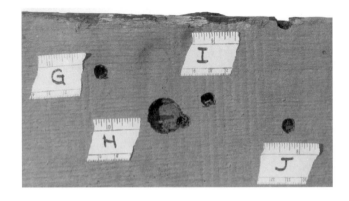

Table 8.1

Nominal Shot Pattern Diameters. This table gives the diameter of the shot pattern in inches at various ranges and chockes.

Choke	Amount of constriction (in.)	Common name	Range (yards)						
			10	15	20	25	30	35	40
Cylinder bore	None	Cylinder bore	19	26	32	38	44	51	57
Quarter choke	.010	Improved cylinder	15	20	26	32	38	44	51
Half choke	.020	Modified	12	16	20	26	32	38	46
Three-quarter choke	.030	Improved– modified	10	14	18	23	29	35	43
Full choke	.040	Full choke	9	12	16	21	26	32	40

and they reach a maximum distance of travel. A summary of maximum range for various sizes of shot calculated from Journee's formula is provided in Table 8.2. Maximum distance traveled, as suggested by Haag and Haag (2004, p. 100), has reconstructive value in cases in which the potential for cause of injury from shot pellets striking victims is in dispute, such as when a shooter claims to have fired in the direction of another person or persons but the pellets failed to strike them. Tests can be conducted with the shotgun in question and the same ammunition involved to determine the maximum range. If the maximum range is less than the reported distance between complainant and defendant, then there may be merit to the defendant's claim.

Note that the previous observations are approximate and should be used only as a general guideline in estimating muzzle-to-target distances (see Fig. 8.69 for a graphic representation of maximum distances of fired shotshell components). Additionally, these observations are only applicable for patterns produced with smooth bore shotguns. Shotguns equipped with rifled

Shot size	Diameter (in.)	Maximum range (yards)	Shot size	Diameter (in.)	Maximum range (yards)
12	.05	110	2	.15	330
11	.06	132	Air rifle	.175	385
9	.08	176	BB	.18	396
8.5	.085	187	#4 buck	.24	528
8	.09	198	#3 buck	.25	550
7.5	.095	209	#1 buck	.30	660
6	.11	242	#0 buck	.32	704
5	.12	264	#00 buck	.33	726
4	.13	286	#000 buck	.36	792
Rifled slugs	All gauges	Approx. 1500			

Table 8.2

Maximum Ranges for the Various Sizes of Shot[a]

[a]Calculated from Journee's formula, which gives the maximum range (in yards) as the product of the shot diameter (in inches) multiplied by 2200 ($r = 2200d$, where r is the range and d is the diameter of shot).

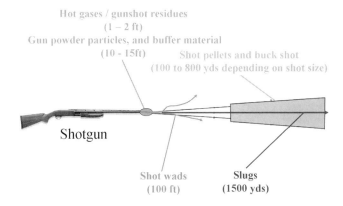

Hot gases / gunshot residues (1 – 2 ft)
Gun powder particles, and buffer material (10 - 15ft)
Shot pellets and buck shot (100 to 800 yds depending on shot size)
Shotgun
Shot wads (100 ft)
Slugs (1500 yds)

Figure 8.69

This illustration provides a general guideline of maximum distances that shotshell components can travel. These distances will vary to some extent depending on the type of shotgun, the length of the barrel, and the type of ammunition used. The reader is cautioned that these distances are approximate in nature and should be used only as a general guideline in estimating muzzle-to-target distances in the field. Testing with the responsible shotgun and ammunition used, if available, should be conducted whenever possible to ensure the most reliable estimate of muzzle-to-target distance.

bores (designed for use with rifled slugs) produce dramatically different patterns than smooth bores when shotshells are fired. Besant-Mathews et al. (1992) characterize these patterns as unconventional in their appearance and significantly larger than those for smooth bore shotguns given the same ammunition and distance. Patterns formed generally resemble "hollow circle," "double doughnut," or "circle-and-central" configurations. It is theorized that the shot load engages the rifling, creating a rotation and thereby imparting a centrifugal (tangential) force on the pellets, causing them to spread outward more rapidly than when fired from smooth bore shotguns (Fig. 8.70).

Estimating muzzle-to-target distance is most useful when an entire load of pellets/buckshot has struck a surface of interest. However, this will not

Figure 8.70

Shotshells containing shot pellets fired from rifled shotgun bores (normally designed to fire slugs) produce dramatically different patterns than when fired from smooth bores. The patterns formed resemble "hollow circle" or "doughnut"-like patterns with significantly more spread (right) at the same given distance as patterns from smooth bores (left), as seen in this example of buckshot fired into a wooden gate. Also, note the impact of shot wads (arrows).

always occur in a shooting incident. Even with partial patterns, it is possible to estimate range of fire by studying the distances between individual pellets. Studies have demonstrated that such separations between individual pellets with distance traveled are predictable (Haag, 2002). In addition, some interesting characteristics of double aught (#00) buckshot patterning are also useful in estimating muzzle-to-target distances when partial patterns are encountered. Double aught buckshot is typically contained within the shotshell in stacked sets of three. The buckshot produces a series of triangular configurations within an overall circular pattern. The distances between these triangles are also repetitive and predictable with distance. Even partial patterns exhibiting these triangular "subpatterns" can be used as a basis for estimating distance by direct comparison of test patterns.

Shotgun loads fired at flat surfaces at angles other than perpendicular will produce an elliptical pattern that can be used as a basis for estimating angle of impact by dividing the oval width by the length and calculating the arc sin value of this ratio (Fig. 8.71). The same approach can be used to calculate the impact angle from the entrance holes produced by individual shot pellets when dealing with incomplete shot patterns. Probing pellet/buckshot holes to empirically estimate impact angle can be used as a cross-check to the calculated estimate derived from the overall pattern shape.

DIAGRAMS AND ILLUSTRATIONS

Field sketches are an important supplement to photographic documentation in accurately locating items of evidence, the direction of projectile paths, establishing the relationship of items to each other, and other significant observations. The degree of attention given to this form of documentation will often dictate the degree of success when considering reconstruction issues in shooting incidents. Field sketches and illustrations

Figure 8.71

Shotgun loads fired at flat surfaces other than perpendicular angles will produce an elliptical pattern that can be used as a basis for estimating angle of impact by dividing the oval width by the length and calculating the arc sin value of this ratio. Note the characteristic pinch points on the left edges of the defects produced by nine buckshot balls and boat wave fractured edges of the paint surrounding them, indicting a left-to-right direction of travel at a low incident angle.

documenting bullet path directions do not have to be works of art, but they should be adequate enough to ensure that the reviewer of the diagram will be able to clearly determine the location of projectile defects and the direction of the responsible projectile(s) that created those defects. The documentation should be adequate to facilitate the preparation of formal crime scene diagrams, CAD scale diagrams, and, in some cases, three-dimensional computer-drawn reconstructions (see Fig. 8.61). Two types of sketches are especially useful for documenting shooting scenes and facilitating CAD and three-dimensional reconstruction diagrams.

OVERHEAD PROJECTION DIAGRAM

The overhead projection diagram provides a bird's-eye view of evidence item locations and projectile paths (Figs. 8.72 and 8.73). These diagrams are useful in depicting not only the location of firearms-related physical evidence items, such as firearms, fired bullets and cartridge cases, bullet holes, and other projectile impact sites, but also their positional relationship to each other. Just as important, they illustrate the relationship of firearms-related evidence to other forms of physical evidence that contribute to the overall reconstruction of a shooting incident. Additionally, the location and position of objects at the scene that have bearing on the circumstances of the shooting incident, such as furniture, doorways and windows, and areas of disturbance in indoor scenes, are easily viewed in the overhead projection diagram. This view is also conducive to the plotting of the azimuth directions of bullet paths passing through the scene and is especially useful for providing reconstructive information related to the location of shooters and participants receiving gunshot wounds along these bullet paths. The

Figure 8.72

Finished drawings such as the illustrated bullet path in this residence can be prepared from a hand-drawn sketch but are not essential to the successful outcome of the shooting scene investigation. They can, however, be quite useful for informing a jury in court. I prepared this projection diagram for this purpose using an easy-to-use Broderbund Home Architect 3D drawing program and then annotated it using PowerPoint.

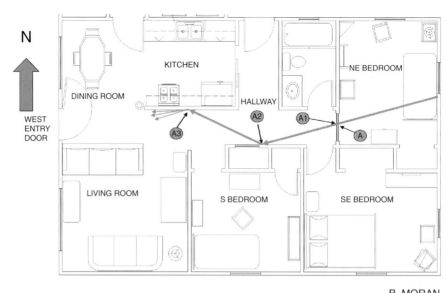

Ⓐ Ⓐ1 = ENTRY/EXIT HOLES

Ⓐ2 Ⓐ3 = RICOCHET SITES

5858 _____ Dr.
ESTIMATED BULLET PATH

B. MORAN
9-30-02
LAB NO. 02-
SSD NO. 02-

Figure 8.73

This finished diagram illustrates various bullet paths in a vehicle prepared by scanning in a generic vehicle diagram into PowerPoint and using the simple drawing tools of this software program to annotate it.

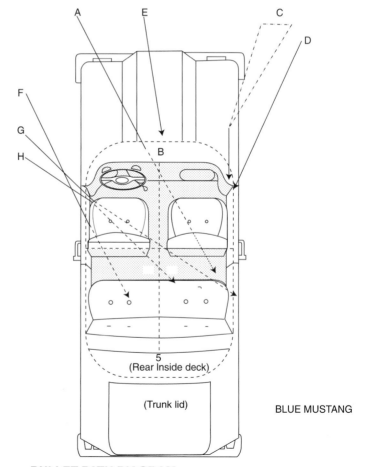

BULLET PATH DIAGRAM
(NOT TO SCALE)
Drawn by: B. MORAN, 9-24-99
Lab No.

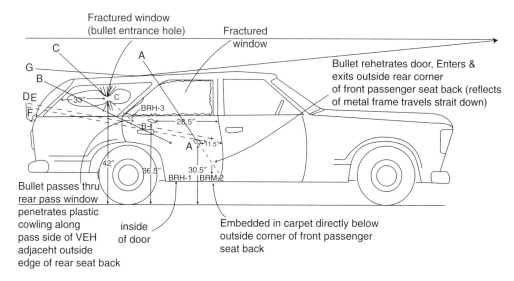

Figure 8.74

Elevation diagrams provide height perspective views of a shooting scene and are an essential form of documentation for reconstructing bullet paths. This hand-drawn example depicts several bullets that have entered at the rear and right rear of a station wagon and one bullet that has deflected off the roof of the vehicle.

diagram is also very useful in orienting the reconstructionist to the overall layout of the scene and facilitating the correlation of crime scene photographs to specific locations and perspective views.

ELEVATION DIAGRAM

Elevation diagrams provide height perspective views of a shooting scene (Fig. 8.74). These views provide valuable elevation information, such as the height of bullet holes and bullet impact sites relative to objects they have struck and their relation to the height of other objects at the scene. Moreover, this diagram is useful for plotting the inclinational direction of bullet paths in the scene as well as any relative ground slopes or contours that could potentially play a significant role in resolving reconstructive issues. Diagrams drawn to scale can be effectively used for illustrating the potential location of a shooter along plotted bullet paths as a function of the shooter's height, as discussed previously.

Three-dimensional (3D) diagrams prepared with the aid of computer drawing programs are effective tools for illustrating aspects of a shooting scene from any perspective. A variety of CAD and 3D drawing programs are available that allow the reconstructionist to prepare illustrations that can then be manipulated in real time to view a scene from any vantage point

Figure 8.75

This 3D perspective diagram of the bullet path in a shooting scene was prepared with the Broderbund Home Architect 3D drawing program and then annotated in PowerPoint. 3D drawing programs allow the reconstructionist to view the crime scene in any perspective.

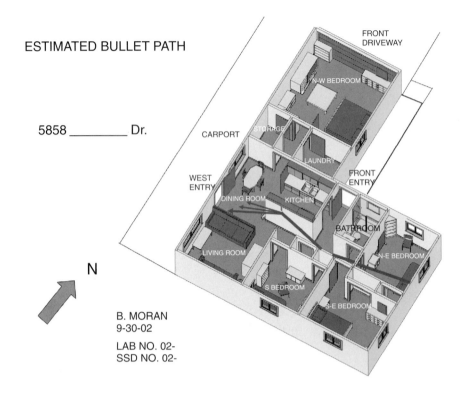

ESTIMATED BULLET PATH

5858 _____ Dr.

B. MORAN
9-30-02

LAB NO. 02-
SSD NO. 02-

(Fig. 8.75). Additionally, programs are also available to construct anatomically accurate human figures in any position. Bullet paths can also be plotted through these models as well. Some of these programs allow for importation of these figures into 2D and 3D reconstructed crime scenes and preparation of 3D models from 2D photographs (Fig. 8.76). I have used some of these programs to great effect in illustrating reconstructed events in shooting incidents (Figs. 8.77 and 8.78). Computer animations have also been used with increasing frequency to illustrate both prosecution and defense theories as this technology has advanced in its sophistication as well as affordability.

CLOTHING OF THE PARTICIPANTS

Clothing of the participants involved in a shooting incident offers a receptacle for a variety of useful information because it retains evidence such as projectile holes that may exhibit sufficient morphology/trace evidence to decipher entrance from exit, gunshot residue patterns, blood patterns, and damage that can provide significant clues with regard to specific events that have taken place in a shooting incident. Thorough photographic documentation of any blood or gunshot residue patterns is mandatory prior to

Figure 8.76

This 3D rendering from an aerial photo taken over the scene of a shooting incident was produced using the Canoma software program. This software allows the reconstructionist to create a 3D model of a shooting scene from a 2D photograph. The model can then be manipulated into any viewpoint and zoomed in and out to any distance. An animated "fly-through" of the 3D scene can also be produced using this software. These models can also be helpful for reconstructing specific viewpoints of key witnesses/participants involved in a shooting incident to either corroborate or refute their statements.

Figure 8.77

This photo depicts a patio area just outside of a kitchen doorway where a fatal shooting occurred with the use of a shotgun. Critical to the case was the position and orientation of the victim and shooter at the moment the fatal shot was fired. The male victim's dress jacket and personal items are observed in the foreground. An expended shotgun shell is just inside the doorway. Spattered, dripped, and trailed bloodstains are also evident.

I prepared this perspective view of the most probable position/orientation of the shooter and victim at the instant the fatal shot was fired after (1) investigating/processing the original shooting scene, (2) examining numerous items of evidence, (3) reviewing the autopsy report, (4) conducting numerous tests with the shotgun and ammunition used, (5) interpreting numerous bloodstains, and (6) considering statements made by witnesses. The shooter and victim were created using Poser superimposed over this perspective view of the patio area created with the Broderbund Home Architect 3D drawing program.

packaging and transport. These patterns and their relationship to other items in the scene are significant observations that can be easily lost without such documentation prior to the collection and transport of the garment. It is also recommended that permission from the coroner or medical examiner be obtained to remove clothing items from any deceased victims to prevent contamination of pattern evidence. In certain cases, bullets will have sufficient energy to perforate the body but insufficient energy to perforate the clothing and may be found inside of clothing.

REVIEW OF THE AUTOPSY REPORT

A review of the postmortem examination report and photographs is a valuable source of information for integration with other observations made at the shooting scene for reconstructive purposes. The pathologist's findings in regard to (1) the locations and direction of projectiles that have penetrated or perforated the deceased; (2) distance estimations of muzzle to entrance wound(s); (3) the nature of the projectile associated with each wound tract, if any; (4) the presence of any significant pattern evidence in the form of wounds, marks from wads or sabots, tattooing, or cylinder gap patterns; and (5) opinions as to the effect of incapacitation from wounds received can add important information to facts established from the examination of the shooting scene.

The reconstructionist often incorporates gunshot wounds and their respective paths into or through the victim with bullet path information gathered at the shooting scene (Fig. 8.79). However, the reader is cautioned that there are some inherent limitations and uncertainties associated with wound paths through the human body. Generally, projectiles penetrating

Figure 8.79

A portion of jacketing recovered from the perforating leg wound of a participant during a postmortem examination was physically matched to the bullet recovered in the floorboard of a vehicle after having passed through the driver's seat cushion. This combined information made it possible to position the gunshot victim in the vehicle at the time the wound was received.

or perforating human bodies travel over very short distances prior to striking the victims. Additionally, bullets striking the body may follow straight paths but may deviate as they pass through tissue, organs, and, most notably, bone. High-powered rifle bullets, due to their length and rearward center of gravity, are more prone to deviation from their initial path when penetrating tissue than short pistol bullets that more closely approach a sphere. Consequently, pistol bullets tend to follow straight paths in tissue unless previously destabilized by contact with an intermediary target prior to striking the body or unevenly deformed during penetration of the tissue (Haag and Haag, 2004, p. 80). Additionally, the recipient of a gunshot wound may likely be in some contorted position at the moment the wound is received and then placed in the standard anatomical position on the autopsy table. For a general understanding of wound profiles, the reader is referred to Roberts (1998) and Fackler (2001), who provide a good general background pertaining to the dynamics involved in wounding effects and incapacitation as well as a variety of diagrammatic examples of wound profiles for various rifle, pistol, and shotgun projectiles.

With these considerations in mind, Haag and Haag (2004, pp. 80–82) emphasize four general sources of information for estimating bullet paths in a gunshot victim: the forensic pathologist's descriptive narrative of the wound path; autopsy photographs; the forensic pathologist's description of bullet entry, exit, recovery site, and organs perforated by the projectile; and additional information such as X-ray films (radiographs).

DESCRIPTIVE NARRATIVE OF THE WOUND PATH

Descriptive narratives of the wound path are typically provided in the main body of the forensic pathologist's postmortem report. Some pathologists will include angle references relative to the vertical and horizontal planes of the body, such as "the projectile enters the lower right back directed back to front, upward 30°, right to left 10° and exiting at the anterior midline of the sternum." These descriptors can be extremely useful for integrating with bullet paths established within the shooting scene to assist in locating/orienting the victim at the moment the gunshot wound was received.

AUTOPSY PHOTOGRAPHS

Obtaining a set of photographs of the postmortem examination is recommended in addition to obtaining the forensic pathologist's report. The photographs should be carefully examined in general and referenced to all observations described by the pathologist. Autopsy photographs depicting probes inserted into the wound track can also be used to estimate the horizontal and vertical angles provided that the photographs have been taken from the proper perspectives (Fig. 8.80). In the event that inappropriate

Figure 8.80

Autopsy photographs depicting probes inserted into the wound track can be used to estimate the horizontal and vertical angles provided that they have been taken from the proper perspective. The perspective of this photo is taken at eye level and perpendicular to the plane of the decedent's back, making it possible to estimate the angle of the bullet path.

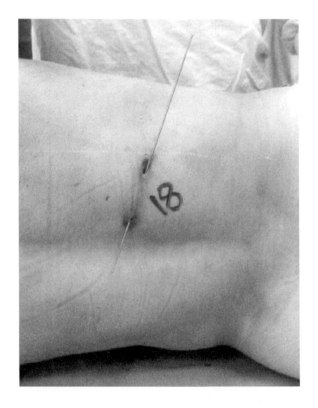

views of the probes are the only photos available, it may be difficult, if not completely unreliable, to make estimates of such angular components of the bullet path in the decedent. If this is the case, the reconstructionist should consult the forensic pathologist who performed the postmortem examination to solicit concurrence with any estimates made (Fig. 8.81). It should also be kept in mind that the wound path represented by the probe may not be a true representation of the actual bullet path if the decedent was in some position other than the supine position on the autopsy table.

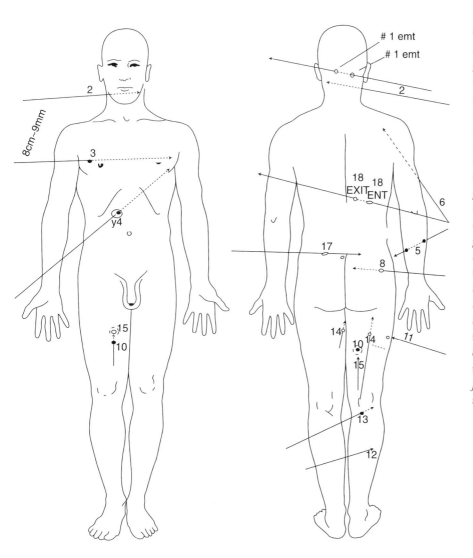

Figure 8.81

In this case, the pathologist narratively described the bullet paths but did not provide any illustrations or photos of the bullet paths. In order to obtain a clearer understanding of the various bullet paths, I plotted the bullet paths using this anatomical diagram based on the pathologist's narrative descriptions of the wounds received by the decedent. I then presented the diagram to the pathologist to verify the accuracy of the represented bullet paths before drawing reconstructive conclusions from this source of information.

Figure 8.82

This anatomical model, produced by the author using Poser, depicts a decedent who suffered three gunshot wounds. The model can be viewed from any viewpoint using the software program and images can be exported for illustration and study. In this case, the left arm of the victim was raised at the instant a bullet passed through the triceps muscle and into the left chest (black probe depicted). When the decedent is lying on the autopsy table, this observation is not apparent, but it can be effectively illustrated using such models.

DESCRIPTION OF BULLET ENTRY, EXIT, RECOVERY SITE, AND ORGANS PERFORATED

With rare exception, forensic pathologists will document the location of bullet entry wounds, exit wounds, and recovery locations of any projectiles found in the body. These locations are typically referenced with measurements to a common point such as the top of the head and direction of the anterior or posterior midline of the body. Using the length of the bullet track and the measured locations of the entry and exit wounds, it is possible to trigonometrically calculate the vertical and horizontal angles of the bullet path. The measured bullet entry and exit wound locations can be plotted on an anatomical diagram or within a computer model depicting a human body of similar size and weight. I have had success producing such anatomical computer models and then viewing the model from various viewpoints and/or importing such models into photographs or 3D diagrams of the scene (Fig. 8.82).

X-RAY FILMS (RADIOGRAPHS)

X-rays of the body can provide useful information, such as a visual trail of small bullet fragments (most commonly lead fragments) along the bullet track and any projectiles. Bones that have been struck or fractured can also be revealed. Additionally, it is possible to identify/characterize projectiles and other ammunition components in X-rays of surviving victims who have not had them surgically removed (Figs. 8.83 and 8.84).

Just as a fired bullet that passes through a shooting scene records a snapshot of time within a sequence of events including the instant a victim is struck, in some cases this momentary recording may indicate the posture of the decedent and/or the orientation of body parts to each other at the time the gunshot wound(s) was received. Additional information that can be obtained from the autopsy report might include the number and types of firearms responsible for striking the decedent with projectiles and the distance of the decedent to the shooter or shooters.

It is advisable to consult the pathologist who performed the examination to confirm, clarify, or expound on the conclusions stated in his or her report if any of the previously discussed possibilities becomes apparent from this source of information. I routinely ask the pathologist about the ability of the victim to perform tasks before expiring and the length of time required for the victim to perform tasks before expiring. This subtle but important information may have a bearing on the feasibility of certain theories that may be brought forward during the investigation.

MEDICAL RECORDS AND PHYSICIAN REPORTS

To a much lesser degree, it is possible to obtain useful information from doctors' reports made during medical intervention of shooting incident participants. However, typically physicians are not trained to make forensic observations. Furthermore, the goal of the physician is to save lives and any observations made concerning the detailed nature of wounds, projectile paths, and distances are secondary to that goal. Reports are often sparse, vague, and confusing. If potential significant observations can be made from medical reports, it is strongly suggested that the physician who prepared the report be consulted for confirmation and/or clarification of conclusions.

REVIEW OF CRIME SCENE PHOTOGRAPHS, DIAGRAMS, AND REPORTS

In many cases, the reconstructionist will be consulted well after the shooting incident has occurred. When there is no opportunity to examine the

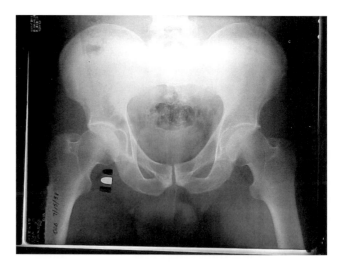

Figure 8.83

A police officer was shot through the pelvic region while attempting to apprehend a suspect wanted for several murders. The bullet was not removed from the officer for medical reasons, and it became important to know if the officer was shot by the suspect or a fellow officer during the incident. This X-ray depicts a bullet that transversed the hips of the wounded officer and lodged in the right hip area. The X-ray was taken in such an orientation that a clear profile of the bullet shape could be seen.

Figure 8.84

The side profiles of the bullets associated with ammunition used in the suspect's gun and police officer's service weapons were compared. The suspect was using ammunition with full metal jacketed round-nose bullets, whereas the police officers were using jacketed hollowpoint bullets. The profiles of sample bullets from these two sources of ammunition were directly compared to the profile of the shadow created by the bullet in the X-ray. I was able to eliminate the police officers' ammunition but not the suspect's ammunition.

original shooting scene, any visual data recorded at the scene therefore becomes the next best alternative to the visual walk-through. It is paramount that a thorough review of all crime scene photographs (including Polaroid photos and snapshots taken by responding officers), crime scene video, crime scene diagrams, and crime scene investigative reports be conducted.

It is my practice to begin familiarizing myself with the scene by first organizing the photographs into a logical order by specific locations within the overall scene and correlating them with any crime scene sketches and/or diagrams that are submitted. The photos are then inserted into clear plastic photo album pocket organizer pages and assembled in a three-ring binder. This facilitates the ability to scan through the photographs as many times and in as much detail as required to gather as much information as possible to assist in resolving whatever questions have been posed or will be posed as the review process develops. The clear plastic protecting the photographs allows me to make notations using an assortment of colored fine-tipped indelible marking pens without damaging the original photographs. Emulsion-based photographs of special interest are typically scanned and/or imported into various media programs, such as Adobe Photoshop, PowerPoint, and Microsoft Word, allowing for enhancement of certain details in the photographs and/or preparation or annotation of notes or observations and/or court exhibits that can be more readily reviewed by any interested party.

With the significant advancements in digital photography, a rapidly increasing percentage of crime scene and evidence documentation is being conducted with this media. Digital images captured with equipment available today are approaching the resolution of emulsion-based photos and are a viable means of crime scene documentation. These images may be rapidly screened on the computer and/or printed out in catalogue form and reviewed in the same manner as described for emulsion-based photographs. Additionally, digital images are very conducive for import into word processing program documents for the purposes of annotation, note taking, supporting conclusions, and report writing. The images may also be used with a presentation program for presenting observations to others. Caution should be taken when relying on such photographs for estimating distances or relationships of items to each other. As previously discussed, field sketches and diagrams are of great importance in supplementing crime scene photographs because they greatly aide in accurately locating items of evidence, establishing their spatial relationship to other items in the scene, documenting the specific location of bullet holes and impact defects that can later be used to ascertain the direction of projectile paths, etc. Additionally, crime scene sketches or diagrams are very useful in correlating item and/or photographic reference numbers depicted in specific photographs when organizing the crime scene photo review binder and orienting the reconstructionist to the shooting scene.

I carefully review reports of crime scene personnel and investigators who have specifically described the condition of the crime scene. These sources of information typically bring attention to significant observations relative to the reconstructive problems at hand as well as direct the reconstructionist to conditions of the scene that may or may not be obvious in the photographs, such as lighting conditions, locked and unlocked doors, settings on appliances, room/atmospheric temperatures, and wet stains.

I also purposely review lists and descriptions of specific items collected at the scene that provide details about items not described in the narrative crime scene report or depicted in photographs. These lists can also be correlated against any evidential examination conducted in the laboratory. Ultimately, the degree of the reconstructionist's success will be directly dependent on the quality and thoroughness of the crime scene documentation. The value of photographic evidence is maximized when the photographs taken at the scene include overall orientation views, medium-view/approach views, and close-up view photographs that include some sort of scale. The reconstructionist can make detailed observations about the appearance and condition of individual items of evidence (with close-up photos), relate the position and orientation of specific items to the environment immediately surrounding them (with medium or approach views), and locate the items in the overall shooting scene (overall views).

The review of any videotape recordings of the crime scene is also highly recommended because it offers an excellent supplement to still photographs. Often, shooting scene videotapes recorded in a systematic fashion with good use of the overall, medium view, and close-up view approach provide an excellent perspective of the scene second only to examining the original scene first-hand. Additionally, videotapes may be the only visual source for filling in the photographic gaps created by failure to record coordinated overall, medium view, and close-up still photos. Although, in general, the resolution of videotape is inferior to still photos, this visual source of information often records details either purposely or coincidentally that can be of great significance in providing important clues to the investigation. If such observations are significant, these frames may be captured and converted into still photos.

REVIEW OF FIRST RESPONDING POLICE OFFICER REPORTS

A review of police reports can provide significant findings, most notably observations made by first responding officers to a shooting incident. Observations made by such personnel are often the only source of information detailing the original condition of the shooting scene. It is inevitable that any postincident activity will alter any crime scene, no matter how diligent efforts are to protect it. As a result, subtle but significant conditions are changed prior to their documentation that may have significance in resolving reconstructive issues. Examples include lighting conditions; the position of doors, windows, and furniture; the status of appliances (on, off, settings, etc.); and the position of small items, such as fired cartridge cases, that can be moved.

Polaroid photographs, 35-mm film, or digital snapshots taken by first responding officers can be very important in establishing original conditions of shooting scenes including positions of wounded or deceased participants, bloodstain patterns, and locations of firearms and fired cartridge cases, which are vulnerable to inadvertent change during the course of the crime scene investigation. Officers assigned to accompany the transport of shooting victims to the hospital for emergency medical treatment may occasionally take photos of the victims during transport and treatment as well and thereby record the appearance of wounds and clothing items that will likely be significantly altered during such treatment. Lighting conditions and the positions of doors and windows may only be recalled by first responding officers and/or emergency medical personnel. If such issues become significant and are not recorded in official reports, it may be necessary to interview first responding officers, firefighters, and emergency medical personnel.

REVIEW OF INVESTIGATIVE REPORTS, INCLUDING VICTIM, SUSPECT, AND WITNESS STATEMENTS

Statements made by victims, suspects, and witnesses and conclusions rendered in investigative reports by investigative personnel can provide information as the basis for the development and testing of scenarios and theories. Additionally, observations by these participants and witnesses can direct significance to certain items of physical evidence that might not otherwise be apparent to investigators at the time the statements are made. However, the reader is cautioned that such statements should be considered only for this purpose, and they should not be relied on as fact. Consequently, physical evidence and observations made at the shooting scene should be consciously correlated with participant statements to either support or refute them.

It is my experience that eyewitness information in many instances is incomplete or falls short of the truth, even when offered in good faith. Witness's recollections can fade with time, be altered due to stressful conditions, be made deceitful for personal benefit, and conflict with other statements. For example, descriptions of firearms observed during a shooting incident are often vague at best and totally inaccurate at worst. So too are statements about the location or posture of shooting scene participants. Notorious for their inaccuracy are "earwitness" statements of the number of shots fired or the caliber of the firearm by the sound heard. It is more the exception than the rule that physical evidence fully supports the accounts of such recollections. Physical evidence, however, when properly documented and interpreted, does not fade in memory and can serve to clarify these ambiguities created by witness statements. Investigative reports may also offer theories of how incidents occurred. These theories, as previously suggested, should neither be believed nor disbelieved but, rather, considered as possibilities that can later be included or excluded when cross-referenced with all sources of physical evidence and crime scene documentation. In this spirit, the reconstructionist should maintain an objective and unemotional demeanor regardless of how far-fetched some theories may seem. It may well be the case that what seems outlandish as a possibility cannot be proven wrong and may therefore be the correct reconstruction of the events being studied.

REVIEW OF LABORATORY PHYSICAL EVIDENCE EXAMINATION REPORTS

Physical evidence examination reports prepared by forensic scientists, including tool mark evidence, footwear and tire track evidence, trace evidence, serology/DNA results, blood pattern interpretation, and toxicological findings, are invaluable tools that can be used to attach additional significance to observations and determinations from firearms-related evidence in the shooting scene and thereby add greatly to the big picture approach of the shooting scene reconstructionist. The reconstructionist is at a great advantage if he or she has at minimum a generalist background in as many of the forensic disciplines as possible to take advantage of these additional sources of information. The reconstructionist should take advantage of the expertise of specialists who have examined the physical evidence or visited the shooting scene. Consultation with forensic scientists who have conducted such examinations is often fruitful in gaining additional insight from the perspective of the analyst that might not be apparent in the written report. Additionally, a review of photographs and notes prepared by the analyst during such consultations may also provide significant observations that would otherwise go unnoticed. The following are examples:

- Tool mark evidence may assist in establishing location and modes of entry and exit within a shooting scene. Additionally, tool marks caused by unconventional items that come into contact with each other, such as impressed damage to a wall by the corner of a sliding table, can provide associative information relating items or events to each other.

- Footwear impression evidence may assist in establishing movements made by participants during the course of a shooting incident.
- Tire track impression evidence may assist in establishing movements of vehicles used by participants in a shooting incident.
- Blood patterns may assist in establishing the location and specific activities of victims wounded or killed during a shooting incident or postshooting activities of surviving participants who have come into contact with sources of blood.
- Fingerprint evidence may assist in establishing locations of participants in a shooting incident and establish certain associations with the shooting scene or the manner in which items were handled during the course of a shooting incident.
- Trace evidence may assist in establishing contact between participants, location of participants within the scene, and association of participants to the shooting incident. Additionally, trace evidence on fired components and firearms may serve to associate these items with other important surfaces they may have come into contact with during the course of the shooting incident. For example, fibers collected from a firearm that can be associated with the pocket lining of a suspect's jacket may serve to suggest this person as the most likely possessor of the firearm in situations in which multiple shooters are involved, or blue paint transfers on the side of a fired bullet might strongly suggest the bullet to be the source of a bullet ricochet observed on a blue vehicle present at the shooting scene.
- Serological/DNA evidence may be valuable for associating participants with a shooting incident, associating specific projectiles with through and through wounds received by participants, or identifying individuals who may have operated a firearm or handled certain ammunition components.
- Toxicological findings may provide a better indication of the ability of surviving participants as well as decedents to perform certain tasks prior to, during, and after a shooting incident.

REVISITING THE SHOOTING SCENE

A visit to the shooting scene even well after the fact, when feasible, is highly recommended if for no other reason than to gain a real-life perspective for the layout of the shooting scene environment. On numerous occasions, I have visited the scenes of shooting incidents for this purpose and/or to conduct follow-up examinations that have become necessary to address specific questions that have developed during the reconstructive process.

Additionally, I have returned to the scene to reconstruct parts of the shooting scene for the purpose of testing various theories that have been developed during the case review.

Typical revisits to the scene have been for purposes as simple as the recovery of fired projectiles that have been left inside walls or inaccessible objects. A return to the shooting scene may also be for the purpose of locating bullet holes and impact sites previously documented and using this information to reconstruct the paths of bullets responsible for creating these defects. More involved revisits to the scene have been done for the placement of items damaged by gunfire, such as vehicles examined in the laboratory, back into their original positions at the shooting scene using crime scene photographs and measurements obtained during the original investigation. Bullet paths that have been predetermined by such laboratory examinations can be extrapolated throughout the extent of the overall shooting scene, taking advantage of the original crime scene environment/terrain. Subsequent documentation of shooter position possibilities along the extrapolated paths is then demonstrated as previously described and documented using photography and the construction of additional crime scene diagrams for either supporting or refuting theories that have been or will be offered.

TESTING OF PROPOSED THEORIES AND OFFERING THE BEST SOLUTIONS THROUGH ROLE PLAYING

Ultimately, the gathering of information results in the ability to test proposed scenarios offered by participants and witnesses or theories offered by police officers, investigators, and attorneys. I suggest that the reconstructionist take a methodical approach to testing these offerings by formulating theories as they are proposed and including as many variations of scenarios that are feasible that might account for the physical evidence gathered at the shooting scene, regardless of how absurd some may seem.

I also encourage the practice of active discussions and role playing with other investigative and forensic science professionals to more rapidly develop any alternate theories that might be feasible and to attempt to disprove as many of the proposed theories as possible. On more than one occasion, this power of multiple thinking has proven quite effective in eliminating all but a few or even one scenario that is fully supported by the physical evidence. It has been my experience that, occasionally, after working laboriously without the benefit of input from others, it becomes increasingly difficult to view the problems at hand with the imaginative thinking so necessary for maximum success. Then in a single moment, a fresh pair of eyes and/or perspective offered by a colleague has resulted in suggestions that have led to solutions that are fully supported by the physical evidence.

CLOSING COMMENTS

In 1991, Bell offered a rather concise definition for reconstruction as a "process of utilizing information derived from physical evidence at the scene, from analyses of physical evidence, and from inferences drawn from such analyses to test various theories of the occurrences of prior events" and that "the above definition indicates that reconstruction is neither an art nor a science, but a process" (p. 741). Reconstruction is indeed a process of elimination conducted with the information that is available. Critiques of the reconstruction process may suggest that it is not possible to reconstruct events in a particular case because changes had been made subsequent to the crime and prior to the crime scene preservation by investigative personnel or due to a lack of physical evidence at the crime scene. Under the previous definition, such a suggestion would not necessarily be true. Due to the lack of information available, the reconstruction will simply be less refined than otherwise. Even in such cases, it may be possible to answer questions to a certain point. For example, it may not be possible to reconstruct the exact position of a shooter, but there may be sufficient information to indicate a general direction such that all but one participant may be excluded as having been in the area suggested.

Given sufficient information, more definitive conclusions can be drawn. For example, in a shooting involving two shooters and a decedent who has received a single perforating wound, the question may be who was responsible for firing the fatal shot. Several bullets are recovered from an adjacent wall near the decedent that are identified as having been fired by the shooters' two guns. The information gathered so far is insufficient to answer the question; however, the presence of blood and tissue containing the decedent's DNA profile on one of the identified bullets provides strong support to implicate the suspect in possession of the firearm responsible for firing the bullet as the responsible party for delivering the fatal shot.

This chapter has been offered as an introduction to the subject of shooting scene reconstruction. Any party involved in a shooting incident investigation can better utilize physical evidence when he or she understands that physical evidence can do more than simply place a person at the scene. To stop at this point and not utilize physical evidence to help establish a record of the events that occurred during the course of the shooting incident is missing a valuable aide. The advantage of physical evidence at shooting scenes is that it can be used to support or refute witness statements, provide undisputable evidence of certain events, as well as associate participants with the shooting incident. The stories offered by participants can be cross-checked and compared and contrasted with the position or condition of items at the scene or patterns produced by actions of physical activities. This is where the process of shooting incident reconstruction makes its greatest contribution.

A comprehensive approach to the evaluation of physical evidence, investigative information, and witness statements from a multidisciplinary standpoint is highly recommended in resolving issues in shooting incidents. Following a logical, methodical, and thorough approach to shooting scene investigation with big picture thinking and grounded in the application of the scientific method will maximize the chances of a successful investigative outcome and be well worth the effort. Finally, it is my hope that those experienced in this area, having read the information in this discussion, will view their next shooting incident with a different eye and see it from a new perspective that will enhance their ability to both identify reconstructive questions and resolve them effectively. For those who have little or no experience, I hope that you will be inspired to pursue the tools necessary to perform such work.

ACKNOWLEDGMENTS

I thank John Murdock and John Thornton for their encouragement to write this chapter and for their support during its preparation.

REFERENCES

Barr, D. "Modification to the Common Trigonometric Method of Bullet Impact Angle Determination," *AFTE Journal*, 33(2), 116–121, Spring 2001a.

Barr, D. "The Trig-Elliptical Method of Bullet Impact Angle Determination," *AFTE Journal*, 33(2), 122–124, Spring 2001b.

Bell, P. "A Proposed Definition of Homicide Reconstruction," *AFTE Journal*, 23(2), April 1991.

Besant-Mathews, P. E., Thompson, E. J., Hamby, J. E., et al., "The Rifled Shotgun Barrel Effect," *AFTE Journal*, 24(3), 246–252, July 1992.

Di Maio, V. J. M. *Gunshot Wounds.* (2nd ed.). Boca Raton, FL: CRC Press, 1999.

Dillon, J. H. "The Sodium Rhodizonzte Test: A Chemically Specific Chromophoric Test for Lead in Gunshot Residues," *AFTE Journal*, 22(3), 251–256, July 1990a.

Dillon, J. H. "The Modified Griess Test: A Chemically Specific Chromophoric Test for Nitrite Compounds in Gunshot Residues," *AFTE Journal*, 22(3), 243–256, July 1990b.

Fackler, M. L. "Wound Profiles," *Wound Ballistic Review Journal*, 5(2), 25–38, Fall 2001.

Garrison, D. H., Jr. "Reconstructing Drive-by Shootings from Ejected Cartridge Case Location," *AFTE Journal*, 25(1), 15–20, January 1993.

Garrison, D. H., Jr. "The Effective Use of Bullet Hole Probes in Crime Scene Reconstruction," *AFTE Journal*, 28(1), 57–63, January 1996.

Garrsion, H. *Practical Shooting Scene Investigation: The Investigation and Reconstruction of Crime Scenes Involving Gunfire.* Universal Publishers/uPUBLISH.com, 2003.

Grzybowski, R., Miller, J., Moran, B., Murdock, J., Nichols, R., and Thompson, R. "Firearm/Toolmark Identification: Passing Reliability Test under Federal and State Evidentiary Standards," *AFTE Journal*, 35(2), 209–240, Spring 2003.

Haag, L. C. "Bullet Ricochet from Water," *AFTE Journal*, 11(3), 27–34, July 1979.

Haag, L. C. "Cartridge Case Ejection Patterns," *AFTE Journal*, 30(2), 300–308, Spring 1988.

Haag, L. C. "A Microchemical Test for Copper-Containing Bullet Wiping," *AFTE Journal*, 21(2), 298–303, April 1989.

Haag, L. C. "Hornady Vector Ammunition: A New Tool in Studying Selected Exterior and Terminal Ballistic Events of Forensic Interest," *AFTE Journal*, 32(1), 32–40, January 1996.

Haag, L. C. "The Average Pellet-to-Pellet Distance for Estimating Range of Fire in Cases Involving Partial Pellet Patterns," *AFTE Journal*, 34(2), 139–143, Spring 2002.

Haag, L. C. "Sequence of Shots through Tempered Glass," *AFTE Journal*, 36(1), 54–59, 2004.

Haag, L. C. "Firearms for Attorneys." In *Forensic Evidence*, pp. VII–21. California District Attorney's Association, 731 K Street, Third Floor, Sacramento, CA, 95814-3402, 1997.

Haag, L. C., and Haag, M. G. *Forensic Shooting Scene Reconstruction Course—Training Manual*, November 8–12, 2004, Prescott, AZ, pp. 1–104.

Hueske, E. E. "Recognition and Documentation of Bullet Ricochet Characteristics and Predicting Shot Directionalities," *SWAFS Journal*, 25(2), 35–45, July 2003.

Kirk, P. L. *Crime Investigation*, (Ed.). J. I. Thornton. (2nd ed.), pp. 262–263. New York: John Wiley, 1974.

Lastrucci, C. L. *The Scientific Approach—Basic Principles of the Scientific Method.* Cambridge, MA: Schenkman, 1967.

MacPherson, D., and Fincel, E. "Windsheld Glass Penetration," *Wound Ballistics Review*, 2(4), 35–39, 1996.

Mitosinka, G. T. "A Technique for Determining and Illustrating the Trajectory of Bullets," *Journal of the Forensic Science Society*, 11(1), 55–61, January 1971.

Moran, B., and Murdock, J. "Zen and the Art of Motorcycle Maintenance—Contribution to Forensic Science—An Explanation of the Scientific Method," *AFTE Journal*, 35(2), 234–240, Spring 2003.

Murdock, J., Goldman, G., and Schorr, R. "The Examination of Suspect Bullet Holes and Related Impressions, The Collection of Bullets at Crime Scenes and the Evaluation of BB Angle of Incidence on Glass," *CAC News Lettter*, 9–13, October 1987.

Patty, J. R., McJunkins, S. P., and Murdock, J. E. "Associating Recovered Projectiles with Ricochet Sites," *AFTE Journal*, 7(2), 28–32, July 1975.

Prendergast, J. M. "Determination of Bullet Impact Position from the Examination of Fractured Automobile Safety Glass," *AFTE Journal*, 26(2), 107–118, April 1994.

Rathman, G. A. "Bullet Ricochet and Associated Phenomena," *AFTE Journal*, 19(4), 374–387, October 1987.

Rathman, G. A. "Bullet Impact Damage and Trajectory through Auto Glass," *AFTE Journal*, 25(2), 79–86, April 1993.

Rathman, G. A., and Ryland, S. G. "Use of the SEM-EDXA as an Aid to the Firearms Examiner," *AFTE Journal*, 19(4), 388–392, October 1987.

Roberts, G. K. "The Wounding Effects of 5.56mm/.223 Law Enforcement General Purpose Shoulder Fired Carbines with 12 GA. Shotguns and Pistol Caliber Weapons Using 10% Ordinance Gelatin as a Tissue Simulant," *Wound Ballistics Review Journal*, 3(4), 16–28, 1998.

Roberts, J. L. "Windshield Glass Crack Propagation Resulting from Additional Bullet Passage," AFTE 36th Annual Training Seminar, Indianapolis, IN, June 19–24, 1998, (james.Roberts@ventura.org)

Thornton, J., and Cashman, P. J. "The Effect of Tempered Glass on Bullet Trajectory," *Journal of Forensic Sciences*, 32(2), 743–746, April 1986.

Van Arsdale, M. "Determining Bullet Trajectory from a Ricochet off Windshield Glass," *AFTE Journal*, 30(2), 309–315, Spring 1998.

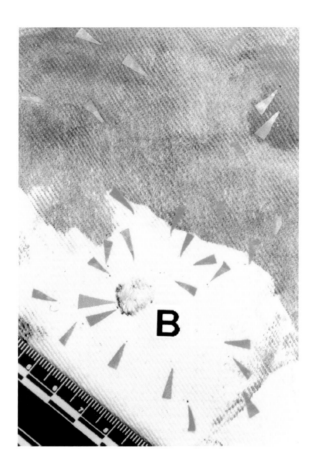

Figure 8.18

The bullet entry hole displaying classic "bullet wipe" favoring the left edge of the defect is depicted in the material of a pair of light-colored pants. Green arrows indicate the locations of gunpowder particles. The orange arrow indicates the location of a microscopic fragment of copper. These observations suggest that a copper jacketed bullet struck the garment at an angle from left to right fired from a gun at a distance of approximately 1 or 2 feet.

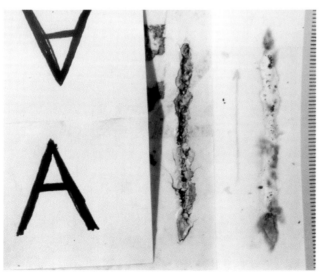

Figure 8.19

This gouge in a linoleum floor is actually a bullet ricochet site. Note the strong rosy-red color reaction associated with the presence of lead (a common constituent of bullets) along the margins of the defect as represented by the filter paper transfer treated with sodium rhodizonate reagent. This reagent can be useful in the field for detecting obscure defects that might not be recognized as damage caused by bullet impact.

Figure 8.33

Brightly colored red string was used to extrapolate the paths of buckshot that passed through a wooden sign and continued into the vehicle while the door was in the open position. This reconstruction was conducted while the vehicle was in its original position at the scene.

Figure 8.34

This photograph illustrates the bullet path from the perspective of the shooter. Colored string with colored Post-it notes attached at 2-feet intervals for increased visibility in the photograph represent these two bullet paths.

Figure 9.3

The red areas are lividity; the light band across this woman's back and on her hips is where the weight of the body was as she was lying on her back. The compression of the tissue kept the blood from draining into these areas.

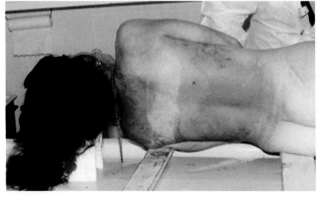

CHAPTER 9

RECONSTRUCTION USING BLOODSTAIN EVIDENCE

W. Jerry Chisum, BS

Blood will tell, but often it tells too much.
—Don Marquis (1878–1937), *A Roach of the Taverns*

The examination and use of bloodstain evidence in criminal investigations and court proceedings is not new, even to this past century. Neither is an appreciation of its multiplicity. As explained by Andrew Fleming, MD (1830–1896), who wrote about the importance of examining and identifying bloodstains at the time of the Civil War (1861, p. 1):

> In the trial of criminal cases, especially where the evidence is of circumstantial character, it is frequently of the greatest importance to determine of what certain spots are composed, in order to fix the guilt or attest the innocence of the accused.
>
> . . .
>
> The blood is an almost homogenous fluid, endowed, while under the catalytic influence of the vessels, with a property closely resembling vitality, and bearing the elements out of which the various structures are to be developed or sustained, and from which the glands elaborate their special secretions. The variety of its numerous attributes indicates the complexity of its nature. Owing to its complexity, and the absolute certainty required in a medicolegal investigation, arises the difficulty of the examination of suspicious stains.

Though Fleming was concerned primarily with the chemistry and composition of blood, he was ultimately interested in the purpose of our current work: crime reconstruction. As such, his worthy sentiments remain relevant.

Bloodstains are among the most useful forms of physical evidence in the reconstruction of a crime. They are present in almost all cases involving violence where there is bloodshed. They may also be present in burglaries, hit-and-runs, and many other crimes. Most recognize their present value for the identification and comparison of the blood, often with DNA testing, which assists in determining whose blood is present and where. However, bloodstains can also provide reconstruction information that far exceeds their identification through DNA and other technologies. Bloodstain patterns—their existence, shape, volume, and location—may be of tremendous reconstructive value. In other words, there may be no question about whose blood it is, but the nature and causes of the patterns left behind may give a great deal of information about what events took place and how.

Bloodstain patterns are the visible record of the bloodshed at a crime scene. *Bloodstain pattern analysis* is the examination of the shapes, locations, and distribution patterns of bloodstains for the purpose of interpreting the physical events that caused them. It is premised on the assertion that all bloodstain patterns are characteristic of the forces that created them.

This chapter is not intended for the bloodstain pattern novice, although certain basic information is discussed. It is written for the reconstructionist who has attended bloodstain courses by qualified forensic scientists, studied bloodstain texts, and further conducted his or her own experiments to learn what blood actually does. This chapter is intended to provide such reconstructionists with further tips and applied information about how to approach the problem of interpreting bloodstains.

For those unfamiliar with the subject, several competent volumes have already been written about bloodstain pattern analysis. I recommend studying at least the following three:

- James, S. *Scientific and Legal Applications of Bloodstain Pattern Interpretation.* Boca Raton, FL: CRC Press, 1998.
- James, S., and Eckert, W. *Interpretation of Bloodstain Evidence at Crime Scenes,* 2nd ed. Boca Raton, FL: CRC Press, 1998.
- Bevel, T., and Gardner, R. *Bloodstain Pattern Analysis: With an Introduction to Crime Scene Reconstruction,* 2nd ed. Boca Raton, FL: CRC Press, 2001.

SHORT COURSE PITFALLS: RECOMMENDATIONS FOR FURTHER STUDY

In addition to reading the recommended publications, it is advised that anyone interested in crime reconstruction take a course in bloodstain analysis from a qualified forensic scientist. These courses can be useful for providing certain basic overviews of fundamental concepts. However, depending on the scientific background of the instructor, they may be lacking in certain crucial areas. A true scientist will find that a majority of the short bloodstain classes are lacking with regard to a discussion of accuracy, precision, and significant numbers. Appreciating these deficiencies is the difference between the technician's pedantic understanding of blood-stains and the forensic scientist's interpretive role in the reconstruction of the crime.

A great deal of time in these classes will be spent on single drop analyses and the review of basic bloodstain types and terms. The following terms that are introduced in these classes include primarily those recommended by the International Association of Bloodstain Pattern Analysts (IABPA). It is not an all-inclusive list:[1]

[1] For a complete list, go to www.**iabpa**.org/Terminology.pdf

- *Angle of impact*: The acute angle formed between the direction of a blood drop and the plane of the surface it strikes.
- *Arterial spurting*: Bloodstain pattern(s) resulting from blood exiting the body under pressure from a breached artery.
- *Back spatter*: Blood directed back toward the source of energy or force that caused the spatter.
- *Castoff pattern*: A bloodstain pattern created when blood is released from a blood-bearing object in motion.
- *Directionality*: The directionality of a bloodstain or pattern that indicates the direction the blood was traveling when it impacted the target surface. Directionality of a blood drop's flight can usually be established from the geometric shape of its bloodstain.
- *Drip pattern*: A bloodstain pattern resulting from blood dripping into blood.
- *Expired blood*: Blood that is blown out of the nose, mouth, or a wound as a result of air pressure and/or airflow, which is the propelling force.
- *Flow pattern*: A change in the shape and direction of a bloodstain due to the influence of gravity or movement of the object.
- *High-velocity impact spatter*: A bloodstain pattern caused by a high-velocity impact/force to a blood source such as that produced by gunshot or high-speed machinery.
- *Impact pattern*: Bloodstain pattern created when blood receives a blow or force resulting in the dispersion of smaller drops of blood.
- *Low-velocity impact spatter*: A bloodstain pattern that is caused by a low-velocity impact/force to a blood source.
- *Medium-velocity impact spatter*: A bloodstain pattern caused by a medium-velocity impact/force to a blood source.
- *Perimeter stain*: A bloodstain that consists of only its outer periphery, the central area having been removed by wiping or flaking after liquid blood has partially or completely dried. Also called a "ghost stain."
- *Point of origin*: The common point (area) in three-dimensional space to which the trajectories of several blood drops can be retraced.

- *Spatter*: That blood which has been dispersed as a result of force applied to a source of blood. Patterns produced are often characteristic of the nature of the forces that created them.
- *Swipe pattern*: The transfer of blood from a moving source onto an unstained surface. The direction of travel may be determined by the feathered edge.
- *Target*: A surface on which blood has been deposited.
- *Transfer/contact patterns*: A bloodstain pattern created when a wet, bloody surface comes in contact with a second surface. A recognizable image of all or a portion of the original surface may be observed in the pattern.
- *Void*: An absence of stains in an otherwise continuous bloodstain pattern.
- *Wipe pattern*: A bloodstain pattern created when an object moves through an existing stain, removing and/or altering its appearance.

These terms will allow you to communicate with other bloodstain analysts and are important for that reason.[2] However, there are mathematics and physics components necessary to make certain bloodstain interpretations. Without this background, the reconstructionist is insufficiently prepared to perform bloodstain pattern analysis. The mathematics are seldom included in short bloodstain classes, and this should be noted by all concerned.

For example, seldom does anyone but a scientist question the measuring devices used. It is well-known that all measuring devices have limitations. The accuracy of any instrument used should be determined and accounted for in all interpretations. For example, a reticule in a hand lens cannot be used to measure micrometer distances. It is at best ±0.2 mm, yet there have been cases in which the second decimal place or 0.01 mm was claimed. In teaching classes and enlarging the drops to five times their size we enlarged photo copies of the drops to 5 times their size. Thirty students measured the drops using stereomicroscopes and reticules. There was considerable variation in the measurements. Yet drops at a scene are measured one time, and the results are used to calculate the angle at which the drop strikes a surface. The variation in measuring is not calculated. There is a range associated with all measurements, and accounting for it is a significant but seldom discussed interpretive limitation.

Another issue is significant numbers. When using the formula for calculating the angle, which involves taking the arc sine or arc cosine, a calculator will give the answer to 12 or more places. These numbers are not meaningful. The concept of significant figures is not normally taught. The result cannot have more figures (or places past the decimal) than the lowest number of figures. That is, if a measurement is 2.2×0.5 cm, then the result can only be one significant figure: $80 \pm 5°$, not $79.863°$ ($\alpha' = \text{cosine}^{-1} 0.5/2.2$).

[2] One term found in the IABPA list refers to "draw back." This is a physical impossibility because there is no negative pressure when a bullet is fired. This was someone's quick explanation, without thought, that became ingrained in the definitions.

Figure 9.1

1. The laser is used to shine along the long axis of a drop from the rounded end to the point to get the direction in two dimensions. This is repeated for several drops. Where the lines cross will be the approximate two-dimensional point of origin (POI).

2. Then the pen is raised above that point and the laser is pointed toward the drops so that the projected circle approximates the oval or ellipse of the drop. The pen is shown on several drops to get the best fit for the ellipses. This will give the third dimension of the POI of the blood.

Bloodstain classes must learn to incorporate these concepts before any subsequent blood drop analyses can be valid.

The angle of impact is more easily approximated using a circular hologram in a laser pointer, and more accurate, than rigid mathematical calculations.

More important, in actual casework, bloodstains are very seldom limited to a single drop. Consequently, the reconstructionist is concerned not with individual drops but, rather, their overall pattern. The short courses that exist do tend to cover general patterns, and this is perhaps their greatest value. But the approach to interpretation tends to be parochial as opposed to holistic, and it betrays a misunderstanding of the variation that can exist in actual casework. Analysts who are trained to look at and interpret single drops in a rote and technical fashion tend to miss the forest for concentrating on the individual trees with respect to their conclusions.

Also of utmost importance, yet often forgotten by the technical bloodstain analyst, is that blood flow is controlled by gravity. Unless there is another force acting on the blood, it will run down. It may fill a space, or it may pool, but then it will follow the contours like a river traveling along its bed, always flowing toward the earth.

WHAT KNOWLEDGE IS NEEDED?

Before interpreting bloodstains, the reconstructionist should have some basic information about the case. They should understand the bloodstain patterns and their limitations; they should know the types of injuries sustained by the parties involved; they should know some basics about the victim; they should know something about the dimensions of the scene and the placement of any furniture; and they should know what type of instrument was used to cause the bloodshed. If the reconstructionist simply looks at the bloodstains without the other background, he or she can make serious errors. First, we consider various types of injuries.

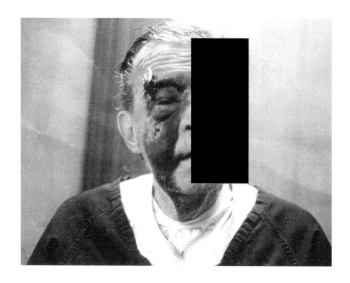

Figure 9.2

This man was struck above the right eye. He had a small abrasion and bruise when he went to the hospital. However, he was on blood thinners and he continued to bleed from the injury. This blood ran under the surface of the skin. Two days later, when this photo was taken, he had a massive bruise extending from his right eyebrow to his right shoulder.

BLOOD IN THE BODY

BRUISING

Blood patterns occur in the body as well as when shed from the body. In a live person, the blood is being pumped through the arteries and into the capillaries, returning to the heart through the veins. Blows delivered to a body can break capillaries, veins, and even arteries. Blood will then leak under the skin and be exhibited as a bruise, or hematoma. This blood is no longer directly affected by the heart. It is now under the control of gravity and the firmness of the tissues. For example, a bruise will migrate down the body. In a young healthy person, this migration is very limited but can show that the person was lying down or standing up for a long period right after the incident. In an older person, when the skin is loose, the bruise can look much worse as the blood will flow under the skin, causing a much larger bruise than expected. This effect is intensified if the person is taking a blood thinner (Fig. 9.2).

LIVOR MORTISE

Livor mortise is the settling of blood by gravity to the lowest part of the body, provided there is no restriction. Since gravity is always working, livor mortise starts immediately upon the heart stopping. The time it takes to become visible is dependent on how much it causes contrast with the normal skin color of the decedent. The darker the skin, the longer it takes to become

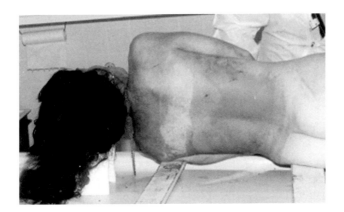

Figure 9.3

The red areas are lividity; the light band across this woman's back and on her hips is where the weight of the body was as she was lying on her back. The compression of the tissue kept the blood from draining into these areas. See color plate.

visible. Over time, the blood that has seeped through the walls of the capillaries or ruptured those capillaries will congeal. The blood cannot flow from that region if the body is now moved. This is when livor is said to be "fixed." This phenomenon is useful in determining if the body was moved after death. Pressure will prevent the blood from settling in the area; therefore, there are areas where the body is touching the surface or clothing is tight that do not show any change (Fig. 9.3).

BLOOD FROM THE BODY

Blood that is out of the body flows under the influence of gravity. It can be pumped from a vein or it can be spurted from an artery, but as soon as it leaves the body gravity is acting upon it. When the heart is no longer beating, the blood flow is dependent solely on gravity. The primary rule to remember in examining bloodstains is, again, "gravity works!" Gravity always pulls the blood toward the earth. It may pool or flow around a high point due to the contour of the object it is on, but it always moves down. If the stain is not in a downward direction, then the blood pattern indicates that the object it is on was moved since the time the blood was deposited (Fig. 9.4).

ARTERIAL SPURTING

The signs of arterial spurting are not common phenomena at crime scenes. Spurting only occurs when the artery is close to the surface and is not covered with clothing. The aorta may be severed and the blood is pumping from the heart in great gushes; however, it is 2–5 inches inside the chest.

Figure 9.4

This woman was supposedly sleeping when a "burglar" shot her. The blood on her side runs counter to gravity. This fact, combined with other evidence, was used to build a case against the husband for her murder.

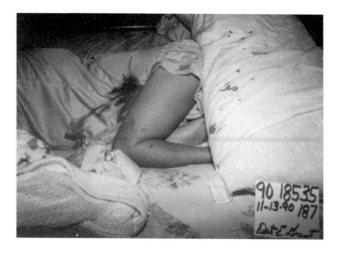

Figure 9.5

This man accidentally shot himself in the face (he thought the chamber was empty). The blood pumped out of the hole for a distance of approximately 4 feet.

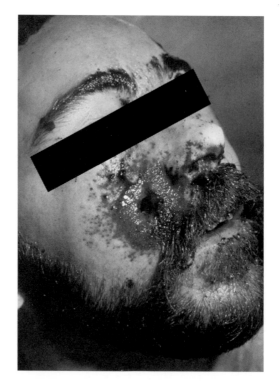

With that much tissue to transverse, it will not escape the body unless the wound is the lowest point. The blood goes for the path of least resistance, which is to fill the chest, collapsing the lungs and stilling the heart. On the other hand, a shot to the face may reach the major arteries in the neck (carotid). The hard tissue of the head (skull) keeps the hole open, through which the blood may pump (Fig. 9.5).

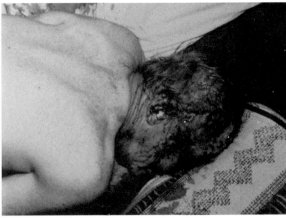

B

Figure 9.6

A. These are drops from the head of a man beaten with a pool cue, causing arterial spurting. He went into the bathroom and bled on the shower curtain, wall, and mirror. Note that the blood drops do not go on the ceiling but stop near the top of the mirror. This case caused a great deal of concern because it was difficult to believe that the man was not beaten in the bathroom. The defense contended that he had tried to doctor himself. B. If the initial crime scene respondents had been observant, they would have seen the clean (i.e., not bloodstained) cotton in his ear proving the defense's contention.

A

The arms, legs, and neck have arteries close to the surface. These arteries will spurt blood when cut. However, clothing will absorb the energy associated with these spurts; as the cloth absorbs the blood, less spurting will be exhibited. The scalp is covered with many small arteries. A blow to the head may cut one or more of these arteries. A very thin stream of blood can be spurted from the scalp for a distance up to 3 feet. The stream is similar to one squirted from a syringe with a large bore needle (Fig. 9.6).

Several reported instances of arterial spurting have turned out to be castoff blood resulting from injuries sustained during a fight. It is important that the reconstructionist not assume that just because blood is in a trailing pattern it must be the result of arterial spurting.

CASE EXAMPLE

I was asked to assist a police laboratory that was documenting a crime scene involving a great deal of arterial spurting. The criminalist siad there was arterial spurting all over the house. When asked how he knew it was arterial spurting, he replied that he had taken a course in which he learned to recognize it and he had no doubt that he was right.

The criminalistics laboratory shared quarters with the coroner's office, so I inquired about the autopsy that had been performed on the victim. We interviewed the doctor. When asked if there were any major arteries cut, he replied, "No, none of significant size." Then he was asked if there were major veins cut, and he replied with the same answer.

Once we got to the scene, the castoff nature of the stains was recognized. This case illustrates that assumptions can cause you serious embarrassment when you report or testify about your findings. If the criminalist had documented the scene and testified about arterial spurting, the defense could have asked the doctor the same questions I did and discredited the criminalist's entire testimony.

To reiterate, before you reach any conclusions regarding bloodstains, you need to determine

- The injuries sustained by the participants (victim and suspect)
- The location of the crime scene(s)
- What weapon(s) was used
- The bloodstain patterns
- The relative sizes of the participants
- The health/fitness issues that may affect the blood flow or patterns

INJURIES

The location of the injuries to the body and the type of injury sustained will affect the bloodstain patterns. The importance of the location, as it relates to arterial spurting, was discussed previously. A location that will cause confusion regarding patterns is the hands. In a stabbing or cutting incident, the hands may be cut. These cuts are commonly called "defense" wounds, but they may be sustained for reasons other than putting out the hands to stop an attack. The arms waving in an attempt to resist or fight back will cause castoff. Do not assume that all castoff is from a weapon; defensive castoff patterns are quite common.

Cautionary: Do not assume that hand castoff patterns will be different from knife castoff patterns. The edge of the hand is narrow and the blood comes off in a thin stream. Also, only one finger may be involved.

Injuries resulting in blood flow can be classified as

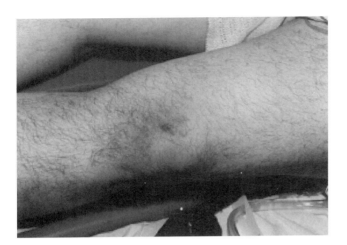

Figure 9.7
An abrasion.

- Abrasions or scrapes
- Incisions
- Lacerations
- Punctures
- Avulsions
- Amputation

An *abrasion* can be a simple scraping of the knee, like all of us did as children, or it can be a serious road burn resulting in a considerable amount of skin and tissue being removed. Abrasion patterns correspond to the object that the skin has brushed or scraped across and provide directionality with regard to the piling of the epithelium. They are also a potential source for trace evidence (Fig. 9.7).

Incisions are cuts with a sharp instrument. The edges are usually not ragged but, rather, well-defined. The amount of blood resulting from incisions is determined by several factors, including the location, direction, size, and depth of the cuts (Fig. 9.8).

The depth of the cuts will determine which blood vessels are damaged. Although not always true, it is normally expected that a deeper cut will result in more blood flow. The larger the cut, the more blood vessels cut.

The shape of any incision wound can vary widely, depending on whether it is along the axis of, or perpendicular to, Langer's lines. These are the natural anatomical grain of the skin surface. If a cut is made across Langer's lines, or other areas in which the skin grows, it will be more open, resulting in more exterior bleeding. In other areas, Langer's lines and the muscle tissue fibers, which are arranged relative to the axis of force generation of

Figure 9.8

This man had these slight incisions made by "the same gang that stabbed his wife 87 times." He was arrested for her murder.

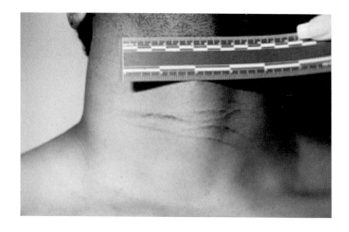

Figure 9.9

These lacerations to the back of the head were caused by a large crescent wrench.

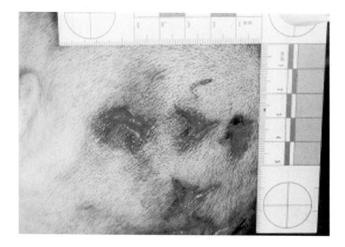

the muscle, do not line up in the same directions. The muscle tissue will spread the cut even further if the cut is across these fibers. If it is parallel to the fibers, the cut will essentially seal shut, resulting in very little blood flow but more bleeding internally.

A *laceration* is a breaking of the skin and tissues. Blunt trauma results in lacerations. This can be by clubbing or throwing something at the surface of the body. Lacerations do not have clearly defined edges and may show some associated bruising. The flow of blood is also affected by the muscle fibers and Langer's lines but not to the same extent. Because when the fibers are crushed, even if parallel to the blow, blood will come to the surface (Fig. 9.9).

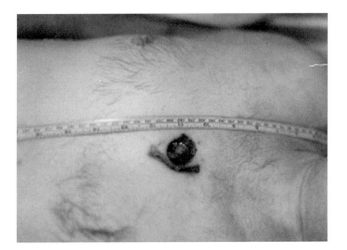

Figure 9.10

This is penetration by a shotgun. The shotliner opened just before contact.

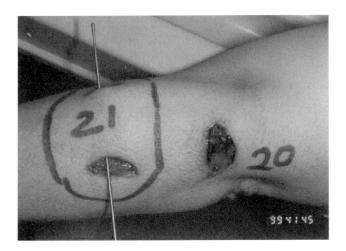

Figure 9.11

This stab wound perforated the knee.

Punctures are classified as penetrating or perforating wounds. *Penetrating* refers to entering or forcing into, whereas *perforation* refers to passing all the way through. Penetration results in one hole as a blood source (Fig. 9.10). Perforation results in two or more holes (a bullet may fragment) as blood sources (Fig. 9.11).

Avulsions occur when a piece of tissue is suddenly and unintentionally lost from the body. This may be from cutting but is more common in crushing blows. There is a lot of blood associated with avulsions. Extreme avulsions occur in traffic accidents when someone is run over by a vehicle. Parts of the body, or tissue, may be "squirted out" for some distance (Fig. 9.12).

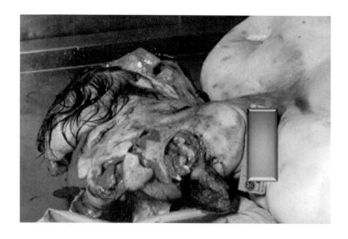

Figure 9.12

This woman's head was crushed by a truck.

Amputation is the intentional removal of a part of the body. Amputation will result in considerable loss of blood. Although generally thought of in terms of the extremities, the head can also be amputated, as has been seen on terrorist videos.

CASE EXAMPLE

In 1978, Larry Singleton raped 15-year-old Mary Vincent, chopped off her arms at the wrists, stuffed her into a culvert, and left her to die in Stanislaus County, California. I was director of the California Department of Justice laboratory located in Stanislaus County at the time.

Due to her age, her arteries were still elastic. Cutting them off allowed them to retract up the arms. When she bent her arms, the blood was sealed in at the elbows.

She managed to make it to I-5, where she was found by a passing motorist. She survived this ordeal and testified against Singleton.

One of her hands was recovered by a fisherman from the Alameda Estuary. An X-ray of the arm and the hand showed a physical match of the bones.

Singleton was convicted, but only of assault. He served 8 of 14 years and was released. He moved to Florida, where he was convicted of murdering a prostitute. He died on death row from cancer in 2001.

It should not be assumed that all blood at the crime scene is from the victim. The suspect may also have an injury if there is a fight or if repeated stab wounds are inflicted. Frequently, the hand becomes bloody and slips onto the blade of the knife, causing a cut to the hand of the perpetrator (Fig. 9.13).

Figure 9.13
Injury to perpetrator from a knife slip.

THE CRIME SCENE

Bloodstain patterns can be found on walls, floors, ceilings, objects in an environment such as telephones and furniture—basically just about anywhere. However, each environment uniquely limits the precise activities of the persons involved in the incident and the subsequent patterns that may be left behind. They cannot walk in certain areas because of fixed objects within the scene; the blood can only go so far because of the walls; intervening objects can intercept parts of the pattern; and the composition of each surface in the scene varies with regard to accepting and retaining patterns (smooth and rough, wet and dry, etc.). The environmental qualities of each scene are different. They must be studied before a reconstruction is undertaken. The physics and blood dynamics remain the same, but the variables that exist within the environment must be incorporated into the analysis. Often, bloodstain interpretations of greatest confidence are offered without consideration of these highly influential variables.

If possible, it is always preferable to go to the crime scene. This allows the reconstructionist to visualize the actions that he is trying to reconstruct in their actual environment. The scene may have changed due to time passage, but the reconstructionist still gains an understanding of the dimensions and spatial relationships in the area. Of course, if the reconstructionist is employed by law enforcement, he should go to the scene prior to any evidence collection. There is often information present that cannot or will not likely be properly recorded.

However, it is not enough to simply visit the crime scene. The documentation of the crime scene must also be studied and scrutinized. Ideally, photos and videos will provide the reconstructionist with a scene's general dimension and character at the time it was discovered. They give context and provide close-ups of items, areas, and patterns that may be of particular interest. A competent diagram of the crime scene is necessary to understand where items were found and should enable the reconstructionist to put the items back in place if needed. It shows the pertinent evidence and its relationship to other evidence and objects at the scene. The measurements must include the dimensions of the area and the measurements to the items of interest, including their height. Unfortunately, a proper crime scene sketch or diagram is an investigative rarity. When one is available, it is often incomplete, inaccurate, or illegible. This is an area in which many crime scene technicians need extensive additional training—both in terms of agreeing that scene diagrams are important and in terms of developing the skill to complete them so that they may be of use to others.

If the scene cannot be visited, the documentation with complete diagrams and photos of the crime scene becomes all the more important.

CASE EXAMPLE

A man on a bicycle approached a man in a Jeep Cherokee and demanded money that he was owed. The window of the Jeep was broken out, with only a little glass remaining in the door at the bottom of the window. The man on the bike was stabbed in the left side just above the hip. He went to the hospital; the driver drove to the police and reported the assault.

The stories are different. The man on the bike says the driver got out of the car, stabbed him, got back in, and prepared to drive off. He grabbed the window and it broke as he pulled it out.

The driver claims the bicyclist hit the window with his fist and broke it inward. The bicyclist then climbed in the window hitting at him and forcing him over the console where he had a knife. He picked it up and stabbed the bicyclist in the side in self-defense.

There were no cuts on the biker's stomach from the window glass. The steering wheel is in the way of any stabbing motion to the side of the biker. The height and angle of the stab wound were consistent with the version given by the man on the bike.

A reconstruction using the dimensions and structure of the vehicle and the location of the wound shows that the driver's story was false.

Some violent crimes occur in places where crime is no stranger, such as certain bars and buildings (crack houses, etc.). In these places, there may be bloodstains, bullet holes, and who knows what else from previous incidents and activity. These can confuse an interpretation if not recognized up front. In such crime scenes, the interpretation of bloodstains should not be completed until the laboratory results are received, identifying the bloodstains as having originated from the actors in the case being worked.

THE WEAPON

To understand subsequent wounds and bloodstain patterns, the reconstructionist should study various weapons and how they are used. This will help with reconstructing how they may have been used in the case at hand or at least provide alternatives for theory testing and elimination. Sometimes, determination of the type of weapon is not possible at the crime scene but can be approximated at the autopsy.

As any weapon is wielded (e.g., a knife, tire iron, or bat), the blood on its surface is subjected to centrifugal forces (moving or directed away from a center or axis), causing the blood to flow along its length. Blood is cast off from those points on the weapon that prohibit further flow. The surface tension is overcome and the blood leaves these points in a series of drops. The quantity and size of the drops depend on the surface area of the weapon that was covered in blood because that defines the volume that can be present. A pocketknife will produce a smaller pattern than a machete, for example. The length of the weapon also affects the pattern; the longer the weapon, the further potential distance of any castoff as a result of greater forces acting on the blood. The longer the weapon, the greater the centrifugal forces, and the further blood will travel when cast off.

High-speed video has shown that the way the blood leaves an object is not always from a point source.[3] Hatchets, knife blades, and clubs each have a sheet of blood come off when they are stopped by striking a surface. This sheet breaks up into drops. The head of a hammer and the claws both have sheets come off; however, because the drops of blood are deposited in similar patterns, it would be difficult to determine for certain from which side the blood originated by examination of the bloodstain pattern.

Beating a blood-soaked sponge is frequently done to demonstrate the way in which blood spatters when hit by various objects. The pattern is not truly the same as that left by beating a person. As it is repeatedly struck, the sponge has less blood; a living body actually has more blood for subsequent blows. In such exercises, more blood should be added after each blow to a sponge, starting with a small amount, to realistically produce a bloodstain pattern.

Blood is neither spattered nor cast off from the weapon until it is present where the blow is landing. The capillaries are compressed and the veins are sealed when the blow lands; it takes time for the bleeding to start, during which the instrument is removed. Several bloodletting blows can be

[3] A high-speed video was made at the California Criminalistics Institute. It was shown at a California Association of Criminalists Seminar in 1995 and the IABPA/ACSR joint meeting in Albuquerque in 1996.

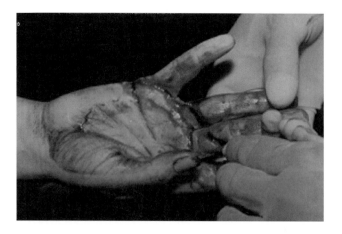

delivered to different portions of the head, for instance, without hitting blood. Subsequently, there would be no spatters or castoff from the weapon. There would, of course, be castoff from the head as the subsequent blows land and cause sudden movement of the head.

It is commonly held that in order to determine the number of blows delivered by a weapon, the reconstructionist need only count the number of castoff patterns related to a series of blows and then add one for the first blow. The logic is that the first blow occurs in the absence of blood. However, the previous example belies that theory, and a crushing blow with penetration, such as with a hammer, will result in immediate blood on the weapon. In such instances, there will be castoff from the first blow.

Contrary to popular fiction, knives used to stab a person do not have much blood on them. The tissue wipes off any blood as it is removed from the victim, leaving an oily film with just trace amounts of blood. It is only when an area already covered with blood is stabbed through that blood is able to coat the blade of the knife.

Cuts across the palms and fingers occur when someone grabs onto the blade of a knife. It is subsequently pulled out and slices across the skin. These are not "defense wounds" in the classic sense. Commonly, these kinds of injuries occur when there has been a close relationship between the victim and the knife wielder. The victim in such cases does not believe that the other person is serious and foolishly tries to take the knife from him or her (Fig. 9.14).

BLOODSTAIN PATTERNS

The reconstructionist must understand the nature and occurrence of bloodstain patterns. For this, there is reason to attend at least a 1-week course on bloodstain analysis. The IABPA Web site (www.IABPA.org) lists different basic classes that will suffice. There are also some experiments provided at the end of this chapter. These experiments are designed to increase your knowledge regarding bloodstain patterns beyond what the basic classes teach.

The patterns that are present in a crime scene must be recorded in their entirety for the reconstructionist. In many cases, scene technicians document only the drops and not the overall pattern, either out of ignorance or for having misread the scene. Interpreting any stain under such circumstances is like looking at a single tree to understand the nature of a forest. It is the overall patterns that the reconstructionist must concentrate on. Consequently, it is of greatest value to see the entire stain patterns present at the crime scene, as they were originally found.

Again, when possible, the reconstructionist should go to the crime scene and see everything before it is disturbed. If this is not possible, then everything should be documented or saved in its original condition. In a homicide, the clothing on the body should be photographed showing all the stains before the body is moved. Then the clothing should be removed at the scene and packaged in paper so that no two stains touch and transfer. This will preserve the stains and any trace evidence that is present on the clothing. The normal practice of leaving the clothing on the body while it is placed in a body bag and transported to the morgue causes contamination and loss of evidence. The information associated with these stains is destroyed by such practices.

THE VICTIM AND SUSPECT

The more the reconstructionist knows about the participants, the more she will be able to understand and explain about the bloodstains. Their health, fitness, activities, medications, and diseases all work to influence the manner in which their blood flows, and the likelihood of the acts that may or may not have taken place. Reconstructionists should therefore get as much information as possible regarding the victim, including the following:

- Age
- Height
- Weight
- Toxicology/medications
- Health/medical diagnoses
- Fitness
- Activities (schedule of typical day, sports, hobbies, exercise, etc.)
- Addictions (drugs, alcohol, etc.)

For example, some medications will cause the blood to flow more freely. Aspirin, coumadin (warfarin), and other drugs keep the blood from clotting so that a minor wound will bleed more than normal. In older people, the use of coumadin to prevent clots is common. People with arterial fibrillation may also be on coumadin, so checking the Medic-Alert bracelet or necklace is a must.

Figure 9.2, which shows the man with the large bruise, illustrates the extreme difference that blood thinning medicine and age can cause. This will also cause bruising to be more common and to flow more. When blood does not clot, it can result in death or far more bleeding than would be expected from the wounds inflicted.

Illness can also be the reason for death or injury. Advanced cases of cirrhosis of the liver can cause weakened capillaries and veins. Even the simple act of helping someone with this condition to stand will cause him or her to bruise.

CASE EXAMPLE

A woman's body was found in her living room. She had bruises on most of her body. The bruises were of different ages. There was no sign of the cause of death. The scene was "frozen" until the cause of death was determined at autopsy. The liver was straw colored; this was advanced cirrhosis. She was a secret alcoholic, and when we returned to the scene we found vodka bottles hidden in several locations throughout the house. The husband claimed to be unaware of his wife's drinking problem.

CASE EXAMPLE

An elderly woman's body was found by a friend in her home. There was an injury to the head and blood trails throughout the residence. There was no pattern of violence. We were able to finally determine the starting location of the blood; it was at a corner near the floor. It was learned that she was epileptic. She had apparently fallen in a seizure and struck her head on this corner. Her confused state when she recovered was such that she had not called for assistance. This was ruled a natural death.

It is common for an entire home to be processed as a death scene with little or no attention paid to the contents of garbage cans and medicine cabinets. The medicine cabinet must be checked to determine what type of medicines/drugs the victim may be taking. The reconstructionist should also direct investigators to inquire about the medical condition from the victim's doctor, if possible.

A person in good health is going to be potentially more difficult for an attacker to overcome than a person in poor health. If they are runners or exercise a great deal, their heart rate will be less than that of sedentary people. Knowing the lifestyle signs will assist you in determining these factors. Look for exercise equipment, gym membership cards, pools, bikes, etc.

The victim's age is also a factor to consider. As a person grows older, the skin becomes thinner and is easily torn and bruised. This is true even without taking coumadin or similar medications. An older person may not have the strength to thwart the actions of a perpetrator. A person with a heart ailment may have a heart attack due to the bloodletting event. This may result in less blood at the scene than would be expected from the nature of the wound.

The height of the victim relative to the suspect will determine where and at what angle wounds can be inflicted. The same effect can be caused by the victim being in other than a standing position. Knowledge of the relative heights allows the reconstructionist to take this fact into account when assessing the wounds.

The activities or hobbies of the victim should also be checked. For example, a martial arts student is less likely to succumb to a direct attack. The defensive and offensive moves he makes will also be different than those of a noncombatant-type individual.

To reiterate, the reconstructionist needs to examine and understand the following to make an informed bloodstain pattern interpretation:

- The injuries sustained by the participants (victim and suspect)
- The crime scene
- What weapon(s) was used
- The bloodstain patterns
- Information about the participants

If the reconstructionist has not thoroughly considered at least three of these areas of consideration, she is essentially guessing with regard to any subsequent interpretations.

SUMMARY

With the previous considerations in mind, the bloodstain analyst is better prepared to interpret the stains and present a reconstruction. However, as stated elsewhere in this text, bloodstains are only part of the evidence. Other types of evidence may give even more information and must be considered in any reconstruction. If the hypothesized explanation of the stains is in disagreement with any of the other types of evidence, then the interpretation is disproved and a different hypothesis must be found that will fit all the evidence.

REPORTING

In reporting bloodstain pattern interpretations, the use of digital photography is invaluable. Including digital photos of the pattern in your text will direct readers to examine the pertinent photos, to see an enlarged version, and better understand your report. It is difficult to describe stains; a photograph is truly worth a thousand words.

All reconstruction conclusions must be justified. That is, the logic and reasoning must be clearly evident in the reconstruction report—not only the conclusion but also the reasons why other interpretations have been eliminated. This is particularly true if you are reexamining evidence that someone else has examined.

A "sanitized" report is provided as Attachment 1. It concerns a rivalry over a man. The "victim" claims that the man's new girlfriend and several of her friends attacked her. The tragedy in the case is that the suspect was arrested and spent 18 months in jail awaiting trail because she could not afford bail. The local crime lab had not examined this case because it was a "minor incident" that did not qualify for lab analysis.

ATTACHMENT 1: CASE REPORT

I was requested to examine the physical evidence and photos involved in the case. I was also asked to read the police reports, which included statements by the alleged victim, Ms. H. These examinations were for a reconstruction of this incident.

STATEMENTS

The following excerpts from the Police Department Crime Incident Report are Ms. H's statement as to what occurred:

Discovery page: 13
Police report page: 5
Paragraph 4 line 2
"pushed her to the ground"

Discovery page: 14

Police report page: 6

Paragraph 1

". . . after she was pushed to the ground on her back by the suspect, she was turned over by a female."

". . . once she was flipped over onto her stomach, the other two females got out and held her legs."

Paragraph 2

". . . when she was placed on her stomach, she felt her shirt being cut and then felt sharp pains in her upper back area."

". . . she was trying to get away from the females and during this time she had the front of her shirt slit by the suspect."

"She said she never saw it (the weapon), but that she knew it was cutting her as her (sic) as could feel the blood dripping down her shoulder area."

Paragraph 3

". . . said after she was cut an unknown number of times, she was able to free herself from the suspects."

The initial report gives the time the incident was called in as Thursday at 1340. The officer was dispatched at 1508. The time of report to time of discovery of the wounds was approximately $1\frac{1}{2}$ hours. Yet according to Officer Y's report on page 4, 2nd paragraph: "I saw that there was fresh blood dripping from these, but that none of them appeared life threatening as it was not deep laceration, but shallow lacerations."

ALTERNATIVES

In crime reconstruction, we test alternative explanations of an incident and determine if the physical evidence supports or refutes those explanations. The other explanation of these injuries and damage to the shirt is that the attack did not occur but the cuts were self-inflicted or inflicted in some manner other than what the "victim" described to the police. This other theory is that the crime was "staged."

EXAMINATIONS

I examined the Xerox copies of the photos and had several questions regarding what I saw. I then asked for copies made from the negatives. I still could not resolve some of the questions I had about the shirt. I examined the shirt in the property room of the police department approximately 16 months after the incident.

The following summarizes my findings:

- I found no visible bloodstains inside the back of the garment.
- I found no soil on the front or back of the garment.
- One of the holes in the back lines up with one of the holes in the front.
- The cut does not cut the collar or the label area but stops at this point.
- The cut is not smooth but is jagged.
- The bottom of the cut is smoother than the top.
- The cut is approximately 15 inches long, almost half the length of the garment.

In examining the photographs of the wounds, I noted two patterns. One is single parallel lines in a "V" shape on both sides of the back; the spacing of these is similar to the spacing between fingers. The other pattern is of three or four parallel lines that are more vertical and horizontal. These have a spacing similar to a dinner fork. There are also single lines.

These injuries could have been made by either the "suspects" or the "victim." None of the injuries are deep but appear to be scratches (see police report).

The victim states she felt the blood running down her shoulder on her back. However, there is no blood on the shirt. There are no blood streaks on the "victim's" back or shoulder represented in the photos of the injuries.

The officer stated that the wounds had "fresh blood dripping" when he saw the "victim" approximately $1\frac{1}{2}$ hours after the call to the police department. If the "victim's" statements were true, the wounds would not be "dripping" blood because blood would clot or dry within the stated time period. She could have reopened the wound by her actions when the officer arrived; however, if the blood was "freshly dripping" then it should be on the shirt. The photographs taken of the injuries do not show "fresh blood dripping."

The interpretations of this lack of blood and the "fresh blood dripping" are as follows:

1. The injuries were done while the shirt was off and the blood dried before the shirt was put back on.
2. Officer Y mistook clotted blood for freshly dripping blood.
3. The injuries were made just prior to the arrival of Officer Y; however, this would still result in blood on the shirt unless the "victim" held herself in such a manner that the shirt did not contact the back.

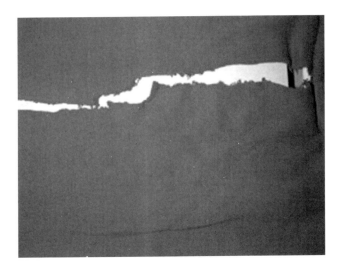

Figure 9.15
The cut in the back of the victim's shirt.

The cut in the shirt is jagged toward the top. This is caused by the shirt being "bunched" or folded over in this area. The top of the cut stops at the neck seam. If a sharp instrument (razor blade) was used, I would expect an indication of a cut on the fabrics at the collar and the entire cut would be smooth. The jagged cut is more consistent with scissors being used (Fig. 9.15).

The "victim" states she was pushed to the ground on her back and then flipped over onto her stomach while two more females held her legs. She states she was held down by four females. The front of the shirt is grease stained from her work; if those areas had come into contact with soil, it should have adhered. No soil was noted on the front or back of the shirt (Fig. 9.16).

The "victim" states she was "trying to get away from the females" and during this time she had the front of her shirt slit by the suspect (Fig. 9.17). It would be expected that the clothing would be abraded where she was moving and struggling in contact with the cement of the sidewalk. There are no abraded areas on either the front or the back of the shirt. The pants do not show abrasions in the areas of the knees or buttocks in the photographs; however, the pants were not collected for examination. There do not appear to be any abrasions or bruises present on the "victim" that would support her version of the incident.

The victim states that she fought the "four suspects" holding her down. If she had fought, she should have abrasions of her clothing where it moved while in tight contact with the cement. No abrasions were found. The hole through the shirt suggests that the person may have cut the shirt while it was off the body (Fig. 9.18).

Figure 9.16
No soil on victim's
clothing.

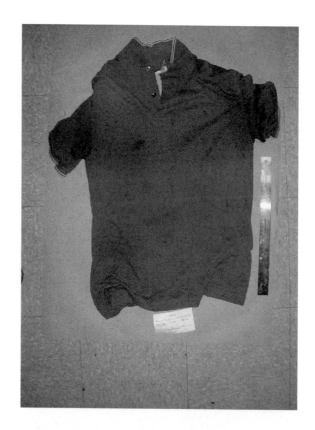

Figure 9.17
No abrasions on victim's
clothing.

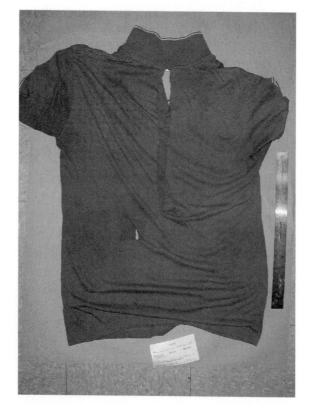

You now have the approximation of the amount of blood deposited at the scene. This should always be approached as a last resort; you should have a very good reason for trying to determine the quantity of blood present. This is only an approximation because blood has differing amounts of solids in different people. Getting an exact equal piece of carpet, bedding, or whatever is never going to happen; it is approximately equal.

Questions

1. How much water was lost from the blood?
2. Does this agree with the published ranges?
3. Do you have enough experiments to calculate a "standard error" in a controlled situation?

ACKNOWLEDGEMENTS

Eric Lawrence and Faye Springer, coworkers at vastly different times, suggested some of the experiments described in this chapter.

REFERENCES

Fleming, A. *Blood Stains in Criminal Trials.* Pittsburgh, PA: W. S. Haven, 1861.
Pizzola, P. A., Roth, S., and DeForest, P. R. Blood Drop Dynamics—II, *Journal of Forensic Sciences*, 31(1), January 1986.

CHAPTER 10

FIRE SCENE RECONSTRUCTION

John D. DeHaan, PhD

THE CHALLENGE OF FIRE SCENE RECONSTRUCTION

The reconstruction of fire scenes is considerably more difficult than the reconstruction of a typical homicide scene because of the changes and destruction wrought by the event being investigated. Imagine taking a homicide scene with its myriad evidence and ripping portions of the walls and ceiling down, flooding the room with water, and then spraying every visible surface with gray or black tempera paint (Fig. 10.1). Heat alone causes surfaces to discolor, melt, or char. Smoke or pyrolysis products coat most exposed surfaces, especially at higher levels in a room. Fire chars or consumes furnishings, bodies, and wall- and floor-coverings, sometimes to the point of structural collapse; however, the processes of combustion, ventilation, and heat transfer produce much of the evidence on which the reconstruction depends. Those processes must be understood before their effects can be correctly interpreted. Water is used in great abundance in the extinguishment of most fires, diluting, moving, obscuring, or even washing away critical evidence. Exposure to the elements (rain, wind, heat, and sun), sometimes prolonged, adds to the destruction. Yet, despite all the difficulties, by applying appropriate protocols in a thoughtful analytical process, gathering appropriate data, and using knowledge of the fire processes and fire engineering principles, we can accomplish a great deal in accurately reconstructing fire events and defending those conclusions in courts of law. Due to the complexity of the topic, this chapter focuses on the reconstruction of fires in residences and small businesses. Explosions and fires in manufacturing or industrial premises, aircraft, vehicles, or wildlands require extensive specialist information and will not be discussed in this chapter. The interested reader is referred to the specialist literature for information on such fires [Cole, 1992; DeHaan, 2002; National Fire Protection Association (NFPA), 2004].

The objective of a fire scene reconstruction is to provide reliable and defensible answers to the following questions:

Figure 10.1

Typical room fire scene. Fire damage patterns on the wall paneling, ceiling, and furniture are all used to re-create the movement of the fire (from left to right in this fire) and intensity (more damage to the sofa in the left rear corner). Photo courtesy of Jamie Novak, Novak Investigations, Lindstrom, MN.

1. Where did the fire begin—that is, where was the origin of the fire?
2. What was the first fuel involved in the fire (and what fuels supported its spread)?
3. What was the cause of the fire—that is, what circumstances brought an ignition source into contact with the first fuel such that a fire resulted?
4. Who, if anyone, was responsible for the fire occurring?
5. What factors contributed to the ignition and growth of the fire?
6. What other events occurred (and in what order) in connection with the fire—death, injury, forced entry, or burglary?

Fires can be accidental in origin. Although accidental events are not a primary focus of this text, fires are nearly unique as investigation targets because each requires at least some investigation before it can be determined that the fire was accidental or intentional in causation. In fact, sometimes extensive investigation and analysis has to be carried out before that call can be made with any authority. Because in many U.S. jurisdictions all fires must be "investigated" and a cause "established" by the responding fire agency, a superficial examination and summary judgment may result. Once a fire is established to be accidental, the public agencies need only secure the building and turn it over to the owner or his or her insurance representative. If a fire is thought to be deliberately set, a criminal investigation must be carried out by a police agency (or fire marshal) having investigative and arrest powers. Some agencies are reluctant to become involved in the more complex police investigations and will write off as many fires as accidents as they can. This is a dangerous and pernicious practice because many fires that at first appear to be simple accidents are in fact deliberately set. The common "fat fire on the stove" may be set to meet the perceived needs of the "cook"—whether that is to justify a remodeled kitchen, to call attention to household or personal crises, or attempt to intimidate or kill another person in the house. Once a fire is thought to be accidental, a more relaxed and less thorough investigation takes place, evidence is overlooked, and less documentation is carried out. If later information suggests the fire was set, critical evidence may be lost forever. Every fire deserves a systematic examination, but pressures of insufficient resources and excessive demand mean many do not receive proper attention from public authorities. Fire scenes should be secured, access controlled, and documented as would any possible crime scene, at least until reliable evidence demonstrates an accidental causation. This practice must be balanced against the danger of assuming that a crime has definitely occurred and developing a bias to exclude accidental causes. It is more important for the fire scene examiner to keep an open mind as to all the possibilities of both accident and crime while conducting the initial examination and developing the evidence to prove one or the other.

Fires can be intentionally set for their own purposes—to kill someone, to destroy property, or to gain a monetary or psychological end. The crime of arson requires three basic elements of proof:

1. There had to be some physical destruction by the fire.
2. The fire had to be deliberately set.
3. The fire had to be set with some specific intent.

That specific intent can be murder, monetary gain, psychological advantage, or to fulfill a need identifiable only to the perpetrator. The existence of a "fire bug" who sets fires in response to an uncontrollable need has been largely discredited by recent research. Fires can also be set as part of another crime—to conceal or destroy evidence (of murder, burglary, or fraud) or as part of a ritual or fantasy (particularly in sexually driven homicides). The reader is referred to other texts for additional information on motives (Icove and DeHaan, 2004, Chapter 5; Sapp et al., 1995).

When there has been a death associated with a fire, the investigation must be three-pronged: What caused the fire? What caused the death? and What circumstances connected those two events? Fires can be the result of accidental, natural, or deliberate events. Deaths can occur by natural, accidental, suicidal, or homicidal means. Either may be undetermined, as seen in Figure 10.2.

The connections between the fire and the death may not be obvious. A death caused by heart attack may be triggered by the stress of a response to an accidental fire or an intentional one. A suicide victim may trigger an

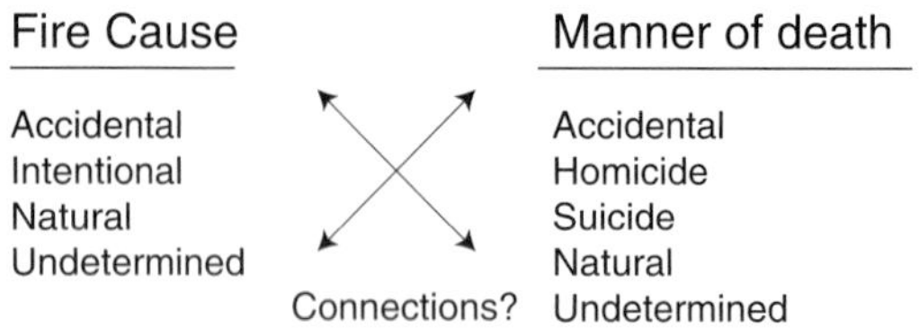

Figure 10.2

The accurate reconstruction of a fatal fire requires a determination of the cause of the fire, the cause of death, and the connections between those two events since an incendiary fire can cause an accidental death as can an accidental fire.

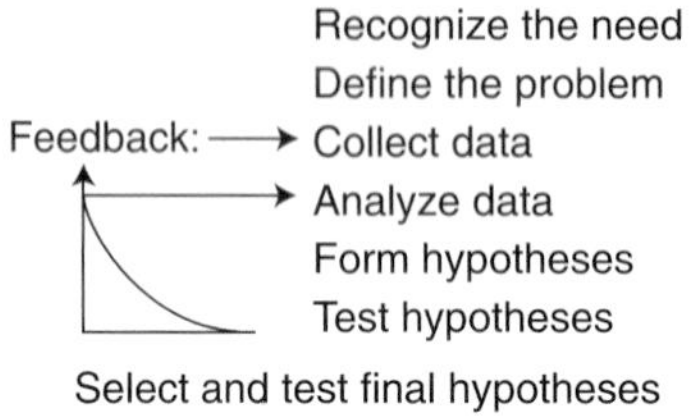

Fire Cause		Manner of death
Accidental		Accidental
Intentional		Homicide
Natural		Suicide
Undetermined		Natural
	Connections?	Undetermined

Recognize the need
Define the problem
Feedback: ⟶ Collect data
⟶ Analyze data
Form hypotheses
Test hypotheses
Select and test final hypotheses

Figure 10.3

The scientific method is a system of logical analysis and interpretation that is the best basis for any scientific inquiry or fire investigation.

accidental fire by actions taken to end his or her life. A natural death may trigger an accidental fire. A homicide may be accompanied by a deliberate fire or by an accidental one. The cause and manner of death must be reliably established by a full forensic postmortem, and then the circumstances of the fire and death must be examined together in a critical manner.

SCIENTIFIC METHOD

Although the "scientific method" is familiar to all of us who have had an education in one of the physical sciences, it is only recently that many fire investigators have been faced by judicial decisions to employ it and defend it as the basis for a properly conducted fire investigation. The "steps" of the scientific method are well-known, as shown in Figure 10.3.

The scientific method has really been the basis for all successful approaches to fire investigation for more than 50 years, but its practitioners simply did not recognize it as such. Recently, fire investigators have been forced to explain and defend their decision-making process and the scientific method is now widely cited in investigation protocols. Obviously, it forms the basis for forensic fire scene reconstruction as well, since it relies on data collection, analysis, hypothesis testing, and the feedback loop for more data.

THE BASIC INVESTIGATION

Investigative approaches to fire scenes are described in nationally recognized protocols such as those in the *Guide to Fire and Arson Scene Evidence* (National Institute of Justice, 2000), *NFPA 921: Guide for Fire and Explosion Investigation* (NFPA, 2004), and *Kirk's Fire Investigation* (DeHaan, 2002). Every good scene investigation begins with an initial noninvasive survey of the immediate scene and its surroundings. This hands-in-pockets walk-through allows the investigator to

1. Establish the nature and extent of fire damage versus the extent of the structure itself
2. Evaluate possible means/routes of entry/exit
3. Establish sight lines to adjoining properties (to aid in canvassing for witnesses and evaluating witness statement reliability)
4. Conduct a preliminary search for evidence outside the fire scene—items discarded or left at some distance from the target property, including fuel cans, shoe prints, stolen property
5. Evaluate the size and location of a security perimeter to control access to the scene and what type of barrier is going to be needed—barrier tape, rope, barricades, or manned checkpoints

The scene perimeter is secured according to the results of the survey and available resources. Every fire scene deserves protection from unauthorized persons entering, moving, destroying, or removing evidence, however inadvertently.

A forensic fire scene reconstruction proceeds in the following six general steps, which may overlap and, depending on scene circumstances, may not occur in the same sequence in every investigation:

Document the fire scene and its processing
Establish the starting conditions
Evaluate the heat transfer damage observed
Conduct a fire engineering analysis
Correlate human observations and factors
Formulate and test hypotheses about the fire

DOCUMENTATION

Documentation is the most critical step of the investigation and reconstruction. The more complete the documentation, the more accurate and defensible the reconstruction can be. Photography is the most critical tool. Photos should be taken of the overall site and then of the exterior of the building (from all available directions). Photos should also be taken looking outward toward nearby roads or buildings from where someone could have seen events. External photos must include undamaged portions of the building. Aerial views are often helpful (pre- and postfire). Exterior photo documentation can begin even while the fire is still in progress before safe entry can be made or while smoke and steam are clearing from the interior. Some fire and police units have point-and-shoot cameras in their vehicles so that they can capture events early on in the response.

Once conditions are suitable for entry, interior photographic documentation takes place. Photos should be taken of all rooms in a structure, even those not damaged by the fire. At least six photos are needed of each room, area, or corridor—one from each corner plus ceiling and floor views. The condition of walls and ceilings can change after a fire as water-logged plaster or drywall collapses, so every effort should be made to take interior photos as soon as possible. Rekindles sometimes occur and subsequent damage may obscure or destroy patterns that survived the initial fire and suppression.

Photos must include patterns of heat and smoke damage on interior and exterior surfaces and visible indicators of intensity and direction of movement. Localized areas protected from heat or smoke may also be useful for putting fuel packages or furniture back into their prefire locations and should also be photographed.

Specialized photographic techniques such as panoramic photography may be needed to capture fire patterns on large surfaces. The human visual field is nearly 180 degrees, but that of a standard 50-mm camera lens is approximately 80 degrees, so multiple overlapping photos are needed to capture wall-sized patterns. These photos can be merged using PC programs such as Roxio Photosuite™ (Roxio Corporation, www.roxio.com) or PTGui™ (www.ptgui.com).

Photos must be taken of the undisturbed scene, as layers of debris are removed revealing buried or concealed evidence and patterns. All photographs must be accompanied by notes in the form of a photographic log listing photo number, object description, location, and direction of camera. This log can be supplemented with a floor plan or plan view diagram of the scene with numbered arrows showing the location and direction of each photo. Scales should be included if size is a critical feature of the evidence.

Notes are important documentation because they help record descriptions of position and condition that may not be discerned from photos alone. Observations such as temperature, wind, weather conditions, odors,

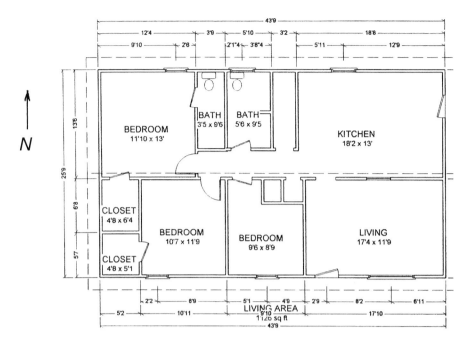

Figure 10.4

A simple plan (overhead) view of a structure fire scene is the best way of capturing room dimensions, window and door locations, and connections between adjoining rooms. All of these data are critical to a proper reconstruction. Courtesy of Dr. David Icove, Knoxville, TN.

and information from responding firefighters or police can only by captured by written notes.

Accurate dimensions of all rooms, including length, width, and ceiling height and size, sill and soffit height of all windows, doors, or other ventilation openings are essential for fire engineering calculations or modeling to be accurate and relevant to the scene. Such dimensions can be captured on simple elevation or plan view drawings or diagrams, as shown in Figure 10.4.

Diagrams must be accompanied by a compass orientation and designation of side A, B, C, etc. Proper documentation should also include notes of observations of police and fire personnel and other witnesses; the nature, condition, and response of alarm or fire protection systems; the actions of firefighting crews; the nature and locations of contents, particularly major fuel packages; and weather conditions (temperature, wind, and precipitation) at the time of the fire. Many alarm system panels can be "queried" (on-site or at a remote monitoring location) to establish recent activations.

Interviews with firefighters should include their observations as to fire, smoke, and ventilation conditions upon their arrival (and time estimate); where fire and smoke were visible; and which windows and doors were open, closed, or broken prior to or during suppression. They should also be asked what tactics were used to attack the fire, from where, and what effects were observed.

ESTABLISH STARTING CONDITIONS

Documentation of the interior of the structure for later analysis or modeling may be aided by a form for each room involved in the fire, such as that shown in Figure 10.5 (NFPA, 2004, pp. 232–233). Note that it includes wall, floor, and ceiling structural materials as well as coverings and also fuel package assessment. The ignition, growth, and contributions of any fuel package are the combined result of that fuel's chemical composition, its geometry, physical state, and mass. To ensure accurate identification, a comparison sample of the combustible portions of any major fuel package or suspected first fuel ignited should be collected and preserved. This includes carpet and pad, wall paneling or other covering, ceiling covering, and upholstery and padding (fabric, liner, and padding). A sample 4–12 inches square (10–30 cm square) would be ample for laboratory identification of material, detection of flame retardants, and simple fire tests, if needed later. Prefire photographs and videos can often be of great help in establishing the starting conditions—structural, furnishings, and decorations—that may play a role in fire ignition, spread, and pattern formation. These may come from family, owners, tenants, or public authorities. Aerial photos are often used by agencies for property tax assessments on both residential and commercial properties.

BASIC FIRE CHEMISTRY

Before we proceed to the evaluation of thermal damage patterns and fire engineering analysis, we must discuss basic fire chemistry and fire dynamics. Fire can be defined as a sustained exothermic oxidation (combustion) of a fuel sufficient to produce readily detectable heat and light. Combustion can occur either as a gaseous flame in which gases or vapors mix with air and then are ignited or as glowing (smoldering) combustion where oxygen combines directly with the solid surface of the fuel, producing little or no flame. The heat from this combustion is in part absorbed by nearby fuel, causing it to pyrolyze or evaporate to continue the process. Very few solid or liquid fuels can burn without pyrolytic action to break down their molecular structure to support combustion (reactive or combustible metals, such as sodium, potassium, iron powder, or magnesium, are the most common exceptions). Heat applied to a surface (by convective, radiative, or conductive heat transfer mechanisms) causes the temperature of that

ROOM FIRE DATA

Room _____ Room # _____

Length _____

Width _____

Height _____

    Note ceiling height changes _____

Floor Plan

Walls: Structure/material _____ Thickness _____ Covering _____ Sample? Y/N

    Structure/material _____ Thickness _____ Covering _____ Sample? Y/N

Ceiling: Structure/material _____ Thickness _____ Covering _____ Sample? Y/N

Floor: Structure/material _____ Thickness _____ Covering _____ Sample? Y/N

Openings (door, window, other vents) into room (number on plan above):

Height (bottom to top of opening)	Sill Height	Soffit Depth (above opening)	Width	Open or Closed? Changes During Fire?
1.				
2.				
3.				
4.				
5.				
6.				
7.				

HVAC System:

    Description _____

    On/off prior to/during fire? _____

Furnishings (descriptions of major fuel items, including floor and wall coverings, draperies):

_____

_____

_____

_____

_____

_____

_____

Figure 10.5

A form such as this reminds the investigator to record all information needed to conduct an accurate fire engineering analysis and reconstruction.

surface to rise [the rate of rise being controlled by the thermal conductivity (k), heat capacity (c), and density (ρ) of the material or by the multiplicand of all three, called the thermal inertia ($k\rho c$)].

Modest heating (to cause surface temperatures up to 100°C) causes no visible or permanent changes to the material. More rapid heat transfer (higher heat flux) causes higher surface temperatures. Temperatures between 100 and 150°C will cause many thermoplastics to soften, shrink, or melt but will not affect most natural fibers or materials (cotton, wool, paper, or wood, unless very prolonged). Higher temperatures will cause many materials to start to degrade or pyrolyze, and this is evidenced by permanent discoloration of the surface as the fuel is degraded (scorched). Further heating to higher temperatures will cause charring or carbonization. Eventually, the surface or the gases generated by the pyrolysis can be ignited by the external heat being applied. This is called *autoignition*. If a preexisting flame is nearby, the ignition of the pyrolytic vapors can occur at a lower temperature, called the piloted ignition temperature. Flames then spread across the surface of the fuel depending on its flammability, thermal inertia, and orientation. Downward vertical flame spread does occur in most solid fuels, but at a rate 1/100 to 1/1000 the upward vertical spread (Quintiere, 1997, pp. 88–91). Outward horizontal spread occurs at a rate in between (but closer to the downward rate).

BASIC FIRE DYNAMICS

The predominant driving forces that produce fire patterns are heat transfer and the buoyancy of the hot combustion gases. The buoyant hot gases rise and form a vertical fire plume. This plume is visible to the unaided eye when it is hot enough to be luminescent (more than ~500°C/1000°F). This is the flame plume. The gases and products that rise above the flame plume are the smoke plume, as shown in Figure 10.6. The movement of gases causes the entrainment of air that brings oxygen into the combustion zone and cools, dilutes, and diffuses the fire plume, as shown in Figure 10.7. Heat is lost from all portions of the plume by convective transfer to the surrounding air (aided by entrainment) and radiative losses mostly from solid carbonaceous soot particles or aerosols (droplets) of pyrolysis products. A fuel that burns very clearly with little or no soot or intermediate pyrolysis products (e.g., methanol) produces very little radiant heat. Very sooty fires (e.g., a crude oil pool fire) produce so much soot that much of the heat is absorbed by the plume. The effect of either circumstance is to reduce the radiant heat effect on target materials while maintaining very high combustion temperatures in the plume.

Smoke

Flame

Fuel surface

Figure 10.6

A burning chair cushion displays three major components of the fire plume: the continuous flame plume (of constant flame temperature), the intermittent flame plume (where the buoyant gases are cooling but still hot enough to support some flame), and the smoke plume above that. Smoke has also accumulated to form the ceiling layer. Photo courtesy of Jamie Novak, Novak Investigations, Lindstrom, MN.

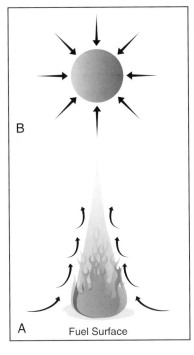

B

A   Fuel Surface

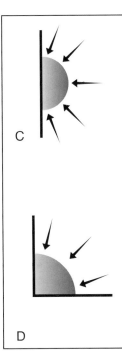

C

D

Figure 10.7

Entrainment of room air into a fire away from any walls forming an axisymmetric plume: (A) Side view. (B) Overhead view. Entrainment of room air. (C) fire near wall and (D) fire in corner.

Figure 10.8

(A) Estimating radiant heat flux ($\dot{q}''$) onto a surface some distance from a small (point) source ($r \gg a$ or b) $\dot{q}'' > X_r\dot{Q}/4\pi r^2$, where $\dot{Q}$ is the heat release rate of source, X_r is the radiant heat fraction, and r is the distance. (B) Radiant heat flux $\dot{q}''$ on a surface close to a large radiant heat source ($r \leq a$ or b) depends on the view factor F_{12} related to the geometry of the exposure. In general, $\dot{q}'' > \varepsilon\sigma T_1^4 F_{12}$, where ε is the emissivity of the hot surface, σ is the Stefan–Boltzmann constant, T_1 is the temperature of the hot surface, and F_{12} is the view factor.

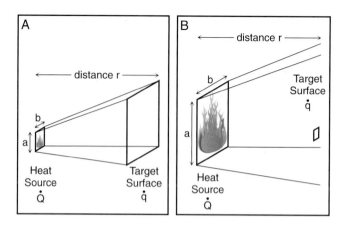

The intensity of heat radiating from a source at temperature T is a function of temperature, namely,

$$I = \varepsilon\sigma T^4$$

where ε is the emissivity of the surface, and σ is the Stefan–Boltzmann constant. Note the intensity is a function of T (in Kelvin) to the fourth power. The nature of the source determines ε, but most sources (e.g., wood flames) are approximately 0.4–0.6.

Convective heat transfer from a gas to solid surfaces plays a much smaller role, in general. The heat flux via convective transfer is expressed as

$$\dot{q}'' = h(T - T_a)/A$$

where h is the convective heat transfer coefficient, T is the temperature of the gas (°C), T_a is the ambient temperature, and A is the area over which transfer occurs (m²). For most materials, h is a function of the gas flow and the nature of the solid surface. For a raw wood surface with a buoyant hot gas flow, h is on the order of $5\,W/m^2 \cdot °C$.

Radiative heat flux can be expressed as

$$\dot{q}'' = X_r\sigma T^4 F_{12}$$

where F_{12} is the view factor between the source and the target surface, as shown in Figure 10.8, and X_r is the radiative function (0.4–0.6 for most fires).

If the source can be treated as a point source (relatively far away from the target), the relationship can be simplified to

Total heat flux (kW/m²)	Source	Surface temperature (°C)	Effect
1	Sunny summer day	40	Warm sensation to skin
2–4	1.0 m from bonfire	50	Pain after 30 seconds
4–6	0.5 m from bonfire	60–80	Skin blisters after 8 seconds
10	0.2 m from bonfire	100–200	Thermoplastics melt; some scorching of cellulosics
20	0.1 m from bonfire	200–400	Scorching, charring, many materials autoignite
50	Contact with flames	500	Rapid onset of charring and ignition
150	Post-flashover room fire	>700	Almost immediate ignition

Table 10.1

Radiant Heat Fluxes and Effects on Common Non-metallic Materials

$$\dot{q}'' = X_r \dot{Q}/4r^2$$

where r is the distance and $\dot{Q}$ is the total heat release rate (HRR) of the source. Note that $\dot{q}''$ falls as the inverse square of the distance.

We can relate heat flux to physical damage to a target surface (if we assume a $k\rho c$ of 0.4, typical of polystyrene plastic, wood, gypsum board, or human skin) by the examples shown in Table 10.1.

EVALUATE HEAT TRANSFER PATTERNS

Some of the effects observed (and the time of onset) will be controlled by the thickness of the material. Thin materials (<1 or 2 mm in thickness) will be affected in a shorter exposure time than will thermally thick materials. Loose sheets of paper (wall calendar pages), thin draperies, wallpaper blistered or separated from plaster, and the like will be affected more than thicker (or firmly attached) materials. Thermoplastics will soften, distort, and melt long before thermosetting materials will start to decompose. If we calculate the convective heat transfer from a buoyant flame at 800°C in room air, we find that the flux $\dot{q}'' = (5\,\text{W/m}^2 \cdot °\text{C})(800 - 20°\text{C}) = 3.9\,\text{kW/m}^2$. The radiant heat from a similar flame adjacent to a surface is on the order of 50 kW/m², so we can see that radiant heat normally plays a dominant role in affecting nearby materials. If a line fire is small, however, such as a match flame or a flame in a small wastebasket, the radiant heat effects are much less pronounced and most of the energy is in the buoyant flame plume. (It is much easier to scorch paper by holding it above a match flame than holding it alongside it.)

Direct contact between a flame and a surface maximizes the heat transfer by both convection and radiation, so fuels in direct contact (direct flame

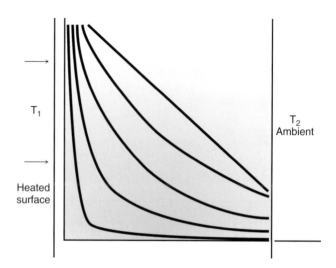

impingement) quickly rise to their maximum surface temperatures, char, and ignite (if sufficient oxygen is available and the piloted ignition temperature of the fuel is exceeded long enough to establish a self-sustaining combustion).

As a general rule, the longer the duration of exposure to heat, the deeper the resulting damage will be. To a limited extent, the more intense the heat flux, the faster the penetration will be. All materials, even good thermal conductors, have a finite thermal penetration time. Application of heat to one side of a slab of material always produces a temperature curve that reflects a high temperature on the exposed side and a much lower temperature on the opposite side, as shown in Figure 10.9. If the heat is applied to an edge or corner, there is less material behind the heated surface, and the temperature of the heated edge is higher than would be observed if the same heat were applied to a flat surface. That is why it is always easier to ignite the edge of a piece of fuel (or very finely divided fuel) than a solid surface of the same fuel. One will observe greater damage to such corners and edges than to the flat surfaces adjacent. The demarcation between damaged and undamaged areas of a flat surface denotes the area where the heat flux was enough to induce thermal damage to the surface. These demarcations record the locations of hot gas layers or fire plumes.

Since flaming combustion (and, to a large extent, smoldering combustion) is a surface phenomenon, the conditions induced on the surface of a fuel are what drive the combustion. The rate at which a fuel burns away from a surface (called the mass flux, measured in $g/m^2 \cdot sec$) is dependent on the nature of the fuel and on the radiant heat flux that is falling on the

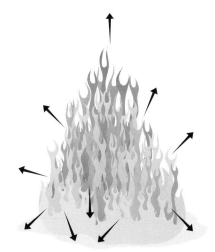

Figure 10.10

In an isolated fire, radiant heat from the flames produces a steady radiant heat flux onto the surface of the fuel below, which is dependent on the fuel being burned.

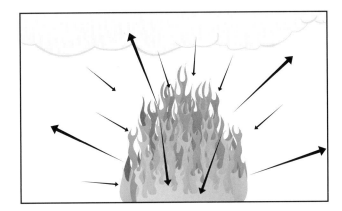

Figure 10.11

In a fire in an enclosure, the surface of the fuel is receiving radiant heat from the flames, from the ceiling layer, and reflected from nearby walls. These fluxes are additive and increase the burning rate of the fuel.

burning surface. If a piece of wood burns in isolation, the radiant heat falling onto the wood is from the flames being generated and so reaches an equilibrium, as shown in Figure 10.10.

If a piece of wood burns in a compartment, the radiant heat reflected from wall and ceiling surfaces can usually reach the burning surface and add to the total heat flux, increasing the combustion rate (as long as there is enough air getting in to support the burning), as shown in Figure 10.11.

If a hot smoke layer forms in the room, or if there are other fuel packages burning in the room nearby, the radiant heat created adds further to the radiant heat impacting the fuel surface. The effects of such additional heat sources must be considered when evaluating thermal effects.

A fire developing in a room produces a quantity of buoyant hot gases (at a rate controlled by the heat release rate, $\dot{Q}$, of the fire). If these gases cannot escape, they form a layer at the ceiling of the room, deepening as the fire burns. The temperature of this layer is determined by the size of the room (especially ceiling height) and the heat release rate of the fire. The larger the fire, the taller the flame plume and the greater the volume of gases being produced. If a fire is located away from walls, the height of the visible flame plume is approximated by the relationship

$$Z_f = 0.23\dot{Q}^{2/5} - 1.02D$$

where Z_f is the height of flame plume, $\dot{Q}$ is the heat release rate of the fine (in kilowatts), and D is the equivalent diameter of the fire, by the Heskestad equation (Drysdale, 1985, p. 133).

When Z_f approaches the ceiling height of the room, the fire gases have not had a sufficient opportunity to cool off and still have a temperature in the range of 500–600°C. If a fire is built against a wall, the entrainment of cooling air is limited and there is some heat reflected from the wall toward the fuel. As a result, the flames are taller for a fire of the same heat release rate. If built in a corner, the effects are more pronounced and the result is even taller flames from a fire of the same heat release rate. This effect is reflected in the relationship

$$Z_f = 0.17(kQ)^{2/5}$$

Where "z > height of flame plume (m), $\dot{Q}$ is the heat release rate of the fire" and where $k = 1$ for an axisymmetric fire away from walls, $k = 2$ for a fire against a noncombustible wall, and $k = 4$ for a fire built in a 90-degree corner (NFPA, 2004, p. 29).

As the temperature of the ceiling layer increases, the intensity of radiant heat originating from it increases (as a function of T^4). Experimental results have shown the relationship between the temperature of the ceiling (hot smoke) layer and the heat flux impacting the floor of the compartment (Fig. 10.12). Since a radiant heat flux of approximately 20 kW/m² is enough to ignite many common materials, it is considered a critical threshold. As seen in Figure 10.12, smoke layer temperatures of approximately 600°C produce radiant heat fluxes of approximately 20 kW/m² on the floor of a compartment with a 2.5-m ceiling height. Since this condition can trigger full room involvement (flashover), it is a critical threshold. Until flashover occurs, the atmosphere in a fire room is divided into two zones, the hot smoke (ceiling) layer overlying a layer of normal room air, as shown in Figure 10.13. As the fire continues, this layer deepens, balanced against losses through the tops of window or door openings and ceiling vents. If the fire increases in size, the temperature of the

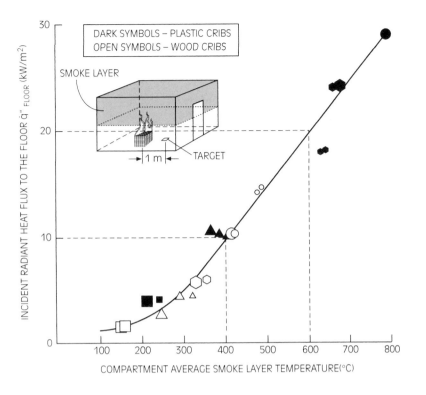

Figure 10.12

These data demonstrate the relationship between the temperature of a ceiling layer in a room fire and radiant heat flux onto the floor. Since radiant heat flux of 20 kW/m² is considered sufficient to ignite most floor coverings and furnishings, the corresponding layer temperature of 600°C is considered critical to triggering flashover. Reproduced from Quintiere, J.G., and McCaffrey, B. J. "The Burning of Wood and Plastic Cribs in an Enclosure: Vol. 1," NBSIR 80-2054, p. 118. Gaithersburg, MD: National Bureau of Standards, September 1980.

Figure 10.13

Chair fire producing a hot smoke (ceiling) layer in a room. Depending on the size of the room and size of vent openings (doors and windows) that can lose heat, the minimum size of the fire needed to trigger flashover can be calculated. Photo courtesy of Jamie Novak, Novak Investigations, Lindstrom, MN.

Figure 10.14

Typical buoyant flow of smoke from room to room produces a stair-step pattern to smoke horizons. The lowest horizon usually corresponds to the room of origin.

Figure 10.15

Buoyant flow along a ceiling produces an acute angle to the heat pattern on adjacent walls. Momentum flow produces a piling effect (sometimes called mushrooming) against vertical barriers on the upstream side and eddy flow (reduced flow or dead airspace) near the base of the downstream header above the opening.

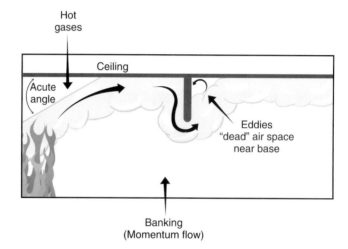

layer increases and transfers more heat to the upper walls and ceilings. Soot, water vapor, and pyrolysis products in this layer condense out on the cooler ceiling, walls, and windows, producing a visible surface effect. In a typical accidental fire, there is usually very little mixing between the layers. These processes give rise to a heat or smoke horizon. As hot gases spill from door openings, the hot buoyant gases begin to fill adjacent rooms, giving a stairstep effect (Fig. 10.14), with the room of origin having the deepest layer (i.e., closest to the floor). Hot gases flowing horizontally have a characteristic acute angle to the "front" of the wave, as shown in Figure 10.15. If flowing hot gases strike a vertical surface, their momentum causes a piling-up effect (like waves against a breakwater or seawall). Flow over an object causes eddies and protected areas on the downstream side.

The most intense heat effects are in the vicinity of the highest temperatures (i.e., near the fuel packages ignited), and the fire progresses from one

Figure 10.16

Vertical fire growth on bedding and draperies (from wastebasket) is very rapid. The depth and temperature of the hot smoke layer will both increase rapidly. Photo courtesy of Jamie Novak, Novak Investigations, Lindstrom, MN.

fuel package in the room to the next by direct flame contact or by radiant heat to nearby surfaces. The damage observed may be limited to a few items, and the logical progression from one item to the next can be deduced. (See Fig. 10.16 for an example of item-to-item growth.) If a fire in a room becomes large enough, the radiant heat from the ceiling layer causes ignition of all the exposed fuel surfaces in the room, leading to full room involvement. This transition is called *flashover*. It is usually (but not always) preceded by flaming ignition of the combustible gases (mostly CO), soot, and pyrolysis products in the smoke layer. This flaming ignition of the smoke layer is referred to as *rollover* or *flameover* and produces very high temperatures that accelerate the radiant ignition of fuels throughout the room (Fig. 10.17A).

After flashover, there are extremely high temperatures (800–1000+°C) and very high heat fluxes (120–150 kW/m^2) everywhere throughout the room (Fig. 10.17B). All fuel packages are burning as quickly as air can reach them. The areas of most intense burning are no longer the vicinity of fuel

Figure 10.17

(A) Nonaccelerated fire in furnished cubicle approaches flameover or rollover as the smoke layer begins to ignite into open flame. (B) Same fire 1 minute later: Radiant heat has ignited all furnishings and carpet throughout, completing the flashover transition. Post-flashover fire is burning most intensely where ventilation (fresh air) supply is best. Note intense fire in the doorway.

A   B

packages but the areas nearest ventilation points where oxygen can best reach the fuels involved. In a post-flashover room, the maximum total heat release rate may be limited by the size of the ventilation openings. Assuming 100% efficiency, the maximum fire size will be controlled by the relationship

$$\dot{Q}_{\max} = 1500(A_o \sqrt{h_o})$$

where A_o is the area of a ventilation opening (m^2), and h_o is the height of that opening (DeHaan, 2002, p. 47). These relationships are roughly additive, so the areas and heights of individual openings can be added together. Each room has a minimum heat release rate necessary to produce flashover in that room. This rate can be calculated by several different relationships that estimate the effects of heat losses through walls, floors, ceilings, doors, and other openings. Using three of the most common relationships, one may calculate a range of 2–4 megawatts (MW)—typical for large 4×5 m rooms with two doors and a 2.5-m ceiling). If the size(s) of opening(s) cannot accommodate a fire of that size (e.g., a single 1×1 m window opening will permit a maximum of a 1 MW fire in a typical real-world room), then flashover could not have occurred by normal fire progression. It is possible to induce temporary full room involvement without forming a hot gas

Figure 10.18
The exposed carpet and ½-inch plywood floor of this test cubicle were consumed by exposure to a post-flashover fire of duration of less than 6 minutes.

layer. If a quantity of gasoline is spread throughout a room and ignited, enough heat and direct flame can be produced to ignite all ordinary combustibles before the oxygen in the room is depleted. Under these conditions, full room involvement can be produced in less than 20 seconds as the oxygen in the room is consumed, but it will only be sustained by whatever air can get in through window and door openings once that supply is exhausted.

Post-flashover fires produce charring of all exposed surfaces (floors, ceilings, walls, and furnishings) as a result of the extremely high combustion temperatures, high heat fluxes, and turbulent mixing that occurs in such a room. The combustion of all surfaces is not a uniform process, however, because complex materials melt, shrink, and decompose. The resulting postfire patterns can be highly irregular in outline and depth. Some irregular floor patterns induced by post-flashover burning of floors, carpets, and pads have been mistakenly identified as "flammable liquid patterns," as shown in Figure 10.18. The investigator must be careful to test hypothesized "flammable liquid" involvement against other possible explanations.

FIRE SCENE RECONSTRUCTION

Forensic fire scene reconstruction, when properly applied, can aid in the hypothesis testing that is so critical to defending conclusions in court. This goes far beyond the physical reconstruction of putting furniture back in its prefire location based on burn patterns and protection patterns. This reconstruction involves a fire engineering analysis of the elements of the fire (fuels, ventilation, and heat sources) to evaluate direction of fire spread, intensity of fire exposure, duration of exposure, effects on materials, effects on people in the fire environment, and time lines of events. The fire engineering analysis can be carried out by "thought" experiments, mathematical relationships, laboratory analysis, simple or complex computer models, or empirical "live-burn" tests in either full scale or reduced scale. Sometimes, several different analyses are required to validate conclusions reached or inferred. In fact, the best solutions are those that can be shown to be correct from several different independent avenues of testing.

AREA OF ORIGIN

The observations of witnesses to early stages of the fire, surveillance camera recordings, or fire, smoke, or burglar alarm activations may give indications of the area within the room or building where the fire began. More commonly, assessment of the fire patterns will yield sufficient indications of the direction of fire spread to make at least a preliminary determination. Sometimes called vector analysis, the process relies on the physics of flow of buoyant gases, smoke and heat layering, heat transfer, and heat effects to develop a set or pattern of directional indicators: hot gases losing heat to a surface and doing less thermal damage in the direction of spread; layers being deeper in the room of origin (lower heat/smoke horizons) than in subsequent rooms; edges and corners being "beveled off" or faces being charred deeper by thermal effects on the side facing the oncoming fire; and smoke being deposited on the eddy (downwind) side of projections into the flow. Like a movie being run backwards, these indicators pointing in the direction of propagation are used to point "back" toward the source. The documentation described previously (supported by interviews of occupants, staff, or owners, when necessary) should establish the appearance and function of structural elements of the building as it existed at the time the fire started; doors, windows, transoms, vents, and HVAC system operations can all affect the buoyant flow of hot gases and smoke. Firefighters need to be interviewed regarding the tactics used to fight the fire and the effects those tactics produced. Opening ceilings or roof vents, positive pressure ventilation, even hose streams can change the flow of hot gases inside a building.

Heat transfer patterns to walls and (often) ceilings can reveal the location of burning fuel packages, with the most intense damage (both temperature and penetration) revealing the hottest part of the flame plumes. Fire patterns can be conveniently classified as surface deposits (no chemical change to actual surface; smoke or soot condensates), surface changes (paint or wallpaper blistered or scorched, plastic coatings melted), penetration (physical and chemical changes within the matrix), and consumption (or destruction). Physical effects such as calcination (dehydration of plaster or gypsum drywall), spalling (differential thermal expansion causing loss of surface material) on concrete or brick, or crazing of glass (complex partial fracture patterns caused by sudden cooling of hot glass) can also be used as indicators of heat transfer.

As a starting premise, the area with the deepest or most widespread thermal damage is likely to be an area of origin. However, the investigator must be aware of fuel load and ventilation considerations (either of which can dramatically affect the heat release rate generated in that room). A well-fueled, well-ventilated fire can do a lot of damage in a shorter period of time than a poorly fueled or inadequately ventilated fire in an adjacent room. Suppression may be successful in one room and not in another. In such cases, the premise that the fire always burns longest, and therefore does the most damage, in the area of origin does not hold up. Alternative hypotheses must be tested even for the simplest cases if later problems are to be avoided.

CAUSATION

Once a suspected area of origin is established, examination can proceed toward locating a point of origin where the heat source came into contact with the first fuel ignited. Identification of first fuel and heat source (and the circumstances in which the contact occurred) constitutes the establishment of the cause of a fire. Ignition sources can range from appliances (matches, lighters, candles, stoves, ovens, etc.) that are designed to produce heat to items that produce heat as a by-product of normal use (current-carrying wires, incandescent lamps, and motors) and items that produce heat as a result of misuse or failure. The circumstances of the heat production and how the heat ignited the first fuel are the bases for establishing responsibility for the fire. The time factors involved are also part of the reconstruction. These include time to develop the heat, time required for that heat to ignite the first fuel, time for that first fuel to become fully involved, and the time for the fire to grow to the point at which it was detected or observed (time to be extinguished). Very few of these times will be "hard" times (i.e., have an accurate clock time recorded). Alarm activation, 911 call time, and on-scene arrival of fire department may be the only hard times. The others will be based on data from a variety of sources, including live-burn tests or heat release curves of test fires in laboratories (and available through published or Web site sources), as shown in Figures 10.19–10.22.

As a general rule, the weaker the initial heat source (the lower its heat release rate), the longer it will take for that source to ignite a fuel (and the

Figure 10.19

Heat release rate signature of bedroom fire with bedclothes ignited by match (at t = 0). Flashover at ~1100 seconds triggered by involvement of "boxspring" under mattress igniting adjacent dresser. Figure courtesy of the Bureau of Home Furnishings & Thermal Insulation, California Departmentt of Consumer Affairs.

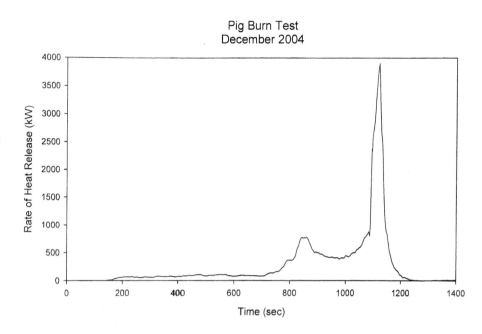

Figure 10.20

Heat release rate curves of 2 liters of camping fuel on carpet (padded and unpadded). Note the rapid growth after ignition at 30 seconds (ultrafast t^2 fire) and rapid decay with a duration of the major fire of less than 1½ minutes. Originally appeared in "The Dynamics of Flash Fires involving Flammable Hydrocarbon Liquids," by John DeHaan, American Journal of Forensic Medicine and Pathology, Vol. 17, pp. 24–31, 1996. Reprinted with permission from Lippincott Williams & Wilkins.

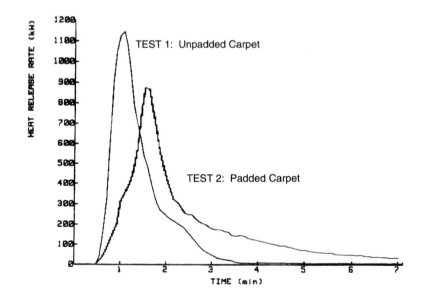

closer the proximity of the source to fuel). A glowing cigarette has a very hot central "coal" (800–900°C), but it is only a 5 W fire. It has to be in contact with a suitable fuel to cause ignition. A wooden match or a candle may have a portion of its laminar flame with a temperature of 1200°C, but it is still only a 50 W fire that must be very close (2–4 cm) to even a susceptible solid fuel. A wastebasket fire of 150 kW can be considerably further from a target

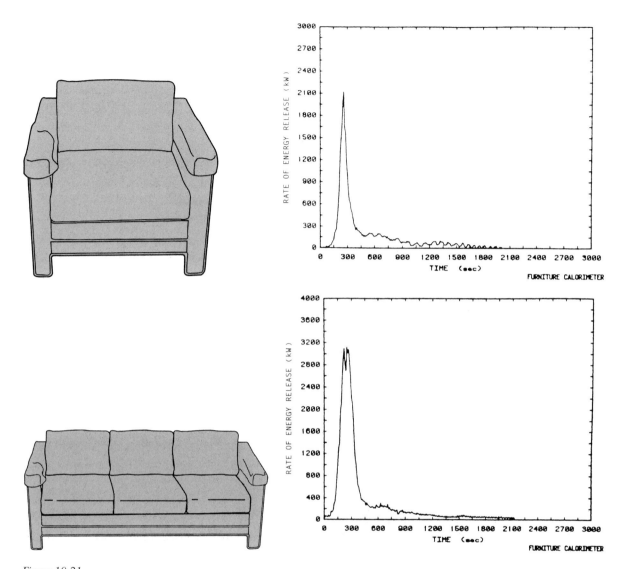

Figure 10.21

Heat release rates of typical modern chair and sofa with flame ignition. Note the rapid growth (ultrafast t² fire), rapid decay, and short duration. Figure courtesy of the National Institue of Standards and Technology.

fuel and still cause ignition. A Christmas tree fire of 3 or 4 MW can cause radiant ignition of materials more than 1 m from the outer margin of the tree. The relationship between heat output of a source, radiative fraction, distance, and radiative heat flux was explored previously, and it plays an important role in analyzing the competence of ignition sources.

If the first fuel ignited is a flammable gas or vapor, even a weak source of energy (the minimum ignition energy of most flammable gases or vapors

Figure 10.22

Figure 10.22

(A) Temperature curve of test fire started in traditional chair with a cigarette. Note the prolonged initiation phase (incipient fire) of 52 minutes and minimal change in ceiling temperature (T1 and T2) until then. After the onset of flaming fire, fire growth is very rapid. The apparent decrease in floor temperature (T3) is due to faulty electrical connection to thermocouple. (B) Temperature data for a fire started with a flame in a wastebasket under a desk (at t = 0). T1 and T2 were ceiling (upper layer) thermocouples, and T3 and T4 were floor-level thermocouples. Note the minimal change in upper layer temperature until the desk ignited at 13:30, followed by extremely rapid onset of flashover. Post-flashover temperatures ranged from 1400 to 1850°F (700–900°C). Figures courtesy of Washington State Patrol, Region 8, Fire Investigation Team.

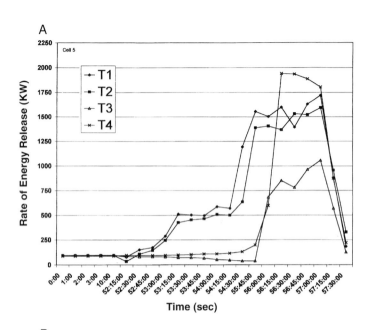

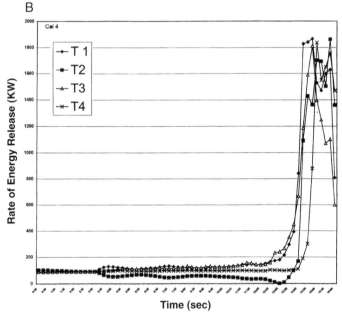

is less than 0.3 mJ) can be adequate, but the source must be in direct contact with the fuel, the fuel must be in its flammable range, and the contact has to be prolonged enough to allow enough energy to transfer. Vapors produced by the evaporation of any flammable liquid are significantly heavier than air and will form a discrete layer at floor level, with only slow diffusion occurring unless there is mechanical stirring (fans, vehicles, or people moving about) or thermal currents mixing the vapors and air. Only methane, carbon monoxide, and acetylene are lighter than air (and only methane will rise perceptibly when released in still air).

Every fire, whether it is a single match, a wastebasket of paper, a sofa, a pool of gasoline, or an entire room, will develop along a characteristic HRR/time curve called its fire signature, as shown in Figure 10.19, with four phases—incipient, growth, fully developed, and decay.

A gasoline pool fire will have a very short incipient phase, a very rapid growth phase (often called ultrafast), and fully developed phase (with HRR controlled by the size of the pool, the maximum mass flux for gasoline, and, possibly, a ventilation limit). As the gasoline pool is exhausted, the onset of decay is very rapid and there is no decay phase smoldering, seen in Figure 10.20. Modern furnishings are easily ignited by open flame and will support extremely large and fast-growing fires (as shown in Fig. 10.21) that behave very much like accelerated fires.

A smoldering ignition in a traditional chair will look very different, as shown in Figure 10.22A. It will have a long incipient phase, a much slower growth phase with a transition to flame, and a prolonged decay phase with considerable smoldering. Timescales vary for the transition to flame, sometimes occurring in as little as 22 minutes from cigarette contact to as long as 3 or 4 hours, or it may never occur.

The flame height above a given fuel package is useful for evaluating fire patterns. The two most common formulas for calculating such values were discussed previously. With a large, rectangular fuel package such as a sofa, the "diameter" correction of the Heskestad formula is useful. The equivalent diameter [D_{eq}] of any non-circular fuel surface of area A is calculated by estimating or measuring the horizontal surface area and solving for r using the familiar

$$A = \pi r \quad D_{eq} = 2(A/\pi)^{1/2}$$

Flame height will be revealed by thermal effects on vertical walls adjacent to the flames (keeping in mind the wall effect). If a flame appears to have been much larger than it should have been based on the estimated HRR of the fuel package thought to have been present, then the investigator should evaluate the possible causes. Was it a stack of chairs and not just one, was it an upholstered armchair and not a simple desk chair, was there an accelerant placed on the chair (Styrofoam packing, a urethane cushion, or a flammable liquid)?

Radiant heat ignition or thermal damage will occur when the radiant heat flux striking a surface causes the temperature of that surface to reach a critical point (to cause it to soften, melt, scorch, char, or ignite). If a fire can be treated as a point source (i.e., its distance, d, from the target surface is much greater than its height or width), the simple relationship

$$\dot{q}'' = X_r \dot{Q} / 4d^2$$

can be applied to test hypotheses about fire progression. Knowing what the "target" surface is (thermoplastic, cellulosic, wool, thermosetting resin, etc.) allows us to predict the effects of various fire sizes ($\dot{Q}$) at various distances. If the critical radiant heat flux needed to ignite a surface is $20\,kW/m^2$, a fire of at least $500\,kW$ is going to be needed to ignite a surface just 1 m away (and this assumes full frontal exposure). If the first fire is a chair, the geometry of the chair and where the fire is burning on it will greatly affect the lateral ignition. Babrauskas observed in his extensive furniture tests that a modern armchair has to be less than 1 m away from a similar burning chair (with a typical $\dot{Q}_{max}$ of $1000\,kW$) if it is to be ignited by direct radiant heat (Krasny et al., 2001). The larger the vertical burning surface in proportion to the distance, the easier it is for distant radiant ignition to occur as the intensity no longer falls off with $1/d^2$ (see Fig. 10.8). Anyone who has attempted to stand in front of a burning wooden wall or tall wooden cabinet can attest to the intensity of radiant heat even 2 or 3 m away.

The fire engineering analysis is carried out to test hypotheses and confirm the reliability of data and predictions in a fire scene reconstruction. In the past, fire investigators relied on experience (often as line firefighters, or as post-fire investigators who rarely saw the actual fire in progress) as the basis for predictions. These cause-and-effect pronouncements were sometimes based on limited (or no) data, erroneous information, or so-called "common sense" and led to wrongful conclusions. Using fire engineering analysis, the investigator can look to enormous bodies of data gathered and tested under controlled conditions by such fire researchers as the National Institue of Standards and Technology (NIST), the University of Maryland, Fire Research Station, Factory Mutual, and others in the public and private sectors. For instance, data show that the heat release rate from a modern sofa can easily exceed that produced by a $1\,m^2$ pool of gasoline burning in the same room and can reach that rate in only 2 or 3 minutes after ignition by open flame. So, short of overpressure (explosion) effects, the end result in a room can look identical (and nearly equal in growth rate). Further testing shows that neither the gasoline nor the modern synthetic-upholstered sofa can be ignited directly with a discarded cigarette. Either first fuel requires an open flame (or an electric arc) to ignite, so the "witness" information that a cigarette was left burning in the room just before the fire can be excluded as unreliable. Fire engineering analysis can help solve puzzles of fire behavior, growth, and effects on humans exposed to it.

CASE STUDY

An elderly man was found unconscious in his upstairs bedroom when firefighters were ventilating smoke and steam from his apartment after extinguishing a large paper and cardboard trash fire on the stairs leading to his bedroom hallway (Fig. 10.23). The fire never extended past the stairs but did damage the adjacent walls and had spread to clothing and other household furnishings adjacent to the stairs. The man, who suffered from emphysema and a heart condition, also had a blood alcohol content of 0.12% (he was a "moderate" alcoholic). He had first- and second-degree burns (blisters) on his face, upper chest, and arms. The door to his room at the end of the upstairs hallway was found partly open, and his room was charged with steam and smoke (to the point the firefighter did not see the victim in bed until the windows were opened and he heard the labored breathing). The man was removed from the apartment and recovered consciousness briefly as he was put on oxygen by the rescue unit, but he lapsed into unconsciousness and died the next day. Upon admission, the victim had a carboxyhemoglobin (COHb) saturation in the hospital of 23% (after approximately 40 minutes on oxygen). He was seen to have soot in his nostrils on admission. Heat effects in his room were limited to softening of a plastic wall clock and lampshade. Smoke levels in the room were estimated to have been 1.5–1.8 m from the floor (by staining on walls). He was found in bed in his underwear at a height estimated to be 0.5 or 0.6 m from the floor. There were unmelted plastic trash bags of clothing on the floor of the room. The issue here was how did the victim sustain his injuries when the fire never extended past the landing of the stairs. Using the pattern of thermal damage on the stairwell walls [showing flame damage to approximately 2.7 m from the foyer floor (base of the stairs)], the maximum heat release rate was calculated from the relationship

$$H_f = 0.174(k\dot{Q})^{2/5}$$

where $k = 2$ (walls). Solving for $\dot{Q}$, using $H_f = 2.7$ m, $\dot{Q} \approx 500$ kW. Using the Zukowski method for smoke production rate,

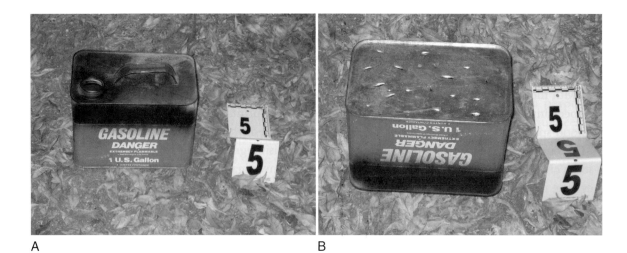

A   B

Figure 10.24

(A) A scorched and smoked gas can appears normal from above, but careful examination shows repeated punctures from a knife blade (B), proving that the can was used to distribute the liquid fuel in an intentional fire.

the fracture pattern and margins may be useful in establishing the sequence of events. The direction and relative speed of mechanical force may also be determined. These reconstructions are most useful when all (or at least a large majority) of the fragments can be recovered and the interior/exterior sides of a window glass can be identified and documented.

TRACE EVIDENCE

Glass, soil, construction materials, fibers, paint, and hairs can all serve to aid the reconstruction of events preceding a fire (and sometimes during it). Fire investigators, however, tend to overlook such trace evidence and need to be reminded of its potential value, particularly early in an investigation before tools, shoes, clothing, or vehicles can be changed or cleaned.

FIRE DEATHS AND INJURIES

PROBLEMS AND PITFALLS

There are several problem areas that can complicate fatal fire investigations and compromise the accuracy and reliability of the conclusions reached.

1. Prejudging the fire and its attendant death as an accident, and automatically treating the scene investigation accordingly, is a major problem. Fires can be

intentional, natural, or accidental in their cause, and deaths can be accidental, homicidal, suicidal, or natural. The linkage between the two events can be direct, indirect, or simple coincidence. The responsibility of the investigation team in fatal fire cases is to establish the cause of both the fire and the death and to determine the connection (if any) between the two.

2. Sudden violent deaths are assumed to be instantaneous exposure to insult followed by immediate collapse and death (a shot is fired and the victim collapses to die shortly afterward), and many forensic investigations are considered (and successfully concluded) in this light. Fires, however, occur over a period of time, creating dangerous environments that vary greatly with time and can kill by a variety of mechanisms. A person may be killed nearly instantaneously by exposure to a flash fire or only after many hours of exposure to toxic gases. Investigators must have an appreciation of the nature of fire and its lethal products and not treat the event as a single exposure to a single set of conditions at a precise moment in time that results in instant collapse.

3. There is little accurate information available to detectives and pathologists about the temperatures and intensities of heat exposure that occur in a fire as it develops.

4. In most violent deaths, the victim offers a fight-or-flight response to the threat, suffers an injury, and collapses and dies. In fires, in addition to flight or attempting to fight the fire, potential responses include going to investigate; simply observing; failing to notice or appreciate the danger; failing to respond due to infirmity or incapacitation from drugs or alcohol; and returning or delaying escape to rescue pets, family, or purses. This variability of response can vastly complicate answering the critical question, Why did this person fail to escape the fire (and perhaps others escaped)?

5. Fires can kill in seconds or the death can occur minutes, hours, days, or even months after the victim is removed from the scene. The longer the time interval between the fire and the death, the more difficult it is to keep track of the actual cause (the fire) and the result (the death). Evidence is lost when a living victim is removed from a scene, and when the victim dies later, away from the scene, it may be too late to recover or document that evidence.

6. There can be conflicts between the perceived or mandated responsibilities of police, fire, medicolegal, and forensic personnel who are often involved in fire death scenes.

7. After death, there can be severe postmortem effects on the body that can vastly complicate the investigation by obliteration of evidence. The body can bear fire patterns of heat effects and smoke deposits that can be masked by exposure to fire after death. The body can be incinerated by exposure to flames, such that evidence of pre-fire wounds or even clinical evidence such as blood samples is

destroyed. There can be structural collapse and the effects of fire fighting hose streams and overhaul that induce additional damage.

8. A major problem is the premature removal of a deceased victim from the fire scene. The compulsion to rescue and remove every fire victim is a very strong one, particularly among dedicated firefighters. However, once the fire is under control and unable to inflict further damage to the body of a confirmed deceased, there is nothing to be gained and much to be lost in the way of burn pattern analysis, body fragments (especially dental evidence), projectiles, clothing and associated artifacts (keys, flashlight, dog leash, etc.), and even trace evidence by the undocumented and hurried removal of the remains.

WHAT KILLS PEOPLE IN FIRES?

Structural fires can achieve their deadly result in a number of ways—heat, smoke, flames, soot, and others—but fire conditions change continually as a fire grows and evolves and the conditions of exposure of a would-be victim can vary from "no threat or injury" to almost instantly lethal. We can isolate the major lethal agents as follows.

Heat

The human body is capable of surviving exposure to external heat as long as it can moderate its temperature by radiant cooling of the blood through the skin and, more important, by evaporative cooling. This occurs internally via evaporation of water from the mucosal linings of the mouth, nose, throat, and lungs and sweat from the skin. If the body temperature exceeds 109°F (43°C), death will occur. Prolonged exposure to high external temperatures (175–250°F, 80–120°C) with low humidity can trigger fatal hyperthermia. Exposure to lower temperatures accompanied by high humidity (which reduces the cooling evaporation rate of the water from the skin or mucosa) can also be lethal. Fire victims can die of exposure to heat alone, even if they are protected from carbon monoxide, smoke, and flames. This may result in victims with minimal postmortem changes, although skin blistering and sloughing ("sleeving" or "gloving") may occur after death.

Inhalation of Hot Gases

Inhalation of very hot gases causes edema (swelling and inflammation) of mucosal tissues. This edema can be severe enough to cause blockage of the trachea and asphyxia. Inhalation of hot gases may also trigger "laryngospasm," in which the larynx involuntarily closes up to prevent entry of foreign material, or "vagal inhibition," in which the breathing stops and the heart rate drops.

Rapid cooling of the inhaled hot gases occurs as the water evaporates from mucosal tissues, so thermal damage usually does not extend below the larynx. If the hot gases include steam or are otherwise water saturated, evaporative cooling is minimized and burns/edema can extend to the major bronchi.

If inhaled gases are hot enough to damage the trachea, they will usually be hot enough to burn facial skin and singe facial or nasal hair.

Smoke

Soot is agglomerations of carbon from incomplete combustion to produce solid particles. These particles may be very hot and are not cooled readily as they are inhaled, so they may induce edema and burns where they lodge in the mucosal tissue of the respiratory system. Soot particles are active absorbents, so they may carry toxic chemicals and permit their ingestion or inhalation (with direct absorption by the mucosal tissues). Soot can be inhaled in sufficient quantities to physically block airways and cause mechanical asphyxiation. Soot in smoke can also obscure the vision of victims and prevent their escape.

Toxic Gases and Chemicals

Products of combustion can include a wide variety of chemicals depending on what is burning and how efficiently it is burning (temperature, mixing, and oxygen concentration are all important variables in determining what species are created). Materials can be classified generally into three basic categories: acidic, toxic, or irritant.

Acidic: HCl, H_2SO_3, H_2SO_4—cause edema and chemical burns when inhaled and absorbed into the water of the mucosal tissues.

Toxic: CO, HCN (hydrogen cyanide), and free radicals (reactive chemical "fragments" that occur at high temperatures)—all have a deleterious effect on tissues, nerves, or biological processes.

Irritants: HCl and acrolein (2-propenal, C_3H_4O) (produced by combustion of wood)—cause tearing of eyes and coughing (possibly to incapacitation).

Carbon Monoxide

Carbon monoxide (CO) is produced in fires by the incomplete combustion of any carbon-containing fuel. It is not produced at the same rate in all fires. In free-burning (well-ventilated) fires, it can be as little as 0.02% (200 ppm) of the total gaseous product. In smoldering, post-flashover, or underventilated fires, CO concentration ranges from 1 to 10% in the smoke stream (Golovina and Khaustovich, 1960, p. 784).

When inhaled and absorbed into the bloodstream, it forms a complex (COHb) with the hemoglobin that is approximately 200 times more stable than the hemoglobin complex formed with either oxygen or CO_2. (There is no measurable diffusion from an external atmosphere rich in CO into the blood or tissues of a dead body.)

The stability of the COHb means that it replaces the O_2 carrying capacity of the blood with a virtually inert complex. CO has both an asphyxiant effect (by starving cells of O_2) and an anesthetic effect as it interferes with energy production in cell functions (Feld, 2002).

Although COHb saturation (the percentage of blood that is "tied up" with CO) is considered lethal by itself at 50%, the actual "lethal" concentration varies widely from as low as 20% in some extreme cases to 80% or higher. Controlling variables are health and age of victim, the presence of other toxic materials, concentration of CO in the air being breathed, and especially physical activity. If no demands are being made on the voluntary muscles (e.g., if the person is asleep), higher concentrations can be accumulated before death occurs. If a person is in good health, with good heart and lung function, higher concentrations can be tolerated. The very old and the very young are most susceptible to death at relatively low concentrations (<40%). Respiratory or cardiac illnesses can compromise oxygen exchange and cardiac function to the point at which saturations of 20–25% can be lethal.

The mere presence of CO in the blood is not a sign of breathing fire gases. The normal body has COHb saturations of 0.5–1% as a result of degradation of heme in the blood (Penney, 2000, Chapter 2). Higher concentrations (up to 3%) may be found in non-fire victims with anemia or other blood disorders. Smokers can have levels of 4–10% since tobacco smoke contains a high concentration of CO coming from a smoldering fire. People in confined spaces with emergency generators, pumps, and compressors can have elevated, sometimes dangerous, COHb concentrations.

When a victim is removed from a CO-rich environment of fresh air, the CO is gradually eliminated (Penney, 2000). The higher the partial pressure of O_2, the faster the elimination:

In fresh air: Initial concentration will be reduced by 50% in 250–320 minutes (approximately 4 or 5 hours).

In O_2 via mask: 50% reduction in 65–85 minutes (approximately $1\frac{1}{4}$ hours).

In O_2 at hyperbaric pressures (3 or 4 atm): 50% reduction in 20 minutes.

The time at which a blood sample is drawn from a subject must be noted as well as the nature of any medical treatment (e.g., O_2). The COHb saturation of blood in a dead body is very stable, even after decomposition is progressing. CO poisoning kills many fire victims before they are ever exposed to fire. It can kill victims even some distance from a fire when they are not exposed to any heat or flames, but it is not the only factor in many fire deaths. CO is not absorbed by a dead body, only by inhalation.

Anoxia

Anoxia is the condition of inadequate oxygen to support life. This can occur when air is displaced by another inert gas such as nitrogen or carbon dioxide, by a fuel gas such as methane, or even by benign products of combustion (e.g., CO_2 and water vapor). Normal air contains 21% O_2. At concentrations down to 15% O_2, there are no readily observable effects. At concentrations between 10 and 15%, disorientation (similar to intoxication) occurs and judgment is affected. At levels below 10%, unconsciousness and death will occur. Hypoxia is aggravated by high levels of CO_2, which accelerate breathing rates.

Flames (Incineration)

When heat is applied to a surface, the rate at which it penetrates that surface is determined by the thermal inertia of the material (the numerical product of thermal capacity, density, and thermal conductivity). The thermal inertia of skin is not much different from that of a block of wood or polyethylene plastic. The pain sensors for human skin are in the dermis, approximately 2 mm (1/10 inch) below the surface. If heat is applied very briefly, there may not be any sensation of discomfort or pain. The longer the heat is applied, the deeper it will penetrate. The higher the intensity the heat applied, the faster it will penetrate. Pain is triggered when skin cells reach a temperature of approximately 120°F (48°C) and cells are damaged if their temperature exceeds 130°F (54°C) (Besant-Matthews, 1993; Stoll and Greene, 1959).

Exposing skin to 2–4 kW/m² radiant heat for 30 seconds will cause pain.
Exposing skin to 4–6 kW/m² radiant heat for 8 seconds produces blisters (second-degree burns).
Exposing skin to 10 kW/m² radiant heat for 5 seconds causes deeper injuries.
Exposing skin to 50–60 kW/m² radiant heat for 5 seconds produces third-degree burns.

Burns

Even in the absence of fire or flames, prolonged exposure of body parts to raise their temperature over 130°F (54°C) will cause desiccation, sloughing, and blistering (which can also be caused by exposure to caustic chemicals). Even in the absence of fire, prolonged exposure to higher temperatures causes desiccation and shrinkage of muscle tissue and tendons, which causes flexion of joints ("pugilistic posturing"). Exposure to flames can cause combustion of muscle and fracturing of major limb bones where the bone is exposed.

Blunt Trauma

Blunt force trauma can also cause or contribute to the death of fire victims. Structural collapse or explosions can produce direct impact of solid materials onto victims. Falls or impact with stationary surfaces (furniture or door frames) during escape attempts can induce blunt trauma that only careful examination can distinguish from the result of an assault. Wound patterns, bloodstains, or even trace evidence can be used to interpret blunt trauma injuries and establish whether they resulted from assault or were inflicted as a result of the fire.

TIME INTERVALS

One of the problems outlined previously is the time interval between exposure to a fire and its fatal aftermath. Death can occur nearly instantaneously or minutes or hours later. Under these conditions, it is not difficult to connect the death to its actual cause. When a person dies weeks or even months after a fire, the cause can still be the fire, but the linkage can be obscured by the extensive medical events in between.

Instantaneous death:
   Vagal inhibition of laryngospasm upon inhalation of flames and hot gases, causing cessation of breathing
   Explosion trauma
   Incineration by exposure to a fully developed fire as a result of structural collapse
Seconds to minutes:
   Hyperthermia—exposure to very hot but nonlethal gases or steam
   Anoxia—lack of oxygen
   Toxic gases—hydrogen cyanide or pyrolysis products (free radicals)
   Asphyxia—inhalation of carbon monoxide or blockage of airways by soot
   Exposure to flames (shock)
   Physical trauma—loss of blood, internal injuries, brain injuries

Hours
    Carbon monoxide
    Edema from inhalation of hot gases
    Burns (shock)
    Brain or other internal injuries
Days
    Burns—dehydration, shock
    Infections
Weeks or months:
    Infections
    Organ failure

It should be remembered that the *cause* of death can be defined as the injury or disease that initiates the sequence of events leading to death. In a fire, the cause may be inhalation of hot gases, CO, or other toxic gases; heat; burns; anoxia (hypoxia); asphyxia; structural collapse; or blunt trauma. The *mechanism* of death is the biological or biochemical derangement incompatible with life. Mechanisms can be respiratory failure, exsanguination, or cardiac arrest. The *manner* of death is an assessment of the circumstances under which the cause was brought about. In the United States, these are most often homicide, suicide, accident, natural, or undetermined. (There are some jurisdictions that recognize death by misadventure and by medical intervention.)

As one can appreciate, the longer the interval between the cause (the fire) and the onset of the mechanism of death (organ failure, septicemia, etc.), the more likely it is that the connection will be lost. This is especially true when the victim has been moved from trauma care hospitals to long-term care facilities, sometimes in other geographical areas. The investigator must be diligent to ensure that the cause of death is not listed on the final death certificate as some generic mechanism, such as respiratory failure, cardiac arrest, or septicemia.

SUMMARY OF POSTMORTEM TESTS DESIRABLE IN FIRE DEATH CASES

Although not all of the following may be needed in all cases, it can be appreciated that once the body is released for embalming or cremation, it will be too late. The complexity of many fire death cases may necessitate finding the answers to problems or questions that were not apparent earlier. Having comprehensive samples and data is the best route to a successful and accurate investigation.

Blood (taken from a major blood vessel or chamber of the heart, not from the body
　　cavity)
Tested for:
　　COHb saturation
　　　　Hydrogen cyanide
　　　　Drugs (therapeutic and abuse)
　　　　Alcohol
Tissue (brain, kidney, liver, lung)
　　Tested for
　　　　Drugs
　　　　　　Poisons
　　　　　　Volatile hydrocarbons
　　　　　　Combustion by-products
　　　　　　CO (as a backup for insufficient blood)
Tissue (skin near burns)
　　Tested for vital chemical or cellular response to burns
Stomach contents
　　Tested to establish activities before death and possible time of death
Airways
　　Full longitudinal transection of airways from mouth to lungs to examine and
　　　　document the extent and distribution of edema, scorching/dehydration, and
　　　　soot
Internal body temperature
　　Should be measured at the scene; may be elevated due to hyperthermia ante-
　　　　mortem or unusually low if death preceded the fire by several hours or more
X-rays
　　Full body (including associated debris in body bag)
　　Details of teeth and any unusual features discovered (fractures, implants)
Clothing
　　Remove and preserve all clothing remnants and associated artifacts
Photographs
　　General and close-up of any burns or wounds, in color, with scale

It is very useful for the fire investigator to be present when the post-mortem is conducted, not only to ensure that all appropriate observations are made but also to answer any questions that arise during the examination. Few pathologists have extensive knowledge of fire chemistry or fire dynamics, so the investigator is in a good position to advise the pathologist as to the fire conditions in the vicinity of the body.

POSTMORTEM DESTRUCTION

A body exposed to fire can support combustion, the rate and thoroughness of which depend on the nature and condition of exposure of the body to the flames. The skin, muscles, and connective tissues will shrink as they dehydrate and char (causing flexion of joints and pugilistic posturing of the body) (Bohnert et al., 1998). If exposed to enough flame, they will burn and yield some heat of combustion, although quite reluctantly. The relatively water-logged tissues of the internal organs must be dried by heat exposure before they can combust, and that dehydration step increases their fire resistance and delays their consumption. Bones have moisture and a high fat content, especially in the marrow, so they will shrink, crack, and split and contribute fuel to an external fire. The subcutaneous fat of the human body provides the best fuel, having a heat of combustion on the order of 36 kJ/g. Like candle wax, however, it will not self-ignite nor smolder and will not support flaming combustion unless the rendered fat is absorbed into a suitable wick. This "wick" can be provided by charred clothing, bedding, carpet, upholstery, or wood in the vicinity (as long as it forms a porous, rigid mass). The size of the fire that can be supported by such a process is controlled by the size (surface area) of the wick. Depending on the position of the body and its available wick area, fires supported by the combustion of a body will be on the order of 20–130 kW (smaller than that of a small wastebasket fire) (DeHaan et al., 1999). The flames will be 800–900°C and if they impinge on the body surface, they can aid the destruction of the body. The process, if unaided by an external fire, is quite slow, with a fuel consumption rate on the order of 3.6–10.8 kg/hr (7–25 lbs/hr). It is possible, given a long enough time (5–10 hours), that a great deal of the body can be reduced to bone fragments (DeHaan and Nurbakhsh, 2001). If a body is exposed to a fully developed room fire, however, the rate of destruction will be much closer to that observed in commercial crematoria. In those cases, flames of 700–900°C and 100 kW/m^2 heat intensity envelop the body and reduce it to ash and fragments of the larger bones in 1½–3 hours (Bohnert et al., 1998).

CONCLUSIONS

In a fatal fire, the cause of death and the cause of the fire are independent but linked by circumstances. Each must be established, and only then can the link between them be determined.

Accidental fires can accompany deaths by accident, suicide, homicide, or even natural causes. Incendiary fires can be associated with homicide (as a direct cause of death or simply as part of the crime event) but also with accidental or natural-cause deaths. For there to be a successful (i.e., accurate and defensible) fire death investigation, there must be the following elements:

1. Every fire with a death or major injury should be treated as a potential crime scene and not prejudged as accidental. The scene should be secured, preserved, documented, and searched by qualified personnel acting as a cooperative team.

2. Documentation is essential. This includes accurate floor plans with dimensions and major fuel packages included and comprehensive photographic coverage. Photos must include presearch survey; photos during search and layering; and all views of the body prior to removal, during removal, and during postmortem examination. This documentation is essential to proper reconstruction.

3. The body must not be moved until it has been properly examined by the fire investigator and the pathologist or coroner's representative and thoroughly documented by photos and diagrams. The debris under and within 3 feet of the body should be carefully layered and sifted. All clothing or fragments should be preserved.

4. The fire investigator has to do his or her job correctly, especially in the assessment of fuels already at the scene (structure as well as furnishings), the role fuels played in ignition, flame spread, heat release rates, time of development, and creation of flashover conditions.

5. Every fire death deserves a full forensic postmortem, including toxicology and x-rays. Toxicology samples should be tested for alcohol and drugs as well as CO, and they should include both blood and tissue. The clothing should remain with the body and be documented and evaluated *in situ* before removal, if possible, then properly preserved. The internal (liver) body temperature should be taken as soon as possible (preferably at the scene).

6. Deceased pets should be x-rayed and necropsied. Injuries to living pets should be noted and documented.

7. "Nonfatal" burn victims should be photographed and blood samples taken for analysis later if needed. External clothing (pants, shoes, and shirt) should be saved and properly preserved.

8. Pathologists and homicide detectives must appreciate the fire environment—temperatures, heat and its transfer, flames, and smoke—and the distribution of fire products and the variables of human response to those conditions. In best practice, the pathologist visits the scene and sees the body *in situ* to appreciate

its conditions of exposure (to flame, heat, and smoke), the nature of debris, and its location and position.

9. A full reconstruction may involve criminalistics evidence such as blood spatter or transfers, fingerprints, tool marks, shoe prints, and trace evidence. The criminalist should be part of the scene team along with the homicide detective, fire investigator, and pathologist.

As we have seen, a death involving fire is not a simple exposure to a static set of conditions at a single moment in time. Fire is a complex event, and a fire death investigation is even more complex and challenging. A coalition of talents and knowledge working together as a team is the only way to get the correct answers to the major questions: What killed the victim? Was the fire accidental or deliberate? and How did those two events interact?

The fire engineering principles described previously also play an important role in reconstructing fire deaths and injuries. Thin materials such as hair or loose, lightweight fabrics will be affected by short-duration exposures to fire (such as the 1-second durations of flash fires or combustion explosions) where thicker materials will not. Skin and underlying tissue has about the same thermal inertia as pine wood or polyethylene plastic and will react to heat flux in much the same way. Very brief exposure (1 or 2 seconds) to flame can induce reddening and separation of the epidermal layers (first-degree burns and peeling) but not pain (Stoll and Greene, 1959). The longer the duration of exposure, the deeper the injury. Fire injuries involving the dermal layer [where the skin cells grow from the germinative (basal) layer] cause third-degree burns that usually require replacement of the skin via skin grafts. Partial-thickness or second-degree burns involve the interface between the epidermal and dermal layers, causing cell death and disintegration, fluid loss, and blisters. Such injuries leave the basal layer of the dermis intact, and the skin will grow back without grafts.

The radiant heat flux from established fires can be calculated to evaluate the likelihood of skin burns at various distances from the fire. The layering effect in a room described previously will also control exposure of a person to heat and toxic gases in the smoke layer. If a person is positioned low in a room (e.g., reclining on a bed or on the floor), he or she may be able to exist in a room with a developing fire for an extended period of time and not suffer any ill effects. If the person stands up (or the smoke layer descends to the person's level), he or she will be exposed to convective heat and inhalation injuries. The intake of CO from smoke can be estimated from the Stewart equation (Icove and DeHaan, 2004, p. 234):

$$\% \text{ COHb} = (3.317 \times 10^{-5})(\text{ppm CO})^{1.036}(\text{RMV})t$$

where ppm CO is the concentration of CO in the air being inhaled, RMV is the respiratory minute volume in liters per minute (lpm), and t is the time of exposure. The RMV, of course, varies with the sex, age, and level of physical activity of the person exposed. In the case study described previously, the time of exposure of the elderly victim could be roughly calculated as follows:

$$t = \frac{(3.015 \times 10^4)(\%COHb)}{(ppm^{1.036})(RMV)}$$

The RMV for an adult at rest is 7.5 lpm. in the case study described previously, the victim's COHb at hospital admission was 23% after ~40 minutes on oxygen. We know that COHb saturation is reduced by 50% by 65–86 minutes, so in 40 minutes his COHb would have been reduced from 50–36% at the time of removal. If the COHb is estimated at 30% and if we estimated that CO concentration at bed level was 5000 ppm (a typical level in light smoke), the time of exposure would be approximately 17 minutes. In this case, this time fits the other information about the start of the fire, response and suppression time for the fire department, fire and smoke conditions observed by the firefighters, and time needed to search for and recover the victim. (The accused landlady never informed anyone that her lodger was still in the apartment, so a rescue search was not conducted. The victim was discovered only during routine post-fire venting operations.)

Very low COHb saturations indicate the victim died of other causes before being exposed to the fire or succumbed to massive external burns (thermal shock), inhalation of flames that stopped further inhalations, or hypoxic conditions as a result of a flash fire. When a flammable hydrocarbon fuel burns explosively in a room, very little or no CO is produced initially, and so much of the oxygen is consumed in the room that the atmosphere is unable to support life (O_2 core below 10%) (DeHaan, 1996). If the victim is trapped, particularly in a closed room, and if he or she survives the flash of intense heat, the victim can die of hypoxia (enhanced by high concentrations of CO_2 produced by the combustion) before he or she is exposed to high concentrations of CO produced by combustion of other combustibles burning in the room. Death by hypoxia cannot be detected postmortem because the O_2 and CO_2 saturations are not stable after death and cannot be measured. The finding of a negligible COHb saturation (<3%) alone is not proof that the victim was dead prior to the fire. There are several other mechanisms. The entire event deserves careful reconstruction and assessment before such a conclusion is reached.

FIRE TESTING

Data to test various hypotheses and defend conclusions derive from a variety of sources. Fire tests can range from simple field tests requiring no specialized equipment to lab (bench-scale) tests involving dedicated equipment and large-scale tests with actual furnishings, scale models or full-scale recreations of a particular room, or even a building. The American Society of Testing and Materials (ASTM) offers a number of bench-scale tests that can provide useful information about what contribution a fuel might make in a real fire (given that the test conditions do not duplicate real fire conditions). Some tests include:

ASTM D1230: Standard Test Method for Flammability of Apparel Textiles (ASTM, 1994a)

ASTM D2859: Standard Test Method for Ignition Characteristics of Finished Textile Floor Covering Materials (Methenamine Pill Test) (ASTM, 1996a)

ASTM E1352: Standard Test Method for Cigarette Ignition Resistance of Components of Upholstered Furniture (ASTM, 1998a)

ASTM E648: Standard Test Method for Critical Radiant Flux of Floor-Covering Materials (ASTM, 1997a)

ASTM E659: Standard Test Method for Determining Autoignition Temperature of Liquid Chemicals (ASTM, 1994b)

ASTM D1929: Standard Test Method for Determining Ignition Temperatures of Plastics (ASTM, 1996b)

ASTM E84: Standard Test Method for Determining Surface Burning Characteristics of Building Materials (Steiner Tunnel Test for Horizontal Surfaces) (ASTM, 1998b)

ASTM E1321: Standard Test Method for Determining Material Ignition and Flame Spread Properties (Vertical Fuel Surfaces) (ASTM, 1997b)

The reader is referred to the ASTM *Fire Test Standards* (2000) for a complete listing. There are also a number of standard bench-scale tests for flammability of apparel as defined by the U.S. Code of Federal Regulations (CFR) (DeHaan, 2002, Chapter 11). The following are examples:

16CFR1610—Flammability of Clothing Textiles

16CFR1611—Flammability of Vinyl Plastic Film

16CFR1630—Flammability of Carpets and Rugs

16CFR1632—Flammability of Mattresses and Pads

16CFR1615 and 1616—Flammability of Children's Sleepwear

Calorimetry is used (in a variety of scales) to establish the heat release rate of some fuels, fuel packages, and even entire rooms. If electronic weighing of the fuel is conducted, the mass loss rates and effective heat of combustion can also be measured. Classical bomb calorimetry is typically used for small quantities of pure fuels (described in *ASTM D240-92*; ASTM, 1997c). Oxygen depletion calorimetry is more commonly used for complex materials. The cone calorimeter was developed by Babrauskas at NIST (described in *ASTM E1354*; ASTM, 1997d. It exposes a $10 \times 10\,cm$ sample to a known radiant heat flux (from a cone-shaped heater), provides a flame ignition source, and then monitors the airflow, O_2, CO_2, and CO concentration in the airstream of the exhaust duct from the chamber. Since combustion of almost all common fuels produces approximately $3\,kJ/g$ of air "consumed" ($\sim13\,kJ/g\ O_2$), if one knows how much oxygen is consumed, the heat released can be derived directly. The sample is continuously weighed by a sensitive load cell. This method has been shown to be widely applicable for assessing the real fire behavior of a wide range of fuels. The same principle is applied in the furniture calorimeter, in which a fume-hood-sized exhaust system is used and the same data are captured by analysis of the exhaust gases and a load cell beneath the item being tested. Very large calorimeters, such as the $20\,MW\ 30 \times 30\,m$ system installed at the ATFE Fire Research Lab in Ammendale, Maryland, can accommodate very large fires, such as those of vehicles or multiroom structures.

Typical test data from a room-size calorimeter at the California Department of Consumer Affairs, Bureau of Home Furnishings showing the development of a fire in a bedroom mock-up was shown in Figure 10.19. Data from such tests on a variety of household and commercial fuel packages are available in printed versions or online from NIST.

Scale models have been used to study fire, and especially smoke, development in structures. Scale models (often 1:4 scale) must allow for dynamics (ventilation, smoke velocity, etc.) that do not scale down in a linear fashion, and thermal responses of lining materials must be calibrated to the scale of the test (Ingason et al., 2001). One successful variant is the construction of a clear plastic scale model of the building, inverting it in a tank of clear liquid, and using a colored liquid of higher density to replicate the fluid flow of buoyant hot gases through a structure. Scaling factors are important, and the relative densities and viscosities of the liquid have to be calibrated to replicate gaseous flows, but the technique has been used to solve some investigation problems and confirm or reject computational models or hypotheses. Full-scale tests can be based on test cubicles made of wood framing and drywall in $2.4 \times 2.4\,m$ to $4 \times 5\,m$ sizes (Icove and DeHaan, 2004, pp. 273–284). They can be constructed to include windows, doors, observation ports, and even operational electricity. They can be constructed "on demand" and use only new materials to minimize toxic hazards from

Fire Testing

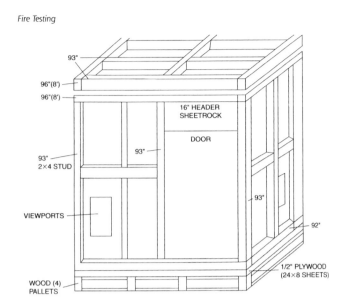

Figure 10.25

Typical cubicle for fire testing. They can be made in larger sizes with or without windows. View/camera ports are simple glass panes glued to the inner surface of drywall.

paint or floor tile and injuries from floor collapse [since they are usually built on grade (concrete slab) or on wood pallets]. (See Fig. 10.25 for a typical design.)

The reconstruction of some fires may require an architecturally accurate re-creation of the original fire scene; however, this is very uncommon and very expensive, especially if more than one hypothesis needs to be tested. More often, donated or abandoned buildings are used and modified to make them similar to the subject property (DeHaan, 1992). Such tests have been used successfully, especially if one fire can be extinguished quickly and the structure rehabilitated so that two or more tests can be completed. Special preparations have to be made to ensure the safety of attending fire-fighters, such as reinforcing floors, removing windows, pre-venting roofs and attics, limiting fuel types, and removing floor coverings (per *NFPA 1403*; NFPA, 2002). Some of these changes make replication of a real fire incident impossible, so alternative solutions need to be sought.

COMPUTER MODELING

In the past 20 years, a variety of computer-based models of fire behavior have been developed as an aid to fire research. Some are very simple and make generous assumptions about fuels, ventilation, geometry, fire growth, and other factors. Others are more complex and allow variables such as a choice of initial fire or changes in ventilation to be built in. Recent models are very sophisticated and can accommodate many variables and predict many factors. No matter how sophisticated these models may be, it must be remembered that none of them can prove how a particular fire occurred. They can best be used to test various hypotheses about a fire to demonstrate which are feasible and which are not. Because they are based on real fire data and validated for reliability in making certain predictions, they can be used to evaluate the effects of changing particular variables without the expense and difficulty of repeating full-scale fire tests.

Fire models can include calculations such as those included in FPETOOL, developed by H. E. Nelson at NIST. It is a collection of analytical tools about fire behavior and properties with simplifications and assumptions to offer approximations rather than exact predictions (Nelson, 1990). It consists of three main elements:

Fireform (fire formulas)—a collection of fire safety calculations

Makefire—a series of procedures to produce fire input data files for use with Fire Simulator

Fire Simulator—an integrated set of equations (i.e., a model) designed to allow the user to create a fire case study in a Lotus format with specifications of room and vent dimensions; fuel characteristics; ceiling, wall, and floor materials; and input fire to predict layer temperature, flashover, and tenability factors

The first successful fire models were called zone models because they treated a room fire as two zones—the hot smoke (ceiling) layer overlying a normal room air layer. These models assume no mixing occurs between the two layers and there is only one localized fire "pumping" hot gases into the ceiling layer. An input fire of known HRR and duration represents the fire (since such models are not capable of predicting fire spread). ASET-B (Available Safe Egress Time—Version B) and CFAST (Consolidated Model of Fire Growth and Smoke Transport) are the two most commonly used zone models. DETACT-QS is a zone model developed for predicting smoke detector and sprinkler activation that has also been frequently used. As long as the user understands the limitations, underlying assumptions, and nature of data obtained, such models can be run by the average computer user using a PC or laptop.

Due to the limitations of zone models, more sophisticated models with better predictive powers and more flexibility were developed using the principles of computational fluid dynamics. Such field models break the room or building into hundreds or thousands of cells, six-sided "boxes," and then calculate the heat energy, mass, and momentum moving into and out of each surface of each box. Such models can predict fire growth, smoke and heat movement, and concentrations of individual chemical species as the fire grows. The most widely used field model is the Fire Dynamics Simulator developed by NIST. It uses a graphical interface called Smokeview to demonstrate data regarding temperatures, smoke densities, chemical species, and gas distribution as a color-coded static or dynamic display. This model requires extensive training and familiarity with fire (and computer) processes, considerable time to set up and input data for the problem, and a moderately fast computer to accomplish its calculations. It is not unusual for a multiroom problem to require days to input data and weeks of continuous computing to conduct one "run." Such data can be used to answer a wide variety of questions (e.g., predicting the actual CO concentration at 0.6 m height in the bedroom of the elderly fire victim) (Christensen and Icove, 2004).

There are numerous guidelines for evaluating the applicability and reliability of computer fire models. There are ASTM guides that deal with critical modeling issues such as evaluation, validation, and documentation. These include:

ASTM E1355-97: Standard Guide for Evaluating the Predictive Capability of Deterministic Fire Models (ASTM, 1997e)

ASTM E1591-00: Standard Guide for Obtaining Data for Deterministic Fire Models (ASTM, 2000a)

ASTM E1895-97: Standard Guide for Determining Uses and Limitations of Deterministic Fire Models (ASTM, 1997f)

ASTM E1472: Guide for Documenting Computer Software for Fire Models (ASTM, 2000b)

TESTING COMPLEX COMPUTER MODELS

One of the major differences between zone and field models is that field models often include routines that calculate the growing fire based on first principles of thermal response, heat flux, and flame spread. Of course, this requires that the initial fuels be identified and their physical and thermal properties carefully defined as input data.

The limitations of this text are such that detailed descriptions of complex fire models cannot be included here. The reader is referred to the references or to the firemodelsurvey.com Web site.

The following questions should be answered by an investigator when considering using a model:

Appropriateness—Is the model's output useful and applicable?

Limitations to the model (time, ventilation, output)

Resources—Computer speed and capacity needed

Operator experience needed

Input data needed—Is there sufficient documentation to supply all of it? What default conditions apply if input data are incomplete?

Sensitivity—What happens to output when input data are changed?

Accuracy

Are the results/outputs realistic? Would they occur that way in a real fire?

Has the model been used to predict the outcome of a test burn, such as tenability, temperatures, or time to flashover? How accurately did it predict the actual fire results?

Was the model "fine-tuned" to make its predictions more accurate? (Was the program run multiple times with different data to slightly "tweak" the result?)

How was the data collected in the test burn? Direct observation, thermocouple measurements, radiometers?

Where were the measurement/observation points for the test fire?

(The fire environment can be so complex that temperature or radiometric data collected in one location may not be representative of the entire room, leading to possible variations of as much as $\pm30\%$.)

Reproducibility

If the program is run with the same data by the same person, does it give the same answer?

If the program is run with the same data by a different person, does it give the same answer?

Robustness

Is the program applicable to different situations? Has it been tested and validated (demonstrated to give accurate results) if starting conditions are very different?

Has it been shown to give reliable results for

Small fire in a large room vs large fire in a small room?

Adequate ventilation vs underventilated?

"Ultrafast" t^2 fire vs "medium" t^2 fire?

Analysis

What features of fuel, starting conditions, and initial fire size are input data and what assumptions have been made by the analyst based on personal judgment or "bias"?

One of the primary considerations before relying on computer model results is verification that the model is appropriate for the situation being modeled. Its documentation must include the "real fire" data against which the model was tested. Before using a model in a fire reconstruction, the investigator must carefully evaluate the following:

Accuracy—The accuracy of input data (initial fire HRR and growth rate) is critical to the accuracy of the final result. "Garbage in–gospel out" is the risk with computer models. Are data arbitrary? Are they correct for the scenario in question?

Assumptions—What assumptions were made by the user to fill the gaps? Incompleteness of data from the scene is the major reason for most failed computer model attempts. What default values does the model insert if data are not available? Will those default values make a difference (i.e., what is the model's sensitivity to those values)?

Impression—How is the data presented? Is it in the form of reviewable printed output or a single dramatic action cartoon? Smokeview will show "movement" of flames and smoke that is a stop-action representation of a "temperature" surface or smoke concentration. Other models (or users) refrain from showing smoke or flame movement because it is, to some extent, too complex and too random to show accurately.

Correctness—Is it the right model for the job? What is the question the investigator wants to answer? What is the question the model was intended to answer (temperature, smoke filling, or species concentration)? What are the limitations of the model—the number of rooms, fire growth, size of fire, ventilation, and time? Will this model address those issues correctly in the problem at hand? Is information about conditions in a specific location at a specific time needed? If so, a zone model may not be able to give an appropriate answer.

Evaluation/validation—Was the model created and validated for a particular scenario (small fire in a large room), and is it being used here for a very different scenario without proper (published) evaluation?

Fine-tuning—When a comparison to a test fire is offered, the number of model runs should be evaluated. Was the model run with changes in input data to get the model to "match" the real fire?

User qualified?—Does the user have the correct documentation (user's guides and technical manuals)? How much experience does the user have with this model? Were other models considered or used? What steps can the user take to make sure the model is correct and correctly used (e.g., reviewing published evaluations)?

LABORATORY TESTS

In many fire investigations, the only analysis the forensic lab is asked to do is the testing of fire debris to determine the presence and identity of ignitable liquid residues. Although this information is critical to some investigations, a proper fire reconstruction may require a much wider variety of analyses. Before many of the predictive fire engineering analyses can be carried out, the investigator must have reliable identification of the materials involved. Carpets may be nylon, acrylic, cotton, polypropylene, or wool (or mixtures of two or more). Each material has very different reactions to heat—some melt, others char, and some decompose. Some (e.g., acrylic) ignite at very low radiant heat fluxes ($<10\,kW/m^2$); others (e.g., nylon or wool) require very high heat fluxes and then ignite only reluctantly (Quintiere, 1997). Upholstery fabrics represent an even wider range of possible types and reactions to heat and fire. Upholstery padding may be cotton (readily ignited by smoldering sources unless fire retardant-treated) or polyester fiber-fill (not ignitable except by direct flame). Foam rubber may be polyurethane (requiring open flame to ignite), synthetic combustion modified foam (very difficult to ignite), or latex foam (readily ignited by either flame or smoldering cigarette). Melting points of a variety of materials play an important role in evaluating fire patterns.

If liquid fuels are involved, lab analysis is needed to determine their flash points, vapor density, and vapor pressure because these are the factors that control their contribution to fire ignition or growth. These values can be determined directly (using appropriate ASTM methods) or indirectly by identifying the material by gas chromatography or infrared spectrometry and then referring to published data. Elemental analysis may be needed if an inorganic material is involved in ignition (e.g., a pyrotechnic mixture), in fire spread (via a combustible metal), or in producing toxic effects in victims (e.g., heavy metals). Organic fuels can produce highly toxic combustion gases (HCN from nylon plastics or wool, and hydrogen chloride from PVC plastics), and their identification may involve both gas chromatography/mass spectrometry and elemental analysis. Forensic laboratory personnel must never limit their thinking or their analytical services to "just doing the GC" on fire cases.

CONCLUSIONS

Final conclusions about a fire scene reconstruction should be peer reviewed whenever possible. The analysis of data from complex scenes can be very time-consuming, and reviewers may be unwilling or unable to devote much time to review someone else's case. The best most of us can do is to make our report as comprehensive as possible, including descriptions of the data examined, a description of the steps taken in accordance with the scientific method, citation of the evidence that supported elements of the final conclusion, and descriptions of the logic and reasoning by which each of the opinions and conclusions were reached.

ASTM E620: Standard Practice for Reporting Opinions of Technical Experts (ASTM, 2004) outlines suggested practices in such technical reports. *ASTM E678: Standard Practice for the Evaluation of Technical Data* (ASTM, 1998c) offers guidance in applying the scientific method by technical experts. Because these publications are peer-reviewed, professional protocols, they are being cited more often in fire cases as the practices that a fire investigator should follow. Some of the practices described exceed the practicality (and time limits) of many investigators, but we should be aware of their existence and follow them whenever possible.

The bottom line is that the report of a fire scene reconstruction must be comprehensive, listing and describing all of the items, evidence, and materials received; what data were collected; what tests were conducted; what special sources of information the expert relied on; description and evaluation of all hypotheses; and the logic and reasoning behind the final conclusions. The more comprehensive the report, the better the guarantee that the expert has conducted his or her investigation and reconstruction thoroughly and reached reliable, defensible conclusions that will withstand rigorous cross-examination.

REFERENCES

American Society of Testing and Materials (ASTM) *ASTM D1230: Standard Test Method for Flammability of Apparel Textiles.* West Conshohocken, PA: ASTM, 1994a.

American Society of Testing and Materials (ASTM) *ASTM E659: Standard Test Method for Determining Autoignition Temperature of Liquid Chemicals.* West Conshohocken, PA: ASTM, 1994b.

American Society of Testing and Materials (ASTM) *ASTM D2859: Standard Test Method for Ignition Characteristics of Finished Textile Floor Covering Materials (Methenamine Pill Test).* West Conshohocken, PA: ASTM, 1996a.

American Society of Testing and Materials (ASTM) *ASTM D1929: Standard Test Method for Determining Ignition Temperatures of Plastics.* West Conshohocken, PA: ASTM, 1996b.

American Society of Testing and Materials (ASTM) *ASTM E648: Standard Test Method for Critical Radiant Flux of Floor-Covering Materials.* West Conshohocken, PA: ASTM, 1997a.

American Society of Testing and Materials (ASTM) *ASTM E1321: Standard Test Method for Determining Material Ignition and Flame Spread Properties (Vertical Fuel Surfaces).* West Conshohocken, PA: ASTM, 1997b.

American Society of Testing and Materials (ASTM) *ASTM D240-92: Test Method for Heat of Combustion of Liquid Hydrocarbon Fuels by Bomb Calorimeter.* West Conshohocken, PA: ASTM, 1997c.

American Society of Testing and Materials (ASTM) *ASTM E1354: Test Method for Heat and Visible Smoke Release Rates for Materials and Products Using an Oxygen Consumption Calorimeter.* West Conshohocken, PA: ASTM, 1997d.

American Society of Testing and Materials (ASTM) *ASTM E1355-97: Standard Guide for Evaluating the Predictive Capability of Deterministic Fire Models.* West Conshohocken, PA: ASTM, 1997e.

American Society of Testing and Materials (ASTM) *ASTM E1895-97: Standard Guide for Determining Uses and Limitations of Deterministic Fire Models.* West Conshohocken, PA: ASTM, 1997f.

American Society of Testing and Materials (ASTM) *ASTM E1352: Standard Test Method for Cigarette Ignition Resistance of Components of Upholstered Furniture.* West Conshohocken, PA: ASTM, 1998a.

American Society of Testing and Materials (ASTM) *ASTM E84: Standard Test Method for Determining Surface Burning Characteristics of Building Materials (Steiner Tunnel Test for Horizontal Surfaces).* West Conshohocken, PA: ASTM, 1998b.

American Society of Testing and Materials (ASTM) *ASTM E678: Standard Practice for the Evaluation of Technical Data.* West Conshohocken, PA: ASTM, 1998c.

American Society of Testing and Materials (ASTM) *Fire Test Standards.* (5th ed.). West Conshohocken, PA: ASTM, 1999.

American Society of Testing and Materials (ASTM) *ASTM E1591-00: Standard Guide for Obtaining Data for Deterministic Fire Models.* West Conshohocken, PA: ASTM, 2000a.

American Society of Testing and Materials (ASTM) *ASTM E1472: Guide for Documenting Computer Software for Fire Models.* West Conshohocken, PA: ASTM, 2000b.

American Society of Testing and Materials (ASTM) *ASTM E620: Standard Practice for Reporting Opinions of Technical Experts.* West Conshohocken, PA: ASTM, 2004.

Besant-Matthews, P. E. "Deaths Associated with Burns, Fire and Arson," Lecture, Dallas, TX, 1993.

Bohnert, M., Rost, T., and Pollak, S. "The Degree of Destruction of Human Bodies in Relation to the Duration of the Fire," *Forensic Science International*, 95, 11–21, 1998.

Christensen, A. M., and Icove, D. J. "The Application of NIST's Fire Dynamics Simulator to the Investigation of Carbon Monoxide Exposure in the Deaths of Three Pittsburgh Fire Fighters," *Journal of Forensic Sciences*, 49(1), 104–107, January 2004.

Cole, L. S. *Investigation of Motor Vehicle Fires.* Novato, CA: Lee Books, 1992.

DeHaan, J. D. "Fire—Fatal Intensity," *Fire & Arson Investigator*, 43(1), 55–59, September 1992.

DeHaan, J. D. "The Dynamics of Flash Fires Involving Flammable Hydrocarbon Liquids," *American Journal of Forensic Medicine and Pathology*, 17(1), 24–31, 1996.

DeHaan, J. D. *Kirk's Fire Investigation.* (5th ed.). Upper Saddle River, NJ: Pearson/Brady, 2002.

DeHaan, J. D., Campbell, S. J., and Nurbakhsh, S. "The Combustion of Body Fat and Its Implications for Fires Involving Bodies," *Science & Justice*, 39, 27–38, 1999.

DeHaan, J. D., and Nurbakhsh, S. "The Sustained Combustion of an Animal Carcass and Its Implications for the Consumption of Human Bodies in Fires," *Journal of Forensic Science*, 1076–1081, September 2001.

Drysdale, D. D. *An Introduction to Fire Dynamics.* Chichester, UK: Wiley, 1985.

Feld, J. M. "The Physiology and Biochemistry of Combustion Toxicology," Proceedings of Fire Risk and Hazard Assessment Research Applications Symposium. FP Research Foundation, July 2002.

Golovina, E. S., and Khaustovich, G. P. Eighth International Symposium on Combustion. San Francisco, CA, 1960.

Icove, D. J., and DeHaan, J. D. *Forensic Fire Scene Reconstruction.* Upper Saddle River, NJ: Pearson/Brady, 2004.

Ingason, H., Weckstrom, V., and Van Hees, P. "The Gothenburg Discotheque Fire Investigation." In *Proceedings: InterFlam,* pp. 965–976. London: Interscience Communications, 2001.

Krasny, J. F., Parker, W. J., and Babrauskas, V. *Fire Behavior of Upholstered Furniture and Mattresses.* Park Ridge, NJ: Noyes, 2001.

National Fire Protection Association (NFPA) *NFPA 1403: Standard on Live Training Evolutions.* Quincy, MA: NFPA, 2002.

National Fire Protection Association (NFPA) *NFPA 921: Guide for Fire and Explosion Investigation.* Quincy, MA: NFPA, 2004.

National Institute of Justice. *Fire and Arson Scene Evidence: A Guide for Public Safety Personnel,* NCJR 181584. Washington, DC: National Institute of Justice, 2000.

Nelson, H. E. FPETOOL: Fire Protection Engineering Tools for Hazard Evaluation, NISTIR 4380. Gaithersburg, MD: U.S. Department of Commerce, NIST, October 1990.

Penney, D. G. (Ed.). *Carbon Monoxide Toxicity.* Boca Raton, FL: CRC Press, 2000.

Quintiere, J. G. *Principles of Fire Behavior.* Albany, NY: Delmar, 1997.

Sapp, A. D., Huff, T. G., Gary, G. P., and Icove, D. J. *A Motive-Based Offender Analysis of Serial Arsonists.* Quantico, VA: FBI National Center for the Analysis of Violent Crime, U.S. Department of Justice, 1995.

Stoll, A. M., and Greene, L. C. "Relationship Between Pain and Tissue Damage Due to Thermal Radiation," *Journal of Applied Physiology,* 14(3), 373–382, 1959.

CHAPTER 11

RECONSTRUCTING DIGITAL EVIDENCE

Eoghan Casey, MA

Information is flowing through wires and air all around us, from one computing device to another, frequently finding a resting place on storage media along the way. Given the ubiquity of digital data, criminal activity today often leaves digital traces stored on or transmitted using computers. Law enforcement and regulatory agencies have recognized that they cannot afford to overlook these traces and are therefore devoting resources to the collection and forensic examination of digital evidence. The resulting evidence provides an abundance of information that can be useful when investigating a crime. Even if digital evidence does not contain the "smoking gun," it can reveal actions, positions, origins, associations, activities, and sequences useful for reconstructing the events surrounding an offense.

Forensic examiners of computer systems are called on to answer both simple and complex questions relating to crimes. Investigators may need to know something as simple as whether a particular document can be located on a computer or when the document was created or printed. In some cases, digital evidence may provide a decisive lead, such as the floppy diskette that was sent by the Bind Torture Kill (BTK) serial killer to a television station and contained data that led investigators to a computer in the church where Dennis Rader was council president. Computers also have physical properties that can be embedded in the digital evidence they produce. The electronics in every digital camera has unique properties that specialized forensic analysts can utilize to link digital photographs to a specific device (Fridrich et al., 2005; Geradts et al., 2005). Some color printers place their serial number on pages in millimeter-sized yellow dots that are only visible under certain light frequencies, enabling investigators to associate an item with a particular printer (Tuohey, 2004). A person's Internet communications and digital documents contain verbal evidence that forensic linguists can analyze to learn more about a victim or offender (Chaski, 2005).

The information stored and created on computers can be used to answer fundamental questions relating to a crime, including what happened when (sequencing), who was responsible (attribution), and the origination of a particular item (evaluation of source). At the same time, the complexity of computer systems requires appreciation that individual pieces of digital evidence may have multiple interpretations, and corroborating information may be vital to reaching a correct conclusion. Forensic examiners need to understand, and make regular use of, the scientific method to ensure that conclusions reached are solidly based in fact. Familiarity with the limitations of forensic examinations of digital evidence will help investigators and attorneys exculpate the innocent and apprehend modern criminals.

This chapter presents the use of digital evidence to reconstruct actions taken in furtherance of a crime, providing case examples to demonstrate key concepts. The focus of this chapter is on how digital evidence can be useful in violent crime investigations. Specifically, this chapter describes how digital evidence that is properly handled and interpreted can be used to apprehend offenders, authenticate documents, assess alibis and statements, and determine intent. Other approaches to analyzing digital evidence, and underlying technical details are beyond the scope of this text. For more in-depth, technical coverage of how forensic science is applied to computers and networks, see Casey (2004).

OVERVIEW OF DIGITAL EVIDENCE

Computers can be directly involved in many types of criminal activity, including terrorism, organized crime, stalking, and child exploitation. For example, sex offenders and obsessional harassers use computers to threaten and control victims, making the computer an instrument of the crime as well as the storage container of evidence relating to the crime. For forensic purposes, it is generally not computers themselves that are of primary interest but, rather, the data they contain. *Digital evidence* is defined as any data stored or transmitted using a computer that support or refute a theory of how an offense occurred or that address critical elements of the offense, such as intent or alibi (Casey, 2004). Homicide, sexual assault, and other violent crimes can involve digital evidence from a wide range of sources, including personal computers, handheld devices, servers, and the Internet, helping investigators reconstruct events and gain insight into the state of mind of individuals.

The digital footprints we leave as we move through the world create "cybertrails" that investigators can retrace to determine what we were doing, where, and when. Third parties, such as mobile telephone providers, banks, credit card companies, and electronic toll collection systems, can reveal significant information about an individual's whereabouts and activities. The computers we use at home and work contain remnants of documents, photographs, Internet communications, and other details that generally reveal a great deal about our daily life, inner thoughts, and motivations. Data that have been "deleted" often remain on a computer indefinitely, and technically savvy individuals can store data in unused areas of a hard disk. A victim's handheld device may contain entries or photographs that indicate where she was or who she met at a particular time. Records from a missing person's mobile telephone provider or car navigation system may indicate where he went. Computers could contain details about a murder plot, from a to-do list in a personal digital assistant to communications between co-conspirators. A trained forensic examiner can recover and use these data to reveal evidence that a criminal sought to hide and glean a great deal about an individual and his activities.

When a large quantity of digital evidence is involved, forensic examiners employ key word searches and other data reduction techniques, as well as reconstruction tools such as time lines and link charts. Some link analysis tools can import e-mail and other digital data to help investigators identify patterns and relationships. Figure 11.1 depicts an example of how the contents of a short message service (SMS) message found on the victim's phone could lead to a suspect and how the locations of mobile telephones could be used to place the suspect at the crime scene.

Some forms of digital evidence contain additional information, called metadata, that specialists can extract to aide an investigation. Consider the following data embedded in a Microsoft Word document extracted using Metadata Assistant (www.payneconsulting.com), which reveals when the document was originally created, when it was last modified and printed, the various file names of the document, and the names of the last 10 authors:

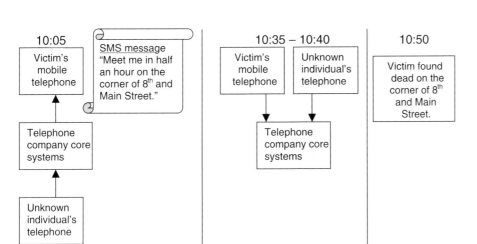

Figure 11.1

Links between victim and suspect established using a SMS message and the location of the mobile telephone at given times.

Document Name: suicide-note.doc

Path: C:\Documents and Settings\ Jane Doe\Desktop

Document Format: Word Document

Built-in document properties:

Built-in Properties Containing Metadata: 3

Title: Note

Author: John Doe

Company: personal

Document Statistics:

Document Statistics Containing Metadata: 6

Creation Date: 7/22/2005 4:31:00 PM

Last Save Time: 6/19/2005 1:58:00 PM

Time Last Printed: 6/19/2005 1:44:00 PM

Last Saved By: Jane Doe

Revision Number: 3

Total Edit Time (Minutes): 5 Minutes

Last 10 authors:

Has Last 10 Data

Author: John Doe Path: A:\note.doc

Author: John Doe Path: C:\Documents and Settings\ John Doe\Application
    Data\Microsoft\Word\AutoRecovery save of note.asd

Author: John Doe Path: A:\note.doc

Author: Jane Doe Path: A:\note.doc

Author: Jane Doe Path: C:\Documents and Settings\ Jane Doe\Desktop\
    suicide-note.doc

Track Changes:

Tracked Changes: 1. Tracked Changes are On.

1 Type: Delete Author: Jane Doe

My husband did not kill me.

Location: Main Text

This type of embedded metadata can answer a variety of questions regarding a document, including its provenance and authenticity. For instance, although this document appears to have been last printed and saved on 6/19/2005, the original creation date suggests that it was not created until more than one month later on 7/22/2005. This date sequence is explained through examination of the last 10 authors, which reveals that the document named "note.doc" was originally created on a floppy diskette using John Doe's computer (corresponding to the "Creation Date" of 7/22/2005) and was subsequently transferred to Jane Doe's computer, where it was saved as "suicide-note.doc" and given a "Last Saved Time" on 6/19/2005, possibly because the clock on Jane Doe's computer had been backdated. The metadata also shows that the line "My husband did not kill me" was deleted from the document at some time. A forensic examination of the computers and floppy diskette would likely uncover remnants of the note on the husband's computer, additional temporal information showing when the document was actually created and transferred onto the wife's computer, and other data that would help determine who wrote the note and gain insight into the author's intent.

As another example of the investigative usefulness of digital evidence, e-mail and AOL Instant Messages provided the compelling evidence to convict Sharee Miller of conspiring to kill her husband and abetting the suicide of the admitted killer (an ex-cop named Jerry Cassaday), whom she had seduced. Miller used their Internet correspondences to control Cassaday's perception of her husband, as demonstrated in the following excerpt from one of their online chat sessions (Bean, 2003).

> [Sharee Miller] twice told Cassaday she was pregnant with his babies—even though she'd had her tubes tied after her third child. In a chat session on Sept. 23, 1999, Miller wrote, "This next part will be hard—I lost my baby, Jerry."
>
> "No," Cassaday replied.
>
> "I never thought I would ever tell you that he hits. I got in trouble because I was with you," she continued. Cassaday wanted to know more.
>
> "Sharee, you can tell me now, or in person when I beat it out of him."
>
> "It made me start having bad thoughts of killing him," she wrote.
>
> "Where did he hit you?" Cassaday asked.
>
> "Jerry, I can't tell you." But Cassaday insisted.
>
> "He didn't hit me, Jerry; he raped me—I lost the baby because of the force."

In another case, the murderer's work computer revealed his intent to commit a crime, and his home computer contained a fake suicide note created after his wife's death (*State of South Dakota v. William Boyd Guthrie*, 2001). On May 14, 1999, Doctor Guthrie, a Presbyterian minister, called 911 for emergency assistance because his wife Sharon was unconscious in the bathtub. Sharon later died in the hospital. Based on the amount of temazepam and other agents in her system, a forensic pathologist determined that her death was not natural and not accidental, but from the autopsy alone he could not resolve whether it was suicide or homicide. A computer specialist examined the contents of the computer in William Guthrie's church office and found evidence of numerous Web searches on subjects related to household accidents, bathtub accidents, and prescription drugs. Some of these Internet activities occurred at approximately the same times as earlier suspicious accidents in the Guthrie household. In April 1999, two days after Web pages describing various drugs including temazepam were viewed on the computer in the church office, William Guthrie visited his doctor complaining of insomnia and persuaded the doctor to prescribe him temazepam. The defense argued that Sharon Guthrie had committed suicide and produced a purported suicide note that Guthrie claimed he discovered in his church office three weeks after Sharon drowned. The unsigned note was dated the day before Sharon's death and was addressed to her daughter. The note, replicated here with its spacing and typographical errors, was apparently created on a computer:

May 13,1999
Dear Suzanne,

   I am sorry I ruined your wedding, Your dad told me about your concerns of my Interfering in Jenalu's and the possibility I might ruin hers. I won't be there so Put your mind at ease. You will understand after the wedding is done. I love you all Mom.

There was insufficient time for experts to examine all of the fingerprints on the note, so only four fingerprints were analyzed, none of which could be attributed to a specific individual. The computer specialist was called on again, this time to examine Guthrie's home computer, and he found an earlier draft of the suicide note. However, the file on the computer had been created on August 7, 1999. William Guthrie denied that he created this note but admitted to creating another note on August 11 that was found on his home computer with Sharon again as the purported author. It listed various grievances Sharon addressed to Guthrie, including one line that stated, "I'm upset that you have had an affair and have not come clean with me, I have thought of ending my life and you would have to face up to it. Believe me I known how to do it." Guthrie claimed that he wrote this note to work through the emotional trauma of Sharon's death. William Boyd Guthrie was convicted of first-degree murder for the killing of his wife.

   William Guthrie was evidently unaware of the digital traces he was leaving behind. As criminals become more aware of these cybertrails, however, they are taking steps to conceal their digital footprints. This concealment behavior includes changing their computer clock to hamper reconstruction, encrypting data to restrict access, and using disk cleaning tools to destroy digital evidence. One disk cleaning tool, Evidence Eliminator (www.evidence-eliminator.com/product.d2w), is specifically advertised as a program that defends against digital forensic examination tools such as EnCase.

Other forms of evidence dynamics can make crime reconstruction using digital data more difficult. Digital evidence can be lost if it is not seized in a forensically sound or timely manner because any use of a computer can overwrite existing data. Relevant network data may be similarly volatile because businesses only keep logs for a limited time. Therefore, it is critical to have digital crime scenes processed by qualified professionals to ensure that the evidence is preserved properly and examined thoroughly.

DIGITAL CRIME SCENE INVESTIGATION

Computers and networks should be considered an extension of the crime scene, even when they are not directly involved in facilitating the crime. It is useful to think of them as secondary crime scenes. Like a physical crime scene, digital crime scenes can contain many pieces of evidence and it is necessary to apply forensic principles to preserve, document, and search the entire scene. A single computer can contain e-mail communications between the victim and offender, evidence of intent to commit a crime, incriminating digital photographs taken by the offender as trophies, and software applications used to conceal digital evidence.

Untrained individuals commonly make the mistake of turning on a computer and looking for a particular item of evidence. The act of turning on and operating a computer is comparable to trampling a crime scene, thereby destroying useful evidence and making it more difficult to reconstruct the crime. To preserve the state of a digital crime scene, professionals make a duplicate copy of the evidence using tools that do not alter the original. At the same time, they document the context of the evidence by making notes and photographs and by calculating hash values of the evidence. A hash value is a formula that reads the data comprising a piece of digital evidence and calculates a unique "fingerprint" that can be used to identify and verify the evidence. The verification process is accomplished by recalculating the hash value of the evidence at any time and ensuring that it is the same as the originally calculated value. After preserving and documenting the digital crime scene, forensic professionals perform their examination on the duplicate copy to locate relevant items, determine their provenance, and answer other questions of interest to investigators.

Only searching for a particular piece of evidence on a computer is like walking into a victim's home just to collect a suicide note without examining the scene for signs of staging. In the United Kingdom case involving Dr. Harold Shipman, changes he made to computerized medical records on his medical office computer system were instrumental in convicting him for killing hundreds of patients. Following Shipman's arrest, police made an exact copy of the hard drive from his computer, thus preserving a complete and accurate duplicate of the digital evidence. By analyzing the computer application Shipman used to maintain patient records, investigators found that the program kept an audit trail, recording changes made to patient records. This audit trail indicated that Shipman had lied about patients' symptoms and made backdated modifications to records to conceal the murders. Had the investigators accepted the patient records without digging deeper into their authenticity, they would have missed this key piece of evidence about the cover-up attempt. During his trial, Shipman claimed that he was familiar with this audit trail feature and was sufficiently knowledgeable about computers to falsify the audit trail if he had actually been trying to hide these activities. However, the court was convinced that Shipman had altered the records to conceal his crimes and sentenced him to life in prison.

INTERPRETATION OF DIGITAL EVIDENCE[1]

Although computers can provide investigators with many tantalizing leads, digital evidence is not always what it seems and can be misinterpreted. At its basic level, digital evidence exists in a physical medium, such as a magnetic disk, a copper wire, or a radio signal in the air. Forensic examiners rarely scrutinize the physical medium and instead use computers to translate the data into a form that humans can interpret, such as text, audio, or video. Therefore, examiners rarely see the actual data but only a representation, and each layer of abstraction can lose information and introduce errors. For instance, analyzing the magnetic properties of a hard drive may reveal additional information useful for some investigations (e.g., overwritten data and the cause of damage to the disk). The risk of examining media at this low level is that the act of observing may cause changes that could destroy or undermine the evidence.

As described in the previous section, it is considered best practice to examine an exact replica of digital evidence to avoid altering the original.

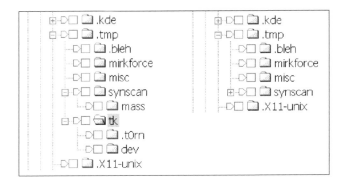

Figure 11.2

A folder named "tk" contained important evidence. The tk folder is visible using a newer version of a digital evidence examination tool (left) but not an older version containing a bug (right).

However, it can be difficult to obtain an exact and complete copy of a magnetic disk, Random Access Memory (RAM), a copper wire, or a radio signal. For instance, programmatic mistakes (a.k.a. bugs) have been found in tools for collecting digital evidence from hard drives, resulting in only a portion of the data being copied. Bugs have also been found in tools for examining digital evidence on computers, resulting in an inaccurate representation of the underlying data, as shown in Figure 11.2.

There are many other potential sources of error in digital evidence between the time data are created by a system and the time of preservation and analysis of the evidence. For instance, system malfunction can result in erroneous or missing log entries. Also, as with other forms of evidence, poor training or lack of experience can lead forensic examiners to mishandle or incorrectly interpret digital evidence. In one case, a failure to adjust for the local time zone caused a defense expert to incorrectly conclude that police had operated the suspect's computer (Forster, 2004).

Digital evidence should always be interpreted in context. For example, the mere presence of an incriminating file on a person's computer may not be sufficient to demonstrate guilt if there is strong indicia that the file was placed on the system by a virus, intruder, or via a Web browser vulnerability without the user's knowledge. An analysis of the file, its location, security vulnerabilities, artifacts of system usage, and other contextual clues may help determine how a file came to be on a given system.

Similarly, a file with a creation date that is after its last modified date may be incorrectly interpreted as evidence that the system clock was backdated. In fact, the last written date of a file does not necessarily imply that the file was modified on the computer on which it is found. Copying a file onto a computer from removable media or another system on a network may not change the last written date, resulting in a file with a modified date prior to its creation date.

[2] Every computer on the Internet is assigned an IP address to enable delivery of data.

There are many other nuances to digital evidence caused by the intricacies of computer operations that can cause confusion or misinterpretation, and the same holds for networks. The Internet Protocol (IP)[2] address in an e-mail header may lead investigators to a particular computer, but this does not necessarily establish that the owner of that computer sent the message. Given the minor amount of effort required to conceal one's identity on the Internet, criminals usually take some action to thwart apprehension. This may be as simple as using a library computer or as sophisticated as inserting someone else's IP address into the e-mail header, requiring investigators to take additional steps to identify the culprit.

Consider a harassment case in which the offender sends the victim threatening e-mail via an intermediate server. Normally, the e-mail message would contain information about the computer used to send the message. Specifically, the e-mail header would contain the IP address of the sender's computer. However, because the harasser sent the message via an intermediate server, the e-mail header will contain the IP address of that server and conceal the actual source. For example, headers in the following e-mail sent from a Yahoo! account indicate that the message was sent from an IP address in Japan (210.249.120.210):

To: Count Rugen
From: "Inigo Montoya" < inigo_montoya@yahoo.com >
X-Originating-IP: **210.249.120.210**
Date: Wed, 04 Jun 2003 03:51:45 -0000
Subject: Prepare to die!

However, the sender merely connected to Yahoo! via this computer in Japan. Therefore, additional investigation would be required to determine the actual source of the message. Log files from the intermediate computer, such as those shown next, might contain the IP address of the actual sender's computer (172.16.34.14 in this example):

172.16.34.14, anonymous, 6/4/03, 03:43:24, 210.249.120.210, GET, http://mailsrv.yahoo.com/login.html, 200
172.16.34.14, anonymous, 6/4/03, 03:44:02, 210.249.120.210, GET, http://mailsrv.yahoo.com/inigo_montoya/inbox.html, 200
172.16.34.14, anonymous, 6/4/03, 03:45:27, 210.249.120.210, GET, http://mailsrv.yahoo.com/inigo_montoya/compose.html, 200
172.16.34.14, anonymous, 6/4/03, 03:51:36, 210.249.120.210, GET, http://mailsrv.yahoo.com/inigo_montoya/sent.html, 200

To mitigate the risks of evidence being missed or misinterpreted, experienced forensic examiners employ a variety of techniques, including comparing the results of multiple tools, validating important findings through contextual reviews, and analyzing corroborating evidence for inconsistencies.

The scientific method provides the final bulwark against incorrect conclusions. Simply trying to validate a theory increases the chance of error—the tendency is for the analysis to be skewed in favor of the hypothesis. This is why the most effective investigators suppress their personal biases and hunches, and they seek evidence and perform experiments to disprove their working theory. Experimentation is actually a natural part of analyzing digital evidence. Given the variety and complexity of hardware and software, it is not feasible for forensic examiners to know everything about every software and hardware configuration. As a result, it is often necessary to perform controlled experiments to learn more about a given computer system or program. For instance, one approach is to pose the questions, "Was it possible to perform a given action using the subject computer, and if so, what evidence of this action is left behind on the system?" Theories about what digital evidence reveals in a particular case may be tested by restoring a duplicate copy of a subject system onto similar hardware, effectively creating a clone that can be operated to study the effects of various actions. Similarly, it may be necessary to perform experiments on a certain computer program to distinguish between actions that are automated by the program and those performed by a user action.

One useful by-product of this type of analysis is exemplars of files or other artifacts created by certain actions. Comparing an item of evidence to an exemplar can reveal investigatively useful class characteristics or even individual characteristics. In one case, the offender claimed that he could not remember the password protecting his encryption key because he had changed it recently. By experimenting with the same encryption program on a test system, the forensic examiner observed that changing the password updated the last modified date of the file containing the encryption key. An examination of the file containing the suspect's encryption key indicated that it had not been altered recently as the suspect claimed. Faced with this information, the suspect admitted that he had lied about changing the password.

In addition to presenting the facts in a case, investigators are generally expected to render an opinion about the evidence. For instance, when a program such as Evidence Eliminator is found on a suspect's computer, the forensic examiner will generally be asked if there is any evidence of its use.

It is not sufficient for a forensic examiner to conclude that Evidence Eliminator was used simply because it was installed on a computer. The following is an example of how this finding might be phrased:

> Evidence Eliminator was almost definitely run on this system. The presence of a folder named "eetemp" and a detailed log file named "EElog.txt" created by Evidence Eliminator, indicate that this program was used on the subject system and was last run on 3/07/05 at 19:29. Many files referenced in the "EElog.txt" log file were altered or overwritten on 3/07/05 at 19:29, which supports the finding that Evidence Eliminator was run on the subject system at this time. Furthermore, file slack and portions of unallocated space were overwritten with random data, which is consistent with the use of a wiping program.

Analysis of digital evidence requires interpretation that forms the basis of any conclusions reached. Investigators should assess the level of certainty underlying each conclusion in order to help the fact-finder determine what weight to attach. The C-Scale (Certainty Scale) described in Casey (2004, Chapter 7) provides a method for conveying certainty when referring to digital evidence and qualifying conclusions appropriately. Some digital investigators use a less formal system of degrees of likelihood that can be used in both the affirmative and the negative sense: (1) Almost definitely, (2) most probably, (3) probably, (4) very possibly, and (5) possibly.

Whenever possible, investigators should support assertions with available sources of relevant evidence. Clearly state how and where the digital evidence was found to help fact-finders interpret the findings and to enable another competent examiner to verify the results. Presenting alternative scenarios and demonstrating why they are less reasonable and less consistent with the evidence can help strengthen key conclusions. Explaining why other explanations are unlikely or impossible is a respected facet of the scientific method that can be applied to examination of digital evidence and demonstrate that a particular conclusion withstood critical scrutiny. If there is no evidence to support an alternative scenario, state whether it is more likely that relevant evidence was missed or simply not present. If digital evidence was altered after it was collected, it is crucial to mention this in the report, explaining the cause of the alterations and weighing their impact on the case (e.g., negligible or severe).

Two similar scenarios are presented here to demonstrate that apparently minor differences in the circumstances can lead to significantly different conclusions, with different levels of certainty.

EXAMPLE CONCLUSION 1

At 17:57 EDT on 05/16/2005, shortly after the incriminating activities occurred on the computer, Evidence Eliminator appears to have been run. Although Jack Smith and Jane Doe were the primary users of this computer, a password was not required and it was in a location that was accessible to many people in the building. Evidence Eliminator was run at a time when both Mr. Smith and Ms. Doe were at another location and could not have accessed the computer remotely. The subject computer does not maintain a record of clock changes and there is no evidence to prove or disprove that the clock was tampered with. It is possible that Mr. Smith or Ms. Doe changed the computer clock to make it appear that Evidence Eliminator was run at a time when they would not be implicated. It is also possible that an unknown third party accessed the computer and ran Evidence Eliminator.

EXAMPLE CONCLUSION 2

Although Evidence Eliminator appears to have been run on the subject computer shortly after the incriminating activities occurred on the computer at 17:57 EDT on 05/16/2005, there is evidence that the clock was tampered with. Based on temporal discontinuities in the Windows Event log, Evidence Eliminator was actually run at 11:45 that morning. Jack Smith and Jane Doe were the primary users of this computer, and they each had their own username and password. Windows Event logs show that Jane Doe's account was used to log into the computer at 11:24 on the date in question and logged out at 11:50. The computer was located in a room that required a key card to access, and the security logs show that Jane Doe's card was used to access the room at 11:20. Furthermore, security cameras show Jane Doe walking through the hall leading to the room at 11:19 and walking away from the room at 11:53. Therefore, it was almost definitely Jane Doe who committed the crime, altered the clock, and ran Evidence Eliminator on the subject computer.

ATTRIBUTION USING DIGITAL EVIDENCE

Digital evidence can play a direct role in identifying and apprehending offenders, helping investigators establish linkages between people and their online activities. This attribution process can be challenging using digital evidence alone, but when combined with traditional investigative techniques, these data can provide the necessary clues to track down criminals. For instance, a lead developed during a serial homicide investigation in St. Louis when a reporter received a letter from the killer. The letter contained a map of a specific area with a handwritten "X" to indicate where another body could be found. After investigators found a skeleton in that area, they inspected the letter more closely for ways to link it to the killer. The FBI determined that the map in the letter was from Expedia.com and immediately contacted the site to determine if there was any useful digital evidence. The Web server logs on Expedia.com showed only one IP address (65.227.106.78) had accessed the map around May 21, the date the letter was postmarked. The ISP responsible for this IP address was able to provide the account information and telephone number that had been used to make the connection in question. Both the dial-up account and telephone number used to make this connection belonged to Maury Travis (Robinson, 2002).

In short, the act of downloading the online map that was included in the letter left traces on the Expedia Web server, on Travis's ISP, and on his personal computer. Investigators arrested Travis and found incriminating evidence in his home, including a torture chamber and a videotape of himself torturing and raping a number of women and apparently strangling one victim. Travis committed suicide while in custody and the full extent of his crimes may never be known.

In another case, Dartmouth professors Susanne and Half Zantop were stabbed in their homes with SOG Seal 2000 knives. Investigators tracked purchases of this type of knife through Internet sites, leading them to two local teenagers, James Parker and Robert Tulloch. A forensic examination of the boys' computers revealed that, after being interviewed by police, they contacted each other over AOL Instant Messenger and agreed to flee to California. Two knives were found in Tulloch's bedroom with blood matching the Zantops, and the boys were apprehended and confessed to the killings (CBS News, 2001).

However, attributing computer activities to a particular individual can be challenging. For instance, logs showing that a particular Internet account was used to commit a crime do not prove that the owner of that account was responsible since someone else could have used the individual's account. Even when dealing with a specific computer and a known suspect, some investigative and forensic steps may be required to place the person at the keyboard and confirm that the activities on the computer were most likely those of the suspect. Considering the mobile telephone example at the beginning of this chapter (see Figure 11.1), it may only be possible for the forensic examiner to state that the suspect's phone was used to send the victim a SMS message at 10:05, and that the suspect's phone was in the same vicinity as the victim at the time of the murder. Other evidence would be required to establish that the suspect was in possession of his phone at these times and to place him at the crime scene.

Attributing a crime to an individual becomes even more difficult when a crime is committed via an open wireless access point or from a publicly accessible computer, such as at an Internet cafe or public library terminal.

In one extortion case, investigators followed the main suspects and observed one of them use a library computer from which incriminating e-mails had been sent (Howell, 2004; Khamsi, 2005).

Using evidence from multiple independent sources to corroborate each other and develop an accurate picture of events can help develop a strong association between an individual and computer activities. This type of reconstruction can involve traditional investigative techniques, such as stakeouts. For instance, a man accused of possessing child pornography argued that all evidence found in his home should be suppressed because investigators had not provided sufficient probable cause in their search warrant to conclude that it was in fact he, and not an imposter, who was using his Internet account to traffic in child pornography (*U.S. v. Grant*, 2000). During their investigation into an online child exploitation group, investigators determined that one member of the group had connected to the Internet using a dial-up account registered to Grant. Upon further investigation, they found that Grant also had a high-speed Internet connection from his home that was used as an FTP server—the type of file-transfer server required for membership in the child exploitation group.

Coincidentally, while tapping a telephone not associated with Grant in relation to another child pornography case, investigators observed that one of the participants in a secret online chat room was connected via Grant's dial-up account. Contemporaneous surveillance of the defendant's home revealed that both his and his wife's car were parked outside their residence at the time. The court believed that there was enough corroborating evidence to establish a solid circumstantial connection between the defendant and the crime to support probable cause for the search warrant.

DIGITAL DOCUMENT AUTHENTICATION

The author of a document and the date it was created can be significant, as demonstrated in the Guthrie case described at the beginning of this chapter. In that case, the offender was not technically savvy enough to change his computer's clock to an earlier date to give the impression that the document was created prior to his wife's death. Such staging can make it more difficult to determine who wrote a document and when it was created. However, there are various approaches that forensic examiners can use to authenticate a digital document.

Forensic examiners can use date stamps on files and in log files to determine the provenance of a document such as a suicide note even when the digital crime scene is staged. For instance, it is possible to detect staging and document falsification by searching for chronological inconsistencies in log files and file date stamps. Nuances in the way computers maintain different date stamps can help forensic examiners reconstruct aspects of the creation and modification of a document. In addition, certain types of files, such as Microsoft Word, contain embedded information that can be useful for authenticating a document. This embedded information may include the last printed date and the last 10 file names and authors, as shown previously.

EXAMPLE

According to Joe Smith, he created the questioned document in January 2005. However, dates associated with this document show that it was actually created in May 2005 and subsequently backdated to January. This fact is supported by dates in file slack of this document from April 2005 and by dates in a temporary copy created while the document was being edited using Microsoft Word in May 2005. Furthermore, Windows Security Event log entries from May 2005 show that the clock was backdated to January 2005 and subsequently returned to the correct date (Figure 11.3). In conclusion, the questioned document was created in May 2005 and not in January as claimed by Joe Smith.

The arrangement of data on storage media (a.k.a. digital stratigraphy) can provide supporting evidence in such forensic examinations. For instance, when a forensic examiner finds a questioned document that was purportedly created in January 2005 lying on top of a deleted document that was created in April 2005, staging should be suspected since the newer

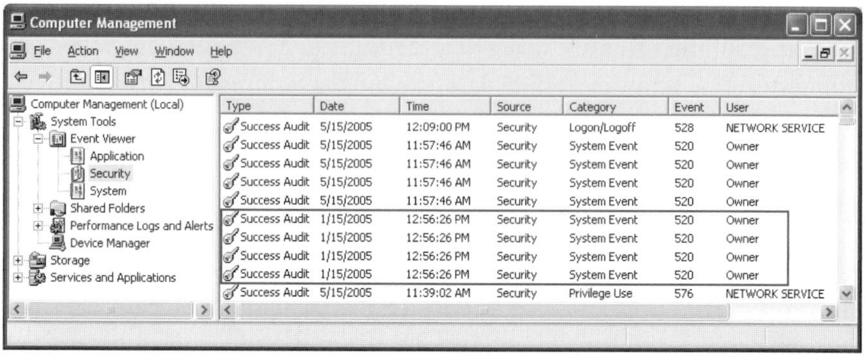

Figure 11.3

Windows Security Event log from May 2005 contains entries with January date stamps, indicating that the clock was backdated.

file should not be overwritten by an older one. Although the usefulness of digital stratigraphy for document authentication can be undermined by some disk optimization programs that reposition data on a hard drive, it can also be aided by the process. In one case, the suspect defragmented his hard drive prior to fabricating a document. The forensic examiner determined that the defragmentation process had been executed in 2003, causing all data on the disk to be reorganized onto a particular portion of the disk. The questioned documents that were purportedly created in 1999 were the only files on the system that were not neatly arranged in this area of the disk, which added weight to the conclusion that the questioned documents were actually created after the defragmentation process had been executed in 2003 (Friedberg, 2003).

EVALUATION OF SOURCE

Different file formats have characteristics that may be associated with their source. As shown previously, Microsoft Office documents contain embedded information, such as printer names, directory locations, names of authors, and creation/modification date–time stamps, that can be useful for determining their source. These embedded characteristics can be used to associate a piece of evidence with a specific computer. Earlier versions of Microsoft Office also embedded a unique identifier in files, called a globally unique identifier, which can be used to identify the computer that was used to create a given document (Leach and Salz, 1998). More subtle evaluations of source involve the association of data fragments with a particular originating file or determining if a given computer was used to alter a piece of evidence.

When a suspect's computer contains photographs relating to a crime, it may not be safe to assume that the suspect created those photographs. It is possible that the files were copied from another system or downloaded from the Internet. Forensic analysis of the photographs may be necessary to extract class characteristics that are consistent with the suspect's digital camera or flatbed scanner. The scanner may have a scratch or flaw that appears in the photographs, or the files may contain information that was embedded by the digital camera, such as the make and model of the camera and the date and time the photograph was taken. This embedded metadata could be used to demonstrate that a photograph was likely taken using a suspect's camera rather than downloaded from the Internet.

If these kinds of metadata are not available in a digital photograph, it may be possible to use other characteristics of a photograph to determine its source. For instance, Europol's Excalibur system uses image recognition technology to search a database of photographs from past investigations for similarities with a given image. If two photographs contain a common component, such as a piece of fabric with a distinct design, this may indicate that they were taken in the same place, providing investigators with a lead.

If incriminating files found on a computer were downloaded from the Internet, investigators may want to locate the originating computer and search it for evidence relating to the crime. This can involve reconstructing the computer user's Internet activities to determine where the files were obtained. It may also be necessary to examine e-mail headers, logs, and other artifacts of network activity to determine where digital evidence came from.

ASSESSING ALIBIS AND STATEMENTS

Offenders, victims, and offenders may mislead investigators intentionally or inadvertently, claiming that something occurred or that they were somewhere at a particular time. By cross-referencing such information with the digital traces left behind by a person's activities, digital evidence may be found to support or refute a statement or alibi. In one homicide investigation, the prime suspect claimed that he was out of town at the time of the crime. Although his computer suffered from a Y2K bug that rendered most of the date–time stamps on his computer useless, e-mail messages sent and received by the suspect showed that he was at home when the murder occurred, contrary to his original statement. Caught in a lie, the suspect admitted to the crime.

As another example, data relating to mobile telephones were instrumental in the conviction of Ian Huntley for the murder of Holly Wells and Jessica Chapman in the United Kingdom. The last communication from Jessica's mobile phone was sent to a cell tower several miles away in Burwell rather than a local tower in Soham (BBC, 2003). The police provided a mobile telephone specialist with a map of the route they thought the girls would have taken, and the specialist determined that the only place on that route where the phone could have connected to the cell tower in Burwell was from inside or just outside Huntley's house (Summers, 2003). In addition, Huntley's alibi was that he was with his friend Maxine Carr on the night the girls went missing, but Carr's mobile phone records indicated that she was out of town at the time.

Investigators should not rely on one piece of digital evidence when examining an alibi: They should search for an associated cybertrail. On many computers, minimal skills are required to change the clock or the creation time of a file. Also, people can program a computer to perform an action, such as sending an e-mail message, at a specific time. In many cases, scheduling events does not require any programming skill—it is a simple feature of the operating system. Similarly, IP addresses can be changed and concealed, allowing individuals to pretend that they are connected to a network from another location. In addition, the location information associated with mobile telephones is not exact and does not place an individual at a specific location. As noted previously, it can also be difficult to prove who was using the mobile telephone at a specific time, particularly when telephones or subscriber identity module cards are shared among members of a group or family.

DETERMINING MOTIVATION AND INTENT

Clear evidence of intent, such as an offender's diary, may be found on a computer. Other pieces of digital data might not be useful on their own, but patterns of behavior can emerge when the pieces of digital evidence are combined with other information about a person's actions. Examples of this were observed in Shipman's modification of patient records and in Guthrie's Web searches described at the beginning of the chapter. In another case, prosecutors upgraded the charge against Robert Durall from second-degree to first-degree murder based on Internet searches found on his computer with key words including "kill + spouse," "accidental + deaths," "smothering," and "murder" (Johnson, 2000). In child exploitation cases, an offender's computer may contain evidence of soliciting and grooming victims over the Internet.

In David Westerfield's homicide trial, the prosecution claimed that Westerfield's digital pornography collection reflected his fantasies relating to kidnapping and killing 7-year-old Danielle van Dam and, in closing arguments, insinuated that the pornography motivated Westerfield to victimize the child (*California v. Westerfield*, 2002):

> Not only does he have the young girls involved in sex, but he has the anime that you saw. And we will not show them to you again. The drawings of the young girls being sexually assaulted. Raped. Digitally penetrated. Exposed. Forcibly sodomized. Why does he have those, a normal 50-year-old man? Those are his fantasies. His choice. Those are what he wants. He picked them; he collected them. Those are his fantasies. That's what gets him excited. That's what he wants in his collection. . . . When you have those fantasies, fantasies breed need. He got to the point where it was growing and growing and growing. And what else is there to collect? What else can I get excited about visually, audibly?

Forensic examinations of computers can reveal other behavior that can be very useful for determining intent. For instance, evidence of clock tampering may enable a forensic examiner to conclude that the computer owner intentionally backdated a digital document. Also, the use of disk cleaning or encryption programs on a computer can be used to demonstrate a computer owner's conscious decision to destroy or conceal incriminating digital evidence. However, these same actions may have innocent explanations and must be considered in context before reaching a definitive conclusion.

CONCLUSIONS

Digital evidence can help answer many questions in an investigation, ranging from the whereabouts of a victim at a given time to the state of mind of the offender. Therefore, evidence on computers and networks should be included whenever feasible in crime reconstructions. At the same time, care must be taken when interpreting the abstracted behavioral evidence that is stored on computers. People use technology in creative ways that can complicate the reconstruction process, particularly when attempts are made to conceal digital evidence. Computers also have many subsystems that interact in ways that can complicate the reconstruction process. In all cases, given the malleability and multivalent nature of digital evidence, it is necessary to seek corroborating evidence from multiple independent sources. The risk of missing or misinterpreting important details highlights the importance of utilizing the scientific method to reach objective conclusions that are solidly based on the evidence.

ACKNOWLEDGMENTS

I thank Jessica Reust and my other colleagues at Stroz Friedberg LLC for their assistance with the development of this chapter.

REFERENCES

BBC "Soham Trial: 'Crucial' Phone Evidence," November 6, 2003. Available at news.bbc.co.uk/1/hi/england/cambridgeshire/3246111.stm

Bean, M. "Mich. v. Miller: Sex, Lies and Murder," Court TV, 2003. Available at www.courttv.com/trials/taped/miller/background.html

California v. Westerfield. Case No. CD165805, Superior Court of California, County of San Diego Central Division, 2002.

Casey, E. Digital Evidence and Computer Crime: Forensic Science, Computers, and the Internet. (2nd ed.). London: Academic Press, 2004.

Casey, E. "Computer Crime and Digital Evidence." In *Encyclopedia of Forensic and Legal Medicine*, Vol. 1–4. London: Elsevier, 2005.

CBS News. "Teen to Plead Guilty in Prof's Death," CBS News, December 2001. Available at www.cbsnews.com/stories/2001/12/03/national/main319894.shtml

Chaski, C. "Who's at the Keyboard? Authorship Attribution in Digital Evidence Investigations," *International Journal of Digital Evidence*, 4(1), 2005. Available at www.ijde.org/docs/chaski_spring_05.pdf

Forster, P. "Time and Date Issues in Forensic Computing," *Journal of Digital Investigation*, 1(1), 2004. Available at www.compseconline.com/digitalinvestigation/tableofcontents.htm

Fridrich, J., Goljan, M., and Lukáš, J. "Proceedings of the SPIE, Vol. 5685: Determining Digital Image Origin Using Sensor Imperfections," *Multimedia on Mobile Devices Journal*, January 16–20, 2005, pp. 249–260.

Friedberg, E. "To Cache a Thief: How Litigants and Lawyers Tamper with Electronic Evidence and Why They Get Caught," *The American Lawyer*, January 2004. Electronic Publication; url: http://www.americanlawyer.com/newcontents0104.html

Geradts, Z., Vrijdag, D., Alberink, I., Goos, M. I., and Ruifrok, A. "Questions About the Integrity and Authenticity of Digital Images," American Academy of Forensic Sciences Workshop Presentation, 2005.

Howell, B. "Ambiguities in U.S. Law for Investigators," *Journal of Digital Investigation*, 1(2), 106–111, 2004.

Johnson, T. "Man Searched Web for Way to Kill Wife, Lawyers Say," *Seattle Post-Intelligencer*, June 10, 2000. Available at seattlepi.nwsource.com/local/murd21.shtml

Khamsi, R. "Dusting for Digital Fingerprints," *The Economist Technology Quarterly*, March 12, 2005.

Leach, P., and Salz, R. "UUIDs and GUIDs," Network Working Group, Internet draft, 1998. Available at www.webdav.org/specs/draft-leach-uuids-guids-01.txt

Robinson, B. "Taking a Byte out of Cybercrime," ABC News, July 15, 2002.

State of South Dakota v. William Boyd Guthrie, 2001 SD 61, 2001. Available at caselaw.lp.findlaw.com/scripts/getcase.pl?court = sd&vol = 2001_061&invol = 1

Summers, C. "Mobile Phones—The New Fingerprints," BBC News Online, December 18, 2003. Available at news.bbc.co.uk/1/hi/uk/3303637.stm

Tuohey, J. "Government Uses Color Laser Printer Technology to Track Documents: Practice Embeds Hidden, Traceable Data in Every Page Printed," Medill News Service, Monday, November 22, 2004. Available at www.pcworld.com/news/article/0,aid,118664,00.asp

U.S. v. Grant. U.S. Court of Appeals, 1st Cir., 2000. Available at laws.lp.findlaw.com/1st/992332.html

CHAPTER 12

STAGED CRIME SCENES

W. Jerry Chisum, BS and Brent E. Turvey, MS

> A clever murderer may very well arrange an accident,or make the death appear to be due to a suicide. Such a murderer has every opportunity of arranging matters to deceive those who treat the task of investigating the circumstances too lightly. But a systematic and accurate investigation will reveal the homicidal intent.
> —Svensson and Wendel (1974, p. 293)

A *simulated* or *staged* crime scene is one in which the physical evidence has been purposefully altered by the offender to mislead authorities and/or misdirect the investigation. Despite their regular occurrence, the majority of the professional literature has failed to devote adequate efforts to their study or interpretation. There are a number of works that have addressed the subject, but few have gone beyond superficial coverage (Douglas and Munn, 1992; Geberth, 1996; Gross, 1924; O'Connell and Soderman, 1936; Svensson and Wendel, 1974).

The formal recognition of crime scene staging as a discrete subject in the literature began with the work of Dr. Hans Gross (Gross, 1924). His insights, provided more than a century ago, resonate through the literature with conspicuous agreement: In each case, examine the forensic evidence carefully, reconstruct the crime meticulously, corroborate/compare victim and witness statements with the evidentiary findings, and assume nothing.

A greater depth of review is necessary.

GROSS

The Austrian jurist, Dr. Hans Gross (see Chapter 1), wrote (1924, p. 439):

> So long as one only looks on the scene, it is impossible, whatever the care, time, and attention bestowed, to detect all the details, and especially note the incongruities: but these strike us at once when we set ourselves to describe the picture on paper as exactly and clearly as possible.
>
> . . . The "defects of the situation" are just those contradictions, those improbabilities, which occur when one desires to represent the situation as something quite different from what it really is, and this with the very best intentions and the purest

belief that one has worked with all of the forethought, craft, and consideration imaginable.

Here, Gross is referring to the critical role that exact, deliberate, and patient efforts at written, scientific crime reconstruction can play in the investigation and resolution of simulated, or staged, crime. Specifically, he is stating that just looking at a crime scene is not enough, and that there is utility in reducing one's opinions to the form of a report. Furthermore, he is discussing the regular fallibility of offenders' efforts to stage crime scenes by virtue of their failure to leave behind the necessary and logical evidence of the crime. This occurs, Gross observes, even when an offender has carefully planned the staging. One is left to infer that this may occur from a lack of actual experience with crime on the part of the unskilled offender, but as we will address later, this may not be entirely the case.

Early in his text, Gross (1924, pp. 13–15) warns strongly against investigators being lulled in by what he refers to as their *preconceived theories* about a case. He discusses those who provide false reports of rape, assault, or injury, who may even engage in self-mutilation, for the purpose of extorting damages or concealing consensual sexual activity that has led to pregnancy. He then opines on the variety of staged crimes, the eventuality of false reports, and the subsequent duty of the investigator, stating (p. 14):

> Among wrongs to property, theft and arson are the most frequently simulated. In the first case, loss of fortune and breach of trust are most frequently sought to be accounted for by the pretence of theft; as a rule it is not very difficult to prove the falsity. The most important point is for the investigating officer to remind himself continually that the theft may have been a sham. In many cases the point must be elucidated; it is not necessary to make a noise about it straight away, but let him keep this idea ever before him and examine from this aspect each of the circumstances. After considering what any fact would signify if there had been a real theft, let him ask himself what the fact would signify if the theft were only concocted. The investigating officer ought never to permit himself to abstain from making this examination by the rank and situation of the supposed victim of the theft, by the cleverness of the *mise-en-scene*, or by any other consideration. Not only must the self-made victim be exposed, but innocent people who may be suspected must be protected.

Later, Gross provides readers with several illustrative examples of what he refers to as simulated crime scenes. These include a suicide altered to appear as a homicide for profit (p. 432), a homicide altered to appear as suicide to conceal the homicide (p. 437), and a natural death altered to appear as a suicide to conceal caregiver neglect (pp. 439–440). The case studies are presented outside of the context of formal research, as anecdotal evidence of the existence of various simulated crime scenes.

The work of Gross stands out as formative to the subject, built upon without direct in-text citation by O'Connell and Soderman (1936) and Svensson and Wendel (1974).

O'CONNELL AND SODERMAN

In their text on the various methods of criminal investigation, written primarily for the police detective, O'Connell and Soderman (1936) dedicate a section of Chapter 17 on the "Investigation of Homicide" to the question of distinguishing suicides from homicides (pp. 260–277). Here, they discuss the simulation of a suicide by hanging to conceal the crime of homicide, stating, "By hanging a murdered person practically the same marks as those caused by a strangulation may be produced" (p. 264). They specifically discuss the importance of carefully reconstructing crime scenes to establish the facts of a case, including the employment of Goddefroy's method in hanging cases:

> The examination of the rope used may reveal most important information. This question has been studied by the Belgian Detective, E. Goddefroy, and such examinations have led, in the last few years, to the solution of quite a few crimes on the Continent. The fibers of the rope will lie in the opposite direction of that of the pulling. If the person slides down a rope the fibers will be directed downwards. If what appears to be a voluntary strangulation is in fact a murder and the murderer has pulled the body up, the fibers will be directed upwards on that part of the rope which was pulled by the murderer, because of the contact of the rope with the substructure.

O'Connell and Soderman (1936) go on to relate the importance of investigating inconsistencies in injuries and wound patterns, stating (p. 266), "Traces of violence found on other parts of the body [other than the part normally associated with the apparent suicidal act] and not brought on by previous, unsuccessful attempts at suicide indicate homicide."

O'Connell and Soderman (1936) do provide readers with brief examples of what they have referred to as simulated crime scenes. These include a simulated fall from a height staged to conceal a homicide (pp. 269–270) and a short section on simulated burglaries (pp. 322–324).

SVENSSON AND WENDEL

In their text on the various methods of examining crime scenes, written primarily for detectives and forensic scientists, Svensson and Wendel (1974) discuss simulated burglaries and the question of distinguishing suicides, homicides, and accidents. Primarily, they are concerned with the systematic analysis and comparison of the different kinds of physical evidence involved in each type of crime.

On the subject of the simulated burglary, Svensson and Wendel (1974, p. 265) state, harkening back to Gross, "To create a successful imitation of a burglary, which will deceive the police officers, the simulator must strive to carry it out as naturally as possible. Otherwise there will be gaps in the sequence of events." This passage seems to suggest that meticulous and dedicated investigators will set upon every crime scene. These investigators will then reconstruct the physical evidence, establish the facts, and discern the truth. Thus, "simulators" must be equally meticulous and dedicated in their alterations to the evidence in a crime scene.

On the subject of distinguishing suicides, homicides, and accidents, Svensson and Wendel (1974, p. 293) make a similar statement:

> A clever murderer may very well arrange an accident, or make the death appear to be due to a suicide. Such a murderer has every opportunity of arranging matters to deceive those who treat the task of investigating the circumstances too lightly. But a systematic and accurate investigation will reveal the homicidal intent.
>
> . . . The following questions must be answered immediately: 1. What are the causes of death? 2. Could the person himself have produced the injuries or brought about the effect which caused death? 3. Are there any signs of a struggle? 4. Where is the weapon, instrument, or object which caused the injuries, or traces of the medium which caused death?

These authors then provide a detailed discussion of the importance of crime reconstruction as it relates to answering the previous questions and others. Topics range from bloodstain pattern analysis to wound pattern analysis and the importance of determining the movement and/or disturbance of furniture.

DOUGLAS AND MUNN

Douglas and Munn (1992, p. 251) define the concept of staging in a way that none of the other literature agrees is acceptable—that is, they include the actions of those altering evidence to protect the victim's reputation or that of their family:

Staging is when someone purposefully alters the crime scene prior to the arrival of the police. There are two reasons why someone employs staging: to redirect the investigation away from the most logical suspect or to protect the victim or the victim's family.

What makes this definition problematic is that the actions of those individuals protecting the victim or the victim's family do not have criminal intent.

For staging to occur, implicit in the historical literature reviewed here, a whole new set of circumstances must be intentionally suggested or rendered through the actions of an offender, not merely the concealment of evidence or circumstances. For example, if an offender rapes and strangles a victim to death and then burns the victim's body inside the victim's own vehicle at the end of a dirt road, this would generally be referred to as a *precautionary act*.[1] If that same offender, rather than using fire, places the victim inside the victim's vehicle, loosens the brake line, and then pushes it over a cliff to make it appear like a single vehicle accident, then this would be referred to as *staging*, which is a particular kind of precautionary act.

Douglas and Munn (1992) offer their own checklist to assist with the identification of staged crime scenes, which includes the following (adapted from p. 253):

[1] *Precautionary acts* are behaviors committed by an offender before, during, or after an offense and consciously intended to confuse, hamper, or defeat investigative or forensic efforts for the purposes of concealing his identity, his connection to the crime, or the crime itself (Turvey, 1999, p. 445). It is a general term, inclusive of many different types of actions that may be taken by an offender.

Questions
1. Did the subject take inappropriate items from the crime scene?
2. Did the point of entry make sense?
3. Did the perpetration of this crime pose a high risk to the offender?

Red Flags
4. Fatal assault of the wife and/or children by an intruder while the husband escapes without injury or a nonfatal injury.
5. The offender does not first target the person posing the greatest threat.
6. The person posing the greatest threat to the offender suffers the least amount of injury.

Douglas and Munn (1992) present no data to support any of the previously mentioned red flags; rather, they adduce case examples as needed. They also engage in a similar presentation on the subject of staged arson crime scenes (pp. 255–257). No internal citations are offered for this chapter or for any of the chapters presented in this text. Rather, all generally referenced works for all chapters are presented in one alphabetized list at the end of the text (Burgess et al., 1992, pp. 357–360), unassigned to ideas or subjects.

It is of interest that Douglas and Munn (1992), when discussing how to apply these investigative red flags, state (p. 253):

> An offender who stages a crime scene usually makes mistakes because he stages it to look the way he thinks a crime scene should look. . . . Inconsistencies will begin appearing at the crime scene, with forensics, and with the overall picture of the offense. These contradictions will often serve as the "red flags" of staging and prevent misguidance of the investigation.

This language is highly reminiscent of Gross (1924), who also discussed at length identifying "contradictions" of the scene and rendering a picture of the scene through physical evidence.

TURVEY

In Turvey (2002), an entire chapter is dedicated to the subject of crime scene staging, from which some of the material in this chapter has been drawn. That chapter also presents data from the first published empirical research on the subject, originally published in Turvey (2000). Using parameters that identified a total of 25 usable cases involving crime scene staging, with 33 offenders and 31 victims between the years 1980 and 2000, that study reported the following:[2]

2 The database used for the selection of the cases in this study was Westlaw (www.westlaw.com), a nationwide database of state and federal court decisions. Both civil and criminal cases were considered.

1. In the 25 cases studied, staging was used to conceal the crime of domestic homicide. This is certainly not the only type of criminal act or event that staging may be used to conceal, as shown by Gross (1924) and Adair and Dobersen (1999). However, it may be the one that investigators are most familiar with, and subsequently the most prepared to recognize.

2. Not surprisingly, given that the sample is composed exclusively of domestic homicides, the motives involved anger, profit, or both. This includes 15 (60%) cases involving an anger motivation and 12 (48%) cases involving a profit motivation.

3. Eleven (44%) cases involved a confession by the offender, and six (24%) cases involved a confession by a co-conspirator or confidante of an offender. Only three (12%) cases studied involved a confession by both. This means that a total of 14 (56%) cases involved some form of confession. In almost every case, the confession was achieved in no small part through the confrontation of the offender or co-conspirator with the inconsistencies of their statements in relation to the physical evidence at the scene. That is, crime reconstruction

played a major role in identifying the factual inconsistencies and "defects of the scene" and subsequently assisted greatly in achieving a reliable confession of some sort. This also means that 11 (44%) cases studied did not involve a reliable confession. In those cases crime reconstruction was ultimately used to prove, through the testimony of police officers and forensic experts, that staging had occurred, again demonstrating its importance in such cases.

4. The findings provide preliminary support for the hypothesis that crime scene staging is most commonly used to conceal an offender's close relationship with the victim(s). It would be a mistake to conclude from this that every case of staging is the result of an offender trying to conceal a close relationship with his victim based on the data presented here. However, viewed as an investigative tool, this finding can be used to place that possibility at the top of the list of investigative possibilities and narrow the initial suspect pool.

5. The most popular form of staged offense remains the stranger burglary gone wrong, involving 13 (52%) of the cases. Suicide was a distant second, involving four (16%) of the cases. Most commonly, the staging would occur with the body found in the bedroom, present in 17 (68%) of the cases. It is difficult to refrain from speculating that this is a functional effect as opposed to something deliberately planned in advance. That is, the type of staging most commonly seen may be born of an association with a domestic homicide.

6. In 18 (72%) of the cases studied, the offender was the one who initially "discovered" the victim's body. In more than a few of these cases, this involved elaborate presentations of shock and grief, and even the enlistment of others to "discover" the body with them. This finding is in direct conflict with the common notion that offenders who commit such crimes wish to leave the body to be found by others and dissociate themselves from the scene entirely.

7. Seven cases (28%) involved valuables that were removed from the scene. This becomes more significant when we consider that this accounts for only 43.73% of the 16 total staged burglaries and robberies. A reasonable person might imagine that in order to effectively stage a crime in which the offender was interested in stealing valuables, those staging the scene would think to remove valuables from it to help complete the illusion. This was not the case.

8. Only two (8%) of the cases studied involved the transportation of the victim's body to a secondary scene.[3]

9. Five (20%) of the cases involved an offender who was currently, or had recently been, in law enforcement.

[3] A secondary scene is any location where there may be evidence of criminal activity outside of the primary scene, such as a disposal site. A primary scene is the location where the offender engaged in the majority of the attack or assault on the victim or victims.

It is evident from this body of work, including the study published in Turvey (2000, 2002), that the determination of whether a crime scene has been staged should hinge primarily on a scrupulous and scientific reconstruction of the physical evidence.

AD HOC RECONSTRUCTION

Based on what they have seen and gathered at the crime scene, detectives and even crime scene technicians will theorize about a case relentlessly. What happened, who did it, and why? These questions push and plague the conscientious investigator. But there must be a mechanism in place to screen bare investigative theory, separating belief, rumination, and speculation from demonstrable scientific fact. Fortunately there is, and it is called forensic science.

As discussed in previous chapters, approximately three-fourths of the forensic scientists working in public labs do not routinely respond to crime scenes (U.S. Department of Justice, 2005, p. 4). Rather, those who are charged with investigative or evidence collection duties are more often in attendance (although not in every case). Their presence at the crime scene during the evidence-processing interval has led some to conclude that investigators and technicians must also be proficient at evidence interpretation (a.k.a. reconstruction). Subsequently, law enforcement officers and crime scene investigators have been allowed by numerous courts to serve as ad hoc reconstructionists and even as experts in the determination of whether or not scene staging is present.

Criminal profilers have also made a bold foray into this area and are commonly brought in by the prosecution so that they may legitimize these and similar law enforcement theories, conferring upon them a false aura of independent expertise. Prosecutorial agencies most commonly consult with and proffer expert testimony from law enforcement criminal profilers who usually have little or no experience in crime reconstruction. Perhaps recognizing this shortcoming, a growing number of profilers have openly expropriated crime scene reconstruction from the forensic sciences as an investigative function. As discussed in Baker and Napier (2003, p. 538):

> Crime scene reconstruction is a process within CIA [Criminal Investigative Analysis] and crime analysis that provides the investigator an understanding of how the victim was reached and controlled, as well as the likely interactions between the offender and the victim.
>
> . . .
>
> A special part of crime analysis is the ability to reconstruct and sequence criminal acts as they occurred in the interaction between the victim and offender.

The specific methods and burdens of the CIA reconstructionist, and requisite educational/training backgrounds, are not mentioned in this half-page

treatment of the subject. Crime reconstruction is simply described as a practice specifically associated with the CIA process that helps "interrogate suspects with authority, and thereby gain a genuine confession which outlines
how and why the crime occurred" (p. 538). There is no mention of science,
forensic science, or the scientific method when forming CIA reconstruction
conclusions; rather, there is reference to the "special abilities" of CIA analysts (p. 538).

These and similar circumstances have combined to result in the perhaps unintentional but ultimately inevitable consequence of removing the
science from the majority of staged crime scene analysis efforts. That is, this
form of crime reconstruction is almost always a function of experience-
driven observation, intuition, and surmise (i.e., the "special abilities" of
the analyst), as opposed to an application of forensic science, analytical
logic, and the scientific method. It should be of no surprise that this form
of nonscientific reconstruction is also routinely offered when the physical
evidence on its own cannot support the inferences needed to warrant a
prosecution.

In the defense of nonscientific examiners, they may or may not have the
first notion that their reconstruction opinions are unqualified and incomplete. They may also believe that presenting investigative theories in court
as though they are reliable conclusions is an acceptable practice. Failure to
distinguish between investigative opinions and forensic opinions (i.e., opinions that are "court worthy" or probative) is a major problem in many areas
of court testimony and represents a significant training need.

CASE EXAMPLES

Expert opinions on the issue of crime scene staging have become a feature
of courtroom testimony. Perhaps the most notorious case in recent years
was *Estate of Sam Sheppard v. State of Ohio*, in which one of the authors
(Turvey) participated as a consulting expert. The state hired a retired FBI
profiler to testify that the crime scene had been staged (Figs. 12.1 and 12.2).
Despite his testimony that he "hasn't been wrong yet in his analyses of crime
scenes," the judge determined that his opinions were not sufficiently reliable. The judge instructed that the profiler could talk about staging in
general, but he could not offer the conclusion that the Sheppard murder
scene had been staged (McKnight, 2000). In other words, he was barred
from giving an expert opinion on the subject.

To better understand the nature of these types of expert opinions, and
their basis, a review of several court decisions may be instructive.

Figure 12.1

The body of Marilyn Reese Sheppard as photographed by the first responders to the crime scene.

Figure 12.2

The home office of Dr. Samuel Sheppard. The removal of these drawers was interpreted as evidence of crime scene staging.

THE DEATHS OF SANDI STEVENS AND MYRTLE WILSON (1997)

This case involves the prosecution of William R. Stevens for two counts of first-degree premeditated murder and one count of aggravated robbery, arising out of the deaths of his wife, Sandi Stevens, and his mother-in-law, Myrtle Wilson. For each of his murder convictions, he received the death sentence (*Tennessee v. Stevens*, 2001).

Both Sandi Stevens and Myrtle Wilson [her mother] were found dead in their home in their respective bedrooms on December 22, 1997. Sandi Stevens was found laying on her bed nude, with pornographic magazines around her head and a photo album containing nude photographs of her on the bed. Myrtle Wilson was also found laying on her bed; her nightgown had been pulled up and her underwear was on the floor. The medical examiner determined that Myrtle Wilson died from stab wounds and manual strangulation, and Sandi Stevens died from ligature strangulation. Several items of Sandi Stevens were taken from the trailer, giving rise to the robbery charge. The Defendant's convictions for these crimes were based on the theory of criminal responsibility for the actions of another. The State's proof at trial established that the Defendant hired his 18-year-old neighbor and employee, Corey Milliken, to kill his wife and mother-in-law and to make it look like a robbery. The Defendant's theory was that Corey Milliken fabricated a "murder for hire fantasy" and that he killed Sandi Stevens and Myrtle Wilson in the perpetration of a sexual assault.

Detective Brad Corcoran, also with the Metro Police Department, testified that he was assigned to the identification section as a crime scene investigator in December 1997. He, along with Officer Ray Radar, was assigned to investigate this crime scene. Detective Corcoran testified that he . . . observed pornographic magazines displayed and opened on the bed around Sandi Stevens' body in the master bedroom. He also observed a photo album containing nude photographs of Sandi Stevens on the bed. He and Officer Radar attempted to obtain fingerprints, and they lifted about 30 latent fingerprints from the crime scene, including prints from the magazines and the photo album. . . .

Detective Corcoran . . . identified the photographs of the contents of the green canvas bag which was found under a nearby trailer; the bag contained an eight-inch kitchen or butcher knife with what appeared to be bloodstains on it, a white tee-shirt with blood on it, various articles of jewelry, numerous pills, and a 35 millimeter camera.

On cross-examination, Detective Corcoran testified that the crime scene was consistent with other sex crime scenes that he had worked in that the victims were either nude or partially nude, but he was unable to determine whether any sexual activity had occurred from looking at the crime scene. However, he stated that "the entire scene appeared to be staged in my opinion." He explained that the Christmas tree was laying on its side, but none of the glass balls on the tree were broken, indicating that the tree was laid down rather than knocked down. In Myrtle Wilson's room, the contents of a purse had been dumped out on the floor, but it did not appear as though the contents had been rifled through or removed. Also in Ms. Wilson's room, the drawers of a dresser had been opened, but it did not appear as though anything had been "moved hastily or pulled out." In Sandi Stevens' room, clothes had been taken from the closet and simply placed on the floor, and the items on the bed appeared to have been placed there. Detective Corcoran testified that there was no evidence of forced entry.

Note that the detective has given reasons for his conclusion that the scene appeared staged. He does not just state that in his opinion the scene was staged; he supports his opinion with facts and observations.

A second detective testified that there were signs of a struggle in Myrtle Wilson's room in and about the bed area, but the living room area appeared to have been staged. He said that the Christmas tree was laying on its side, but none of the balls were broken or scattered about the room. . . .

The lead detective on the case also testified about staging. He said that when he arrived on the scene, he did a walk-through. He did not see any signs of forced entry. He believed that someone had attempted to disguise the scene to make it seem like a burglary. He testified that in Ms. Wilson's room, drawers were pulled open but nothing was disturbed inside the drawers. In the living room, the tree was knocked over and the paper was removed from the Christmas presents, but the presents were not taken. Items were taken out of the closet and placed on the floor still on the hangers. In some areas, things did not appear to be disturbed at all, such as the office area, which looked like a valuable area of the trailer.

The defense in this case hired a former FBI profiler "to conduct a criminal investigative analysis of the crime scene in this case, which involves analyzing the crime scene, studying the victims to determine what might have elevated their risk for becoming victims, looking at underlying forensic reports, and looking at how the crime was committed."

In this case, the profiler testified that he was provided with "photographs and a videotape of the crime scene, as well as the medical examiner's report" (*Tennessee v. Stevens*, 2001). At a hearing to determine the admissibility and reliability of his evidence, he testified that:

the crime scene was sloppy and in disarray. The crime scene showed a lack of control. There was a general trashing of the crime scene—clothes were thrown down, purses and pills were dumped, things were scattered, the Christmas tree was knocked over—all of which was unnecessary to commit the murders.

Mr. [Gregg O.] McCrary testified that based on the crime scene, it is possible that there could have been more than one offender. First, different weapons were used to kill the victims: Ms. Wilson was stabbed, and Ms. Stevens suffered ligature strangulation. Second, there was not a lot of transfer blood in Ms. Stevens' room where you would expect it to be. In addition, the "staging" of the crime scene seemed to have been accomplished without transferring any blood to the items that were thrown about the trailer. Mr. McCrary testified that there was a feeble attempt at "staging" to make the scene look like a burglary. He said that burglars do not necessarily throw clothes and other items around.

. . .

During a jury-out offer of proof, Mr. McCrary testified that he was asked by the defense to conduct a crime scene analysis in which he would examine the evidence at the crime scene in order to determine the likely motive for the crime. He said that he specifically requested that he not be given any information regarding the suspect and that he was not engaging in criminal profiling, which is trying to determine the profile of an unknown suspect. Mr. McCrary described this crime scene as a "disorganized sexual homicide." He determined that Sandi Stevens was the primary target and was the focus of a sexual assault. He thought that Myrtle Wilson was simply a victim of opportunity who was in the wrong place at the wrong time. Mr. McCrary explained that in a disorganized homicide the victim and location are known to the offender, and there is minimal interpersonal contact between the victim and offender. He stated that usually a "blitz attack" or sudden violence is used. The crime scene is sloppy and in disarray. There is minimal use of restraints. Sexual acts tend to occur after death, and there is postmortem injury to the victim and indications of postmortem sexual activity. He stated that the body is left at the scene, typically in view, and a great deal of physical evidence is left at the scene. The murder weapon is usually a weapon of opportunity obtained at the scene. There is generally a precipitating stressor that triggers the violent event in a disorganized homicide, and the crime usually involves transferred aggression from the person or persons who precipitate the stressing event to the victim.

Mr. McCrary contrasted a disorganized crime scene to an organized crime scene, such as the typical "contract killing," which usually involves a victim and offender who are strangers. There is some interpersonal contact prior to the crime, such as a con or ruse to lure a victim out. In an organized crime scene, the scene reflects an overall sense of control; restraints are often seen; there are aggressive acts prior to the death; the body is usually hidden, though sometimes it is left propped up or displayed for shock value; the murder weapon is a weapon of choice brought to the scene and taken away after the crime; offenders are more "evidence conscious," and there is usually transportation of the body.

Mr. McCrary was asked whether a potential accuracy rate had been established, and he reported that the FBI had conducted one survey and determined that its agents were 75 to 80% accurate on crime scene analysis and profiling. He explained that this type of analysis is "not a hard science where you can do controlled experiments and come up with ratios in all this," but the increased demand for such services exemplifies its effectiveness. Mr. McCrary testified that there were seven agents in the FBI unit when he first entered the unit, there were 12 agents when he left the unit, and there are currently about 40 agents in the unit. He said, "the proof . . . [that] there is validation and reliability in the process is that it's being accepted. Uh—it's being used and the demand is just outstripping our resources to provide it."

As a result of the defense expert's testimony in this evidentiary hearing, the court disallowed much of his testimony for use at trial, determining that it dealt with the "behavior aspect of an offender and not the crime scene." The trial court stated that testimony regarding the behavioral aspects of suspects would not comply with Tennessee Rule of Evidence 702 "in terms of substantially assisting the tr[ier] of fact because there is no trustworthiness or reliability" (*Tennessee v. Stevens*, 2001).

The trial court did permit the expert to testify generally about the crime scene, the staging, the possibility that there were two offenders, and the things that should have been done by the police. However, it did not permit him to testify as to what he believed to be the motive for the crime (*Tennessee v. Stevens*, 2001):

> Most of McCrary's proffered testimony dealt with conclusions he reached after analyzing the scene of the crime. For instance, he concluded that the manner in which various household items had been carefully moved, displayed, damaged, or destroyed indicated that the perpetrator had staged or altered the scene in an effort to confuse the authorities. The Court found this type of testimony to be sufficiently reliable to present to the jury. However, McCrary's testimony regarding the perpetrator's motivation, although based in part on the physical evidence at the scene, appeared to be much more speculative.

The profiler in this case offered a reconstruction of events based on his experience with other similar crimes rather than a scientific examination of the evidence in the case. He concluded not that alternative theories had been considered and carefully eliminated but, rather, that the scene simply looked wrong to him, in terms of what he believed the offender should have done at the scene based on a subjective sense of what is "expected," "usual," and occurs "often." In other words, he gave an opinion about staging based entirely on his own beliefs and experience.

THE DEATHS OF DONALD AND MARY ANN DUVARDO (1999)

In this case, a jury convicted defendant Jeffrey Lee Duvardo of murdering his parents in 1999. He was sentenced to life in prison without possibility of parole. In his appeal, he argued that the circumstantial evidence in his case was insufficient to support the murder convictions, and that the trial court erroneously admitted expert testimony of crime scene reconstruction from a profiler.

According to the record (*California v. Duvardo*, 2004):

Donald and Mary Ann Duvardo were retired and lived on a cul-de-sac in the small town of Nice in Lake County. They were last seen on Tuesday, March 30, 1999. Their bodies were discovered in their home on Tuesday, April 6, 1999. They had been brutally stabbed and beaten to death. The prosecution contended that defendant killed his parents on March 31, driving from his home in Valencia, near Long Beach, to Nice and back—a round trip of some 14 to 16 hours. Defendant claimed his parents were killed a few days *after* March 31, a time when other evidence suggested—or, according to defendant, "indisputably demonstrated"—that defendant was in Southern California with insufficient time to make the round trip by car.

Deputy Morshed looked upstairs and saw that the bedroom closets and chests of drawers had been ransacked, with clothing and linens strewn about. But valuable items normally taken in burglaries, such as camera equipment, had not been taken—and the manner in which the chests and closets had been ransacked suggested to Morshed that the intruder had not searched for any valuable items.

Detectives and a criminalist responded to the scene. They found no signs of forced entry. Burke testified that the Duvardos habitually kept their doors locked.

The body of Mary Ann Duvardo was face down in the living room, near a computer desk a few feet from the front door. The computer was off, as was the television and stereo. Videotapes had been pulled out from underneath the television cabinet. The computer desk had been ransacked, with some drawers opened and some pulled entirely out. A large pool of blood was on the carpet beneath Mary Ann's body. The blood pool was somewhat dry on top but still wet on the bottom. Mary Ann's sweatshirt was still wet with blood.

The body of Donald Duvardo was in the laundry room near the washer and dryer. Donald's head was against the wall, and his feet were pointed toward the door into the living room. Some cabinets in the laundry room had been opened. Two plastic buckets filled with firewood were on the floor.

In the kitchen, most of the cupboards and some of the drawers had been opened. One of the burner plates from the electric stove was in the sink, along with a scrub brush. There was a water ring around the sink. Some items which would have been in Mary Ann's purse, such as a lipstick and keys, were on the kitchen counter. The coffeepot was unplugged but had not been cleaned. Two used coffee mugs sat near the pot. There was mold growing on the remnants of coffee left in the pot and one of the mugs. In the criminalist's opinion, the mold meant that the coffee remnants "had been there for some time." A plant was on the windowsill. A piece of it, along with some soil, had fallen onto the kitchen counter.

There was no kitchen towel to be seen except for a decorative one buttoned to the oven handle.

In the dining room connected to the kitchen, the doors and drawers of the liquor cabinet and the hutch had been opened. Two wristwatches, a man's and a woman's, sat on a shelf of the hutch. In the downstairs bedroom, papers and file folders were scattered on the floor and camera equipment was on the floor by the bed. A dresser leaned against the bed, its drawers open. A rifle could be seen leaning against the wall inside the partially open closet. A clock had fallen to the floor and had stopped because of a bent second hand. The clock read 10:25.

No lights were on in the downstairs of the Duvardo house. A living room light was on a timer. The living room and kitchen clocks were an hour slow. Daylight savings time started Sunday, April 4. Obviously, the Duvardos had not turned their clocks ahead one hour to synchronize with daylight savings time.

The Upstairs

The only lights that were on in the house were in the area of the stairs and the upstairs hallway. In the hallway a linen closet had been emptied onto the floor. In one bedroom boxes and suitcases were on the bed and the floor. In another room the drawers of a file cabinet had been pulled out.

The master bedroom had been ransacked. The bedclothes had been moved to one side. Jewelry, shoe boxes, and clothing were scattered on the floor and the bed. The dresser drawers had been pulled out and stacked one atop the other. The nightstand drawer was open. One of the dresser drawers contained a coin collection and unopened jewelry boxes. In the master bathroom, the drawers and cabinet doors had all been opened.

The police found a wadded up kitchen towel in the master bathroom sink. Janet testified the towel came from Mary Ann's kitchen. The towel was stiff, as if it had been wet and had air dried. It did not appear to have been laundered. The towel was stained with blood, which DNA testing showed to be the defendant's. The blood could not have come from Donald or Mary Ann.

The DNA testing involved testing of nine locations known as "short tandem repeats." Defendant's DNA profile matched the blood on the towel at all nine locations. The probability that someone other than defendant left the blood on the towel ranged from one in 8.3 trillion to one in 120 trillion, depending on ethnicity. The population of Earth is about six billion.

Fingerprint evidence at the crime scene was inconclusive, except that defendant's fingerprints were not found.

Detective Paulich concluded the Duvardo house was a staged crime scene. He saw no indications of an actual burglary. Many valuable items normally taken by burglars were left behind. The only items taken were Donald's wallet and Mary Ann's purse, both of which contained credit cards—which no one had tried to use.

An FBI profiler, whose background consisted of working as a police investigator for a small town in northern California and then on a Native American reservation for the FBI and whose education consisted of a BS in human physiology, was brought in to validate the police investigator's theories of the case. He qualified as an expert in crime scene analysis (*California v. Duvardo*, 2004):

> The Special Agent, after extensive voir dire by both counsel and review of his curriculum vitae, was qualified by the trial court as an expert in crime scene analysis. . . . He had interdisciplinary training including forensic pathology and psychiatry and criminal behavior. He would "look at the behavior that occurs at a crime [scene] and assign certain personality characteristics to that behavior." He had investigated or reviewed over 3000 homicides.

Note that homicides reviewed and homicides investigated are lumped to enhance the picture of experience. As provided in *California v. Duvardo* (2004):

> The agent reviewed the investigative reports of the Duvardo murders, photographs and diagrams of the crime scene, autopsy photographs and protocols, evidence analyses, and maps of the area of the Duvardo home. He also visited the crime scene. He came to a number of conclusions.
>
> First, he opined that the Duvardos knew their killer and let him in the house.
>
> That the sliding glass door was not locked seems to have been overlooked as it could have been the entry point without leaving evidence of "forced entry."
>
> Second, he concluded from the crime scene and the front-to-back direction of the knife wounds, that Mary Ann was sitting at the computer desk and was attacked from behind: "She didn't realize the threat until it was too late." She was grabbed and thrown to the floor. The fractured ribs indicated "that the assailant landed on top of her." By contrast, Donald was attacked from the front because all his wounds were on the front of his body.
>
> Third, from his analysis of the crime scene and the blunt force trauma, he concluded that Mary Ann was attacked first. Had Donald been attacked first, Mary Ann would not have been sitting unsuspectingly at the computer desk.

In this case, the physical evidence can only provide that Mary Ann did not react by getting up, and that perhaps she was attacked first. It cannot, however, speak to her mental state so precisely and offer such a specific version of events. If it was the defendant, she would not necessarily have suspected that her son was planning to kill her. Moreover, there may have been an argument first. Or the offender may simply have approached her carefully from behind. There are numerous possibilities. As with any final conclusion, there needs to be consideration of alternatives and demonstrated attempts at falsification to withstand scrutiny. Otherwise, such opinions are unguarded speculation.

> The agent suggested that Donald came in from the garage, possibly bringing in wood for the stove. [Special Agent] Safarik emphasized that "we never know . . . the exact sequence of everything that happens," but believed that Donald was confronted by his killer in the laundry room: "I think that when Don[ald] walked in, he looked through the doorway not ten feet away . . . saw his wife [lying] on the floor. Dropped the buckets, and of course now perceiv[ed] the threat, as the offender moves toward him. He back[ed] up, and he backs up into the laundry area, which is only about four feet away. There's no escape from this area. And now he's trapped. Probably pleading for his life. And the offender comes at him and now starts stabbing to the front."

> Fourth, like Detective Paulich, he concluded the crime scene was staged to make it look like the killer was a burglar. The agent saw through the staging because numerous items of valuable property in plain view were not taken, the ransacking was "excessive," and areas were searched that typically were not searched by burglars. He concluded the killer was not motivated by financial gain. In his opinion, a stranger to the Duvardos would not bother to stage a burglary: "When you see a staged crime scene, it is an attempt by the offender to misdirect law enforcement into another direction. That's because the offender perceives . . . that they will be the focus of a law enforcement investigation."

> Fifth, he concluded from the number and nature of the wounds that the killer was enraged at the Duvardos.

It is clear from the record that the profiler was brought in to help prove the state's case by ratifying the detective's theories through nonscientific reconstruction based on observation, intuition, and surmise. The problem is that the witnesses lacked sufficient education and training in the forensic sciences and the scientific method to see the limitations of the evidence, explore alternate case theories, and show interest in theory falsification. This is demonstrated by the speculative nature of their inferences, the lack of evidentiary basis (experience is cited repeatedly), and the inappropriate certainty with which conclusions are given. The analyst, for example, purports to give a detailed version of events that is not unlike viewing the crime through a video camera. Although he claims there are breaks in the evidence, he goes on to fill them in with untested, intuition-oriented speculation. He further testifies to things that he "believes" to be true as opposed to conclusions that have been demonstrated through the evidence. The failure to make this important distinction is more than just a little misleading in the overall art that is expert witness testimony.

The question may be asked as to whether the analyst was ultimately correct in his opinion that this was a staged crime scene. This is unknown from the testimony given at trial. It can only be said that the analyst did not prove crime scene staging through the physical evidence. Rather, he gave an opinion that the crime scene was staged, or rather looked similar to other supposedly staged scenes he had seen, based on a highly speculative and ultimately untested version of events.

What is most important to the question of accuracy, and can be readily answered, is whether or not the analyst showed his work when reaching conclusions. In this case, he did not. Summoning experience to explain conclusions and filling in the gaps of evidence with hypothetical guesswork is intellectually bankrupt regardless of whether or not anyone agrees that the final conclusions are correct—they may very well be. But the forensic reconstructionist has a burden to show how she arrived at her conclusions, and to follow clearly articulated practice standards, so that her findings may be evaluated by the trier of fact.

The analyst in this case also continually resorts to fallacies of relevance (supporting opinions and conclusions with something other than actual evidence), such as appeals to the authority of the one (himself) and the select few (his organization). This includes the use of phrases such as "experientially," "it is the organization's opinion," "we would offer," and "we believe" intended to allow the analyst to speak and then testify on behalf of his entire organization (the FBI's Behavioral Analysis Unit). When such fallacies of relevance appear in the examiner's reports, it signals a weakness in an argument due to a lack of any evidence, requiring the buttress of collective experience. According to Thornton (1997, pp. 15–17), experience is very subjective and difficult to evaluate. When an expert substitutes experience for defensible scientific fact,

> no practical means exists for the questioner to delve into the extent and quality of that experience. . . .
>
> Testimony of this sort distances the witness from science and the scientific method. And if the science is removed from the witness, then that witness has no legitimate role to play in the courtroom, and no business being there. *If there is no science, there can be no forensic science.*
>
> Experience is neither a liability nor an enemy of the truth; it is a valuable commodity, but it should not be used as a mask to deflect legitimate scientific scrutiny, the sort of scrutiny that customarily is leveled at scientific evidence of all sorts. To do so is professionally bankrupt and devoid of scientific legitimacy, and courts

would do well to disallow testimony of this sort. Experience ought to be used to enable the expert to remember the when and the how, why, who, and what. Experience should not make the expert less responsible, but rather more responsible for justifying an opinion with defensible scientific facts.

The previous quote appears more than once in this text, and it will keep appearing due to its importance. Testimony that does not explain its reasoning, and hides behind poorly constructed logic and questionable experience, deprives the trier of any mechanism for gauging its quality. It also telegraphs an overall ignorance of crime reconstruction and the limits of the physical evidence.

As previously mentioned, throughout this particular analyst's reports, the word "believe" is regularly used to qualify opinions and conclusions. A belief is something akin to faith, or knowing and accepting something without proof. The use of this term signals a lowered confidence in the opinions being expressed. We are at a loss as to why something that is merely believed would be relied on in a forensic report as the basis for any conclusion. A forensic report should contain conclusions supported by the evidence. If there is uncertainty, this should be explained and the opinion should not be used to support further conclusions or opinions (although one may certainly use them to develop hypotheses). Moreover, when a reconstruction is not based on evidence but, rather, faith in one's experience, it may be appropriate for examiners to provide a disclaimer such as "there is no actual proof that the events occurred as outlined below," much like some crime reenactments on television display "Dramatization—may not have actually happened" at the bottom of the screen while actors show a version of events. To do otherwise only facilitates the promulgation of an imprecise and uninformed vanity reconstruction that really has no place in a courtroom.[4]

[4] A *vanity reconstruction* is an interpretation of events based on an inflated sense of one's abilities, without regard for scientific method, analytical log, the physical evidence, or the results of forensic testing. It is, in essence, reconstructing based on personal belief or experience.

THE CASE OF LANNY BRAYBROOK

Much like the previous example, this involves a reconstruction of events based on bare observation and surmise by nonscientific law enforcement personnel.

Lanny Braybook, the defendant, claimed that he shot the victim, his neighbor, in self-defense (*Michigan v. Lanny Braybrook*, 2002):

> Defendant gave two consistent statements to the police about the incident, in which he described how the victim lunged at him following an argument in defendant's garage about a land deal that had soured. In his statements to the police, defendant explained that he was afraid of the victim, who had a history of assaultive

behavior and allegedly had threatened defendant and his wife if they did not go ahead with the land transaction, and how the victim would respond when defendant attempted to back out of the land deal. Thus, defendant purportedly began preparations to move away from the victim, who was his next-door neighbor and, in anticipation of meeting with the victim, defendant went to the police station on the day of the shooting to seek advice on how to deal with the situation. That same day, defendant bought a handgun and registered it with the sheriff's department.

. . .

Detective Miller, who investigated the incident, testified on behalf of the prosecution that he believed the knife found near the victim's body had been planted by defendant to make the shooting appear as if it were committed in self-defense. His theory was based on three observations. First, defendant claimed that he had used the knife earlier that day to cut some insulation, but defendant's garage had been finished for some time, except for the area around the fuse box, making it suspicious that defendant had chosen that day instead of anytime in the past few years to insulate around the fuse box. Second, there were no visible cut marks on the cardboard on which the insulation was resting, thereby undermining defendant's claim that he had used the knife to cut the insulation. Third, the tape measure was locked in the open position, which was suspicious because most people, when finished measuring, would allow the tape measure to return to the retracted position. From these observations, the detective concluded that the scene had been staged.

Also, the detective testified that after the tape recorder was turned off during defendant's interview, defendant said, "I shouldn't tell you this, but now that you've got this turned off, I'll tell you. He never saw the gun." Detective Miller opined that this contradicted defendant's earlier statements that he told the victim he had a gun and raised it to a level where the victim should have seen it. Thus, Detective Miller concluded that, although defendant may have been legitimately afraid of the victim, he overreacted to the situation and planted the knife as an afterthought to explain the shooting.

Detective Miller testified that his skepticism about defendant's account was further fueled by defendant's claim that the victim held the knife in his right hand, when the victim was in fact left-handed. The victim's daughter and one of his ex-wives testified that he had only limited use of his right hand, although he was admittedly not so disabled as to prevent him from holding a knife. The detective concluded that it was unlikely that the victim would have attempted to use the knife in his nondominant, partially disabled hand.

Again, the question is not whether we believe the scene was actually staged but whether or not the analyst (in this case the detective) was able to use the evidence to prove it.

Although it is of greatest interest that the detective had certain theories regarding the case, and was suspicious of certain circumstances, these theories and suspicions were not subjected to any manner of scientific inquiry. Alternate explanations for the three indications of staging were not eliminated; rather, the suspicious nature of the circumstances, viewed through the subjective experience of the detective, was inappropriately used to conclude that staging had occurred. Subsequently, this untested reconstruction theory of evidence planting and crime scene staging was allowed in court without a voire dire that looked at more than the detective's police qualifications. Suspicion is not a bad thing; police investigators are in fact paid to be suspicious. But investigative suspicion should lead to further investigation and not be used as the basis for forensic conclusions.

It is important to note that when this type of testimony is offered by a forensic examiner, to suggest that law enforcement has planted an item of evidence, the witness must be qualified as an expert, there is significant voire dire, and there is a question as to whether the judge will actually allow it. The judge may in fact disallow it for a variety of nonscience related reasons. It is a curious discrepancy.

USE OF CRIME RECONSTRUCTION TO DETERMINE STAGING

It should be clear by now that we are concerned with preserving the science in the application of forensic science, as well as in any reconstruction-oriented examinations and testimony. As shown in the previous section, far too often reconstructions are allowed in court absent these considerations. For the forensic reconstructionist, we offer several suggestions.

The crime scene is full of information that can be used to detect staging, but even experienced investigators can miss it. Staging is undoubtedly present in more cases than it is found; however, the *evidence dynamics* (influences on the crime scene; see Chapter 6) can alter, obscure, or obliterate evidence and render it impossible to detect. In order to see through the evidence dynamics in a staged crime scene or any other, keen observation of the bloodstains, clothing, hair, body position, trajectories, and other evidentiary relationships is necessary. The knowledge, skills, and ability to interpret these evidentiary relationships are precisely the arena of the forensic generalist and reconstructionist.

However, the proper mind-set is also necessary. The easy road, followed by many, is to fit the evidence to one's theory of the crime. This is an approach that will lead to wrongful convictions and professional/departmental embarrassment. If the evidence does not fit the theory, then the theory must be reworked. None of the physical evidence may be excluded or ignored. This is especially true when witness statements and physical evidence differ. A witness' statement, like an investigator's theory, represents one person's view of the crime that may or may not be accurate. In other words, the witness statement is one more description of events to test against the physical evidence.

Staging needs to be considered as a possibility in every case. However, the forensic reconstructionist does not set out to prove that a crime scene has been staged, or to prove anything else for that matter. We set out to disprove the known possibilities. Like investigative theories and witness statements, staging is one more explanation for the crime that must be repeatedly tested against any and all known evidence.

The scientific method demands that all of the known evidence in a case must fit a reconstruction theory, not just some, or the theory must be discarded. As stated better by noted historian Peter Novick (1988, p. 46), "The value of an interpretation is judged by how well it accounts for the facts; if contradicted by the facts, it must be abandoned."

What kind of evidence does the reconstructionist look for in order to detect staging efforts in a crime scene? Generally, we must look for any evidence that does not fit the acts suggested or represented by the overt circumstances. In some cases, it may be just one piece of evidence, or its absence, out of necessary step with a particular event or series of events. In others, staging may be evidenced by a system of interrelated evidentiary inconsistencies. Each case is different and must therefore be examined scrupulously.

Although not all-inclusive, the following topics are meant to help the reconstructionist begin to tackle the staging issue. The questions provided are intended to stoke the fires of reconstructionists' imagination and then lead them to new areas of inquiry. They are not meant to be exhaustive.

POINT OF ENTRY/ POINT OF EXIT

Among the most commonly staged crime scene elements is the open or broken window (Turvey, 2000). In the mind of the crime scene simulator, this creates the illusion that an offender could possibly, if not certainly, have entered the scene at that location. Examination of the point of entry and point of exit is therefore of greatest consequence to the reconstructionist. The following general guide is helpful:

- Establish all points of entry and exit throughout the scene (doors, windows, paths, roads, etc.).

- Establish whether or not these locations were passable at the time of the crime (e.g., some windows and doors may be barricaded or permanently sealed, and some windows may be too high).
- Determine their involvement in the crime by virtue of documenting transfer evidence (blood, fingerprints, broken glass, dropped items, etc.) and negative transfer (the absence of footwear impressions in mud outside a window, the absence of any signs of forced entry, etc.).
- Determine whether or not entry and exit were possible in the manner required for the crime at hand, in terms of breaking in from the outside, removing any valuables, and the existence of requisite transfer evidence—this may require some experimentation by the reconstructionist.

Determining whether or not there is sufficient evidence that an offender could have entered and exited the crime scene in the manner required, with the evidence that must necessarily be altered or transferred at that location, is often the single most dispositive feature with respect to establishing crime scene staging. Most staged homicide scenes are domestic homicides committed in the victim's home. The stranger offender needs to get in, and the stranger offender needs to get out. In disproving this possibility, by virtue of an entry/exit point that is a locked double dead-bolted door, or a window that is covered with undisturbed dust, what remains is the possibility of staging.

EXAMPLE

One of the authors (Turvey) was asked to help investigate the crime scene in a potential fetish burglary/death threat case. The fact summary from the author's final report reads as follows:

According to the complaint report number •• filed on 9/13/•• by Det. No. 1, a 24 year old white female living in an apartment at ••, returned home from her place of work at 2200 hours to find that her apartment had been "ransacked." As well, some of her personal belongings were broken, and others are thought to be missing. No items of value were apparently taken.

She is currently employed by an off track betting facility, as well as having been a confidential informant for narcotics (contact: Det. No. 2, Narcotics) at the time of the complaint.

According to the victim's account and the account given by Det. No. 2, the victim first had two friends come over and help her investigate the apartment. Then, per her procedure as a confidential informant, she paged her contact from a pay telephone on the street. Det. No. 2, her contact, arrived at the scene shortly and spoke with her in his vehicle before he performed a canvass of the area.

According to information provided to this examiner, the offender appears to have entered the apartment through the front (living room?) window from the outside. Apparently, the front window was forced open from the outside and then laid down on the floor inside of the apartment. Attempts made by Det. No .2 at the scene to reinstall the window were not successful. A tennis shoe footwear pattern was found on this window.

According to the victim's account, the victim's dog (a pitbull) was left secured to her front door. When she returned, she found it in the bedroom. It is apparent from the amount of damage and behavior described at this scene that the offender spent a significant amount of time there (perhaps as much as an hour). It is also apparent, given that the dog was moved that the offender preferred to spend time in the front room and bedroom without the dog present.

According to Det. No. 1, he and the victim searched the 2nd floor rooftop of the victim's building for evidence on 9/24/••. They found several seashells on the rooftop, which had belonged to a collection owned by the victim, that lead from above the victim's window to an area on •• Street above a Blimpies restaurant. A blue pen, which is consistent with the type used to write the note and damage the photos, was found outside of the victim's bathroom window. A cut was found in the shade of one of the windows.

Given these facts, it [has been argued that it is] likely that the offender exited though the front window, climbed up to the roof, then walked over the area near or above Blimpies and made his exit from the rooftop. It is also likely that he exited the same way he entered. It is further possible, though not established, given the dropped pen and the cut shade, that the offender waited for the victim to arrive home and

surreptitiously viewed her reaction to his activities before finally leaving.

The offender allegedly broke into the victim's home, cut up or otherwise defaced many of her personal photographs with pen marks through her neck, left a number of pornographic videos behind, and wrote a death threat that was left on her pillow.

After being called in to the case and examining the evidence, Turvey, with the assistance of police investigators, established the following:

- The window could not be removed from the outside of the building.
- Even if the window could be removed from the outside, it would have to be dropped into the apartment and likely would have broken; it was unbroken.
- Even if the window could be removed from the outside, and then could have been dropped into the apartment without breaking, the act of stepping on it would have cause breakage.
- The victim's dog hated strangers, yet the offender moved it from the front door area to the bedroom and shut it inside without incident.

Shortly, this information led to other inconsistencies in both the evidence and the alleged victim's timeline, as well as that of Det. No. 2. Ultimately, it was learned that the alleged victim and her handler, Det. No. 2, who was married, were involved in a personal relationship, and that she had staged the scene to get his attention. The detective came to her aid as requested, and they spent 2 or 3 days in her apartment reviewing the evidence (the aforementioned tapes) before contacting anyone else and filing a police report.

WEAPONS AT OR REMOVED FROM THE SCENE

Of every weapon found at a crime scene, ask at least the following: Is the weapon found with the victim the one that caused the injury, and, if not, what was its purpose at the scene? Was there another weapon found at the scene? Does it have a known purpose?

EXAMPLE

A rifle was found beside an apparent suicide. Dr. John Thornton (personal communication, 1988) brought a class of students to the scene as part of an educational exercise. After the police had "finished with the scene," one of the students looked at the rifle and noted spider webs in the barrel.

The suicide theory was abandoned and the investigation was reopened as a possible homicide.

In this example, the suicide theory hinged on the rifle being used by the victim to inflict the fatal injury. Because the victim had died of a gunshot wound, and the rifle was the only weapon found at the scene, disproving its involvement in the victim's death was the only step necessary to cast doubt on the theory of suicide and suggest that the scene had been altered.

Sometimes there is evidence of weapons use at a crime scene but no weapon can be found there. For each crime scene it must be asked whether there exists evidence that a weapon has been removed and, if so, what purpose could its removal have served? If the answer to the first part of the question is no, answering the second part of the question becomes unnecessary.

FIREARMS

A firearm of some kind is the most likely weapon of choice in a staged crime scene (Turvey, 2000). It follows that the reconstructionist must be prepared to ask of each firearm certain basic questions in order to determine its involvement in the crime.

First, are the wounds consistent with the story presented? In suicides, could the victim have shot himself or herself? (See Fig. 12.3.)

Then we must ask whether the firearm is loaded correctly, in a manner consistent with the evidence and the statements of witnesses.

STAGED CRIME SCENES 467

Figure 12.3

In this case, a young male's deceased body was found in his vehicle, engine on, in an open field, with a single fatal gunshot wound to the head. A 20-gauge shotgun was found across his lap, pointing toward a broken window with a round hole in it. However, an expended shotgun shell was found outside the broken window on the ground along with several cigarette butts. Furthermore, there was no brain, blood, or hair material inside or outside the shotgun barrel or on the victim's hands and wrists. Also, there was brain and bone material on the stock of the shotgun in such a manner as to suggest that it was delivered to that surface in situ. Add to this the fact that the victim's truck had suffered new damage to the front end, as though it had struck something, and was still leaking radiator fluid when discovered by authorities. The inescapable conclusion is that the decedent could not have fired the shotgun without some resulting transfer. Nor could he leave behind a spent shell to be discovered outside of the vehicle. This case was closed as a suicide, the cigarettes were not collected, and the body was cremated without autopsy.

EXAMPLE

A man claimed to have been sleeping in the bedroom when his wife shot herself with a shotgun using a bent coat hanger. The shotgun was found to be loaded to capacity with a live round in the chamber (Tulare County, W. Jerry Chisum and David Burd, 1969).

Next, is the hammer down on an empty casing? And is it the right casing? Furthermore, is the rotation of the cylinder consistent with the way the shots were fired?

EXAMPLE

The perpetrator in a particular case fired two shots into the head of the victim. He then reloaded the chamber and fired one more to "put gunshot residue" on her hand in an attempt to stage the scene as a suicide.

Apparently, the perpetrator became confused when reloading at the scene and put one of the empty casings in the wrong chamber. Note that the pen tip in Figure 12.4 indicates where the hammer was resting, and the arrow indicates the direction of rotation. The firing pin impression is wrong on one casing (Tehama County, Joe Rynearson, 1994).

Another question to consider is whether the firearm found at the scene is defective or not? Is it capable of chambering rounds and firing them?

EXAMPLE

A man claimed that his 25 ACP could not have been used to shoot his wife as it was actually defective. He had taken it to a gunsmith a few days before the shooting because it would not work. The gunsmith testified that it would take at least four hours for him to correct the problem. The reconstructionist removed a screwdriver from his pocket, moved a screw, and showed that the gun was fully functional (Imperial County, W. Jerry Chisum and Ted Elzerman, 1968; Ted testified).

Figure 12.4

This cylinder was reloaded incorrectly by the perpetrator when he was staging a suicide. The pen marks the casing under the hammer and the direction of rotation is indicated by the arrow. In this case, the cylinder was marked with an indelible marker prior to picking up the gun.

These questions are designed to establish a firearm's involvement in a particular case, and they should be answered in every reconstruction in which firearms are involved—not just those concerned with staging.

GUNPOWDER DEPOSITS

Gunpowder deposits are composed of carbon, soot, unburned gunpowder, and the components of gunshot residue (GSR). Burning powder comes out of a gun barrel (and elsewhere, depending on the firearm design) and will, upon contact with skin, cause powder burns. These deposits must be consistent with the supposed act.

Most suicides are contact or near contact shots. The powder distribution must be something that can be caused by the person holding the gun. A lack of powder indicates that there is a greater distance or that there was an intervening target.

EXAMPLE

A woman shot her sleeping husband on the couch. She used a throw pillow to muffle the sound. Then she placed the gun in his hand and placed the pillow under his head. There was no powder on the head, but it was present on the bottom of the pillow under the exit wound (Tuolumne County, W. Jerry Chisum, 1978).

Powder can be carried for as much as three feet from a person into the wound. A forensic pathologist must examine the bullet track to determine if powder particles are present. A single particle is insufficient proof of close range because fired bullets can have a particle stuck in the lubricating grease that will remain on the bullet for some distance.

To get GSR on the hand of the victim, the gun may be held close to the hand and fired. If it is close enough, gunpowder deposits will result and there may even be powder burns. The resulting pattern may not be consistent with the manner in which the gun can be held. In other words, the presence of the gun in the hand creates a void in gunpowder deposits that must be evident. If these patterns are different, it may indicate staging.

MOVEMENT OF THE BODY

It is not at all common for staged crime scenes to involve movement of the victim's body to a secondary scene or "dumpsite" (Turvey, 2000). Typically, the scene is staged at the location where the body has fallen, perhaps even because of where the body has fallen, out of convenience. This may include the inability to move the body or the inability to sufficiently clean the scene

Figure 12.5

Female victim's nude body found on a steep riverbank. Law enforcement crime scene investigators and detectives insisted that the victim was rolled down the hill from the road above. Note the drag trail in the vegetation leading up from the water below and the victim's outstretched arms. Upon close analysis, duckweed from the river was identified on the victim's body.

before the body may be discovered. To determine whether this is the case, care must be taken to examine the conditions and circumstances that best address this issue. In each scene, this will depend on the interaction between the victim and the victim's environment, and the expected transfer evidence. This can include consideration of (but is certainly not limited to):

- Evidence of drag trails and drag stains on the ground and against environmental surfaces (i.e., bunched carpet, heels dragged across mud, bloodstains leading in from another room, etc.) (Fig. 12.5)
- Bunched or rolled up clothing on the victim's body
- Livor mortis inconsistent with the final resting position of the body (blood pooling against gravity)
- Rigor mortis inconsistent with the final resting position of the body (joints stiffened against gravity)
- Blood evidence in places where there should not be any
- Trace evidence on the body from locations unassociated with the crime scene

CLOTHING

Is the clothing pulled or rolled in a particular direction? A person being pulled by the feet will have their shirt pulled up, with the most deviation being on the side that was in contact with the surface. A person pulled by the hands will have the pants pulled down and the shirt stretched tight, and the legs will be extended. The hands may be placed in a "normal" position.

Consider also the following:

- Has the clothing been removed from the victim or the scene? What purpose may this have served?
- Have the pockets been searched? Are they pulled out even partway?
- Has the body been rolled, causing the clothing to be unevenly distributed?
- Are there smears of something on the clothes that indicate the body was dragged through (soil, vegetation, water, etc.)?
- Is there anything unusual about the clothing? Is anything inside out or backwards?
- Does it appear as though the victim may have been redressed after being attacked? If so, why were the clothes off in the first place, and why would the offender bother to redress the victim—what purpose would that serve?

The reconstructionist may need to conduct experiments in order to determine how the clothing got the way that it did.

SHOES

In traffic accidents, the bottoms of the shoes will have parallel scratches indicating the direction and location of the injuries to the body and the foot on which the victim was standing. If these scratches are missing, either the accident was at very low speed or the body was dumped at this location.

Consider the following:

- Are the shoes on the correct feet?
- Do the shoes have any transfer evidence inconsistent with the scene?
- Was the victim wearing them during the commission of the crime? Or do the bottoms of the victim's feet indicate that the shoes may have been off (blood, injury, or scene transfer such as mud or gravel).
- Where are the knots in the strings?

A person tying his own shoes will bend over and tie them in the middle or lift the leg, cross it over the other, and tie the shoe so the knot is on the inside. A mother tying a child's shoe may tie it so that the knot is on the outside. When putting the shoes on a dead person, this mistake is easy to make.

BLOODSTAINS

Bloodstains are a record of actions that occurred when blood was shed. The one rule that is always in effect with blood is that gravity works. Blood runs down, only going in a different direction if acted upon by another force. Again, blood runs down, never horizontal.

First, is the blood going in the direction it should, given the position of the body and gravity?

EXAMPLE

A man shot his wife while she was sitting on the bed. He lowered her to the bed and drove to a distant city. He called the police because she was not answering the telephone. He was sure a burglar had killed his wife in her sleep. The blood from the chest wound runs toward her feet, showing she was upright at the time of the shooting (Fig. 12.6; Tulare County, CA 1998).

Next, are the bloodstains consistent with the purported actions of the victim and the suspect?

EXAMPLE

A woman was found by her husband with her head almost completely exploded from a 12-gauge shotgun contact blast. Most of the brains and tissue only went to the side out about five feet; however, two pieces of brain with scalp attached went out the door and struck the wall. The brains were responsible for two of the bloodstain patterns. The other originated approximately a foot from the corner of the opposite wall. Examination of the blood spatters on this wall showed that there were three separate acts that produced these stains. Two large stains were from the brains striking the wall, and the other was a castoff stain that did not originate from the area of the gunshot. There was a prior act that killed or seriously injured the victim, who then "committed suicide" (Tulare County, 1984).

Figure 12.6

This woman was shot "by a burglar while she slept" claimed the husband. Note that the blood is running toward her feet, not the bed. The husband was convicted of homicide.

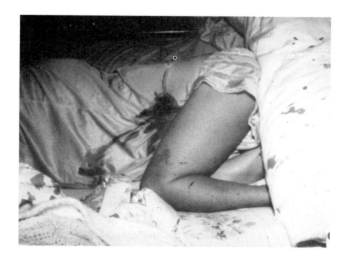

HAIR

The position of the hair is a frequently overlooked clue. Decedent hair can frequently show how the person came to the position in which she was found. This is particularly true with longer hair but not exclusively, because shorter hair may also show movement (Figs. 12.7–12.12).

When a person is dragged, her hair will extend in the direction from which she came. If the head is raised and then lowered, then hair will be in

Figure 12.7

Small person falling face down; note the hair.*

*Thanks to Julia and Kyra Chisum (the author's granddaughters) for assisting in illustrating the manner in which hair can be used to reconstruct activities.

Figure 12.8

Note how the hair flairs out when a person with long hair falls to the ground.

Figure 12.9

The hair does not flair out as much on a small child.

Figure 12.10

When a person is dragged by the feet, her hair will trail pointing back to where she started. Note how the shirt has been pulled up due to friction.

a "pompadour" style, and in fact, it may be on just one side if only one arm was used to pull with. A person with long hair who falls backwards to the ground will have her hair flare out away from the head in a halo-like array. If falling to the front, the hair will also flare out from the head. It should not be under the face.

Hair also obeys the law of gravity. It will hang down unless something is acting on it. An injury that occurs sometime before death can cause hair to stick to the side of the head in drying blood. Drying blood can also capture hair movement on flat surfaces. Hair makes a pattern of very fine streaks.

Figure 12.11

The person was dragged by her arms, then she was laid down and her arms put by her sides. Note the puffed up hair that was trapped by the head. The pants (not shown) will be pulled down at the waist due to friction.

Figure 12.12

The hair shows that the person was rolled from her side or stomach onto her back over her right (the side with the hair) side.

In discussing all of these clues, one must know how the body can bend and move, and one must accept that gravity works.

"APPEARS STAGED"

Each investigator and forensic examiner has his own subjective sense of those elements that, when discovered at a crime scene, indicate staging. Or at least, that is what they say in court. These can include such circumstances as:

- No sign of forced entry.
- Forced entry is evident.
- The drawers in a room have been removed and carelessly dumped out to give a "ransacked" appearance.
- The drawers in a room have been removed and carefully stacked to protect or preserve the content.
- No search for valuables is apparent.
- Only particular items have been stolen.
- No items have been stolen.
- The victim had life insurance.
- The victim's death profited a family member, household member, or intimates in some way other than life insurance (anger, revenge, trust fund, unfettered access to a large bank account, etc.).

Any or all of these circumstances may raise the suspicion of the alert investigator, and there is nothing inherently wrong with suspicion. However, these circumstances also occur in cases in which there is no staging. Careful readers will note that they are not even useful as red flags because they cover almost all possibilities with respect to each particular circumstance (i.e., the point of entry will either be forced or not, items of value will either have been stolen or not, and the scene will either be ransacked or not).

Suspicion justifies further investigation; it tells the investigator where to look for more evidence. Suspicious circumstances are not themselves evidence, however. They are hypotheses that must be tested with the evidence; they do not signal the end of inquiry but rather its beginning. If forensic examiners do their long division and work to disprove these theories, they may discover that what appears to be evidence of staging may ultimately be something else.

Let us consider the issue of "ransacking." If the crime scene "appears ransacked," and this is used to support the inference of staging, at least the following must be established:

- That the ransacked appearance is a departure from the normal appearance of the scene.
- That the ransacked appearance is the direct result of offender activity, and not crime scene personnel.
- That the ransacked appearance was unrelated to a search by the offender for items of value (cash, checkbooks, jewelry, firearms, etc.).
- That the ransacked appearance was unrelated to a search by the offender for a specific item of interest (vehicle keys, illicit drugs, prescription medications, personal items of a fetishistic value, etc.).

If the forensic examiner can eliminate these possibilities, then it can be argued that ransacking may support the inference that the scene was staged. We emphasize *may* because it is only one indication and must be considered in context with all of the other evidence.

Let us also consider the issue of "valuables." The issue of whether or not valuables have been taken from the crime scene is often a major consideration with respect to establishing the elements and motive of a crime. Some examiners are quite comfortable assuming that the offender took valuables, despite having evidence that the item even existed, because it is helpful to promoting their theory of a case. For those examiners and all others, a certain threshold line of inquiry for each item of value is required:

- What was the item? What is its value?
- Where was the item located in the scene?
- Who knew of the item's existence?
- Who knew where the item was located?
- What barriers did the offender overcome to locate and remove the item (was it hidden or in a safe; was it in plain sight on the kitchen table)?
- What evidence demonstrates that it was actually removed from the scene?
- What evidence demonstrates that it was the offender who removed it from the scene? Has forensic testing established a clear association of any kind?
- Has the item been located? If so, where?

As already discussed, it is common for those who have staged crime scenes to appear as burglaries gone awry to forget their purpose and not remove valuables. Or they may simply remove a few items of value to create a superficial illusion. Or the scene may not have been staged at all. For example, the following are all possibilities when considering why there are items of obvious value remaining in the scene:

- The offender was interested in items of a personal or fetishistic nature; they may be removed from the scene undetected in many cases.
- The offender was under the influence of controlled substances during the crime and was fixated on locating something specific.
- The offender was not there to steal anything but, rather, entered to satisfy other desires, such as rape or fetish burglary, for which there may or may not be clear indications, depending on the level and quality of scene documentation.

In any case, neither circumstance is entirely dispositive. Furthermore, in order to use this finding to support an inference of staging, the crime scene documentation has to be sufficiently exclusory with respect to negative documentation of offender scene activity.

As with any circumstance at the crime scene, the removal of valuables must be considered in context with all of the other evidence. Cash in particular is difficult because proving its existence is not always easy, although it is certainly not impossible. Seeking to answer the previous questions will set the reconstructionist on the right path and help to establish the relevance of the items of value that have been stolen from the scene or that may have been left behind.

What appears to be ransacked, what appears to be missing, and what appears to have been left behind tend to be of primary concern to investigators who testify regarding crime scenes that "appear to be staged." As this section indicates, appearances may be deceiving. This is especially problematic when investigative theories and suspicions are offered in court as pseudo-expert conclusions.

Forensic reconstructionists have an obligation to test their theories against the known evidence and to do their reconstruction homework. In their final analysis, they should not be interested in how the scene appears based on their experience but, rather, in what can be established about its appearance through the physical evidence.

CASE EXAMPLE

The victim was 9 months, 1 day pregnant. Her husband left for work at 6:15 a.m., arrived at 7, and had several witnesses putting him at the work site approximately 35 miles from home. The daughter went to her second grade at 9 a.m. Mommy was fine then.

The daughter came home from school at 2 p.m. The door was locked; she assumed her mother had gone to the hospital. She went to get the key from the garage but saw "someone" in the garage. She ran to her grandparents' house approximately two blocks away. The grandfather found his daughter in the garage with her head split down the middle by a shotgun blast (Figs. 12.13 and 12.14).

With the shotgun at her feet and her shoes off, it looks as though she had pulled the trigger with her toe. However, Figures 12.13 and 12.14 show several discrepancies with the theory of suicide. Some are subtle, whereas others are easily determined.

First, the blood on her arms, hands, legs, and front is not the way blood would come from a shotgun shot to the head. The heart would only pump a couple of times and the blood would run down the back of the chair onto the ground. Second, the angle of the shot is almost level, as determined by the location of the blood, brains, etc. that went into the cabinet instead of up on the ceiling.

Third, the woman's belt is above her breasts. This indicates that she was carried to this location and set into this chair. Also, her gown is pulled up so that her legs are on the chair instead of on her gown.

This looks like a planned "suicide" by other persons. It is staged as shown by the inconsistencies listed previously. When the search warrant was issued and the house entered, bloodstains were found throughout the kitchen, dining room, and family room. There were two bloody cast-iron frying pans with triangles broken from the centers and a bloody saucepan with the handle broken off. Another saucepan was also bloody. The stains showed that these pans had been used to strike a bloody object.

Her husband had hired a friend to kill her. The plan was to knock her out, put her in the garage, and set up the suicide. The plan did not work; she fought to stay alive.

The following evidence in this case points to staging:

1. The blood pattern is not consistent with the injury.
2. The direction of the shot is not consistent with self-infliction.
3. The clothing is not in the normal position.

The primary clue here is the bloodstains. If the plan had worked, and the victim had been rendered unconscious with one blow, would the responding officers have been astute enough to recognize the subtle clues associated with the shotgun angle and the belt? With the proper training and enthusiasm, perhaps (San Joaquin County, CA 1986).

CONCLUSION

Any interpretation of the physical evidence that suggests an action, an event, or a series of events, such as staging, is a form of crime reconstruction. This is the domain of the forensic scientist, preferably the forensic generalist, as we have shown here. Although it is important for investigators to theorize and speculate as to what happened and how a crime may have occurred, these theories must ultimately be tested against the physical evidence. Investigators who proceed with a confirmatory mind-set, and seek to interpret the available evidence in the light most favorable to their theory, will have no trouble convincing themselves that theirs is the correct and only explanation for events. As provided in previous chapters, we can easily prove any theory so long as we go back through the evidence and ignore everything that would tend to disprove it. This is a common habit among nonscientists

Figure 12.13

Suicide or homicide? The head is split open and there is a shotgun at the feet.

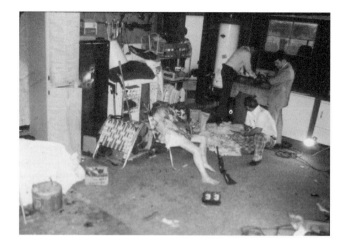

Figure 12.14

This woman was 9 months 1 day pregnant. The blood on her clothing is not consistent with a shotgun blast to the head. She was beaten unconscious first and then carried to the garage and shot to stage a suicide. The husband hired the killer; both were convicted of two counts of first-degree murder.

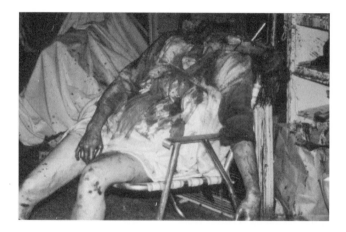

and is one of the reasons that the forensic scientist exists—as a filter for unfounded, untested, and ultimately unproven theories.

Staging is a possibility in every case. Therefore, in every case, it must be considered and excluded before entirely abandoned as an explanation. It cannot be proven, however, through mere observation, intuition, and surmise. The evidence must be reliably established, the conclusions must be empirically tested and logically rendered, and alternative explanations must be eliminated. Only then may staging be considered as the most viable explanation for events.

REFERENCES

Adair, T. W., and Dobersen, M. J. "A Case of Suicidal Hanging Staged as Homicide," *Journal of Forensic Sciences*, 44(6), 1307–1309, November 1999.

Baker, K., and Napier, M. "Criminal Personality Profiling." In S. James, and J. Nordby, (Eds.) *Forensic Science: An Introduction to Scientific and Investigative Techniques*, Boca Raton: CRC Press, 2003.

Burgess, A., Burgess, A., Douglas, J., and Ressler, R. *Crime Classification Manual.* New York: Lexington Books, 1992.

California v. Jeffrey Duvardo, No. A098935 (Lake County Super. Ct. No. CR 5090), November 3, 2004.

Douglas, J., and Munn, C. "The Detection of Staging and Personation at the Crime Scene." In A. Burgess, A. Burgess, J. Douglas, and R. Ressler (Eds.). *Crime Classification Manual.* New York: Lexington Books, 1992.

Geberth, V. *Practical Homicide Investigation.* (3rd ed.). New York: CRC Press, 1996.

Gross, H. *Criminal Investigation.* London: Sweet & Maxwell, 1924.

Kirk, P., and Thornton, J. (Eds.) *Criminal Investigation.* (2nd ed.). New York: John Wiley, 1974.

McKnight, K. "Expert's Opinion Challenged," *Ohio Beacon Journal*, April 1, 2000.

Michigan v. Lanny Braybrook, Court of Appeals of Michigan, No. 223088, April 19, 2002.

Novick, P. *That Noble Dream.* New York: Cambridge University Press, 1988.

O'Connell, J., and Soderman, H. *Modern Criminal Investigation.* New York: Funk & Wagnalls, 1936.

Svensson, A., and Wendel, O. *Techniques of Crime Scene Investigation.* (2nd ed.). New York: Elsevier, 1974.

Tennessee v. William Stevens. No. M1999–02067-CCA-R3-DD, May 30, 2001 (2001 WL 579054), 2001.

Thornton, J. "The General Assumptions and Rationale of Forensic Identification." In D. L. Faigman, D. H. Kaye, M. J. Saks, and J. Sanders (Eds.). *Modern Scientific Evidence: The Law and Science of Expert Testimony*, Vol. 2. St. Paul, MN: West, 1997.

Turvey, B. *Criminal Profiling: An Introduction to Behavioral Evidence Analysis.* London: Academic Press, 1999.

Turvey, B. "Staged Crime Scenes: A Preliminary Study of 25 Cases," *Journal of Behavioral Profiling*, 1(3), December, 2000.

Turvey, B. *Criminal Profiling: An Introduction to Behavioral Evidence Analysis,.* (2nd ed.). London: Elsevier, 2002.

U.S. Department of Justice "Census of Publicly Funded Forensic Crime Laboratories, 2002," *Office of Justice Programs Bureau of Justice Statistics*, NCJ 207205, February 2005.

CHAPTER 13

SURVIVING AND THRIVING IN THE COURTROOM

Raymond J. Davis, BS

One of the many privileges afforded the expert witness in the criminal justice system is the opportunity to present his or her work in a court of law. Contrary to popular belief, going to court is not something to be dreaded but anticipated. Testifying is the ultimate expression of your work product. It allows you to inform and educate jurors on your training, education, experience, test results, and opinions.

In ancient times, the solons of Rome entered the Forum to give voice to their beliefs and ideas, from the arguing of senatorial resolutions on matter of state, to the resolution of legal conflicts between injured parties, to the debate over specific laws and the meaning of their language. The spirit of this process continues today through our legal system. The sworn testimony of investigative and forensic professionals, from police officers to crime scene investigators to criminalists, gives voice to their work, not unlike the senators of Rome more than 2000 years ago.

Next to the defendant, the witness is the most important person in the courtroom. Not the attorneys nor the judge, not the jurors nor court personnel, but the witness gives oral and demonstrative evidence before a captive audience. Every utterance is recorded, in some cases videotaped, to preserve the testimony and ultimately the integrity of the trial system. Expert witnesses are given the opportunity to hold forth while lawyers, judges, and jurors are made to pay attention while they unravel the mysteries of forensic science.

No matter how great the privilege to testify may be, there are two fundamental reasons why some expert witnesses would rather endure a root canal operation than testify in court: the fear of public speaking and the fear of the legal system. This chapter covers in detail these two issues, which have caused more angst among forensic scientists than any single challenge in their careers.

FEAR OF PUBLIC SPEAKING

Medical researchers know that the human brain begins to work at the moment of birth and only stops working when a person is called on to give a speech. In fact, one of the great fears shared by most people is the fear of public speaking. Not even the specter of death or an IRS audit can compete with the gnawing fear produced by giving a speech. The following is a short but not complete list of fears commonly shared by most everyone who has ever been called on to speak in front of a room or give expert testimony:

- I might say something stupid and get ridiculed.
- I might do something stupid and be humiliated.
- I will forget something important.
- I will run out of time before I run out of material.
- Worse, I will run of material before I run out of time.
- My audience will not like me. I see them talking to each other.
- I don't think I have anything important to say.
- I'll go blank and appear a fool.
- I don't know as much as my audience does.
- I'll look nervous and embarrass myself in front of everyone.
- Someone in the audience thinks they can do a better job than me.

All of these feelings and more are racing through the speaker's mind as he or she moves toward the podium or takes the witness stand. The fear mounts as adrenaline surges through the body, blocking all reason and calmness. By the time they have reached the front of the room, their anxiety level has ramped to a near unmanageable level. Once the fear takes hold, a person's ability to access information and appear calm and relaxed has all but disappeared. The ridicule and embarrassment most people feel when ask to give a speech soon teaches them that public speaking is something to be avoided at all costs. This fear is so great that no amount of coaxing will get people to accept another invitation to speak in public. Some forensic experts even request reassignment within the laboratory in order to avoid going to court.

As much as people fear the thought of giving a speech, the speaker is greatly admired by the audience. The primary reason for this admiration is that the person dreading public speaking does not have to get up and speak. As he looks to the front of the room, he is relieved to see that someone else is doing it. All he has to do is sit back comfortably in his chair, not subjected to a sea of eyes staring back at them.

When the time or occasion presents itself to give a speech, the act of forcing oneself through the experience does not build confidence in the speaker. The only thing produced is a wariness that keeps most people from the opportunity to share their knowledge and wisdom with their audience. There are many ways to overcome this dreadful feeling or fear of public speaking. The method that I have found successful involves a few concepts that will be explained in detail here. The first and most important factor in overcoming this fear is to believe that your audience is pulling for you to be successful in front of the room. This is the fundamental tenet for overcoming the fear of public speaking. If you were absolutely assured that your audience was behind you 100%, wouldn't you race to the front of the room or to the witness stand? Remember, the speaker is greatly admired for doing the speaking while the audience gets to sit comfortably in their chairs content to listen. Another reason why your audience is pulling for you is a purely selfish one. They would rather you do the talking, allowing them to remain seated, and they want your presentation to be so captivating, inspiring, and informative that they will actually enjoy it. Recall the last time you heard someone testify or give a technical paper or teach a class. Didn't you want that person to be compelling, interesting, and informative? In fact, you found yourself so involved with the presentation that you wished it would have continued a little longer. In effect, you, as part of the audience, were directly supporting the speaker to do well.

Your active participation was to show the speaker that you were paying attention, laughing at the funny places, asking questions at the right places, and clapping enthusiastically at the conclusion. Think of those times when you were captivated by the speaker or the presentation that your time in the audience was as much fun as being in the theater. In order to achieve this sense of comfort when presenting a paper or giving testimony, there are some helpful suggestions that will assist you. The following set of guidelines or rules will aid you during those times when you are called on to present a technical paper, be a moderator or emcee, or give expert testimony. These are not the only rules that work—just the ones that have worked for me and for many others. Follow these rules or ideas and they will lead you to overcome the fear of public speaking.

This rule requires a small leap of faith on your part. Remember the times when you sat in the audience and wished that the speaker would not get lost or stumble through her presentation, have her PowerPoint presentation fail, suddenly drop unnumbered index cards, or begin to mumble, run over time, and apologize for omitting large portions of her presentation. When it is your turn to stand in front of the room or take the witness stand, your audience is fully engaged to support you. They are on your side. Even

RULE 1

Your audience is always on your side wishing you to do well. Furthermore, they are grateful that you are the one in front of the room and not them.

if they believe that someone else can do a better job of presenting the material, your audience is pulling for you because they want your presentation to be a pleasant learning experience.

The Roman statesman Horace said, "Well begun is half completed." Do not fret about memorizing your whole presentation. It is an unnecessary task. Just practice the beginning or the introduction. A rule of thumb that I employ for a 50-minute talk is to practice the first 10 minutes, going over it time and again until it's letter perfect. With this great start I can see my audience relax noticeably and I find myself relaxing along with them. From this relaxed state I have easier access to information that will assist me in my presentation. Any miscues I make after the first ten to 15 minutes go largely unnoticed. For a 30-minute speech or presentation, I practice the first five to seven minutes. For a ten-minute speech, I have a perfect audience-captivating one-minute start. Some of the main reasons for not memorizing your whole presentation are that while you are talking you are also thinking about not getting lost, not wanting to leave anything out, finishing on time, and being able to address and answer questions.

One of the best ways to practice the beginning of your courtroom testimony is to present the information contained in your resume or curriculum vitae. This is something you are quite familiar with. When you are asked questions during the qualification period, seize this opportunity to deliver a sterling presentation of your credentials that allows you to capture the jurors' attention while at the same time calming any nervous energy. Practice going over your qualifications to the point of perfection and watch the rest of your courtroom testimony flow smoothly to the delight of everyone in the courtroom.

There are two things to consider here. First, your audience has not heard your qualifications before and they are interested in you. They were made aware of your participation by the attorney during his opening statement to the jury. Second, do not make your testimony sound like a tape recording, repeatedly using the same words and phrases. The added benefit to you will be to avoid sounding bored through repetition. Vary it from time to time, finding words that best illustrate your training and level of proficiency. You may even wish to change how you lay out your qualifications just to keep it interesting, especially when you find yourself testifying in the same courtrooms. Make your qualifications more than a recital of data. After all, it is your professional career that you are talking about.

Another fact to aid in your courtroom presentation is that jurors hold experts in high regard. It is a confidence booster to know that jurors already think highly of me as I make my way to the witness stand. I can increase that level of confidence by looking at them as I pass by. Notice their nods of

Summary of Rule 1

Your audience is awaiting your presentation and is delighted to hear from you while sitting in rapt attention.

RULE 2

"A great start makes for a superior presentation."

recognition and appreciation for your role in the judicial process. Your confidence will be greatly increased by the support you will receive from jurors as you take the witness stand and offer your expert testimony.

Your audience does not want you to read from a typed text or from a PowerPoint presentation. They want to hear from you as if you were talking to them personally. If you plan on reading from a script, make a copy of it and hand it out to them and avoid going up to the lectern. The visual technique I use is called the mind map method. It is a method for capturing all the material I need to present to my audience and only requires one sheet of paper. No matter how long or short the presentation, all the information I plan on delivering is contained on this one sheet of paper. I never get lost and always get the information out in the time allotted. Because I do not have to worry about whether I will get all the information out, I can devote more of my mind to the delivery of my presentation.

The following is a short primer on how to use the mind map method for the qualification portion of your testimony. Take a piece of blank paper and write your name in the center and circle it. In any order you choose, start placing elements of your resume around your name: Education, Formal Training, Area of Expertise, Professional Societies, Cases Worked, Number of Times Testified, Military Service, Honors/Awards, Papers Published, Classes Taught, and Journals Subscribed To. By utilizing these major topics, it will be easier to recall the specifics of your qualifications without having to read from your resume. Provide a copy to the prosecutor or defense attorney and it will prompt them to ask some follow-up questions should you leave something out or they want a deeper treatment.

The pretrial conference is your first opportunity to show the prosecutor the mind map of your qualifications. Most attorneys are loath to read from printed text and flip through pages while examining the witness. There is no time to read and listen at the same time. Also, this mind map affords them the opportunity to quickly glance at your qualifications, allowing them to conduct a smooth direct examination. This method is thorough, complete, and ensures that nothing is kept from the jurors favorable impression of you. Following is a typical mind map resume.

Be sure to keep the information brief and avoid writing a narrative to fill in the various circles. Find the words or acronyms that catch the eye while providing the highest level of information. There are several books available that outline the advantages of this fast, elegant, and comprehensive tool (Konieczka, 1995).

Being granted this latitude on nervousness provides you a brief respite while you take the witness stand or the podium. One of the ironies of being nervous is that most people only manifest about ten percent of their

Summary of Rule 2

Practice to perfection the first part of your presentation and observe how well the rest flows smoothly and effortlessly.

RULE 3

Prepare a visual picture of your presentation in order to avoid reading it and boring your audience to numbness.

Summary of Rule 3

Do not read your presentation. Instead, create a visual picture of the information you wish to present and then talk to your audience.

RULE 4

Your audience knows that public speaking can be nerve wracking and will grant you some latitude (but only for a short period of time).

488   CRIME RECONSTRUCTION

nervousness to their audience. You may be experiencing a variety of physical calamities, such as shaking, fidgeting, perspiration running down your neck, and your face turning beet red, but only you will be aware of this. Unless you broadcast your nervousness by shouting to your audience, "I hate public speaking," "I'm really nervous up here," or "I'd rather be somewhere else," they will not be aware of your discomfort. Even though you may be feeling uncomfortable in the extreme, your audience will not be aware of your discomfort.

Although they will not be aware of your heightened level of discomfort, that knowledge alone will not make the nervousness disappear. The best way to make it disappear is to channel or direct the nervous energy during a presentation that will assist you in looking and feeling better. Some of the ineffective ways of displaying nervousness are pacing back and forth in front of the room, playing with a key chain attached to the belt or rattling coins in one's pant pockets, the clasping and unclasping of hands, and a speech filled with nonwords such as "ums" and "ahhs."[1] These negative traits detract from a persuasive presentation and courtroom testimony.

Also, the inappropriate use of the laser pen that some speakers use as a pointer reflects their nervous behavior, as does unconsciously banging on the lectern or fiddling with the microphone while delivering a speech. These traits do not serve the speaker.

A more effective way to channel nervous energy is through eye contact, gestures, and a confident voice. Let's begin with eye contact. This method of channeling nervous energy with the audience is the best way to begin the calming process. As previously mentioned, they are pulling for you and wish to learn something from you. As the speaker begins to receive feedback from the audience through eye contact, her level of nervousness begins to decrease. There is an inverse relationship between the amount of eye contact and the level of nervousness. As the amount of eye contact increases, the level of nervousness decreases. Avoid the old advice of looking over their heads. It is eye contact that produces the greatest results, both for the speaker and for the audience.

The second way to channel nervous energy is through the use of gestures. The appropriate use of gestures lends a visual component to a person's presentation. Most people are visually oriented and gestures help facilitate understanding. In addition, the physical act of gesturing transfers much of the nervous energy into the presentation. An animated and relaxed speaker or witness is much admired.

The third and most effective way to channel nervous energy is through one's voice. This is the most important quality a speaker can possess in capturing his audience's attention. A fundamental requirement of the speaker

[1] During a 50-minute presentation to law enforcement officers by a criminalist in 1996, I counted 175 "ums" and "ahs." I have a vague memory of the topic but clearly remember how I spent my time counting the nonwords.

is that he must be heard, and the quality of the voice must sound confident and persuasive. Also, the use of repetitive words or phrases such as "basically," "you know," "as I said before," and "like" erodes the speakers credibility. Being able to speak with a compelling and confident voice gives the audience the impression that the speaker knows his material well and enjoys being in front of the room. Through constant practice and by receiving feedback, a person can improve his delivery. Some of the greatest actors who ever performed found success and fame only after discovering their optimum voice. Through practice, coaching, and feedback, you will find your optimum, audience-captivating voice.

It helps to focus on these three qualities for channeling nervous energy: voice, eye contact, and gestures. Just remember the acronym VEG to access the ways to increase your delivery style while appearing calm and relaxed. Remember that nervous energy can be harnessed for a more effective presentation.

A final thought about public speaking. You must practice constantly. You cannot go to court and practice on jurors. You cannot go to a scientific symposium and practice on your peers. There are many places where you can practice and receive feedback that will inspire you to improve your presentation skills. There are many public and private service organizations, such as Kiwanis and Rotary, that are looking for forensic scientists and other law enforcement personnel to come and speak to them. Junior high and senior high schools have career day events seeking forensic experts to speak about careers in the criminal justice system. You can be a moderator at a scientific symposium or give classes to law enforcement personnel or train others in your laboratory or workplace. There are opportunities to give talks through your church or other charitable service organizations.

There are many companies that train people to be more effective communicators. Look for these classes and sign up to take them. Some are one day long, and others are two or three days. This is a small investment that will pay great dividends. One nationwide organization that will improve your presentation skills immeasurably is Toastmasters. Virtually every city in the United States has a Toastmasters that offers new members the opportunity to enter at their own proficiency level. The skills learned in Toastmasters have produced great results in people's careers. In addition, there are financial benefits to being an effective public speaker.

It is important to practice your presentation skills long before you testify in court. If you fail to hone your communication skills, you may see your work fall on deaf ears as jurors begin to lose interest in you. Law enforcement personnel and attorneys have put a great deal of work into their case and your testimony is part of that work. Too much is riding on the outcome

Summary of Rule 4

No matter how you feel in front of the room or how nervous you may be on the witness stand, your audience will not be aware of how nervous you are. Remember this important caveat: Do not tell them.

to fail in conveying your work results and opinions. You must be prepared so that there is no risk of any one juror not understanding your testimony. If this one juror fails to follow or understand your testimony due to your inability to convey your information, then the process may result in a hung jury.

There are two final suggestions for improving your presentation skills. The first is to watch others speak or testify. Record the skills you find particularly interesting and incorporate them into your next presentation. If the techniques or skills you observed do not seem to work for you, then drop them and learn some new ones. Some experimentation is required before one develops his or her own unique style. The second suggestion is to practice, practice, and then practice some more. It is only through employing the skills and techniques mentioned previously that one eventually becomes a confident and persuasive public speaker.

THE LEGAL PROCESS FOR EXPERT TESTIMONY

This chapter covers the process that the expert witness undergoes when called to testify in a jury trial. There are some slight differences in a bench trial, in which the judge becomes the trier of fact instead of jurors. The most significant difference for the expert in a bench trial is that he should endeavor to direct some of his testimony toward the judge. Some judges find the forensic evidence interesting and will follow your every word. It is important to include them in your answers and it gives you the opportunity to determine if they are following you. Some judges are not as interested and you may find yourself only glancing at them from time to time. Generally, judges signal early on in your testimony whether they are interested or not. Follow their lead. The following discussion will lead the reader through the process from the subpoena to posttrial review.

Before witnesses are called to testify at trial, there are administrative matters requiring action by the court. The prosecutor and defense attorney may have motions before the court ranging from a request to dismiss all charges to seeking further discovery or having evidence excluded from the trial process. These legal matters may be taken up prior to empanelling a jury or just after according to custom or policy. After these matters are resolved, the attorneys are permitted to begin jury selection. All jurors go through a process of *voir dire* before being allowed to serve as a witness. Their voir dire is different from an expert's voir dire process. They are challenged on their knowledge, bias, or familiarity with the participants in a particular trial. Attorneys have challenges they can exercise to eliminate certain jurors who they believe would not support their position. Judges may grant more challenges in capital murder cases than they would in a drunken driving case. At the conclusion of this process, jurors are asked to stand and be sworn in.

Once they take an oath as jurors, they are given specific instructions on how to conduct themselves during the trial process. Jurors are instructed not to discuss the case among themselves until instructed by the judge. They may not read about the case in the newspaper or watch news programs about the case on television. They may not conduct independent research or experiments to answer questions they may have about the evidence. In some cases, jurors may be sequestered to avoid any influences that might affect their deliberation. Alternates may be chosen in the event a juror falls ill or is removed for misconduct. These alternates may sit in the jury box along with the regularly empanelled jury. Custom may dictate the exact location where the alternates will sit.

As soon as this process is completed, the prosecutor will make an opening statement. The prosecutor is required to outline the criminal case for the jury, giving them a time line of the events leading up to, during, and after the crime. In addition, the prosecutor will list the witnesses who will appear on behalf of the State. The defense attorney may choose to make her opening statement immediately after the prosecutor or at a later time that best suits her case. Generally, this will occur before she presents her case to the jury.

It is my intention to allay some of the concerns that experts have about testifying through this overview. It will assist forensic experts on those occasions when they find themselves reporting on the results of their work. This guide focuses on courtroom testimony. Becoming familiar with the legal jargon heard in the courtroom will alleviate many of the concerns witnesses have while in the courtroom.

The prosecutor assigned to a criminal case will issue a legal document, called a subpoena, requesting a witness's attendance at trial. An expert witness may receive dozens of subpoenas throughout the year and only testify in a small percentage of trials. The prosecutor or district attorney directs a member of her staff to send the subpoena to the laboratory. The date of appearance is usually the date the trial commences. It may be days or even weeks before the expert is required to present his testimony.

It is highly recommended that the expert contact the prosecutor after receiving the subpoena to request a pretrial conference if one has not already been arranged. The expert should find out approximately when he will be needed to testify and whether his testimony will be challenged on cross-examination. Occasionally, the evidence may not be vigorously challenged by defense counsel, which may alleviate some concern on the part

Pretrial note

A meeting with the prosecutor is vital to your success and comfort on the witness stand. Whether by phone or in person, this is your opportunity to find out as much as possible about the case. This meeting will allow you the opportunity to see how your work, conclusions, and interpretations fit into the prosecutor's presentation of his case. You can provide a copy of your qualification mind map at this time. Additionally, if you are unfamiliar with the court you will be testifying in, it is recommended to arrive early and become acquainted with the layout prior to your testimony. Check to see if there is a place to post your visual aid, whether there are any push pins, and whether there are marking pens in the event you need to write on your visual aid. Check to see if there is a microphone and how close or how far away you will be from the jury box.

Strategy 1

Place tabs on important sections of your case file for quick and easy access to information. This will prevent thumbing back and forth looking for data when called upon to do so. Your ability to quickly reference information at a moment's notice is impressive and much appreciated by everyone in the courtroom.

of the witness. That does not mean that the defense attorney will avoid cross-examining the witness. It just means that the evidence is not contentious and the witness may not be vigorously challenged in court. The expert should also determine whether the evidence has been independently reviewed or reexamined by another expert.

Prior to trial the expert should review her case file and take a thorough inventory of the information and data to ensure completeness. In particularly difficult cases, in which other members of the laboratory may be working on the same case, they will have their notes and test results in the same folder. The expert should make three copies of everything contained in the file relating to her work only. It is advised not to take the original file to court because it may end up being submitted as evidence and never seen again. The three copies are for the prosecutor, the defense attorney, and the court should they request one. Being prepared by having additional copies sends an important message to everyone in the courtroom that the witness is prepared.

One of the most important qualities of successful expert witnesses is that they know their communication requires them to speak at a level of understanding possessed by their audience—that is, the jurors. Since the expert witness cannot always be certain of the audience's knowledge level, he should endeavor to err on the side of their knowing much less than the expert. An expert witness should not assume that his audience knows as much as he does or that the audience even cares to know about the technical details. This is especially true with police officers, judges, and attorneys.

With the popularity of several TV series such as *CSI*, *Forensic Files*, and *Law and Order*, more people are aware of what forensic scientists, latent print examiners, and crime scene investigators do. They believe they have an understanding of the work conducted in the modern crime laboratory. Furthermore, they think that they comprehend the nature of the work and the types of results that can be obtained through scientific investigation. In reality, they do not possess the training and skill to fully comprehend and appreciate the work conducted by forensic examiners.

As much as people seem to know about forensic science and crime scene investigation, their understanding is extremely limited. It is imperative for the expert witness to avoid the use of technical terms and acronyms without explaining them. Some professional organizations have ethical standards for expert testimony that go to the heart of explaining the work in the jurors' common experience (California Association of Criminalists Handbook, 1957). Even experts in the same discipline find themselves unable or unwilling to communicate to other members in the same field.[2]

If experts are unable to communicate their technical ideas to one another, then they certainly will not be able to communicate those ideas and principles in a court of law. To solve this problem, it is incumbent upon the expert to practice her testimony on nonscientists. Another solution is to speak to a colleague in a different discipline to catch offending phrases, acronyms, and technical concepts that might surpass the jurors' level of understanding.

The opening statement allows each attorney the opportunity to present their respective cases and the steps they plan to take to complete their task. Generally, the prosecutor's case will be presented in a chronological fashion, taking careful steps to ensure that each witness builds the preceding witness. Sometimes, a witness may be taken out of order for any number of reasons, which can create some confusion for jurors. The judge will endeavor to explain to jurors why a particular witness is testifying out of order.

Included in the prosecutor's opening statement are the introductions of the various witnesses who have been subpoenaed to testify. All witnesses are subpoenaed to court in order to ensure their timely appearance. Prior to the expert's appearance at trial, the jurors will have been informed about the expert's credentials, examinations, and findings. Jurors will be told how the expert's results and opinions will play in the prosecutor's case.

Presenting the expert's work before a court and jury follows an age-old process. First, the witness gives a brief self-introduction—that is, name, position/title, employer, and business address. The next step is the presentation of the witness's resume or credentials that allow him to be "qualified" by the court to testify as an expert witness. This process allows the expert witness the opportunity to present his work as well as his opinions in a court of law. An expert's qualifications include his formal education—that is, where he received his university education and the degree(s) he obtained. Next comes the specific training courses in his area of expertise, any specialized training he has received, seminars and workshops attended, forensic study group meetings attended, and professional societies of which he is a member. The witness should endeavor to be as thorough as possible when providing her qualifications. These qualifications can also include other nonrelated degrees, training classes sponsored by her agency, military service, papers presented at seminars, and articles written to peer-reviewed journals.

In addition, the expert should be able to provide exact training dates, length of courses, instructors' names and credentials, as well as an overview of each training course. Rarely is an expert witness required to provide this level of detail in an ordinary criminal proceeding, but this may be the case

[2] Sitting through a technically challenging DNA presentation at a California Association of Criminalists meeting in 1995, I turned to a well-respected DNA expert sitting beside me and whispered, "Well at least you know what he is talking about." I was shocked when he replied, "I have no idea what the speaker is talking about!"

Strategy 2

It is an advantage to cite the names of these popular TV shows to bridge the gap between you and your audience. Their familiarity with the profession of forensic science will assist you in relating to them and finding common ground. In addition, by mentioning these successful programs you might be able to bask in their reflective glow.

Strategy 3

Prepare a brief statement of your credentials and give it to the prosecutor prior to trial. He can use it to properly introduce you to jurors prior to your arrival, and they will have an accurate assessment of who you are and the type of work you conducted as well as your role in the case.

in a high-profile or a highly contentious case. Being able to provide this level of detail when requested will not go unnoticed by attorneys and jurors alike. When the prosecutor believes he has presented sufficient information to qualify the expert, he may begin to ask direct examination questions.

If the defense attorney wishes to voir dire the witness, she must do so at this juncture. The defense attorney is under no obligation to proceed in a similar chronological fashion as the prosecutor should she wish to voir dire the witness. She may elect to conduct voir dire and cross-examination in a random manner. She may start at the end of the witness's account and move backward in time. She may start at some advantageous point for her case and move in either direction. The experienced expert witness tends to fare better during the voir dire process due to his previous courtroom experience.

Voir dire (French for "to see it and speak it") is a process utilized by opposing counsel to determine the merits of the witness's credentials and whether to permit the witness to testify as an expert. This allows for opposing counsel to "cross-examine" the witness on his qualifications. This process begins after the prosecutor has finished with the witness's qualifications, and it is the responsibility of the opposing counsel to ask the judge if they can voir dire the witness. It is not an automatic process. They either have to ask or in some cases the judge will make it a point to ask the defense attorney if she wishes to voir dire the witness. It is her decision to voir dire the witness or not. Rarely, the judge may ask additional questions of the expert witness to satisfy any concerns the court may have about the expert's credentials or ability to offer opinion evidence. It is usually the young and less experienced experts who get challenged in the voir dire process. On the other hand, opposing counsel may challenge an experienced witness through voir dire if that person proffers some fringe expertise or has had prior difficulties in court.

Opposing counsel may stipulate to the witnesses qualifications—that is, agrees that the witness is qualified to testify. This is generally not a favorable strategy for the experienced witness who may be deprived of the opportunity to present the full extent of his qualifications. Therefore, it is important to present a full and complete picture of your qualifications in the event opposing counsel chooses not to voir dire you.

Usually, voir dire is designed to plumb the depths or lack thereof regarding the witness's training and experience. This part of the expert's time on the witness stand should not be dreaded but anticipated. It is an opportunity to look even better in the eyes of jurors and attorneys by describing in detail the breadth and depth of the expert's training and experience. Prior to the expert's testimony and while stating her name for the record, it is important that she connect with the members of the jury.

Strategy 4

Although it is vital to present a complete picture of your qualifications to the court, it is advised not to go into such extensive detail that there is nothing to add in the event opposing counsel wishes to voir dire the witness. Therefore, you must judge how much information you want to present in the event there is no challenge to your qualifications. If there is a challenge, then jurors will be impressed by the extent of your qualifications as you thrive during voir dire.

Strategy 5

Align your chair slightly toward the jury panel. Then turn slightly back toward counsel and be ready to receive the question. After the question has been posed, begin your answer with the attorney and then slightly turn and face the jury. By facing them, you are now in the most comfortable and relaxed position for

Continues

After completing voir dire, the prosecutor may ask some follow-up questions. This may occur if opposing counsel has raised some concerns or doubts regarding the expert's level of competency or if the prosecutor wishes to have some information clarified for the benefit of the court. After completing qualifications, the prosecutor may ask the court to have the witness confirmed or declared as an expert within his discipline. Opposing counsel may or may not object at this point. If opposing counsel does take this opportunity to object, they will do so by stating that the witness should not be confirmed as an expert. Opposing counsel must cite a reason or reasons for denying permission to testify. They may cite a general lack of experience and training as the reason, or they may have some documentation reflecting the witness's bias or the witness's failure to qualify in a previous case as the basis for denying the expert permission to testify in court. Unless there is some egregious cause for denying an expert witness the right to testify, most judges overrule the attorney's objections and allow the witness to testify. In some cases, the judge may inform the jury that the court finds the expert well qualified to testify.

This strategy by opposing counsel may be to simply send a signal to jurors that he does not believe the witness is qualified and that the jurors should not believe the witness is qualified. Sometimes, this is done to "rattle the expert witness," to "get them off their game," or to "see how well they handle themselves" when confronted with this unsettling circumstance. Rest assured that 99.9 times out of 100 the judge will confirm the witness's expertise by stating, "The court rules (or finds) that the witness is an expert in the field of. . . ." By this statement, the judge is informing jurors as well as the witness that he or she is qualified to testify as an expert.

The most important element of being qualified as an expert witness is the ability to render opinion testimony and to be able to circumvent the hearsay rule. Experts are permitted to rely on scientific treatises and the opinions of others when offering their own opinions at trial. Seldom are witnesses granted permission to state an opinion that is routinely afforded technical experts.

It is well to remember that this confirmation of expertise only applies in the matter at hand. Every time an expert witness is called to testify, he must repeat the same process prior to giving expert (opinion) testimony. Witnesses may be asked in a casual manner if they consider themselves to be an expert. It is advised to avoid falling into this trap because only the court can confer "expertise" on a witness. The following is a good response to this question: "Based on my formal education, practical laboratory experience, crime scene experience, and previous courtroom testimony, I believe I am qualified to give expert testimony." Another good response is, "I do have

Continued

relaying information. Prior to completing your answer, turn back to the attorney as you finish your answer. This is your signal that you have completed your answer and are now ready for the next question. This technique is most useful during narrative portions of the testimony and should not be used when answering "yes" or "no" to questions.

Trial note

The expert witness should not be alarmed at this point. Opposing counsel has an absolute duty to ensure that each expert is well qualified to present fairly and accurately all scientific and technical information in court. Voir dire, cross-examination, and other challenges are part of the opposing attorney's job. They are expected to elicit as much information as possible. They are simply doing their job and you should take no offense. Junk science and poorly trained and unqualified experts are vigorously challenged in court. The best strategy for the witnesses is to maintain their composure during this phase of their testimony. The expert's equanimity on the witness stand will not go unnoticed by opposing counsel.

Strategy 6

At this point, the witness can breathe an inaudible sigh of relief and continue to maintain his composure. This is a routine courtroom procedure and should not be viewed as a reflection on the witness's credibility. Maintaining one's composure at this juncture is a sure sign of confidence not lost on opposing counsel and jurors.

Trial note

Do not be concerned at this point either. In most jurisdictions, the prosecutor may not feel the need to have the court confirm that the witness is an expert. Again, this is just a routine courtroom procedure.

more knowledge than a lay person in this field," or "It is a matter for the court to decide on my expertise." These responses allow you to answer the question without encroaching upon the court's authority. This respect for and deference to the court process will keep you in good stead with the judge and jurors.

In many cases, the prosecutor does not even bother asking the court (the judge) to have the witness declared an expert in her respective field or discipline. The prosecutor begins by asking direct examination questions about when the witness received the evidence, the work the witness was asked to perform, and the results or findings the witness has reached. This transition from qualifications to direct examination appears seamless to everyone in the courtroom. Only the witness is acutely aware of the fact that no definitive statement has been made confirming that the witness is an expert.

Just because the prosecutor does not ask to have the witness declared an expert witness in a case does not mean that the witness cannot testify to her examinations and findings. The witness's confirmation that she is indeed the expert comes with the first question on direct examination. When experts become adept at testifying and developing excellent communication skills, it becomes obvious to everyone in the courtroom that the witness is indeed the expert.

After qualifications have been completed, the prosecutor begins direct examination. This is the point in the trial at which the expert witness is asked to describe how and when he received the evidence, the work he was asked to perform, the results obtained, and the interpretations made. The expert is required to present his testimony with clarity, using understandable language employing examples and analogies in the jurors' common experience. The California Association of Criminalists (1990, Article IV, p. 22) has incorporated into its code of ethics a requirement that:

> Where the expert must prepare photographs or offer oral "background information" to the jury in respect to a specific type of analytical method, this information shall be reliable and valid, typifying the usual or normal basis for the method. The instructional material shall be of that level which will provide the jury with a proper basis for evaluating the subsequent evidence presentations, and not such as would provide them with a lower standard than the science demands.

The expert witness is encouraged to provide visual aids to assist in explaining her analytical results and interpretations. The visual aid should have a clear title or heading for jurors to follow and that assists in the expert's presentation of the evidence. The visual aid(s) has the added benefit of leaving something behind for jurors' consideration during their deliberations. Visual aids may be made at the prosecutor's prompting or by the witness. They may be made ahead of time or done at a moment's notice. If you are going to bring in a visual aid, it is recommended not to take it to the witness stand with you. There is a possibility that you may not be able to use it and jurors will wonder why you brought it with you. Also, if you are carrying your case file along with several visual aids, you might look over-burdened. Leave it with counsel ahead of time and they will bring it out when you request them to do so.

During direct examination you will be asked about the evidence you examined or tested and it is important to cite the court exhibit number. Being prepared ahead of time by cross-referencing your case item numbers with the court's exhibit numbers will facilitate your testimony and avoid any confusion during the trial process. Also, avoid using phrases such as "this package," "the white powder," and "this part here" without first referring to the exhibit number. The court recorder does not know what you are refer-ring to and will ask the judge to interrupt you for clarification. Your ability to smoothly transition from your case item numbers to the court's exhibit numbers will make you appear more professional.

During the course of testimony, whether direct or cross-examination, sit-uations arise in which the witness can take advantage and inject some humor. On these rare occasions, humor will and should be a part of the courtroom process. Incredibly funny things happen in the courtroom just because people are involved in the asking and answering of questions. To be effective, this humor should be spontaneous and directed back at the expert witness. The following are examples:

A toxicologist was asked about his DUI experience and mentioned that he spent several nights in the drunk tank at the county jail. Then realizing what he had just said quickly added, "As an observer of course." To everyone's delight.

An expert was performing a calculation on the board in front of the jury and when he multiplied two times three and came up with five, one of the juror's spoke up and said "you mean six." The expert turned around and said, "Well, so much for being an expert!" Everyone laughed, noting the expert's self-possession.

An expert witness lost some focus during voir dire and asked the defense attorney to rephrase the question. "Certainly, what is your name?" Everyone burst out laughing, including the witness, who exclaimed, "I guess I need to pay more attention here."

After the witness has completed direct examination, the prosecutor usually states to the court, "I have no further questions at this time your Honor." The judge then turns to opposing counsel and asks, "Counselor, do you have any questions for the witness?" If yes, then it is time for

Trial note

Always remember this vital fact about jurors: They are not forensic scientists, latent print examiners, or crime scene investigators. Even if they possess some scientific training or knowledge in another scientific field, they do not really understand the work that is conducted at the crime scene or in the crime laboratory. It is up to you to help them understand the science you used and the significance of your findings. Visual aids, demonstrative evidence, role playing, and other techniques are used to assist the jurors' understanding. There may, of course, be a scientist on the jury. That juror may or may not explain things to the other jurors, but he will know if you are following good scientific practices.

Strategy 7

Self-effacing humor spontaneously uttered is greatly appreciated by jurors. Humor reduces the tension in the courtroom, which many jurors struggle with during a trial. In addition, humor confirms a high regard upon the witness for her ability to appear "normal" and acting cool under fire. Avoid telling jokes or funny stories in order to get a laugh. Humor always works when it is spontaneous and used on the witness.

opposing counsel to cross-examine the expert on his work, findings, and interpretations. They may try to put the expert's work in an unfavorable light. They may try to minimize the forensic significance of the expert's findings, or they may suggest other possibilities or outcomes for the witness's results. They will challenge the objectivity of the witness and whether his "collusion" with the police and the prosecutor may have created a bias in his results, or that there may be some financial gain for his testimony.

It is vital that the expert witness not view this period as a personal attack but, instead, view it as opposing counsel's responsibility to present their case in the light most favorable for their client. Remember, attorneys have their agendas and expert witnesses are only a small part of the trial process. Do not assume you know the entire case along with the testimony of all the witnesses. In order for attorneys to be successful in the courtroom, each witness must tell the truth in the most objective manner possible. Sometimes the questions are ambiguous. Sometimes the questions make absolutely no sense, and other times the questions have already been asked and answered. Your ability to calmly and professionally answer difficult and nettlesome questions with aplomb goes to your credibility as a witness.

Opposing counsel may go over the same question several times, hoping for a different answer or to see if the expert becomes impatient and upset. They do not care if they make the witness angry or break down in tears. In fact, they would not mind at all if the witness became upset and angry. Once a witness loses his calm demeanor on the witness stand, the opposing attorney has effectively neutralized his effectiveness as an expert. More often than not, attorneys are looking at "how" witnesses respond to their questions as well as the answers themselves.

Occasionally, there may be no cross-examination. Do not be surprised if the opposing counsel states, "No questions, your Honor." If the expert's testimony is not contentious, there may be no need to challenge the witness on her findings. Sometimes, the witness's testimony is required to make a legal record in case of a future appeal or a mistrial. Technically, opposing counsel is not allowed to ask about anything not presented during direct testimony. The attorney may ask the court to allow him the opportunity to cover some material outside the scope of direct examination. Depending on the nature of the trial, some judges may grant some latitude to opposing counsel but keep them on a short leash.

After cross-examination, the prosecutor may only go over points raised by opposing counsel. This is called redirect examination. The prosecutor cannot conduct redirect based on topics he failed to raise on direct. Should he wish to do so, he can ask the judge to grant him permission to ask about new material on redirect. Occasionally, judges may allow the prosecutor

Trial note

It is a common practice for attorneys to meet with their respective witnesses prior to trial. After all, they need to know ahead of time what their witnesses will testify to. The expert witness who meets with the prosecutor prior to trial attends a "pretrial conference." This is not collusion unless the witness intends or allows the attorney to cause her to alter her findings in order to support one side or the other in the trial. The same applies to defense counsel who meet with their expert to go over his anticipated testimony. Neither expert is allowed to adjust their work product, conclusions, or opinions in order to obtain a desired verdict.

Strategy 8

One way to counter this tactic is to carefully listen to the question and then state, "Counsel, as I said before . . ." to send a message to the judge, jury, and counsel about the repetitive nature of the questions. It is also helpful to have the opportunity to repeat an answer but not to the point of frustrating the witness.

some latitude in presenting his case, granting him some flexibility due to the burden he faces in proving the defendant's guilt beyond a reasonable doubt.

The prosecutor may take this step for several reasons. Perhaps something opposing counsel brought up needs more clarification or needs deeper treatment, or the prosecutor may find a need to rehabilitate the witness if she believes that opposing counsel has taken some liberties with the witness's credibility or with the significance of the evidence. To employ a metaphor here, the prosecutor will heal the witness's wounds, apply a new coat of paint, and make the witness sparkle like the knight in shining armor he started out as. This has happened to many experts, young and old alike, and will continue to happen as scientists provide technical expertise in courts of law.

Occasionally, opposing counsel may re-cross-examine the expert witness. The witness should be patient and understanding as she continues to be examined on points she believes were made perfectly clear earlier in her testimony. At this point, if the expert finds herself repeating answers to questions she has already answered during cross-examination, she should avoid making statements such as "As I've already said . . ." or "As I've previously stated. . . ." Repeating one's answers, without pointing out the repetition, is an opportunity for jurors to remember and recall the expert's testimony. This repetition increases the audience's retention of the technical information being provided. Take advantage of this opportunity to drive home the importance of the work conducted. The expert should consider not only repeating the answer but also rephrasing it so that jurors will have a deeper understanding. Jurors do not mind some repetition of the testimony, particularly when that testimony deals with scientific principles, analytical testing, and opinion testimony. It can be trying when counsel repeatedly asks the same question hoping for a different answer.

Finally, the witness will know when his time on the witness stand has come to an end when the attorneys state to the judge, "No further questions, your Honor." The judge, being a thorough professional, will ask if there are any further questions of the expert witness. Hearing none, the judge informs the witness that he may step down and that he is excused from the courtroom. That is the witness's cue to leave the witness stand and depart. Alternatively, the judge may ask the witness just to step down from the witness stand. This directive does not imply that the witness is allowed to leave the courtroom. It just means he is asked to step down but not leave the courtroom.

The prosecutor may wish to have you hear the testimony of another witness. The exception to this directive is if there is a court ruling to exclude witnesses. The expert must ask the judge for permission to leave the

Trial note

Restating an important fact about trial attorneys: They have an absolute duty to present their evidence in the light most favorable to their respective clients, whether it is for the government or for the defendant. They are not required, bound, or obligated to present the evidence the way the expert sees it.

Strategy 9

Take this brief period of rehabilitation in a relaxed, self-confident manner and allow jurors to see you in the most favorable light possible. After all, it is the prosecutor's responsibility to make you look and sound like the professional you aspire to be.

Strategy 10

As you leave the witness stand, remember to smile at the jurors as you pass them on your way out of the courtroom. You will notice them smiling back and giving you a final nod of approval. Then depart with purpose.

Strategy 11

All witnesses, particularly expert witnesses, should always be gracious and accommodating in the courtroom. Remember that everyone is watching how you behave and observing your overall courtroom demeanor. From the time you arrive at the courtroom, through your testimony, to your departure from the courthouse, you are being observed.

Trial note

The expert witness should remember this final and important fact about testifying in court: You are a guest in the courtroom. You have been invited into their home (the courtroom). As a good guest, you should at all times play by the rules of your host. It does not mean you have to like the rules. It is the expert's opportunity to be informative, helpful, clear, patient, cheerful, and respectful at all times. This behavior is much admired and appreciated by all the participants in the courtroom. The expert's decorum will be remembered long after he has left the courtroom by both the judge and counsel. This respectful behavior will make life a little easier the next time the witness testifies.

courtroom if the judge does not make it clear that the witness can leave. Also, you may be asked to step down and wait outside subject to recall. That means you are not to leave the courthouse until instructed to do so. Again, if you are "excused" you may remain because you are finished as a witness in this case; if you are "excused, subject to recall" you must leave the courtroom. If you are not certain of what to do, turn to the judge and ask, "May I be excused your Honor?"

Occasionally, the prosecutor may want to shake the witness's hand and commend her on doing a fine job in front of the jury. The expert should offer her hand in return and say, "You're welcome." There is no need to make any comments such as "I'm just doing my job" or "It was a pleasure to serve as a witness." Just shake his hand and leave. In some cases, opposing counsel may want to shake the witness's hand and commend her on doing a fine job. Opposing counsel may want to seem like a nice person to jurors, especially after having grilled the witness during cross-examination. Again, the witness should offer her hand in return and say, "You're welcome." The fact that defense attorneys have less than wholesome, credible clients does not imply that they are cut from the same cloth. They are professionals, well schooled, trained, and licensed to practice law and to represent their clients in a court of law. Without them, there would be no criminal justice system. Remember, they are doing their job, and by your fair and impartial testimony, you are doing yours.

When the expert returns to the laboratory, she should debrief with a colleague or supervisor about her courtroom experience. Perhaps the expert was challenged with some difficult questions and she is curious how another colleague would have handled them. Also, after the trial, the expert is advised to get some feedback from the prosecutor and then incorporate all the feedback, especially that from her colleagues, into her next courtroom experience.

It is also a good idea to get some feedback from the defense attorney should the opportunity arise. If the defense attorney is willing to offer some feedback, it can have an immeasurable impact the next time the expert goes to court. This is particularly true when expert witnesses face off with the same defense attorney time and time again. This is how successful expert witnesses build their reputations in the legal community.

Although the expert's duty has been completed and he has returned to work, the trial is still proceeding toward a verdict. The trial may go on for another day, week, or perhaps even months before there is a verdict. Additionally, newly discovered evidence, a defense expert's report, or some other problem may arise during the trial requiring the expert witness to assist the prosecutor, either by phone or by testifying again in the same matter. Until the case has been adjudicated, it is important that the expert witness not disclose the details of the trial to the public. When asked to retake the witness stand, the judge will remind the expert witness, the court recorder, as well as the jurors that the expert is still under oath. The judge may ask the witness if she discussed her testimony with anyone. The witness should respond truthfully. For example, the witness might say, "Yes, your Honor there were certain questions posed during my cross-examination that I shared with a colleague and I wanted her to evaluate my responses." Do not elaborate any further. Let the judge inquire as to the depth of the discussion. If it seems imperative, then reassure the court that you did not discuss any elements of the case with the public.

At the conclusion of the trial, the judge will make a general statement regarding the credibility of the witnesses who gave their testimony and the weight that should be given to their testimony during the jurors' deliberations.[3] Just because you were sworn in as an expert witness and gave truthful testimony does not mean that jurors will give any more consideration to your testimony than that of any other witness. Judges instruct jurors that expert testimony is not an absolute. They can consider the testimony during their deliberations or completely disregard it.

The expert should add a page to his case file indicating that he testified on the case. He should record the date, time, and place of testimony. It is also helpful to add the counsel's names along with that of the judge. There are occasions when the expert is called back to testify in the same case perhaps years later as a result of an appeal or a mistrial. Another reason for adding these data is that another colleague in the same laboratory may be working on the same case. Generally, laboratories use one case file even though they may have more than one person assigned to it. It is important

Strategy 12

Always address the judge as "your Honor" in the courtroom, even if the judge is an old friend or you knew him when he worked in the district attorney's office. Show respect to both attorneys as well. You can call them "sir" or "madam," "counselor," or, more formally, "Mr." or "Ms." Maintain this level of decorum outside the courtroom as well.

Strategy 13

It is vital to build on your experience. Avoid repeating the same formula even if it is working for you. Keeping the testimony fresh and your interest level high will send a powerful message to everyone in the courtroom that you enjoy testifying and that jurors should give due consideration to and place a high value on your work.

Posttrial note

Expert witnesses are permitted, even encouraged, to discuss their testimony with another colleague regarding the questions that were posed to them and their responses. They are discouraged from discussing the facts in the case and any information provided by the prosecutor that could create a problem for both the prosecutor and the witness at some future date.

[3] Superior Court County of Sacramento California CALJIC 2.20 Credibility of Witness:

Every person who testifies under oath is a witness. You are the sole judges of the believability of a witness and the weight to be given the testimony of each witness.
In determining the believability of a witness you may consider anything that has a tendency in reason to prove or disprove the truthfulness of the testimony of the witness, including but not limited to any of the following:
The extent of the opportunity or ability of the witness to see or hear or otherwise become aware of any matter about which the witness has testified;
The ability of the witness to remember or to communicate any matter about which the witness has testified
The character and quality of that testimony
The demeanor and manner of the witness while testifying
The existence or nonexistence of a bias, interest, or other motive
Evidence of the existence or nonexistence of any fact testified to by the witness
The attitude of the witness toward this action or toward the giving of testimony
A statement previously made by the witness that is (consistent) or (inconsistent) with the testimony of the witness
The character of the witness for honesty or truthfulness or their opposites
An admission by the witness of untruthfulness

Strategy 14

Keep a record of every trial in which you testify. That record should include the name of the defendant, where it was held, and the nature of the testimony (e.g., toxicology, drugs, rape, and firearms). Experts are often asked about their prior courtroom experience and the nature of the cases in which they have testified. Include any pretrial testimony, depositions, civil and grand jury appearances, and military court martial trials.

that everyone assigned to a particular case be aware of another colleague's testimony in that case.

In the event the expert is subpoenaed to testify in a retrial, the expert is advised to obtain a copy of the trial transcript containing her testimony. That testimony should be reviewed and any mistakes or errors corrected and noted. Often, an errata sheet will be provided along with a copy of the witness's transcript. This sheet is designed to register any errors for later correction. These errors are created when the court recorder tries to write down technical terms and scientific concepts that are not well-defined or spelled out. Then the expert should have a follow-up discussion with the prosecutor prior to trial to go over these errors. This is particularly true if a new analytical technique or methodology has been implemented since the last testimony or a scientific journal article casts doubt or supports the techniques used. It is vital that the testimony the second time around mirror the testimony from the first trial as much as possible. Any significant differences may result in a challenging cross-examination. The expert can be assured that the opposing attorney will have a copy of the expert's previous testimony and will use it to his advantage should there be any significant differences.

An expert's courtroom experience will ultimately be as valuable as her university degree when in the courtroom. A note of caution: It is not important to specify the exact nature of the cases in which you have testified. Simply state that "I have previously testified on the examination, identification, and interpretation of physical evidence." If counsel requires specifics about the cases in which you have testified, then you will be prepared to provide them because you have kept an accurate account of your courtroom experience. Your courtroom experience becomes invaluable to you because you know what to expect. The fact that you have qualified once or 100 times does not qualify you to testify on any particular case. You must go through the process every time you take the witness stand. If for some reason you fail to qualify in a particular case or in a particular area of your expertise, you can expect vigorous challenges in the future. It is imperative that you determine the reasons behind any disqualifications because they will certainly follow you throughout your career.

Testifying to one's work is the most compelling reason to be a forensic expert. To have the opportunity to provide information that will assist jurors in rendering decisions without confusion is the ultimate challenge and reward. Testifying can also be the most perilous event in one's career if the witness fails to communicate the precise nature and impact of his work on a particular case.

A final call to arms: Give as much effort to become the most effective witness you can be as you do in the work you are called on to perform.

QUALIFICATION QUESTIONS FOR THE EXPERT WITNESS

The following are typical questions most experts encounter at trial. For the less experienced expert, both the prosecutor and the defense attorney may utilize most of the questions listed here. The prosecutor will ask the types of questions that show the breadth of the witness's expertise, whereas the defense attorney will ask the types of questions that plumb the depths of the witness's expertise. For the more experienced experts, a much more abbreviated version may be utilized. In some cases, opposing counsel may not voir dire the witness at all. Your qualifications can be divided into four general areas. This courtroom procedure will ensure that each witness passes the court's requirement of "expert witness" and is therefore qualified to testify to his or her analytical results and interpretations and to offer opinion testimony. This process also serves to introduce the witness to the jurors.

Qualifications (Direct Examination of Expertise)

Area 1: Identification/Associations

What is your name?

By whom are you employed?

How long have you been employed by _____?

What is your business address?

What is your position or title?

What is your area of expertise?

Do you have other areas of expertise in addition to the current one?

What are they?

How long have you practiced in your area of expertise?

Were you previously employed by another law enforcement agency?

If yes, for whom and how long?

Area 2: Expertise

Would you please state your qualifications for the court/jury? (formal education, on-the-job training, specific training courses within the discipline, workshops taken, seminars attended, continuing education classes, university graduate programs, etc.)

Do you belong to any professional organizations?

Have you previously qualified as an expert in this field? In other fields?

How many times?

Do you present and/or publish technical papers to your peers? When and where?

Do you train other technical members of your staff?

Please specify areas of training.

What is the most recent training you've received in your area of expertise?

What was the last article you read in your discipline?

Area 3: Laboratory

Is your laboratory accredited?

If yes, by what organization and for how long?

Does your laboratory participate in an independent proficiency testing program? Which one(s)?

Do you routinely undergo proficiency testing yourself?

If so, what types of proficiency tests have you been assigned?

How many proficiency tests have you participated in the past _____ years?

What have been the results of your proficiency tests?

Are your case reports peer/supervisory/administratively reviewed? By whom?

Area 4: Personal

Have you received any awards or commendations for your work? (employee of the month, top case producer, meritorious service award, etc.)

Have you received any honors from the university you attended? (summa cum laude, etc.)

Are you undergoing any continuing education programs? (master's degree, etc.)

Are you a military veteran? (Which of the armed forces and for how long?)

Did you have a previous or related career prior to joining your agency? (former chemistry teacher, Peace Corps volunteer, pharmacist, etc.)

Voir Dire (Cross-Examination of Expertise)

Area 1

Are you currently on probation?

Were you placed on probation when you began your career?

How long were you on probation?

Is that standard for all employees to be placed on probation?

Why does your agency put its employees on probation?

Are you a law enforcement officer?

Did you leave your former employer on favorable terms?

How long did you work for your former employer?

Why did you leave your former employer?

Are you being paid to testify today?

If no, then are you here on your own time?

Have you ever failed to qualify as an expert? When and where?

Area 2

Do you consider yourself an expert?

Did you take any specific courses during your university studies in your area of expertise?

Who were the principal instructors in the following courses you took: _____?

When did you take these courses?

How long were they?

Were tests given to assess your level of comprehension?

What grades did you receive for these courses?

How long have you been a member of your professional organization?

Why are you not a member of any professional organization?

Have you attended any meetings?

Do you only attend meetings your agency pays for?

Do you participate in any of the committees of your organization?

Who pays for your dues?

Do you receive any literature from your organization(s)?

What was the last article you read in your discipline?

Who were the authors?

Are you qualified to train other experts?

What are your qualifications to be an instructor?

Isn't it a fact that you have never qualified as an expert before?

How much time do you devote to reviewing journal articles?

Area 3

Isn't it a fact that your laboratory/agency is not accredited?

Why has the laboratory not been accredited?

Does your agency plan on being accredited in the near future?

Do you participate in a proficiency testing program?

Why have you not participated in a proficiency testing program?

How do you know if you are conducting your examinations properly?

Have you ever made a mistake on a proficiency test?

If so, please describe your mistake and the steps you took to correct it.

Have you ever made a mistake in any case you have worked?

How was the mistake brought to your attention?

How can this jury be assured that you did not commit an error in this case?

Did you meet with the prosecutor to go over your testimony?

When did you meet?

If yes, then what did the prosecutor tell you to say?

What did the prosecutor want you to testify to?

Did he/she give you any explicit instructions prior to your testimony?

Area 4

You don't have any advanced degrees do you?

You're not a doctor are you?

Do you plan on obtaining an advance degree? If so, when?

You didn't graduate with honors did you?

You're not a published author are you?

Do you have any work-related hobbies outside your employment?

What is your current salary?

How much are you being paid to testify today?

As a government witness, how can you be a fair and unbiased witness?

Redirect on your qualifications may occur if the attorney believes more detail is required to meet the court's standards for qualifying you as an expert witness.

REFERENCES

California Association of Criminalists, *Code of Ethics*. California Association of Criminalists, 1990.

California Association of Criminalists Handbook, *Code of Ethics, Section III, Ethical Aspects of Court Presentation*. pp. 11–13, California Association of Criminalists, 1957. Available on-line at http://www.cacnews.org/pdfs/Membership%20Handbook.pdf

Konieczka, R. The 59-Second Mind Map. Seattle, WA: Hara Publishing Group, 1995.

CHAPTER 14

RECONSTRUCTIONISTS IN A POST-*DAUBERT* AND POST-DNA COURTROOM

Craig M. Cooley, MS, JD

> In order to preserve the integrity of the criminal justice system . . . particularly in the face of rising nationwide criticism of forensic evidence in general . . . state courts . . . must . . . cull scientific fiction and junk science from fact.
> —*Ramirez v. State* [810 So. 2d 836, 853 (Fla. 2001)]

> Time after time it was the expert witness, learned or ignorant in forensic medicine, careful or perfunctory, concerned or casual, who in effect determined whether the accused perished on the gallows, were transported for forced labor in the colonies, or went free.
> —Forbes (1985, pp. 1–2)

Forensic science, in the broadest sense, is the "application of scientific principles and technological principles to the purposes of justice in the study and resolution of criminal, civil, and regulatory issues" (Sapir, 2002, p. 2). In particular, forensic science attempts to uncover the actions or happenings of an event, typically a crime, by way of (1) identification (categorization), (2) individualization, (3) association, and (4) reconstruction of the physical evidence (Inman and Rudin, 2000, pp. 75–79). For more than a century, prosecutors, defense attorneys, and trial judges have relied heavily on these four aspects of forensic science to help establish a criminal defendant's guilt or innocence (Mitchell, 1911; Thorwald, 1964). From Alphonso Bertillon's system of anthropometry (Bayle, 1931; Rhodes, 1956) to the present-day utilization of DNA technology (Connors et al., 1996; National Institute of Justice, 2002), the legal system has faithfully called upon forensic scientists, including reconstructionists, to help answer the questions that beset our criminal justice system. To the forensic community's credit, history has shown that even complex evidentiary issues can be answered when qualified and ethical forensic scientists using validated methods, techniques, and technologies examine physical evidence.

Although reconstructionists and other forensic examiners are influential players in the criminal justice system, their roles at trial and subsequent expectations regarding their findings have rapidly evolved during the past 20 years, principally in the past decade. This evolution can be directly linked to a number of factors, but there are two in particular: the DNA revolution and the *Daubert* insurgency in regard to admitting expert testimony at trial. This chapter's primary objective is to educate the reconstructionist as to how these revolutionary changes and other converging circumstances have transformed the various forensic science working environments and how they will continue to impact the nature of reconstruction methods and courtroom presentations. It also recommends specific reforms vital to the reconstructionist's survival as an expert forensic witness.

It is important to understand that this chapter is written from the perspective of a practicing defense attorney who also holds a number of advanced forensic credentials. It is therefore not an uninformed shot at the forensic community, nor is it intended to help zealous advocates unilaterally bar all forensic experts from court testimony. Rather, it is meant to realistically educate the reconstructionist regarding the nature and measure of the toughest challenges that will confront his or her evidence at the gates of the court in its attempt to screen for fraud and error.

If the reconstructionist believes that he has a firm grasp of all relevant courtroom issues, and that he is well prepared to answer challenges from any of the lions at the gate of expert testimony, then I understand why he may not be inclined to read further. However, if the reconstructionist believes that this is an area in which he lacks preparedness, or in which he wishes to do better by virtue of advancing his craft through good scientific practice, then he is encouraged to read on.

FORENSIC SCIENCE UNDER SCRUTINY

For much of the 20th century, judges, prosecutors, and attorneys infrequently scrutinized the individualizing and reconstructive claims and qualifications of forensic experts.[1] Although various reasons subsist as to why these legal actors did not forcefully and repeatedly challenge such evidence, it is undeniable that this lack of scrutiny has permitted the forensic community to operate below the radar. Left unchecked by the courts, too many in the forensic community have grown and evolved believing that they are immune to error, and therefore free from it. Subsequently, there have been more than a few forensic examiners, and disciplines, that have felt justified in portraying themselves as essentially infallible.[2] This portrayal has in turn perpetuated the apathetic approach that courts, prosecutors, and defense attorneys have historically taken. These circumstances have also fostered an unsettling and nonscientific atmosphere in which much of the forensic community does not feel obligated to conduct research and substantiate the certainty of their claims.[3] Moreover, these circumstances have created a culture

[1] Berger (1994, p. 1353) noted that "considerable forensic evidence made its way into the courtroom without empirical validation of the underlying theory and/or its particular application."

[2] This campaign continued into the early 1990s with DNA technology. As Professor William C. Thompson and Dan E. Krane (2004, p. 68) note, "Promoters of forensic DNA testing have done a good job selling the public, and even many defense attorneys, on the idea that DNA tests provide a unique and infallible identification." Even in the face of rising criticism stemming from notable misidentifications (e.g., Brandon Mayfield and Stephen Cowans), the fingerprint community's infallibility campaign seems stronger than ever. See Simon A. Cole (2005).

[3] Adina Schwartz (2005) noted that "the discipline of firearms and tool mark examination has not developed the requisite statistical empirical foundations for identity claims." Sargur N. Srihari et al. (2002, p. 856) stated, "The individuality of writing in handwritten notes and documents has not been established with scientific rigor."

in which forensic examiners feel justified in attesting to statistics, reenactments, and interpretations that often have little, if any, foundation in science or logic. Until recently, the defense community, which is in no small part responsible for checking the findings of state forensic personnel, has taken little notice of this.

The winds of change have been steadily accelerating during the past decade, as an increasing number of legal actors (e.g., defense attorneys, judges, and scientists) have started to investigate and question the accuracy of forensic methodologies, as well as the nature of testimony regarding evidence interpretations. There are at least eight reasons why this tidal wave of scrutiny has come crashing down on the forensic community, including the following:

The advent of DNA technology
Noticeable correlation between forensic misidentifications and wrongful convictions
Crime lab crisis
Escalating discovery of forensic fraud
Escalating discovery of forensic incompetence
The media's impact on potential jurors
Increased forensic awareness of criminal defense attorneys
Daubert revolution in regard to the admission of expert testimony

Reconstructionists are obligated to understand the context of each of these items because they directly affect their work. This section therefore provides a discussion of the issues and their interrelation.

DNA TECHNOLOGY AND THE DNA WARS

The advent of DNA technology was (and has been) a double-edged sword for the forensic science community. Although DNA represents an individualizing technique that has a legitimate foundation in science, it has inadvertently exposed the forensic community's many shortcomings. Despite the aforementioned century-long public relations pitch that proclaimed that forensic techniques were infallible and premised on established scientific principles, it has become clear that neither is true. This undisclosed reality began surfacing when DNA scientists were hired by defense attorneys to litigate the "DNA wars" of the late 1980s and early 1990s (Thompson, 1993). Defense attorneys, along with trial courts, learned that Ph.D. educated geneticists and DNA experts approached forensic issues, particularly the question of individuality, in a radically different manner than "police scientists" (e.g., fingerprint, tool mark, and handwriting examiners). Rather than approaching forensic issues (e.g., individuality) in an experienced-based, binary manner ("it is a match or it is not a match because my experience says so"), these scientists relied on statistics and controlled empirical proficiency studies to qualify their opinions as to whether a DNA sample from a crime scene could have originated from a particular criminal defendant. This new approach to dealing with associative forensic evidence, in which actual scientists provide qualified probabilistic opinions premised on hard research and experimentation, led many legal commentators and observers to question why police scientists had yet to endorse such an approach.[4]

This was the time when defense attorneys, and the courts, began to attenuate themselves to the differences between science, reconstructions based on scientific evidence, and evidentiary interpretations based merely on unchallenged or unqualified examiner experience.

FORENSIC MISIDENTIFICATIONS AND WRONGFUL CONVICTIONS

Aside from revealing a persistent lack of actual science and scientific methodology in the forensic identification sciences, the DNA revolution unquestionably debunked the notion of forensic examiner infallibility.[5] To

[4] Saks and Koehler (1991) comment on the stark difference between the DNA community and the "police sciences." For example, consider how the Florida Supreme Court described this binary, experienced-based process:

The State's experts testified that an identification under this procedure is a subjective judgment that is based entirely on the examiner's experience and training. For instance, at the Frye hearing below, Hart testified as follows [Ramirez v. State, 810 So. 2d 836. 851 n.45 (Fla. 2001)]:

THE COURT: But it is not— you keep using the word criteria, but from what you are telling me, there isn't a criteria. There is a sense that you have enough training, you look at it and you say this is a match, this is not a match. Is that it?

THE WITNESS: Basically that is correct. There is not a numerical count score. . . .

[5] The "infallibility" claim is still routinely made by publicly employed forensic examiners. See, for example (Koehler, 1993, quoting a number of similar statements from DNA analysts), *United States v. Crisp*, 324 F. 3d 261, 268 n.4 (4th Cir. 2003) ("Brannan, the [Government's] fingerprint expert, testified to achieving perfect scores on all of her proficiency tests."); *United States v. Havvard*, 260 F. 3d 597, 599 (7th Cir. 2001) ("[FBI examiner] Meager . . . testified that the error rate for fingerprint comparison is essentially zero."); *United States v. Ewell*, 252 F. Supp. 2d 104, 113 (D.N.J. 2003) ("The [FBI] has demonstrated the scientific method [of DNA analysis] has a virtually zero rate of error."); *United States v. Sullivan*, 246 F. Supp. 2d 700, 703 (E.D. Ky. 2003) (noting that the FBI examiner "asserts that the rate of error for the ACE-V methodology is essentially zero."); *United States v. Lewis*, 220 F. Supp. 2d 548, 554 (S.D.W.Va. 2002) ("There were aspects of Mr. Cawley's testimony that undermined his credibility. Mr. Cawley testified that he achieved a 100% passage rate on the proficiency tests that he took and that all of his peers *always* passed their proficiency tests. Mr. Cawley said that his peers *always* agreed with each others' results and *always* got it right."); *United States v. Allen*, 207 F. Supp. 2d 856, 862 (N.D. Ind. 2002) ("[Examiner] Vanderkolk testified that the error rate of the [footprint identification] process . . . is zero."); *United States v. Llera Plaza*, 179 F. Supp. 2d 492, 511 (E.D. Pa. 2002) ("[Fingerprint Examiner] Meagher's response to the question whether 'you have an opinion as to what the error rate is for the work that you do, latent print examinations': 'As applied to the scientific methodology, it's zero.'"); *United States v. Trala*, 162 F. Supp. 2d 336, 347 (D.Del. 2001) ("The FBI methodology has been developed to result in a zero error rate within acceptable measurement error conditions (error being understood as yielding an incorrect result), if the methodology is followed and properly calibrated instruments are used."); *United States v. Gaines*, 979 F. Supp. 1429, 1437 (S.D. Fla. 1997) ("Dr. Tracey testified that he was familiar with some of the proficiency tests that had been performed on FBI agents and examiners in other laboratories, and that all of the FBI proficiency tests with which he was familiar were error-free."); *United States v. Peters*, 1995 U.S. Dist. LEXIS 20950 *54 (D.N.M) ("Dr. Budowle testified that the FBI lab's error rate for declaring false positives or false negatives is zero."); *State v. Proctor*, 595 S.E. 2d 480, 482 (S.C. 2004) ("[South Carolina Law Enforcement Division lab] produced an affidavit from SLED Lt. Ira Jeffcoat that outlined the general test procedures, and stated that the SLED examiners have never made an incorrect 'match' in any proficiency test."); *State v. Payne*, No. 02AP-723, 2003 WL 22128810, at 13 (Ohio Ct. App. Sept. 16, 2003) (quoting a fingerprint examiner's testimony that "the error rate [of fingerprinting] is essentially zero"); *Ramirez v. State*, 810 So. 2d 836, 851 (Fla. 2001) (noting that the State's tool mark expert in a death penalty case "testified that the method [of tool mark identification] is infallible, that it is impossible to make a false positive identification."); *Commonwealth v. Teixeira*, 662 N.E. 2d 726, 728 (Mass. App. Ct. 1996) (noting that Agent Quill testified "that the error rate was reduced to zero by reason of his lab's method of multiple-sample [DNA] analysis."); *State v. Jones*, 922 P. 2d 806, 809 n.1 (Wash. 1996) (crime lab examiner "testified that the Washoe County laboratory is subject to external blind tests and proficiency testing and presently has a tested lab error rate of zero."); *Commonwealth v. Blasioli*, 685 A. 2d 151, 165 n.29 (Pa. Super. Ct. 1996)

date, there have been at least 182 convictions thrown out or overturned because postconviction DNA tests conclusively exonerated a previously convicted felon or cast such doubt on the State's case that the State moved to have the defendant released and all charged dismissed.[6] Although a certain number of these flawed convictions stemmed from eyewitness misidentification (Koosed, 2002), false confessions (Drizin and Leo, 2004), jailhouse snitches (Zimmerman, 2001), and incompetent defense counsel (Scheck et al., 2001), a perceptible correlation has surfaced between these cases and forensic misidentifications (Cooley, 2004a). Of these problems with the physical evidence, Dr. Michael J. Saks (2001, p. 423), legal evidence expert and professor of law and psychology at the Arizona State University College of Law, notes:

> If the criminal justice community and the public were startled to learn that numerous innocent people were convicted of serious crimes and sentenced to long terms of imprisonment and sometimes even to execution, they will be even more surprised to learn that *forensic science has played a large part in those erroneous convictions* [italics added].[7]

In many of these cases, forensic identification examiners or police scientists offered opinions that were later proven to be inaccurate by DNA evidence (see www.law-forensic.com, which lists and discusses many of the wrongful conviction cases). For instance, scores of convicted defendants, who were originally linked to a victim or crime scene by way of microscopic hair analysis, garnered their freedom when DNA tests on the hair conclusively excluded them or the victim as the donor.[8] Likewise, an increasing number of defendants who were initially associated to a victim via bite mark identifications have walked free from prison due to DNA technology, which is able to test the cells transferred to the victim from the offender's mouth during the act of biting via saliva.[9]

More notably, fingerprinting and DNA analysis, the gold standards of forensic science, have not been immune from acting as causal agents in erroneous convictions. Three of the more noteworthy wrongful conviction

[6] See Cardozo Law School's Innocence Project at www.innocenceproject.org (accessed July 15, 2006); Gross et al. (2005) (noting that of the 328 exonerations between 1989 and 2003, 145 were exonerated with DNA analysis).

[7] Possley et al. (2004, p. 1) noted, "A [*Chicago*] *Tribune* examination of the 200 DNA and death row exoneration cases since 1986—including scores of interviews and a review of court transcripts and appellate opinions—found that more than a quarter involved faulty crime lab work or testimony."

[8] Connors et al. (1996) note that out of 28 erroneous convictions, six had hair comparison testimony supporting the original conviction.

[9] For instance, consider Dan Young Jr. and Harold Hill's cases. Young and Hill were convicted and sentenced to life in prison for raping and strangling Kathy Morgan in October 1991. The key piece of forensic evidence used to link Hill and Young to Morgan's murder were bite marks discovered on Morgan's body. According to the State's forensic odontologist (Dr. John Kenney), Hill and Young were responsible for the marks on Morgan. In closing arguments, a Cook County prosecutor told the jury, "The biggest piece of evidence that backs up [the State's theory], ladies and gentleman, is Dr. Kenney's testimony about the bite mark evidence" (Main, 2003, p. 12). When new DNA testing was performed in 2005, the results excluded Hill and Young as potential contributors. As a result, the Cook Country State's Attorneys Office dropped all charges against Young and Hill. See Mills and Coen (2005). See also Weinstein (2002), who discusses Ray Krone's wrongful capital conviction; Krone's capital conviction, like Dan Young Jr.'s and Harold Hill's, was premised on the testimony of a forensic dentist who opined that Krone's teeth marks matched a bite mark on the murder victim's breast. DNA tests in 2002, however, excluded Krone as a possible donor. Krone was released from prison in April 2002.

(crime lab director "testified that the Pennsylvania State Police lab had an error rate of zero: No errors had ever been detected."); *State v. Johnson*, 905 P. 2d 1002, 1012 (Ariz. 1995) "[State's DNA expert] testified that the laboratory had undergone several proficiency tests and that its laboratory error rate was currently zero."); *Hicks v. State*, 860 S.W. 2d 419, 423 (Tex. Crim. App. 1993) ("Dr. Kevin McElfresh, Ph.D. . . . testified . . . that the [RFLP] procedures utilized had the ability to exclude suspects absolutely and that a false positive result was impossible."); *People v. Wesley*, 589 N.Y.S. 2d 197, 200 (N.Y. App. Div. 1992) ("It was unrefuted that it is impossible under the RFLP procedure to obtain a false positive result, i.e., to identify the wrong individual as the contributor of the DNA being tested."); *People v. Shi Fu Huang*, 546 N.Y.S. 2d 920, 921 (N.Y. Crim. Ct. 1989) ("Dr. Baird [the State's DNA expert] testified that it is impossible to get a false positive reading. Environmental effects could at worst result in 'no result,' but never in a false positive reading."); *Cobey v. State*, 559 A. 2d 391, 392 (1989) ("[A]n incorrect match is an impossible result.").

and accusation cases of the recent past have dealt with fingerprint and DNA evidence (Liptak, 2003a; Saltzman and Daniel, 2004; Stacey, 2005a). The Brandon Mayfield misidentification (discussed later), for example, has been dubbed by some as "the most highly publicized fingerprint error ever exposed" (Cole, 2005, p. 985). These cases make clear that "[b]old statements or broad hints that [forensic] testing is infallible . . . are not only irresponsible, they border on scientific fraud" (Burk, 1990, p. 80). As Professor Max Hirschberg (1940, p. 34) noted more than 60 years ago, "A real student of science is too well aware of the fallibility of scientific knowledge to presume infallibility, while a charlatan tries to force his infallibility on his public." His cautionary words have never been more appropriate.

It should be noted that the overwhelming majority of exonerations, DNA or otherwise, are non-capital. However, non-capital cases infrequently suffer the consistent level of appellate attention or post-conviction review afforded capital cases for lack of funds and lack of exigency. Given this state of affairs, one is lead to surmise that if the DNA lens could be pointed at more of the identifications in non-capital convictions, the frequency of exonerations might just explode.

The reconstructionist has a duty to understand the limits of her evidence and not extend her interpretations beyond established science (as discussed thoroughly in Chapters 2–4). This should include a refusal to render conclusions that prefer to sell an image of forensic infallibility and certainty. It should also include a willingness to admit the historical existence and current possibility of error and to further embrace the necessary component of independent peer review that is required to uncover it. That the courtroom has two sides is not an accident—it is by design.

THE CRIME LAB CRISIS

Another reason why the forensic community is under intense scrutiny is because there has been persistent trouble with "one of the foundations of the modern criminal justice system—the crime lab" (Tanner, 2003, p. A18).[10] As discussed in the preface and Chapter 3, during the past decade there have been numerous audits of publicly funded laboratory systems. These audits have repeatedly identified systemic problems within crime labs throughout the United States.[11] One fundamental issue can be traced back to many, if not all, of these problems—a pervasive lack of funding.[12] Inadequate funding prevents crime labs from performing the following necessary tasks and functions:

[10] A *U.S. News & World Report* article commented, "In recent years, the integrity of crime labs across the country, including the vaunted FBI crime lab, has come under attack for lax standards and generating bogus evidence" (Roane, 2005, p. 48).

[11] Possley et al. (2004, p. 1) noted, "Revelations of shoddy work and poorly run facilities have shaken the criminal justice system like never before, raising doubts about the reputation of labs as unbiased advocates for scientific truth."

[12] The National Institute of Justice (2001, p. 55) noted, "Public crime laboratories historically have suffered from low funding." For instance, in 1967, the President's Commission on Law Enforcement and Administration of Justice (p. 255) commented that "the great majority of police department laboratories have only minimal equipment and lack highly skilled personnel able to use the modern equipment now being developed and produced by the instrumentation industry" (A later commission concluded, "Too many police crime laboratories have been set up on budgets that preclude the recruitment of qualified, professional personnel" (National Advisory Commission on Criminal Justice Standards and Goals, 1974).

- Hiring a sufficient number of staff
- Hiring adequately educated staff
- Adequately paying current staff (which results in high turnover)
- Purchasing up-to-date-technology
- Purchasing basic supplies and equipment
- Properly training both new and experienced lab examiners
- Implementing congressionally or statutorily mandated quality assurance programs[13]

The current state of U.S. crime labs, and their regular lack of qualified personnel, has forced Barry Scheck (2004, p. 4), defense attorney, DNA expert, and co-founder of the *Innocence Project*, to conclude:

> Everyone should know our crime laboratories are in a crisis, reeling from an epidemic of scandals reflecting decades of shoddy work, usually from bad actors producing incompetent or fraudulent results, but sometimes from methodologies that have been exposed as unreliable.

Although some may argue that Scheck's comments must be viewed through a cautious lens, given his allegiance to the criminal defense bar, it must be conceded that his position is actually reinforced by numerous high-ranking forensic practitioners and administrators. For instance, Milton E. Nix, director of the Georgia Bureau of Investigation's crime lab, admitted to Congress, "You may find this an unusual statement, but I am in total agreement with the National Association of Defense Attorneys when it comes to quality and accuracy of crime lab examinations and analysis" ("Crime Lab Modernization," 2001). Similarly, Barry Fisher, director of the Los Angeles County crime lab, made the following comment regarding the lack of crime lab oversight (as quoted in Graham, 2001, p. 10): "I don't think anyone can tell you what's really going on [in the nation's crime laboratories]. . . . The truth is, we don't know."

Although we cannot know the entire picture, we do know that there are well-documented, recurring cases of forensic fraud, ineptitude, and error that have been steadily uncovered at the FBI's crime lab, and that's just since 1997 (Associated Press, 2001; Buchanan, 2003; "The FBI Laboratory," 1997; Pitsch, 2003; Solomon, 2003; Willing, 2003). Far from being the exception, these same kinds of problems have also been identified and exposed across the numerous careers of individual examiners, and within more than a few major police laboratory systems. This includes publicly investigated crime

[13] The National Institute of Justice (2003, p. 2) states, "Most . . . crime labs lack sufficient numbers of trained forensic scientists. . . . State and local governments with shrinking budgets lack adequate resources to hire trained scientists." Martinez (2002, p. 001) notes, "Massachusetts law enforcement teeters on the brink of disaster due to a seriously underfunded, understaffed, and overworked corps of state medical examiners and other forensic investigators." *CBI Labs Need a Boost* (2002, p. E-6) discusses several reasons why evidence is stockpiling at the Colorado Bureau of Investigation's crime laboratory; also arguing that "Gov. Bill Owens and the legislature should make increased CBI funding a priority so this crime-fighting organization can expand its inadequate staffing and facilities. That would be money well spent and send an unmistakable message to the bad guys." Bailey (2003, p. E-06) discusses how the Alabama Department of Forensic Sciences has "a backlog of 9000 drug cases, 2000 DNA cases, 900 toxicology cases, and 500 firearms cases, a shortage of at least three forensic pathologists and a budget with about 2.5 million fewer dollars than last year's." Silver and Lash (2003, p. A-1) discuss how Pittsburgh's crime laboratory has a DNA backlog of 350 cases, 1100 drug cases, 900 firearms case, and 400 fingerprints case because of inadequate funding. *Labs Hope to Get Funds Requested* (2003) notes that the Louisiana legislature approved a $1 million appropriation for the Louisiana crime labs for three years, but the funding is not in the proposed state budget. Upshaw (2003, p. 1) discusses how Arkansas investigators have "been forced to rely mostly on old-fashioned police work to solve [cold murder cases] and other cases since the state crime laboratory shut down its mitochondrial DNA testing section earlier this year because of a lack of money."

[14] The Seattle Post-Intelligencer has conducted an in-depth investigation into the Washington State Patrol Crime Lab system, documenting recurring problems with poor oversight, DNA contamination, errors, and unqualified or discredited forensic personnel. See: http://seattlepi.nwsource.com/specials/crimelab/.

[15] Hamilton (2001) discusses the systemic origins of the Joyce Gilchrist scandal, which spans at least 21 years and more than 1400 criminal cases. The Oklahoman also maintains a database of public documents regarding the ongoing investigation at: http://newsok.com/news/gilchrist.

[16] Carroll and Sowers (2003) note how Phoenix Police Department crime lab technicians have overstated the probability of a suspect's genetic material in at least nine criminal cases since 2001, resulting in the need to review of hundreds of cases.

[17] Ryckaert (2003) notes that at least 64 cases were called into question because a DNA technician bypassed crucial steps that would have verified the accuracy of his work. This has resulted in the need to review of hundreds of cases.

[18] As the result of an ongoing investigation into the Texas Department of Public Safety (DPS) crime lab system, Boyd (2003) and McDonald (2002) note that a Fort Worth Police Department senior DNA analyst was fired for failing proficiency tests and for submitting a questionable and unsolicited DNA report that forced prosecutors to drop the death penalty in a case. So far The Office of the Independent Investigator, who maintains an archive of reports at: http://www.hpdlabinvestigation. org/, has uncovered numerous instances of drylabbing, poor evidence storage, false or misleading testimony, and unqualified personnel. The Houston Chronicle also maintains an archive of public findings at: http://www.chron.com/content/chronicle/special/03/crimelab/.

labs and crime lab systems such as those in Washington,[14] Oklahoma,[15] Phoenix,[16] Indianapolis,[17] Texas,[18] and Virginia.[19]

Add the astounding revelations brought to light by the Houston Police Department (HPD) crime lab investigation to this list as well. According to forensic experts, the HPD crime lab "has been something akin to a crime lab from hell for the past several years" (McVicker, 2003, p. A15). The HPD crime lab services Harris County, which has the dubious distinction of being the county that has sent the most defendants to death row in the United States. At least 1000 cases, including approximately 20 death penalty cases, have been under review for approximately 2 years. In May 2005, the independent auditing team brought in to inspect the crime lab publicly disclosed that it had uncovered four separate incidences of "drylabbing," which is perhaps "the most egregious form of scientific misconduct that can occur in a forensic science laboratory" because it is essentially the "fabrication of scientific results" (Bromwich, 2005).

Far from being the case of a few bad apples spoiling the barrel, the crime lab crises is nationwide, and it reflects a particularly negative image of the current state of forensic science.

FORENSIC FRAUD AND INCOMPETENCE

As already suggested, interwoven with the crime lab crisis are the problems of forensic fraud and scientific incompetence. As former Illinois Governor George Ryan's 2002 capital punishment commission report noted, "[I]n some highly publicized cases, it has been alleged that *incompetence* or even *intentional misconduct* [italics added] has resulted in defendants being accused or convicted of crimes they did not commit" (*Report of the Governor's Commission on Capital Punishment*, 2002, p. 52). An analogous remark was made in Massachusetts Governor Mitt Romney's 2004 death penalty council report: "Serious problems, including both inadvertent errors of omission and commission, as well as *deliberate and conscious acts of wrongdoing* [italics added], have arisen in crime laboratories, medical-examiner offices, and forensic-service providers around the country" (*Report of the Governor's Council on Capital Punishment*, 2004, p. 24).

[19] Virginia's crime laboratory has erred in at least three separate DNA tests in a capital case (Dao, 2005). According to an independent investigation by the American Society of Crime Laboratory Directors, the Virginia crime lab's internal review process was flawed, and found that lab employees had felt pressured by their superiors, as well as the office of the governor, to produce quick results with bad evidence in high profile cases. As a result of this audit, the crime lab was separated from the Department of Criminal Justice Services (law enforcement) and restructured under the auspices of Governor's Secretary of Public Safety as the Department of Forensic Science. A laboratory audit report can be found at the Innocence Project's Web site: www.innocenceproject.org/docs/VA_ASCLD_Audit_Report.pdf (accessed July 30, 2005).

With respect to forensic fraud, a 2005 *U. S. News & World Report* article highlighted this reoccurring problem (Roane, 2005, p. 48): "Dozens of coroners, crime lab technicians, police chemists, forensic anthropologists, crime-reconstruction experts, and other forensic specialists . . . have been fined, fired, or prosecuted for lying under oath, forging credentials, or fabricating evidence."

According to Paul C. Giannelli, a professor of law at Case Western Reserve University School of Law who has conducted and published extensive research on the subject of forensic experts and evidence, a number of "world-class fabricators have surfaced" within the forensic science community (Giannelli, 2002; see also Giannelli, 1997). Professor Giannelli's sentiments are echoed by former FBI trace evidence examiner Max Houck, who says (as quoted in Roane, 2005, p. 48), "For some reason, the forensic sciences have always had their fair share of charlatans."

Instances of forensic fraud during the past few decades have included fabricating fingerprints,[20] testifying to autopsies that were never performed,[21] knowingly excluding information from a forensic report that is unmistakably exculpatory,[22] providing knowingly false testimony,[23] testifying to forensic analyses that were never conducted (i.e., drylabbing),[24] data dredging,[25] testifying beyond the limits of acceptable science or beyond one's expertise,[26] and presenting testimony based on unsubstantiated techniques.[27] Similar to unintentional forms of errors, forensic fraud has played a significant role in various wrongful conviction cases.[28] More significantly,

[20] Roth (1997) details the largest fingerprint fabrication scandal in U.S. history. According to Charlie Stuart (as quoted in Midkiff, 2004, p. 67), former head of the New York State Police Troopers Union, New York State troopers regularly fabricated evidence: "There were a lot of fingerprints found in places where they never should have been found. . . . The feeling was, if you had a good suspect, it wouldn't hurt to have a few more things against him." In regard to the New York State Police fingerprint fabrication scandal, Stuart added, "They'll never get to the bottom of this, it's too big, it's too deep and it's been going on way too long." Gerald Aurenberg, executive director of the National Association of Chiefs of Police, reinforced Stuart's fabrication claims: "These things happen every single day on the street and if you don't believe that, you're living in a crystal palace" (as quoted in Hansen, 1994, p. 22). Well-respected fingerprint examiner Pat Wertheim "believes these cases number in the hundreds or even thousands" (Wertheim, 1994, p. 653; see also Geller et al., 1999).

[21] Ralph Erdmann, the now discredited Texas forensic pathologist, immediately comes to mind (see Campbell, 1993). Fricker (1993, p. 46) quotes a law enforcement official as stating Ralph Erdman treated autopsies as if they were "kindergarten classes or show and tell."

[22] Midkiff (2004, pp. 55–60) discusses Chicago Police Department crime lab forensic serologist Pamela Fish's willingness to exclude plainly exculpatory evidence from her lab reports. Herguth (2001, p. 5) states, "[Pamela] Fish . . . provided false or incomplete testimony in nine cases, including one involving Billy Wardell and Donald Reynolds, who were wrongly convicted of the 1986 rape of two University of Chicago students. They were exonerated through DNA testing." Possley (2000) suggests that Fish's misleading testimony presumably resulted in John Willis' wrongful conviction.

[23] Former FBI metallurgist, Kathleen Lundy, pled guilty to intentionally providing false testimony about the FBI's comparative bullet lead analysis technique in a Kentucky murder case (see Pitsch, 2003).

[24] Khanna and McVicker (2005) discuss how two Houston crime lab examiners drylabbed results in four cases. Maier (2002) discusses how a former Wisconsin State Police fingerprint analyst skipped tests and then claimed in his reports that he had conducted the tests. Osborne (2001) discusses how a former Texas Department of Public Safety crime lab analyst falsified fingerprint reports. Thornton (1997) discusses how a San Diego Police crime lab DNA analyst falsified reports.

[25] According to forensic evidence expert Gil Sapir (2002, p. 35), "All too often the [crime] laboratory [examiner] states a conclusion, then gets data to support it after being challenged, thereby supplying the facts post hoc."

[26] Joyce Gilchrist, once again, comes to mind. The Oklahoma Court of Criminal Appeals overturned Curtis Edward McCarthy's first-degree murder and death sentence because of Gilchrist's misconduct. According to the Court [*McCarty v. Oklahoma*, 2005 Okla. Crim. App. LEXIS 9, *11–12 (June 14, 2005)],

> Ms. Gilchrist, while acting as an agent of the State and in relation to her role as an expert in Petitioner's case, withheld evidence, most likely lost or intentionally destroyed important and potentially exculpable (or incriminating) evidence, provided flawed laboratory analysis and documentation of her work, *testified in a manner that exceeded acceptable limits of forensic science* [italics added], and altered lab reports and handwritten notes in an effort to prevent detection of misconduct; and . . . as a result of Ms. Gilchrist's actions, Petitioner did not receive a fair trial and resentencing proceeding.

[27] Drs. Michael West and Louise Robbins best exemplify this category. See Murr (2001), who questions Dr. West's dubious, and as yet substantiated, ability to identify imperceptible bite marks with an ultra-blue light. Quade (1985) describes Dr. Robbins' remarkable ability to individualize indecipherable footprints or shoeprints.

[28] See Cooley (2004a, pp. 401–408), who discusses forensic fraud problems and wrongful convictions, and Giannelli (2002), who discusses various forensic fraud wrongful convictions.

[29] For instance, see the Florida Supreme Court's comment (*Ramirez v. State*, 2001) regarding the increased skepticism of forensic science and examiners. Likewise, Inman and Rudin (2000, p. x) hit the nail on the head when they commented that the "reputation of the forensic science community has been significantly tarnished" because of these "unethical, unprofessional, and immoral acts."

[30] Only in the past decade has the question of forensic science competence and literacy been raised from within the forensic science community in a meaningful way. In 1999, for example, the NIJ sponsored a report into the general standing of the forensic community with respect to training, technology, methods, and quality of services. In the foreword, past ASCLD president Kevin Lothridge wrote (NIJ, 1999; p. 1):

It has been more than 20 years since the last status and needs of the forensic sciences were studied. The need for a document that not only addressed the current challenges facing the forensic science profession, but offered possible solutions, became obvious.

This report spurred the NIJ's creation of the technical working group for education and training in forensic sciences (TWGED), and the AAF's creation of the Forensic Science Education Programs Accreditation Commission. As of this writing, these have yet to gain national acceptance, or bear significant fruit.

however, when each new instance of forensic fraud has surfaced, it has further eroded an already diminished confidence in all the forensic sciences, and forensic institutions, regardless of whether the science is legitimate and the institution is competent.[29]

Injustices originating from the forensic sciences and reoccurring crime lab scandals have also provided considerable evidence that an alarming percentage of forensic practitioners have a questionable understanding of science and the scientific method. For instance, according to David L. Grieve (2000, p. 148), one of the nation's top fingerprint examiners, an intolerable number of forensic practitioners are in fact scientifically illiterate:

What is usually not taught is the protocol of the scientific method, how to formulate a hypothesis, the prudent value in the formulation of a counter or null hypothesis, the way in which experimentation and comparative analysis are used to prove or disprove the stated theory and the means by which evaluation and validation are applied to the results. In short, students are usually not properly taught about sameness and difference, at least not in a way that enables them to understand what each truly is, how each is caused and to what extent each may be recognized.[30]

Grieve's comments come on the heels of a similar opinion offered by forensic science pioneer (and co-contributor) Dr. John Thornton (1997, pp. 484–485), who stated the following about the state of scientific awareness within the forensic science community:

Daubert may . . . serve a useful adjustive purpose for the forensic science profession. . . . Forensic scientists may be nudged in the direction of learning more about the scientific method. . . . Science is often viewed as a *product* rather than in terms of *process*, and it certainly couldn't hurt to have the forensic scientist more attentive to the process. I find that many forensic scientists, even those who are entirely competent in their profession, have an exceedingly poor grasp of what constitutes the scientific method. . . . [My experience] has convinced me that many, perhaps even most, forensic scientists are not just inattentive to the scientific method, but ignorant.

In light of this mounting evidence, as well as the permeation of the previous sentiments among legitimate forensic scientists, many prominent forensic practitioners are conceding that a number of purported forensic scientists are actually technicians,[31] or non-degreed law enforcement officers, performing scientific functions without any actual science background.[32] Unfortunately, it is common in the forensic science community to label any individual who works for a crime lab or handles evidence as a forensic scientist despite the limits of their role or education.[33] For example, it is not only likely, but indeed usual, "that a person with a bachelor's degree in chemistry, geology, biology, or other scientific discipline, has not had a single college lecture on precisely how the scientific method works" (Thornton and Peterson, 2002, p. 15).[34] This is to say nothing of the fact that a percentage of forensic technicians and police scientists have yet to obtain an undergraduate degree of any sort.[35] Thus, forensic science is not always being practiced by qualified forensic scientists, although their education or title may suggest otherwise.

The problems of forensic fraud and forensic incompetence arise most commonly from unchecked professional bias and scientific ignorance made worse by inadequate funding. These subjects have been discussed in previous chapters. Reforms that may help the reconstructionist address these issues will be discussed later.

CSI OR CS-LIES? THE CSI EFFECT

Forensic fraud and forensic incompetence may only intensify in the future in response to the so-called "CSI effect." This is a "phenomenon in which actual investigations are driven by the expectations of the millions of people who watch fake whodunits on TV. It has contributed to jurors' desire to see more forensic testimony from the stand" (Hempel, 2003, p. 13). In a Nielsen's rating poll, seven of the top 20 TV shows were premised on forensic investigations and courtroom dramas, meaning that more than 120 million viewers, many of whom are prospective jurors in criminal cases, watch these shows each week (Salmon and O'Brien, 2005). Regrettably, Hollywood's portrayal of forensic science is far from accurate, as these "shows tend to embellish and exaggerate the science, ignore actual time

[31] A scientist is a researcher devoted to the scientific method, which is "the persistent critique of arguments, in the light of tried canons for judging the reliability of the procedures by which evidential data are obtained, and for assessing the probative force of the evidence on which conclusions are based" (Nagel, 1961, p. 13). To guarantee objectivity, scientists regularly design "blind" tests to discover whether a certain outcome is a legitimate by-product of the expected amalgamation of variables or by the chance intrusion of an impurity. Technicians, on the other hand, "merely follow prescribed routines, and [are] not expected to understand their underlying fundamentals." The technician "knows how, but not why" (Kirk, 1964, pp. 393–394). See also Kirk (1947, pp. 165–166), who states, "A technician is understood to be a person who is incapable of doing independent work but is skilled in the routine performance of laboratory operations according to a predetermined routine established and supervised by others." As Professor Moenssens (1993, pp. 5–6) also explained,

[Technicians] have been taught to use the complex instruments, such as the infrared spectrophotometer, or the gas chromatograph, or a whole host of other delicate scientific apparatus or even "simple" breathalyzers, as "bench operators" who have only a superficial understanding of what the instrument really does, and how the read-out is generated.

[32] Selavaka (2005, p. 74) states, "In our nation, most of the examinations for forensic purposes of fingerprinting and guns *are performed by law enforcement officers* [italics added], who were hired for one thing but became an expert in another." Dr. Selavaka is the Director of the Massachusetts State Police crime lab.

[33] The National Institute of Justice (2004, p. xi) states, "[N]ew hires who analyze drugs, DNA, trace, and toxicological evidence in forensic science laboratories typically have a degree in chemistry, biochemistry, biology, or forensic science." See also Furton et al. (1994).

[34] As one forensic science commentator noted, "While some have gone on to earn advanced degrees, possession of such a degree is usually not characteristic of the laboratory criminalist" (Lindquist, 1995, p. 64).

[35] The National Institute of Justice (2004, p. 8) reports that

although forensic scientists involved in the recognition and comparison of patterns (such as latent prints, firearms, and questioned documents) historically may not have been required to have a degree, the trend in the field is to strengthen the academic requirements for these disciplines and require a baccalaureate degree, preferably in science.

[36] As an Illinois state's attorney complained, these CSI-type shows "[project] the image that all cases are solvable by highly technical science, and if you offer less than that, it is viewed as reasonable doubt. . . . The burden it places on us is overwhelming" (Peoria County State's Attorney Kevin Lyons as quoted in Roane, 2005, p. 48). Another prosecutor emphasized this concern by commenting, "The jurors' expectations of criminal prosecutions have been altered by these shows. . . . They expect fingerprints. They expect all the DNA evidence. The prosecution has to bring the jury home in that what they see on 'CSI' does not typically happen in a real case." (Allegheny County Common Pleas Judge John Zottola as quoted in Newhouse, 2005). The most brazen prosecutorial disparagement of jurors came from Los Angeles District Attorney Steve Cooley, who called jurors "incredibly stupid" for acquitting Robert Blake (the actor) of murdering his wife. Mr. Cooley claimed that the jurors fell for the "C.S.I. effect" and said that the show "create[s] false expectations" (as quoted in Winton, 2005, p. 1). Andrew Blankstein and Jean Guccione (2005, p. A1) quote Joshua Marquis, an Oregon prosecutor and member of the board of directors of the National District Attorneys Association, as stating, "There is no doubt that there's increasing expectation by jurors of [the evidence] they're going to see. . . . Prosecutors across the country are very concerned about this." McMahan (2005, p. 1A) states, "Prosecutors worry jurors develop impossibly high expectations about how easily and conclusively criminal cases can be solved with DNA analysis and other forensic science."

[37] Some forensic watchdogs, conversely, take issue with this claim. Simon Cole, for instance, wrote that "to argue that 'C.S.I.' and similar shows are actually raising the number of acquittals is a staggering claim, and the remarkable thing is that, speaking forensically, there is not a shred of evidence to back it up" (Cole and Dioso, 2005).

lines for testing and raise expectations of the general public, law enforcement, and judicial system to an extremely absurd and totally unrealistic level" (Wecht, 2003, p. D03).

The CSI effect may exacerbate the forensic fraud problem in two respects. First, according to many prosecutors, the CSI effect has raised their burden of proof[36] to such an extant that it is "killing" legitimate prosecutions (Terrence Farley, a prosecutor in Ocean County, New Jersey, as quoted in Coscarelli, 2005).[37] For instance, the Delaware Supreme Court held that a trial judge abused his discretion when he failed to reprimand a prosecutor who complained to a jury that the standard for guilt was no longer "beyond a reasonable doubt." The prosecutor argued that the new standard is "the TV expectation that [criminal defendants] hope folks like you want. Can they meet 'C.S.I.'? If they don't have fingerprints, he can't be guilty. On TV, they would have found fingerprints. But this isn't TV, this is real life" (*Boatswain v. State*, 2005 Del. LEXIS 168 at *3; the error was ruled harmless because "the evidence introduced at trial produced overwhelming proof of guilt").

The prosecutorial perception that these shows will or have already raised the prosecution's burden of proof may cause otherwise ethical prosecutors to request or even demand the unreasonable and the impossible from their crime scene investigators and forensic scientists (e.g., physical evidence or statistics that do not exist or that are minimally or greatly exaggerated). It is conceivable that this, in turn, may lead even the most objective and neutral crime scene investigator or forensic examiner to fabricate physical evidence or massage forensic reports to ensure that a murderer or child molester is not able to "walk" because the State's case lacks the requisite CSI-type of evidence.[38] In the DNA era, such conduct can prove to be even more detrimental to innocent defendants because refuting an accurate DNA identification from a planted, fabricated, or misrepresented piece of physical evidence is difficult or even impossible.[39]

[38] Starrs (1985, p. 299) notes that "the pressures upon the expert to give the prosecutor or [law enforcement] what they want . . . is sometimes overpowering, even when to do so will convey the misleading notion that the impossible is, in fact, possible."

[39] Consider Odell Barnes' case in Texas. Barnes was convicted and sentenced to death for brutally murdering his next-door neighbor Helen Bass. The strongest pieces of physical evidence against Odell were two small bloodstains that were allegedly discovered on his overalls by forensic examiners from the Southwestern Institute of Forensic Science (SWIFS) in Dallas. Barnes, however, proclaimed his innocence from the very beginning and thus could not account for the two small bloodstains on his pants. Curious at whether the blood evidence may have been planted by SWIFS lab examiners or someone else working for the prosecution, Barnes' postconviction attorneys had potions of one bloodstain sent to blood-preservative expert Kevin Ballard. Ballard tested the spot of blood found on Barnes' overalls. Ballard's DNA tests confirmed that the blood came from the victim and thus, from the looks of it, clearly inculpated Barnes. Barnes' story, nevertheless, did not end at this point. Since Ballard was a blood-preservative expert, Barnes' attorneys asked Ballard to examine whether the blood spot found on Barnes' overalls had a high concentration of any type of blood preservative. If the results indicated a high concentration of a blood preservative, it would bolster Barnes' claim the blood was planted onto Barnes' overalls. To

Second, the entertainment media's distorted representations of the forensic sciences (i.e., forensic science has all the answers and can deliver them fast) places the forensic community's credibility in serious jeopardy in that jurors will be (and already are) more antagonistic toward forensic evidence and testimony that does not measure up to the images portrayed on shows such as *CSI* or *Crossing Jordan*. To blunt any potential attacks to their façade of infallibility, and to bolster their image to correspond with the public's enhanced perception of forensic science, forensic examiners on their own volition (and not at the behest of an aggressive attorney), may resort to unethical tactics such as fabricating physical evidence, misrepresenting findings, or exaggerating the significance of their conclusions.[40]

The CSI phenomenon may also exacerbate the forensic incompetency issue. Shows such as *CSI* and *Crossing Jordan* have ignited an unprecedented interest in forensic science at all levels of education. Indeed, one survey by student lender Sallie Mae suggests that forensic science is the fastest growing college major (Sappenfield, 2003). Although increased interest in forensic investigation may speak volumes about Hollywood's ability to lure students into believing in the existence of "hip" and high-tech crime labs, and may represent a financial windfall for innumerable universities and colleges throughout the country, it may also have a negative impact on the quality of work generated in crime labs in the future.

Even before Hollywood turned the crime lab examiner into a "sexy" pop culture icon, the adequacy of forensic education was a reoccurring problem. A variety of factors, which were outlined in a groundbreaking and controversial article on the subject by Randolph N. Jonakait (1991a), a professor of law at New York Law School, led to the unfortunate yet undeniable reality that would-be forensic scientists and examiners were not being adequately educated in the principles and practices of science.[41] These educational inadequacies were correlated to the "substandard performance[s]" of crime labs during the 1970s, 1980s, and early 1990s (Jonakait, 1991a, p. 124).[42]

[40] As Professor James E. Starrs (2002, p. v) insightfully wrote:

Soon, if we are not exceedingly careful to rein in the public portrayals of the forensic sciences to a more realistic scientific level, the forensic sciences will be found to be wanting in credibility by juries for failing to measure up to public image. Worse yet, forensic scientists, to keep pace with this public misperception of forensic science, will render opinions as experts in courts by expressing more scientific assurance than they should or can.

Jon J. Norby (2003, p. 6) offers a similar insight:

Forensic scientists must be prepared to battle dubious cultural expectations, either inappropriately elevating or denigrating the powers of science. Such expectations are usually generated though crime novels, popular theatre, movies, and television. These inappropriate expectations when found among jurors, lawyers, and even judges can negate conservative scientific testimony.

[41] Unfortunately, Professor "Jonakait's critique of crime laboratories [and forensic education] was passionately attacked by forensic scientists despite the validity of most of his observations" (Giannelli, 2003, p. 245). Consequently, throughout the 1990s very little was done in terms of rectifying the educational inadequacies in forensic science.

[42] Lindquist (1995, p. 66) notes, "Some of these programs lacked specialized instrumentation and . . . a large number of the instructors had neither a strong science background nor crime laboratory experience."

his astonishment, Ballard's test revealed that the blood from Barnes' overalls contained an unbelievable amount of blood preservative. Ballard's conclusion was that the blood was either accidentally spilled from a vial onto Barnes' overalls by the state crime lab or deliberately planted there. According to Ballard, "This is the most blatant case of tainted evidence I've ever seen" (as quoted in Burtman, 2000). Even with Ballard's blood-preservative evidence and other evidence pointing strongly toward Barnes' innocence, Barnes' was executed in March 2000. (See A&E, *Forensic Fraud*, originally aired on December 2, 2002.) Immediately prior to his execution, the district attorney who prosecuted Barnes said he was 100% certain Barnes killed Bass. Why was he 100% certain? Because of the DNA evidence. Thus the reason for this example: It is very difficult to rebut DNA evidence even when you have your own forensic expert and testing. See also Phoebe Zerwick (2005, p. A1), who quotes Rich Rosen, a law professor at the University of North Carolina at Chapel Hill and a member of the North Carolina Actual Innocence Commission, as stating, "The revolution in forensics . . . provides a real opportunity for resolving cases accurately, but it also presents us with some real dangers. . . . For instance, if you get a wrong DNA result presented to a jury, it's far worse than faulty eyewitness identification because everyone believes the DNA is the absolute answer."

[43] Roane (2005, p. 48) notes, "Forensic practitioners say the popularity of the field may make things even worse, noting that new forensics-degree programs are cropping up all over the place, some turning out questionable candidates."

[44] Brian A. McGaw and Jon Hanna (2003, p. 15) state, "Many courses with forensic in the title may indeed have insufficient science content." *Stink Tanks* (2003) notes," Most of the 360-plus undergraduate forensic science courses offered are of dubious worth. Most are taught by academic chemists with no forensic science training or experience."

[45] Sapir (2002, p. 3) states, "Most lawyers and judges are scientifically unaware if not uninformed. They are ill equipped and underprepared by training and experience to handle the complexities of scientific evidence." Faigman et al. (2002a, p. v) write, "Judges and lawyers . . . are not known for [their] expertise in science. . . . Nor is science a subject given significant attention in American law schools."

Key factors identified by Professor Jonakait and others, such as inadequate funding, lack of instrumentation, and an insufficient quantity of qualified hard science professors, still exist today. Despite these shortcomings, many colleges and universities throughout the country have jumped into the forensic science business by creating inadequate and uninformed forensic science curriculums and programs.[43] As one forensic science scholar explained, many of these "so-called fly-by-night programs . . . are pretty poor. . . . [So poor that] people don't even hire their [own] graduates" [Professor Joe Mascarenhas, State University of New York at Albany, as quoted in *Crime Labs* (2003)].[44]

That an increasing number of potential forensic examiners are graduating from these questionable programs should give rise to concern. As already shown, the occurrence of questionably educated forensic examiners currently employed in public crime laboratories is already unsettling, demonstrated in the wrongful convictions and lab scandals already discussed. However, this number may pale in comparison to that of the coming generation of forensic examiners. The more low-quality forensic science programs, the more low-quality job applicants will flood the community.

It should be noted that the first steps towards national forensic science education standards have been taken with the June 2004 publication of "Education and Training in Forensic Science: A Guide for Forensic Science Laboratories, Educational Institutions, and Students" (available at http://www.aafs.org) by the Technical Working Group for Education and Training in Forensic Science (TWGED). A major problem with this important effort is that it fails with respect to establishing a hard science degree requirement for practicing forensic scientists. Rather, it suggests a trend in that direction without any discussion as to why it might be important.

The reconstructionist's duty in this regard is to not only achieve a solid education in the sciences, which includes receiving an actual degree, but also to know and practice the scientific method, and thereby learn to recognize a lack of scientific rigor in the work of others.

AN EDUCATED DEFENSE

Another reason why reconstructionists and other forensic examiners are under much more scrutiny these days is that the criminal defense bar is becoming increasingly educated regarding forensic science and its limitations. As already discussed, throughout much of the 20th century most attorneys were ill equipped to deal with scientific or forensic evidence.[45] Not having the scientific or forensic wherewithal to understand and confidently cross-examine forensic examiners, defense attorneys rarely attempted to deconstruct their methods, assertions, or data.[46] This passive and even fearful stance toward forensic evidence and testimony allowed a surprising number of novel (but unsubstantiated) techniques and dubiously qualified examiners to influence the outcomes of more than a few criminal prosecutions.[47]

The playing field, as mentioned, has considerably changed during the past decade. Out of ingenuity and necessity, an increasing number of attorneys have become more in tune with the relevant assumptions, premises, and practices that characterize the various forensic sciences. This increased forensic awareness has had two salient effects. First, it has enabled defense attorneys to independently identify potential issues and problems related to the forensic evidence allegedly linking their client to a charged offense. Second, defense attorneys are better prepared to perceive and then contact the most appropriate forensic expert. Subsequently, they are more likely to get the specialized expertise needed to effectively review, cross-examine, or even deconstruct the State's physical evidence.

As a result, experienced criminal defense attorneys are now more likely to file comprehensive exclusionary motions regarding forensic evidence or vigorously attack the lack of science in the forensic sciences. According to the (past) president of the American Academy of Forensic Science (AAFS), Graham R. Jones (2002, p. 437):

Defense lawyers have also become more critical and aggressive in challenging forensic evidence and are more willing to hire qualified forensic experts to assist them. At one time challenges to forensic science evidence were based largely on nonscientific issues and the legal admissibility of the evidence. Now, increasingly, the scientific validity and reliability of every major forensic science discipline is being challenged. Even the reliability of fingerprinting, previously accepted with little comment, has recently undergone a major challenge in the courts and continues to be challenged.[48]

Ronald L. Singer (2004, p. 1), another (past) president of AAFS, made a similar observation:

Trying cases involving forensic evidence has changed dramatically. . . . The recognition that not all science is necessarily good science, appellate court decisions such as *Daubert* and *Kumho Tire*, and the potential of DNA to essentially identify

[46] According to Professor Jonakait (1991b, pp. 348–349):

Many lawyers and judges feel unable to deal with issues raised by forensic science. Perhaps as a group, attorneys are reasonably bright people who became lawyers partly because they were afraid of science and math. Perhaps when lawyers lie awake in the dark of night, they fear that scientists are smarter than they are. If so, lawyers will not examine the scientific evidence with as much skepticism as they would other information. As a result, the jury will not be as completely informed as it ought to be.

[47] Giannelli (1980, p. 1243) states, "A surprising number of novel techniques have gained admissibility without the presentation of defense expert testimony."

[48] Hansen (2000, p. 20) notes, "In the last year alone, more than a dozen so-called *Daubert* challenges to the admissibility of fingerprint identification evidence have been filed in state and federal courts around the country. In the three cases that have been decided so far, the courts have all admitted the fingerprint evidence. But critics say the battle isn't over yet."

individuals are but a few examples that have caused trial strategies and techniques to evolve into something quite different than was previously known. In criminal trials, the prosecution can no longer call expert witnesses to the stand and expect them to go unchallenged, and more and more defense attorneys are utilizing experts not only to review what has already been done but also to delve into areas not addressed by the state.

Appellate or postconviction defense attorneys have also been able to use their newly acquired forensic knowledge to expose embellished forensic reports and junk forensic science. In fact, most of the wrongful convictions in which forensic science played a role have come to light not because the forensic community was policing itself but because dogged appellate defense attorneys refused to accept a forensic examiner's testimony or reports at face value.

The defense bar's full-throttle approach to attacking forensic examiners and their evidence is not entirely unanticipated, especially when one considers the shortcomings and lack of reform in the forensic and reconstructive communities during the past 40 years. In the 1960s, for example, James W. Osterburg (1966, p. 269), a preeminent forensic scholar of his day, foresaw a time when the defense bar would have more than enough ammunition to wholly expose the inadequacies of forensic science: "Unless measures are taken to correct . . . pervasive shortcoming[s] in many areas of criminalistics, the day is not far off when the legal profession will become sufficiently sophisticated in science to make cross-examination a justifiably harrowing experience."

For reconstructionists, this means expecting, being prepared for, and even inviting a thorough voire dire and cross-examination of their credentials and findings. Ultimately, there needs to be an acceptance of this process so courts can separate legitimate from junk science for the triers of fact. If their findings can withstand legitimate scrutiny, then reconstructionists and the court alike can be better assured that what they are presenting is the best evidence possible, as opposed to the most helpful evidence for their client or employer.

ACTUAL ADMISSIBILITY

In *Frye v. United States* [293 F. 1013 (D.C. Cir. 1923)], the Court of Appeals for the District of Columbia affirmed the exclusion of a psychologist's finding, based on blood pressure measurements, that the defendant was being truthful when he denied committing a murder. The *Frye* Court required a showing that the psychologist's novel scientific test for deception be generally accepted by the relevant scientific community. According to the court (293 F. 1013):

> Just when a scientific principle or discovery crosses the line between the experimental and demonstrable stages is difficult to define. Somewhere in this twilight zone the evidential force of the principle must be recognized, and while courts will go a long way in admitting expert testimony deduced from a well-recognized scientific principle or discovery, the thing from which the deduction is made must be sufficiently established to have gained *general acceptance* [italics added] in the particular field in which it belongs.

Although many courts throughout the United States embraced *Frye*'s general acceptance standard [see *United States v. Addison*, 498 F. 2d. 741 (D.C. Cir. 1974); *Reed v. State*, 391 A.2d 364 (Md. 1978); and *People v. Kelly*, 549 P.2d 1240 (Cal. 1976)], it still had numerous admitted shortcomings (Giannelli, 1980). In 1975, the Federal Rules of Evidence were signed into law. Rule 702 revolutionized expert testimony by sweeping away the restrictive doctrine that curtailed expert testimony under the common law. Rule 702 employed a "helpfulness" test that departed from the common law's more strict standard requiring an expert's testimony to be "beyond the ken" of an ordinary trier of fact. Rule 702 stated:

> [I]f scientific, technical, or other specialized knowledge will assist the trier of fact to understand the evidence or to determine a fact in issue, a witness qualified as an expert by knowledge, skill, experience, training, or education, may testify thereto in the form of an opinion or otherwise.

Legal scholars and courts characterized this rule as a "relevancy test" (Giannelli, 1994).[49] As applied, this test often meant that once a court qualified a witness, so too was his or her technique automatically qualified (Giannelli and Imwinkelried, 1999). Ironically, neither the advisory committee's commentary nor Rule 702 mentioned *Frye*. The failure to clarify whether Rule 702 superseded *Frye* produced confusion among federal (and even state courts) during the 1970s and 1980s.

In *Daubert v. Merrell Dow Pharmaceuticals, Inc.* (509 U.S. 579, 1993), the Supreme Court held that Rule 702 superseded *Frye*. *Daubert* stressed that trial judges were obligated to utilize their "gatekeeping" capacities when screening expert testimony to make certain that it is "not only relevant, but reliable" (509 U.S. 589). In carrying out their gatekeeping respon-

[49] As Professor McCormick (1954, pp. 363–364) explained:

> Any relevant conclusions which are supported by a qualified expert witness should be received unless there are other reasons for exclusion. Particularly, its probative value may be overborne by the familiar dangers of prejudicing or misleading the jury, unfair surprise, and undue consumption of time.

sibilities, the Supreme Court instructed trial judges to assess not merely whether a technique or theory was generally accepted but also whether it was testable, falsifiable, and whether it possessed an identifiable error rate and had undergone the rigors of peer review (509 U.S. 589). *Daubert's* primary gatekeeping function was to ensure experts were testifying to "good science" (509 U.S. 593). Thus, *Daubert* generally focuses on four factors:

Error rate
Peer review
Testability (or falsifiability)
General acceptance

Daubert, nevertheless, left open the question of whether "technical" and "specialized knowledge," the two other forms of expert testimony identified in Rule 702, fell within the parameters of *Daubert's* reliability standard.

In *Kumho Tire Co. v. Carmichael* (526 U.S. 137, 1999), the Supreme Court held that *Daubert* "applies not only to testimony based on 'scientific' knowledge, but also to testimony based on 'technical' and 'other specialized' knowledge" (526 U.S. 141). The Supreme Court believed it would be an administrative nightmare if trial judges were required to apply different admissibility standards to areas of knowledge where "there is no clear line that divides . . . one from the other" (526 U.S. 148). *Kumho Tire* put forth another significant, although less overt, principle that the gatekeeping decision must focus on the "task at hand" and not the standard reliability of a generally and broadly defined vicinity of expertise (Risinger, 2000).

Rule 702 was amended in 2000. The amendment codified the Supreme Court's decisions in *Daubert, Kumho Tire,* and *General Electric Co. v. Joiner* (522 U.S. 136, 1997, holding that abuse of discretion is the proper standard of review for district court evidentiary rulings). Rule 702 now reads:

> If scientific, technical, or other specialized knowledge will assist the trier of fact to understand the evidence or to determine a fact in issue, a witness qualified as an expert by knowledge, skill, experience, training, or education, may testify thereto in the form of an opinion or otherwise, if (1) the testimony is based upon sufficient facts or data, (2) the testimony is the product of reliable principles and methods, and (3) the witness has applied the principles and methods reliably to the facts of the case.

Like *Daubert* and its progeny, newly amended FRE 702 forces courts to question the empirical underpinnings of all expert testimony and to exclude those opinions that are "connected to existing data only by the *ipse dixit* of the expert" (*General Elec. Co. v. Joiner*, 522 U.S. 136, 146, 1997).[50]

Since *Daubert* was handed down, courts and legal observers have expressed trepidations that *Daubert*'s emphasis on empirical testability, scientific falsifiability, and error rates poses serious trouble for the forensic sciences.[51] For example, Judge Louis Pollack's initial opinion in *United States v. Llera Plaza* [179 F. Supp. 2d 492 (E.D. Pa. 2002) vacated by *United States v. Llera Plaza*, 188 F. Supp. 2d 549 (E.D. Pa. 2002)], in which he barred the government's fingerprint experts from testifying that they were able to match the defendant's prints to a crime scene print, illustrates these various shortcomings. Although Judge Pollack ultimately "changed his mind" when he vacated his original opinion [*United States v. Llera Plaza*, 188 F. Supp. 2d 549, 576 (E.D. Pa. 2002)],[52] both opinions unmistakably indicate that many of the professed forensic sciences have much work ahead of them if they wish to continue influencing the criminal process.[53]

In short, although many of the forensic sciences are still routinely admitted even under intense legal jousting, chinks in the armor of forensic science have begun to show due in large part to the *Daubert* revolution. Moreover, the forensic science community is discretely aware that *Daubert* continues to offer criminal defense attorneys a powerful weapon to effectively attack many of the forensic fields that have a tenuous relationship with science and the scientific method. This includes crime reconstruction.

[50] As the district court in *United State v. Hines* wrote, *Daubert* and its offspring "plainly invite a reexamination even of 'generally accepted' venerable, technical fields" [55 F. Supp. 2d 62, 67 (D.Mass. 1999)].

[51] See, generally, Fradella et al. (2004); *United States v. Mikos*, No. 02 CR 137, 2003 U.S. Dist. Lexis 22069 *16 (N.D. Ill. Dec. 9, 2003) ("There is no body of data to corroborate the government's (comparative bullet lead analysis) expert's further opinion that from this finding it follows that the bullets must or even likely came from the same batch or melt."); *United States v. Crisp*, 324 F. 3d 261, 269–70 (4th Cir. 2003) (Michael, J., dissenting) ("Nothing in the history of the use of fingerprint and handwriting evidence leads me to conclude that it should be admitted without the scrutiny now required by *Daubert*."); *United States v. Lewis*, 220 F. Supp. 2d 548, 553 (S.D. W.Va. 2003) ("The Government had the burden of establishing by a preponderance of the evidence that Mr. Cawley's [handwriting] testimony was sufficiently reliable to be admissible under Rule 702. The court found that the Government did not meet its burden."); *United States v. Hidalgo*, 229 F. Supp. 2d 961, 967 (D. Ariz. 2002) ("The Government offers the uniqueness of handwriting as a scientific principle. But there is no evidence before me to support the thesis that handwriting is unique. . . . We therefore find and conclude that the principle of uniqueness of handwriting or handprinting fails to satisfy a *Daubert/ Kumho* analysis."); *United States v. Llera Plaza*, 188 F. Supp. 2d 549, 560 (E.D. Pa. 2002) ("ACE-V—the system of fingerprint identification . . . is not, in my judgment, itself a science."); *United States v. Horn*, 185 F. Supp. 2d 530, 549 (D. Md. 2002) ("The doctrine of judicial notice is predicated upon the assumption that the source materials from which the court takes judicial notice are reliable. Where, as here, that reliability has been challenged, the court cannot disregard the challenge, simply because a legion of earlier court decisions reached conclusions based on reference to the same then-unchallenged authority. For the reasons that will be explained below, on the record before me, I cannot agree that the HGN, WAT and OLS tests, singly or in combination, have been shown to be as reliable as asserted by Dr. Burns, the NHTSA publications, and the publications of the communities of law enforcement officers and state prosecutors."); *United States v. Starzecpyzel*, 880 F. Supp. 1027, 1038 (S.D. N.Y. 1995) ("Forensic document examination, despite the existence of a certification program, professional journals, and other trappings of science, cannot, after *Daubert*, be regarded as 'scientific . . . knowledge.'").

[52] For a critique of Judge Pollack's second opinion, see Kaye (2003).

[53] For instance, Professor Simon Cole (2003, p. 74) notes,

While fingerprint identification has thus far emerged from the controversy unscathed in a strictly legal sense—in that forensic fingerprint evidence remains unconditionally admissible—the terms of its admissibility have, in fact, changed greatly in ways that have profound implications for other areas of forensic science.

WHAT IS EXPECTED FROM THE RECONSTRUCTIONIST?

> Reforms in [forensic science] are desperately needed and long overdue.
>
> —Senate President Robert E. Travaglini (as quoted in Klein, 2003, p. B4)

As the previous section makes clear, it is a "brave new world" in terms of evaluating and deconstructing opinions premised on forensic technology, scientific interpretations, and reconstructions of the physical evidence. Accordingly, reconstructionists must be equipped with the requisite technical and scientific comprehension to survive in the 21st-century courtroom. This section suggests various related reforms that the reconstruction community needs to embrace, from a defense attorney's perspective. Implementing these reforms would go a long way to blunt the intense scrutiny being directed at the forensic and reconstruction communities because they would help substantiate the reliability, validity, and proficiency of interpretive forensic conclusions in the eyes of the criminal justice system.

A caveat is that these suggested reforms are not all-inclusive. They are a start, but only start, and will not cure all ills. A comprehensive overview of forensic reform is needed, and that is a subject large enough to fill another whole textbook.

EDUCATION AND TRAINING

> [I]t is the responsibility of all forensic scientists to keep up to date on not only their area(s) of specialty, but to continually seek out knowledge and training that will maximize the application of their specialty within the totality of forensic science.
>
> —Moran (2002, p. 697)

Education reforms should be considered the most essential and necessary in each of the forensic sciences. The crime lab problems during the past decade have demonstrated that an alarming number of forensic examiners are inadequately trained in science, the scientific method, statistics, and ethics. The reconstruction profession is susceptible to the dangers of diminished education, and this is made worse because of the move toward forensic specialization (for a discussion, see the Preface).[54] Under a "specialist" model, forensic examiners are predominately trained in one area of analysis (e.g., DNA, toxicology, firearms, tool marks, or fingerprints).[55] Although "specialists" may take short courses in other forensic disciplines, the bulk of their training is devoted to mastering one area of evidence. Even though it may be desirable in other professions, and it may even enhance the professional status of the forensic science community in some ways, specialization nevertheless spells disaster for the reconstruction community.

[54] According to Moran (2001, p. 698), "In light of technical advancements in the field of forensic science and in our zeal to pursue a greater degree of professionalism, we have moved toward increased specialization."

[55] Kirk and Bradford (1965, p. 50) note, "By definition, the specialist is someone who, by reason of training or experience, may be assumed to know much more about a limited subject than he does about related subjects in the same general field."

This text has been written from the perspective that evidence interpretation and crime reconstruction are functions of objective forensic scientists. Crime reconstruction in particular should be the domain of forensic generalists, working separate from the direction and influence of the police investigation. This is in conflict with the notion that reconstruction should be a function of police crime scene investigators who by and large lack a scientific background and, in many instances, a formal education.

FORENSIC GENERALISTS VS. LAW ENFORCEMENT–CSIs

Forensic examiners who become forensic specialists often have a novice-level understanding of science and the scientific method. This is the case because few forensic science programs require budding forensic specialists to partake in a rigorous physical science curriculum that includes extensive laboratory work.[56] Similarly, forensic specialists are commonly uninformed with regard to statistics because they are "rarely forced to take one statistics course, let alone an entire series of classes, during their undergraduate or graduate education" (Cooley, 2004a, p. 698). Thus, although the mantle of specialist may be used to imply that a particular forensic professional has a deep and highly technical understanding of a narrowly defined area of science, evidence suggests this implication is misleading (e.g., crime lab mishaps, proficiency testing programs, and wrongful convictions cases). Put simply, many of today's forensic specialists are poorly trained "technicians" who follow mandatory laboratory procedures and are not expected to comprehend the underlying forensic fundamentals that comprise their chosen area of expertise.

If forensic specialists or technicians do not fully understand the fundamentals underlying their own area of forensic expertise, they surely cannot have an all-inclusive appreciation of the methods and practices of forensic science subjects in general. As Robert Adamo and his American Board of Criminalistics colleagues (Adamo et al., 2000, p. 749) wrote, "Many of these individuals do not have a sufficient understanding of the basic principles of criminalistics." This has disturbing implications for the reconstruction profession. As forensic scientist Bruce Moran (2002, p. 698) explains, crime scene reconstruction "requires a *comprehensive understanding* of all forensic science disciplines." Mr. Moran further notes (p. 698):

> [Because of the specialization movement] we are steadily increasing the risk of reducing independent and innovative thinking in regards to conducting [reconstructive] casework. The generalist is indeed a vanishing breed, and with it, the "big picture thinking" and holistic approaches necessary to provide a comprehensive approach to casework is fading.[57]

[56] As Keith Inman and Norah Rudin (2000, p. 302) note:

Although a number of programs can be found that list themselves as forensic science programs, a closer look shows that the majority of these programs . . . provide only a general curriculum most appropriate for an overview or introduction to forensic science in the broadest sense. Rarely are they combined with a rigorous physical science curriculum, including laboratory work.

[57] Adamo et al. (2000, p. 749) note, "The trend in most forensic laboratories is toward increased specialization and away from the generalist or 'holistic' approach to problem solving."

Paul Kirk and Lowell Bradford, two pioneers of the forensic generalist movement who, in essence, predicted the current crime lab crisis, support Mr. Moran's modern-day comments and concerns. According to Kirk and Bradford (1965, pp. 53–54):

> Every criminalist in the laboratory should be capable of dealing with evidence otherwise belonging to another's specialty, in order that illness, vacations, and other unforeseen interruptions do not disrupt the entire laboratory output. . . . [In short], [n]o specialist can be assumed to recognize fully the potentialities of every type of evidence.

Consequently, not only have the shortcomings of the forensic specialist model inadequately prepared forensic specialists to practice in today's crime labs, they have also effectively brought the generalist–reconstructionist to the brink of extinction. The pool of qualified reconstructionists is currently so diminished that nonscience professionals, such as CSIs, detectives,[58] and police profilers,[59] have enthusiastically rushed to pick up the slack in the reconstructive arena. In fact, the three largest organizations devoted to crime reconstruction and/or evidence interpretation are composed of individuals who can best be described as law enforcement investigators (or CSIs) turned reconstructionists. The professionals who inhabit these organizations regularly proclaim that reconstructive work is an intuitive process based on special training and special abilities that defy explanation; that conclusions may be premised on an investigator's special training or bare experience, which is the source of these special abilities; and that reconstruction is best left to those with special law enforcement CSI training, not forensic scientists.

Given that the CSI–reconstructionist model runs contrary to the forensic generalist–reconstructionist model, a turf war appears to exist between CSIs and forensic generalists. Consider the exchange between two such practitioners on a public discussion forum for forensic professionals, particularly CSIs. One advocates the forensic generalist (scientific) approach, whereas the other is an advocate of the CSI (intuitive) approach. The CSI argued the following, in favor of the CSI-reconstructionist model:

- Crime scene interpretation and reconstruction is best done by qualified CSIs, not scientists.
- The scientific analysis of evidence is extremely important and should be done by scientists at the crime lab.

[58] Brant (1998) details how a detective with a nonscientific background and no experience in firearms reconstruction carried out a reconstructive study to determine the relative distance of a revolver from a victim when fired.

[59] See Greg McCrary's (former FBI profiler) reconstruction of the Sam Sheppard case at www.courtv.com/national/2000/0131/mccrary-ctv.html. For a more detailed analysis of why profilers should not conduct reconstructions, see Inman and Rudin (2000, pp. 182–188).

- Scientist supply facts to the investigator or CSI.
- The CSI or investigator is the one who is actually interpreting the crime scene based on facts derived from the scene, not just the evidence.
- Scientists must stick to their jobs, and not falsely proclaim how they reconstruct or interpret a crime scene, because they lack the knowledge and experience to do so—primarily because they are too academic, and lack experience processing evidence.[60]

[60] Transcripts of this June 3, 2005, Web-based discussion are on file with the author.

Because the rest of this textbook has effectively delineated the various reasons why properly educated forensic generalists, rather than CSIs, should be performing reconstructions, there remains only the need for a short discussion of these issues from a defense attorney's perspective.

If the reconstruction community wishes to remain legitimate in the eyes of the courts and establish scientific credibility with the public, it must exist separately from law enforcement–CSI investigative efforts, both physically and philosophically. There are several reasons for this.

First, law enforcement investigators and scene responders regularly approach their job with a confirmatory mind-set because they attempt to prove (or confirm) that a particular individual committed a certain offense in a particular fashion. Scientists (or reconstructionists), on the other hand, are obligated to approach their tasks with a skeptical (or disconfirmatory) perspective because they are trained to disprove all hypotheses before rendering an opinion that only supports (but does not categorically prove) a specific inference. These two competing mind-sets cannot co-exist. If forced together, the confirmatory mind-set generally wins out because the CSI–reconstructionist, in essence, has learned his methods and habits in a nonscientific setting.[61] The independence and objectivity needed to master the scientific method and apply it to crime reconstruction techniques cannot be accurately and effectively learned in an environment that suffocates skepticism and rewards compliance and certainty.

Second, simply working at or in hundreds of crime scenes does not turn a crime scene responder into a reconstructionist. There is a fundamental distinction between crime scene processing and evidence interpretation (i.e., crime reconstruction). The former is often accomplished with little or no interpretive skills, whereas the latter is completely dependent on a forensic generalist's interpretative dexterity. As offered candidly by the aforementioned advocate of the CSI–reconstructionist model (and in contrast to his earlier position that only CSIs should be reconstructionists), "the main job of a CSI is to document, identify, and collect physical evidence at a crime scene" (Baldwin, 2005, http://icsia.org/faq.html). Again, it is

[61] For instance, Baldwin (2005), a prominent promoter of the CSI model of reconstruction, stated the following about "cops" doing reconstructive work:

I am a cop. I have been one all my career and still feel that I am. I do not understand why anyone wants to be a CSI without being a cop first. It just doesn't make sense to me. It is like wanting to be a brain surgeon but not wanting to be a doctor first. It just doesn't make sense to me. But then I am not 21 anymore and the world and job market is different. If you want to be a CSI I think that is great! But being a cop first will give you more experience than you can ever imagine. Plus there are several avenues in law enforcement that opens up new areas to find a career in."

important to understand that crime scene processing (documenting, identifying, collecting, and transporting physical evidence), as it is currently practiced by the majority of law enforcement-employed crime scene technicians, does not actually require any scientific interpretation. One is only required to have good visual and handwriting skills to successfully fulfill a CSI's duties, which is reflected in the low CSI hiring requirements in many police departments throughout the country (e.g., most do not require college education of any kind, emphasizing prior law enforcement experience or affiliation and a valid driver's license).

On the other hand, determining whether the fibers found on a victim originated, or could have originated, from a suspect's van is all about scientific and probabilistic interpretation. The generalist–reconstructionist must not only consider alternative hypotheses as to how the fiber became affixed to the victim (scientific interpretation) but also consider the fiber's frequency or commonness within the environment (statistical interpretation). Ascertaining the associative value of each piece of evidence must take place before a reconstruction can even be attempted. Without attending to these and other related considerations, the reconstructionist risks misunderstanding the strength of her evidence and misleading the trier of fact.

A generalist–specialist analogy is appropriate here. As previously mentioned, many forensic specialists do not have a comprehensive background in criminalistics or any of the other numerous disciplines within forensic sciences. Frequently, however, as Robert Adamo and his American Board of Criminalistics colleagues point out, "laboratories confer the title of 'criminalist' upon these technical specialists" (Adamo et al., 2000, p. 749). They find this disturbing because a "technical specialist does not become a criminalist by virtue of title or by working in a forensic laboratory but rather by the knowledge, skills, and abilities (KSAs) needed to be a criminalist" (p. 749). This same analogy and reasoning can be employed to deconstruct the "I've worked hundreds of crime scenes" rationale used by law enforcement-trained CSIs. The title of reconstructionist should not be conferred on someone merely because he has processed or investigated numerous crimes scenes but, rather, because he has repeatedly demonstrated his ability to accurately and competently follow established practice standards and incorporate scientific methods of inquiry and analytical reasoning into his analyses. Similarly, as discussed in more detail later, that an examiner has testified in numerous prosecutions resulting in numerous convictions does not establish an examiner's accuracy or analytical ability.

Third, in the CSI–reconstructionist model, the influences of observer effects and examiner bias are far greater (see Chapter 3). CSI–reconstructionists are not just influenced by law enforcement personnel; they are often embedded with them in both task and spirit. This does tremendous if not irreversible damage with respect to their "professional chastity" (see Chapter 2) and may even entirely prevent them from offering truly neutral and objective reconstructions.

Fourth, the CSI–reconstructionist model endorses, like most forensic subspecialties, the nonscientific habit of supporting one's opinion with his or her experience rather than scientifically verifiable facts, analytical logic, and critical thinking. This issue was discussed in Chapter 4 and will be discussed at greater length later.

Fifth, CSI–reconstructionists, like many law enforcement-based forensic identification examiners, often claim that their reconstructions or interpretations must be correct because they have resulted in "X" number of arrests or convictions that have yet to be overturned.

A CSI's reference to "sustained arrests and convictions" is aimed at strengthening claims that she is better equipped to perform reconstructions by virtue of a demonstrable track record of success for the prosecution. This argument is unpersuasive for several reasons. First, as any legitimate forensic scientist will attest, whether an arrest is made or a conviction is obtained (and sustained) is absolutely irrelevant. The primary and singular interest of the forensic scientist, including the reconstructionist, is to provide the fact finder with accurate information so he may appropriately infer the cause of the evidence, the relationships between items of evidence, or a sequence of events. More important, an examiner's accuracy and analytical ability cannot be gauged by merely calculating the number of times an examiner has testified and then determining what percentage of those cases resulted in convictions or acquittals. This claim, in effect, deflects attention away from the real source of accuracy or inaccuracy—the reconstructionist's proficiency.

The aforementioned CSI's reference to convictions as a point of pride is similar to statements made by other "police scientists," who try to prove the quality and accuracy of their techniques, or inculpatory identifications, by referencing other allegedly inculpatory evidence in a criminal case. Consider the following (Stafford-Smith and Goodman, 1996, p. 259):

> Apologists for the technique of forensic hair comparison analysis may argue that their trade does not occur in a vacuum, and that their conclusions are buttressed by other evidence. This is correct when a confession confirms pubic hair evidence of a rape. However, real life can also cut the other way, enhancing the probability of an error, with the technician's belief that the "right" person has been arrested

tainting the approach to the hair comparisons. *If it is to be accepted as probative of anything, hair analysis must stand or fall on its own merits, without reference to other evidence in an actual criminal* case [italics added].

The italicized portion says it all, in that if a reconstructionist's analysis is to be probative of anything, it must live or die on its own intrinsic worth.

Sixth, the CSI–reconstructionist model is too often premised on completing a series of short courses. For instance, many investigators attend 5-day (40-hour) workshops or courses on bloodstain pattern analysis, trajectory analysis, or crime scene reconstruction. Some may even attend advanced 2-week (80-hour) courses in these subjects. Attending these courses does not automatically transform an investigator into a bloodstain or trajectory analysis expert (see Chapter 8).[62] As Stephen Bright, director of the Southern Center for Human Rights and forensic watchdog, explains (as quoted in Wrolstad, 2002, p. 1A):

> [W]hat you have in many laboratories are police officers who have been sent up to the FBI training facility in Quantico, VA, and come back after 2 weeks claiming to be experts. . . . They tend to embellish, to make statements not supported by science, that often go unchallenged because defendants are poor and don't have the resources to hire independent experts.[63]

Using the short course model rationale, I could justifiably claim expertise in forensic pathology. Not only have I attended various 40-hour (5-day) seminars on forensic pathology and medicolegal death investigation, I also participated in a 3-month forensic pathology/medicolegal death investigation course in graduate school at the University of New Haven. Moreover, considering my area of criminal defense (i.e., death penalty cases), I have also viewed and read innumerable autopsy reports, autopsy photos, crime scene photos, and crime scene reports.

However, I am fully aware that such a claim of expertise is ridiculous because there is more to developing ability than acquiring knowledge. There is refinement through application and error, there is experimentation, there is proficiency at following established practice standards when engaging in analysis, there is keeping current with trends within the relevant disciplines, and much, much more.

In their crime laboratory management treatise, Kirk and Bradford (1965, p. 58) scoffed at the notion that examiners or reconstructionists can acquire expert levels of knowledge simply by attending only short or "correspondence" courses:

[62] See, for example, *Commonwealth v. Miller*, 532 A. 2d 1186, 1189 (Pa. Super. 1987) ("In the instant case, the Commonwealth did not present expert testimony regarding general acceptance of the scientific principle (i.e., consumption of alcohol causes nystagmus) upon which the HGN test is based. Rather, the only testimony concerning the validity of the HGN test came from Officer Arnold Duck, Jr., whose only specialized training in this area was a two day course on the proper use of the HGN test and other field sobriety tests. We find that this was an inadequate foundation for the admission of the testimony regarding the results of the test. Though Officer Duck's testimony mentioned the scientific principle underlying the HGN test, his brief training session on how to properly administer the test was insufficient to qualify him to testify either about the scientific principle that consumption of alcohol causes nystagmus or about the principle's general acceptance in the appropriate scientific communities."); *People v. Knox*, 459 N.E. 2d 1077, 1082 (Ill. App. Ct. 1984) (Stouder, J., dissenting) ("I do not believe that Officer Ganda's three-week training course in New York qualified him as an expert in blood spattering.").

[63] Stephen B. Bright (as quoted in Liptak, 2003b, p. A5) states, "So many of the people who give DNA testimony . . . went to two weeks of training by the F.B.I. in Quantico . . . and they are miraculously transformed from beat policemen into forensic scientists."

A degree in science from a college or university ordinarily falls far short of meeting the minimum requirements. Except in the most unusual instances, such *a college degree must be considered an essential,*[italics added] but not sufficient in itself. Directed laboratory and theoretical work in the field of *criminalistics itself* [italics added] is the other essential requirement for the absolute minimum training.

Correspondence and extension courses are occasionally helpful, but generally totally inadequate except as a supplement to sounder training. The student does not learn the subject—he learns a little about it. It does not truly become part of him, either technically or philosophically. For the same reasons, reading of books, however helpful and relevant they may be, is likewise inadequate by itself to meet minimum requirements. The reading and supplementary study should accompany, not replace, the laboratory training. All of this, including the laboratory training, is still inadequate without sound groundwork in basic sciences, such as can be obtained in the colleges and universities.

Again, mastering the many scientific and technical skills needed to properly carry out a reconstructive analysis cannot be acquired in a 2- or 3-week time span. An undergraduate or graduate science degree, combined with broad-based knowledge of the forensic sciences, and a demonstrated proficiency in reconstructing crimes using analytical logic, critical thinking, and the scientific method are essential.

The short course model is just one example of how the law enforcement community has "oversimplified" a process, which by its very nature is scientifically complex, to serve its own self-interests. As one of the co-contributors to this text (Casey) has said on quite a few occasions, "The less you know about something the simpler it seems." Unfortunately, this is how generations of CSI–reconstructionists have been educated or trained. They are taught superficial kernels of truth regarding the professed principles and practices of forensic science. Then they are told that these principles and practices are so simple that anyone can apply them to forensic or criminal investigations. James W. Osterburg and Charles E. O'Hare (1949, p. x) expressed their frustration with law enforcement's desire to oversimplify complex forensic concepts and procedures more than a half century ago:

The student entering the field of scientific crime detection finds himself confronted by an odd assortment of texts. Most of these are popularizations which explain away the difficulties of subject matter in terms of facile analogies. The most serious works are optimistically written with a view to making a scientist out of a detective; but here again, the road to a true understanding of the principles of criminalistics is blocked by the necessity for oversimplification. A few texts meet squarely the major problem: To make a detective out of a science student, i.e., to develop from the scientist the scientific investigator of crime, by showing how the principles and techniques which he has studied can be applied to the peculiar problems of examiner clue materials.

Once more, "The less you know about something the simpler it seems." The simpler a concept seems, the more persuasive one appears when he or she is trying to explain it to someone else—for instance, a juror assessing guilt or a district attorney contemplating whether to file charges. Consequently, it may be argued that nonscientific investigators, with their foray into reconstruction, have steadily helped remove science from forensic science to ease the State's burden. As one of the co-editors of this text (Turvey) remarked in a discussion of these and other forensic issues, "Science without science? What's next? Books without words?"

It bears mentioning that the disagreements between generalists–reconstructionists and CSI–reconstructionists are strikingly analogous to the turf wars of the 1920s and 1930s between up-and-coming "self-styled scientific detectives" and so-called "true detectives." For example, in 1931 Captain Duncan Mathewson, Chief Detective of the San Francisco Police Department, said the following about so-called "scientific" detectives (p. 322):

> [There] seems to be a pretty well-defined controversy raging in this country between some of the exponents of science on the one side and a few of the old-time detectives on the other science. . . .
>
> Much has been said and published about the educated college policeman and detective and it is all bunk. Give me the practical detective with actual experience in handling criminals and criminal cases and with ten such men I will do more work than any college professor or so-called expert can do with one hundred of his trained nuts. Most of those that I have seen couldn't put a harness on a mule, let alone catch a crook. . . . There is an overabundance of self-styled scientific detectives and crime experts in this country. They would have a gullible public believe they are so scientific that the crooks would respond to engraved invitations to visit police headquarters and surrender. Just how long the public will stand for this rot is a question.
>
> No sane person should care to underestimate the value of any scientific means for solving crime problems. Science in all its branches should be called into play wherever there is a possible use for it. . . . This does not mean, however, that we should go still further, as the public has been led to believe, and substitute scientific detectives with college diplomas for experienced men who show a natural

aptitude for the work of criminal investigation, men of initiative, courage, and good judgment who know their business and can be depended upon to get results. . . . It is almost axiomatic that any person is better off with a college education than without one, but unless a man is endowed by nature with the true detective instinct, all the college training in the world will not make him a successful crime investigator. In the language of Shakespeare, you can't make a silk purse out of a sow's ear.

Clearly, the disagreement over who is best qualified to reconstruct crime has been going on for generations. Currently, through sheer numbers, the nonscientific CSI–reconstructionist model dominates the field. For this to change, there must be resurgence in the educating of forensic generalists and employing them separate from that community (see Chapter 3).

ENDORSING A GENERALIST APPROACH

If practicing criminalists Keith Inman and Dr. Norah Rudin (2000, p. 303) were correct when they begrudgingly admitted "specialization is here to stay," what must the reconstruction community do in order to escape extinction and to legitimize their status in the eyes of the criminal justice system?

In its simplest terms, the solution is to (1) move away from the CSI–reconstructionist model with regard to courtroom testimony and then (2) work at improving the quality of our nation's science and forensic science programs, both undergraduate and graduate. This can be accomplished by developing undergraduate and graduate forensic science programs that emphasize learning and applying the natural and physical sciences in a forensic context, and by requiring extensive laboratory work, forensic science experimentation, and crime scene investigation. As the National Institute of Justice's (NIJ; 2004, p. 11) report on forensic science education explained:

> Forensic science is an applied science that covers an array of disciplines. Regardless of the area of forensic science pursued, an undergraduate degree in forensic science should be interdisciplinary, combining a strong foundation in the natural sciences with extensive laboratory experience.
>
> A model undergraduate forensic science degree program should provide a strong and credible science foundation that emphasizes the scientific method and the application of problem-solving in both classroom and laboratory setting.

Inman and Rudin (2000, p. 302) concur with the NIJ:

> Now, more than ever, the onslaught of technology obligates the criminalist (and the reconstructionist) to draw on a strong background in the physical sciences, including an understanding of statistics and logic. The scientific background cannot be only theoretical, it must include copious laboratory experience.

Requiring this kind of educational background for prospective forensic scientists and reconstructionists would, in theory, increase the likelihood that these individuals would have a fundamental grasp of science and the scientific method as it applies to crime reconstruction. Specifically, it would minimize the chance that future forensic analysts would confuse the concepts of inductions and deduction. As John Thornton and Joseph Peterson (2002, p. 14) have pointed out:

> Forensic scientists have, for the most part, treated induction and deduction rather casually. They have failed to recognize that induction, not deduction, is the counterpart of hypothesis testing and theory revision. They have tended to equate a hypothesis with a deduction, which it is not. As a consequence, too often a hypothesis is declared as a deductive conclusion, when in fact it is a statement awaiting verification through testing.

A scientist or generalist–reconstructionist can conjure up a hypothesis about the natural world through various means—systematic study, enthused conjecture, or a rambling imagination. But others must in due course subject that hypothesis to controlled tests that are reproducible. Only if the tests support the hypothesis can the hypothesis be accepted. There must be multiple tests and the results of these tests can only support a particular hypothesis. Inman and Rudin (2000, p. 180) provide an excellent illustration of this problem as it pertains to reconstructionists:

> It is common, particularly when attempting a reconstruction, for criminalists to try to re-create or simulate the circumstances he thinks led to the scenario found at the crime scene. This kind of experimentation can be informative, but its limits must be well understood. All too often, having set up conditions that appear to duplicate the physical observations, the investigator will then conclude that he has discerned what happened. Doing an experiment is a good idea, but it is crucial to understand that an experiment can only tell you that the evidence could have been produced using your simulated conditions. It does not tell you either that this is the only way to produce the evidence, or that the incident happened in the way you envision. . . . A simulation supports a reconstruction, it does not prove one.

Likewise, endorsing a scientific approach that produces actual scientists as opposed to technicians has the potential of minimizing pro-prosecution bias. For instance, according to Professor Andre Moenssens (1993, p. 7), pro-prosecution bias

> is even more prevalent among some "technicians" (nonscientists) in the crime laboratories, for whom the presumption of innocence disappears as soon as police investigative methods focus on a likely suspect. These individuals, who are frequently trained to do forensic work on the job after obtaining an undergraduate degree in chemistry or biology, are bestowed with the job title of "forensic scientist" after only a short time in their crime laboratory function. Their pro-police bias is inconsistent with being a scientist. In fact, the less of a scientific background a lab person has, the less critical that person is likely to be in terms of investigating the validity of claims made by other laboratory personnel. These are the "experts" who typically jump on the bandwagon of anything new that comes down the pike, and will staunchly advocate its reliability, even in the absence of any objective investigation and validated experimentation. . . . Again, many of these individuals do good work in the field in which they have been trained, but their bias is often so strongly pro-prosecution that they may lack the kind of objectivity and dispassionate judgment that one expects of a true scientist, be it forensic or otherwise.

Although improving our nation's forensic science programs is a step in the right direction, particularly for forensic specialists such as DNA analysts or trace evidence analysts, it does not completely solve the problem. Forensic generalists and specialists need additional science and laboratory training given the varied nature of their work. This is not only difficult to obtain with an undergraduate degree but also very difficult to acquire once someone has started at a crime lab as a specialist. As Inman and Rudin (2000, p. 303) explain,"Unless one comes up through the ranks in a full-service laboratory, it's not a simple matter to acquire this generalist background once one starts working. It is not impossible, but it does require a measure of dedication and discipline." Moreover, generalists also need schooling in crime scene processing, investigative techniques, and the ways in which these intersect with the forensic sciences. Unfortunately, there are very few forensic science programs that offer a mixture of hard science, lab study, and crime scene work.

Thus, the fundamental dilemma for the near-extinct forensic generalist is how do up-and-coming generalists go about acquiring the broad skill set needed to perform reconstruction work? Inman and Rudin (2000, p. 303) offered what appears to be one of the more intelligent solutions:

A more realistic approach is to include this information (e.g., crime scene work) as part of a complete criminalistics program, along with the necessary physical science courses and associated laboratory work. As a minimum or interim solution, a criminalistics specialization could be offered as a fifth year after a more standard university curriculum. A certification program in criminalistics might culminate in the opportunity to take the General Knowledge Exam (GKE) offered by the American Board of Criminalistics (ABC).

Who will win the 21st-century turf war is anyone's guess. Nonetheless, if reconstructionists wish to be taken seriously by the courts and the public, it would be advantageous for them to embrace an educational agenda that emphasizes science and objectivity rather than arrests and convictions.

RESEARCH

Ms. Kelly's inability to cite such studies, given her high standing within the FDE community and the substantial period of time that the government had to prepare both its case and its witness, leads to an inference that there are few useful scientific studies relevant to forensic document examination.

—*United States v. Starzecpyzel* [880 F. Supp. 1027, 1034 (S.D.N.Y. 1995)]

The government did not offer any record of testing on the reliability of fingerprint identification. Indeed, it appears that there has not been sufficient critical testing to determine the scientific validity of the technique.

—*United States v. Crisp* [324 F. 3d 261, 273 (4th Cir. 2003) (Michaels, J., dissenting)]

One of the major criticisms directed at forensic science, and by inference crime reconstructions based thereon, is the lack of empirical research supporting fundamental theories or conclusions. Criticisms regarding forensic research, and its absence, did not appear out of the blue after *Daubert* was handed down. Rather, forensic watchdogs have for years claimed that many forensic disciplines are scientifically bankrupt because they are buttressed by almost no empirical data or research. James W. Osterburg (1966, p. 261) commented on the lack of research in forensic science:

Intimately connected with the question of interpretation is the problem of basic data, upon which objective criteria for the evaluation of physical evidence must be based. If the research work had been done and had been published, the problem would be relatively simple and such an evaluation possible. This indispensable, laborious work was started long ago and continues at a fantastic pace in the established sciences. In criminalistics, however . . . [published data] is almost non-existent. Testimony reported in the [Warren Commission] hearings emphasizes unintentionally the scarcity of published data through failure to mention any journals in which such vital information is available.

Although four decades have passed since Osterburg made these comments, it still appears that there is a dearth of research to support a number of the claims made by forensic scientists and reconstructions. *Daubert's* impact has only intensified these criticisms because two of the four factors identified by the Supreme Court (i.e., has or can the claim be tested and what is the technique's or examiner's known error rate) can only be gauged if empirical testing has been performed.

Accordingly, if reconstructionists want to appease *Daubert* and to quiet the critics, it would behoove them to conduct and publish research that substantiates the underlying assumptions of crime reconstruction. The following passage from Inman and Rudin (2000, p. 177) captures the current state of affairs with respect to reconstructive research:

Very little literature has been written about reconstruction as an autonomous process. Almost no scientific research has been performed, and no universal principles have been articulated. Further, the age of specialization in criminalistics has decreased the number of criminalists that are both competent and willing to undertake a true reconstruction. The state of the practice today is such that this area is the least understood procedure in forensic science.

Forensic evidence scholar, Professor Edward J. Imwinkelreid (1999, p. 516), wrote similar comments with respect to the research (or lack thereof) surrounding bloodstain pattern analysis:

While bloodspatter analysis relies on many well-accepted propositions in physics . . . it rests on a limited body of empirical research. . . . Given the limited amount of empirical research, in *Daubert* jurisdictions a particular opinion might be vulnerable to an admissibility attack. Even in a *Frye* jurisdiction, by exposing the limited underlying database, an opponent might succeed in persuading the trier of fact to attach little weight to the opinion.

Furthermore, many claim Locard's notion of transfer is the "generally acknowledged *law* of forensic science" (Knupfer, 2000, p. 1049). This claim is misleading because Locard's transfer theory is just that—an untested theory or concept awaiting verification. According to Inman and Rudin (2000, p. 94), "As much as the Locard transfer theory has been invoked, no peer-reviewed literature exists that proffers it, *tests it, or refutes it* [italics added]. It is axiomatic in forensic science; *it is accepted as true without proof* [italics added]."

A concept or theory does not become a scientific law (or principle) simply because a community of experts has repeatedly proclaimed its legitimacy but, rather, it does so through rigorous empirical testing. In the end, the reconstruction community, like the forensic science community in general, has developed concepts rather than scientific laws or principles.[64] Inman and Rudin's (2000) research supports this contention as it relates to Locard's transfer theory (p. 85):

> After reviewing Locard's writings, it seems to us far more likely that, rather than intentionally articulating a global principle, he was merely reflecting on the reasons a careful scrutiny of the crime scene, including victims, suspects, and witnesses, was worth the effort. Frequently (or perhaps, in Locard's mind, inevitably) contact between two objects will be indicated by small traces of each left on the other. Find the traces, and contact is established.

If science could be premised merely on repetitive assertions about a concept's professed legitimacy, then astrologists would have a strong argument that they too are engaged in science because so many believe in astrological concepts. As Nagel (1961, p. 2) explains:

> Many men take pride in being "scientific" in their beliefs and in living in an "age of science." However, quite often the sole discoverable ground for their pride *is a conviction* [italics added] that, unlike their ancestors or their neighbors, they are in possession of some alleged final truth.

Again, simply because a community of experts strongly believes in a particular notion, concept, or idea does not turn that concept, theory, or idea into a scientific law or principle.[65] This is explained thoughtfully by the late Imre Lakatos (1998, p. 21), a Hungarian philosopher of science and Jewish survivor of the Holocaust in Nazi Germany:

> The cognitive value of a theory has nothing to do with its psychological influence on people's minds. *Belief, commitment, understanding* are states of mind. But the objective, scientific value of a theory is independent of the human mind which creates it or understands it. Its scientific value depends only on what objective support these conjectures have in facts.

With these thoughts in mind, what are the parameters of individuality, Locard's exchange theory, and crime reconstruction in general? Are non-

[64] Inman and Rudin (2000, p. 76) note:

Over the last several decades, a theoretical framework of sorts has . . . evolved. These fundamental precepts provide a philosophical and rational framework for the application of scientific knowledge to the forensic arena. They are *concepts that guide a forensic analysis in a logical progression,* [italics added] starting with understanding the origin of evidence, and culminating in a statement of the significance of the analytical result. Unfortunately, these concepts have evolved in a fragmented manner and, in fact, no published record of a comprehensive organized paradigm exists.

[65] Lakatos (1998, p. 20) argues that "a statement may be pseudoscientific even if it is eminently 'plausible' and everyone believes in it."

human, mass-manufactured objects uniquely identifiable? Do individuals actually leave a perceivable trace of themselves everywhere they go, or are there certain requirements, technological limits, or environmental circumstances that dictate when traces are left and when they can be detected? Can a reconstruction be performed even though fire suppression activity contaminated and altered every conceivable piece of physical evidence? Ultimately, these are questions to be answered through empirical testing and scientific inquiry, not concepts to be assumed for reconstructive convenience.

ELIMINATING THE "EXPERIENCE" SHIELD

Science endeavors to explain how and why circumstances, observed and unobserved, occur as they do. To answer these questions in an empirical fashion, scientists put forth statements, or systems of statements, which they methodically test (Popper, 1959). Testing produces empirical data that form the foundation of scientific inferences. In short (Faigman et al., 2002b, p. 120), "God does not whisper the answers into the ears of scientists, as though they were members of a modern priesthood. The only way a scientist can reach an answer to an empirical question is to conduct an empirical inquiry."[66]

When testing is conducted, the scientist is engaged in a structured and disciplined form of observation. Accordingly, although casual observation is an aspect of the scientific method, it is not enough, standing alone, to draw valid and reliable inferences. The methodology behind the observation is what distinguishes valid and invalid inferences.[67] Thus, for traditional connoisseurs of science, the fundamental word in the phrase "scientific method" is the word "method." A finding of fact is only as sound as the method used to discover it.

Forensic practitioners, regrettably, have frequently disregarded formal methodology by basing their conclusions or inferences on the accumulation of casual observations they have accrued over years of experience.[68] Quite often, "laboratory practices are based on intuitions and deductions, not empirical proof" (Jonakait, 1991a, p. 137). Forensic scientists and others openly and even proudly admit that this is what regularly occurs, and too often confuse it for good science. For example, according to Thornton and Peterson (2002, pp. 16–17),

> [E]xperts exploit situations where intuition or mere suspicion can be voiced under the guise of experience. When an expert testifies to an opinion, and bases that opinion on "years of experience," the practical result is that the witness is

[66] As Jon J. Nordby (2003, p. 5) wrote, "Reaching the truth, or as close as one can come to it, depends upon the available evidence combined with a reliable method and *not upon the rhetoric of persuasion* [italics added]."

[67] Faigman et al. (2002b, p. 120) state, "Methodology . . . is the engine that generates knowledge that is scientific."

[68] Faigman et al. (2002b, p. 120) note, "Some people or groups who call themselves scientists do not use the scientific method. . . . Their own and their field's beliefs are based on casual observation, or intuition, or faith, or the authority of past generations of members of their field exercising their intuition."

immunized against effective cross-examination. When the witness testifies that "I have never seen another similar instance in my 26 years of experience . . . ," no real scrutiny of the opinion is possible. No practical means exists for the questioner to delve into the extent and quality of that experience. Many witnesses have learned to invoke experience as a means of circumventing the responsibility of supporting an opinion with hard facts.

Notwithstanding the constant questions and concerns that have been directed at hair identification, "a hair technician may testify that over many years of analysis, he or she has never seen two hairs that have 'falsely matched'" (Stafford-Smith and Goodman, 1996, p. 260). For example, in Robert Milford's homicide trial, an FBI examiner testified that a strand of hair located at the crime scene perfectly matched Milford's pubic hair. He testified, "It would be highly unlikely for . . . anybody else to have hairs exactly like the hairs of Mr. Milford." The Department of Justice (DOJ) criticized his testimony by first claiming that he did not perform his tests in a scientifically acceptable manner. In addition, the DOJ claimed the examiner overstated the hair evidence's significance when he testified to statistical probabilities about hair comparisons. According to the DOJ, there is (and still are) no statistical database(s) to determine the likelihood that a specific hair originated from one person and not from someone else. In his rebuttal, he argued his statistics were supported by his years of experience as an FBI examiner (Freedberg, 2001).

Similarly, in *State v. Pierce* [786 P. 2d 1255 (Okla. Ct. App. 1990)], the criminalist "testified . . . that in the years during which she had been involved with hair analysis, she had never seen hair from different people that were microscopically similar in all characteristics" (786 P. 2d 1265).[69] Likewise, in *State v. Butler* [24 S.W. 3d 21 (Mo. App 2000)] the State's chemist was permitted to testify that "she did not recall having ever seen a match with this characteristic before in her [years working as a chemist] . . . [and that] it was *very* [italics added] rare to find not only two . . . unknown head hairs that happen to match somebody else, but also two hairs from totally different body regions that match the individual" (24 S.W. 3d 24).[70] Lastly, during a 1988 Texas murder trial, an FBI examiner testified, "From my 21 years of experience doing bullet-lead analysis, I can determine if bullets came from the same box of ammunition" (Piller and Mejia, 2003, p. 1).[71]

Although the value of experience cannot be denied, forensic scientists and reconstructionists need to support their opinions by reference to logical reasoning and an established corpus of scientific knowledge. If the previously discussed analysts' findings were based on evidence produced by empirical research, they should have been able to produce it at trial.

[69] It should be noted that this dubious hair identification testimony was used to convict Jeffery Todd Pierce of rape and robbery in 1986. Due to DNA testing, though, Pierce was able to prove his innocence in 2001. Pierce's exoneration triggered a massive investigation into Joyce Gilchrist's trial testimony and lab results. Gilchrist was ultimately fired by the Oklahoma City Police Department crime lab in 2001. See Luscombe and Bower (2001).

[70] *State v. Magouirk*, 539 So. 2d 50, 61 (La. Ct. App. 1989) (special agent testified that "over . . . 12 years . . . I've looked at hair for about 10,000 different divisions, I've only had two occasions out of the 10,000 where I had hairs from two different people that I could not tell apart. Again, it's not a fingerprint, but it's normally a strong association."); *Bivens v. State*, 433 N.E. 2d 387, 389 (Ind. 1982) (hair expert testified that on only two occasions out of 1500 did hair samples from two different individuals have identical characteristics); *State v. Hazley*, 428 N.W. 2d 406, 411 (Minn. Ct. App. 1988) ("Although hair analysis cannot conclusively identify a hair as belonging to a particular person, the technician who performed the analysis testified that in analyzing 2400 hairs per year for 16 years, she had never found a coincidental identical match.").

[71] The FBI's comparative bullet lead analysis has since been called into serious question. See National Research Council (2004), Finkelstein and Levin (2005), and Imwinkelried and Tobin (2003).

More important, although experience, training, and common sense are critical in any scientific endeavor, they cannot provide the valid and informative answers that surface when a belief or assertion is systematically and empirically tested. For example, "experience tells us that children resemble their mothers in some ways and their fathers in others, and that manure increases crop yield" (Black et al., 1994, p. 755). Experience or common sense, however, "does not provide *explanations* [italics added] for these phenomena" (p. 755). Furthermore, even though common sense shares certain similarities with science, it fails to methodically discover the relations between incidences that are not obviously related (p. 754). The following passage from Ernest Nagel (1961, pp. 3–4), a prominent philosopher of science, encapsulates the fundamental distinction between commonsense convictions and scientific conclusions:

> A marked feature of much information acquired in the course of ordinary experience is that, although this information may be accurate enough within certain limits, it is seldom accompanied by an explanation of why the facts are as alleged. Thus societies which have discovered the uses of the wheel usually know nothing of frictional forces, nor of any reasons why goods loaded on vehicles with wheels are easier to move than goods dragged on the ground. Many peoples have learned that advisability of manuring their agricultural fields, but only a few have concerned themselves with the reasons for so acting. The medicinal properties of herbs like the foxglove have been recognized for centuries, though usually no account was given of the grounds for their beneficent virtues. Moreover, when "common sense" does attempt to give explanations for its facts . . . *the explanations are frequently without critical tests of their relevance to the facts.* Common sense is often eligible to receive the well-known advice Lord Mansfield gave to a newly appointed governor of a colony who was unversed in law: "There is no difficulty in deciding a case— only hear both sides patiently, then consider what you think justice requires, and decide accordingly; but never give your reasons, for your judgment will probably be right, but your reasons will certainly be wrong."

As Nagel's passage implies, it is the yearning for explanations that are at once methodical and manipulated or controlled by factual evidence that generates science and legitimate scientific inferences.

When forensic examiners or reconstructionists are trained to use or rely on common sense or experience as a proxy for empirical research, this eventually blunts an examiner's intellectual and analytical growth. Nagel (1961, p. 5) offers an informative example:

> Few who know them are capable of withholding admiration for the sturdy independence of those farmers who, without much formal education, are equipped

with an almost endless variety of skills and sound information in matters affecting their immediate environment. Nevertheless, the traditional resourcefulness of the farmer is narrowly circumscribed: He often becomes ineffective when some breaks occur in the continuity of his daily round of living, for his skills are usually products of tradition and routine habit and are not informed by an understanding of the reasons for their successful operation. More generally, commonsense knowledge is most adequate in situations in which a certain number of factors remain practically unchanged. But since it is normally not recognized that this adequacy does depend on the constancy of such factors—indeed, the very existence of the pertinent factors may not be recognized—commonsense knowledge suffers from a serious incompleteness. It is the aim of systematic science to remove this incompleteness, even if it is an aim which frequently is only partially realized.

Forensic examiners who depend heavily on their experience or common sense to answer critical questions presented to them will generally be unable to think outside the box when they are presented with novel questions. Their inability to think beyond the four corners of their own experience stems from the fact that they have rarely been forced to engage in a form of critical thinking that would have shed light on the fundamental reasons and explanations that make up their particular area of expertise or science. These forensic examiners "suffer from a serious incompleteness" because they are usually incapable of connecting the dots that comprise their own area of expertise or science. Reinforcing this sentiment is Thornton and Peterson's comment regarding experienced-based testimony (as quoted in Cooley, 2004b, p. 403):

> [E]xperience-based testimony dissociates the witness from science and the scientific method. Accordingly, once science has been eradicated from the forensic *scientist* [italics added], then he or she has no justifiable function to perform in the courtroom, and no business being there. . . . *If there is no science, there can be no forensic science* [italics added].

Furthermore, Ian W. Evett (1996, p. 121), a well-known and respected forensic scientist, stated the following about using one's "experience" to substantiate a particular conclusion:

> Believing something to be so just because of something called "experience" is, in my view, essentially unscientific. And the toughest fights I have had have been with those who could call on many years' experience to justify their position! I believe that we have to be very wary of this thing called "experience." I believe . . . that it

is fundamentally unscientific for one scientist to attempt to finish a debate with another by citing length of experience. The statement "when you've been doing the job as long as I have" always strikes me as unconvincing. How do we know that the person who has been doing the job for 30 years is any better than he was after five years? I'd only be convinced if I could see some evidence from performance in regular proficiency tests.

Evett (Evett 1996, p. 121) goes on to note that, according to his research, the claim that accuracy increases with experience is illusory:

Once I was involved in running a collaborative study to evaluate performance in identifying human hairs where . . . the participants were asked to match up unknowns with control samples from individuals. They were asked to attach numerical weight to their conclusions so it was easy to devise a simple scoring system of positive marks for correct identifications, negative marks for an incorrect identification, and zero score for no opinion. Participants also recorded their length of experience. Was there an association between performance and experience? Yes. The less experienced participants performed better! In [a] fingerprint study . . . there was [likewise] no association between number of identifications and length of experience.

In the end, although experience has its place in science, it does not define it. Science attempts to recognize and identify the underpinnings of natural phenomena through systematic empirical testing. It endeavors to complete the incomplete by identifying relationships between seemingly unrelated variables. These newly identified relationships add clarity to previously recognized explanations or they create entirely new elucidations that have the potential to bring lucidity to areas of science that were once characterized as eternally incoherent. Regardless of whether it is the former or latter, the hunt for explanations (or wholeness) is what separates science from common sense or experience.

Case Examples: The Misinterpreted Burn Pattern Cases

Todd Willingham's capital conviction, death sentence, and execution provide an excellent example of how experience-based testimony can lead to wholly inaccurate results, which can produce the "quintessential miscarriage of justice . . . the execution of a person who is entirely innocent" [*Schlup v. Delo*, 513 U.S. 298, 324–25 (1995)]. In 1991, Willingham's three daughters were killed in a fire that engulfed their house. Willingham was charged with capital murder after fire investigators concluded an accelerant had been used to start three separate fires inside the one-story, wood-frame home. Their findings were based on what they described as more than 20 indicators of arson (Mills and Possley, 2004).

At trial [*Willingham v. State*, 897 S.W.2d 351, 354 (Tx. Ct. Crim. Apps. 1995)], an expert witness for the State testified that

> the floors, front threshold, and front concrete porch were burned, which only occurs when an accelerant has been used to purposely burn these areas. This witness further testified that this igniting of the floors and thresholds is typically employed to impede firemen in their rescue attempts.

The fire/arson expert's testimony was introduced to establish that Willingham "poured a combustible liquid on the floor throughout his home and intentionally set the house on fire, resulting in the death of his three children" (*Willingham v. State*, 897 S.W. 2d 351, 354). Specifically, one of the fire experts testified, "The fire tells a story . . . I am just the interpreter. I am looking at the fire, and I am interpreting the fire. That is what I know. That is what I do best. And the fire does not lie. It tells me the truth" (Deputy State Fire Marshal Manuel Vasquez as quoted in *Willingham v. State*, 897 S.W. 2d 351, 354). This same expert not only claimed that of the 1200–1500 fires he had investigated, nearly all had been arson, but also made the extraordinary claim that he had never been wrong in any of these prior cases (*Willingham v. State*, 897 S.W. 2d 351, 354). Due in large part to the expert's testimony, Willingham was ultimately convicted and sentenced to death.

Although Willingham steadfastly proclaimed his innocence, he was executed in February 2004. Immediately before being put to death, Willingham angrily stated (as quoted in Mills and Possley, 2004, p. 1), "I am an innocent man, convicted of a crime I did not commit. . . . I have been persecuted for 12 years for something I did not do." Remarkably, an increasing number of individuals, particularly fire science and arson experts, truly believed Willingham was not misstating the truth when he uttered his final words. For instance, at the *Chicago Tribune*'s behest, three of the country's top fire scientists (Gerald Hurst, John Lentini, and contributing author of this text book John DeHaan) were asked to review the arson testimony presented during Willingham's trial (Mills, 2005; Mills and Possley, 2004). All three experts were extremely critical of the arson testimony because much, if not all, of the testimony was based on nothing more than pure conjecture that was causally developed through years of experience investigating suspicious fires. According to Lentini (National Public Radio, 2005):

> Their training was faulty and their judgment was faulty as a result of their poor training. *They relied entirely on experience* [italics added]. They relied on what their

mentors had taught them. And unfortunately, what the mentors taught them *had no basis in science* [italics added]—crazed glass, spalled concrete, shiny alligator blisters. All of these have been over the years written down as indicators of a fire that moved too fast or burned too hot. And you can be totally confused about where the fire started, and you can also be totally confused about how the fire started.[72]

As Lentini, Hurst, and DeHaan repeatedly stressed, most of the beliefs about arson indicators, the very same indicators that led to Willingham's execution, were arrived at without the benefit of empirical testing.[73] Eventually, however, fire scientists tested these beliefs—by burning down buildings in which they had simulated both intentional and accidental fires—with the goal being to determine whether the indicators correlated with the manner in which the fires began. The results of the simulated fires led to the startlingly and unsettling discovery that many of their experienced-based beliefs about arson indicators were entirely without merit.[74]

Remarkably, even after Hurst, Lentini, and DeHaan voiced their grave concerns about the arson testimony, Chief Deputy State Fire Marshall Doug Fogg, who testified the fire was purposely set by Willingham, once again turned to his experience to substantiate his investigation and testimony. In a December 2004 interview with the *Chicago Tribune*, Fogg professed, "Fire talks to you. The structure talks to you. . . . You call that years of experience. You don't just pick that knowledge up overnight" (Mills and Possley, 2004, p. 1).

Although Fogg's comments are undoubtedly discouraging, a glimmer of hope has surfaced for other defendants, particularly capital defendants who

[72] Gerald Hurst, a Cambridge University educated chemist, commented (as quoted in Mills and Possley, 2004, p. 1), "There's nothing to suggest to any reasonable arson investigator that this was an arson fire. . . . It was just a fire." Louisiana fire chief Kendall Ryland, another expert hired by the *Chicago Tribune*, said that when he attempted to re-create the conditions the original fire investigators described, he could not. When he could not, he said (as quoted in Mills and Possley, 2004, p. 1) that it "made me sick to think this guy was executed based on this investigation. . . . They executed this guy and they've just got no idea—at least not scientifically—if he set the fire, or if the fire was even intentionally set." Edward Cheever, one of the fire marshals who aided in the original investigation in 1991, acknowledged that Hurst's criticism was entirely legitimate. According to Cheever (as quoted in Mills and Possley, 2004, p. 1), "At the time of the Corsicana fire, we were still testifying to things that aren't accurate today. . . . They were true then, but they aren't now." Cheever's claim that the arson indicators were "true" in 1991 is disingenuous and mischaracterized in such a way to minimize the accountability or negligence of the initial arson investigators who concluded that the fire was purposely set. Scientific "truth" can only be uncovered through empirical research; if no such research was performed, then the suspected indicators cannot be considered "true" or "false"— rather, they can only be described as untested hypotheses awaiting verification. Any legitimately trained fire scientist or engineer in 1991 would have known this critical distinction between hypotheses and empirically generated scientific truths.

[73] As Professor Moenssens and colleagues (1995, pp. 459–460) wrote a decade ago:

Many of the arson indicators that are commonplace assertions in arson prosecutions are deficient for want of any established scientific validity. In many instances, the dearth of published material in the scientific literature substantiating the validity of certain arson indicators should be sufficient grounds to mount a challenge to the general scientific acceptability of such indicators. It is clear, from the cases, however, that arson indicators are given a talismanic quality that they have not earned in the crucible of scientific validation.

Similarly, two other fire/arson experts have written (Brannigan and Torero, 1999, p. 60):

The debate over whether fire patterns could be reliably interpreted has simmered over a number of years. The major problem has been a serious lack of high-level research. The entire arson field has a low level of qualification. In the typical case, an arson investigator is a fire officer with a very limited technical education. Unlike some other areas of forensic science, fire pattern research was rarely funded, and educational programs were limited to in-service training of fire personnel.

[74] The "old investigators' tales" that were not substantiated included wide V's versus narrow V's (which were misinterpreted to reflect the "speed of fire"); crazing of window glass (which was incorrectly considered to indicate rapid cooling; it actually indicates rapid heating); char blister and speed of fire (large, shiny blisters were believed to signify a rapid fire, whereas small blisters were thought to denote a slower fire); window sooting/staining (previously considered to suggest the type of fuel that had burned); and color of smoke and flame (likewise considered to imply the kind of fuel that was burning). See Federal Emergency Management Agency, U.S. Fire Administration (1997) and Lentini (2002).

have been unjustly convicted and, worse, sentenced to death based on these dubious theories about fire dynamics. The scientific research cited by Hurst, Lentini, and DeHaan in Willingham's case has played a significant role in exonerating two death row inmates, Ernest Willis and Kenny Richey, whose initial convictions and death sentences were also tainted by what can properly be called "arson witchcraft."

In Ernest Willis' case, Willis was convicted and sentenced to death in 1987 for purposely setting a 1986 fire that led to two deaths [*Willis v. State*, 785 S.W. 2d 378 (Tex. Crim. App. 1989)]. After unsuccessfully attacking his conviction for nearly 20 years based on his "actual innocence," Willis was granted a writ of habeas corpus in August 2004 [*Willis v. Cockrell*, 2004 U.S. Dist. LEXIS 15950 (W.D. Tex., Aug. 9, 2005)].[75] Once granted, the State of Texas had two options: It could appeal to the Fifth Circuit Court of Appeals, or it could retry Willis. The Texas Attorney General's capital crimes section decided against appealing to the Fifth Circuit, whereas Pecos County District Attorney, Ori White, declined to reprosecute Willis after he reviewed reports completed by Gerald Hurst and another arson expert. As in Willingham's case, Hurst and the other expert concluded that the State's theory that the burn patterns were caused by a liquid accelerant equated to "voodoo" science. Hurst opined (as quoted in McCollum, 2005, p. 98) that the State's fire expert's testimony was "worse than merely absurd; it [was] unconscionable."[76] The other expert similarly found that "there [was] not a single item of physical evidence . . . which support[ed] a finding of arson" (as quoted in McCollum, 2005, p. 98).[77] Thus, after spending nearly 20 years on Texas' death row, Willis walked away a free man in October 2004 (Gold and Hart, 2004, p. A14).

Like Willis, Kenny Ritchey was granted a writ of habeas corpus by the Sixth Circuit Court of Appeals [*Richey v. Mitchell*, 395 F. 3d 660 (6th Cir. 2005)]. Prior to the Sixth Circuit's grant, Richey had spent 16 years on Ohio's death row after being convicted of starting a fire that killed two-year-old Cynthia Collins in 1986 [*State v. Richey*, No. 12–87–2, 1989 WL 156562 (Ohio Ct. App. Dec. 28, 1989)]. Assistant State Fire Marshall Robert Cryer initially concluded that a malfunctioning electric fan accidentally caused the fire. During the trial, nevertheless, Cryer opined the fire was intentionally set. Cryer changed his preliminary opinion for two reasons. First, the crime lab reported traces of accelerants were detected in the victim's living room carpet (*State v. Richey*, No. 12–87–2, 1989 WL 156562, *6). Second, the "burn or pour patterns on the cement floor beneath the carpet and on the wooden porch . . . led him to conclude that the fire was arson related" (*State v. Richey*, No. 12–87–2, 1989 WL 156562, *6). Several facts, though, surfaced after Richey's conviction that raised serious questions about the validity of the

[75] Mr. Willis' writ of habeas corpus was not granted on his "innocence" claim based on the faulty arson testimony presented at trial. Under Fifth Circuit law, a standing claim of "actual innocence" is not a cognizable claim for relief in federal habeas proceedings. See *Willis v. Cockrell*, 2004 U.S. Dist. LEXIS 15950 *42–47 (W.D. Tex., Aug. 9, 2005)]; see also *Lucas v. Johnson*, 132 F. 3d 1069, 1074 (5th Cir. 1998) (holding that "the existence merely of newly discovered evidence relevant to the guilt of a state prisoner is not a ground for relief on federal habeas corpus."); *Robison v. Johnson*, 151 F. 3d 256, 267 (5th Cir. 1998).

[76] Hurst added (as quoted in Gold and Hart, 2004, p. A14), "I couldn't find any trace of evidence that this was arson. It was a joke. It kind of blew me away." Hurst also noted (as quoted in Gold and Hart, 2004, p. A14), "All of their indicators [that it was arson] are basically old wives' tales by today's standards. . . . Those were the bad old days of fire investigation, and it's just really unfortunate that he wound up on death row because of it."

[77] According to District Attorney Ori White (as quoted in Gold and Hart, 2004, p. A14), "[Willis] simply did not do the crime. . . . The justice system actually worked in this case. But admittedly, it worked very slowly. I'm sorry it wasn't quicker. I'm sorry this man was on death row for so long and that there were so many lost years."

crime lab tests.[78] First, the State failed to produce any physical evidence linking Richey to the fire.[79] Furthermore, top fire scientists, retained by Richey's postconviction attorney, opined that "no evidence exists that meets with the best scientific practice to prove there were traces of either petrol or paint stripper used in the house" (the attorney paraphrased his experts' opinions, quoted in Macgregor, 2003, p. 16). In addition, the experts cast significant doubts on Cryer's testimony. For instance, during the trial, Cryer opined that given the depth and breadth of the burn patterns, Richey probably used a quart of accelerants. According to the fire scientists, at least ten gallons would have been required to create the patterns Cryer described (Macgregor, 2003).[80]

DEVELOPING AND ENFORCING STANDARDS

Perhaps the most important issue in forensic science is the establishment of professional standards. An assessment is needed of standards of practice in the collection, examination, and analysis of physical evidence.

—Lee (1993, p. 1124)

[F]orensic science require[s] adherence to standards of operation and of performance.

—Thornton and Peterson (2002, p. 18)

Developing and enforcing practice standards is crucial to reconstruction because the scientific method is premised in part on the value of replication.[81] Standards must therefore be clearly articulated and represent the consensus of opinion among a profession's members (Thornton and

[78] For instance, at some point subsequent to the fire, the carpet was removed from the victim's residence by the manager of the apartment complex and was taken to a dump site. Investigators retrieved the carpet from the dump site 36 hours after the fire. Moreover, samples from the carpet were not taken until two or three weeks later. Lastly, in the course of obtaining the samples, the carpet was laid out in the sheriff's department parking lot.

[79] *Richey v. Mitchell*, 395 F. 3d 660, 686 (6th Cir. 2005) notes:

[Richey's] experts' attacks on the State's evidence would have been all the more powerful given the absence of corroborating physical evidence. Neither Richey's clothing, boots, or bandage revealed the presence of accelerants. No empty canisters of flammable liquids were found at or around the scene. And the owner of the neighboring greenhouse—from which the State theorized Richey stole the accelerants—was unable to determine whether anything was missing.

[80] The Sixth Circuit's opinion highlights further inadequacies surrounding Cryer's work product and opinion [*Richey v. Mitchell*, 395 F. 3d 660, 686 (6th Cir. 2005)]:

Had counsel made the effort to find a qualified expert, rather than blindly hiring DuBois, the expert would have had the expertise and wherewithal to undermine the State's evidence that the fire was caused by arson. Custer and Armstrong [Richey's postconviction fire science experts] highlighted a litany of irregularities in the State's scientific evidence. First, Custer revealed alternative explanations for the circumstances that led Cryer to finger arson as the culprit, and surmised that the fire was more consistent with an accidental outbreak. Second, Armstrong opined that "there is no evidence of an identifiable ignitable liquid in any of the samples from the fire scenes." Moreover, the blunders that Armstrong highlighted—the State's failure to use accepted methodology, use control groups, and eliminate other explanations, to name a few—would likely have led the fact finder to adopt the defense's understanding of the science.

In November 2005, the United States Supreme Court vacated the Sixth Circuit Court of Appeals' opinion because the Sixth Circuit failed to determine whether Richey defaulted his ineffective assistance of counsel claim by failing to raise certain facts in state courts. [*Bradshaw V. Richey*, 126 S. Ct. 602 (2005)]

[81] McNamee and Sweet (2003, p. 382) state, "Establishing a consensus of a standard protocol . . . aids in the unity and reliability of [any] profession." Derry (2002, p. 204) notes, "[Scientific] judgments are made within the context of agreed upon methodological standards that allow us to employ nature as a reliable . . . guide." As one commentator explained (Dribben, 1994, p. 110), "It is this replication of results that is the heart of science."

Peterson, 2002, p. 18). Regrettably, other than those published in the current work (see Chapter 4), the reconstruction and forensic science communities have yet to establish standardized protocols for an assortment of forensic techniques (Robertson, 1999).

Reconstructionists are disadvantaged when it comes to the lack of standards because reconstructions can only be performed once identifications, comparisons, associations, and individualizations have been determined. That is, many of the forensic subspecialties that focus on identification, association, and individualization lack empirically derived standards. For instance, fields such as odontology (I.A. Pretty & D. Sweet, 2001), hair and fiber identification (Stafford-Smith and Goodman, 1996), firearm and tool mark identification (Miller and McClean, p. 20),[82] Jerry Miller & Michael McClean, (1998) and fingerprinting (Epstein, p. 610) Robert Epstein (2002). have yet to identify, through empirical research, specific protocols or criteria that can assist forensic examiners in determining whether individuality has been attained.[83] Note, however, that both firearms and fingerprints have large computerized databases at their disposal. What both need is someone versed in statistics to analyze the data and develop meaningful identification/individualization criteria. This has yet to occur. Accordingly, reconstructionists risk taking some of the factual basis for their analyses on faith that good science has actually been performed.

Additionally, reconstructionists are hampered by the lack of standards that govern (or at least should govern) death and crime scene investigations and evidence collection. With respect to death investigations, as the National Institute of Justice (1999, p. 1) admits, "There is no 'system' of death investigation that covers the more than 3000 jurisdictions in this country. No nationally accepted guidelines or standards of practice exist for individuals responsible for performing death-scene investigations."

As many cases have demonstrated, "even the most sophisticated forensic instrumentation cannot remedy errors made during the identification, collection, preservation, and transportation of evidence from the scene to the forensic laboratory" (Hanley and Clark, 1999, p. 27). Thus, contrary to popular belief, the "seemingly simple task of collecting evidence from a crime scene . . . requires a scientific approach and scientific knowledge" (DeForest, 1998, p. 1). Without any investigative or evidence collection standards, as forensic scientist Dr. Peter DeForest (2005) notes, the collection and preservation of physical evidence is severely jeopardized because it is left to the tendencies of questionably trained and educated crime scene technicians.

[82] Miller and McClean (1998, p. 20) state, "AFTE has not established specific criteria for a tool mark identification, and describes it as 'based on the examiners' training and experience.'"

[83] With no standardized criteria, forensic experts often disagree among themselves whether a match has been properly or sufficiently identified. For example, there have been various cases in which forensic dentists have been at odds whether a particular mark on a victim was, in fact, a bite mark or not. See Davis v. State, 611 So. 2d 906 (Miss.1992) (state and defense experts disagree about whether mark was human bite mark); People v. Smith, 63 N.E. 2d 879 (N.Y. 1984) (same); State v. Kendrick, 736 P. 2d 1079 (Wash. App. 1987) (same); Kinney v. State, 868 S.W. 2d 463 (Ark. 1994) (same); State v. Holmes, 601 N.E. 2d 985 (Ill. App. 1992) (same); Sperry and Campbell (1990).

A complete lack of standards from evidence collection to identification and individuation provides reconstructionists and other forensic practitioners substantial discretion in selecting the methods of analysis they wish to use. When unfettered discretion is coupled with the absence of empirical testing, a significant likelihood exists that reconstructionists and forensic examiners will fail to embrace the most accurate and discriminatory tests available. Worse, the lack of operational norms and proficiency testing may lead rogue forensic examiners to endorse radical techniques or interpretations (for articles concerning Drs. West and Robbins, see footnote 27). Courts, lawyers, and unsuspecting innocent defendants may fall prey to these untested interpretations or techniques simply because the relevant forensic community has failed to delineate the appropriate standards for demonstrating proficiency and governing interpretations.

Not only must the reconstructionist and forensic communities develop practice standards, they must also ensure that these standards are continually enforced. For example, consider the so-called "one dissimilarity doctrine" in fingerprinting (Thornton, 1977, p. 89). According to this generally accepted doctrine (or standard), even if only one indisputable dissimilarity is observed between two prints, the prints cannot be attributed to the same finger or individual (Thornton, 1977, p. 89). Although well recognized by the fingerprint community as a necessary tool to prevent false-positive identifications, according to fellow Federal Defender Robert Epstein (Epstein, 2002, p. 640), "it is effectively ignored in practice."[84] For instance, according to Thornton, once a fingerprint examiner trawls over the prints and comes across what he or she believes to be an adequate quantity of corresponding points of similarity to make an inculpatory identification, the examiner will simply disregard any dissimilarities by explaining them away as either being a manifestation of distortion or artifact. As Thornton (1977, p. 89) wrote:

[84] Mr. Epstein was the first defense attorney to make an all-out *Daubert* attack on fingerprinting, as he spearheaded the litigation that led to one of the most comprehensive opinions regarding fingerprinting's admissibility. See *United States v. Mitchell*, 365 F. 3d 215 (3rd Cir. 2004).

> Faced with an instance of many matching characteristics and one point of disagreement, the tendency on the part of the examiner is to rationalize away the dissimilarity on the basis of improper inking, uneven pressure resulting in the compression of a ridge, a dirty finger, a disease state, scarring, or superimposition of the impression. How can he do otherwise? If he admits that he does not know the cause of the disagreement then he must immediately conclude that the impressions are not of the same digit in order to accommodate the one-dissimilarity doctrine. The fault here is that the nature of the impression may not suggest which of these factors, if any, is at play. The expert is then in an embarrassing position of having to speculate as to what caused the dissimilarity, and often the speculation is without any particular foundation.

The practical implication of this is that the one-dissimilarity doctrine will have to be ignored. It is, in fact, ignored anyway by virtue of the fact that fingerprint examiners will not refrain from effecting an identification when numerous matching characteristics are observed despite a point of disagreement. Actually, the one-dissimilarity doctrine has been treated rather shabbily. The fingerprint examiner adheres to it only until faced with an aberration, then discards it and conjures up some fanciful explanation for the dissimilarity.

Reconstruction conclusions work in much the same way: A theory not supported by all of the facts and evidence must be abandoned. However, in practice, reconstructionists often pick and choose from the evidence that supports their conclusions and may explain away or outright ignore that which does not. Developing and enforcing articulable practice standards that address this and other issues is a good start. In my estimation, adherence to those standards discussed in Chapter 4 as well as the ethical canon suggested in Chapter 2 would be a welcome sign that the reconstructionist is making honest efforts to perform solid, reliable work.

THE NEED FOR INDEPENDENT CASE-BASED PEER REVIEW

There were aspects of Mr. Cawley's testimony that undermined his credibility. . . . Mr. Cawley said that his peers always agreed with each others' results and always got it right. Peer review in such a "Lake Woebegone" environment is not meaningful.

—*United States v. Lewis* [220 F. Supp. 2d 548, 554 (S.D. WV 2002)]

Forensic examiners often claim on the witness stand that their results are accurate because a colleague (or peer) has reviewed the final report and has subsequently agreed with the methods and results contained within. In this fashion, the occurrence of peer review is used to create the impression that conclusions or identifications suffered a systematic critique that was specifically designed to ensure the accuracy of their conclusions.[85] This is not necessarily the case because much of the forensic community embraces a form of peer review that can best be described as "formalistic" peer review.

Formalistic peer review is the type of peer review advocated by American Society of Crime Laboratory Directors (ASCLD, 2000) standard 1.4.2.16. This ASCLD standard states that the function of a laboratory's peer review process is "to ensure that the conclusions of its examiners are reasonable and within the constraints of scientific knowledge." Under formalistic peer

[85] *United States v. Havvard*, 260 F. 3d 597, 599 (7th Cir. 2001) ("Meager also testified that the error rate for fingerprint comparison is essentially zero. Though conceding that a small margin of error exists because of differences in individual examiners, he opined that this risk is minimized because print identifications are typically confirmed through peer review."); *United States v. Rogers*, 26 Fed. Appx. 171, 173 (4th Cir. 2001) (unpublished opinion) ("The possibility of error was mitigated in this case by having two experts independently review the evidence.").

review, the reviewer, in effect, simply functions as a shallow check on the procedures utilized by the initial examiner; making certain the report adequately documents and explains its findings and conclusions. The reviewing examiner is, in effect, simply ensuring that the initial examiner's report contains all the necessary formalities (e.g., what techniques were used and whether the examiner thoroughly documented his findings to explain his conclusion). This form of peer review should not be mistakenly interpreted or presented as an independent verification of the initial conclusions' accuracy (D. Michael Risinger et al., 2002).

Often, this form of peer review is inappropriately presented to prosecutors, courts, and defense attorneys as a process that ensures the accuracy of the initial examiner's conclusions. This is intellectually dishonest because this form of peer review is easily susceptible to subconscious context effects (i.e., observer effects; see Chapter 3). For instance, even if the peer reviewer(s) is not exposed to contaminating information, like the initial examiner may have been, the reviewer(s) knows the original examiner's conclusions, which, as mentioned, is a strong impurity that can influence the reviewer's evaluation. What we have under this fact pattern, then, is an examiner (albeit a second one) who is made privy to an expected outcome before he or she evaluates an ambiguous stimulus. Thus, from a practical perspective, we have one examiner going to another examiner and saying, "Look, I found 13 points of similarity and concluded that the crime scene fingerprint without question came from the defendant's right index finger; all need you to do is review my identification so I can take this information to the district attorney." Under this fact pattern, we are again at square one because the initial examiner's conclusions will, without question, influence (consciously or subconsciously) the reviewing examiner's conclusion(s). In short, the reviewing examiner is, without question, vulnerable to a specific kind of observer effect—" confirmation bias."

To complicate matters even more, consider the scenario in which the initial examiner is the reviewing examiner's superior or supervisor who presumably has more experience than the reviewing examiner. In this scenario, the reviewing examiner's ultimate conclusion will be impacted by two irrelevant, yet powerful, factors—the initial examiner's conclusion and rank. The latter factor (i.e., the initial examiner's rank or title) may cause the reviewing examiner to minimize or withhold any criticisms or concerns regarding the initial examiner's conclusion or identification for fear that any criticisms may harm his or her future advancement. Moreover, the less experienced reviewing examiner may internalize legitimate concerns or shortcomings regarding the initial examiner's results. For example, a less experienced reviewing examiner may feel very strongly that the more experienced fingerprint examiner misidentified various points of correspondence. Thus, from the less experienced examiner's review, there are only six points of similarity rather than 13. However, rather than being candid with the more experienced fingerprint examiner, the less experienced reviewing examiner may convince himself or herself that the reason he or she is unable to identify all 13 points of similarity is his or her lack of experience. ASCLD and its stable of certified crime labs continue to claim that formalistic peer review ensures accuracy. However, given these influences and scenarios, it is clear that this is not the case. The reviewers involved are too easily tainted or otherwise vested in the outcome.

Case Example: The Brandon Mayfield Misidentification

Consider the FBI's fingerprint misidentification with respect to the train bombing in Madrid, Spain. On March 11, 2004, a bomb exploded in a Madrid train station that killed 191 and injured approximately 2000 people (Sciolino, 2004). Spanish authorities discovered a bag of detonators in close proximity to the site of the explosion with a fingerprint on it that did not match any in their databank (Schmidt and Harden, 2004). Spanish authorities forwarded the print to several law enforcement agencies, including the FBI. After searching its fingerprint database, the FBI located a possible match to the prints of Mr. Brandon Mayfield, an attorney in Portland, Oregon (Schmidt and Harden, 2004).

From the outset, there were disconcerting and curious aspects about the FBI's professed match. For instance, Mr. Mayfield had converted to Islam, his wife was Egyptian, and he represented one of the "Portland Seven," a group of Muslim men convicted of terrorist conspiracy, in a child custody case. However, there was no evidence that Mr. Mayfield had been out of the United States in many years (Schmidt and Harden, 2004). Nevertheless, three highly qualified FBI examiners (current and retired) concluded that the print was a "100 percent positive identification" and so informed the Spanish authorities on April 2, 2004 (FBI, 2004; Stacey, 2005b). Mr. Mayfield was arrested on May 6, 2004.

The FBI's identification of Mr. Mayfield was incorrect. Spanish authorities eventually came across an Algerian suspect named Ouhnane Dauod whose prints more closely "matched" the prints found on the bag (Schmidt, 2004). The final piece of evidence came when the Spanish authorities "found traces of Daoud's DNA in a rural cottage outside Madrid where investigators believe the terrorist cell held planning sessions and assembled the backpack bombs used in the attack" (Tizon et al., 2004, p. A13). Mr.

Mayfield was ultimately released after spending two weeks in jail and received a rare apology from the FBI (Heath and Bernton, 2004).

In the aftermath of the Mayfield misidentification, an international review committee was commissioned to determine how and why three highly trained FBI fingerprint examiners mistakenly linked the fingerprint to a wholly innocent person. The committee's report, which ironically was written by an FBI employee, Robert Stacey of the FBI's Quality Assurance and Training Unit, rather than the committee itself,[86] offered a variety of explanations why Mr. Mayfield was wrongly inculpated. A primary explanation offered by the FBI was that the reviewing examiners fell prey to "confirmation bias (or context effect)." Specifically, the FBI's report noted that (Stacey, 2005b):

the power of the IAFIS match, coupled with the inherent pressure of working an extremely high-profile case, was thought to have influenced the initial examiner's judgment and subsequent examination. This influence was recognized as confirmation bias (or context effect) and describes the mind-set in which the expectations with which people approach a task of observation will affect their perceptions and interpretations of what they observe.

The apparent mind-set of the initial examiner after reviewing the results of the IAFIS search was that a match did exist; therefore, it would be reasonable to assume that the other characteristics must match as well. In the absence of a detailed analysis of the print, it can be a short distance from finding only seven characteristics sufficient for plotting, prior to the automated search, to the position of 12 or 13 matching characteristics once the mind-set of identification has become dominant. This would not be an intentional misinterpretation of the data, but it would be an incorrect interpretation nevertheless.

Once the mind-set occurred with the initial examiner, the subsequent examinations were tainted. Latent print examiners routinely conduct verifications in which *they know the previous examiners' results without influencing their conclusions*. However, because of the inherent pressure of such a high-profile case, the power of an IAFIS match in conjunction with the similarities in the candidate's print, and the knowledge of the previous examiners' conclusions (especially since the initial examiner was a highly respected supervisor with many years of experience), it was concluded that subsequent examinations were incomplete and inaccurate. To disagree was not an expected response.

Additionally, this erroneous individualization was not made by an examiner alone, but by an agency that for many years has considered itself, rightfully so, as one of the best latent print units in the world. Confidence is a vital element of forensics, but humility is too. It was considered by the committee that when the

[86] As Professors Thompson and Cole (2005, pp. 42–43) have correctly noted, having the agency that actually made the mistake write the official "audit" report pertaining to their own lapses or errors raises legitimate concerns as to whether Mr. Stacey and the FBI were entirely forthright about the extent of the problems they identified in the report pertaining to the FBI's fingerprinting methodology and its examiners. Thompson and Cole insightfully analogized this fact pattern to a bank that is being audited: "By analogy, imagine a bank audit in which the conclusions are written by one of the bank's managers rather than the auditors themselves."

individualization had been made by the examiner, it became increasingly difficult for others in the agency to disagree. This is supported because the Latent Print Unit immediately entered into a defensive posture when the Spanish National Police issued its statements that the FBI was wrong.

"Independent" peer review in the identification sciences involves having another examiner who is entirely unaware of who the original examiner is and the original examiner's conclusions.[87] In these circumstances, the reviewing examiner cannot be persuaded by related extraneous information or expectations. Independent confirmation, in effect, involves evaluating all of the underlying documentation to determine whether the reviewing examiner can re-create the initial examiner's conclusions. If the reviewing examiner cannot replicate the initial conclusions, then the validity of the original examiner's conclusions must be called into question. Again, it needs to be stressed that independent confirmation is a blind-testing procedure in that the reviewing examiner has no active knowledge with respect to any superfluous data or anticipated outcomes.

Consequently, reconstructions based on identifications and associations developed through formalistic peer review may be presented with an unearned level of confidence and certainty. This is to be avoided. Furthermore, reconstructionists who seek to bolster their own findings through peer review have an obligation to understand, and make clear to the court, its actual nature and limitations.

THE RESPONSIBILITY OF PROFESSIONAL ASSOCIATIONS

There is a real need for tightening of requirements for membership in professional forensic societies to make member quality more significant than member quantity.
—Midkiff (2004, p. 77)

Reconstructionists and other forensic examiners have an individual measure of responsibility, but so to do those professional organizations that confer credentials upon them. According to the (past) president of the AAFS, Kenneth E. Melson (2004, p. 1), "While forensic science organizations, like the (American) Academy (of Forensic Sciences) and some certifying organizations, have ethics codes, there is no universally recognized applicable, and enforceable code of professional responsibility for forensic scientists." With no "universally recognized" ethical standards, identifying and sanctioning unethical behavior has been left to the professional organizations that have conferred forensic credentials and established codes of ethics (e.g., American Academy of Forensic Science, American Board of Crimi-

[87] That means nonmatches and supposed matches be submitted routinely. Otherwise, they would know that someone else had made a match.

nalistics, California Association of Criminalists, International Association of Identification, and Association of Crime Scene Reconstruction). These professional organizations have the ability to send harsh and swift admonishments to their members when they engage in unethical behaviors (e.g., purposely misrepresent their qualifications, testify beyond the realm of their expertise, provide contradictory testimony in various cases, or knowingly fabricate evidence).

At a time when the criminal justice system's view of forensic science is fairly low, these professional organizations have the extraordinary ability to change how the justice system perceives forensic evidence and forensic examiners. Immediately reprimanding or, in extreme cases, exiling unethical individuals would give the refreshing appearance that the forensic science community is genuinely interested in policing itself. Likewise, it would demonstrate to forensic watchdogs that the organization is extremely concerned with the fact that its members are competent, objective, and ethical. Actions such as these would perhaps even begin the slow process of reconciliation because, as it currently stands, the relationship between forensic science and the criminal justice system is not what it used to be (i.e., courts are no longer turning a blind eye to questionable science). In short, professional organizations must not bury their heads in the sand when it comes to enforcing their high ethical standards. As one past president of the AAFS emphatically stressed (Joling, 1976, p. 746):

Ethical principles cannot be ignored. Indeed, they must not be ignored! The misapplication of forensic science is a possibility and is part of the realities of human frailty. Indifference to these actualities can only result in the immediate disrespect for the entire discipline and the forensic science organization that umbrellas that discipline. A wrongful act can be condoned by inactivity, silence, "stonewalling," or by ignoring professional ethics. Flagrant disregard for truth and justice can be noted by disinterest as well as by active participation in its propagation.

Unfortunately, forensic science organizations seem to be taking a back seat when it comes to enforcing their own ethical codes by turning a blind eye to behavior that is inappropriate under any fact pattern. In his chapter in Richard Safterstein's *Forensic Science Handbook*, Charles Midkiff (2004, pp. 77–78), a retired ATF forensic examiner, stated the following about the lack of ethical oversight in forensic science professional organizations:

When faced with a threatening situation, the box turtle retracts its head, closes its trap door, and sits quietly until sufficient time has passed for the threat to have receded. When faced with a threat such as dealing with charges to serious ethical violations by one of their members, forensic organizations seem to find the turtle model appropriate. The turtle is aware that he is unlikely to outrun the threat, so he doesn't even try. He sits patiently and waits, hoping against hope that when he slowly opens his shell, the ogre will be gone. Ethics committees of forensic societies and even the certifying boards much prefer to sit and wait as well. Even when they initiate action, it moves even more slowly than the turtle, and the delay is sufficiently lengthy that the miscreant, aware he is a target, simply neglects to pay his dues and renew his membership. He doesn't even have to write a letter of resignation. At the next encounter of members of the ethics committee, we may hear, "Whew! He's gone. Now nobody can expect us to do anything; why he's not even a member anymore." After all, we don't have any authority to take action against nonmembers. If the organization truly believes in swift justice, maybe a bit of it would be useful. Retention of an identified fraud among the membership is hardly a public relations success for the organization or the field. There is a need for teeth in ethics policies of forensic professional organizations and for those policies to be put to work promptly when a fraud is exposed.

Case Example

I received discovery materials detailing a litany of gross ethical misconduct by a well-known reconstructionist and bloodstain expert. The expert's unethical behavior was detailed as follows:

- In numerous cases, the expert gave contradictory opinions about whether expectorated blood from the nose or mouth can make high-velocity impact spatters. The expert's opinion always favored the prosecution's theory.
- The expert repeatedly misrepresented whether he had ever worked for the defense. In some cases, he testified he had previously worked as a defense expert; in other cases, he testified he had not.
- In various cases, the expert testified he received graduate training at the University of Virginia (UV) (this information was also on his resume). This was materially untrue because UV never had a "graduate school in police management and administration."
- In various cases, the expert testified he did postgraduate work at Cal State Fullerton (CSF) (this information was also on his resume). This again was materially untrue because CSF does not have any record that he ever attended CSF.
- In certain cases, the expert testified he was a "forensic scientist" and that he clearly understood elementary chemistry and physics because he took college-level courses in chemistry in physics. On other occasions, however, the expert testified he had no education in physics or chemistry.

- In one case, the professed "forensic scientist" testified he did not understand the fundamentals of Newtonian physics, viz., force = mass × acceleration (without a firm grasp of physics, one cannot be a competent bloodstain analyst).

- In one case, the expert testified that he had conducted bloodstain research with real blood. In a later case, however, the expert testified he had never carried out any bloodstain research and that all his experience was "real-life" experience.

- One well-respected forensic pathologist stated the following about the expert after reviewing his analyses and opinions in a particular case:[88]

> In my opinion, [the expert] misrepresented facts and evidence. He overinterpreted and reached conclusions on scientific evidence that were pure conjecture yet he led the jury to believe that he was more than just certain of his opinions, that he was in some cases one hundred and ten percent sure about facts which had various possibilities as to their interpretation and probative values to the case. I read a number of sworn testimonies given by [the expert] in the Utah case. I was so appalled by his testimony that it was all that I could do to continue to read what he was saying. All I can say is that in the 20 years that I have practiced as a forensic pathologist which includes dealing with and being involved in cases from all over the country and other countries as well, my exposure to [the expert] was one of the most frightening things which has occurred to me in my career.

Considering these factual claims, it is not surprising that an individual filed an ethics complaint with the AAFS against this expert, since he is an AAFS fellow and prominent member. In a letter to the individual who filed the complaint, the AAFS stated:[89]

> [The AAFS] did receive a more detailed response from Hon. Haskell Pitluck, Chair of the Ethics Committee, which was distributed to the members of the executive Committee prior to our meeting last month. The matter was thoroughly discussed (in Executive Session) at our recently completed meeting, and after considerable debate, it was decided that no further action on the part of the Executive Committee or the Board of Directors was warranted.
>
> The Executive Committee saw two major issues in this case—one involving entries on the C.V. of the accused, and the other involving testimony given by the accused. Both issues hinged on whether or not the actions on the part of the accused could be proven to be deliberate. In the first case, the accused agreed to correct the offending portions of their C.V. while claiming no impropriety. The

[88] Quoting Chief Medical Examiner for Fulton County (Atlanta) Georgia, Joseph Burton, M.D. This quote was extracted from a relief from judgment motion in *Michigan v. David E. Duyst*, S.Ct. No. 124548, Cir. Ct. No. 00–9779-FC (motion on file with the author).

[89] AAFS memo on file with author.

Ethics Committee was subsequently provided with a copy of the corrected version. Obviously, should the accused continue to provide uncorrected copies of their C.V., or make the same representation as before the hearing, there would no longer be an issue of intent.

The second issue is a somewhat different matter. After having reviewed the materials provided to me, I was also troubled by some of the testimony given. However, as you know, this is basically opinion testimony, and under our current Bylaws, it is not unethical to be ignorant. Also, as Haskell pointed out in his memo these issues were subject to cross-examination at the time of trial. Barring any positive proof that the testimony was deliberately intended to misrepresent the facts of the case, there is really nothing that the Ethics Committee can do at this time.

The AAFS sent the expert a cease-desist notification. The ethics committee ruling seems at odds with its *Code of Ethics and Conduct* (CEC) which states:

> Every member . . . shall refrain from providing any material misrepresentation of education, training, experience, or area of expertise. Misrepresentation of one or more criteria for membership in the AAFS shall constitute a violation of this section of the code.

Consider this reasoning: There can be no question that ignorant practice will invariably result in incompetent work product. In this case, if the examiner demonstrates he is ignorant of the fundamental sciences (e.g., physics and chemistry) that comprise his field of expertise (i.e., bloodstain interpretation), then it stands to reason he is not an expert at all. If he is not an expert, then he is ethically bound to refrain from offering expert services to anyone—defense or prosecution. That he continues to testify with AAFS approval runs counter to the AAFS's CEC and its overall objective.

Additionally, under the CEC, "Every member of the American Academy of Forensic Science shall refrain from exercising personal or professional conduct adverse to the best interests and purposes of the Academy." The suggestion that repeated incompetence does not constitute "conduct adverse to the best interests and purposes of the Academy" hardly seems defensible.

Moreover, according to the AAFS (bylaws, section III of the Preamble), its objective is

> to promote education for and research in the forensic sciences; to encourage the study, improve the practice, elevate the standards, and advance the cause of the forensic sciences; to promote interdisciplinary communications; and to plan,

organize, and administer meetings, reports, and other projects for the stimulation and advancement of these and related purposes.

The failure of the AAFS to enforce its own ethical guidelines is as frustrating as it is disappointing. This being the case, those on the AAFS ethics committee, as well as those in other forensic professional organizations, should perhaps recall the words written three decades ago by the AAFS's (then) president (Joling, 1976, p. 745):

> The day has arrived when the Academy can no longer hide its scientific light under a bushel basket. We have been and are now within the public domain. As time passes more and more of our members will be involved in matters of great public debate, controversy, and importance. We cannot remain isolated as a national organization while having our members intimately involved in scientific determinations and judicial utilizations of our individual and collective expertise. Consequently, the American Academy of Forensic Sciences has present national obligations—and it will continue to exert an influence locally, statewide, and nationally in the future. As a result, we can no longer escape into scientific seclusion, but rather we must face our greatly increased role of responsibility in the advocacy of issues which have public overtones. Invidious, unusual, or paramount problems of public as well as private concern for the rights of individual members of society or society as a whole have been placed upon our doorstep—and they will be placed there again.

CONCLUSION

As this book, in general, and this chapter, in particular, clearly demonstrate, every field in forensic science is under siege. Attacks are coming from not only the defense bar but also prosecutors, judges, and other critical criminal justice advocates who, until recently, faithfully and blindly believed in the forensic scientist's "special knowledge" and infallible interpretations. Consequently, the forensic science community (reconstructionists included) is at a critical crossroads. Forensic professionals can do one of two things: (1) They can stand tall, admit to the community's obvious problems and shortcomings, and then work to solve them, or (2) they can continue to disregard the mounting evidence of incompetence, poor science, and fraud by portraying all those who cast a critical eye on the forensic sciences as ignorant outsiders who do not have the faintest clue of how forensic science is truly practiced.

If forensic professionals continue to travel the second course, there is no question that their courtroom role will continue to be embattled and continue to suffer decline. Preferably, forensic professionals will choose the former rather than the latter. By critically evaluating those factors that have precipitated the decline of forensic science, and by developing the means to change them, forensic practitioners may begin to regain their "professional chastity."

This textbook has highlighted a number of causal factors leading to the decline of forensic science—the most important being access to high-quality forensic and scientific education (or the lack thereof). Forensic science and crime scene reconstruction reform must therefore begin with education, and this textbook can be an important part of that process. As the various contributors to this text have identified, there is much room for improvement in the forensic sciences and in the field of crime reconstruction. Taken all at once, the task may seem too daunting, even overwhelming. Taken one problem at a time, over time, and by a community of concerned practitioners, it is perhaps an attainable objective.

In any case, various courts have shown that they notice, and expect, more from forensic examiners than has been asked in the past—more in the way of demonstrating competency and proficiency, more in the way of demonstrating objectivity, and more in the way of showing one's work. The true forensic reconstructionist will not only meet these expectations when possible but also work to exceed them. In this way, he or she will show that the court has not been misled in qualifying him or her as an expert witness.

REFERENCES

Adamo, R., et al. "Commentary on the American Board of Criminalistics (ABC) Certification Process," *J. Forensic Sci.*, 45, 749 (2000).

Associated Press "Rape Verdict Reversed for F.B.I.'s Bad Science," *The N.Y. Times*, p. A13, December 15, 2001.

American Society of Crime Laboratory Directors, *Laboratory Accreditation Board Manual*, American Society of Crime Laboratory Directors/Laboratory Accreditation Board, Garner, North Carolina, 2000.

Bailey, S. "Crime Lab Chief Faces Immense Backlog," *Birmingham News*, January 3, 2003.

Baldwin, H. B. *How to Become a CSI*. Available at http://icsia.org/faq.html. Accessed June 4, 2005.

Bayle, E. "The Scientific Detective," *Am. J. Police Sci.*, 2, 158 (1931).

Berger, M. A. "Procedural Paradigms for Applying the Daubert Test," *Minn. L. Rev.*, 78, 1345–1353 (1994).

Black, B., et al. "Science and the Law in the Wake of Daubert: A New Search for Scientific Knowledge," *Tex. L. Rev.* 72, 714–755 (1994).

Blankstein, A., and Guccione, J. "'CSI' Effect or Just Flimsy Evidence? The Jury Is Out," *L. A. Times*, p. A1, March 18, 2005.

Boyd, D. "Scientist at Crime Lab Is Fired," *Ft. Worth Star-Telegram*, p. 1, April 22, 2003.

Boyd, D., and McDonald, M. "Boost in Funding Needed to Put Lab Back on Track," *Ft. Worth Star-Telegram*, p. 29, June 9, 2002.

Brannigan, V., and Torero, J. "The Expert's New Clothes: Arson 'Science' after Kumho Tire," *Fire Chief*, 60 (July 1999).

Brant, M. D. "Determining the Distance of Gunshot Wounds to the Head by Appearance and Physical Evidence," *J. Forensic Identification*, 48, 133 (1998).

Bromwich, M. R. Second Report of the Independent Investigator for the Houston Police Department Crime Laboratory and Property Room, 12 May 31, 2005. Available at www.hpdlabinvestigation.org

Buchanan, E. "Did FBI Help Send Wrong Man to Death Row?" *Miami Herald*, p. 1, May 31, 2003.

"Budget Cuts Mean State Will Stop DNA Testing," *Providence Journal*, p. A-01, June 20, 2002.

Burk, D. L. "DNA Identification: Possibilities and Pitfalls Revisited," *Jurimetrics*, 31, 53–80 (1990).

Burtman, B. "Odell Barnes Awaits Execution on March 1 Despite New Evidence That He Didn't Commit the Crime," *Houston Press*, January 27, 2000.

Campbell, G. A. "Erdmann Faces New Legal Woes: Pathologist Indicted for Perjury in Texas Murder Trial," *ABA J.* (1993, November).

Carroll, S., and Sowers, C. "DNA Flaws Called Unlikely to Jeopardize Police Cases," Arizona Republic, p. 1B, May 7, 2003.

"CBI Labs Need a Boost" [editorial], *Denver Post*, p. E-06, March 31, 2002.

Clouse, T. "State Police Lab Fights Crime, Backlog of Cases; Swamped Technicians Hope Legislature Will Fund Expansion," *Spokesman Review* (Spokane, WA), p. A1, April 6, 2003.

Cole, S. A. "Fingerprinting: The First Junk Science?" *Okla. City U. L. Rev.*, 28, 73 (2003).

Cole, S. A. "More Than Zero: Accounting for Error in Latent Fingerprint Identification," *J. Crim. L. Criminology*, 95, 985 (2005).

Cole, S. A., and Dioso, R. "Law and the Lab; Do TV Shows Really Affect How Juries Vote? Let's Look at the Evidence," *The Wall St. Journal*, May 13, 2005.

Connors, E., et al. *Convicted by Juries, Exonerated by Science: Case Studies in the Use of DNA Evidence to Establish Innocence after Trial.* Washington, DC: National Institute of Justice, 1996.

Cooley, C. M. "Reforming the Forensic Community to Avert the Ultimate Injustice," *Stan. L. Pol'y Rev.*, 15, 381 (2004a).

Cooley, C. M. "Forensic Individualization Science and the Capital Jury: Are Witherspoon Jurors More Deferential to Suspect Science Than Non-Witherspoon Jurors," *S. Ill. L. J.*, 28, 273–310, no. 232 (2004b).

Coscarelli, K. *The "CSI" Effect: TV's False Reality Fools Jurors*, Newhouse News Service, April 21, 2005.

Crime Labs, Nat'l Pub. Radio, May 15, 2003.

Dao, J. "Lab's Errors in '82 Killing Force Review of Virginia DNA Cases," *The N.Y. Times*, p. 1, May 7, 2005.

Davis, D. "Plenty of Cases, Not Enough Resources for Crime Lab," *Santa Fe New Mexican*, April 21, 2002.

DeForest, P. R. "Proactive Forensic Science," *Sci. Just.*, 38, 1 (1998).

DeForest, P. R. "Crime Scene Investigation," in *Encyclopedia of Law Enforcement*, New York: Sage Publications, eds. L. E. Sullivan and M. S. Rosen, pp. 111–116, 2005.

Derry, G. N. *What Science Is and How It Works*, Princeton University Press: Princeton, NJ, 2002.

Dribben, S. "DNA Statistical Evidence and the "Ceiling Principle": Science or Science Fiction," *Mil. L. Rev.*, 146, 94–110 (1994).

Drizin, S. A., and Leo, R. A. "The Problem of False Confessions in the Post-DNA World," *N.C. L. Rev.*, 82, 891 (2004).

Dunlap, A. "Science versus Practical Common Sense in Crime Detection," *Am. J. Police Sci.*, 2, 322 (1931).

Epstein, R. "Fingerprints Meet Daubert: The Myth of Fingerprint 'Science' Is Revealed" *Southern California Law Review*, 75, 605–658 (2002).

Evett, I. W. "Expert Evidence and Forensic Misconceptions of the Nature of Exact Science," *Sci. Just.*, 36, 118–121 (1996).

Faigman, D. L., et al. *Science in the Law: Forensic Science Issues*, West Group, St. Paul, MN. (2002a).

Faigman, D. L., et al. "Scientific Method: The Logic of Drawing Inferences from Empirical Evidence." In *Modern Scientific Evidence: The Law and Science of Expert Testimony*, (2nd ed.). West Group: St. Paul, MN, 2002b.

The FBI Laboratory: An Investigation into Laboratory Practices and Alleged Misconduct in Explosives-Related and Other Cases, USDOJ/OIG Special Report, Washington, DC: USDOJ Office of the Investigator General, April 1997.

Federal Bureau of Investigation. *Statement on Brandon Mayfield Case*, Press release, May 24, 2004.

Federal Emergency Management Agency, U.S. Fire Administration, *USFA Fire Burn Pattern Tests—Program for the Study of Fire Patterns*, FA 178, 1997.

Finkelstein, M. O., and Levin, B. "Compositional Analysis of Bullet Lead as Forensic Evidence," *J. L. Pol'y*, 119 (2005).

Forbes, T. R. *Surgeons at the Bailey: English Forensic Medicine to 1878*. Yale University Press: New Haven, CT, 1985.

Fradella, H. F., et al. "The Impact of Daubert on Forensic Science," *Pepp. L. Rev.*, 31, 323–325, (2004).

Freedberg, S. P. "Sloppy Lab Work Casts Doubt on Some Florida Cases," *St. Petersburg Times*, p. 8A, March 5, 2001.

Fricker, R. L. "Grave Mistakes," *ABA J.*, p. 46 (1993, December).

Furton, K., et al. "What Educational Background Do Crime Laboratory Directors Require from Applicants?" *J. Forensic Sci.*, 44, 128 (1994).

Geller, B., et al. "A Chronological Review of Fingerprint Forgery," *J. Forensic Sci.*, 44, 963 (1999).

Giannelli, P. C. "The Admissibility of Novel Scientific Evidence: *Frye v. United States*, A Half- Century Later," *Colum. L. Rev.*, 80, 1197–1243 (1980).

Giannelli, P. C. "*Daubert*: Interpreting the Federal Rules of Evidence," *Cardozo L. Rev.*, 15, 1999 (1994).

Giannelli, P. C. "The Abuse of Scientific Evidence in Criminal Cases: The Need for Independent Crime Laboratories," *Va. J. Soc. Pol'y L.*, 4, 439 (1997).

Giannelli, P. C. "Fabricated Reports," *Crim. Just.*, 16, 49 (2002, Winter).

Giannelli, P. C. "Expert Evidence and Criminal Justice," *Jurimetrics J.*, 43, 243–245 (2003).

Giannelli, P. "Scientific Evidence" *Criminal Justice Magazine*, 18(1), Spring 2003.

Giannelli, P. C., and Imwinkelried, E. J. *Scientific Evidence*. (3rd ed.). Lexis Publishing: Charlottesville, VI, 1999.

Gold, S., and Hart, L. "Inmate Freed after 17 Years on Death Row," *L. A. Times*, p. A14, October 7, 2004.

Graham, J. "Crime Labs Contaminate Justice: Poor Science, Quality Control Jailing Innocents," *Chicago Tribune*, p. 10, June 21, 2001.

Grieve, D. L. "The Identification Process: SWGFAST and the Search for Science," *J. Forensic Identification*, 50, 145–148 (2000).

Gross, S. R., et al., Exonerations in the United States: 1989 through 2003," *J. Crim. L. Criminology*, 95, 523 (2005).

Hamilton, A. "Chemist's Errors Stir Fear: Were Innocent Executed?" *Dallas Morning News*, p. 1A, October 22, 2001.

Hanley, B. H., and Clark, S. C. "Developing National Guidelines for Death Scene Investigations," *Crim. Just.*, 14, 27 (1999).

Hansen, M. "Troopers' Wrongdoing Taints Cases," *ABA J.* 80, 22 (1994).

Hansen, M. "Dusting for Daubert: Several Defense Lawyers Argue Fingerprint Evidence Is Not Scientific. So Far, the Courts Aren't Buying It," *ABA J.*, 86, 20 (2000).

Heath, D., and Bernton, H. "Portland Lawyer Released in Probe of Spain Bombings," *Seattle Times*, p. A1, May 21, 2004.

Hempel, C. "TV's Whodunit Effect: Police Dramas Are Having an Unexpected Impact in the Real World," *Boston Globe*, p. 13, February 9, 2003.

Herguth, R. C. "Report Slams 80s Police Lab," *Chicago Sun-Times*, p. 5, January 14, 2001.

Hirschberg, M. "Wrongful Convictions," *Rocky Mtn. L. Rev.* 13, 20–34 (1940).

Imwinkelreid, E. J. "Forensic Science: Bloodspatter Analysis," *Crim. L. Bull.* 36, 509–516 (1999).

Imwinkelried, E. J., and Tobin, W. A. Comparative Bullet Lead Analysis (CBLA) Evidence: Valid Inference or Ipse Dixit? *Okla. City U. L. Rev.*, 28, 43 (2003).

Inman, K., and Rudin, N. *Principles and Practice of Criminalistics: The Profession of Forensic Science*. Boca Raton, FL, 2000.

Joling, R. J. "Problems of Freedom and Responsibility in the Forensic Sciences," *J. Forensic Sci.*, 21, 743–746 (1976).

Jonakait, R. N. "Forensic Science: The Need for Regulation," *Harv. J. L. Tech.*, 4, 109 (1991a).

Jonakait, R. N. "Stories, Forensic Science, and Improved Verdicts," *Cardozo L. Rev.*, 12, 343–349 (1991b).

Jones, G. R. "President's Editorial—The Changing Practices of Forensic Science," *J. Forensic Sci.*, 47, 437 (2002).

Kaye, D. H. "The Nonscience of Fingerprinting: *United States v. Llera-Plaza*," *Quinnipiac L. Rev.*, 21, 1073 (2003).

Kennedy, D. "Forensic Science: Oxymoron?" *Science*, 302, 1625 (2003, December 5).

Khanna, R., and McVicker, S. "Crime Lab Faked Results in 4 Cases, Probe Finds," *Houston Chronicle*, p. A1, June 1, 2005.

Kirk, P. L. "The Standardization of Criminological Nomenclature," *J. Crim. L. & Criminology*, 38, 165–166 (1947).

Kirk, P. L. "The Interrelationship of Law and Science," *Buffalo L. Rev.*, 13, 393–394 (1964).

Kirk, P. L., and Bradford, L. W. *The Crime Laboratory: Organization and Operation*. Charles C Thomas Publishing: Springfield, IL, 1965.

Klein, R. "Senate Leaders Massachusetts Seeking Increase for Crime Lab," *Boston Globe*, p. B4, May 14, 2003.

Koehler, J. "Error and Exaggeration in the Presentation of DNA Evidence at Trial," *Jurimetrics* 34, 21 (1993).

Knupfer, G. C. "Crime-Scene Sciences." In J. Siegel et al. (Eds.). *Encyclopedia of Forensic Science*, Vol. 3, p. 1049, 2000. Academic Press, New York, New York.

"Labs Hope to Get Funds Requested," *Baton Rouge Advoc.*, p. 7B, June 5, 2003.

Lakatos, I. "Science and Pseudoscience." In M. Curd, and J.A. Cover, (Eds.). *Philosophy of Science*, p. 20, 1998.

Lee, H. C. "Forensic Science and the Law," *Conn. L. Rev.*, 25, 1117–1124 (1993).

Lentini, J. "The Scientific Basis of Expert Testimony on Fires, Arsons, and Explosion." In D. L. Faigman et al. (Eds.) *Science in the Law: Forensic Science Issues*, West Group: St. Paul, MN, p. 359, 2002.

Lindquist, C. A. "Criminalistics Education and the Role of the Criminalistics Educator," *Forensic Sci. Rev.*, 7, 61–64 (1995).

Liptak, A. "Houston DNA Review Clears Convicted Rapist, and Ripples in Texas Could Be Vast," *The N.Y. Times*, p. A14, March 11, 2003a.

Liptak, A. "You Think DNA Evidence Is Foolproof? Try Again," *The N.Y. Times*, p. A5, March 16, 2003b.

Luscombe, B., and Bower, A. "When the Evidence Lies," *Time*, p. 38, May 21, 2001.

Macgregor, F. "New Bid to Prove Richey Is Innocent of Killing," *Evening News* (Edinburgh, Scotland), May 7, 2003.

Maier, T. W. "Federal Judge Slams Fingerprint 'Science,'" *Insight on the News*, p. 20, March 18, 2002.

Main, F. "Inmates Seek New Trials in 1990 Rape, Murder," *Chicago Sun-Times*, p. 12, November 25, 2003.

Malkin Koosed, M. "The Proposed Innocence Protection Act Won't—Unless It also Curbs Mistaken Eyewitness Identifications," *Ohio St. L. J.*, 63, 263–272 (2002).

Martinez, J. "Bay State Crime Labs in Dire Straits; Report: State Crime Labs Underfunded, Overworked," *Boston Herald*, p. 001, April 15, 2002.

McCollum, D. "The Accidental Defenders," *The American Lawyer*, Januray 1, 2005.

McCormick, C. *Handbook of the Law of Evidence*, St. Paul, MN: West Publishing Co., 1954; pp. 363–364.

McDonald, M. "DNA Test Sways Prosecutors," *Ft. Worth Star-Telegram*, p. 1, October 10, 2002.

McGaw, B. A., and Hanna, J. "Stiff Standards," *Times Higher Education Supplement*, p. 15, May 9, 2003.

McMahan, T. "Real Life Meets 'CSI'; Television Dramas Leave Fingerprints on Local Juries' Expectations," *Daily Oklahoman* (Oklahoma City), p. 1A, May 2, 2005.

McNamee, A. H., and Sweet, D. "Adherence of Forensic Odontologists to the ABFO Guidelines for Victim Evidence Collection," *J. Forensic Sci.*, 48, 382 (2003).

McVicker, S., and Khanna, R. "House Hearings on HPD Crime Lab to Focus on Audit," *Houston Chronicle*, p. A15, March 3, 2003.

Melson, K. E. "President's Message," *Academy News*, 1 (2004, January) (newsletter of the American Academy of Forensic Science).

Midkiff, C. R. "More Mountebanks." In R. Saferstein (Ed). *Forensic Science Handbook*, (2nd ed.), Vol. 2, p. 67, Academic Press: New York, New York, 2004.

Miller, J., and McLean, M. "Criteria for Identification of Toolmarks," *AFTE Journal*, 1998;30(1):15–61.

Mills, S. "Texas May Have Put Innocent Man to Death, Panel Told; Nobody Would Listen, Lawyer, Expert Say," *Chicago Tribune*, p. 7, April 20, 2005.

Mills, S., and Coen, J. "12 Years Behind Bars, Now Justice at Last," *Chicago Tribune*, p. 1, February 1, 2005.

Mills, S., and Possley, M. "Texas Man Executed on Disproved Forensics; Fire That Killed His 3 Children Could Have Been Accidental," *Chicago Tribune*, p. 1, December 9, 2004.

Mitchell, A. C. *Science and the Criminal*. Little, Brown: and Company, Boston, MA, 1911.

Moenssens, A. A. "Novel Scientific Evidence in Criminal Cases: Some Words of Caution," *J. Crim. L. Criminology*, 85(1) (1993).

Moenssens, A. A., et al. *Scientific Evidence in Civil and Criminal Cases* (5th ed.). Foundation Press: Westbury, NY, 1995.

Moran, B. "Commentary on: Max M. Houck, Review of Principles and Practice of Criminalistics," *J. Forensic Sci.*, 46, 1263 (2001); *J. Forensic Sci.* 47, 697 (2002).

Murr, A. "A Dentist Takes the Stand," *Newsweek*, p. 24, August 20, 2001.

Nagel, E. *The Structure of Science: Problems in the Logic of Scientific Explanation.* Harcourt, Brace & World, Inc.: New York, New York, 1961.

National Advisory Commission on Criminal Justice Standards and Goals, *Police*, 304 (1974).

National Institute of Justice. *Death Investigation: A Guide for the Scene Investigator.* Washington, DC: National Institute of Justice, 1999.

National Institute of Justice. *Forensic Sciences: Review of Status and Needs.* Washington, DC: USDOJ, NCJ 173412, February 1999.

National Institute of Justice. *A Resource Guide to Law Enforcement, Corrections, and Forensic Technologies.* Washington, DC: National Institute of Justice, 2001.

National Institute of Justice. *Using DNA to Solve Cold Cases.* Washington, DC: National Institute of Justice, 2002.

National Institute of Justice. *Report to the Attorney General on Delays in Forensic DNA Analysis.* Washington, DC: National Institute of Justice, 2003.

National Institute of Justice. *Education and Training in Forensic Science: A Guide for Forensic Science Laboratories, Educational Institutions, and Students.* Washington, DC: National Institute of Justice, 2004.

National Public Radio, "John Lentini Discusses the Science of Arson," Weekend Edition, April 30, 2005.

National Research Council. *Forensic Analysis: Weighing Bullet Lead Evidence*, 2004. Available at www.nap.edu/catalog/10924.html

Newhouse, M. "Real-Life Investigators Indict 'CSI' for Perjury," *Pittsburgh Trib. Rev.*, April 13, 2005.

Newman, A. "Fingerprinting's Reliability Draws Growing Court Challenges," *The N.Y. Times*, p. 8, April 7, 2001.

Nordby, J. J. "Here We Stand: What a Forensic Scientist Does." In S. H. James and J. J. Nordby *Forensic Science: An Introduction to Scientific and Investigative Techniques*. (Eds.). CRC Press, Boca Raton, FL, 2003.

O'Hara, C. E., and Osterburg, J. W. *An Introduction to Criminalistics: The Application of the Physical Science to the Detection of Crime*. Indiana University Press: Bloomington, IN, 1949.

Osborne, J. "Perry to Decide If DPS Lab Must Face Legislative Inquiry," *Austin American-Statesman*, p. B7, January 4, 2001.

Osterburg, J. W. "A Commentary on Issues of Importance in the Study of Investigation and Criminalistics," *J. Forensic Sci.*, 11, 261–269 (1966).

Piller, C., and Mejia, R. "Science Casts Doubt on FBI's Bullet Evidence," *L. A. Times*, p. 1, February 3, 2003.

Pitsch, M. "Ex-FBI Scientist Pleads Guilty," *Courier-Journal* (Louisville, KY), p. 1B, June 18, 2003.

Popper, K. *The Logic of Scientific Discovery*. Routledge: New York. 1959.

Possley, M. "Ex-Inmate Exonerated of Rapes Tries to Get His Life in Order," *Chicago Tribune*, p. 4, June 29, 2000.

Possley, M., et al. "Scandal Touches Even Elite Labs; Flawed Work, Resistance to Scrutiny Seen across U.S., *Chicago Tribune*, p. 1, October 21, 2004.

President's Commission on Law Enforcement and Administration of Justice, *The Challenge of Crime in a Free Society*, 1967.

Pretty, I. A., and Sweet, D. "The Scientific Basis for Human Bitemark Analysis—A Critical Review" *Sci. Just.*, 2001;41(2):85–92.

Quade, V. "If the Shoes Fits: Footprint Expert Testifies," *ABA J.*, 34 (1985, July).

Report of the Governor's Commission on Capital Punishment, 2002.

Report of the Governor's Council on Capital Punishment, 2004.

Rhodes, H. T. F., *Alphonse Bertillon: Father of Scientific Detection*. George G. Harrap & Co. Ltd.: London, England, 1956.

Risinger, M. "Defining the 'Task at Hand': Non-Science Forensic Science after *Kumho Tire Co. v. Carmichael*," *Wash. & Lee. L. Rev.*, 57, 767 (2000).

Risinger, D., Saks, M., Thompson, W., and Rosenthal, R. "The Daubert/Kumho Implications of Observer Effect in Forensic Science: Hidden Problems of Expectation and Suggestion". *California Law Review*, 90, 1–56 (2002).

Roane, K. R. "The CSI Effect," *U.S. News & World Report*, p. 48, April 25, 2005.

Robertson, J. "Integrity Issues Impacting on the Provision of Forensic Services," *Austl. J. Forensic Sci.* 31, 87, 93–94 (1999).

Roth, N. E. *The New York State Police Evidence Tampering Investigation: Report to the Honorable George Pataki, Governor of the State of New York*, 1997.

Ryckaert, V. "Crime Lab Tech Was Disciplined; Murder Case DNA Testing Questioned," *Indianapolis Star*, p. 1A, July 19, 2003.

Saks, M., and Koehler, J. "What DNA 'Fingerprinting' Can Teach the Law about the Rest of Forensic Science," *Cardozo L. Rev.*, 13, 361 (1991).

Saks, M. J. "Merlin and Solomon: Lessons from the Law's Formative Encounters with Forensic Identification Science," *Hastings L. J.*, 49, 1069, 1082–1090 (1998).

Saks, M. J. "Scientific Evidence and the Ethical Obligation of Attorneys," *Cleveland St. L. Rev.*, 49, 421–423 (2001).

Salmon, R., and O'Brien, P. "Jurors Tuning in to TV's Influence; Popular Crime and Forensics Programs Are Changing Courtroom Perceptions, Lawyers Say," *Press Enterprise* (Riverside, CA), p. A1, May 1, 2005.

Saltzman, J., and Daniel, M. "Man Freed in 1997 Shooting of Officer; Judge Gives Ruling after Fingerprint Revelation," *Boston Globe*, p. A1, January 24, 2004.

Sapir, G. "Legal Aspects of Forensic Science," in *Forensic Science Handbook*, ed. R. Saferstein, 2nd edn., 2002. (Academic Press, New York, New York)

Sappenfield, M. "From Lindbergh to Laci, a Growing Forensics Fancy," *Christian Science Monitor*, p. 01, April 24, 2003.

Scheck, B., et al. *Actual Innocence: When Justice Goes Wrong and How to Make It Right.* Singnet, New York: New York, pp. 237–249, 2001.

Scheck, B. C. "The Need for Independent Forensic Audits Now," *Champion*, 28, 4 (2004, October).

Schmidt, S. "Oregon Lawyer's Status Remains Murky," *Washington Post*, p. A2, May 22, 2004.

Schmidt, S., and Harden, B. "Lawyer's Fingerprint Linked to Bombing Bag, Detonators Found in Stolen Van in Spain," *Washington Post*, p. A3, May 8, 2004.

Schwartz, A. "A Systemic Challenge to the Reliability and Admissibility of Firearms and Toolmark Identification," *Colum. Sci. Tech. L. Rev.*, 6, 2–12 (2005).

Sciolino, E. "Ten Bombs Shatter Trains in Madrid, Killing 192," *The N.Y. Times*, p. A1, March 12, 2004.

Selavaka, C. M. "A Scientist's Perspective on Forensic Science," *Indiana L. J.*, 80, 72–74 (2005).

Siegel, J. A. "Discussion of 'Criminalistics—A Look Back at the 1970's, a Look Ahead to the 1980's," *J. Forensic Sci.*, 25, 269 (1980).

Silver, J. D., and Lash, C. "U.S. Targets DNA Backlog," *Pittsburgh Post-Gazette*, p. A-1, March 12, 2003.

Singer, R. L. "President's Message," *Academy News*, 34, 1 (2004, May/June) (newsletter for the AAFS).

Solomon, J. "Crime Lab Chief in Bombing Investigated," *Miami Herald*, p. 3, August 29, 2003.

Sperry, K., and Campbell, Y. H. R., Jr. "An Elliptical Incised Wound of the Breast Misinterpreted as a Bite Injury," *J. Forensic Sci.*, 35, 1126 (1990).

Srihari, S. N., et al. "Individuality of Handwriting," *J. Forensic Sci.*, 47, 856 (2002).

Stacey, R. B. "Report on the Erroneous Fingerprint Individualization in the Madrid Train Bombing Case," *Forensic Sci. Communications*, 7 (2005a).

Stacey, R. B. "A Report on the Erroneous Fingerprint Individualization in the Madrid Train Bombing Case," *J. Forensic Identification*, 54, 706–710 (2005b).

Stafford Smith, C. A., and Goodman, P. D. "Forensic Hair Comparison Analysis: Nineteenth Century Science or Twentieth Century Snake Oil," *Colum. Hum. Rights L. Rev.*, 27, 227 (1996).

Starrs, J. E. "In the Land of Agog: An Allegory for the Expert Witness," *J. Forensic Sci.*, 30, 289–299 (1985).

Starrs, J. E. "Foreword." In S. H. James and J. J. Nordby (Eds.). *Forensic Science: An Introduction to Scientific and Investigative Techniques*, CRC Press: Boca Raton, FL, 2002.

"Stink Tanks," *The Economist*, May 3, 2003.

Tanner, R. "Crime Labs Stained by a Shadow of Doubt," *L. A. Times*, p. A18, July 13, 2003.

Thompson, W. C. "Evaluating the Admissibility of New Genetic Identification Tests: Lessons from the 'DNA War,'" *J. Crim. L. Criminology*, 84, 22 (1993).

Thompson, W. C., and Cole, S. A. "Lessons from the Brandon Mayfield Case," *Champion*, 29, 42–43 (2005).

Thompson, W. C., and Krane, D. E. "DNA in the Courtroom." In J. C. Moriarty (Ed.). *Psychological & Scientific Evidence in Criminal Trials*. West Publishing: St Paul, MN, §11:42, pp. 11–68, 2004.

Thompson, W. C., et al. "How the Probability of a False Positive Affects the Value of DNA Evidence," *J. Forensic Sci.*, 48, 47–48 (2003).

Thornton, J. I. "The One-Dissimilarity Doctrine in Fingerprint Identification," *Int. Crim. Police Rev.*, 306, 89 (1977).

Thornton, J. I. "Courts of Law v. Courts of Science: A Forensic Scientist's Reaction to *Daubert*," *Shepard's Expert Sci. Evid. Q.*, 1, 475, 484–485 (1997).

Thornton, J. I., and Peterson, J. L. "The General Assumptions and Rationale of Forensic Identification." In D. L. Faigman et al. (Eds.). *Science in the Law: Forensic Science Issues*, West Publishing: St. Paul, §1–5.4, p. 15, 2002.

Thornton, K. "Police Lab Accused of Sloppy Work, False Data," *San Diego Union-Tribune*, p. A-1, May 24, 1997.

Thorwald, J. *The Century of the Detective*. Harcourt, Brace & World, Inc., New York, New York, 1964.

Tizon, T. A., et al. "Critics Galvanized by Oregon Lawyer's Case," *L. A. Times*, p. A13, May 22, 2004.

Upshaw, A. "Budget Cuts Shelve DNA Tests; Crime Laboratory Shuts down Unit Devoted to Old Cases," *Arkansas Democrat-Gazette* (Little Rock), p. 1, May 26, 2003.

Wecht, C. H. "Science Fiction; TV Programs Fail to Show Busy, Overworked Forensic Labs," *Patriot-News* (Harrisburg, PA), p. D03, May 4, 2003.

Weinstein, H. "Death Penalty Foes Mark a Milestone," *L. A. Times*, p. 1A, April 10, 2002.

Wertheim, P. A. "Detection of Forged and Fabricated Latent Prints: Historical Review and Ethical Implications of the Falsification of Latent Fingerprint Evidence," *J. Forensic Identification*, 44, 652–653 (1994).

Willing, R. "Mueller Defends Crime Lab after Questionable DNA Tests," *USA Today*, p. A3, May 1, 2003.

Winton, R. "Blake Jurors 'Stupid,' D.A. Says; Despite the Acquittal, Steve Cooley Contends the Evidence Showed the Actor Killed His Wife," *L. A. Times*, p. 1, March 24, 2005.

Wrolstad, M. "Hair-Matching Flawed as a Forensic Science: DNA Testing Reveals Dozens of Wrongful Verdicts Nationwide," *Dallas Morning News*, p. 1A, March 31, 2002.

Zimmerman, C. S. "From the Jailhouse to the Courthouse: The Role of Informants in Wrongful Convictions," in *Wrongly Convicted: Perspectives on Failed Justice*, eds. S. D. Westervelt and J. A. Humphrey, pp. 55–76, 2001. (Rutgers University Press, New Brunswick, New Jersey)

INDEX

Page numbers noted with "f", "t", or "n" indicate related figures, tables, and notes.